DATE DUE

SOCIETY AND SELF

A Reader in Social Psychology

SOCIETY

AND

SELF

EDITED BY

Bartlett H. Stoodley

THE FREE PRESS OF GLENCOE

For information, address: The Free Press of Glencoe
A Division of The Macmillan Company, The Crowell-Collier Publishing Company
60 Fifth Avenue, New York 11
Library of Congress Catalog Number: 62-11864

To My Mother and
the Memory of My Father

"THE OBJECTIVE STRUCTURE of a society provides a framework within which an individual's non-interchangeable and singular characteristics will develop and find expression, depending on the greater or lesser possibilities which that structure allows."

Georg Simmel

Preface

A STUDY of the readers in the field of social psychology over the last few decades shows a trend. The biological frame of reference has lost some of the earlier stress and social factors have received increased consideration. This shift has naturally brought about a change in theoretical perspective. Concepts such as drive and instinct have retired a little toward the wings of the stage and interaction has moved steadily front and center.

The present Reader takes a further step. Although it does not dismiss either biology nor interaction it places a central importance on the concept of social structure. This emphasis reinstates an earlier enterprise. In 1930 Kimball Young opened his textbook in social psychology with a section called, "The Social Setting of Human Behavior." In his introduction to this section he states, "Perhaps the commonest fallacy of the psychology textbook lies in the assumption that the beginnings of social behavior exist only in the individual. It is because of this misconception that we introduce the material in this book with two chapters bearing on the social-cultural background of human personality." The present Reader attempts to maintain the focus of social structure in view of the wealth of studies now available that round out the perspective. To this end it is advisable to avoid head-on collision with many concepts, such as motivation, that are now going through a period of agonizing reappraisal.

One of the difficulties with the "culture-personality" studies has been their tendency to seek to exhaust both categories, culture and personality. It is clear at this stage of our knowledge that we must favor one or the other categories and explore the region of its influence. By postulating social structure as the major focus, this Reader does not seek to exhaust personality but to explore the significance of social structure for the individual enterprise. Man will not be exhausted by our specializations, nor can he be appropriated by one of them. But our specializations can gradually round out his complexity if they cannot sum him.

The Reader starts from the premise of social structure and examines some modes of its relations to the individual, but in later sections some of the important forms of individual reaction back upon social structure are presented. This procedure makes it possible to round up those empirical insights that rise from an explicit concern with social organization, and at the same time to recognize not determinism but interdependence in the relations between society and self. Increasing emphasis on this interdependence in the later sections makes it possible for the self, in limited dimensions, to rise empirically in the material rather than as a set of preconceived molds into which data must be fitted.

The studies are reprinted in their entirety without deletions of any sort. Their subject matter throws considerable light on the contemporary social scheme. Recent material has been favored throughout. It serves no purpose to saturate the field with older, standard work, however excellent, that is already within the sociological domain and generally available. The same principle has been followed with the selected readings. Teachers, of course, are encouraged to introduce other readings to salt and season the Reader to their tastes, and to develop fields in which they have a particular interest.

A reader should have certain long-term goals. It should try to bring together in one volume a selection of outstanding work. This would constitute a service to experts and students alike. And this material should be presented within a frame of reference firm enough to give coherence and direction to the order of the studies, but elastic enough to give them elbow room and breathing space. For the studies must be able to speak for themselves. The student must judge to what extent the present arrangement meets these criteria.

The studies present a wide range of sociological methodology which can perhaps convey to the student how methodology is adapted to purpose and subservient to results.

Some have suggested that studies examining the self by a major emphasis on the tool of social structure depart sufficiently from traditional social psychology to require a new name such as psycho-sociology. I would consider that the usual term is quite satisfactory. The field it covers is merely being extended. There is room for more than one room in the house of social psychology.

Bartlett H. Stoodley

Wellesley College
Wellesley, Massachusetts

Acknowledgments

MY THANKS to the authors of the studies presented in this volume. Their permissions to publish their work were often given without clear indication from the editor what precise use he proposed to make of them and so in what light they would appear. I hope they have all appeared in a good light.

My thanks to my students who for some years have stimulated my interest and thinking in this field.

My thanks to Jerry Kaplan, president of *The Free Press of Glencoe, Inc.*, who has the happy faculty of not only being sagacious in himself but of encouraging the roots of sagacity in others. What fails in this Reader must be attributed to roots too small to profit.

B. H. S.

Contents

B. ATTITUDES

C. ASPIRATIONS

D. AUTHORITARIANISM

7 *Self-Feedback Process*

A. SOCIAL MOVEMENTS

B. CHANGE IN SOCIAL STRUCTURE

C. CREATIVE ART

8 *Postulates and Models*

A. OPERATIONAL MODELS

B. ASSUMPTIONS ABOUT THE NATURE OF MAN

SOCIETY AND SELF

1 *The Concept of Social Structure*

SOCIAL STRUCTURE was not invented by sociologists. It has long been known that individuals live in groups and that groups have tradition, morale, and socialization patterns. People must have been talking sociology ever since they talked at all.

Nor did sociologists invent systematic analysis of social systems. In the Western tradition, philosophers, social philosophers, apologists for church and for state, humanists, and polemicists have recognized the existence of the "social organism" at least from the time of the Greeks. The concept of social system has become more sophisticated through the centuries, rising to a point of great complexity with the thought of Riverol, Lamennais, de Maistre, and a legion of thinkers, many of them stimulated by the challenge of the French Revolution, who concerned themselves with the problem of order. The problem of order is the touchstone of sociology.

Not only did these thinkers concern themselves with the social system and the problem of order, they also inquired into the relation between the individual and the state and even into the nature of the individual as related to the state. The state was viewed by many as a moral system, and this moral system was clearly seen to contradict certain obvious tendencies in individuals. The function of religion in maintaining this moral system was rightly emphasized. Authority was analysed in relation to moral order, and sanction was seen to rest on legitimation.

With these facts in mind it is clearly something of a convention to say that sociology started with Comte. Sociology is both a subject matter —and in this regard it shares the stage with thinkers considerably predating Comte—and a method. As a method it does date from Comte's positivism.

But in another sense sociology must be seen as starting with the great French sociologist, Emile Durkheim, for Durkheim can be taken to represent that group of sociologists, working around the turn of the century, who began to inquire closely into the details of social organization and the problems of encompassing them with useful theory. This basic spadework was made necessary as a result of the decline and fall of general ideas that were supposed to explain all the important aspects of social systems. Edmund Burke and John de Maistre relied on religion. Althusius and Jean Bodin employed the concept of natural law. Herbert

Spencer rested his case on the process of evolution and associated with it the idea of progress. When these generalizations proved inadequate, there was need for a new beginning, fresh observations, and careful theorizing. Sociology took form as a discipline under this stimulus, although, of course, the stimulus itself ranged far wider than sociology, influencing not only the other social sciences but the humanities as well.

The sociologist takes social organization or social structure as his main focus. A book of readings in social psychology relies on this main focus, but relates it to different facets of human behavior. First, however, it is necessary to get the feel of social structure as such. Social structure is as objective as a church, a bank, or a school. It is a system of proprieties that define the way things are done in given situations. A church, a bank, or a school are different systems of proprieties. The individual, throughout his life, has both an internal and an external relation to these systems. They immensely enlarge his field of potential experience in some directions, while they make more and more hazardous his ventures into certain other fields. When these systems are all added up, they constitute the way a given society does business, its "way of life."

The studies in this section give us the feel of social structure. "Social Class and Sociability in Fraternity Pledging," by Levine and Sussmann, calls attention to certain class-linked attributes and their importance in gaining entrance into fraternities at Massachusetts Institute of Technology. In this article the aspect of social structure emphasized is social class. In "A Cross-Cultural Study of Structure and Conflict in Social Norms," Stoodley employed a research design originally used by Stouffer. Stouffer used it for a sample of Harvard students, and Stoodley used it for a sample of students at the University of the Philippines. What are the proprieties for a proctor who finds a student cheating? What do others expect him to do? The uniformity of expectations perceived by a proctor in this situation is a measure of the clarity with which that social situation is defined in a given society. This concrete situation is one aspect of social structure in both the United States and the Philippines. The results of the two studies indicate that the experimental situation is defined with more clarity in the Philippines than in the United States.

Charles K. Warriner's "Groups Are Real: A Reaffirmation" sums up the implications of the two articles preceding it and emphasizes the analytical reality of the group. It should be kept in mind that this article does not suggest that the group is the only analytical reality or that relations between the individual and the group realities should not be explored. Warriner's point can perhaps be illustrated simply by the fact that at a funeral ceremony an important group of behaviors are explained by the existence of proprieties perceived as binding in the given situation. Individuals as personalities may differ in every respect except that they perceive and defer to the expectations defining the situation. Thus, the controlling element is the structural component. This element is not always controlling, but it is always important and always analytically separable from the usual type of personality motivation.

GENE NORMAN LEVINE
and LEILA A. SUSSMANN

Social Class and Sociability in Fraternity Pledging

EACH fall Freshmen entering many colleges may choose whether or not to seek membership in Greek-letter, social fraternities. These fraternities, many of which have chapters at scores of colleges, have lately been under some pressure from without and from within to give up their traditional exclusion of Jewish and Negro students. Discriminatory practices are widespread enough, however, to allow Jewish and Negro counterparts still to flourish. Fraternity men proclaim their right to associate with whom they choose—and hence to select only those persons, whatever their racial or religious origins, whom they find congenial.

But, as is well known, personal characteristics—values and attitudes, styles of life, habits of dress, speech, and comportment—are to a great extent class linked. Does this, then, mean that the fraternities, middle class in origin and character, bar from their ranks youths from the working class, apart from religious and racial discrimination?

Whom do the fraternities choose as members? What are the personal characteristics on which they base their selection? Are these traits class linked? What chance does a youth of the working class have to gain entry into these organizations which are so central to the social life of

---

Reprinted from "Social Class and Sociability in Fraternity Pledging," by Gene Norman Levine and Leila A. Sussmann, The American Journal of Sociology, *January, 1960, pp. 391-399, by permission of The University of Chicago Press.*

many college campuses? Data on the behavior of students at a technical college in the East provide quantitative answers to these questions.

In August, 1957, a detailed questionnaire was mailed to 890 prospective Freshmen students in engineering and science. They were asked about their experiences at secondary school, their expectations of the college they were about to enter, their plans for a career, and their social and personal backgrounds. Six hundred and twenty-three youths mailed back completed questionnaires before leaving home, and another 192 filled them out within two weeks of their arrival at college—a total return of 92 per cent. In addition to the questionnaire data, the Office of the Dean of Residence informed us who in the entering class did and who did not seek fraternity membership by attending "Rush Week." The Dean's office also informed us who among the rushees "pledged" fraternities, i.e., accepted invitations ("bids") for membership. Qualitative data of three kinds were collected, too: first, a few of the participants (both Freshmen and brethren) served as informants by keeping journals of Rush Week for us; second, we ourselves recorded events which we observed at fraternity houses at the time; third, several officers and rank-and-file members of fraternities, as well as several Freshmen, were interviewed before, during, and after Rush Week concerning their experiences.

Over two-thirds of the class of 1961 (609 out of 890 Freshmen) attended Rush Week. Of the rushees, roughly half (285 out of 609) became fraternity pledges. In the analysis to follow we concern ourselves with three questions: (1) How do the Freshmen who come to Rush Week differ from those who elect not to come? (2) What happens during Rush Week? (3) How do the rushees who pledge fraternities differ from those who do not?

Some time around the first of August the Freshmen mailing list is made available to the rushing chairmen of the various fraternities. Immediately, a wave of brochures and pamphlets telling about life at the college, the fraternity system, and the specific houses arrives in the Freshman's mail. In addition, or instead, some fraternities delegate to their members the responsibility of contacting by letter, by telephone, or in person a portion of the Freshmen class who live in their own section of the country.

Rushing comes early at this college because an acute shortage of dormitory space makes it necessary for some of the Freshmen to reside in fraternity houses from the beginning of the semester. This situation sometimes makes for intense competition between the brotherly societies in their attempts to identify "good" men early in the game.

There are rules of the game of rushing, and these extend to summer rushing as well. Information concerning the backgrounds and personalities of Freshmen may be obtained through channels of personal communication available to every fraternity. It is legitimate to gain an advantage by investing a great deal of energy to get the most out of these sources—for instance, by paying more personal visits than other fraternities do. It is legitimate to send literature to the Freshman but not to spend money on his entertainment in the summertime. It is legitimate to entertain him lavishly during Rush Week but not to keep him in ignorance of invitations from other houses. An indication that fraternity members care very much about recruiting good pledges is the constant, if mild, pressure to break the rules. As a fraternity man, the member is concerned to see that the rules be enforced; but as a loyal member of a specific fraternity, he cannot help but search for ways to get ahead of the game. This makes for an intense interest in the rules and in violations of them.

Before leaving home the Freshman—personally contacted or not by a fraternity during July, August, or early September—is in the throes of the decision: to rush or not to rush. For the men who definitely perceive themselves as fraternity material and for those who think of themselves in the opposite fashion the problems are few. But between these extremes are the Freshmen who are less sure: Can they afford to join a fraternity? Will the active social life called for in such organizations interfere with the serious pursuit of studies? Will close fraternity relationships help them in their school and later careers?

Who in the class of 1961 was the more likely to journey to college a week early in order to seek fraternity membership? To take a simple question first: Does money enter into the student's decision about Rush Week? Because of the collective use of resources and facilities, fraternity membership at this school, in fact, costs little or no more than living in a dormitory; but if entering students *believe* membership to be more expensive than dormitory life, the less affluent will probably count themselves out of the rushing.

The data show, indeed, that money matters. The higher the annual income of the student's family, the more likely is he to appear for Rush Week (Table 1).[1] (The tables herein contain information only on students who answered the relevant questions.) While only about half the

Table 1. Percentage of Students at Rush Week by Family's Income*

Family's Annual Income	Per Cent Coming to Rush Week	Total No.
Under $5,000	56	127
$ 5,000-$ 8,000	68	254
$ 8,000-$15,000	70	242
$15,000 and over	76	150

*Forty-two out of the 815 who returned the questionnaire neglected or refused to report their families' annual incomes.

1. Respondents were asked: "What is your family's present annual income? (Check one): Under $5,000, $5,000-8,000, $8,000-10,000, $10,000-15,000, $15,000-25,000, Over $25,000?"

students from the families with the lowest income enter into the competition for fraternity membership, eight in ten of those from families with the highest income do so.

Finances enter into the decision to come to Rush Week in indirect as well as direct ways. Some students have summer jobs which help substantially to pay for their first year at college and which they cannot afford to leave until the last possible moment. For others—those who plan to work during the school year—time is literally money. They feel they cannot spare the extra time fraternity activities demand, hold a job, and also give adequate attention to their studies. There are, of course, fraternity men who hold part-time jobs. Nevertheless, these problems deter some Freshmen from even considering a fraternity.

Preferences in styles of living enter into a student's considerations about rushing. Popular images of the "fraternity man" and how he lives are not lacking. The imagery includes elements that in anticipation cannot fail to affect the Freshman's decision. Peering into the mirror of his personality, one Freshman may feel that he "looks like" a fraternity man; another may see no resemblance at all.

What are some elements which enter into his deliberations? The fraternity man is thought to be a person who is gregarious, sociable, party-loving, and easy-to-meet. The fraternity brother also expects *himself* to exhibit these qualities. Part of the role, then, of the good fraternity man, as conceived both by outsiders and by the brethren themselves, is what we shall call the "sociability complex." It entails a set of attitudes and behavior patterns thought to be proper for the fraternity man. And, whether he actually ranks low or high on any hypothetical scale designed to measure gradations of sociability, he strives to live up to the standard set for him. A corollary of the expectation that the brother will be gregarious is that he will not be too competitive, academically. He ought *not* to be a "greasy grind," a man who studies unceasingly to reach the top of his class. And, finally, the fraternity man is considered to be organization minded, eager to give of his time to campus affairs.

The popular image of the fraternity man—his gregariousness, his avoidance of appearing to study "too much," his extracurricular preeminence—definitely enters into the beginning student's judgment about the advisability of coming to Rush Week. First, we find that the more dating and socializing a Freshman did in high school, the more apt he is to come to Rush Week.[2] Sixty per cent of the young men who socialized little in

2. The student was asked to fill out a time budget for a typical week during his Senior year in high school. He had to account for the number of hours a week he spent in school, at study and homework, sleeping and eating, in extracurricular activities at school, dating and socializing, on hobbies and other leisure-time activities, doing chores at home, on a job, and "other activities."

high school (fewer than six hours a week) come to Rush Week; 84 per cent of those who socialized a great deal (twenty or more hours a week) do so. Second, the more an entering student thinks of "having fun generally" as important in his career at college, the more likely is he to "rush": of those who feel that having fun at college is "not important," only 55 per cent come to Rush Week; of those who feel that having fun is "very important," 80 per cent come. Third, the greater the importance the Freshman places on "making close friends" while at college, the more likely he is to rush. Fifty-six per cent of the students who feel that making close friends is "not important" rush, while 75 per cent of those who feel it is "very important" do so. Clearly, these responses support the hypothesis that fraternity men are thought to be gregarious and that this image influences the Freshman. For, the less sociable the Freshman is, the less likely he is to rush.

The less time a student spent on studying and homework in high school, the more likely he is to rush: 64 per cent of the men who studied over twenty hours a week rush, as compared to 76 per cent who studied less than ten hours. Also, the lower his level of aspiration regarding academic performance at college, the more likely he is to come to Rush Week. Of the Freshmen who would only be satisfied to rank "close to the top" of their class, 60 per cent come to Rush Week; of those who would be satisfied to rank "in the top half" or "lower," 76 per cent come. Here again a popular notion of the fraternity man affects the Freshman's willingness to try to "go fraternity." The better he feels he fits the picture, the more often he enters into the competition for membership.

Finally, the data reveal that the greater the importance a Freshman places on achieving extracurricular distinction, the more likely is he to rush; and the more hours a week he plans to devote to extracurricular activities at college, the more likely is he to come to Rush Week. Sixty-four per cent of the young men who feel that achieving extracurricular distinction is "not important" and 80 per cent of those who regard it as "very important" rush; 60 per cent of those who plan to spend fewer than five hours a week on extracurricular activities and 86 per cent of those who plan to devote at least fifteen hours a week to them rush.

The preceding data all point to the same conclusion: the popular picture of the fraternity man affects the Freshman's decision about attendance at Rush Week. The better the Freshman feels he fits this picture, the more likely he is to rush. Conversely, the less the student feels his own personality resembles that of the fraternity man, the more often he decides to stay out of the running.

Thus far we have discovered two conditions that enter into a Freshman's consideration about coming to Rush Week: his family's income and the degree to which he feels he "looks like" a fraternity man. But are these two factors independent? A great body of information which has been collected about the values of the American middle- and lower-income groups would lead us to believe that they are not. It is well known that middle-class Americans tend to have more friends, to join more organizations, and to cultivate more interests and hobbies than Americans in manual occupations.

The personal qualities or values which make up the fraternal ideal are not, then, entirely personal. They are esteemed and cultivated differently in the various occupational and income groups. Does this hold true also among our Freshmen engineers? The Freshmen whose fathers were in manual occupations who come to this technical college are atypical of their group in having chosen middle-class occupations for themselves. They are likely to share more in middle-class values as well. Nevertheless, the anticipated class differences appear (Table 2). For example, the number of hours a week spent in dating and socializing in high school and the importance placed on "having fun" at college are greater in the highest- than in the lowest-income group.

Table 2. Relationship between Family Background and "Sociability Complex"

	FAMILY'S ANNUAL INCOME	
	Under $5,000	*$15,000 or More*
Hours a week spent dating and socializing in high school:		
Under 10	64%	25%
10 or more	36	75
Total	100%	100%
Total number	97	79
Importance of having fun at college:		
Very important	24%	34%
Somewhat or not important	76	66
Total	100%	100%
Total number	126	127

Even though the admired personal values are class linked, we must not overlook the fact that a substantial minority in the lower-income groups possess them. But which factor—family income or sociability—is more important in the entering student's decision to come to Rush Week? Or do they have an equal impact?

In Table 3 we observe the simultaneous effects on the rushing decision of the Freshman's family income and his degree of sociability. Reading down the two columns of the table, it is seen that in the higher-income group resemblance or non-resemblance to the image of the fraternity man makes some, but not a large, difference in the proportion who come to Rush Week. Among those of lower income, however, the difference is more pronounced: those who do not see themselves as matching the image are decidedly less likely to come to Rush Week than those who do.

Table 3. Income and Likeness to the Popular Image of the Fraternity Man

	Per Cent Coming to Rush Week	
	FAMILY'S ANNUAL INCOME	
	Less than $8,000	$8,000 and Over
Hours a week spent studying in high school:		
Fewer than 15	74%	72%
(Base)	182	211
15 and over	55%	72%
(Base)	198	179
Hours a week to be devoted to extracurricular activities:		
10 or more	73%	79%
(Base)	124	111
Fewer than 10	58%	71%
(Base)	226	246
Importance of having fun for career at college:		
Very important	76%	83%
(Base)	82	97
Less than very important	60%	74%
(Base)	284	271
Hours a week spent socializing in high school:		
10 or more	79%	79%
(Base)	86	106
Fewer than 10	61%	70%
(Base)	290	285

It is possible to state the matter another way. Reading across the rows of Table 3, it is seen that students who resemble the fraternity image attend Rush Week in much the same proportions, regardless of family income. Those who do *not* resemble the image, however, come to Rush Week often only if they come from families with higher incomes.

Having elected to come to Rush Week, only about half the rushees end up as fraternity pledges. How does the rushing process select some Freshmen to join the brotherhoods and reject others?

The fraternity men spend many hours before Rush Week converting their sometimes modest, sometimes lavish, residences into showplaces for the Freshmen. The fraternities are about to engage in the annual melee, the outcome of which they hope will be the replenishment of their ranks reduced by the departure of the previous June's graduates. The penalties of a bad showing are heavy: if a house does not succeed in getting the number of men it seeks (or, rather, the number of *good* men it seeks), some years may elapse before its strength and its distinctive character, in the eyes of the members, are restored. "We are fighting for survival," some brothers say.

Who is the "hot" prospect—the likely, as distinguished from the unlikely, prospective member? By what criteria do the fraternity brothers differentiate the "hotter" from the "colder" Freshmen? Let the fraternity men speak for themselves. Among the rushees, they seek:

> The man who can express himself maturely, who has an interest in things outside of books, the one who has a neat appearance.
>
> Likeable guys, ones who know how to talk and who aren't loud. Men who'll fit in here. After all, we've got to live with each other.
>
> The extrovert.
>
> All we want is a sharp group of congenial people. . . . By a good person I mean one who is the all-American-boy type but with brains.
>
> We look for a sharp person who is a bit of an extrovert, conversing well and intelligently.
>
> The type of fellow we are trying to pledge is one that would be apt to glide into the atmosphere of the house very easily. In other words, we are looking for the fellow whom we would be glad to call our friend and whom we would enjoy being with. Now this fellow is not just a "good egg," for he usually needs something to attract our attention to him, and this usually comes in the form of various high school activities he participated in.[3]

On the other side of the coin, the brothers do *not* want:

> The "grind": the boy who is always studying.
>
> The "meatball": someone who is too pushy and aggressive.
>
> Someone who dresses and speaks poorly—a "meatball."

The fraternities seek, in other words, the gregarious youth, already socially poised, interested in and participating in the world outside of himself and his books: "the average American boy"—without evident personality quirks, well and soft spoken, neat and clean, somewhat athletic, and not too overtly intellectual. He is preeminently a "regular guy"—but one with brains. This is the standard the rushee must approach if he is to be among the chosen. It is the standard the fraternity man strives to attain himself.

3. These remarks were made to one of the investigators or recorded by fraternity men who kept journals during Rush Week.

The two types of Freshmen whom the brethren look at with disapproval, the grind and the meatball, are seen as deficient in these qualities. The former is unwilling to give of himself because he is so absorbed in his studies; the meatball because he lacks *savoir-faire*. Either type, if admitted, would presumably make it difficult for the brothers to live and to study cooperatively.

As observed, many of the Freshmen who are unlikely to meet the fraternities' criteria have already eliminated themselves before Rush Week begins. The others, the likely and the less likely, begin arriving at any fraternity's house on Saturday morning. The brothers immediately begin screening the youths, checking them off as to their relative possibilities —first, sheerly on the basis of appearance (Is he neat? Does he dress well? Is his handshake firm? Does he smile?) and then on the basis of his behavior (Is he poised? Is he self-confident? Does he talk well?). That it does not take long to screen a youth is attested by these fraternity men's statements:

> You can tell right away by their faces or the way they shake hands. A cold, clammy handshake as versus a warm, friendly one. Or by the way they are dressed.

> You can see right through them in five minutes.

> First, I'm concerned with how they are dressed. It's not a matter of Ivy League clothes, but looking neat and well-groomed. The next thing is a hearty handshake with a smile to go with it. A cold, clammy handshake and a tense face don't go with me.

At the first "all-friendly" on Saturday morning, the brothers quickly decide whom to ignore and whom to pursue. The main technique of communicating to the rushee that he does not fit into the house is tactful avoidance. He is not admitted to intimate personal contacts. Those who are eliminated in the initial screening are drawn together in groups to whom one or two brothers are assigned as hosts. They converse with the Freshmen and entertain them but do not woo them. Eventually, it is hoped, these rushees will take the hint and depart. Quite different is the treatment of those who pass the initial screening: these men may rarely have an opportunity to speak with a fellow rushee. Writes a brother:

> The actives circulate the good men among the other actives, while the meatballs are kept from the hot men in a group. Of course, the hot men get rushed by more than one person at a time; while the meatballs get left to their own devices (often a pool table).

The initially successful rushee is drawn out in private discussion—on his background, his likes and dislikes, the life he contemplates leading at college. Passing through the second screening, other brothers—preferably those who have the same interests and hobbies (the better to hold the rushee's attention)—are directed to him. Shortly after, he meets and is met by the bulk of the brotherhood. He is pressed to assure them that he will revisit the house soon.

It is not unusual that a rushee, passing the early screening and asked to return, fails in his circulation through the membership to impress anyone favorably. But after the first few visits, these men are decided on one way or the other—either they are weeded out or the doubters revise their estimates.

Typically, the fraternities are satisfied with the men whom they pledge; moreover, differences between one fraternity's pledges and those of any other are more apparent than real. Pledges are both willing and able to live up to the prescribed standards of how a fraternity man ought to behave. In truth, they know before they arrive at school how they ought to act. Their previous social experience—their extra-school activities, their participation in organizations different from fraternities only in that the members are younger—has prepared them for rushing and made them confident. The youth who lacks anticipatory social experience—ignorant of how a prospective fraternity man is expected to behave—stands less chance of faring well in the Rush-Week procedures.

Two things that enter into the Freshman engineering student's decision about whether or not to come to Rush Week have been reported above: the relative affluence of his family and the degree to which he resembles the popular image of the fraternity man. Among rushees, as well, the screening process continues to work in the same directions. The better-off youth and the one who, regardless of financial status, subscribes to values which set him off as fraternity material are the most likely to pledge. The Office of the Dean of Residence, besides knowing who did and who did not rush, had data on which rushees pledged, and we shall use these to validate this statement. It must be noted, however, that the outcome of rushing is in part a *self*-selection process and not solely a matter of whom the fraternity members choose. We do not know how many among the unpledged turned down bids, but we believe they are few if only because a young man so ambivalent about fraternity life would probably not stay on the course long enough to receive a bid.

It is true, as fraternity members say, that many Freshmen come to Rush Week only to see what it is like, without seriously intending to compete for a bid. Others undoubtedly come without having made up their minds where they want to live. When, in August, the Freshmen were asked where they planned to live at school, of 548 youths who came to Rush Week, 37 per cent had said they did not want to join a fraternity. This is a rough measure of the proportion who come to Rush Week "for the ride." Of 347 students who said in August that they wanted to join a fraternity and who subsequently came to Rush Week, 43 per cent did not pledge. This is a rough measure of those who would like to be fraternity members but who receive no bids or none they wish to accept.

What characteristics distinguish rushees who pledge from those who do not? Considering money first, we find that the higher the rushee's family income, the more likely he is to pledge (Table 4).

Table 4. Family Income and Percentage of Rushees Who Pledge

Family's Annual Income	*Per Cent Becoming Pledges*	*Total No.*
Under $5,000	31	71
$ 5,000-$ 8,000	40	174
$ 8,000-$15,000	46	169
$15,000-$25,000	52	65
$25,000 and over	61	49

And what of the "sociability complex"? Is it also true that the more gregarious rushees whose academic hopes are moderate and who aspire to extracurricular eminence are more likely to become fraternity men than their opposites? The data offer a partly affirmative, partly negative, answer: the more time a rushee has spent dating and socializing in high school, the better his chance of pledging a fraternity (Table 5). The greater the importance the rushee places on achieving extracurricular distinction at college and the more hours a week he plans to devote to out-of-class activities, the better his chance of pledging (Table 6).

Table 5. Socializing in High School and Chance of Being Pledged

Hours a Week Dated and Socialized	*Per Cent Becoming Pledges*	*Total No.*
Fewer than 6	32	182
6-10	47	213
11-19	51	102
20 and more	62	58

Table 6. Extracurricular Interests and Chances of Being Pledged

	Per Cent Becoming Pledges	*Total No.*
A. Hours a week planned to spend on extracurricular activities:		
Fewer than 5	36	96
5-9	45	229
10-14	48	142
15 and more	53	45
B. Importance of extracurricular distinction:		
Not important	32	111
Somewhat important	45	333
Very important	58	108

Regarding scholastic performance, however, the data show a discrepancy between the popular image of fraternities and the fraternities at this technical college. Here the fraternities choose the rushee who plans to study a lot and who aspires to high academic rank about as frequently as they do the man who plans to study less and whose aspirations are lower.

Now we may ask with respect to pledges the same question raised previously about coming to Rush Week. Which is more strongly related to a rushee's chance of pledging: family income or sociability? The answer is much the same as before: the rushee from a family with a high income tends to pledge, whether or not he is sociable. Among wealthier students, the more sociable join fraternities only slightly more often than the less sociable. Among students who are financially less well off, however, sociability makes the difference: the sociable will pledge much more often than the less sociable. We present just one of several tables which prove the point (Table 7).

Table 7. Per Cent of Pledging among Rushees by Family Income and Dating and Socializing in High School

	Per Cent Pledging	
	FAMILY'S ANNUAL INCOME	
Hours a Week Dated and Socialized	*Less than $8,000*	*$8,000 and Over*
Fewer than 10	29%	47%
(Base)	172	197
10 and more	53%	56%
(Base)	68	84

The rushee from a family with a lower income who has already come to resemble the fraternity ideal has a good chance of joining a fraternity. How is it that some young men who lack money acquire this when still in high school while others do not? We do have one piece of information which gives a glimpse of the process. This question was put to the Freshmen:

Would you say that compared with most other people you know, you are (check one): closer to your parents; less close to your parents; just about as close as most?

We expected the replies to this seemingly psychological question to show a relationship to fraternity pledging because of the fact that the upwardly mobile—for example, those moving from the working to the middle class—are frequently estranged from their families. In order to be successful in the climb, they have had to unlearn working-class values and to acquire the values of the class they aim at. An unfortunate concomitant of the ascent has often been the rejection of parents and of non-mobile siblings who stand for a way of life that has been abandoned.[4]

This process may be at work among some of the upwardly mobile Freshmen in engineering and science (Table 8): among those who come

Table 8. Percentage of Sons Who Pledge, According to Father's Occupation and Closeness to Family

	PER CENT PLEDGING	
	Sons of Fathers in Non-manual Occupations	Sons of Fathers in Manual Occupations
Closer to parents	47%	19%
(Base)	115	21
Same as others	48%	37%
(Base)	281	62
Less close to parents	45%	43%
(Base)	47	14

to Rush Week whose fathers are in manual occupations, those closest to their parents are least likely to pledge a fraternity, whereas those least close are most likely to do so. Among the others, closeness to family makes no difference at all in the probability of pledging. In order to stand as good a chance of being pledged as a middle-class youth, the Freshman from a working-class home apparently has to be "distant" from his family and should already have acquired, before arriving at college, the external signs (dress and speech) and internal symbols (values and sentiments) of membership in the middle class; the acquisition of these traits has probably implied some alienation from his working-class family. "Distance" from the family has not the same significance for the middle-class Freshmen. For them, lack of cloesness to parents is not a function of moving out of their class and therefore entails neither greater nor lesser adherence to class-related sociability.

Fraternity pledging illustrates some salient aspects of the American status system. Both stratification and mobility exist. Class-linked attributes are conceived as individual traits, so that the credit for what is "desirable" and the shame of what is "undesirable" are borne alike by the individual. The near-universal denial by students that anyone is "hurt" by fraternity rushing testifies that the shame produced in those who fail may be a serious problem but one that is buried. Later on, the fraternities themselves will help prepare their members intensively for adult social life, and some of this (e.g., "pledge training") is thoroughly planned and organ-

4. For a poignant account of this "American tragedy," see Oscar Handlin, *The Uprooted* (Boston: Little, Brown & Co., 1951), esp. chap. ix, "Generations," and chap. x, "Alienation." Handlin discusses the gap between first- and second-generation Americans, but we are observing young Americans of at least the third generation: 79 per cent of them have parents both of whom were born in the United States.

ized. Much more is informal. Forty young men in late adolescence living together for four years can greatly influence each other's values and character. College fraternities represent a powerful agency of near-adult socialization which is accessible to study.

BARTLETT H. STOODLEY

A Cross-Cultural Study of Structure and Conflict in Social Norms

How do individuals in a society perceive the expectations of others about a concrete action? What consistency and range do they attribute to these expectations? What conflicts exist between different sets of expectations both bearing on the same concrete situation? The answers to these questions furnish us with quantitative data about social structure and with indications of how problems for individual action may be generated by aspects of social structure.[1]

Criticisms of Stouffer's study of these questions have concentrated on the allegation that paper-and-pencil tests are no substitute for real situations. These criticisms probably have more force with reference to the hypothetical action in the tests than the perception of the expectations of others. Not only does Stouffer's design for the study of expectations have

Reprinted from "A Cross-Cultural Study of Structure and Conflict in Social Norms," by Bartlett H. Stoodley, The American Journal of Sociology, *July 1959, pp. 39-48, by permission of The University of Chicago Press. Copyright 1959 by the University of Chicago.*

1. Cf. Samuel Stouffer, "An Analysis of Conflicting Social Norms," *American Sociological Review,* XIV, No. 6 (December, 1949), 107-17. Stouffer with Toby tested certain personality hypotheses resulting from the above study in "Role Conflict and Personality," *American Journal of Sociology,* LVI (March, 1951), 395-406. [Both of these articles have been reprinted in Samuel A. Stouffer, *Social Research to Test Ideas,* Chapter 3. New York: The Free Press of Glencoe, Inc., 1962.] See also J. P. Sutcliffe and H. Haberman, "Factors Influencing Choice in Role Conflict Situations," *American Journal of Sociology,* LVII (July, 1951), 48-49; Samuel A. Stouffer, "Reply to Korber" (letter to the editor), *American Journal of Sociology,* LVII (July, 1951), 49; J. W. Getzels and E. G. Guba, "Role, Role Conflict, and Effectiveness: An Empirical Study," *American Sociological Review,* XIX, No. 2 (April, 1954), 164-75.

merit, but it also makes possible cross-cultural comparisons that would hardly be available in real-life situations. The present study analyzes the results of Stouffer's design when adapted to a sample of Filipinos.

Christian Filipinos have a strong, extended family organization that commands the utmost loyalty.[2] Their wider social arrangements emphasize particularistic relations in which the family is advanced through judicious selections of *compadres* and *comadres*. Nepotism, as a system of particularistic obligations, is institutionalized in the local political organization. Particularistic norms, by definition, favor a concrete personal relationship in contrast to all relationships of the same type[3] and since the test forces a choice between a universalistic and a particularistic choice, it would appear probable that Filipinos would favor the particularistic one. However, the Christian Filipino is not oriented *only* to particularistic norms. The evidence on this point, although not conclusive, clearly indicates that particularistic rights and obligations must often conform to wider universalistic norms.[4]

Filipino youth has no culture which is in any way comparable to the one in the United States. There is little or no indication of revolt among adolescents; youth there is clearly an apprenticeship to adulthood. It seems reasonable to hypothesize that Filipinos in conflict between strong particularistic and strong universalistic norms would favor particularistic norms more than Americans would.

To the Filipino the world is a simpler place than it is to the American. This is, of course, markedly true of the rural Filipino, but it is also true of the urban Filipino, who comprises the bulk of our sample. The family is still the major institution in the Philippines; family rights and obligations apply lineally to grandparents on both sides and collaterally to cousins, aunts, and uncles, also on both sides. Thus important rights and obligations, social relationships, and emotional responses are defined by the family structure and persist from the cradle to the grave. The occupational structure in urban areas is only just beginning to break into the web of relationships established by the family. Thus there is far less

2. See Bartlett H. Stoodley, "Some Aspects of Tagalog Family Structure," *American Anthropologist*, LIX, No. 2 (April, 1957), 236-49, and "Normative Attitudes of Filipino Youth Compared With German and American Youth," *American Sociological Review*, XXII, No. 5 (October, 1957), 553-61. "Filipinos" here refers to Christianized Filipinos, who constitute about 92 per cent of the total population.

3. See Talcott Parsons, *The Social System* (New York: Free Press, 1951), p. 63.

4. An interesting finding reported in Stoodley, "Normative Attitudes of Filipino Youth Compared with German and American Youth," and confirmed by personal observation [reprinted in this volume]. The modes of relationship have not as yet been worked out. The emphasis on particularistic and universalistic norms appears traditional.

heterogeneity than in the United States. The relative simplicity of structure appears to be associated with clear structural definitions and adequate communication to individuals. No indications of Filipino attitudes toward the situation in the test were available before it was given. But on the basis of wider observations it was hypothesized that the normative orientation of Filipinos to universalistic and particularistic norms would show a greater modal response and a smaller range than the orientations of Americans and that particularistic norms would exercise more power over Filipinos than would universalistic norms.

The questionnaire employed by Stouffer required the respondent to imagine that he was a proctor at an examination and that he found a student cheating. He did not know the student. He was asked what he would do to this student under three different circumstances, assuming that (1) neither the authorities nor his student friends knew about his decision; (2) the authorities but not the student friends would know; (3) the friends but not the authorities would know. The interviewee was then asked to assume that the cheating student was a roommate and close friend who needed a good mark in the course, and was asked what he would do under conditions 1, 2, and 3, above. For each situation the interviewee was presented a table combining five possible courses of action with four probabilities of choosing each type of action (see Table 1).

Table 1. Choices of Action in Hypothetical Situations*

	CHECK ONE IN EACH VERTICAL COLUMN			
	My Most Likely Action (Check One)	*My Next Most Likely Action (Check One)*	*My Least Likely Action (Check One)*	*My Next Least Likely Action (Check One)*
A. Take away his notes and exam book, dismiss him and report him for cheating	___	___	___	___
B. Take away his notes, let him finish the exam, but report him for cheating	___	___	___	___
D. Take away his notes, but let him finish the exam, and *not* report him for cheating	___	___	___	___
E. Act as if nothing had happened and *not* report him for cheating	___	___	___	___

*This table excludes choice C, as given by Stouffer, for reasons indicated in the text. Choice C was as follows. If he can be led to withdraw from the exam on some excuse, do *not* report him for cheating; otherwise report him.

This part of the questionnaire was designed to reveal the preferred action of the interviewee in the several circumstances and the effect of knowledge by the authorities or the students upon it. These data are, of course, vulnerable in that they involve hypothetical behavior.

Another section of the questionnaire inquired into the interviewee's opinions about the expectations of authorities and friends as to the two situations of the ordinary student cheater and the student cheater who is a friend of the proctor. The interviewee was asked to assume that he took one of the five categories of action in Table 1 and then to indicate whether this action would be approved, first, by the authorities and, second, by the student friends. His opinions about the degree of approval or disapproval of a specific act by authorities and students were indicated on a four-degree scale as shown in Table 2. As Stouffer pointed out, these

Table 2. How Would the University Authorities [or Students] Feel if They Knew You, as Proctor, Did This?

Check One	
______	Would expect one to do something like this
______	Would not necessarily expect one to do this, but would not disapprove
______	Would disapprove
______	Would not tolerate it

are primary data on the structure of expectations of authorities and students.

The writer in adapting the questionnaire added one section. In the Filipino family, younger siblings have clearly defined duties of obedience to older siblings of either sex. It follows that the apex of sibling authority is the eldest child, with slight emphasis on the male. Younger siblings tend to be obedient, and, at the same time, emotionally attached, to older siblings. How would Filipino respondents react to the test situation when friendship solidarities and structured obedience and respect reinforced each other? To find out, the respondent was asked to imagine that the cheating student was his elder brother.

The adapted questionnaire omitted the assumption that the cheating student was a roommate but included the other two elements—that he was a close friend and that he needed a good grade. There is a large commuter population at the University of the Philippines and, therefore, insufficient evidence that the factor, "roommate," would uniformly reinforce the other two.

In the list of categories of possible treatment of the cheating student in Stouffer's questionnaire (Table 1), alternative C was eliminated. Stouffer scaled these alternatives in order of punitiveness; alternative C was variously interpreted among Filipinos, however. Pretesting showed that it was generally considered hardly more punitive than D because the cheater could invent some pretext for leaving the examination and then take it later.

The American and Philippine sample are comparable in that they are drawn from congruent segments of the respective societies. The Philippine sample consists of 235 persons whose names were chosen systematically at random from the roster of the University of the Philippines' undergraduate divisions for the academic year 1954-55. The questionnaire was given to a total of 154 persons who attended a meeting held on the university premises for that purpose. Every precaution was taken to protect anonymity and to make anonymity psychologically real to the interviewees. The questionnaire was in English, which, in the pretest, had proved the most satisfactory language. Forty-nine questionnaires were rejected, mostly for incompleteness, which does not appear to be a high percentage in view of the complexity of the questionnaire. This left 105 questionnaires. A systematic random sample of 40 was drawn from the group, in the original sample, that did not attend the general session, and the individuals were contacted separately by three Filipino instructors in the department of sociology. Measures to convey the reality of anonymity to the interviewees were again stressed. Thirty-seven additional questionnaires were completed in this manner. Fourteen had to be discarded, leaving twenty-five. The data furnished by the original 105 were compiled separately from the data furnished by the 25, and the results in each case were not significantly different from each other. The data were combined for final analysis, and the group of 127 Filipino students is hereafter referred to as the "Philippine sample."

The data were first broken down to show the respondents' opinions on the expectations of the authorities and the students, separately, as to each action when the cheater is an ordinary student (see Table 3). Filipino authorities are seen as somewhat more tolerant than are American. About 20 per cent of the Filipino respondents thought the authorities would approve act D, while only 4 per cent of the American respondents felt that way about the American authorities. There is clearly a better "fit" between the expectations of authorities and students in the Philippine sample than in the American sample in the matter of acts D and E. There was, for instance, a 23 per cent spread between the opinions of Filipino respondents on approval of act D by authorities and students compared to a spread of over 45 per cent on the part of the American respondents. Filipino respondents saw a measure of tolerance of act E by both authorities and students, but it was only 6 per cent in the case of the authorities and 26 per cent in the case of the students. On the other hand, there is a strong universalistic orientation among Filipino authorities and students: 60 per cent thought the students would approve act A, and over 70 per cent felt they would approve act B. Higher percentages, of course, thought the authorities would approve act A or B, although these percentages were not as high as in the case of the American respondents.

The data reveal a similarity in viewpoint among Filipino respondents when the cheater is a close friend of the respondent. The authorities are seen as holding the line, as would be expected. About 10 per cent less of the respondents think that the students would approve act A, but just about the same proportion think that the students would approve act B. In the American sample there is a drop of 36 per cent in the respondents who think that the students would approve act A and a decline of 34 per cent in those who think that they would approve act B. Filipino respondents' opinions about act D are nearly identical with their opinions on the ordinary student. The same holds true for their views on the authorities about act E; but they are somewhat more permissive about act E in the case of the close friend.

The Filipinos' adherence to universalistic norms in the case of the close friend is in contrast to the American respondents. Only 33 per cent of the latter thought that the students would approve act A; a bare majority, act B; but 72 per cent felt that the students would approve act D, and more than half of them thought that the students would support act E, which consists of the proctor doing nothing at all.

Where authorities and students are seen as agreeing on a type of action, regardless of whether approving or disapproving, the area of potential conflict for a specific respondent is cut proportionally. Table 3 shows in

Table 3. Percentage of Filipino and American Respondents Who Think Authorities and/or Students Would Approve Specific Acts

	Percentage Distribution for Each Specific Action										
	A		*B*		*C*	*D*		*E*		*ALL ACTIONS*	
	Am.	*Fil.*	*Am.*	*Fil.*	*Am.*	*Am.*	*Fil.*	*Am.*	*Fil.*	*Am.*	*Fil.*
Case of ordinary student:											
Authorities only	28	35	12	17	3	....	5	....	1	9	13
Both authorities and students	68	56	81	70	19	4	16	2	5	35	36
Students only	1	4	6	8	55	48	28	24	21	27	16
Neither authorities nor students	3	5	1	5	23	48	51	74	73	29	35
	100	100	100	100	100	100	100	100	100	100	100
Case of close friend:											
Authorities only	63	40	44	20	9	1	10	....	3	24	18
Both authorities and students	33	50	53	70	25	6	12	4	3	24	33
Students only	....	5	....	9	49	66	33	48	36	33	21
Neither authorities nor students	4	5	3	1	17	27	45	48	58	19	28
	100	100	100	100	100	100	100	100	100	100	100

Philippine sample, N = 127; American sample, N = 196.

the column of "all actions" that 71 per cent of the Filipino respondents feel that given actions would be approved by neither students nor authorities or by both. Sixty-four per cent of American respondents perceive these areas of agreement by exclusion or inclusion.[5]

5. It should be kept in mind that the Philippine sample has no category C. Because of

When the cheater is a close friend, the situation changes in the expected direction. Sixty-one per cent of the Filipino respondents see given acts as approved by neither students nor authorities or by both. The comparable figure among American respondents is 43 per cent.

In Table 4 is shown the percentage distribution of hypothetical actions, which the respondents say they would be most likely to take as proctors, broken down into private and public acts. Private acts indicate what the

Table 4. Percentage Distribution of Hypothetical Actions Which Filipino and American Respondents Say They Would Be Most Likely To Take as Proctor

	In Case of Ordinary Student				*In Case of Friend*			
Action	*PRIVATE*		*PUBLIC*		*PRIVATE*		*PUBLIC*	
	Am.	*Fil.*	*Am.*	*Fil.*	*Am.*	*Fil.*	*Am.*	*Fil.*
A	21	25	30	30	4	11	6	18
B	47	64	48	59	12	38	34	58
C	16	....	13	....	18	....	31	....
D	15	9	7	8	38	38	18	21
E	1	2	2	3	28	13	11	3
	100	100	100	100	100	100	100	100

Philippine sample, N = 127; American sample, N = 196.

respondents would do if no one knew about it, and public acts indicate what the respondents would do if the authorities knew. With reference to the ordinary student, Filipino respondents show considerable consistency. Eighty-nine per cent of them favor act A or B, whether the act is public or private; 68 per cent of Americans favor act A or B when the act is private, but the percentage increases to 78 per cent when the act is public. The increase of 10 per cent indicates, of course, even in his hypothetical situation, a tendency to feel the pressure of opinion as overruling personal inclination.

In Table 4 we see the distortion cast upon this pattern by friendship: only 16 per cent of the American respondents see themselves as adopting the most punitive act A or B in private; Filipinos show a percentage of 49 per cent. Both groups move far toward conformity when the acts are public. American respondents choosing act A or B under these circumstances increase from 16 to 40 per cent. The comparable figure for Filipinos increases from 49 to 76 per cent. In both situations the Filipinos are more punitive than Americans and thus indicate a stronger allegiance, in the hypothetical situation, to universalistic norms. However, it is clear that claims of friendship are not lightly dismissed among Filipinos: 51 per

this and because Stouffer's American sample was not intended to be a sample of a wider universe, no statistical tests of significance have been made.

cent of them imagine themselves as adopting act D or E in private; 66 per cent of the American respondents see themselves as adopting act D or E in private.

In Table 5 the data in Table 4 are broken down according to the cate-

Table 5. Respondents' Own Most Likely Hypothetical Action as Proctor

	Would Be Approved by							
	AUTHORITIES ONLY		*BOTH AUTHORITIES AND STUDENTS*		*STUDENTS ONLY*		*NEITHER*	
	Fil. Sample	*Am. Sample*	*Fil. Sample*	*Am. Sample*	*Fil. Sample*	*Am. Sample*	*Fil. Sample*	*Am. Sample*
Case of ordinary student:								
Private Act								
A	6	3	17	18	....	....	1	....
B	12	2	44	44	5	1	4	....
C	....	....	....	6	....	9	....	....
D	....	....	4	3	4	10	1	2
E	....	....	....	....	2	2	....	....
	18	5	65	71	11	22	6	2
Public Act								
A	10	5	20	25	....	....	....	....
B	12	2	45	44	2	2	2	....
C	....	....	....	7	....	6	....	....
D	1	....	3	3	1	4	2	....
E	....	....	1	....	....	2	1	....
	23	7	69	79	3	14	5	....
Case of friend:								
Private Act								
A	2	....	10	4	....	....	....	....
B	7	1	27	10	2	....	1	....
C	....	....	....	7	....	9	....	3
D	2	....	8	2	19	31	10	5
E	....	....	2	1	4	20	6	7
	11	1	47	24	25	60	17	15
Public Act								
A	4	1	14	5	....	....	....	....
B	14	7	42	25	2	....	2	1
C	....	2	....	10	....	15	....	3
D	....	....	7	2	11	15	3	2
E	....	....	....	3	1	8	1	1
	18	10	63	45	14	38	6	7

Philippine sample, N = 127; American sample, N = 196.

gories in Table 3, to show the expectations of approval from authorities and/or students of respondents who adopt a certain action. The data disclose the comparative emphasis that Filipinos place on the approval of authorities: 18 per cent felt that their private action in the case of the ordinary student would be approved by the authorities only. The percentage increased to 23 per cent in the case of a public act. Only 5 per cent of the American respondents felt this way about their private acts, and the figure increased to only 7 per cent in the case of public acts. In the case of the close friend, Filipino respondents were not quite so inclined to seek support solely from the authorities. Eleven per cent did so with reference to a private act; and 18 per cent, with reference to a public act. The American figures were about the same as before: 7 per cent for the private act and 10 per cent for the public act. Filipinos were obviously more anxious to be on the safe side.

The Filipinos' bias in favor of the authorities in both private and public acts is balanced by a comparatively smaller reliance on the support of "students only" in their choice of action. And, where this support was relied on for a private action, it withered away in the case of a public action. For the ordinary student, where the act was private, 11 per cent of Filipino respondents felt that they would be supported by the students only. This figure declined to 3 per cent when the act was public. Twenty-two per cent of American respondents relied on the support of students only in a private act, and this figure was reduced to 14 per cent when the act was public. In the case of the friend, 25 per cent of the Filipino respondents relied on students only for support in a private act compared to 14 per cent for the public act. American respondents took the bit in their teeth under the stimulus of friendship. Sixty per cent of them relied on the support of students only for the private act, and 38 per cent of them persisted in this, even under the threat of publicity. Filipino respondents, generally, were more than twice as likely as Americans to entertain hypothetical acts approved by the authorities only, and Americans were more than twice as likely as Filipinos to entertain acts supported by students only.

Filipinos had a "tighter" expectation system than Americans. In Table 6 are presented comparative figures in percentages, with reference to ranges A, B, and AB. Eighty-four per cent of the Filipino respondents

Table 6. Percentages in Which Various Ranges of Acts Are Perceived as Approved by Authorities

	Case of Ordinary Student				*Case of Friend*			
	PHILIPPINE SAMPLE		*AMERICAN SAMPLE*		*PHILIPPINE SAMPLE*		*AMERICAN SAMPLE*	
Range	Auth.	Stu.	Auth.	Stu.	Auth.	Stu.	Auth.	Stu.
A	9	3	7	2	6	2	2	1
B	6	10	3	1	10	7	2	1
AB	69	35	68	19	65	30	61	6

Philippine sample, $N = 127$; American sample, $N = 196$.

thought that authorities' expectations with reference to the ordinary student lay in these ranges, compared with 78 per cent of the American respondents—indicating no significant difference in the universalistic norms attributed to the authorities by both samples. But, among Filipinos, 48 per cent of the respondents placed students' expectations in these ranges, compared with 22 per cent of American respondents.

In the case of the friend, the Filipino authorities are seen as more punitive than American authorities: 81 per cent of the Filipino respondents placed the authorities' expectations within the ranges A, B, or AB, compared with 65 per cent of the American respondents. And, among Filipino respondents, students' expectations were more frequently seen as restricted to these ranges. Thirty-nine per cent of Filipino respondents placed students' expectations in these ranges, compared with 8 per cent of American respondents.

Filipino respondents treated elder brothers in just about the same way that they treated close friends: in fact, 65 of the respondents out of the sample of 127 said that they would take action A or B in private, compared with 62 in the case of the close friend. In public, the comparative figures were 94 and 97. When the students only would know what the proctor did, the Filipinos were a little more punitive with elder brothers than with close friends. Eighty-one of the respondents would take action A or B in these circumstances with reference to elder brothers, as against 68 for the close friend.

The belief that students would be more punitive in their expectations with reference to elder brothers than with close friends is borne out by the expectations that they attribute to authorities and students (see Table 7). Two hundred and twenty-two responses (respondents could pick

Table 7. Frequencies with Which Filipino Respondents See Authorities and Students Approving Specific Acts (N = 127)*

Action	CASE OF CLOSE FRIEND Authorities	CASE OF CLOSE FRIEND Students	ELDER BROTHER Authorities	ELDER BROTHER Students
A	110	69	111	71
B	112	92	111	86
D	27	59	34	54
E	11	50	18	43

*No argument is made, of course, for the statistical significance of differences in these figures. On the contrary, frequencies are reported to emphasize the similarity of responses in actions A and B.

more than one category) indicated that the authorities would approve acts A and/or B for both close friends and elder brothers. One hundred and fifty-seven responses stated students' expectations as within this range for elder brothers, as against 161 for the close friend. With reference to acts D and E, a curious phenomenon occurs in the frequencies which may turn out to have substantive importance, although its statistical significance cannot be established here. Authorities are seen as less punitive with elder brothers than they are with close friends, but students are seen as more punitive. Fifty-two responses indicated that authorities would approve acts D and/or E in the case of the elder brother, as against 38 in the case of the close friend; but only 97 indicated that students would approve these actions in the case of the elder brother compared with 109 with reference to the close friend. Thus it may be supposed that the duty of obedience owed to elder brothers is overruled by universalistic norms and that the family relationship, in the eyes of students, at least, requires more rather than less allegiance to them.

As remarked earlier, Filipinos experience a well-defined and continuous—not discontinuous—socialization within age and sex roles. The evidence in this study suggests that, at least in the university, this integration is maintained. Filipinos perceive the expectations of proper conduct in the test situation with more uniformity than do their opposite numbers in the United States, and they are less deflected from their proper course by the temptations of friendship. Our first hypothesis—that Filipinos would exhibit a larger modal response and a smaller range with reference to both universalistic and particularistic norms—appears to be sustained. The second hypothesis—that the Filipino respondents would see particularistic norms as more binding than universalistic ones, in contrast to American respondents—was not sustained.[6]

The power of universalistic norms bears an important relation to the allocation of authority in the social structure of the Philippines. In the dominant institution—the family—authority is carefully allocated among siblings according to age and culminates in the parents. Obedience in accordance with this ladder of authority is strictly enforced. Furthermore, particularistic relationships extend to the remotest kin on both sides of the family—social and political arrangements reflect them. An observer, as a consequence, is strongly inclined to interpret so strong an authority structure as "authoritarian."

As a matter of fact, however, the authority structure is remarkably leavened by the strong universalistic limits found in this study and by the close affection among family members who are separated by considerable "authority distance."

Who is the legitimate employer of sanctions when there is a transgression? We found that a Filipino student does not hesitate in exercising sanctions against a fellow student. Friendship deflects the needle of probity, but not so much as in the case of Americans. In these relationships,

6. It must be confessed that there was evidence pointing to this result. The writer perhaps, showed some ethnocentric bias in being unwilling to trust the "regnancy" of universalistic norms in situations of great temptation to be particularistic.

however, there is no inequality: students are equal in authority, as are friends.

Who has the right to sanction among those unequal in authority? We must conclude that the subordinate has the obligation to institute sanctions against the superordinate who violates universalistic obligations. Thus Filipinos were as harsh on their eldest brothers when they were cheaters as they were on their friends. This view is supported by the findings in other studies. For instance, Filipino respondents reported in impressively large numbers, considering their duty of obedience, that a Filipino child was entitled to run away from home if his father was cruel and brutal. Some even maintained that the child had the duty to stay home to "correct his father"; some supported the right of a soldier to refuse to carry out the order of a superior officer to shoot an "innocent military prisoner."[7]

The devotion to universalistic principles in the case of eldest brothers is especially noteworthy. Friendship is, of course, an elusive concept, especially when applied cross-culturally. However, the strong emotional solidarity among siblings is a matter of everyday observance in the Philippines. When the elder brother is imagined as a cheater, it should raise for the sibling proctor all the conflicts of friendship. Furthermore, the duty of obedience to the elder brother (so universally observed in Philippine society) should mitigate the obligation to employ sanctions against him. With friendship and fraternal duty reinforcing each other, the chances of the proctor's resorting to strong sanction should be minimal. Yet we observe that there was no mitigation, comparing to the case of the close friend, and it is possible that there is some tightening up —which supports the evidence already given on location of the right and duty to sanction. It is institutionalized in subordinates. It may be questioned perhaps whether our own society, which places such high value on universalistic norms, has, in any comparable manner, established the right to sanction in subordinate roles.

The findings do not indicate fear of retaliation among subordinates or any need for attitudes of submission. The question is therefore raised for further consideration whether the syndrome of authoritarianism may be related not so much to the allocation of strong authority in social roles as to the existence of universalistic limits to the exercise of this authority and the location of the right to sanction in subordinates.

Today, Filipinos stand on the threshold between folk culture and the industrialization and Westernization introduced by American influence. The clarity of expectations which we see in this study appears to extend to other aspects of the social structure, so that we conclude that the Filipinos have a cohesive social structure. The institutionalization of

7. See "Normative Attitudes. . . ."

authority combined with strict universalistic obligations for performance on the part of those exercising authority should preserve stability during the transition to industrialization. Universalism as a normative orientation favors the kind of role structure that has been generally adapted to the industrial revolution in the Western world. The structure of the Filipino family permits radical splintering without the loss of morale. It also favors the introduction of both men and women into the work force, and both sexes have in fact entered the work force in considerable numbers.[8]

The emphasis on universalistic limits to particularistic obligations in the Philippines is interesting in relation to the economic and political "challenge" there. In particularism, of course, the relation between individuals explains the norms that bind them. In universalism, however, the norms which are held applicable to all explain the relations which finally ensue between concrete individuals. The American occupational structure is characterized by universalistic norms. But this abstract structural commitment is mitigated, in behavior, by considerable *de facto* particularism and even by occasional abject personal accommodation, which is a limiting case of particularism.

In the Philippines, particularism is clearly built into the crystallizing political structure and is bound to form an element in the occupational structure. Nepotism—derived from the enduring nature of kinship relations and obligations—is thus institutionalized. Filipinos reverse the trend as we have seen it in the United States: while the American family has been strongly influenced by occupational structure, in the Philippines the family has to date exercised important influence over the structure of politics and occupations. But Filipino political and business roles are not fully formulated. When they are formulated, it is quite possible that they will include a combination of particularistic obligations limited by overriding universalistic norms. The logical incompatibility of such a combination should not conceal one advantage: particularistic relations have not, in fact, been eliminated from American politics or American business. The Philippine "experiment" might bring particularistic relations under institutional control.

It is possible that erosion of the family structure in the Philippines may prevent any clear test of these possibilities. Some of the values of American society, which has high prestige in the Philippines as it emerges from the parochialism of the Spanish era, are accepted on trust, as it were, without awareness of what it may mean eventually for the family, which, at the moment, is able to withstand almost any *direct* attack.

The family, among Filipinos, is the society in microcosm. It enjoys undivided loyalty. But its strength depends on the maintenance of the system of obligations and rights allocated among family roles. American

8. See 1948 *Census of the Philippines.*

individualism is nibbling at the corners. The Filipino is beginning to ask why he should carry out obligations to his younger brothers and sisters before he looks after himself. He is asking why the money that he saves should be spent on the family and members of the kin group when it could be used to send him to college and to help him make his way in the world. Indirect erosion can eventually result in the contraction of the Filipino family to the "nuclear" type and the breakdown of the established hierarchical roles. Since generalized or universalistic values spring from these roles rather than independently of them, their disappearance will probably undermine the generalized concepts of value.

In any event, the Philippines may have the opportunity for some choice or compromise in the change, which is a signal advance in the direction of self-determination. It seems to me that this situation may be found in most "underdeveloped" areas.

CHARLES K. WARRINER

Groups Are Real: A Reaffirmation

THE term "group" is an ancient one in the social sciences, but despite its antiquity there is little agreement on the nature of the reality to which refers—or even if it refers to any reality at all. This problem has been fundamental to many of the arguments of the past. There have been times when we assured ourselves that the issues were resolved only to find that they have arisen again in somewhat different form.

Contemporary writings on the small group—research reports and theoretical statements—exhibit four major orientations to the group and to the question of its reality. Each of these orientations is here presented as a logically consistent point of view. However, it must be remembered that in their concrete representation they are not often so clearly stated or

---

Reprinted from American Sociological Review, *October, 1956, pp. 549-554, by permission of the author and the journal.*

Revised version of paper read at the annual meeting of the Midwest Sociological Society, April, 1956.

consistent. Any particular author may exhibit elements of several of these orientations.

Nominalism. The oldest, and the most extreme position in the light of contemporary knowledge, is the *nominalist* view that the group is not a real entity, but is merely a term used to refer to "an assemblage of individuals."[1] According to this view, the term is reified if it is used to refer to anything more than the behavior of individuals. Since individuals are the only reality, then the only thing which needs to be or can be explained is their behavior, singly or collectively. This point of view has its most favorable climate in a mechanistic type of psychological theory.

The nominalist orientation is implicit in much of the present work on the small group. A recent issue of the *American Sociological Review*,[2] devoted to small group studies, included several research papers in which the total extra-individual phenomenon was to be found in very brief contact between "subjects" with a minimum of interaction.[3] These papers, no doubt, deal with phenomena which have some bearing upon interpersonal relations, but by no stretch of the imagination can they be called studies of *groups*, as some purported to be.

Interactionism. Pure nominalism as an explicit theoretical doctrine has died out during the past thirty years with the rise of the *interactionist* point of view. The focus upon interaction led to a rejection of the group-individual dichotomy intrinsic to the nominalist-realist argument and to a stress upon the concrete indivisibility of the two. Wirth makes these points explicit:

> Rather than settling the issue as to whether the individual or the group is the ultimate unit in terms of which social life must be analyzed, the main stream of sociological and social-psychological thought has forgotten this issue and proceeded to analyze social phenomena as complexes of the meaningfully oriented actions of persons reciprocally related to one another.[4]

According to this doctrine, neither the group nor the individual is real except in terms of the other: that is, you-don't-have-persons-without-a-group and you-don't-have-groups-without-persons. In addition to the stress upon the indivisibility of the two, there is an emphasis upon the study of this whole in its concrete entirety and complexity. Finally, the interactionist doctrine has placed emphasis upon the multiplicity of caus-

1. Bronislaw Malinowski, "The Group and Individual in Functional Analysis," *American Journal of Sociology*, 44 (May, 1939), p. 938. Although Malinowski is quoted, practically identical phraseology may be found in other sources.

2. *American Sociological Review*, "Special Issue on Small Group Studies," 19 (December, 1954).

3. Cf. papers by Hochbaum, Emerson, Kelley and Shapiro, Mills and others, *ibid.*

4. Louis Wirth, "Social Interaction: The Problem of The Individual and the Group," *American Journal of Sociology*, 44 (May, 1939), p. 966.

ative factors needed to account for what happens. It combines biological, cultural, personal, and social explanations.

In much of the interactionist literature there are ghosts of the older nominalist thoughtways, most often found as implicit assumptions of and stresses upon the individual as the greater or more basic reality,[5] and of the more fundamental character of biological and psychological explanations of social life. On the other hand, the pure nominalist orientation could not continue unaffected in the face of the evidence on the social origins of personality and the findings on the interconnectedness of social and personal phenomena.

Neo-Nominalism. However, the interest in persons and the orientation toward the individual remained and formed the basis for a revised nominalist doctrine. The *neo-nominalist* pattern of thought accepts the proposition that the term "group" refers to an objective reality, but claims that the group is less real than persons for it is, after all, made up of persons and of processes which have their locus and immediate origin in the person.[6]

The exact character of the neo-nominalist view depends to a great extent upon the conception of interaction that is held. The most extreme rejection of the equal reality of the group is possible where the interaction is seen in stimulus-response terms. In this view the interaction itself, though being something different from individuals, is explicable only through individual psychological processes.

The basis for the explanation of group phenomena is perhaps the most clearly distinguishing characteristic of the neo-nominalist view. This is an essentially reductionist philosophy which holds that, since the individual is the more fundamental unit, the final and basic explanations of the group are obtained only when these explanations are couched in terms of individual psychology. Allport, the most persistent exponent of this view, says:

> The concept of a causal science on a purely social (non-psychological) plane is untenable, because in all science *explanation* is possible only by drawing upon the concepts of sciences at more elementary levels. . . . The true basis for sociology is the social behavior of the socialized individual, in other words,

5. This is illustrated in the work of Arensberg and Kimball. In their introduction they present a typical interactionist point of view but end with a stress upon the person: "There is no such thing as *the* society or *the* individual. Both concepts are conclusions of relative and limited validity. *There are only persons* behaving in various ways." (Final stress added.) Conrad M. Arensberg and Solon T. Kimball, *The Family and Community in Ireland*, Cambridge: Harvard University Press, 1948, p. xxix.

6. For illustrative statements of this view see, for example, D. Katz and R. L. Schanck, *Social Psychology*, New York: Wiley, 1938, p. 71. Also see Floyd Allport, "Rule and Custom as Individual Variations of Behavior Distributed upon a Continuum of Conformity," *American Journal of Sociology*, 44 (May, 1939), pp. 897-921.

social psychology. The work of sociology is to describe collectivities of social behavior and social change resulting from it in terms of the group, and to explain these phenomena in terms of "the individual."[7]

Realism. The antithesis of these nominalist views has been the realist argument. Realism, like nominalism, has undergone metamorphoses since Durkheim's time, but since the earlier forms of realism are seldom encountered today we shall describe merely what we have called *modern realism.*

This doctrine holds that (1) the group is just as real as the person, but that (2) both are abstract, analytical units, not concrete entities, and that (3) the group is understandable and explicable solely in terms of distinctly social processes and factors, not by reference to individual psychology. In short, modern realism is theoretical, analytical, and anti-reductionist. However, this does not mean that it is non-empirical.[8]

There are relatively few explicit presentations of this orientation. A recent article[9] by two "group psychologists" argues for it and there are occasional incidental papers in the sociological journals.[10] In addition there are occasional research reports which, in an unselfconscious fashion, exhibit this kind of thinking. There are, however, many tendencies in the thoughtways which appear to this author to lead toward the realist orientation.[11]

Of the four doctrines discussed, the neo-nominalist view appears to be in the ascendency today in small group research as well as in other areas of inquiry. Even interactionism has been distorted in this direction.[12]

7. Floyd Allport, *op. cit.*, and "The Group Fallacy in Relation to Social Science," *American Journal of Sociology*, 29 (May, 1924), p. 688.

8. One of the most persistent confusions in modern social science is that of empiricism with concreteness. Chemistry is an empirical science but is not concerned with the concrete, i.e. with substances as they appear in nature in all their complexity and interconnectedness. H_2O does not appear in nature, though water does. Chemistry of course, has an advantage in that it has been able to make many of its abstract analytical entities concrete entities in the laboratory through the manipulation of the materials and conditions.

9. Milton Horowitz and Howard V. Perlmutter, "The Concept of the Social Groups," *American Journal of Social Psychology*, 37 (February, 1953), pp. 69-95.

10. Donald R. Cressey, "Changing Criminals: The Application of the Theory of Differential Association," *American Journal of Sociology*, 61 (September, 1955), pp. 116-20; also Joseph D. Lohman and Dietrich C. Reitzes, "Note on Race Relations in Mass Society," *American Journal of Sociology*, 58 (November, 1952); pp. 240-246.

11. A case in point is the work in social psychology by Coutu, whose approach to the person is based on a realist orientation to the group. Walter Coutu, *Emergent Human Nature: A Symbolic Field Interpretation*, New York: Alfred A. Knopf, 1948.

12. In support of this judgment a recent brief treatment of the character of modern sociology is cited: ". . . most American sociologists have been unwilling to accept this Durkheimian tenet of society as separate and real in itself because their characteristic voluntaristic nominalism has led them to consider society as the sum of individuals in

This stress upon the individual, upon explanations in terms of psychology or psychological processes, and upon the lesser reality and importance of the group and other social phenomena have become the sensible, common-sense point of view. Its acceptance does not need to be defended because it is common-sense and because its doctrines are congenial to a period in which there is a general cultural stress upon individualism and the importance of the person.

But progress in a discipline depends upon getting beyond the common-sense orientations of the time. The purpose here is to make this attempt by calling attention to and defending the legitimacy and validity of the realist position, and to propose that this is the most valid and potentially fruitful sociological approach to the study of the group and society. This follows a long sociological tradition: the work of Durkheim, Simmel, and Radcliffe-Brown, among others.

In order to do this within the scope of this paper it will be necessary to be elliptical and to forego the kind of documentation that might be desirable. However, the intention is not so much to prove a position as to call attention to it and to the bases upon which it can be defended. This effort seems particularly pertinent at this time when sociology, at least as far as its interest in small groups is concerned, is in danger of being displaced by psychologists, some of whom are claiming the field for their own and stressing a psychological orientation as the only valid one:

> We have . . . to establish a branch of psychology concerned with the "personality" of groups . . . in spite of much talk about "culture patterns," methods and concepts simply do not exist. The sociologists, recognizing that a group cannot be defined in merely political or economic terms have turned to the psychologist for a science of the living group entity. . . .[13]

Such excesses could be forgiven if it were not for the fact that many sociologists seem to accept the premises and orientations such a statement implies.

The Arguments against Realism Examined

There are four basic propositions in the thoughtways of contemporary social science that serve as the bases for arguments against the realist position. The propositions are thought to be self-evident and not in need of defense. Such wide-spread uncritical acceptance is itself reason enough for critical scrutiny, but it is our thesis that these propositions are funda-

---

interaction." Roscoe C. Hinkle, Jr. and Gisela J. Hinkle, *The Development of Modern Sociology*, New York: Doubleday, 1954, p. 51.

13. Raymond B. Cattell, David R. Saunders, Glen F. Stice, "The Dimensions of Syntality in Small Groups," *Human Relations*, 6 (November, 1953), pp. 331-356.

mental fallacies in contemporary sociological thought and are a bar to further progress in the sociology of the group. These propositions are:

1. We can see persons, but we cannot see groups except by observing persons.

2. Groups are composed of persons.

3. Social phenomena have their reality only in persons, this is the only possible location of such phenomena.

4. The purpose for studying groups is to facilitate explanations and predictions of individual behavior.

The first proposition, that we can see persons, but not groups, has recently been criticized by several authors[14] who suggest that the argument involves a confusion between the idea of *individual* and that of *person.* They point out that the individual and the person are different "things" and that it is only the former, the biological structure, which we see directly, while the person is observed only through a series of actions and behaviors.

We can, perhaps, define the problem more clearly by stating it as a situation in which we treat a conceptual entity as a perceptual entity. The only thing which we as humans can observe are events within a relatively limited time and space location. Any unity that is microscopic, that extends beyond the scope of our perceptual equipment in space, or whose structural processes are too slow or too fast for our perception must be inferred from partial observations made via instruments or through time series. The fact that we cannot directly perceive their unity does not detract from their essential empirical reality; it merely reflects the human limitation. This appears to be no less true of social phenomena than of physical ones.

Whenever we are dealing with a unity that exceeds our perceptual facility, we postulate that unity from the observation of sequences of events appearing to have a continuity and a degree of causal connection. We create a conceptual unit. When, as a result of the use of this concept, we become fully convinced that it refers to, and essentially coincides with, an empirical, objective unity, we then come to project that conceptual reality upon our limited observations. That is, we call to mind the total thing when we see only a part of it; we come to treat our conception as if it were perception. This appears to be exactly the same kind of process as occurs in the operation of stereotypes except that in the former case we take greater pains, presumably, to make sure that our concept has a sounder basis in empirical fact.

14. Horowitz and Perlmutter, *op. cit.;* Bart Landheer, *Mind and Society: Epistemological Essays in Sociology*, The Hague; Martinus Nijhoff, 1953; and Arthur F. Bentley, *Inquiry into Inquiries: Essays in Social Theory*, Boston: The Beacon Press, 1954.

In any case, our argument here is that we cannot "see" persons any more than we can see groups: both are realities which extend beyond the range of human perception. Both are abstractions from and summaries of our observations of more limited aspects of the reality. The proposition that "we can see persons, but cannot see groups" is then a statement about our relative confidence in and acceptance of these concepts, *not a statement about perception or about what exists in external reality.*

We might note here that this argument is often joined with an assumption that the only *realities* are those which have physical substance. The basis for this belief is undermined by contemporary theory in physics, which proposes the interchangeability of matter and motion. As we inquire more carefully into the nature of what we believe is solid substance, we find that the solidity is more often than not the substance of our perceptual limitations.

The second proposition, that "groups are composed of persons," serves as a basic premise for two distinct conclusions about groups: (1) that they are more abstract, less real than persons, and (2) that really basic explanations of groups are in terms of their components, the persons of which they are composed.

This proposition loses its strength once we accept the idea that persons are no more concrete entities than are groups, but it is an idea that is so widely and unquestioningly accepted that it is worth examining independently of our earlier argument.

First, the proposition ignores the fact of interaction and is incompatible with the fact unless interaction is treated purely as a stimulus-response phenomenon, which can be done only through extreme contortion.[15] There is much evidence to show that interaction results in new phenomena which are emergent in the situation and not explicable by reference to the persons as they exist prior to the interaction. The statement thus ignores the fact that in combination here, as in chemistry, the elements cease to be the same thing they were before and that the characteristics of the compound are not the results of a mere blending or mixing of the components.

There is, however, a much more fundamental problem—a problem that raises the issue of what we mean by components, elements or units and whether there are different orders of components involved in the same concrete phenomenon.

Without going into the lengthy argument necessary we propose that *components*$_1$ (the materials from which a substance is created) have been confused with *components*$_2$ (the structural elements or members unique

15. For a discussion of the limitation of this view of interaction see this author's "Leadership in the Small Group," *American Journal of Sociology*, 60 (January, 1955), pp. 361-369.

to and characteristic of the system or unity with which we are dealing). We can clarify the problem by an analogy from common experience. Suppose we ask, "Of what is a chair composed?" We might get this variety of answers: wood and cloth, steel and leather, metal and organic compounds, atoms and molecules, chemical compounds. Each of these is in some senses a correct statement about some chairs, i.e. about certain observable objects. None of these, however, tells us anything about chairs as chairs, as a unique class of phenomena. Rather the answers tell us about the kinds of materials from which chairs may be created or about physical substances in general. The only answer which makes sense when we are investigating chairs, *qua* chairs—rather than chairs as furniture, or as wood products, or as chemical compounds, or as physical substances—is the answer which defines chairs in terms of their common structural parts and arrangements, the parts and arrangements which set chairs off from all other objects. Thus a chair is composed of a seat, legs, back, frame, etc.

In the language of the general semanticists, we have jumped abstraction ladders when we say that chairs are composed of atoms, of metal, or of chemical compounds. These may be characteristics of some or all chairs, but are not the components of chairs.

It would seem then that the proposition that groups are composed of persons tells us nothing about groups as such, but merely says that persons are characteristic of human social life. It describes a characteristic of groups as one kind of social life, but does not indicate the structural components that are involved in groups as a particular kind of unity and reality.

Our third proposition claims that "the only existence of social phenomena is in the individual." The proposition is an ambiguous one and may have several interpretations. It is frequently taken to mean that culture and other social phenomena are distributive only through the individuals in the group. Hence, for example, culture exists only as a sum or average of the beliefs or habits of the members of the group.

This point of view is fostered by such doctrines as Cooley's that the group is one side of the coin of which the individual is the other, and the perhaps misinterpreted statements of ethnographers that one can often find out all about a primitive culture from the study of a few members. These notions suggest that society and culture are mirrored in each individual member of the group.

The fallacy is the assumption that for a social phenomenon to be real it must be internalized by the individual, and results from a failure to make the distinction between knowing and internationalization. It is clear that a person may know cultural forms, beliefs, and patterns and know when they are appropriate (much in the way an anthropologist knows a culture which he studies) without these becoming an integral part of his own personality.

When we recognize this distinction, we see that it is possible for social phenomena to exist without being a part of the personalities who are the actors in the situation. Just as an anthropologist may participate in a savage rite in which he does not believe in order not to offend his hosts, so may any actor express cultural beliefs or conform to social actions he does not really believe or are not his personal habits. He may do so for a variety of motivations, but from a sociological point of view the character of the motivations is not the important thing, but the fact that he is motivated and that he knows the belief, ideology, or social act called for in the situation. Internalization or mirroring of social facts in the person is thus not a prerequisite to existence of the phenomenon. Because of this, such phenomena take on a reality independent of persons as persons. This means that we cannot discover social facts through a study of persons except in certain extremely stable and limited societies. As a result, to say that social phenomena have their location in the person is misleading. It would be much more appropriate to say that social phenomena have their reality only through expression by actors, in which case we imply the necessity not only for distinguishing person from individual, but also for distinguishing actor from person.

Support for this argument of the independent reality of social phenomena was found in my own study of a small Kansas village. We learned that there was a public, "official" morality regarding the use of alcoholic beverages that was quite different from the morality observed in other contexts. All the members of the community knew what the official morality was and they expressed it in their public behavior, but many of them did not "believe" it and conformed to other patterns in their homes, in small groups, and away from the village. There were a variety of sentiments (i.e. motivations) which led to the expression of this morality. They ranged from a few who *really believed* that drinking was wrong, to those who felt that it was *good for others* to abstain ("my brother's keeper" attitude), to those who merely felt that it was easiest not to go against the official position. Many other situations, which we now explain in terms of ambivalence of persons, bias, etc., are more easily explained by this formulation and support our conclusion.

The final proposition holds that the only purpose for studying groups is to facilitate knowledge of and prediction for persons. In the final analysis this is a value issue and is therefore not amenable to argument. It is in some ways basic to all the other arguments, however, for a thorough commitment to this value renders the realist approach superfluous. The only reason for realism as defined here is to facilitate the study of groups for their own sake. This author believes that anything which is real and observable is worth studying for itself. I am of the knowledge-for-the-sake-of-knowledge persuasion. But for those who judge knowledge and science in terms of "what good is it?" it might be pointed out that we have seldom perceived the ultimate values or applications of new developments in knowledge at their start.

Conclusion

In conclusion we must note that argument against the critics of a position does not prove that position. We have merely suggested that *a priori* rejection of realism is founded upon fallacy and misconception. The proof of the realist doctrine lies not so much in whether its present statement upon ultimate test will prove to be valid, but rather whether the present statement of it leads to fruitful research that would not otherwise be done.

Furthermore, the acceptance of the realist doctrine does not require that other views be rejected as wrong. They, too, reflect some aspects of reality and provide a way of approaching certain problems.

I propose that if we treat groups as real units or systems, if we cease to identify group phenomena with a particular personnel and with personality, if we cease to look for group phenomena in persons, and if we study groups for the sake of learning more about groups, only then will we begin to make real strides in a uniquely sociological problem.

SELECTED READINGS

Charles P. Loomis in *Social Systems* (Princeton, N.J.: D. Van Nostrand Co., Inc., 1960) has a cogent, extended treatment of social structure. Lloyd A. Fallers presents a stimulating, liberalized view of "structural-functional" analysis in *Bantu Bureaucracy* (Cambridge, England: W. Heffer and Sons, Ltd., 1960), especially in Chapter 1, "The Problem: Institutional Conflict and Change."

All of Talcott Parsons' work bears on the central issue of social structure. Two recent publications are *Structure and Process in Modern Societies* (New York: The Free Press of Glencoe, Inc., 1960) and a sourcebook of theories of human society edited by Parsons, Edward Shils, Kaspar D. Naegele, and Jesse

R. Pitts, *Theories of Society* (New York: The Free Press of Glencoe, 1961). Robert K. Merton, Leonard Broom, and Leonard S. Cottrell, Jr., have edited a book of readings, *Sociology Today: Problems and Prospects* (New York: Basic Books, 1959), that examines the whole sociological scene. Seymour Martin Lipset and Neil J. Smelser have edited a series of articles examining the course of sociology in the last decade, *Sociology, The Progress of a Decade* (Englewood Cliffs, N.J.: Prentice-Hall, Inc., 1961). Don Martindale examines the origins of social science and the development and schools of sociology in *The Nature and Types of Sociological Theory* (Boston: Houghton Mifflin, 1960).

Francis L. K. Hsu has a good discussion of basic concepts in "Structure, Function, Content, Process," *American Anthropologist*, 1959, and Fred W. Voget argues well for convergences in social scientific theory in his study "Man and Culture: An Essay in Changing Anthropological Interpretation," *American Anthropologist*, December, 1960.

Some support for the Stoodley paper can be found in "Sexual Differentiation of American and Filipino Children as Reflected in the Draw a Person Test," A. I. Rabin and Josefina A. Limuaco, *Journal of Social Psychology*, 1959.

2 *Aspects of Psychosocial Process*

THE READINGS in the first section indicated the analytical "reality" of social organization or social structure, but individuals are not woodenly tied to this social structure. They encounter social structure both internally and externally. The encounter may result in a variety of responses from the individual. It may result in a routine compliance that scarcely raises a ripple on the surface of personality process. This kind of behavior, as we have said, is not caused in the usual sense by personality processes but by our recognition of the modes of behavior that are current in our society. No issue is raised for the self. On the other hand, to go to the opposite extreme, the individual may make such an issue of the expected behavior that he refuses to follow the mode. Storm warnings are flying within the self. The range runs then from routine compliance to outright rebellion.

A model of psychosocial process must leave room for the dynamics of initiative both in social structure and in the self. The articles in this section all show an interest in this dynamic relation and thus give us a general orientation that can be useful for subsequent readings. The first group of articles indicates the importance for his behavior of the individual's conception of himself with reference to others. The study by Reckless, Dinitz, and Murray, "Self Concept as an Insulator against Delinquency," illustrates this proposition in the field of conforming and nonconforming behavior. Coates and Pellegrin show, with reference to executives and supervisors, not only that each group has an image of itself and of the other group but also that each group has rationalizations justifying one group's position with reference to the other. Melvin Seeman's article, "The Intellectual and the Language of Minorities," shows that the self-conceptions of intellectuals resemble those of Negroes and Jews in their responses to their status in the society. Seeman's undoubtedly rough measure of creativity among intellectuals suggests that these self-conceptions may impair creative behavior. Reeder, Donohue, and Biblarz show the relation between a person's self-conception and his conception of the opinion of others about him. In explaining their data, the authors touch on reference group theory, thus somewhat complicating the model used in the previous papers. This serves as a transition to the next group of studies.

Recent papers dealing with role performance have introduced an important element of dynamism into role performance. This dynamism is obtained by laying emphasis on the situation of action not so much as a stable referent for conformity but as a more or less stable referent for bargaining between relevant actors. Social action thus becomes a matter of negotiation within the field of resources and deprivations that define the situation. A serf in medieval Europe had little room for negotiation in bargaining with his lord, while the lord of the manor, on the other hand, had little need to negotiate, since the situation as defined gave him almost complete power over his serf. In the more usual situation there is ample room for negotiation, although actors in situations are seldom in positions of complete parity. A child in our society is not on a level of parity with the mother, but, nevertheless, has ample resources for bargaining and negotiating within limits. The same is true of the student in relation to the teacher. Goode's article indicates that the decrease of legitimacy in the Caribbean area indicates the need for a reformulation of Malinowski's dictum that societies require a "sociological father." He also suggests that the high rate of illegitimacy is related to important changes in the relevant bargaining position of the courtship partners. The element of bargaining or negotiation is emphasized also by Thompson and McEwen, although they are concerned with large scale organization. They see the defined situation, the organizational environment, as a source of strategy, a fund of alternatives. The analysis of Theodore M. Mills relates to deviance, but his analysis brings him to consideration of generalized models of the self-society relation. The analysis binds society and self into reciprocating systems, but room is made for innovation both on the side of the individual and of the group. Some of the concepts employed in this study, such, for instance, as "domain of demands," may prove useful to the student.

a) THE ROLE IMAGE AND THE SELF-IMAGE

WALTER C. RECKLESS, SIMON DINITZ, and ELLEN MURRAY

Self Concept as an Insulator against Delinquency

This study is concerned with sixth-grade boys[1] in the highest delinquency areas in Columbus, Ohio, who have not become delinquent and who are not expected to become delinquent. What insulates an early teen-age boy against delinquency? Is it possible to identify certain components that enable young adolescent boys to develop or maintain non-delinquent habits and patterns of behavior in the growing up process?

Methodology

In order to study the non-delinquent boy, all 30 sixth-grade teachers in schools located in the highest white delinquency areas in Columbus were asked to nominate those white boys in their school rooms who would not, in their opinion, ever experience police or juvenile court contact. Treating each nominee separately, the teachers were then re-

Reprinted from American Sociological Review, *December, 1956, pp. 744-746, by permission of the authors and the journal.*

Paper read at the annual meeting of the American Sociological Society, September, 1956. This research was supported by a grant from The Ohio State University Fund.

1. Sixth-grade students were selected for study because they represent the threshold age group for entry into legal and social delinquency. In Columbus, Ohio, the delinquency rate doubles between the ages of 11 and 12. For details on age and census tract rates see John S. Ely, *An Ecological Study of Juvenile Delinquency in Franklin County*, Master's Thesis, The Ohio State University, 1952.

quested to indicate their reasons for the selection of a particular boy. Of the eligible students, 192, or just over half, were selected and evaluated by their teachers as being "insulated" against delinquency. A check of police and juvenile court records revealed that 16 (8.3 per cent) of those nominated had some type of law enforcement record, and these boys were eliminated from further consideration. Repeated neighborhood visits failed to locate 51 others. In the remaining cases both the boy and his mother were interviewed.

The 125 "good" boys comprising the final sample were given a series of four self-administered scales to complete. These included, in somewhat modified form, (1) the delinquency proneness and (2) social responsibility scales of the Gough[2] California Personality Inventory, (3) an occupational preference instrument,[3] (4) and one measuring the boy's conception of self, his family and other interpersonal relations.[4] At the same time, though not in the presence of the nominee, the mother or mother-surrogate was interviewed with an open-ended schedule to determine the boy's developmental history, his patterns of association, and the family situation. (Now nearing completion is a comparable study of sixth-grade boys in the same classrooms who were nominated by the same teachers as being likely to come into contact with the police and juvenile court.)

Findings

An analysis of the scores made by these 125 nominees on the delinquency vulnerability (De) and social responsibility (Re) scales seemed to justify their selection as "good" boys. Out of a possible total (De) score of 54, scores ranged from a low of 4 to a high of 34 with a mean

2. For a detailed description of the delinquency proneness scale see Harrison G. Gough, "Systematic Validation of a Test for Delinquency," reprint of a paper delivered at the annual meeting of the American Psychological Association, September, 1954; Harrison G. Gough and Donald Peterson, "The Identification and Measurement of Predispositional Factors in Crime and Delinquency," *Journal of Consulting Psychology*, 16:1952, pp. 207-212; and Harrison G. Gough, "A Sociological Theory of Psychopathy," *American Journal of Sociology*, 53:1948, pp. 359-366. In correspondence with us, Gough suggested the inclusion of the social responsibility scale as a "partial index of the 'social control' factor in personality . . . (and) an index of delinquency proneness based upon both scales would be a better measure for your study." Both scales were used with Gough's expressed permission and consent.

3. This instrument was developed in a study of juvenile vulnerability to delinquency. See James E. Morlock, *Predicting Delinquency in a Homogeneous Group of Pre-Adolescent Boys*, Doctoral Dissertation, The Ohio State University, 1947.

4. This measure was based in part on the Glueck findings concerning family variables and delinquency. See Sheldon and Eleanor Glueck, *Unraveling Juvenile Delinquency*, New York: The Commonwealth Fund, 1950.

of 14.57 and a standard deviation of 6.4. This mean score was significantly lower than that of school behavior problem boys, young delinquents, or reformatory inmates investigated in other studies. In fact, the average De score of the sample subjects was below that obtained in all but one previous study using the same scale.[5]

For a twelve-year-old group, the nominees scored remarkably high on the social responsibility scale. The mean Re score for the group was 28.86 with a standard deviation of 3.60 and a range of 12 to 40 out of a possible 42 points. This mean score was appreciably higher than that achieved by school disciplinary cases, delinquents, and prisoners tested in other studies. The correlation between the two sets of scores was —.605, indicating a significant and negative relationship between delinquency vulnerability and social responsibility as measured by these instruments.

In response to self-evaluation items, the 125 boys portrayed themselves as law-abiding and obedient. Specifically, the vast majority defined themselves as being stricter about right and wrong than most people, indicated that they attempted to keep out of trouble at all costs and further indicated that they tried to conform to the expectations of their parents, teachers, and others.[6] The nominees did not conceive of themselves as prospects for juvenile court action or detention,[7] and they stated that their participation in such activities as stealing had been minimal and that their friends were either entirely or almost completely free of police and juvenile court contact.[8] As part of their conformity pattern, the respondents rarely played "hookey" from school and almost without exception indicated a liking for school. Finally, the "good" boys visualized themselves as being about average in ability, activity level, and aggressiveness. When asked "What do you think keeps boys out of trouble?" the respondents listed parental direction (a good home), non-deviant companions, and work, as well as other conventional answers. It would therefore appear that the internalization of these non-deviant attitudes played a significant role in the "insulation" of these boys.

Nominee perceptions of family interaction also appeared to be highly

5. Based on data furnished by Gough.

6. Nearly 60 per cent of the boys thought they were stricter about right and wrong than most people; 85 per cent tried to escape trouble at all costs; 81 per cent stressed their obedience to their parents' wishes, and 81 per cent were concerned with the reaction of friends and others to their behavior. These and other data were based on responses to items in one or more of the four instruments used.

7. For example, 70 per cent of the boys in answering the questions on the Morlock scale seemed certain that they would never be brought before the juvenile court; only one respondent believed he would have future contact with the court. Two-thirds indicated certainty about never being taken to jail. Some 57 per cent did not rule out the possibility of becoming policemen.

8. In only 12 per cent of the cases had any of the friends of these boys experienced police or juvenile court contact.

favorable. As noted in a previous paper, the 125 families were stable maritally, residentially, and economically.[9] There appeared to be close parental supervision of the boys' activities and associates, an intense parental interest in the welfare of the children, and a desire to indoctrinate them with non-deviant attitudes and patterns. This parental supervision and interest seemed to be the outstanding characteristic of the family profiles. It extended over the entire range of their sons' activities—from friendship patterns, leisure activities, and after school employment to movie attendance and the performance of well-defined duties at home. Thus, as regards companions for example, the mothers almost without exception stated that they knew the boys' friends, that these friends were good boys, and that, in fact, the boys couldn't have chosen better companions. The mothers also knew the whereabouts of their sons at almost all times and many insisted on this knowledge.

Despite this intensive supervision, the boys did not feel themselves to be unduly restricted. In general, the nominees appeared satisfied with the amount of parental affection and attention and with the quality of discipline and punishment given them. They viewed their home life as pleasant and their parents as understanding.

Low and high scorers on the delinquency proneness scale and their respective mothers did not differ significantly in their evaluations of these various aspects of family interaction. Of the 22 home background variables tested—ranging from the percentage of boys from broken homes to parental favoritism—none was found to be significantly related to the delinquency proneness scores. This finding was hardly surprising in view of the non-representative character of the sample group and the relatively small amount of variation in the family settings. It may also well be that in defining his interpersonal and family relationships favorably, the "good" boy, regardless of the degree of his "goodness" as measured by various scales, is in fact expressing the positive attitudes and perceptions that are important components in his "goodness."

While there was no appreciable variation in aspects of family interaction between the low and high scorers, the boys as a group and their mothers as a group did differ significantly in some of their evaluations. These differences were largely centered around the activity level of the boys, the definitions of the fairness and severity of parental punishment, and the amount of bickering in the home. Mothers thought their sons to be more active, punishment to be less frequent and severe, and parental tranquility to be more pervasive than did the nominees. Most significantly, perhaps, the mothers expressed less satisfaction with the role

9. For a complete discussion of the family backgrounds of the nominees see Walter C. Reckless, Simon Dinitz, and Ellen Murray, "The 'Good' Boy in a High Delinquency Area," *Journal of Criminal Law, Criminology, and Police Science,* 48 (August, 1957), pp. 18-26.

played by the boys' fathers than did the boys. Briefly, the mothers pictured their husbands as being relatively aloof and rigid in their affectional relationships with their sons. The nominees, however, could not differentiate between their parents in this regard.

These divergences in perceptions may largely reflect age, sex, and role differences in expectations of what constitutes satisfactory family relationships. Consequently, predictive tables based on the parents' conceptions of the boy and his relationships would necessarily be different in many particulars from those based on the boys' conceptions.

Conclusion

"Insulation" against delinquency on the part of these boys may be viewed as an on-going process reflecting an internalization of non-delinquent values and conformity to the expectations of significant others. Whether the subjects, now largely unreceptive to delinquent norms of conduct, will continue to remain "good" in the future remains problematic. The answer to this question, it is felt, will depend on their ability to maintain their present self-images in the face of mounting situational pressures.[10]

While this pilot study points to the presence of a socially acceptable concept of self as the insulator against delinquency, the research does not indicate how the boy in the high delinquency area acquired his self image. It may have been acquired by social definition of role from significant figures in his milieu, such as a mother, a relative, a priest, a settlement house worker, or a teacher. It might have been a by-product of effective socialization of the child, which had the good fortune of not misfiring. On the other hand, it may have been an outgrowth of discovery in social experience that playing the part of the good boy and remaining a good boy bring maximum satisfactions (of acceptance) to the boy himself. Finally, there is a strong suspicion that a well-developed concept of self as a "good boy" is the component which keeps middle- and upper-class boys, who live in the better neighborhoods, out of delinquency. The point is that this component seems to be strong enough to "insulate" the adolescent against delinquency in the unfavorable neighborhoods.

---

10. See Daniel Glaser, "Criminality, Theories and Behavioral Images," *American Journal of Sociology*, 61 (March, 1956), pp. 433-444.

CHARLES H. COATES
and ROLAND J. PELLEGRIN

Executives and Supervisors: Contrasting Self-Conceptions and Conceptions of Each Other

Cooley's "looking-glass self" and Mead's "taking the role of the generalized other" rank among the foremost concepts in sociology.[1] In spite of their utility and significance, however, these concepts have rarely been exploited in the investigation of why some individuals achieve more vertical occupational mobility and career success than others in the same or similar occupational environments.

Successful executives in business and industry have often been and are continually being studied through self-appraisals obtained by personal interviews and questionnaires.[2] Their success stories are widely publicized, and the top-level business and industrial executive has been popularized as an ideal type of successful American. From such self-appraisals by outstanding executives, so many generalizations have been made about "how to become successful" that it is often erroneously assumed that the means of achieving executive success have universal applicability. What is usually overlooked is that executive success, like leadership and success in other occupational fields, is subject to situational and environmental variability. It would therefore seem logical to study differential executive success situationally by asking top-level executives to appraise their "looking-glass selves," and to take the roles of "generalized others" on the top and bottom rungs of the executive ladder by appraising retrospectively their own personal attributes in contrast with those of subordinates in their own or similar occupational environments. It would also seem logical to compare these top-level

Reprinted from the American Sociological Review *(April, 1957), pp. 217-220, by permission of the authors and the journal.*

Revised version of paper read at the annual meeting of the American Sociological Society, September, 1956.

1. Charles H. Cooley, *Human Nature and the Social Order*, New York: Scribner's, 1902; and George H. Mead, *Mind, Self and Society* (Charles W. Morris, ed.), Chicago: University of Chicago Press, 1934.

2. A recent example of such research is found in W. Lloyd Warner and James C. Abegglen, *Big Business Leaders in America*, New York: Harper and Brothers, 1955.

appraisals oriented downward with similar lower-level appraisals oriented upward.

Essentially, this was the approach employed in a comparative study made in 1954 and 1955 of 50 top-level executives in 30 large and bureaucratically structured business, industrial, governmental, and educational organizations, and 50 first line supervisors in the same or similar occupational environments.[3] The setting of the study was a dynamic Southern community, fictitiously called "Bigtown," which had experienced within a span of 30 years a growth to a population of 200,000 as a result of industrial and business expansion. The confidential personal interview was used in studying the comparative samples of top- and low-level individuals in management, all of whom had long occupational histories. Because of the effective matching of the samples on the basis of age and long occupational histories, the retrospective appraisals had a unique quality of depth in time. The confidential nature of the study made possible considerable interviewer-interviewee rapport, which brought forth a wealth of subjective data. Since standardized interview schedules were utilized, comparative analysis of the data was facilitated.

The following analysis is limited to the executives' and the supervisors' self-conceptions and conceptions of each other. In eliciting these self- and other-conceptions, open-ended questions were utilized on the interview schedule, and no preconceived list of desirable or undesirable attributes was employed. The attributes presented below are derived from a content analysis of equivalent terms most frequently mentioned by interviewees. There was virtually no disagreement concerning the attributes of executives and supervisors, although some respondents listed more attributes than others. Each attribute was mentioned independently by at least 15 of the 50 persons involved in each self- or other-rating.

Results

Most executives conceived of themselves as possessing several of the dynamic personal attributes revealed in Henry's well-known study of 100 executives in the Chicago business community.[4] Among these were:

3. Further information on the scope, method, and content of the study is presented in the following papers by the authors: "Absentee-Owned Corporations and Community Power Structure," *American Journal of Sociology*, 61 (March, 1956), pp. 413-419; "Executives and Supervisors: A Situational Theory of Differential Occupational Mobility," *Social Forces*, 31 (December, 1956), pp. 121-126; and "Executives and Supervisors: Contrasting Definitions of Career Success," *Administrative Science Quarterly*, 1 (March, 1957), pp. 506-517.

4. William E. Henry, "The Business Executive: The Psychodynamics of a Social Role," *American Journal of Sociology*, 54 (January, 1949), pp. 286-291.

strong achievement desire, high mobility drive, sympathetic conception of authority, considerable ability to organize, firm decisiveness, strong self-structure, much aggressive activity, and direct orientation toward reality. Mention of these executive attributes was to be expected, but of more interest were the main distinctions that executives made between themselves, their associates, and first-line supervisors they had known through the years.

These comparative self- and other-appraisals usually began with a statement of qualities that executives possess and that supervisors either lack or possess to a lesser degree. Among the distinctions most frequently made by executives between themselves and supervisors were: more energy, alertness, and initiative; aggressive as opposed to submissive attitudes; more understanding of and ability to get along with and manipulate people; greater willingness to assume responsibilities and make decisions; greater ability to deal with and impress superiors; better judgment and foresight; more magnetic, well-rounded, projective personalities; more tact and poise; better problem-solving ability; more adaptability to changing situations; more determination and strength of personal character; different definitions of the meaning of success; greater ability to sell themselves and their ideas, and to get things done through group effort; more education and training; different occupational and social contacts and opportunities; different loyalties and job interests. Illustrative of the self- and other-conceptions of the executives are the following:

Executive A: Successful executives are not "born," or "made" in college, but are products of their social environments. Compared to low level supervisors they have much more ability, personality, human understanding, and motivation. They have different attitudes and values and different definitions of organizational and personal success. Low level men simply lack the inner determination to climb further up the executive ladder.

Executive B: The main distinctions are: "spark" or lack of it, willingness to accept responsibility and make decisions or the lack of it, ability to handle people or the lack of it. I can't define "spark," but you know it when you see it. Maybe it is a combination of personality and drive.

Executive C: The big difference in the two levels is in the ability to analyze the motives of others and to foresee their reactions. Low level men are unable to realize why people react as they do. Because of this they lack the ability to plant ideas in others and get them to do things.

Like the executives whom Henry studied, these executives placed high values on achievement and self-directedness, but they may also pay a high price for holding these values.[5] The executives were asked to give

5. *Ibid.*, p. 291.

their conceptions of the penalties and sacrifices associated with the achievement of top-level executive success. Among those most frequently mentioned were: adverse effect of a pressure environment on personal health; considerably more worry than the average professional person; lack of time for recreation and leisure; insufficient opportunity for normal family life; a certain amount of loneliness associated with an isolated position; feeling that hard work would lead to even harder work; recurring invasions of personal privacy; forced suppression of personal desires; continuous disruption of personal plans; constant fear of making wrong decisions. One executive stated:

Executive D: This corporation has been reorganized just so I could turn over the presidency to a younger man. I wanted to get rid of all of these responsibilities, worries, and pressures. The ups and downs in the competitive business world are terrific. You're always on the 'phone, days and nights and holidays. I've got to get more time with my family and more time for recreation before it is too late. I haven't had a vacation in four years, and the only way to get one is to just pack up and leave town.

In order to compare the self- and other-conceptions of the executives oriented downward, the supervisors were invited to give similar self- and other-conceptions oriented upward.[6] When asked to make the main distinctions between themselves, their supervisory associates, and executives they had known through the years, the great majority rather surprisingly tended to concede to executives greater amounts of the same personal attributes in which executives had tended to claim superiority. What was of more interest, however, were their reasons for conceding to executives this superiority. Their concessions seemed to have resulted not only from their conceptions of their own personal limitations and those of their associates, but also from their conceptions of the differential role expectations of executives and supervisors. Supervisors tended to be acutely aware of the handicaps of their socio-cultural backgrounds, education and training, and occupational opportunities.[7] As derivatives of these self-conceived personal limitations, they tended to concede to executives: better social and educational backgrounds; more ambition and motivation; higher level attitudes, values and life goals; more energy, alertness, and initiative; better understanding of human nature; better rounded, more magnetic personalities; more ability to handle large numbers of people; more ability to solve problems and make long-range plans; more willingness to delegate authority, accept

6. See Robert Dubin, "Upward Orientation Toward Superiors" in his *Human Relations in Administration*, Englewood Cliffs, N. J.: Prentice-Hall, 1951, pp. 272-273.

7. The effects of these factors upon career patterns are analyzed in the authors' "Executives and Supervisors: A Situational Theory of Differential Occupational Mobility," *op. cit.*

responsibility, and make decisions. Illustrative self- and other-conceptions of the supervisors follow:

Supervisor A: Top men are totally different from supervisors. Top men have better social backgrounds and education and thus have different abilities and goals. Most supervisors want to get so high and no higher because they don't want big responsibilities. They just want to carry out instructions without having to make decisions.

Supervisor B: Top level men are like Army Generals. They sit down, make the plans, and issue the orders, though in doing so they are thoughtful, courteous, understanding, and helpful. Supervisors carry out the orders like Army Sergeants. Some are hard-boiled, and some are soft-boiled. Some are drivers, and some are leaders. It all depends on how they think the boss wants them to behave.

Supervisor C: The top level is better at getting jobs done through group effort because they have more flexible, more magnetic personalities. They are the better planners, organizers, coordinators, decision-makers, and administrators. That's what top men are for, anyway.

To throw further light upon their conceptions of the roles of top level executives, the supervisors were asked the question, "If you could start all over again, would you like to become a top level executive?" The great majority of the supervisors stated emphatically that they would *not.* Usually they gave as their reasons, "too many worries, headaches, and responsibilities." As one veteran supervisor expressed it:

Supervisor D: Who, me? Hell no! Not way up top. Look at our head man. He has a wonderful education, makes a lot of money, and has a big reputation. But that kind of a job commands a man's whole being, day and night, and almost commands his soul. He's always contending with worries, responsibilities, and decisions. The directors hound him to death. With the power and the glory go the headaches and the ulcers. One of my top level friends died the other day of "industrial suicide." As for me, I'd rather have a happy, pleasant life. What's the use of killing yourself?

Thus, there appeared in the self- and other-conceptions of supervisors an acute awareness, not only of their own personal limitations, but also of the penalties and sacrifices associated with top level executive roles.

Implications

1. Superiors tend to judge their subordinates in terms of their own self-images and to appraise low-level role performance by comparing it with their own high-level role performance.

2. Subordinates tend to judge their superiors in terms of their own images of high-level role expectations, and to account for their own personal limitations in terms of socio-cultural backgrounds and conceptions of low-level role expectations.

3. Both superiors and subordinates tend to be aware of the rewards, penalties, and sacrifices associated with high-level roles. Such an awareness differentially influences achievement desires on the two levels.

4. Such self-conceived achievement desires positively or negatively affect role performance and therefore differentially influence life-span career success.[8]

Further study of comparative samples of individuals at different levels in various occupational hierarchies may be helpful in increasing understanding of such factors as differential motivation, role performance, and status striving.

8. On this point, see the discussion in *ibid.* and in our "Executives and Supervisors: Contrasting Definitions of Career Success," *op. cit.*

MELVIN SEEMAN

The Intellectual and the Language of Minorities

I

THE signs of deep concern about the contemporary position of the intellectual in America are not hard to find. To be sure, as Merle Curti has stressed in his presidential address to the American Historical Society, anti-intellectualism—in one form or another—has a long history in American life.[1] But in recent years the situation of the intellectual has not resembled the mere continuation of a somewhat consistent and

Reprinted from "The Intellectual and the Language of Minorities," by Melvin Seeman, The American Journal of Sociology, *July, 1958, pp. 25-35, by permission of The University of Chicago Press. Copyright 1958 by the University of Chicago.*

1. "Intellectuals and Other People," *American Historical Review,* LX (1955), 259-82.

historically routine negativism. The current sense of urgency regarding the definition of the intellectual's role has found expression in a wide variety of places: from *Time* magazine's alarm about the "wide and unhealthy gap" between the American intellectuals and the people to a series of symposiums which have appeared in the *Journal of Social Issues,* in the book edited by Daniel Bell entitled *The New American Right,* and in the thoughtful British journal, *Encounter.*[2]

Yet, in spite of this volume of words, and the talent of those involved, it is still possible to agree with Milton Gordon's remark that "the man of ideas and the arts has rarely been studied seriously as a social type by professional students of society."[3] Whether, as some have argued, this retreat from self-analysis reflects a basic disorder in the scientific study of man is debatable enough; but the fact is clear that the research techniques which have been applied to nearly everybody else—from the hobo to the business elite—have rarely been applied to ourselves.[4]

This paper is a report on one such study of ourselves, its aim being to determine how intellectuals in the current social climate deal with their identity as intellectuals and, beyond that, to suggest what difference it may make if this identity is handled in different ways.

The empirical base for this report was obtained through relatively unstructured interviews (on the average about one hour in length) with all the assistant professors teaching in the humanities and social science departments of a midwestern university.[5] These interviews were not content-analyzed in any statistical sense but were simply examined (as the illustrations in the next section will show) for patterns of response.

The total number of persons interviewed was forty. They came, in

---

2. Cf. S. S. Sargent and T. Brameld (eds.), "Anti-intellectualism in the United States," *Journal of Social Issues,* Vol. II, No. 3 (1955); D. Bell (ed.), *The New American Right* (New York: Criterion Books, 1955); and *Encounter,* Vols. IV and V (1955).

3. "Social Class and American Intellectuals," *A.A.U.P. Bulletin,* XL (1955), 517.

4. The roster of those who have recently written, more or less directly, on the problem of the intellectual would comprise a list of the contemporary great and near-great in a variety of humanistic and social science fields (not to mention the physical sciences): e.g., Schlesinger and Hofstadter in history; Parsons and Riesman in sociology; Tolman and Fromm in psychology. Two well-known older works that embody the spirit of self-study are those by Znaniecki (*The Social Role of the Man of Knowledge*) and Logan Wilson (*The Academic Man*). There have, of course, been many commentaries on the intellectual, especially in the more or less Marxist journals; but I am referring here to the more formally analytic mode of investigation.

5. It seemed wiser, with a limited sample, to hold staff level constant rather than sample all levels of permanent staff. The assistant-professor group was chosen for two reasons: (1) it was large enough to provide suitable frequencies, yet small enough to be manageable without taxing time and finances, and (2) it is, in the institution studied, basically a tenure group like the higher ranks but presumably less involved in official committee work and graduate work and therefore more likely to give the time required for interviewing.

the number indicated, from the following departments: Economics (7), English (6), German (2), History (4), Law (1), Mathematics (3), Philosophy (4), Political Science (2), Psychology (4), Romance Languages (3), and Sociology-Anthropology (4). The sample included no one from the physical or biological sciences, from the engineering and applied fields, or from the creative arts; and, when an appropriate level in the staff hierarchy had been selected, there was no further sampling problem. Cooperation was good: of a total of forty-five persons listed in the university directory at the assistant-professor level, only one refused to be interviewed (and four were unavailable because of assignments out of the city).

The procedure in the interviews was consistent though not standardized. There was no attempt to get answers to preformed questions. We engaged, rather, in a conversation regarding a letter which outlined a plan for exploring the situation of the intellectual today. The letter was not mailed; it was read by the respondent at the start of the interview and served in this way as a common stimulus object. The body of the letter, which carried my signature, follows:

> There is considerable evidence (though debatable evidence, to be sure) that the role of the intellectual has become increasingly problematic in American life. Such evidence includes: (1) the widespread expression of anti-intellectual attitudes; (2) the increasing pressure for conformity in intellectual work; and (3) the typical isolation of the intellectual in community life. These current trends are presumably matters of considerable moment to university people who are uniquely concerned with the social conditions under which intellectual activity is carried forward.
>
> It seems to me that some effort to assess the problem among ourselves is in order; and that such an effort might proceed initially by calling together small, informal groups of faculty members to clarify issues and get an exchange of viewpoints. This letter comes as an invitation to you to participate in one of these discussions on the current situation of the intellectual. The discussion would include four or five other persons from the humanities and social sciences, and would take roughly one hour of your time. Since several discussions are planned, I would consider it part of my responsibility to provide you with some type of analytical summary of the sessions held—in effect, a research report. *Let me emphasize that the purpose of these discussions is not to canvass possible lines of action, but to achieve a clarification of issues on matters which are clearly controversial.*
>
> Would you indicate whether you wish to be included in the list of discussants by returning this letter to me with the appropriate notation?[6]

6. The italicized portion of this letter was underlined in the original; but in one-half of the cases a more action-oriented statement was substituted for the underlined portion given here. The two types of letters were randomly alternated in the interviewing program. In the second version, the underlined sentence read: "*Let me emphasize that the purpose of these discussions is not only to achieve a clarification of issues on matters which are clearly controversial; but also to canvass suitable lines of action.*" In all cases, at the end of the interview, the respondent was asked to comment on what his reaction

After the respondent had read the letter, he was encouraged to comment freely on any aspect of it; then each of the three points listed in the first paragraph of the letter was discussed; and, finally, I raised the question, "Do you classify yourself as an intellectual?"

The latter question raises for us, no less than for the respondents, the matter of definition. As a first approximation, I defined the intellectuals as a group for whom the analysis of ideas in their own right (i.e., for no pragmatic end) is a central occupation. The group I chose to interview was taken as a sample of intellectuals, in spite of the fact that some would surely not qualify on more stringent criteria (e.g., their degree of dedication to the life of the mind or the quality of their intellectual work). The sample is defensible, however, on the ground that by social definition—whether he or his colleagues prefer it or not—the university professor teaching in the humanities or social sciences is probably the prime case of intellectual endeavor (i.e., of nonpragmatic and ideological pursuits). Thus, we are concerned with the self-portrait of those who, by social definition at least, are intellectuals.[7]

---

to the letter would have been if the alternative not presented to him had been used. The variation in letter style is mentioned here for the sake of completeness; it is not directly relevant to the treatment of the interviews reported here. The proposed discussions never took place, owing to both the press of time and a certain lack of enthusiasm—a lack which the remainder of this paper may make more understandable.

7. This assertion, obviously, is an assumption, since the public definition of an intellectual is not a matter of empirical record, so far as I know. One could hold, further, that, if they are not so designated, they should be—that, in the ideal university, the group I have described would be identifiable as intellectuals in the sense of my stated definition. That definition has its difficulties, to be sure. For example, one might ask why an intellectual cannot believe that (or behave as if) ideas are of more than simply aesthetic interest, that ideas have consequences, and that the analysis of them serves a "pragmatic" end. A host of names come to mind of persons who would appear to have indorsed this view and whom we would presumably not wish to dismiss as intellectuals—e.g., Marx, Lenin, Jefferson, among others. The best provisional answer to this, I should think, would be that being an intellectual is not the designation for a person but for a role and that many who play the intellectual role, and play it well, are also deeply involved with the course of societal and individual development. One does not need to say, therefore, that Marx was not an intellectual because he was also a revolutionary.

In any event, though this definition does not thoroughly solve matters, it does suggest a line of approach and clarifies, perhaps, the senses in which our sample may or may not be considered as members of the class. To my mind it is much less important to determine whether they are, so to speak, "in" or "out" of the category than it is to recognize that they are candidates in several senses: (1) in public definitions of them; (2) in their personal self-definitions; and (3) in the definition of a university ideal. The issue is nicely captured in Randall Jarrell's fictional *Pictures from an Institution*, where he says of an academic man: "He had never been what intellectuals consider an intellectual, but other people had thought him one, and he had had to suffer the consequences of their mistake" (p. 110).

II

In a certain sense the chief finding of this study consisted of a "surprise": the unanticipated discovery of the extent to which these intellectuals use the language and mechanisms of minority status to describe themselves and their situation. It may be suggested that this should have been no surprise—that arguments quite consistent with this have been advanced in many places. And to some degree that is true.

In a recent well-publicized paper in *Harper's*, for example, a French writer had this to say:

> It seems to me that the attitude of the American intellectual in comparison with his European counterpart is based on frustration and an inferiority complex. I am continually meeting people who tell me that the intellectual in Europe enjoys a position which, if not happier, is at least more dignified than that of the intellectual in America. . . . Whose fault is this? They go on to tell me that the fault rests with the American people, who have no appreciation for things of the intellect. I wonder whether it is not also in great measure the fault of the American intellectuals themselves.[8]

In a similar vein Riesman and Glazer have commented that "the opinion leaders among the educated classes—the intellectuals and those who take their cues from them—have been silenced more by their own feelings of inadequacy and failure than by direct intimidation."[9] And Marcus Cunliffe, describing the United States intellectual for *Encounter* magazine, concludes: "Altogether, there has been an unfortunate loss of self-respect. Some intellectuals have felt that, wrong about communism, they must be occupationally prone to be wrong about everything."[10]

But the point is that comments of this kind do not constitute evidence; and, indeed, it is possible, if one questions the evidence, to treat such comments themselves as reflections of a kind of minority-style indictment of one's own group. (Like the Jew who agrees that "we" are too clannish, the intellectual says that "we" are too weak in will.) Furthermore, the comments we have cited do not provide a systematic view of the specific forms of minority language which intellectuals employ in discussing themselves. Our empirical task here is to indicate that such minority references are surprising, indeed, in their frequency and to make a start toward a categorization of the forms these references take.[11]

---

8. R. L. Bruckberger, "An Assignment for Intellectuals," *Harper's*, CCXII (1956), 69.

9. D. Riesman and N. Glazer, "Intellectuals and the Discontented Classes," *Partisan Review*, XXII (1955), 50.

10. "The Intellectuals: II. The United States," *Encounter*, XX (1955), 31.

11. A word is in order about the meaning of "minority" and the occasion for

The clearest of these forms may be labeled *the direct acceptance of majority stereotypes.* Like the Negroes who have accepted the whites' definition of color and who choose "light" among themselves, our respondents appear eager to validate the outsider's negative view of them. One need only read these forty protocols to emerge with a collective self-portrait of the soft, snobbish, radical, and eccentric intellectual who is asocial, unreliable, hopelessly academic, and a bit stupid to boot. It is impossible to cite here the evidence for all this; but each of the stereotypes in the previous sentence has a parallel affirmation in the interview material. These affirmations are, to be sure, frequently hedged with restrictions and limitations—we are dealing, after all, with a group of highly trained qualifiers. But the significant thing is that the respondents take this opportunity to affirm the stereotype; and this affirmation is typically set in a context which makes it clear that the stereotype, rather than the qualification, has a competing chance to govern behavior. Let me give some examples:

If there is anti-intellectualism in our community, I feel frankly we are to blame. If we can't throw off our infernal need for preaching and dictating, they have a right to damn us, and we have no answer but our human fallibility [C-1].[12]

It's pretty difficult for the intellectual to mix with people. They feel ill at ease. Many intellectuals are not very approachable; perhaps his training is not

"surprise." On the latter I am aware of the fact that many occupational groups (and certainly "notorious" ones—e.g., policemen, farmers, or traveling salesmen) develop somewhat negative images of themselves. But two special conditions make this case, it seems to me, somewhat different. First, we are dealing with a high status group (note, for example, their generally high placement in the North-Hatt prestige scale); and, second, we are dealing with a group whose very function, in good part, is the objective analysis of society and its products. On these grounds, I would argue that it is not enough to dismiss the problem by saying that all occupations reflect negative self-images or that the problem approach in the stimulus letter occasioned the results obtained. The question is: What occupations have stereotypes about them, in what degree, and how are these stereotypes handled by the incumbents, with what consequences? This is the broader problem to which this paper is addressed.

With regard to "minority": I use it here to designate a group against which categorical discrimination is practiced. A minority, in this view, is determined not by size but by the behavior of being subjected to categorical discrimination. It should be clear, however, that I am not attempting to prove that intellectuals *are* a minority in this sense but that they use the typical language and forms of the classical minority groups in their self-descriptions.

12. The source of each quotation from the interviews is identified by an assigned case number so that the reader may note the spread of the illustrations. Departmental identifications are avoided, though these would be of some interest, to preserve anonymity. There is, I presume, every reason to believe that the frequency and subtlety of minority responses will vary among universities and departments—by region, eminence, and the like. But it also seems reasonable to believe that the bulk of American universities are not substantially different from the one involved here.

complete enough. The intellectual may be more to blame for that than anyone else [C-2].

My general attitude is that some of the intellectuals are so concerned with academic freedom that it kind of tires me. And, I think, this sometimes adds up to wanting more freedom than anybody else—the kind of freedom to be irresponsible. [And later, when asked whether the letter should include the action alternative, this subject said:] It shouldn't be in there, because basically I think that except in the most long-run sense there is not a thing you can do. Maybe we can breed a new line of professors [C-3].

We could go on here, if space permitted, about "the snobbishness we are all guilty of" and about the "queer birds" who "make a profession of being different" and "don't have sense enough to pour sand out of a boot" (these quotations coming from four different protocols). This direct acceptance by intellectuals of the negative stereotype regarding intellectuals follows the pattern of the minority "self-hate" which Lewin has described in the case of the anti-Semitic Jew[13] and which has been clearly expressed in Negro color attitudes.[14]

A second, and somewhat less extreme, variety of minority attitude may be labeled *the concern with in-group purification.* This label points to language and behavior which are guided by the idea that the minority's troubles are rooted in the misguided ways of a small fraction among them. The parallel with traditional minorities reads: for the Jews, it is the "bad" Jew—the one who is, indeed, aggressive and loud—who breeds anti-Semitism; and, for the intellectuals, it is the radical, asocial types who are responsible for the group's difficulty. Thus, on the radical issue, one respondent, speaking of his effort to establish a research contact downtown, said:

I realized we had one or two strikes against us because we were from the university. We had to have people vouch for us. We don't enjoy the best reputation down there; we're blamed for the actions of a few who make radical speeches and seem to overgeneralize [C-4].

Another respondent, speaking of an "extreme liberal" in his college, remarked:

I've got nothing against it, but the average man might translate this [liberalism] over to our college. In this sense, he does a slight disservice to the college [C-5].

---

13. K. Lewin, *Resolving Social Conflicts* (New York: Harper & Bros., 1948), pp. 186-200.

14. M. Seeman, "Skin Color Values in Three All-Negro School Classes," *American Sociological Review*, XI (1946), 315-21.

Similarly, on scores other than radicalism there are expressions of the view that the position of the intellectuals turns on the "impure" behavior of the intellectual himself. One respondent, discussing anti-intellectualism in general, remarked that we could lick the problem:

> If we had people getting out and who really did mix, as speakers and members. . . . I've worried about this: would I be willing to be in an organization if I were only a member? We get to be president and vice-president all the time. It doesn't do any good to be in and be officers; in order to get over the thought of us as intellectual snobs, we have to be satisfied to be just members [C-6].

This quotation highlights one interesting result of this concern with the "impure"—and a result which, again, has a clear minority flavor. The intellectual becomes involved in the need to prove that the impurity really is not there (or, at the very least, that the intellectual in question is not one of the "impure" few). We are familiar with the Jewish person who is inordinately careful to demonstrate in his own behavior that Jews as a group are not what the stereotype says; and Anatole Broyard has nicely described the various forms that Negro "inauthenticity" of the same type may take (e.g., what he calls "role inversion" is a careful and extreme negation of precisely those qualities embodied in the Negro stereotype—"cool" music and passive behavior, for example, being a negation of the primitive, hot, carefree quality in the Negro stereotype).[15]

The interviews reveal a similar concern with disproving the stereotype. Thus, one respondent, discussing possible action alternatives, commented:

> We could, of course, go out and make talks to various groups—show them that intellectuals really aren't bad guys [C-7].

Another, speaking about the isolation of the intellectual, said:

> Well, in neighborhood isolation, there's a lot of it due to their initial reaction —when they find out you're a professor they slightly withdraw, but, if you continue to make connections, then they find out you're a human being [C-5].

Still another person commented:

> If we mixed more, and became known as people as well as college teachers, maybe it would be better. Frequently, the antipathy to college teachers melts when they meet you personally; though we do have a tendency to carry our classroom personality into other areas [C-8].

A third major category of minority-like response may be titled *the approval of conformity*. In a certain sense, of course, the pattern just described is a specialized form of conformity; for its main aim is to

15. "Portrait of the Inauthentic Negro," *Commentary*, X (1950), 56-64.

emphasize the conventional as against the divergent aspects of the intellectual's behavior. But the pressure for conformity goes beyond this. It involves the same kind of passive, conservative, and attention-avoiding behavior that Lewin has described as prototypical for minority leaders, his "leaders from the periphery."[16] And, in the long run, this pressure for conformity leads to assimilationism—to the very denial of any significant observable differences on which minority status may rest. As far as the more traditional minorities are concerned, the classic Adorno volume on prejudice and personality has put one part of the conformist case as follows:

> Since acceptance of what is like oneself and rejection of what is different is one feature of the prejudiced outlook [i.e., of the authoritarian personality], it may be that members of minority groups can in limited situations and for some period of time protect themselves and gain certain advantages by conforming in outward appearance as best they can with the prevailing ways of the dominant group.[17]

As with these minorities, we find that there is considerable commitment to conformity among intellectuals and that this is expressed variously as a need to adjust, to avoid controversy, or to assimilate and deny differences entirely. Thus, one respondent, discussing the conformity question raised in the letter, said:

> On that, I can't say I've experienced it. I'm in a pretty safe field. . . . [He then described a book of readings he had collected and said that there was a short passage from a well-known writer which had been taken out before publication.] Theres no use stirring up trouble. I don't think it was a lack of courage on my part. We thought—that is, the editor and I—that it was too touchy. It's a very beautiful thing, but we took it out [C-9].

Another individual, discussing the community life of the intellectual, noted that they often do not take an active part and added:

> Part of that is good, in that they are lending the prestige of the university when they do take part, and shouldn't be doing that. I don't want to be written up in the paper as Professor X of university holding a certain opinion. I've deliberately refrained from expressing political opinion [C-5].

Still others appear to argue for conformity by denying that there is a difference to which the notion of "intellectual" points:

> I don't feel any different from my electrician-neighbor [C-10].
>
> I get a kind of inferiority complex if they call me "professor"; I know that my work with the intellect is on the same level in the eyes of the man in the street as, say, a chain-store manager [C-11].

16. *Op. cit.*, p. 196.

17. T. W. Adorno *et al.*, *The Authoritarian Personality* (New York: Harper & Bros., 1950), p. 974.

Or else there is insistence that it is important for the intellectual to assimilate or disguise himself more successfully. Thus, one respondent, speaking of occasions when he makes public addresses, said:

> When I go out and meet these people, I try to fit myself into their realm, into the climate of the various groups [C-12].

Another gave, as part of his recipe for the intellectual's behavior, the directive:

> He should adjust his personality so he can mix in better with the person who isn't an intellectual [C-2].

And one I have quoted before, speaking of the intellectual's isolation in community life, said:

> You must make concessions. I would find it pretty hard to have contacts, for example, in places like Wilder's *Our Town* or Anderson's small Ohio town, but I couldn't accuse the people in the town of being anti-intellectual; it's probably my fault. If you make a certain amount of concession, you will find a way [C-11].

There are other comments which are less clear in their conformist implications—for example, more than faintly guilty remarks to the effect that "my neighbors see me home in the early afternoon and wonder just what it is I do in my job" (C-13). On the whole, there is considerable evidence in these protocols that the typical minority response of conformity is found in a variety of forms among intellectuals.[18]

The fourth category of response represents the extreme of minority assimilation from the standpoint of the individual, namely, *the denial of group membership*. Like the name-changing Jew and the Negro who "passes," many intellectuals find means to hide or escape their unwelcome identity. An interviewee nicely described this pattern as follows:

> One consequence of anti-intellectualism is for some intellectuals to deny that they are intellectuals. This is a behavioral denial; it's part of the psycho-

---

18. Two of the respondents themselves commented on this "trimming of sails" in the university setting. One, for example, after noting an increase in anti-intellectual pressures, said:

"If you work at the university, you want the outside to be as non-controversial as possible; to say, 'Look at me, I'm just like anybody else.' This is part of the general line of not hurting the university by getting in the news in negative ways" (C-14).

Another person, in similar vein, remarked:

"The intellectual is assuming more of the role of the non-intellectual and seeks to be a part of the gang—denies that he's different" (C-15).

logical revolution, the adjustment trend. . . . The pressure to be well-adjusted is high, and so he becomes non-intellectual and begins to deny in some respects that he is an intellectual [C-15].

The evidence in the interviews indicates that the retreat from membership is a substantial one and takes many forms. Indeed, one of the real surprises, during the course of these interviews, was the rarity of real acceptance of intellectual status. This non-acceptance is revealed in several ways. First, there is the frequency with which this freely offered remark appears: "Intellectuals, I hate the word!" Second, there are the direct denials to the question, "Do you consider yourself an intellectual?" A complete listing of the protocol responses on this point would reveal a quite consistent, though subtly varied, pattern of maneuvering, all aimed at being counted out—the kind of "Who, me?" response one gets from the obviously guilty.[19] Thus, one respondent said:

> That's a word that always does bother me. I don't think of myself so. It's a self-conscious word that sets us apart from the rest of the population. The only thing that sets us apart, in fact, is that we have gone to school longer than some, and there are doctors who have gone longer and we don't consider them intellectuals [C-10].

Another said:

> I don't apply it to myself. I never use it myself. It's sort of snobbish [C-17].

And still another:

> I would [use the designation "intellectual"] in the professional sense only. . . . Professionally, I suppose we can't avoid it. Only in the very narrow professional sense, in the sense that we are trying to improve the intellect of students, I suppose it applies. I don't see how a university professor can escape the narrow meaning of the term [C-1].

And, finally, one respondent clearly recognized the social definition of himself yet reflected no eagerness in his personal definition:

> I suppose I would [consider myself an intellectual]. . . . I don't know if I am twenty-four hours a day, but still I suppose my work would be classified or considered an intellectual. . . . I teach the best I can, and certainly I'm classified as an intellectual by the community, my neighbors, and my colleagues [C-9].

A third kind of denial of membership is shown in the efforts that are made to avoid having one's affiliation publicly known. Thus, one respondent said:

19. Even where there is acceptance of the "intellectual" label, there is sometimes a suspicious belligerence about it. One respondent, who vigorously denied the validity of the view embodied in the stimulus letter and felt that anti-intellectualism was a fictitious problem, said: "You need to live your life as if you were proud of it—talk it up" (C-16).

When I'm away from the university, I usually have plenty of dirt under my nails, or I'm getting a harvest. Some of us fool ourselves into believing that the stain of our profession doesn't follow us. I can work with a carpenter for several weeks, and he has no notion I'm a university professor. I take a foolish pride, I suppose, in this [C-1].

Another remarked:

By training we get so we show contempt for those who overgeneralize, as in the Rotary, and we don't want to be in arguments all the time so we stay away. And how often do we go out of the way to announce that we're college professors. I don't conceal it; but I don't volunteer it. It would change your relation to the group [C-4].

Thus, in one way or another, many of our respondents indicate that they do not cherish either their name or their identity as intellectuals; and they adopt a language of evasion and anonymity which is minority-like, indeed. Though one may argue that this rejection of the name is not, after all, so terribly important, it seems to me more reasonable, in this case, to see the "naming trouble" as an essential part of the status involved.[20]

The fifth, and last, category of minority-like response can be designated *the fear of group solidarity*. This label indicates behavior whose essential function is similar to the conformist response; namely, behavior calculated to keep the majority's attention off the minority as such. In our intellectuals this typically takes the form of strong resistance to any clearly identifiable group action on the group's problems; the answer lies, rather, in individual goodness. One respondent, in fact, while stating the case against group action, made the minority tie himself:

The notion of action involves the whole place of the intellectual in society. In addition, direct action puts us in the position of special pleading. It's like a Jew going out and talking about anti-Semitism [C-7].

Another said:

Individual action seems more feasible. One has to measure one's forces and deploy them properly. . . . If you try to organize a society for X, Y, or Z, and you have the right people on the letterhead, maybe you're O.K.; but otherwise you're considered radical. Many things can be carried out without anybody knowing there is an organization [C-18].

---

20. On a similar point Everett Hughes has written in an essay titled "What's in a Name": "Words are weapons. As used by some people the word 'Hebrew,' for example, is a poisoned dart. When a word is so expressively used, we are face to face with no simple matter of social politics, but with part of the social process itself. This is, in part, what Durkheim had in mind in his long discussion of collective symbols and concepts. Words, he pointed out, are not merely something that happens along with the social process, but are its very essence. Naming is certainly part of the social process in inter-ethnic and racial relations" (*Where Peoples Meet* [New York: Free Press, 1952], p. 139).

Still another remarked:

> I'm frankly very much afraid of any action that has the label of the organized action of the intellectuals—not afraid of what they might do, but of public reaction. It ought to be unorganized [C-19].

Many of those interviewed seem committed to "having an effect the individual way" and are against "forming an organization that's militant." They wish, in a certain sense, to be (as one respondent [C-20] described himself) "the kind of social actionist who never appears to be one." I am interested here not in asserting that the strategy of organizational effort is a sounder strategy but in noting that the arguments against it frequently reflect a desire—common in other minorities—not to become too visible or too aggressive in one's own interest.

III

Neither the quotations nor the categories given above exhaust the minority language in these protocols. Moreover, I have intentionally failed to analyze or report in any fulness the more "positive" remarks on the intellectual's role in society or on the anti-intellectualism within university life itself (as one person put it [C-21]: "the destruction of the intellectual community within the university"). It was, in fact, only after the interviews were almost completed, and the variability in self-definition became ever more striking, that it was clear we might treat intellectual status directly, as one which presents a standard problem in minority adjustment.

I have argued elsewhere that marginalities of this kind provide the opportunity for the development of perspective and creativity—an opportunity whose realization depends upon the adjustment which is made to marginal status.[21] In this earlier study, using the Jews as a case in point, I found that favorable adjustment to marginality was, indeed, associated with what was called "intellectual perspective"; and it now seemed possible to apply the same general logic to this sample of intellectuals.

Certainly many have asserted that there is an inherent alienative potential—an inescapable degree of marginality—in the intellectual role; and the assertion usually follows that the individual's style of adjustment to this marginality affects his performance as an intellectual. The

21. M. Seeman, "Intellectual Perspective and Adjustment to Minority Status," *Social Problems*, III (1956), 142-53.

usual view, of course, is that those who are "frozen" by this marginality and who retreat into conformity are less creative as intellectuals. Cunliffe, almost incidentally, makes this tie between mode of adjustment and creativity in advancing his distinction between two types of American intellectuals, whom he calls the "*avant-garde*" and the "clerisy":

> So, if there have been many alienated Western intellectuals since 1800, whom I will label the *avant-garde*, there have also been others, [the "clerisy"] of similar intellectual weight, though as a rule of less creative brilliance, who have remained more or less attached to their society.[22]

The discovery, in the interviews, of so many and so varied responses to this marginal aspect of the intellectual's position suggested the possibility of testing, in a small-scale empirical way, such common assertions about the consequences (or correlates) of the intellectual's adjustment to marginality. The hypothesis to be tested parallels that given in the earlier paper on the Jews as a minority; namely, that those intellectuals who have successfully adjusted to the marginal character of their role—those who, let us say, reveal a minimum of our five minority-style attitudes toward themselves as intellectuals—will be, in turn, the more creative workers in their respective crafts.

For a provisional glimpse of such a test, and to illustrate at the same time one possible utility of the descriptive categories developed in the previous section, I attempted to score the forty protocols for evidence of commitment to, or rejection of, each of the five categories. At the same time, I asked a group of persons in the various departments (in all cases, men of higher academic rank than the individual in question) to judge the professional creativity of those interviewed. Creativity here refers to the ability to make the "given" problematic: the ability to challenge the routines and to provide alternatives to the standardized "right answers" in the respective fields.

Unfortunately, though expectedly, the free-response character of the interviews led to some serious limitations as far as the present more quantitative interest is concerned. For example, on two of the five minority categories (No. 2, "concern with in-group purification," and No. 5, "fear of in-group solidarity") more than one-third of the protocols received a score of 3, which indicated a lack of substantial evidence in the interview; and, in addition, among the remaining two-thirds of the cases, there was a very poor numerical split between "high" versus "low" adjustors on these two categories.

In view of these limitations, I shall not attempt to present what would amount to a complete, but premature, account of the adjustment

22. *Op. cit.*, p. 25.

ratings and creativity judgments.[23] But it is of illustrative interest to note what happened on the three remaining "minority response" categories where a more reasonable split between high versus low adjustment was obtained. "High" adjustment refers to a tendency to reject the use of the indicated minority-like modes of response in self-description; "low" adjustment refers to a tendency to embody the indicated minority-type response. Table 1 reveals what was obtained

Table 1. Mean Creativity Scores and Standard Deviations for Individuals Scored High versus Low on Three Categories of Minority Response to Intellectual Status

ADJUST-MENT GROUP	CATEGORY 1—ACCEPTANCE OF STEREOTYPES			CATEGORY 3—APPROVAL OF CONFORMITY			CATEGORY 4—DENIAL OF MEMBERSHIP		
	N	Mean	S.D.	N	Mean	S.D.	N	Mean	S.D.
High	12	3.27	0.65	16	2.74	0.84	13	2.48	1.02
Low	13	2.54	1.19	15	2.53	1.35	15	2.34	1.06

when individuals who scored 3 (no evidence) on each category were eliminated and when the high and low adjustors were compared on their average creativity. The data in Table 1 are read as follows: For the twelve persons who scored either 4 or 5 on category 1 (i.e., whose responses were antithetical to the acceptance of majority stereotypes about the intellectual), the mean creativity score was 3.27, with a standard deviation of 0.65. For the thirteen persons who scored low in adjustment on this same category (i.e., who revealed a clear tendency to accept negative stereotypes), the mean creativity score was 2.54, with a standard deviation of 1.19.

The differences in creativity between adjustment groups are con-

23. I am indebted to Mrs. Frances Mischel, a graduate student in sociology and anthropology, for the two hundred "minority" ratings (five ratings on each of forty protocols). These ratings were "blind" as far as identification of individuals or specialty fields was concerned. They were done as independently as possible, as far as the five categories are concerned, to minimize "halo." A total of 120 creativity judgments by colleagues were secured; and the evidence suggests that there is substantial agreement among them. Both the adjustment and the creativity ratings were made on five-point scales. For minority adjustment, the scale read as follows: 1—very much evidence of this; 2—some evidence of this; 3—no evidence one way or the other; 4—some evidence of rejection of this mode of response; 5—clear evidence of rejection of this mode. The creativity scale ran simply from 1 ("low in creativity") to 5 ("high in creativity") and was accompanied by a full-page explanation of both the meaning of creativity in this context and the method to be used in making the ratings. It should be clear that the term "adjustment" does not refer to the standard psychological meaning of the term; it designates only whether the respondent reflects or does not reflect the five categories of response described here. Thus, "high adjustment" refers to those who secured either 4 or 5 on the given category; "low" refers to a score of 1 or 2 on the category.

sistently in the direction of higher ratings for those who do not use the minority-style response to intellectual status. Though the *N*'s are small, and the differences are not uniformly great, the trend is clear, and the difference between adjustment groups for Category 1 is statistically significant.[24]

I do not take this as an unequivocal demonstration of the hypothesis in question. For one thing, there are other variables of considerable relevance (e.g., the age of the respondent) that cannot be controlled adequately in a sample of this size; and, in addition, questions remain open about the reliability of the adjustment ratings.[25] But for purposes of illustration the trend revealed in Table 1 is of considerable interest, for it suggests that the minority orientations I have attempted to specify here may be treated (provisionally, at least) not simply as categories of description but as relevant factors in the performance of the intellectual role as such.

It is customary, of course, to conclude by noting the need for further research—in this case, research on the forms and consequences of anti-intellectualism. But there is one crucial thing.—To find, as we have, that many intellectuals adopt, without serious efforts to build a reasoned self-portrait, an essentially negative, minority view of themselves and to find, in addition, some plausible ground for believing that this failure in self-conception is not independent of role performance—gives a special cast to the usual call for research. Thus it would seem essential to recognize that this research must include, if we may call it that, an "inward" as well as an "outward" orientation—that is, we must presumably conduct two related research operations: a study of the attitudes that others take toward intellectuals as well as a more intensive study of the intellectuals' attitudes toward themselves. A serious effort along those lines might yield considerably more than the usual research project; it can become an opportunity for self-discovery.

24. A test of the homogeneity of the two variances for the adjustment groups yielded an F ratio which approximated the 0.05 level of significance and raised doubt about the wisdom of pooling the variances of the two groups in computing the t test between the creativity means. The obtained t ratio for the test of Category 1 was 1.841, a figure which is significant at the 0.05 level using a one-tailed test. Neither of the two remaining categories yielded a significant t. The method used to test for homogeneity of variance and for the significance of the difference between means is given in A. Edwards, *Statistical Methods for the Behavioral Sciences* (New York: Holt, Rinehart, Winston, 1954), pp. 271-74.

25. The question of reliability of rating may not be a serious problem. The same judge who did the ratings in this case was also used in the previously mentioned study of Jewish adjustment; and in that case the ratings of two independent judges, completing a task quite similar to the rating task involved here, were quite reliable (see the paper cited in n. 21 above). I have not deemd it essential for purposes of this illustration to compute another reliability figure for the judge in question.

LEO G. REEDER, GEORGE A. DONOHUE, and ARTURO BIBLARZ

Conceptions of Self and Others

THIS paper presents some findings of a study bearing on the Mead-Cooley symbolic interactionist theory. As other investigators have pointed out, it is quite difficult to make empirical tests of the theory, and, consequently, few empirical field studies are concerned with the processes of self-conception.

Miyamoto and Dornbusch summarize the Mead-Cooley theory by pointing out that: (1) the responses of others have an influence in shaping self-definitions; (2) there is a distinction between (*a*) the actual response of the other and (*b*) the subject's perception of the response of the other; (3) the self takes the role of the "generalized other," that is, of "the individual's conception of the organized process of which he is a part."[1] The theory does not specify the nature or extent of the influence of others, and, consequently, a primary task of research is its specification. With reference to the second point, there is another dimension, namely, the individual's own conception of his self based upon (*a*) and (*b*) as well as other psychological determinants. As to the third point, Mead distinguishes three aspects of the generalized other—attitudes of other individuals toward the self, toward one another, and "toward the various phases or aspects of the common social activity or set of social undertakings in which, as members of an organized society or social group, they are all engaged."[2]

The authors were interested in the relation between self-conception and the objective and perceived ratings of members of the group. The subjects of this investigation were enlisted military personnel at a small isolated base, all members of one crew but with different specialties. Nine groups, based upon specialty and ranging from five to seven mem-

---

Reprinted from "Conceptions of Self and Others," by Leo G. Reeder, George A. Donohue, and Arturo Biblarz, The American Journal of Sociology, *September, 1960, pp. 153-159, by permission of The University of Chicago Press. Copyright 1960 by the University of Chicago.*

The authors wish to express their appreciation to Richard J. Hill and Wilfred J. Dixon for their valuable advice on the analysis of the data.

1. S. Frank Miyamoto and Sanford Dornbusch, "A Test of the Symbolic Interactionist Hypothesis of Self-Conception," *American Journal of Sociology*, LXI, No. 5 (March, 1956), 400.

2. *The Social Psychology of George Herbert Mead*, ed. Anselm Strauss (Chicago: University of Chicago Press, 1956), pp. 231-32.

bers, were the source of data. A total of fifty-four participated.[3] These were men who worked together eight hours each day, who lived together on the base, and most of whom had been assigned there for several months. The method employed has a close relationship to analytical schemes frequently used in small-group research, using perceptual responses.[4]

Every member of the crew available on a given day was asked to complete a brief questionnaire, administered to entire work groups assembled in one room at a specific time. In addition to the usual face-sheet data on their social background, they were asked to answer the following questions:

A. Rank the men in your work group on the following point:
"Who is the Best Leader? Who is best able to handle men and new situations?"

Be sure to rank yourself and encircle your own name. The first man you name should have the highest qualities of leadership, the second name should be the man with the next highest leadership qualities, and so on until you have listed every man in your work group. Do not omit anyone.

B. In which of the above positions do you think most of the men in your work group place you as a leader? Indicate your answer by circling one of the numbers below:

The second question was:

"Who is the best worker? Who is the most efficient and useful man to have around?"

The same instructions were used with this question as in the one above. The following variables were measured:

1. *Self-rank* (SR). This variable is construed as a measure of the individual's self-conception. It is assumed that the self-rank is an expression of the individual's self-conception, which involves the three elements of symbolic interaction described above.

2. *Objective group rating* (OGR). An average rank was computed for each individual based upon the rank given him by every other member of his work group. The objective group rating is one of the aspects of Mead's "generalized other"; i.e., attitudes of others toward the self.

---

3. A tenth group was dropped because it consisted of three members only. Also, the total responding to the second question dropped to fifty-one as a result of incomplete information from three subjects.

4. Perhaps the first use of the technique of "perceptual response," or asking the respondent to guess others' response to him, was by R. Tagiuri ("Relational Analysis: An Extension of Sociometric Methods with Emphasis upon Social Perception," *Sociometry*, XV [February-May, 1952], 91-104).

3. *Estimated objective group rating* (EOGR). This variable is based upon the individual's response to the "B" part of each ranking question. It assumes that the individual, in making an estimate of how the group ranks him, is taking the role of the generalized other.

In the analysis the military site was treated as a universe, and the nine work groups were considered as a sample in time of all work groups there. Two statistical measures of the average, the mean and the median, were used in analyzing the data, and, as indicated below, there were minor differences in the results achieved in their use.[5]

In order to separate the total group into categories of ranks, in the five-person groups persons in ranks 1 and 2 were classified as "high," rank 3 as "medium," and ranks 4 and 5 as "low." For the seven-person groups those in ranks 1 and 2 were classified "high," ranks 3 and 4 were "medium," and ranks 5, 6, and 7 were classified "low."

Two interdependent hypotheses were developed; the first states:

I. People with a high self-rating (SR) on a characteristic will have a higher group rating (OGR) and a higher mean estimated group rating (EOGR) on it than will those with a low self-rating.[6] Further, those with a high EOGR will receive a higher group rating (OGR) than those with a low EOGR.

This hypothesis would support the notion that the person's self-conception is related to the responses of others and to the individual's perception of those responses. This hypothesis does not say anything about the extent of the relationship, if any, among the variables given. The second hypothesis is concerned with this problem:

II. A person's self-rank (SR) tends to correspond with the EOGR and the OGR; e.g., if a person places himself in rank 1, he will perceive the group as giving him rank 1 and will likewise be placed in rank 1 by the group.

Where the hypothesized correspondence is not found, it would appear that other factors, in addition to EOGR and OGR, would be related to self-conception; attempts should then be made to specify some of these factors.

To test the first part of Hypothesis I, each group was sorted into high, medium, and low self-raters and compared with the mean group rating (OGR) and with the mean of the individual's estimate of the

5. There is some question as to whether the mean is an appropriate statistic to use with non-interval data (for a discussion of the limitations of the mean with different types of data, see S. S. Stevens, "Mathematics, Measurements, and Psychophysics," in *Handbook of Experimental Psychology*, ed. S. S. Stevens [New Cork: John Wiley & Sons, 1951], pp. 1–50.

6. This hypothesis replicates two tested by Miyamoto and Dornbusch, *op. cit.*, pp. 402–3.

group rating (EOGR) on each characteristic being measured. The results support this part of the hypothesis (Tables 1, 2). Inspection of Tables 1 and 2 shows that the high self-rankers were given a higher average rank by the group. These results provide additional support to the findings of Miyamoto and Dornbusch.[7]

Table 1. Self-Rankings by Objective Group Ratings of "Leadership" and "Worker" Characteristics

	OBJECTIVE GROUP RATING			
	MEAN		*MEDIAN*	
Self-Rating	*Leadership*	*Worker*	*Leadership*	*Worker*
High	3.4	3.8	3.0	4.0
Medium	4.8	4.6	5.0	5.0
Low	6.2	5.6	7.0	6.3

Table 2. Self-Rankings by Estimated Objective Group Ratings of "Leadership" and "Worker" Characteristics

	ESTIMATED OBJECTIVE GROUP RATING			
	MEAN		*MEDIAN*	
Self-Rating	*Leadership*	*Worker*	*Leadership*	*Worker*
High	2.1	1.8	2.0	1.0
Medium	4.1	3.7	4.0	3.0
Low	6.4	5.0	6.0	4.5

Each person was assigned to a high, medium, or low rating group on the basis of his estimation of the group's rating of him (EOGR). Comparisons were then made with the rating given to the persons in each rating group by the work group (OGR). The second part of Hypothesis I, that those with a high EOGR would receive a higher OGR than those with a low EOGR, was supported (Table 3).

Table 3. Estimated Objective Group Ratings by Objective Group Ratings of "Leadership" and "Worker" Characteristics

	OBJECTIVE GROUP RATING	
	MEDIAN	
Estimated Objective Group Rating	*Leadership*	*Worker*
High	3.0	3.5
Medium	5.0	4.0
Low	6.3	7.0

Thus, the data tested by the first hypothesis consistently support Mead's theory, insofar as they indicate a direct relationship between the three variables: self-conception, the perceived generalized other, and

7. *Ibid.*

the actual responses of others.[8] The extent of the relationship, however, as well as its causal direction have been left unspecified. Although these data are static and one cannot make casual analyses, it is possible to investigate in more detail the extent to which a direct relationship between the three variables exists in the groups studied.

Hypothesis II was designed to test another aspect of the relationship between the three variables. The general question asked was: Is there a one-to-one correspondence between self-conception (SR), the perceived generalized other (EOGR), and the actual responses of other (OGR)? The correspondence between SR and OGR was tested by comparing the distribution of persons in the high, medium, and low self-rank groups with respect to their objective group ratings (Table 4). On the

Table 4. Self-Ratings by Objective Group Ratings of the "Leadership" Characteristic

	OBJECTIVE GROUP RATINGS							
	HIGH		MEDIUM		LOW		TOTAL	
Self-Rating	N	Per Cent	N	Per Cent	N	Per Cent	N	Per Cent
High	10	40.0	8	32.0	7	28.0	25	100.0
Medium	1	6.7	4	26.0	10	66.6	15	100.0
Low	....	....	....	....	14	100.0	14	100.0
Total	11	20.4	12	22.2	31	57.4	54	100.0

"leadership" characteristic the data reveals that 40 per cent of the high self-rankers were likewise rated high by their work group, while 26 per cent of the medium self-rankers were given a medium rating, and 100 per cent of the low self-rankers were given a low rating. The hypothesis that those with self-ranks of high, middle, and low, respectively, would also have high, middle, and low objective group ranks, respectively, was supported only in the case of the low self-rankers. It is interesting to observe that more than half of the individuals were given a low rating; on the other hand, almost half ranked themselves high.

A discrepancy revealed by the data is that the percentage of medium self-raters who were also rated medium by the group is less than the percentage of high self-raters who were rated medium by the group. This is probably related to the larger number of high self-raters as compared to medium self-raters and to the large percentage of low group ratings given to the medium self-raters.

With respect to the "worker" characteristic, the findings are approximately the same (Table 5). Again, only those persons with low self-

8. Limitations of the data do not permit the use of tests of significance. The first hypothesis, however, was uniformly supported.

Table 5. Self-Ratings by Objective Group Ratings of the "Worker" Characteristic

	OBJECTIVE GROUP RATING							
	HIGH		MEDIUM		LOW		TOTAL	
Self-Rating	N	Per Cent	N	Per Cent	N	Per Cent	N	Per Cent
High	8	33.3	3	12.5	13	54.1	24	100.0
Medium	2	13.3	5	33.3	8	53.3	15	100.0
Low	1	8.3	1	8.3	10	83.3	12	100.0
Total	11	21.6	9	17.6	31	60.8	51	100.0

ratings were given a corresponding rating by the group. On the other hand, no more than one- third of the high and the medium self-raters were given equivalent rating by the group. As reported in the analysis above, more than half of those ranking themselves high were given a low rank by the group, and, furthermore, 61 per cent of all the subjects were given a low rating by the group.

Hypothesis II was further tested by the relationship between persons with high, middle, and low self-ranks and the perceived generalized-other rankings (EOGR). Comparisons were made between the self-ranks of persons and the estimated objective group ratings, and the hypothesis was supported (Table 6). This hypothesis may be viewed as crucial in

Table 6. Self-Rank by Estimated Objective Group Rating of "Leadership" Characteristic

	ESTIMATED OBJECTIVE GROUP RATING							
	HIGH		MEDIUM		LOW		TOTAL	
Self-Rank	N	Per Cent	N	Per Cent	N	Per Cent	N	Per Cent
High	21	84.0	2	8.0	2	8.0	25	100.0
Medium	0	0	12	80.0	3	20.0	15	100.0
Low	0	0	1	7.1	13	92.9	14	100.0
Total	21	38.9	15	27.8	18	33.3	54	100.0

this examination of Mead's theory, for it is here that the relationship between the self and Mead's "generalized other" is tested. The percentage congruence between the self-rank and the EOGR was 84.0, 80.0, and 92.9 for the high, medium, and low groups, respectively. Again, it will be observed that the low self-rankers had a higher percentage of corresponding rank. In contrast to the high percentage of actual low ranks given by the group in the preceding analyses, here the estimated group ranks are relatively evenly distributed among the three categories.

When the data were analyzed for the characteristic of "best worker," a similar pattern was revealed, lending further support to the hypothesis (Table 7). The highest percentage of correspondence between self-rank

Table 7. Self-Rank by Estimated Objective Group Rating of "Worker" Characteristics

	ESTIMATED OBJECTIVE GROUP RATING							
	HIGH		MEDIUM		LOW		TOTAL	
Self-Rank	N	Per Cent	N	Per Cent	N	Per Cent	N	Per Cent
High	19	79.2	4	16.7	1	4.1	24	100.0
Medium	2	13.3	10	66.7	3	20.0	15	100.0
Low	....	....	3	25.0	9	75.0	12	100.0
Total	21	41.2	17	33.3	13	25.5	51	100.0

and EOGR, however, was not in low rank category but rather in the high rank category.

Finally, the hypothesis was examined with respect to the EOGR and OGR variables; that is, persons with a high, middle or low estimated objective group rank will also have a corresponding high, middle, or low objective group rank. The hypothesis was not supported (Table 8).

Table 8. Estimated Objective Group Rank by Objective Group Rank of "Leadership" Characteristic

	OBJECTIVE GROUP RANK							
Estimated Objective	HIGH		MEDIUM		LOW		TOTAL	
Group Rank	N	Per Cent	N	Per Cent	N	Per Cent	N	Per Cent
High	9	43.0	6	28.5	6	28.5	21	100.0
Medium	1	6.7	5	33.3	9	60.0	15	100.0
Low	1	5.5	1	5.5	16	89.0	18	100.0
Total	11	20.4	12	22.2	31	57.4	54	100.0

Only 43 per cent of the high EOGR group and 33.3 per cent of the middle EOGR group had corresponding OGR ranks. The low-rank EOGR group once more had the highest percentage of correspondence with the objective group rank; as in the preceding analysis, more than half the total group was ranked low.

Analysis of the ranking on the "best worker" characteristic revealed a similar pattern of relationships; 52.4 per cent of those with a high EOGR rank actually were given a low rank by the group; this is similar to the results obtained when self-rank was related to objective group rating on this characteristic (Table 5).

Hypothesis II was concerned with the general question of the correspondence between self-conception (SR), perceived generalized other (EOGR), and the actual responses of others (OGR). The data suggest a close correspondence between self-conception and the perceived generalized other. The correspondence between these two variables and the actual responses of others was close only for those who either ranked themselves low and/or perceived others as ranking them low;

on the other hand, for the high- and medium-ranked groups, SR and EOGR and the actual responses of others correspond in less than 50 per cent of the cases.[9]

The relationship between these findings and the theoretical framework from which the hypotheses were derived can now be assessed. The two major theoretical propositions involved are: (1) that the responses of others have an influence in shaping one's self-definition and (2) that this self-definition is derived chiefly from the perception of the "generalized other." The second of these propositions was consistently supported by the data as shown by the findings in Tables 2, 6, and 7. The first proposition is supported by the findings with respect to Hypothesis I (Tables 1, 3). Thus, it was found that there is a direct relationship between self-conception and the perceived generalized other, on the one hand, and actual responses of others, on the other. Even though this relationship exists, a one-to-one correspondence was found only in the case of low self-rankers and those who expected to be rated low by the group, as shown by the findings for Hypothesis II (Tables 4, 8).

The self-conception of persons who do not think highly of themselves thus appears to be determined largely by the perceived and actual responses of others. For those who think highly of themselves, additional variables are necessary to explain self-conception. Several alternative explanations may be considered.[10]

We can speculate, for example, that the subjects who have high self-rankings are operating with values derived from groups other than the one with which we are here concerned, while those with low self-rankings may judge their performance primarily on the basis of the values of this particular group. Such characteristics as age, urban or rural background, education, and the socioeconomic status of parents may be significant variables. Persons reared in a rural setting, for instance, may have fewer groups of significant others from which to derive their self-conceptions, and these may show them a more consistent concep-

9. It may be questioned whether one could expect medium self-rankers to be ranked low on the basis of chance factors alone, given the definition of medium and low groups. If chance factors alone were operating, of those fifteen persons whose self-ranking was medium, 6.4 would be expected to have received low OGR rankings. The actual number of such persons was ten. Furthermore, eight of these ten persons had a discrepancy of two or more ranks between their SR and OGR statuses. No test of significance was made because of the limitations of sample size. The findings here can only be considered suggestive.

10. R. Tagiuri, J. S. Bruner, and R. R. Blake suggest the possibility that congruency between SR and OGR is a function of mutuality of feelings ("On the Relation between Feelings and Perception of Feelings among Members of Small Groups," in E. E. Maccoby, T. M. Newcomb, and E. L. Hartley [eds.], *Readings in Social Psychology* [3d ed.; New York: Holt, Rinehart, Winston, 1958], pp 110-16).

tion of themselves than is the case for the city-dweller.[11] The latter may be able to select one of several alternative self-conceptions and ignore the others; having experienced the degradation of one group's values by another group, he is familiar with the possibility of legitimately ignoring the values of a particular group. Conceivably, the urban person's conception of himself may be independent of his group at a given time. The rural person, being less likely to feel that he can legitimately ignore the values of a group, may more easily develop a self-conception which reflects the actual response of the group with whom he happens to be in extended and intimate contact. This, of course, requires the test of empirical verification, and additional analyses of the data were made.

Given the above considerations, the general hypothesis was developed that persons whose self-rating disagrees with the objective group rating are likely to have recourse to a greater number of reference groups. Consequently, certain variables—age, marital status, urban-rural background, education, and military rank—were used to construct an index of significant reference groups, differential weights being assigned to each variable. The variables selected were assumued to be probably the most important for reference groups. The weighting scheme was as follows:

Education: Less than high school, 0; some high school, 2; some college, 3

Marital status: single, 0; divorced or married, 1

Urban or rural background: Home in area with population of 10,000 or lower, 0; over 10,000, 3

Age: Under 25 years, 0; 25 years and over, 2

Military rank: Private, private first class, corporal, 0; sergeant, sergeant first class, master sergeant, 3

Each individual's score was summed, and this was called his "index score"; those with a high score were assumed to have more significant reference groups than persons with a lower score. It was assumed that the greater a person's participation in various forms of the social organization, the greater the likelihood of his adopting a larger number of significant reference groups. College education, urban background, and high military rank were treated as more or less equivalent sources of strong reference groups from which the individual could obtain a legitimized self-conception that would withstand the "attacks" of his immediate associates at work. A college education, even when it does not involve the experience of city life, provides the possibility of identi-

11. Some support for our speculations on participation in membership groups and urban-rural background is presented by Basil Zimmer ("Farm Background and Urban Participation," *American Journal of Sociology*, LXI, No. 5 [March, 1956], 470–75).

fying one's self with a group of superior status and, in general, presents a wide variety of reference groups through actual or ideal contact or both. Of military rank it was assumed that, for those who had reached the three highest grades, the rank represented to them status conferred by a reference group with great moral authority, and those who achieve such status could adopt the view that their work groups had relatively less moral authority in comparison with the entire military service.

The next procedure was to divide the sample arbitrarily into two groups based upon their index scores, one with a large number of reference groups and the other with few. The groups were then analyzed to determine if there was a significant relationship between a high score on the index of reference groups and the agreement or disagreement between self-ratings and objective group ratings. A significant relationship was found (Table 9). This supports the general hypothesis that

Table 9. Relationship of Reference-Group Index Scores and Agreement-Disagreement between Self-Rating and Group Rating

Reference Group Index Score	Agree	Disagree	N
Low	19	9	28
High	9	17	26
N	28	26	54

$x^2 = 6.01$; $P < .02$.

persons whose self-rating disagrees with the rating assigned to them by the group (OGR) are more likely to have a greater number of reference groups.

In conclusion, it should be noted that this study tests only a partial aspect of the symbolic-interactionist frame of reference. Further research on the role of number type, of groups, and of personal factors should be encouraged, to define the various conditions under which self-conception may vary. Finally, empirical tests of segments of more comprehensive or dynamic frames are possible in a systematic fashion and may be the most feasible, if not the only, way in which validation of sociological theory may occur.

b) THE "INTERCHANGE" APPROACH

WILLIAM J. GOODE

Illegitimacy in the Caribbean Social Structure

OVER a generation ago Malinowski enunciated a principle which he said amounted to a universal sociological law, that "no child should be brought into the world without a man—and one man at that—assuming the role of sociological father. . . .[1] This rule is not based on the social disapproval of premarital or extramarital sexual freedom. Malinowski's Trobrianders, for example, indulged in considerable sex play before marriage, but were shocked at illegitimacy. Rather, the rule expresses the interest of the society in fixing responsibility for the child upon a specific individual. Marriage, therefore, is not primarily the legitimation of sex, but the legitimation of parenthood.[2] Whether Malinowski's principle is indeed a universal sociological law has not been analyzed, except to the degree that the recurring debate as to whether the "nuclear family" is universal implicitly includes that prin-

---

Reprinted from American Sociological Review, *February, 1960, pp. 21-30, by permission of the author and the journal.*

This paper was completed under National Institute of Mental Health Grant No. M-2526-S.

1. Bronislaw Malinowski, "Parenthood, the Basis of Social Structure," in V. F. Calverton and Samuel D. Schmalhausen, editors, *The New Generation*, New York: Macaulay, 1930, pp. 137-138.

2. Malinowski was puzzled as to how the Trobrianders could be sexually so free without numerous illegitimates, especially since they denied any connection between sexual intercourse and pregnancy and took no contraceptive precautions. It was not until M. F. Ashley-Montagu's *Coming into Being among the Australian Aborigines*, London: Routledge, 1937, that the solution seemed to be clear.

See also M. F. Ashley-Montagu, *The Reproductive Development of the Female*, New York: Julian, 1957.

ciple.[3] It seems safe enough to claim at least that all societies have family systems and that possibly a sociological father is required everywhere.[4]

Illegitimacy in the Caribbean

Malinowski's principle is not refuted by data from the United States or Western Europe, where illegitimacy rates range from perhaps four or five per cent to about eleven per cent.[5] However, in the Caribbean area illegitimacy rates are often over fifty per cent, as Table 1 shows.

Table 1. Illegitimacy Rates in Selected Caribbean Political Units

Political Unit	*Year*	*Per Cent*
British Guiana	1955	35
French Guiana	1956	65
Surinam (excluding Bush Negroes and aborigines)	1953	34
Barbados	1957	70
Bermuda	1957	30
Dominican Republic	1957	61
Guadeloupe	1956	42
Jamaica	1954	72
Antigua	1957	65
Martinique	1956	48
Trinidad and Tobago	1956	47
Grenada	1957	71
Puerto Rico	1955	28
Haiti	—	67-85

All figures except those for Puerto Rico, British Guiana, Surinam, Dominican Republic, Trinidad and Tobago, Grenada, and Haiti were taken from the United Nations Year Book Questionnaire for the years in question. Data were furnished to the U.N. by the statistical offices of the country, and contain all the errors of their own registration procedures. Data for other countries, excluding Haiti and the Dominican Republic, were kindly furnished by the Caribbean Commission. The Dirección General de Estadística of the Dominican Republic graciously sent me the figure for 1957. I have found no recent figure for Cuba; presumably it was 30 per cent in 1939. For Surinam, Rudolf van Lier, *Samenleving in ein Gransgebied*, 's-Gravenhage: Martinus Nijhoff, 1949, p. 287, gives 70 per cent for 1940. The rate has also dropped in British Guiana from the 41 per cent reported in 1946 in *British Guiana Annual Report of the Registrar-General, 1954*, Georgetown, Demerara, British Guiana, 1956, p. 9. I have found no official figure for Haiti. Bastien reports two-thirds for Marbial (Remy Bastien, *La Familia Rural Haitiana*, Mexico: Libra, 1951, p. 85); George E. Simpson reports about 85 per cent for one Haitian area in "Sexual and Family Institutions in Northern Haiti," *American Anthropologist*, 44 (October-December, 1942), p. 664.

---

3. For a recent discussion of this point, see Melford E. Spiro, "Is the Family Universal?" *American Anthropologist*, 56 (October, 1954), pp. 839-846.

4. The most notable case which raises doubts is the Nayar of Malabar Strait. See K. M. Panikkar, "Some Aspects of Nayar Life," *Journal of the Royal Anthropological Institute*, 48 (July-December, 1918), esp. pp. 260 ff; E. Kathleen Gough, "Changing Kinship Usages in the Setting of Political and Economic Change among the Nayar of Malabar," *Journal of the Royal Anthropological Institute*, 81 (Parts I and II, 1951), pp. 71-88. Gough's latest report ("The Nayars and the Definition of Marriage," *Journal of the Royal Anthropological Institute*, 89 [1959], p. 31) asserts that Nayar marriage does establish paternity legally. Another possible case is the Minang-Kabau; see E. N. Loeb, "Patrilineal and Matrilineal Organization in Sumatra, Part 2," *American Anthropologist*, 36 (January-March, 1934), pp. 26-56.

5. In Iceland, illegitimate births constituted 27.9 per cent of live births in 1950, and

Under such conditions, doubt may be raised as to whether a "sociological father" exists, and indeed various writers have spoken of a "matrifocal family."[6] Certainly so high a rate of deviation would suggest that the norm, if it does exist, might have a very different meaning than in a society in which the rate is less, say, than ten per cent. But we must keep in mind that Malinowski was stating a proposition about a *cultural* element: he asserted that the *norm* would always be found, not that the members of the society would obey it under specified conditions.

It is precisely with reference to Malinowski's principle that many students of the Caribbean have taken an opposing position—without developing its implications for family theory. The claim has often been made for various Caribbean lands that when a couple is living together in a consensual union "the family may be said to exist in much the same way as it does in peasant communities throughout the world,"[7] and the child therefore suffers no disadvantage from being illegitimate.[8] Henriques, also writing about Jamaica, comments that there is no moral sanction against "concubinage," by which he means a man and woman keeping house together and raising children, and even claims that respectable black people would rather have their daughter become mistress or concubine to a white or fair colored man than marry a black one.[9] Otherwise put, the consensual union is the marriage form of the lower classes in the Caribbean, and is "sociologically as legitimate" as a legal union. It is, in short, a "cultural alternative," as permissible a way of founding a family as any other.[10] If this interpretation is correct, Malinowski's principle would be erroneous, and one of the apparently major functions of the father would have to be redefined as unessential.

---

the rate in Stockholm and a few other areas in Sweden has remained at about 15 per cent in recent years. Cf. Meyer Nimkoff, "Illegitimacy," *Encyclopaedia Britannica*, 1954.

6. "One of the regularities of social organization, which has appeared in the literature from Herskovits to Henriques, is the concept of the 'matrifocal' family." Vera Rubin, "Cultural Perspectives in Caribbean Research," in Vera Rubin, editor, *Caribbean Studies: A Symposium*, Jamaica: Institute of Social and Economic Research, 1957, p. 117. Such comments are often applicable as well to one period in the development of the Negro family in this country. Cf. E. Franklin Frazier, *The Negro Family in the United States*, New York: Dryden, revised edition, 1948, Part 2, "In the House of the Mother."

7. T. S. Simey, *Welfare and Planning in the West Indies*, Oxford: Clarendon Press, 1956, p. 15.

8. "The fact of illegitimate birth is one completely taken for granted. An illegitimate child does not consider himself disadvantaged. . . ." *Ibid.*, p. 88.

9. Fernando Henriques, *Family and Colour in Jamaica*, London: Eyre and Spottiswoode, 1953, pp. 87, 90.

10. "Thus, the matrifocal family . . . is a subcultural norm. . . ." John V. Murra, "Discussion," in *Caribbean Studies*, *op. cit.*, p. 76.

Comments similar to those given above about Jamaica have been made about other Caribbean areas. Herskovits and Herskovits make a similar claim for Trinidad, noting what a "false perspective on the thinking of the people is given by the application of legal terms such as 'legitimate' and 'illegitimate' to the offspring."[11] Similarly, they assert that "there is no social disability imposed by the community because of legitimacy or illegitimacy."[12] The common-law marriage is for many the accepted form.[13]

With respect to Haitian children of a placée union which is legalized, of a legal union, or of a union outside of an existing marriage the claim is made that "none of these classes of children are at any special social disadvantage."[14] With reference to the forms of Haitian unions: "In the main, especially in the countryside, socially sanctioned matings which do not enjoy the approval of the Church endure as long and hold as respected a place in the community. . . ."[15] In a parallel vein, Bastien remarks that when a man has "good intentions" with respect to a girl, but does not have enough money with which to marry, he may "establish himself" with the girl, with marriage as a publicly acknowledged, later goal, but does not thereby "incur the scorn of the community."[16]

In Martinique, we are told, in place of the rule of legitimacy, which is absent here, other values have emerged such as ingroup solidarity, status equality, and conviviality, which express family organization.[17] There is "no unequivocally preferred type of bond between parents."[18] The legitimate and illegitimate share the same status.

Although the illegitimacy rate in Puerto Rico is lower than in the areas noted above, here too the claim has been made that the rule of legitimacy fails. It is said of the consensual union that it is "a cultural alternative," that is, marriage is split into two culturally permissible alternatives.[19] Similarly, ". . . the prevalence of consensual unions ought

11. Melville J. Herskovits and Frances S. Herskovits, *Trinidad Village,* New York: Knopf, 1947, p. 17.

12. *Ibid.*, pp. 82-83; see also p. 107.

13. Lloyd Braithwaite, "Social Stratification in Trinidad," *Social and Economic Studies,* 2 (October, 1953), p. 125.

14. Melville J. Herskovits, *Life in a Haitian Valley,* New York: Knopf, 1937, p. 118.

15. *Ibid.*, p. 106.

16. Bastien, *op. cit.*, pp. 72-73. However, Bastien also presents the prestige rankings of the three forms of matings.

17. Mariam Kreiselman, *The Caribbean Family. A Case Study in Martinique,* Columbia University, Ph.D. thesis, 1958, pp. 271, 292.

18. *Ibid.*, p. viii.

19. J. Mayone Stycos, *Family and Fertility in Puerto Rico,* New York: Columbia University Press, 1955, p. 110. I assume here the meaning of "culturally equivalent" or "normatively equal."

to be considered in terms of local lower-class conceptions of what is considered 'moral.'" It is not that the lower class prefer illegal behavior, but that consensual unions are not seen as immoral.[20] It is asserted, too, that "the consensual union is considered a binding marriage truly cemented at the birth of the first child."[21]

At first glance, then, Malinowski's rule of legitimacy is refuted. A substantial number of societies in the West appear not to accept the norm. If this is the case, then several fundamental notions in family theory would have to be discarded.

Yet a closer examination of these and other reports prove conclusively that the norm exists, since in fact marriage is the ideal, and those who violate the rule do suffer penalties. The fact that perhaps a majority of certain of these populations do live in unions outside marriage, at some time in their lives, does not change the normative status of the rule. On the other hand, as we shall later indicate, Malinowski's rule must nevertheless be reformulated.

Let us first look more closely at Jamaica. As against the assertion that illegitimacy is not stigmatized, we note the opposing facts. Both upper and middle class opinion is set against "concubinage."[22] The priests may shame the couple about the matter. When a young girl is found to be pregnant, her family is angry.[23] Few men (Rocky Roads) allow their women to bring their illegitimate children into the union, if they do marry.[24] In the same community, illegitimate children are subjected to more physical rejection and pressures of sibling rivalry.[25] Moreover, as individuals move through the life cycle, an increasing proportion are actually married, a phenomenon which would be inexplicable if the consensual unions were backed by a set of alternative norms. This process is illustrated by the proportions of persons ever married by selected ages in the major areas of the British West Indies, as shown in Table 2.[26] Thus, though the average British West Indian ages at marriage are among the highest in the world (for example, for Jamaica, 34.1

20. Sidney W. Mintz, "Cañamelar, The Subculture of a Rural Sugar Plantation Proletariat," in Julian Steward *et al.*, *The People of Puerto Rico*, Urbana: University of Illinois Press, 1956, p. 377.

21. Robert A. Manners, "Tabara: Subcultures of a Tobacco and Mixed Crop Municipality," in *The People of Puerto Rico*, *op. cit.*, p. 144.

22. Henriques, *op. cit.*, pp. 87, 164.

23. *Ibid.*, p. 88. See also Edith Clarke, *My Mother Who Fathered Me*, London: Allen & Unwin, 1957, p. 99; and Kreiselman, *op. cit.*, p. 189.

24. Yehudi Cohen, "Structure and Function: Family Organization and Socialization in a Jamaican Community," *American Anthropologist*, 58 (August, 1956), p. 669.

25. *Ibid.*, p. 672.

26. G. W. Roberts, "Some Aspects of Mating and Fertility in the West Indies," *Population Studies*, 8 (March, 1955), p. 223. The figures for Jamaica in Table 2 presumably refer to 1943.

Table 2. British West Indies: Per Cent of Males Ever Married by Age, 1946

Age	Jamaica	Barbados	Windwards	Leewards
20–24	10.1	8.5	4.1	4.0
25–34	21.0	37.6	27.6	27.3
35–44	41.9	61.7	54.9	53.4
45–54	55.0	70.8	68.2	63.7
55–64	66.3	75.2	78.4	75.5
65 and over	74.7	85.2	83.1	78.9

years for males; for Barbados, 31.7, and for Grenada, 33.0[27]), most individuals do marry. In sum, these various mating forms are "not regarded as alternative forms of conjugal associations between which any individual was free to choose."[28]

Similarly, in Trinidad, a couple may finally marry after living together for some time, "for the position it gives the family." Among other things, "marriage is . . . a prestige phenomenon in terms of social or religious values." Though a couple will usually begin life together as "keepers," "such an episode is outside correct procedure." The unmarried keeper woman wears no ring, and only the married woman is called *Madam*.[29] Many people who rise in class find that their new rank is incompatible with the type of union they once entered. Moreover, when working-class women quarrel, one may point out that the other is not properly married.[30]

Although the case of Haiti seems more complex, the same conclusion seems inescapable. The prestige from the legal, Church union is of sufficient significance to "motivate weddings at which the children and even grandchildren of the principals act as attendants."[31] The legal union cannot be broken as easily as the plaçage. When the unmarried girl becomes pregnant, she is beaten.[32] The woman in a placée union

27. *Ibid.*, p. 205. More fundamental data are the actual expressions of norms and ideals, to be found in Judith Blake's *Family Structure: The Social Context of Reproduction*, Ph.D. thesis, Columbia University, 1959, a study of the lower class Jamaican family [Judith Blake, *Family Structure in Jamaica: The Social Context of Reproduction*. New York: The Free Press of Glencoe, Inc., 1961]. It is the first detailed investigation of the mechanisms through which the norms lose much of their coercive power. For a preliminary report from this study, see Blake, "Family Instability and Reproductive Behavior in Jamaica," *Current Research in Human Fertility*, New York: Milbank Fund, 1955, pp. 24-41.

28. Clarke, *op. cit.*, pp. 77-78. It is significant that Clarke and Blake, who appear to be the only investigators to take seriously the Jamaican's *own* normative statements, assert unequivocally the normative underpinnings of a legal marriage.

29. Herskovits and Herskovits, *op. cit.*, pp. 82, 84, 87, 93-94.

30. Lloyd Braithwaite, "Social Stratification in Trinidad," *Social and Economic Studies*, 2 (October, 1953), pp. 125, 126.

31. Herskovits, *op. cit.*, pp. 106, 107.

32. *Ibid.*, p. 110; George Eaton Simpson, "Sexual and Familial Institutions in Northern Haiti," *American Anthropologist*, 44 (October-December, 1942), p. 665.

cannot demand as much from her man, and her children have no right to the name of the father.[33] Most persons would prefer to marry, and this is especially true of women.[34] Contemporary pressures are increasing the proportion who marry, but some gradations of prestige remain.[35] The plaçage is not stable: "perhaps three-fourths of the peasant men, and possibly more, have or have had at one time one or more mates in addition to a legal wife or *femme caille*."[36] "The consciousness of their social inferiority so troubles . . . [them] . . . that few resist the temptation to explain the cause of their situation . . . "[37]

In Martinique, too, parents are angry at the pregnancy of the unmarried girl, who may have to leave her home. When talking about the consensual relationships of others, the term "concubine" is used. Many men will promise marriage, but deceive the girl. In a few reported cases of girls having babies, the parents pretended that the children were their own.[38] The consensual union is easily dissolved, and no social obligations are incurred by entering it.[39]

Perhaps more conclusive for Martinique is an important finding, which grew out of an effort to understand the *fête*. In possibly every study of illegitimacy in the Caribbean, people are described as saying—most researchers have accepted this assertion—that they cannot marry because they cannot afford the wedding feast, without which the ceremony is a mockery. The couple will be laughed at later. The "cost of the wedding" is not the church expenses; in every country the Catholic Church (or others, where they are important) has offered nearly free weddings—but with rare acceptance. A few observers have doubted that the expense of the *fête* was the crucial item, even though it is substantial, emphasizing rather that the *fête* is an expression of community solidarity, a *rite de passage*, and a community validation of the union. Kreiselman is unique among observers in offering and, within limits, testing the hypothesis that most persons who can afford to live

---

33. Herskovits, *op. cit.*, pp. 116, 119.

34. Simpson, *op. cit.*, pp. 655, 658.

35. Rhoda Métraux, *Kith and Kin*, Ph.D. thesis, Columbia University, 1951, pp. 197, 205-209.

36. Simpson, *op. cit.*, p. 656. The *femme caille* shares her consort's house. Bastien, *op. cit.*, p. 73, gives three main categories of unions, in order of social rank: (1) marriage; (2) a union established with the idea of later marriage; and (3) the ordinary plaçage, some forms of which involve several women living apart from one another.

37. Bastien, *op. cit.*, p. 73.

38. Kreiselman, *op. cit.*, pp. 189, 223, 201, 191, 188.

39. *Ibid.*, p. 231. All unions involve social obligations, of course, but the fact that the investigator makes this observation underlines the lack of community support for this type of union.

en ménage can also afford a *fête* and therefore a marriage, but that most who do not marry early or later do not have the same rank.[40]

Whether the rank differences among people of a lower stratum are so crucial, and whether a broad sample of stable consensual unions would show that it is mainly those of equal status who marry, remains to be seen. But if this is the case even in Capesterre (Martinique), the relationship shows that the rule of legitimacy holds there. For the rule has as a major function the prevention of unions between wrong lineages, and in nearly every society the rules of marriage serve to confine legal unions mainly to men and women of equal rank.[41]

In Puerto Rico, there is social disapproval of the consensual union, even though the sanction does not necessarily lead to conformity. Fathers become angry when their daughters elope, and almost everyone pays "lip service" to the superiority of marriage.[42] People may say that they get married in order to baptize the children.[43] Girls have "idealized feelings" about marriage ceremonies,[44] and often the girls' parents request or insist upon legal unions.[45]

Two-thirds of both men and women in a national sample of Puerto Rico said that a consensual union is a bad life for a man, and over 80 per cent of the respondents made the same assertion for women.[46] Perhaps a more penetrating test of the normative status of the consensual union may be found in the attitudes expressed about a *daughter* entering a consensual union: only 7.4 per cent of the men and 5.5 per cent of the women admitted that this arrangement would either be "all right" or that "it's up to her; doesn't matter."[47]

We are similarly told that in British Guiana the children born outside wedlock "are not sharply differentiated by any stigma of illegiti-

40. *Ibid.*, pp. 221-231. After a long consensual union, may marriage occur because the man and woman come to have the same rank?

41. Perhaps the Natchez were an exception. See Kingsley Davis, "Intermarriage in Caste Societies," *American Anthropologist*, 43 (July-September, 1941), pp. 382 ff. Of course, a "free courtship system" achieves the same end; and one may date a person whom one may not marry without censure.

42. Stycos, *op. cit.*, pp. 108, 110-111.

43. Eric R. Wolf, "San José: Subcultures of a 'Traditional' Coffee Municipality," in *The People of Puerto Rico, op. cit.*, p. 220. In Puerto Rico, the girl is usually a virgin when she enters a consensual union. Bastien makes the same claim for the Marbial area in Haiti, but to my knowledge no observer of other Haitian areas has done so; and Bastien is inconsistent. See Bastien, *op. cit.*, pp. 64, 65, 72.

44. Mintz, *op. cit.*, p. 378.

45. Elena Padilla Seda, "Nocora: The Subculture of Workers on a Government-Owned Suger Plantation," in *The People of Puerto Rico, op. cit.*, p. 293.

46. Paul K. Hatt, *Backgrounds of Human Fertility in Puerto Rico*, Princeton: Princeton University Press, 1952, p. 127.

47. *Ibid.*, p. 64. I would suppose, however, that the percentage would be much less on the mainland of the United States.

macy," while the consensual union is a "socially sanctioned one," and "part of the lower-class tradition."[48] Once again, however, we can note that parents are angry at the daughter and beat her when she becomes pregnant while still in the home. An unmarried mother will usually ask another person to take her illegitimate child to church for baptism.[49] And, although the scholar here quoted agrees with a turn-of-the-century French writer on the Congo who asserted that among the Bavili "birth sanctifies the child," a man's "outside" children in British Guiana do not rank equally with his legitimate children, and not all of a woman's children remain with her in a new marital union.[50] Moreover, only the married woman is called "Mistress," while her marital rights are clearer and more secure.[51] Marriage confers a different status on the woman. Women wish to marry, and after they have begun to have illegitimate children they understand that they can achieve this status only by gambling that a quasi-marital union may develop into a marriage.[52] Finally, most people do marry eventually, and the legal, monogamic union is clearly the ideal.[53]

Differential Intensity of Norm Commitment

Several conclusions and problems emerge from such a confrontation of general assertions with specific observations. In order to proceed to further related propositions, these conclusions may be summarized:

1. Unequivocally, Malinowski's Principle of Legitimacy holds even for these societies, for which various observers have asserted that it did not hold. Birth out of wedlock is not a "cultural alternative." There is no special approval of the consensual union, no "counter-norm" in favor of such a union. Of course, the parental anger aroused by a clandestine pregnancy will not be repeated when the girl has entered a consensual union. Nevertheless, in none of these societies does the unmarried mother of her child enjoy the same status as the married mother and her legitimate children. A union based on a marriage enjoys more respect than do other types of unions.

2. Equally clear, however, is the corroboration of another principle: that the degree of norm commitment varies from one segment of the population to another. Not only do some individuals reject particular

48. Raymond T. Smith, *The Negro Family in British Guiana,* New York: Grove Press, 1956, pp. 109, 149, 182.

49. *Ibid.*, pp. 126, 145, 132.

50. *Ibid.*, pp. 102, 120, 156, 178.

51. *Ibid.*, pp. 179-180; see also pp. 59, 148-149.

52. *Ibid.*, p. 138. The highest illegitimacy rate occurs among births to females 15-19 years of age; British Guiana, *Annual Report . . ., op. cit.*, p. 9.

53. *Ibid.*, Chapter 5.

norms, but the members of some strata are less concerned than those of others about given norms.[54]

3. A more specific inference from the latter principle is also corroborated, namely, that the lower social strata are less committed than the middle or upper strata to a variety of family norms, in this instance that of legitimacy,[55] and also obey them less.

More important, however, is a reformulation of Malinowski's principle. As stated, it gives too little emphasis to the real foundation on which it rests, and ignores the differences in norm commitment among different strata, doubtless because neither problem was important in the societies with which Malinowski was concerned. The principle in fact rests primarily upon the function of status placement, not that of locating a father as "protector": the bastard daughter of a count is still illegitimate even if he "protects" her. Violation of the norm creates some status ambiguity with respect to the child, the parents, and the two kin lines. Consequently:

4. Commitment to the norm of legitimacy will be greater among the strata *or* kin lines which enjoy a higher prestige, or in which concern with the kin relation is higher. Although in general this concern is more marked in the upper strata, in every stratum there will be *some* family lines which possess "traditions," pride, a sense of kin identity, and so on. Illegitimacy rates can be expected to be higher among the lower strata in all societies.

5. Correlatively, to the extent that a given society possesses a high proportion of lower strata families who are concerned little or not at all with their lineage, that society will exhibit a higher total rate of illegitimacy than it would have if the proportion were lower.

Given a high rate of illegitimacy, two further inferences may be made:

6. The actual amount of stigma suffered by the average illegitimate child cannot be great, relative to legitimate children in his same stratum and neighborhood.

---

54. Thus, one can find individuals who specifically reject marriage for one reason or another in all these societies. However, the empirical question is: what percentage of the society or stratum? In our society, too, any public opinion poll will locate a few such individuals.

55. There is substantial literature on this point. See, e.g., William J. Goode, *After Divorce*, New York: Free Press, 1956, Chapters 4 and 5; Ruth S. Cavan, *The Family*, New York: Crowell, 1953, Chapters 5, 6, and 7; and William F. Whyte, "A Slum Sex Code," *American Journal of Sociology*, 49 (July, 1943), pp. 24-31. For other data relevant to the subsequent discussion, see Herbert Hyman, "The Value Systems of Different Classes . . .," in R. Bendix and S. M. Lipset, editors, *Class, Status, and Power*, New York: Free Press, 1953, pp. 426-442.

7. The "matrifocality" of the Caribbean family is merely the result of the mother being left with her children, by either a casual lover, a consensual partner, or husband. The "matriarch" who is in charge has power precisely because no other adult of her generation is there to exercise it. Very likely a different personality configuration as well as a different self-image can and sometimes does develop from this experience.[56] The loyalty of children to the mother is stronger under such a system, since the father is not likely to be around during much of the infancy and youth of the offspring.[57]

On the other hand, early in the union, or continuously when the father remains in the union, the male behaves in a fashion which might be called "patriarchal" in the United States. It is possible that some observers have been misled, in their evaluation of the mother's power, by a false image of male behavior in such patriarchal societies as Japan, China, and India, where in fact the older mother is likely to have great authority in the home even when she pays considerable overt deference to the male head of family.

Role Bargaining and Illegitimacy

An "explanation" of these high rates may properly take two directions. One of these would widen our empirical perspective to include other areas of the world, especially the countries south of the Rio Grande where high illegitimacy rates are found, and locate the cultural elements which are common to them. In a related paper, I am making such an analysis, with special reference to the cultural structure of a society and conformity to its norms. This analysis seeks to answer the question: in what types of societies are high rates found?

The second direction is to focus on the more immediate social forces which create a high illegitimacy rate in the Caribbean. It may be granted that the lower norm commitment in the lower strata of this area would, other things being equal, decrease conformity. Intensity of norm com-

56. Nor should the matter of *self-selection* be forgotten. Given the social option, some individuals will find this role more congenial and choose it against other alternatives.

57. Although almost every writer points to "some" consensual unions which have "lasted as long as" legal ones, the instability of both types seems indubitable, and consensual unions are less stable; see R. T. Smith, "Family Organization in British Guiana," *Social and Economic Studies*, 1 (No. 1, 1953), p. 101; Simpson, *op. cit.*, p. 656; Braithwaite, *op. cit.*, p. 147; Seda, *op. cit.*, p. 293; Mintz, *op. cit.*, p. 375; Stycos, *op. cit.*, p. 119; Simey, *op. cit.*, p. 16. (Kreiselman, by contrast, asserts stability for both types: *op. cit.*, p. 180). That matrifocality is by default has been noted by others, e.g., Kreiselman, *op. cit.*, p. 282; Simey, *op. cit.*, p. 43; Braithwaite, *op. cit.*, p. 147.

mitment, however, is only one element in the decision to risk pregnancy. The social pattern of primary importance is that the young woman in her courtship behavior must make essentially an *individual role bargain.* This apparent contrast with courtship patterns which produce low illegitimacy rates requires only little attention.

By "making an individual role bargain," I refer to the fact that in any role relationship both ego and alter are restricted in what services they may agree to perform for one another, by the expectations of others and thus by the sanctions which others will apply. For example, father and daughter owe and feel they owe, certain obligations to one another, and in part these obligations are met because of the rewards and sanctions which either can direct toward the other. However, even if both of them are willing to agree to a different set of obligations—say, those appropriate to lovers—there is a "third layer" of persons who have role relationships with either ego and alter, or both of them, and who will act to force both of them to perform properly. These actions include pressures on ego or alter to punish the other for improper performance.

All courtship systems are market systems, in which role bargains are struck. They differ from one another with respect to the commodities which are more or less valuable on that market (beauty, personality, kinship position, family prestige, wealth) and who has the authority to do the marketing. Modern Western societies seem to constitute the only major historical civilization in which youngsters have been given a substantial voice in this bargaining (Imperial Rome might be added by some historians). Even in the United States, however, where this trend is most fully developed, numerous studies have shown that youngsters make their choices within a highly restricted market, with respect to age, race, religion, social class, and so on. Precisely because courtship systems are bargaining systems, apparently hypergamous marriages (the woman marries upward in class) usually are, in most societies, unions in which a high ranking on one or more variables (wealth, beauty) is traded for a high ranking on other variables (power, prestige, race).[58] As a consequence, most marriages occur between individuals of like rank, or at least like bargaining power,[59] whether youngsters or their elders have the greater authority to conduct the bargaining process. When one party has much less bargaining power, he may be unable to

58. See Davis, *op. cit.,* p. 386.

59. Of course, the principle of least interest operates in courtship as in marital conflict; the individual who is more deeply in love has less bargaining power. Willard Waller and Reuben Hill, *The Family: A Dynamic Interpretation,* New York: Dryden, 1953, pp. 190-192.

pay as much as the other demands, or will have to pay much more than another family with greater bargaining power.

Although these principles hold with respect to both the choice of marital partner and the decision to marry at all, they are upheld, as is any market system, by a set of community-wide or stratum-wide set of agreements about *what* is valuable and *how* valuable those characteristics are, and a set of corresponding pressures which prevent the individual from paying too much. In our society, for example, even if a middle-class girl is willing to bear a child outside of marriage, usually her parents will oppose this behavior strongly because she would be giving more than need be under the operating market system.

By contrast, what is striking in the Caribbean community studies are the anonymity and isolation within which the decision is made to enter a union, and the fact that under those social conditions the girl has little chance of being married at all unless she is willing to risk a union outside of marriage. Not only does she become pregnant without her parents' knowing that she is courting, but she is also likely to enter the consensual union without any prior ritual or public announcement.[60]

A synthesis of the factors of importance in the decision to marry or to enter a consensual union can be made from the existing studies (although in many cases needed data are lacking because the appropriate questions were not asked[61]). Especially important are the following five points:

1. The class pattern of marriage has been suggested above. This may be clarified here by noting that not only do middle- and upper-class individuals marry (though of course males from those strata may have mistresses whom they do not marry), but that most members of the lower strata also marry eventually. Some lower class persons never enter a consensual union, but begin their conjugal career by a wedding. Others begin with a consensual union, but marry sooner or later, usually after the male has somewhat improved his social position. In certain communities which seem to enjoy a higher social standing, a substantial majority of all marital unions are legal.[62]

2. Kreiselman's finding for Martinique concerning marriages between persons of similar rank can be extended to every Caribbean community. Notwithstanding the frequently voiced assumption to the contrary, many fine distinctions of prestige are made within the lower class, in

60. Smith, *op. cit.*, pp. 101, 137.

61. For Jamaica, as noted in footnote 27, the most complete synthesis has been made by Blake, *op. cit.*

62. E.g., Orange Grove reported in Clarke, *op. cit.;* Better Hope reported in Smith, *op. cit.;* and apparently San José as reported in Wolf, *op. cit.*

spite of its apparent homogeneity to the (usually White) outside observer.[63] If there were no other index, we could rely on the fact that certain members of the lower class do marry without entering a consensual union.[64] However, other data are also available, for example, the higher ranking of unskilled laborers with *steady* jobs. Granted, these differences are less sharp or refined than the gross differences between upper and lower strata, but within the narrower class horizon of persons in the bottom stratum they may nevertheless loom large. From this fact, we can suppose that when marriage does occur, the man and woman are more likely to be "rank equals," within the more generalized terms proposed above—which include not merely family prestige but also personal qualities such as beauty.[65]

3. Given a system in which consensual unions are common, it follows that the punishments for entering them cannot be severe, and the rewards for marrying cannot be great. (This proposition is an inference from a well-known principle of social control.) Consequently, the girl's parents or relatives (there is no extended kin group which acts as a unit) are punished or rewarded very little if, in turn, they make or fail to make her behavior conform to "ideal" norms.

4. In the Caribbean, there is no "free" adolescent courtship system such as our own, in which an as yet ineligible male is permitted to approach an immature girl, under the protection of her relatives and peer group. Many or most of the men she first meets are ineligible because of the great cost of a wedding. Most of them have not accumulated enough wealth to finance the formal union and to support its subsequent requirement of a higher level of living than a consensual union.[66] Consequently, the girl's first love and sex contacts occur away from home, and without the knowledge of the family. These first contacts take place essentially in social anonymity, so that she must make the best bargain she can, without the family's support.[67] Parental anger, reported in most studies, is at least in part a reaction to the knowledge that the girl has entered the world of adulthood without parental permission and has acted independently while presumably still a child.[68]

63. For example, although Smith, *op. cit.*, pp. 218-220 *et passim*, refers to a lack of status differentiation, his detailed descriptions show considerable differentiation.

64. See, for example, Smith's description (*ibid.*, pp. 169-170) of a formal engagement; Seda's comment that parents may insist on a wedding ceremony (*op. cit.*, p. 293); and Clarke, *op. cit.*, pp. 85-88.

65. Here the variable of rank is generalized, of course, and Kreiselman's observation (*op. cit.*, p. 278) from Martinique is extrapolated to the rest of the Caribbean.

66. Cf. Clarke, *op. cit.*, pp. 78, 99; Herskovits and Herskovits, *op. cit.*, p. 84.

67. Kreiselman, *op. cit.*, p. 99; Herskovits and Herskovits, *op. cit.*, p. 88; Smith, *op. cit.*, pp. 109, 137, 145.

68. Smith, *op. cit.*, p. 145, makes this point clearly, citing a common statement, "If you want to play a big woman go find yourself a man."

5. The Caribbean girl with unusual qualities may be able to demand marriage. However, the average girl has little chance at marriage, early or late, unless she is willing to gamble that a more permanent union will grow from one relationship or another. Without reliable data on the number of unions in the average individual's life, we cannot state what these chances are. Motherhood lowers the girl's value in the market, but if she does not produce a child for the man with whom she is living, or with whom she has a liaison, her chance of a stable union is low.[69] The decision to marry, within the existing social structure, is his rather than hers, and she gains more from marriage than he does. Consequently, as noted previously, it is the women who press toward marriage, while they must take the only road which can–and, apparently, eventually does–lead to marriage. Meanwhile, however, a woman may have children by several men, and may leave some or all of them with her parents or relatives when entering a new union[70]–a practice often resulting in the "grandmother" family. The widespread adoption pattern in the Caribbean is in part a method of taking care of these children. Ideally, a man wants only his own children in his home, especially if he is marrying.

Summary

Although Malinowski's Principle of Legitimacy has been called into question by several students of the Caribbean, the detailed descriptions of family and courtship patterns in that area show that it is generally valid. Derived from societies in which conformity to this norm was high, however, the principle requires revision. This should emphasize status placement rather than "paternal protection," and should specify the lower strata as the part of the society in which deviation from the norm is greatest. In addition, revision of the principle should note the weaker norm commitment in these strata, and the resulting lowering of both punishment for deviation and reward for conformity.

The "matrifocal" Caribbean family is a product of an unstable family pattern, in which the mother or grandmother is often in power because no father is there. The courtship pattern is anonymous, so that the young girl must make the best bargain she can, which usually means that she must be willing to risk pregnancy in order to establish a basis for a more stable union. Eventually, most individuals do enter a mar-

69. At the same time a pregnancy may frighten him away, as being too great a burden to assume. Clarke, *op. cit.*, pp. 75, 91, 100-102; Smith, *op. cit.*, p. 138. Blake, *op cit.*, also reports that fact.

70. Herskovits and Herskovits, *op. cit.*, pp. 104-105, 131; Clarke, *op. cit.*, p. 91; Smith, *op. cit.*, Chapter 4.

riage. The girl is not protected by her relatives or peers in this bargaining. Thus, though the Principle of Legitimacy is valid, it must be revised. It has also been shown how courtship relations in the Caribbean may lead to a high illegitimacy rate, even when the norm of legitimacy is accepted.

JAMES D. THOMPSON
and WILLIAM J. McEWEN

Organizational Goals and Environment: Goal-Setting as an Interaction Process

IN the analysis of complex organizations the definition of organizational goals is commonly utilized as a standard for appraising organizational performance. In many such analyses the goals of the organization are often viewed as a constant. Thus a wide variety of data, such as official documents, work activity records, organizational output, or statements by organizational spokesmen, may provide the basis for the definition of goals. Once this definition has been accomplished, interest in goals as a dynamic aspect of organizational activity frequently ends.

It is possible, however, to view the setting of goals (i.e., major organizational purposes) not as a static element but as a necessary and recurring problem facing any organization, whether it is governmental, military, business, educational, medical, religious, or other type.

This perspective appears appropriate in developing the two major lines of the present analysis. The first of these is to emphasize the interdependence of complex organizations within the larger society and the consequences this has for organizational goal-setting. The second is to emphasize the similarities of goal-setting *processes* in organizations with

---

Reprinted from American Sociological Review, *February, 1958, pp. 23-31, by permission of the authors and the journal.*

manifestly different goals. The present analysis is offered to supplement recent studies of organizational operations.[1]

It is postulated that goal-setting behavior is *purposive* but not necessarily *rational;* we assume that goals may be determined by accident, i.e., by blundering of members of the organization and, contrariwise, that the most calculated and careful determination of goals may be negated by developments outside the control of organization members. The goal-setting problem as discussed here is essentially determining a relationship of the organization to the larger society, which in turn becomes a question of what the society (or elements within it) wants done or can be persuaded to support.

Goals as Dynamic Variables

Because the setting of goals is essentially a problem of defining desired relationships between an organization and its environment, change in either requires review and perhaps alteration of goals. Even where the most abstract statement of goals remains constant, application requires redefinition or interpretation as changes occur in the organization, the environment, or both.

The corporation, for example, faces changing markets and develops staff specialists with responsibility for continuous study and projection of market changes and product appeal. The governmental agency, its legislative mandate notwithstanding, has need to reformulate or reinterpret its goals as other agencies are created and dissolved, as the population changes, or as non-governmental organizations appear to do the same job or to compete. The school and the university may have unchanging abstract goals but the clientele, the needs of pupils or students, and the techniques of teaching change and bring with them redefinition and reinterpretation of those objectives. The hospital has been faced with problems requiring an expansion of goals to include consideration of preventive medicine, public health practices, and the degree to which the hospital should extend its activities out into the community. The mental hospital and the prison are changing their objectives from primary emphasis on custody to a stress on therapy. Even the church alters its pragmatic objectives as changes in the society call for new forms of social ethics, and as government and organized philan-

1. Among recent materials that treat organizational goal-setting are Kenneth E. Boulding, *The Organizational Revolution*, New York: Harper and Brothers, 1953; Robert A. Dahl and Charles E. Lindblom, *Politics, Economics, and Welfare*, New York: Harper and Brothers, 1953; and John K. Galbraith, *American Capitalism: The Concept of Countervailing Power*, Boston: Houghton Mifflin, 1952.

thropy take over some of the activities formerly left to organized religion.[2]

Reappraisal of goals thus appears to be a recurrent problem for large organization, albeit a more constant problem in an unstable environment than in a stable one. Reappraisal of goals likewise appears to be more difficult as the "product" of the enterprise becomes less tangible and more difficult to measure objectively. The manufacturing firm has a relatively ready index of the acceptability of its product in sales figures; while poor sales may indicate inferior quality rather than public distaste for the commodity itself, sales totals frequently are supplemented by trade association statistics indicating the firm's "share of the market." Thus within a matter of weeks, a manufacturing firm may be able to reappraise its decision to enter the "widget" market and may therefore begin deciding how it can get out of that market with the least cost.

The governmental enterprise may have similar indicators of the acceptability of its goals if it is involved in producing an item such as electricity, but where its activity is oriented to a less tangible purpose such as maintaining favorable relations with foreign nations, the indices of effective operation are likely to be less precise and the vagaries more numerous. The degree to which a government satisfies its clientele may be reffected periodically in elections, but despite the claims of party officials, it seldom is clear just what the mandate of the people is with reference to any particular governmental enterprise. In addition, the public is not always steadfast in its mandate.

The university perhaps has even greater difficulties in evaluating its environmental situation through response to its output. Its range of "products" is enormous, extending from astronomers to zoologists. The test of a competent specialist is not always standardized and may be changing, and the university's success in turning out "educated" people is judged by many and often conflicting standards. The university's product is in process for four or more years and when it is placed on the "market" it can be only imperfectly judged. Vocational placement statistics may give some indication of the university's success in its objectives, but initial placement is no guarantee of performance at a

2. For pertinent studies of various organizational types see Burton R. Clark, *Adult Education in Transition*, Berkeley: University of California Press, 1956; Temple Burling, Edith M. Lentz, and Robert N. Wilson, *The Give and Take in Hospitals*, New York: G. P. Putnam's Sons, 1956, especially pp. 3-10; Lloyd E. Ohlin, *Sociology and the Field of Corrections*, New York: Russell Sage Foundation, 1956, pp. 13-18; Liston Pope, *Millhands and Preachers*, New Haven: Yale University Press, 1942; Charles Y. Glock and Benjamin B. Ringer, "Church Policy and the Attitudes of Ministers and Parishioners on Social Issues," *American Sociological Review*, 21 (April, 1956), pp. 148-156. For a similar analysis in the field of philanthropy, see J. R. Seeley, B. H. Junker, R. W. Jones, Jr., and others, *Community Chest: A Case Study in Philanthropy*, Toronto: University of Toronto Press, 1957, especially Chapters 2 and 5.

later date. Furthermore, performance in an occupation is only one of several abilities that the university is supposed to produce in its students. Finally, any particular department of the university may find that its reputation lags far behind its performance. A "good" department may work for years before its reputation becomes "good" and a downhill department may coast for several years before the fact is realized by the professional world.

In sum, the goals of an organization, which determine the kinds of goods or services it produces and offers to the environment, often are subject to peculiar difficulties of reappraisal. Where the purpose calls for an easily identified, readily measured product, reappraisal and readjustment of goals may be accomplished rapidly. But as goals call for increasingly intangible, difficult-to-measure products, society finds it more difficult to determine and reflect its acceptability of that product, and the signals that indicate unacceptable goals are less effective and perhaps longer in coming.

Environmental Controls over Goals

A continuing situation of necessary interaction between an organization and its environment introduces an element of environmental control into the organization. While the motives of personnel, including goal-setting officers, may be profits, prestige, votes, or the salvation of souls, their efforts must produce something useful or acceptable to at least a part of the organizational environment to win continued support.[3]

In the simpler society social control over productive activities may be exercised rather informally and directly through such means as gossip and ridicule. As a society becomes more complex and its productive activities more deliberately organized, social controls are increasingly exercised through such formal devices as contracts, legal codes, and governmental regulations. The stability of expectations provided by these devices is arrived at through interaction, and often through the exercise of power in interaction.

It is possible to conceive of a continuum of organizational power in environmental relations, ranging from the organization that dominates its environmental relations to one completely dominated by its environment. Few organizations approach either extreme. Certain gigantic industrial enterprises, such as the *Zaibatsu* in Japan or the old Standard

3. This statement would seem to exclude antisocial organizations, such as crime syndicates. A detailed analysis of such organizations would be useful for many purposes; meanwhile it would appear necessary for them to acquire a clientele, suppliers, and others, in spite of the fact that their methods at times may be somewhat unique.

Oil Trust in America, have approached the dominance-over-environment position at one time, but this position eventually brought about "countervailing powers."[4] Perhaps the nearest approximation to the completely powerless organization is the commuter transit system, which may be unable to cover its costs but nevertheless is regarded as a necessary utility and cannot get permission to quit business. Most complex organizations, falling somewhere between the extremes of the power continuum, must adopt strategies for coming to terms with their environments. This is not to imply that such strategies are necessarily chosen by rational or deliberate processes. An organization can survive so long as it adjusts to its situation; whether the process of adjustment is awkward or nimble becomes important in determining the organization's degree of prosperity.

However arrived at, strategies for dealing with the organizational environment may be broadly classified as either *competitive* or *cooperative*. Both appear to be important in a complex society—of the "free enterprise" type or other.[5] Both provide a measure of environmental control over organizations by providing for "outsiders" to enter into or limit organizational decision process.

The decision process may be viewed as a series of activities, conscious or not, culminating in a choice among alternatives. For purposes of this paper we view the decision-making process as consisting of the following activities:

1. Recognizing an occasion for decision, i.e., a need or an opportunity.
2. Analysis of the existing situation.
3. Identification of alternative courses of action.
4. Assessment of the probable consequences of each alternative.
5. Choice from among alternatives.[6]

The following discussion suggests that the potential power of an

4. For the *Zaibatsu* case see Japan Council, *The Control of Industry in Japan*, Tokyo: Institute of Political and Economic Research, 1953; and Edwin O. Reischauer, *The United States and Japan*, Cambridge: Harvard University Press, 1954, pp. 87-97.

5. For evidence on Russia see David Granick, *Management of the Industrial Firm in the U.S.S.R.*, New York: Columbia University Press, 1954; and Joseph S. Berliner, "Informal Organization of the Soviet Firm," *Quarterly Journal of Economics*, 66 (August, 1952), pp. 353-365.

6. This particular breakdown is taken from Edward H. Litchfield, "Notes on a General Theory of Administration," *Administrative Science Quarterly*, 1 (June, 1956), pp. 3-29. We are also indebted to Robert Tannenbaum and Fred Massarik who, by breaking the decision-making process into three steps, show that subordinates can take part in the "manager's decision" even when the manager makes the final choice. See "Participation by Subordinates in the Managerial Decision-Making Process," *Canadian Journal of Economics and Political Science*, 16 (August, 1949), pp. 410-418.

outsider increases the earlier he enters into the decision process,[7] and that competition and three sub-types of cooperative strategy—*bargaining*, *co-optation*, and *coalition*—differ in this respect. It is therefore possible to order these forms of interaction in terms of the degree to which they provide for environmental control over organizational goal-setting decisions.

Competition. The term competition implies an element of rivalry. For present purposes competition refers to that form of rivalry between two or more organizations which is mediated by a third party. In the case of the manufacturing firm the third party may be the customer, the supplier, the potential or present member of the labor force, or others. In the case of the governmental bureau, the third party through whom competition takes place may be the legislative committee, the budget bureau, or the chief executive, as well as potential clientele and potential members of the bureau.

The complexity of competition in a heterogeneous society is much greater than customary usage (with economic overtones) often suggests. Society judges the enterprise not only by the finished product but also in terms of the desirability of applying resources to that purpose. Even the organization that enjoys a product monopoly must compete for society's support. From the society it must obtain resources—personnel, finances, and materials—as well as customers or clientele. In the business sphere of a "free enterprise" economy this competition for resources and customers usually takes place in the market, but in times of crisis the society may exercise more direct controls, such as rationing or the establishment of priorities during a war. The monopoly competes with enterprises having different purposes or goals but using similar raw materials; it competes with many other enterprises, for human skills and loyalties, and it competes with many other activities for support in the money markets.

The university, customarily a non-profit organization, competes as eagerly as any business firm, although perhaps more subtly.[8] Virtually every university seeks, if not more students, better-qualified students. Publicly supported universities compete at annual budget sessions with other governmental enterprises for shares in tax revenues. Endowed universities must compete for gifts and bequests, not only with other universities but also with museums, charities, zoos, and similar non-profit enterprises. The American university is only one of many organizations

7. Robert K. Merton makes a similar point regarding the role of the intellectual in public bureaucracy. See his *Social Theory and Social Structure*, New York: The Free Press, 1949, Chapter VI.

8. See Logan Wilson, *The Academic Man*, New York: Oxford University Press, 1942, especially Chapter IX. Also see Warren G. Bennis, "The Effect on Academic Goods of Their Market," *American Journal of Sociology*, 62 (July, 1956), pp. 28-33.

competing for foundation support, and it competes with other universities and with other types of organizations for faculty.

The public school system, perhaps one of our most pervasive forms of near-monopoly, not only competes with other governmental units for funds and with different types of organizations for teachers, but current programs espoused by professional educators often compete in a very real way with a public conception of the nature of education, e.g., as the three R's, devoid of "frills."

The hospital may compete with the midwife, the faith-healer, the "quack" and the patent-medicine manufacturer, as well as with neighboring hospitals, despite the fact that general hospitals do not "advertise" and are not usually recognized as competitive.

Competition is thus a complicated network of relationships. It includes scrambling for resources as well as for customers or clients, and in a complex society it includes rivalry for potential members and their loyalties. In each case a third party makes a choice among alternatives, two or more organizations attempt to influence that choice through some type of "appeal" or offering, and choice by the third party is a "vote" of support for one of the competing organizations and a denial of support to the others involved.

Competition, then, is one process whereby the organization's choice of goals is partially controlled by the environment. It tends to prevent unilateral or arbitrary choice of organizational goals, or to correct such a choice if one is made. Competition for society's support is an important means of eliminating not only inefficient organizations but also those that seek to provide goods or services the environment is not willing to accept.

Bargaining. The term bargaining, as used here, refers to the negotiation of an agreement for the exchange of goods or services between two or more organizations. Even where fairly stable and dependable expectations have been built up with important elements of the organizational environment—with suppliers, distributors, legislators, workers and so on—the organization cannot assume that these relationships will continue. Periodic review of these relationships must be accomplished, and an important means for this is bargaining, whereby each organization, through negotiation, arrives at a decision about future behavior satisfactory to the others involved.

The need for periodic adjustment of relationships is demonstrated most dramatically in collective bargaining between labor and industrial management, in which the bases for continued support by organization members are reviewed.[9] But bargaining occurs in other important, if less dramatic, areas of organizational endeavor. The business firm must bar-

9. For an account of this on a daily basis see Melville Dalton, "Unofficial Union-

gain with its agents or distributors, and while this may appear at times to be one-sided and hence not much of a bargain, still even a long-standing agency agreement may be severed by competitive offers unless the agent's level of satisfaction is maintained through periodic review.[10] Where suppliers are required to install new equipment to handle the peculiar demands of an organization, bargaining between the two is not unusual.

The university likewise must bargain.[11] It may compete for free or unrestricted funds, but often it must compromise that ideal by bargaining away the name of a building or of a library collection, or by the conferring of an honorary degree. Graduate students and faculty members may be given financial or other concessions through bargaining, in order to prevent their loss to other institutions.

The governmental organization may also find bargaining expedient.[12] The police department, for example, may overlook certain violations of statutes in order to gain the support of minor violators who have channels of information not otherwise open to department members. Concessions to those who "turn state's evidence" are not unusual. Similarly a department of state may forego or postpone recognition of a foreign power in order to gain support for other aspects of its policy, and a governmental agency may relinquish certain activities in order to gain budget bureau approval of more important goals.

While bargaining may focus on resources rather than explicitly on goals, the fact remains that it is improbable that a goal can be effective unless it is at least partially implemented. To the extent that bargaining sets limits on the amount of resources available or the ways they may be employed, it effectively sets limits on choice of goals. Hence bargaining, like competition, results in environmental control over organizational goals and reduces the probability of arbitrary, unilateral goal-setting.

Unlike competition, however, bargaining involves direct interaction with other organizations in the environment, rather than with a third party. Bargaining appears, therefore, to invade the actual decision process. To the extent that the second party's support is necessary he is in a position to exercise a veto over final choice of alternative goals, and hence takes part in the decision.

Management Relations," *American Sociological Review,* 15 (October, 1950), pp. 611-619.

10. See Valentine F. Ridgway, "Administration of Manufacturer-Dealer Systems," *Administrative Science Quarterly*, 1 (March, 1957), pp. 464-483.

11. Wilson, *op. cit.*, Chapters VII and VIII.

12. For an interesting study of governmental bargaining see William J. Gore, "Administrative Decision-Making in Federal Field Offices," *Public Administration Review,* 16 (Autumn, 1956), pp. 281-291.

Co-optation. Co-optation has been defined as the process of absorbing new elements into the leadership or policy-determining structure of an organization as a means of averting threats to its stability or existence.[13] Co-optation makes still further inroads on the process of deciding goals; not only must the final choice be acceptable to the co-opted party or organization, but to the extent that co-optation is effective it places the representative of an "outsider" in a position to determine the occasion for a goal decision, to participate in analyzing the existing situation, to suggest alternatives, and to take part in the deliberation of consequences.

The term co-optation has only recently been given currency in this country, but the phenomenon it describes is neither new nor unimportant. The acceptance on a corporation's board of directors of representatives of banks or other financial institutions is a time-honored custom among firms that have large financial obligations or that may in the future want access to financial resources. The state university may find it expedient (if not mandatory) to place legislators on its board of trustees, and the endowed college may find that whereas the honorary degree brings forth a token gift, membership on the board may result in a more substantial bequest. The local medical society often plays a decisive role in hospital goal-setting, since the support of professional medical practitioners is urgently necessary for the hospital.

From the standpoint of society, however, co-optation is more than an expediency. By giving a potential supporter a position of power and often of responsibility in the organization, the organization gains his awareness and understanding of the problems it faces. A business advisory council may be an effective educational device for a government, and a White House conference on education may mobilize "grass roots" support in a thousand localities, both by focusing attention on the problem area and by giving key people a sense of participation in goal deliberation.

Moreover, by providing overlapping memberships, co-optation is an important social device for increasing the likelihood that organizations related to one another in complicated ways will in fact find compatible goals. By thus reducing the possibilities of antithetical actions by two or more organizations, co-optation aids in the integration of the heterogeneous parts of a complex society. By the same token, co-optation further limits the opportunity for one organization to choose its goals arbitrarily or unilaterally.

Coalition. As used here, the term coalition refers, to a combination of two or more organizations for a common purpose. Coalition appears to

13. Philip Selznick, *TVA and the Grass Roots*, Berkeley: University of California Press, 1949.

be the ultimate or extreme form of environmental conditioning of organizational goals.[14] A coalition may be unstable, but to the extent that it is operative, two or more organizations act as one with respect to certain goals. Coalition is a means widely used when two or more enterprises wish to pursue a goal calling for more support, especially for more resources, than any one of them is able to marshal unaided. American business firms frequently resort to coalition for purposes of research or product promotion and for the construction of such gigantic facilities as dams or atomic reactors.[15]

Coalition is not uncommon among educational organizations. Universities have established joint operations in such areas as nuclear research, archaeological research, and even social science research. Many smaller colleges have banded together for fund-raising purposes. The consolidation of public school districts is another form of coalition (if not merger), and the fact that it does represent a sharing or "invasion" of goal-setting power is reflected in some of the bitter resistance to consolidation in tradition-oriented localities.

Coalition requires a commitment for joint decision of future activities and thus places limits on unilateral or arbitrary decisions. Furthermore, inability of an organization to find partners in a coalition venture automatically prevents pursuit of that objective, and is therefore also a form of social control. If the collective judgment is that a proposal is unworkable, a possible disaster may be escaped and unproductive allocation of resources avoided.

Development of Environmental Support

Environmental control is not a one-way process limited to consequences for the organization of action in its environment. Those subject to control are also part of the larger society and hence are also agents of social control. The enterprise that competes is not only influenced in its goal-setting by what the competitor and the third party may do, but also exerts influence over both. Bargaining likewise is a form of mutual, two-

14. Coalition may involve joint action toward only limited aspects of the goals of each member. It may involve the complete commitment of each member for a specific period of time or indefinitely. In either case the ultimate power to withdraw is retained by the members. We thus distinguish coalition from merger, in which two or more organizations are fused permanently. In merger one or all of the original parts may lose their identity. Goal-setting in such a situation, of course, is no longer subject to inter-organizational constraints among the components.

15. See "The Joint Venture Is an Effective Approach to Major Engineering Projects," *New York Times,* July 14, 1957, Section 3, p. 1 F.

way influence; co-optation affects the co-opted as well as the co-opting party; and coalition clearly sets limits on both parties.

Goals appear to grow out of interaction, both within the organization and between the organization and its environment. While every enterprise must find sufficient support for its goals, it may wield initiative in this. The difference between effective and ineffective organizations may well lie in the initiative exercised by those in the organization who are responsible for goal-setting.

The ability of an administrator to win support for an objective may be as vital as his ability to foresee the utility of a new idea. And his role as a "seller" of ideas may be as important to society as to his organization, for as society becomes increasingly specialized and heterogeneous, the importance of new objectives may be more readily seen by specialized segments than by the general society. It was not public clamor that originated revisions in public school curricula and training methods; the impetus came largely from professional specialists in or on the periphery of education.[16] The shift in focus from custody to therapy in mental hospitals derives largely from the urgings of professionals, and the same can be said of our prisons.[17] In both cases the public anger, aroused by crusaders and muck-rakers, might have been soothed by more humane methods of custody. Current attempts to revitalize the liberal arts curricula of our colleges, universities, and technical institutes have developed more in response to the activities of professional specialists than from public urging.[18] Commercial aviation, likewise, was "sold" the hard way, with support being based on subsidy for a considerable period before the importance of such transportation was apparent to the larger public.[19]

In each of these examples the goal-setters saw their ideas become widely accepted only after strenuous efforts to win support through education of important elements of the environment. Present currents in some medical quarters to shift emphasis from treatment of the sick to maintenance of health through preventive medicine and public health

16. See Robert S. and Helen Merrell Lynd, *Middletown in Transition*, New York: Harcourt, Brace, and World, 1937, Chapter VI.

17. Milton Greenblatt, Richard H. York, and Esther Lucille Brown, *From Custodial to Therapeutic Patient Care in Mental Hospitals*, New York: Russell Sage Foundation, 1955, Chapter 1, and Ohlin, *loc. cit.*

18. For one example, see the Report of the Harvard Committee, *General Education in a Free Society*, Cambridge: Harvard University Press, 1945.

19. America's civil air transport industry began in 1926 and eight years later carried 500,000 passengers. Yet it was testified in 1934 that half of the $120 million invested in airlines had been lost in spite of subsidies. See Jerome C. Hunsaker, *Aeronautics at the Mid-Century*, New Haven: Yale University Press, 1952, pp. 37-38. The case of Billy Mitchell was, of course, the landmark in the selling of military aviation.

programs likewise have to be "sold" to a society schooled in an older concept.[20]

The activities involved in winning support for organizational goals thus are not confined to communication within the organization, however important this is. The need to justify organization goals, to explain the social functions of the organization, is seen daily in all types of "public relations" activities, ranging from luncheon club speeches to house organs. It is part of an educational requirement in a complicated society where devious interdependence hides many of the functions of organized, specialized activities.

Goal-Setting and Strategy

We have suggested that it is improbable that an organization can continue indefinitely if its goals are formulated arbitrarily, without cognizance of its relations to the environment. One of the requirements for survival appears to be ability to learn about the environment accurately enough and quickly enough to permit organizational adjustments in time to avoid extinction. In a more positive vein, it becomes important for an organization to judge the amount and sources of support that can be mobilized for a goal, and to arrive at a strategy for their mobilization.

Competition, bargaining, co-optation, and coalition constitute procedures for gaining support from the organizational environment; the selection of one or more of these is a strategic problem. It is here that the element of rationality appears to become exceedingly important, for in the order treated above, these relational processes represent increasingly "costly" methods of gaining support in terms of decision-making power. The organization that adopts a strategy of competition when co-optation is called for may lose all opportunity to realize its goals, or may finally turn to co-optation or coalition at a higher "cost" than would have been necessary originally. On the other hand, an organization may lose part of its integrity, and therefore some of its potentiality, if it unnecessarily shares power in exchange for support. Hence the establishment *in the appropriate form* of interaction with the many relevant parts of its environment can be a major organizational consideration in a complex society.

This means, in effect, that the organization must be able to estimate the position of other relevant organizations and their willingness to enter into or alter relationships. Often, too, these matters must be determined or estimated without revealing one's own weaknesses, or even one's ulti-

20. Ray E. Trussell, *Hunterdon Medical Center*, Cambridge: Harvard University Press (for the Commonwealth Fund), 1956, Chapter 3.

mate strength. It is necessary or advantageous, in other words, to have the consent or acquiescence of the other party, if a new relationship is to be established or an existing relationship altered. For this purpose organizational administrators often engage in what might be termed a *sounding out process.*[21]

The sounding out process can be illustrated by the problem of the boss with amorous designs on his secretary in an organization that taboos such relations. He must find some means of determining her willingness to alter the relationship, but he must do so without risking rebuff, for a showdown might come at the cost of his dignity or his office reputation, at the cost of losing her secretarial services, or in the extreme case at the cost of losing his own position. The "sophisticated" procedure is to create an ambiguous situation in which the secretary is forced to respond in one of two ways: (1) to ignore or tactfully counter, thereby clearly channeling the relationship back into an already existing pattern, or (2) to respond in a similarly ambiguous vein (if not in a positive one) indicating a receptiveness to further advances. It is important in the sounding out process that the situation be ambiguous for two reasons: (1) the secretary must not be able to "pin down" the boss with evidence if she rejects the idea, and (2) the situation must be far enough removed from normal to be noticeable to the secretary. The ambiguity of sounding out has the further advantage to the participants that neither party alone is clearly responsible for initiating the change.

The situation described above illustrates a process that seems to explain many organizational as well as personal interaction situations. In moving from one relationship to another between two or more organizations it is often necessary to leave a well defined situation and proceed through a period of deliberate ambiguity, to arrive at a new clearcut relationship. In interaction over goal-setting problems, sounding out sometimes is done through a form of double-talk, wherein the parties refer to "hypothetical" enterprises and "hypothetical" situations, or in "diplomatic" language, which often serves the same purpose. In other cases, and perhaps more frequently, sounding out is done through the good offices of a third party. This occurs, apparently, where there has been no relationship in the past, or at the stage of negotiations where the parties have indicated intentions but are not willing to state their positions frankly. Here it becomes useful at times to find a discreet go-between who can be trusted with full information and who will seek an arrangement suitable to both parties.

---

21. This section on the sounding out process is a modified version of a paper by James D. Thompson, William J. McEwen, and Frederick L. Bates, "Sounding Out as a Relating Process," read at the annual meeting of the Eastern Sociological Society, April, 1957.

Conclusion

In the complex modern society desired goals often require complex organizations. At the same time the desirability of goals and the appropriate division of labor among large organizations is less self-evident than in a simpler, more homogeneous society. Purpose becomes a question to be decided rather than an obvious matter.

To the extent that behavior of organization members is oriented to questions of goals or purposes, a science of organization must attempt to understand and explain that behavior. We have suggested one classification scheme, based on decision-making, as potentially useful in analyzing organizational-environmental interaction with respect to goal-setting and we have attempted to illustrate some aspects of its utility. It is hoped that the suggested scheme encompasses questions of rationality or irrationality without presuming either.

Argument by example, however, is at best only a starting point for scientific understanding and for the collection of evidence. Two factors make organizational goal-setting in a complex society a "big" research topic: the multiplicity of large organizations of diverse type and the necessity of studying them in diachronic perspective. We hope that our discussion will encourage critical thinking and the sharing of observations about the subject.

THEODORE M. MILLS

Equilibrium and the Processes of Deviance and Control

THIS paper explores certain theoretical issues that arise in applying an equilibrium model to processes of deviance and control in human behavioral systems. A number of social scientists have employed

Reprinted from American Sociological Review, *October, 1959, pp. 671-679, by permission of the author and the journal.*

Revision of paper presented at the annual meeting of the American Sociological

one or another of the notions of equilibrium in order to comprehend complex processes in such systems, be they personalities, as in the cases of Lewin[1] and Parsons and Shils,[2] or social systems, as in the cases of Pareto,[3] Chapple and Coon,[4] Homans,[5] and Parsons, Shils, and Bales.[6] With respect to its popularity, Easton recently went so far as to say that ". . . it represents perhaps one of the few analytical orientations common to all social research," and, with implicit uses added to the explicit, ". . . the idea of equilibrium stands as the closest approximation to a general theory that can be found in the whole field" of social science.[7]

But social scientists have not restricted themselves to a single notion of equilibrium.[8] From the variety of models, I select the following special case as appropriate for the study of deviance and control processes: a system is in equilibrium (regarding deviance) when, following an initial period in which the system contains a given potential for deviance and following a disturbance in the form of an increased potential which is manifest in deviance, the sanctions administered by controlling agents of the system in response to the deviance tend to reduce the potential so that it approaches its initial value.

If we let (A B) represent an ordered process with a given potential, *k* represent deviance, and *l* represent sanctions, then the following sequence illustrates one instance of a system in equilibrium:

A B A B A B *k l* A B A B A B

This model can be applied appropriately and meaningfully only under very special conditions. I combine these conditions into an hypothetical

---

Society, August 1957. Some of the points arose in discussions with the late Andrew Henry of Vanderbilt University, Hope Leichter of the Jewish Family Service of New York, and Odd Ramsøy of the Institute for Sociology, Oslo, Norway.

1. Kurt Lewin, *A Dynamic Theory of Personality,* New York: McGraw-Hill, 1935.

2. Talcott Parsons and Edward A. Shils, editors, *Toward a General Theory of Action,* Cambridge: Harvard University Press, 1951, pp. 110-158.

3. V. Pareto, *Mind and Society,* New York: Harcourt, Brace, and World, 1935, Vol. IV, pp. 1435-1442.

4. E. D. Chapple and C. S. Coon, *Principles of Anthropology,* New York: Holt, Rinehart, Winston, 1942.

5. George C. Homans, *The Human Group,* New York: Harcourt, Brace, and World, 1950, pp. 421-423.

6. Parsons and Shils, *op. cit.,* pp. 190-233; Talcott Parsons, Robert F. Bales, and Edward A. Shils, *Working Papers in the Theory of Action,* New York: Free Press, 1953, esp. pp. 99-103 and 111-161, and a revised form of the later analysis in A. Paul Hare, Edgar F. Borgatta, and Robert F. Bales, editors, *Small Groups,* New York: Knopf, 1955, pp. 424-463.

7. David Easton, "Limits of the Equilibrium Model in Social Research," *Behavioral Science,* 1 (April, 1956), pp. 96-104.

8. Cf. *ibid.*

system called the *simple system.* When a concrete case can be shown to correspond to it, the observation that the system is in equilibrium, as well as the observation that it is not, leads to further questions about its variant and invariant properties. When the concrete case departs from the simple one, however, the observation that the system is not in equilibrium may indicate only that we are not asking a reasonable question. The relevant question in this latter instance is not "What are the consequences of sanctions upon the potential for deviance?"—as asked in the model—but "What changes in the system are necessary to bring its conditions into line with the simple system, so that the issue of restoration to an initial potential is a problematical one?" In this way, the concept of the simple system is proposed as an intermediate one, standing between concrete behavioral systems and the equilibrium model. Before explaining its characteristics, certain terms should be defined, and two concepts concerning the boundaries of behavioral systems—the *domain of demands* and the *range of legitimate control*—should be introduced.

Definitions

Deviance. By *deviance* I refer to behavior which violates the norms of a person or a group and which is followed, or is expected to be followed, by sanctions from appropriate controlling agents. By *norms* I refer to a set of ideas as to how a person should behave—is indeed obliged to to behave—under specified circumstances.[9]

For theoretical purposes the *context of deviance* may be either within the personality, as illustrated by a private impulse followed by guilt or self-punishment,[10] or within the group where overt behavior is expected to be followed by overt sanctions of one form or another. Each of these contexts has its own *controlling agent.* The function of the agent in the first case is to maintain internalized norms; in the second it is to maintain the group norms. Of course individuals, as members of groups, may serve in both capacities.

The Domain of Demands. For the most part when we interact with others we commit to them only a small part of ourselves—that part which belongs to *this* relationship, *this* group. Yet, while interacting we bring with us all of ourselves: we are subject to attachments, loyalties, and ties to other relationships; and we are subject to memories and unconscious processes which have their home elsewhere. Much of what we bring to the immediate situation is a stranger to it. This means that to protect the part of ourselves invested in this relationship we must

9. This definition of norms follows Homans, *op. cit.*, pp. 121-125.

10. Parsons and Shils, *op. cit.*, p. 142.

manage a variety of internal demands. The total array of demands operating upon an individual, or upon all individuals organized in a group, I call the *domain of demands.*

Because of man's symbolic capacity, the nature of these demands and the number of groups, societies, persons, and so on, to which they refer seem to be limited only by the life histories of men. The demands may stem from within the immediate group, or they may refer to persons and to groups existing in other places at other times.[11] The demands may stem from conscious needs and wants, or they may exist in the unconscious. This is to say that they may be beyond the awareness not only of other group members but of the person himself. Known or unknown, and whatever their source, their totality in a given context I term the *domain of demands.*

I assume that deviance is causally connected to the configuration of demands in this domain. It is the manifestation of an attempt to manage intractable or fundamentally incompatible demands. In this sense, it has an end and a direction. And though this purpose may not be obvious, I assume that it can be inferred from a knowledge of the underlying demands.

The Range of Legitimate Control. By this term I refer to the set of impulses and acts over which the controlling agents of a system have jurisdiction. Much as local, state, and federal governments each has its respective sphere of authority, controlling agents in social relationships and in groups have a defined realm of control. Similarly, their counterparts within the personality have legitimate control over some but not all internal processes. As the term legitimate implies, the range refers to the authority granted the agents by the norms of the system, not to the actual control exercised, which in the case of usurpation oversteps the legitimate range and in the case of negligence falls short of it.

Examples of spheres of authority in groups and parts of society are commonplace and need not be enumerated, but a brief comment may help to clarify the claim that personality systems possess the same type of boundary. When impulses and thoughts are repressed they are sent beyond the sphere of the governmental authority of the personality—the sphere that is legitimized by the internalized norms. Repressed impulses, like all unconscious processes, exist outside the range of legitimate control. Moreover, from this viewpoint, ego-defences, such as denial, isolation, and projection, function to keep certain matters outside the range.[12] In this sense, I suggest that all behavioral systems possess a boundary

11. Reference groups of course are one source of demands. See Robert K. Merton, *Social Structure and Social Theory*, New York: Free Press, 1957, Chapters 8 and 9.

12. Anna Freud, *The Ego and Mechanisms of Defence*, New York: International Universities Press, 1946, pp. 58-70.

within which their controlling agents have jurisdiction and beyond which they do not.

The Simple System

With these definitions and concepts in mind can we not picture a personality or a group where the problem of controlling deviance is a simple matter? I call such a personality or group a *simple system.* It has three essential characteristics.

The first of these is that, whatever the extent of the domain of demands underlying deviance, the extent of the range of legitimate control is as great. This condition, for example, may be approximated within the personality through a knowledge of one's unconscious processes. As signals from conflicting and intractable demands are received, one works to interpret what is signified and to bring the underlying demands within the government of the personality. Knowing these demands and managing them become legitimate functions of the self. In similar fashion, this condition may be approached in the two-person situation as the therapist, by an ever-increasing knowledge of the demands impinging upon the patient, works indirectly through the patient to help him to become aware of these demands and to extend his management functions to include them. With success, the boundaries of the range of legitimate control spread toward the boundaries of the domain of demands.

As mentioned above, there are two agents of control in the group: one operating on behalf of selves, the others on behalf of the group norms. The jurisdiction of one may be limited while the jurisdiction of the other is extensive. For present purposes, however, this ratio is of secondary importance: *who* or *what* has control is distinct from the primary issue of whether or not control exists at all. Therefore, regardless of jurisdictional ratios, if the combined range of control includes all elements in the domain of demands, the situation meets the first condition of the simple system.

The second characteristic of the simple system concerns the immediate reaction to deviance, which is not to uphold automatically current values, norms, and beliefs. Rather, deviance poses the question: shall the norms be maintained by controlling this deviance or shall this behavior be viewed as innovation and the norms be changed accordingly? Or, as it is put by Parsons, Bales, and Shils: is the system to *maintain* its original state or is it to *learn* from this unexpected behavior?[13]

On the personal level, the question may be: Is this foreign thought,

13. Parsons, Bales, and Shils, *op. cit.*, Chapter 5.

this strange impulse, to be repressed or is it to become part of a new state of integration yet to be worked out? The issue may confront groups as well. For example, as the child grows up, encountering new demands from within and from others and exhibiting new forms of behavior, the family, in effect, chooses either to enforce the established set of relationships, suited perhaps to a baby and nurturant parents, or to rearrange its normative structure so as to accommodate a youth and eventually an adult. In the simple system the issue is raised and faced, not ignored.

The third characteristic of the simple system is that once behavior is defined as deviance, the sanctions in the repertoire of controlling agents, if exercised, penetrate beyond the symptomatic act to the basic demands themselves. The silent member of the group who feels that a hostile word can destroy others and who, instead of being seduced into battle, is reassured to the point where he not only speaks but is not afraid, is one illustration. Another is the case when the interpretation of the therapist, in addition to eliminating a pattern of overt action, opens to the patient the possibility of comprehending and of organizing a set of conflicting demands. Or again, when the idea back of parental sanctions becomes incorporated as a strengthening ingredient within the child who by this means gains access to and management of forces otherwise beyond him.

To summarize, in the simple system the boundaries of the domain of demands are included within legitimate control boundaries, sanctions occur not automatically but only after behavior is defined as deviance rather than as innovation, and sanctions (when exercised) affect not only the symptomatic act but the basic demands. The simple system contains the conditions which must prevail in order to apply, appropriately and productively, the equilibrium model—the model of no deviance—deviance—sanctions—no deviance. This claim rests upon the following reasons:

1. When, contrary to the conditions in the simple system, demands underlying deviance are beyond the scope of legitimate control we may expect either routine application of sanctions, which by definition can not reach the demands, or application of more effective but illegitimate sanctions. In the first instance, there is no reason, beyond chance, to expect the sanctions to counteract or neutralize the conflicting demands. Therefore, the question of reducing the probability of deviance has in the asking its answer: only by chance. Moreover, in the second instance, deviance by a member is followed by deviance on the part of an agent of control, introducing the possibility of a vicious circle. On the other hand, when conditions of the simple system prevail in the respect that underlying demands fall within the scope of control—when,

in other words, control is not impossible—whether normative sanctions actually neutralize the conflict or whether they fail to do so becomes a meaningful question for both controlling agents and social scientists.

2. The second stipulation of the simple system would not be necessary if, on the one hand, internal and external demands upon behavioral systems were in fact constant and, on the other, norms could not be changed. However, since the body, for one thing, varies in the kinds and intensity of its demands, since adaptive exigencies of groups and of societies vary, since individual persons grow and learn, and since cultures change, provision should be made for the possibility that restoration to a previous state of non-deviance may be accomplished by changing the norms. Thus, even though the system is faced with irreducible conflicting demands which inevitably result in deviance, the issue of restoration remains relevant because the norms may be altered to accommodate would-be deviance as acceptable behavior, consequently reducing the potential. In these and similar circumstances, observations as to whether the norms are actually changed lead to further inferences about the system. But no such benefit derives from the question when it can be shown that the existing norms are rigid and applied automatically—none, that is, unless it can also be demonstrated that internal and external demands are in fact constant.

3. Finally, since sanctions which reach the symptomatic act but not beyond do not alter the system's potential for deviance, the pertinent question concerns the new manner in which demands will manifest themselves, not equilibrium. In contrast, since the simple system's repertoire contains sanctions which can affect the causal connections between demands and behavior, there is reason to expect restoration, so that observations as to what sanctions are applied, in what manner, and with what consequences, again, are meaningful.

In short, unlike the situation in more complex systems, in the simple system the tendency toward restoration of a state of low potential for deviance is neither impossible, nor simply by chance, but a reasonable expectation over a wide range of circumstances.

Departures from the Simple System

Major departures from the simple system render the issue of equilibrium inappropriate. This point may be developed by illustrating two types of departures likely to be encountered.

The first type is observed when the range of legitimate control excludes the domain of demands underlying deviant behavior. This may occur because the demands are unknown, as in the conspicuous case of the psychotic, but also in the case of the family whose child simply goes "out" to do "nothing," as well as the case of diplomatic negotiations when personal loyalties and cross-loyalties are far less understood than home instructions. In these instances, *some* of the demands making themselves felt are beyond the intelligence of all participants—certain forces are unknown to anyone in the system.

In other cases, even though the demands are thought to be known, they are inaccessible because the jurisdiction of controlling agents is limited. In attempting to treat the juvenile offender, for example, the court and its agencies may have formed a tentative diagnosis of the complicated internal and external forces confronting him, but are prevented by law from investigating and treating, beyond clearly defined limits, either the social world or the personal domain of the offender. His privacy and the privacy of his gang are protected by laws which insure individual rights for all of us.

In cases of this kind ignorance and inaccessibility complicate readjustment processes. So much so, in fact, that if controlling agents feel compelled to recapture a previous balance before they understand what is going on, their sanctions are not only likely to miss their mark but, by beclouding the true demands, by creating new ones, and by creating an illusion that the matter is understood, to compound the state of ignorance and inaccessibility. Practically and theoretically, the expectation of restoring a previous low potential for deviance by means of existing sanctions is misplaced.

The second type of major departure occurs when the simple system contains subparts each of which is organized to maintain itself largely in its own terms.[14] Such is the case of the foreman in his well known role conflict: his relation to the workers is one sub-system, his relation to management a second, and the relation between his role and himself as a person is another. Although the context is quite different, a similar complexity exists in the case of Bateson's "double-bind," illustrated by the relation between mother and child: if the child responds with affection the mother becomes anxious and withdraws; if the child withdraws, increased anxiety within the mother again leads to a demand for signs of affection.[15] One sub-system focuses on the mother's need to be a good mother, the other on her desire not to be a mother, and these two conflicting sub-systems impinge upon the child. A similar complexity exists when, within the personality, feelings of what one *wants* to be are at war with feelings of what one *should* be.

---

14. For a general discussion see Odd Ramsøy, "System and Subsystem: A Study in Sociological Theory," mimeographed, Oslo: Oslo University, 1958.

15. Gregory Bateson, D. D. Jackson, J. Haley, and J. H. Weakland, "Toward a Theory of Schizophrenia," *Behavioral Science,* 1 (October, 1956), pp. 251-264.

These systems are complex, in the first place, because they contain sub-systems each with its own controlling agent; in the second place, because the sanctions proscribed by the norms of the sub-systems tend to intensify the conflict of demands originally leading to deviance. For example, in the case of the foreman, if management punishes a "workingman's foreman," if workers negatively sanction a "management-foreman," and if the foreman punishes himself for unsuccessfully maintaining some non-existing middle ground, the original conflict is intensified. This intensification is shown in the case of the double-bind for, if Bateson is correct, the built-in sanctions on the part of the child result in the creation of a new type of communication and eventually of schizophrenic mental processes. The normal controlling activities guided by the norms within the sub-systems tend to increase, not to decrease, the probability of deviance. In this respect, whether or not sanctions will restore a previous low potential for deviance is not one of the more fruitful questions that might be raised.

The Complexity of Behavioral Systems

While we may use the set of conditions called the simple system in order to separate those concrete cases for which the equilibrium model is appropriate from those for which it is not, two questions remain: How likely, and under what conditions, are we to find concrete systems corresponding to the simple one? How are we to analyze deviance and control processes in more complex cases?

With respect to the first question—notwithstanding our limited knowledge of behavioral systems; indeed partly because of such limitations—I suggest that simple systems are rare. Moreover, as I shall indicate below, there are reasons to believe that departures result not from incomplete evolution, for example, but because positive forces operating to preserve other features of the system create a complex state and tend to keep it complex. Simple systems are rare because complicating factors are strong and, possibly, universal.

Are there not tendencies, for instance, which keep the domain of demands beyond the range of legitimate control? With respect to the personality, as noted above, psychoanalytical mechanisms describe how certain impulses, thoughts, and so on are excluded from the psyche's governmental jurisdiction. The mechanisms serve a positive need to maintain the integrity of the self. Impulses, once beyond the boundary of control, are kept there by resistance, which serves the same positive need. Active demands are kept beyond the range of direct control, not because they are weak or inconsequential, but by forces operating on behalf of the self. This discrepancy serves to preserve the self.

With respect to the group, the first obvious, though often overlooked, source of a similar discrepancy is that in groups when individuals meet they bring their individual defenses, thereby introducing into the group-system sets of active demands beyond personal boundaries of control. The new aggregation of demands extends beyond the aggregation of realms of control and tends to be kept there by the members' defenses. Moreover, and quite apart from this source, the discrepancy is widened by two factors associated with the group as an organized unit. The first is the group's resistance to cultural change; the second is its resistance to adding to its responsibilities. By what it recognizes and does not recognize to exist, a group's culture selects the phenomena that can be acknowledged to be within the domain of demands. If not omniscient, it will fail to recognize certain demands and will tend to account for them in terms consistent with the accepted images, beliefs, and explanations. When these explanations are internalized members have a positive investment in ignoring demands not acknowledged by the culture and in explaining away those which contradict it. Various mechanisms are employed to keep unknown demands unknown and to deny incompatible ones; they serve the end of preserving the basic values and beliefs as they are.[16] In performing this function, however, they create and maintain a gap between the domain of actual demands and the group's range of control.

The discrepancy may be widened even further by the group's conception of its responsibility. Paralleling the right to sanction is the obligation to control effectively, so that one consequence of acknowledging a demand as a cause of deviance is to extend the responsibility of controlling agents to cover the demand. Unless resources are unlimited in this respect, and in order to avoid negligence, groups tend to define, to limit, and to protect their realms of responsibility.[17] Therefore, in general we can expect some demands to be beyond the range of control, not simply because they are unknown, nor because they are incompatible with cultural beliefs, but, from the group's point of view, because they are within the province of some other controlling body.

To the extent, then, that there is a need for groups to maintain their

16. A pathological development in this direction is illustrated and discussed by Lyman C. Wynne, Irving M. Rycoff, Julian Day, and Stanley Hirsch in "Pseudomutuality in the Family Relations of Schizophrenics," *Psychiatry*, 21 (May, 1958), pp. 205-220.

17. Groups vary, of course, in their scope of responsibility. One way of characterizing these variations is by using Parsons' pattern variables: a narrower scope is expected where role-expectations are universalistic and specific, for example, than where they are particularistic and diffuse. See Parsons and Shils, *op. cit.*, pp. 76-88.

cultures and their spheres of responsibility, like individuals, they have a vested interest in surrounding themselves with a set of active demands which are either kept unknown or are defined as some other body's responsibility. As a part of an answer to our initial question, therefore, I suggest that while other things are equal, the stronger these protective factors the less likely a concrete system will correspond to the simple one.

Even though demands are accessible concerning jurisdiction, ignorance of the causes of deviance is another factor which prevents a system from becoming simple. The stringent requirement, it will be recalled, is that sanctions penetrate beyond the symptomatic act to the underlying demands. Under what conditions does this occur? Because of the incidence of deviance through time, its prevalence, and the positive part culture plays in proscribing sanctions,[18] I believe that we can justifiably rule out the possibility that demands are neutralized or counteracted by some automatic means. Moreover, although we may be encouraged in finding a system with an effective repertoire, acquired through a long history of trial and error, we should not conclude that the system is simple—for unless it can be shown that demands are constant and will remain so, we have no reason to expect the repertoire to handle future contingencies. An alternative to trial and error, and to mechanical restoration, is an understanding, on the one hand, of the causal links between demands and deviance, and, on the other, between sanctions and demands. This alternative requires enough knowledge to form an accurate diagnosis, an expert prescription, and the freedom to administer the sanction effectively. I suggest that this alternative presumes more knowledge than we possess—more knowledge than that of either controlling agents or social scientists—at least at present. In fact, it is largely from our realization of how little we know in this respect that increasing efforts are being made to discover the causes of deviance and the effectiveness of treatments. Until we know more, on what basis can we expect to find a simple system? Meanwhile, as our understanding improves, should we not expect a gradual increase in the number of simple systems and, consequently, more cases for which the equilibrium model is appropriate?

In summary, I have suggested that the following factors tend to counteract simplification tendencies: (1) the need to protect the integrity of the self; (2) the need to preserve the culture at its current level of integration; (3) the cost in extending the realm of responsibility; and (4) ignorance of the causal relations between demands, deviance, and

18. Clyde Kluckhohn, "Culture and Behavior," in Gardner Lindzey, editor, *Handbook of Social Psychology*, Reading, Mass.: Addison-Wesley, 1954, Vol. II, Chapter 25.

sanctions. If, empirically, it is found that these complicating factors outweigh to a significant degree the simplifying ones, it means not only that the utility of the equilibrium model is severely limited but that behavioral systems, as a type, tend to be unstable. It means that they fail to maintain a boundary, as shown by the discrepancy between demands and range of control, and that lacking effective sanctions, they fail to absorb internal disturbances.[19] To the degree that they are unstable, we are confronted with a difficult task in formulating general principles regarding deviance and control processes, for in an unstable system even though we observe an instance of restoration, for example, it provides no basis for anticipating a future instance nor for generalizing from one unstable system to another. For these reasons, empirical investigations of such properties as the domain of demands, the range of control, and the consequence of sanctions are important not merely in applying the equilibrium model but for our general understanding of behavioral systems.[20]

Transitions from Complex to Simple

Granting the argument so far, we reach an impasse. The simple system must prevail if we are to apply the equilibrium model fruitfully, yet this kind of system seems unlikely to exist. At best, behavioral systems seem to be complex; they may be inherently unstable. What course from the impasse might we follow? How, in general, might we conceive of processes of deviance and control?

My proposal is, first, that we postpone the issue of restoration, second, that in considering reactions to deviance we take into account more than sanctions, and third, that we use the conditions of the hypothetical simple system as that state which tends, or not, to be approached as a consequence of reactions to deviance. The central issue would shift from the question of whether or not systems are in equilibrium to the question of whether or not changes in the system, following deviance, bring the system closer to the hypothetical simple system, which we might expect to be in equilibrium. Simplification may be marked by a wide variety of changes in the concrete system. I call attention to only one of these, but do so because of its relevance to the two major departures described above, namely, the discrepancy between demands and the range of control and the existence of sub-systems.

19. Parsons and Shils, *op. cit.*, pp. 107-109.

20. Cf. Lewin, *op. cit.*, p. 58, where in reference to studying the personality as a whole, he suggests that "Indeed, the concrete task of research will often consist precisely in the search for [the] determinative system, its boundaries and its internal structure."

Returning to the foreman, the double-bind, and unconscious conflict as illustrations of complex systems, and asking what will reduce the probability of deviance in these cases, it can be seen that reduction has nothing directly to do with the deviant events themselves, nor with an application of a specially devised sanction. Instead reduction calls for a reorganization of the system. This may take the form of negotiations between workers and management in the case of the foreman; it may be accomplished in the case of the double-bind by a redefinition of the situation to the effect that the mother is ill; it may be achieved in the case of an unconscious conflict between *wants* and *shoulds* by a strengthening, or an extension, of ego functions. The shortest path (however long it may be) to a lower probability of deviance is by way of developing a new system, not by applying new energy in administering sanctions in the service of old norms. For this reason, we need to include in our model the addition, subtraction, and re-organization of diverse parts of the system, not merely sanctions. In so far as the negotiations between workers and management create an over-arching range of legitimate control, encompassing the originally conflicting demands, the system surrounding the foreman is simplified. Since the child's realization of the mother's illness is in Bateson's terms a meta-communication about the situation, or a comprehension of previously unrecognized connections between various demands, the intensity of the conflict caused by the mother's contradictory behavior diminishes and to this extent the system shifts toward a simpler state. And the personality system is simplified when the ego takes on new mediating functions in handling the intra-psychic conflict between *wants* and *shoulds.*

The first point illustrated by these changes is that when, in addition to sanctions, we incorporate into the model any modification which might result in either simplification or complication, our analysis involves the total structure of the system, how it is differentiated, how the different parts function, and how they are interrelated. The second point is the important distinction between simplicity of structure and simplicity of control, between the undifferentiated system and what I have defined as the simple system. They are not only different, but under certain circumstances they are inversely interrelated. In this way, because of the wider scope of functions it is able to perform, a personality with a highly differentiated ego is more likely to approach the simple state than one with a primitive ego; similarly, a highly differentiated group, particularly a group with various specialists who learn the demands, adjudicate conflicts, and consider the causes and effects of group events, is more apt to approximate the simple state than a group with a minimum division of labor. Although this correlation exists only within certain limits, it leads us to include the addition of roles and functions as one of the possible means by which systems shift from the complex to the simple type.

A case in point is illustrated by the history of the diagnosis and treatment of mental illness, which shows a progressive extension and elaboration of roles: from the biologically oriented physician to the psychiatrist, the analyst, the social worker, the psychiatric social worker, the medical sociologist or anthropologist, and now in certain mental hospitals an increasingly elaborate and administratively complicated team. One aim of the team is to learn more about the demands pressing upon patients from many quarters, another is to extend therapeutic control beyond the single hour to "the other 23 hours of the day." As it has been realized that the demands underlying mental illness are illusive and extensive and that treatment may come from many quarters, new roles, functions, and so on have been added in the hope that the range of therapeutic control will encompass them. While these changes may complicate the system organizationally, from the viewpoint of deviance and control processes they can simplify it.

In terms of elegance and the power of an over-arching theory, the proposal to use the simple system as a set of conditions standing between concrete cases and the equilibrium model is a conservative move. But I believe that it is a timely and appropriate one. It has an advantage in admitting complexities into behavioral systems—complexities increasingly substantiated by social science research—but at the same time allowing for those instances when a system might possibly be in equilibrium. In this way it may help avoid the illusion that systems must be in or near equilibrium to be of concern to a general theory of deviance and control processes. The proposal may in fact contribute substantially to the understanding of how far systems are from the state in which equilibrium is expected, on the one hand, and, on the other, of the factors that keep systems away from that state. Yet, it presents a challenge and a sense of direction to the empirical investigation of system processes for, like the equilibrium model, its application calls for improved techniques in identifying more precisely the domain of demands, the norms, the range of control, and the causal connections between sanctions and demands, as well as those between structural changes and the underlying demands.

SELECTED READINGS

The use of concepts like self-image, role image, or self-conception has proved useful in relating the self to the social system. The following studies indicate this: "Self Conceptions as the Reactions of Others," Richard Videbeck, *Sociometry*, December, 1960; "The Psychiatric Attendant: Development of an Occupational Self-Image in a Low-Status Occupation," Richard L. Simpson and Ida Harper Simpson, *American Sociological Review*, June, 1959; "Men's and Women's Beliefs, Ideals and Self Concepts," John P. McKee and Alex C. Sheriffs, *American Journal of Sociology*, January, 1959; "Self Conception and Ward Behavior in Two Psychiatric Hospitals," Thomas S. McPartland, John H. Cummings, and Wynona S. Garretson, *Sociometry*, June, 1961; "Images of Class Relations among Former Soviet Citizens," Alex Inkeles, *Social Problems*, January, 1956; "Social Images in East and West Germany: A Comparative Study of Matched Newspapers in Two Social Systems," Richard Conrad, *Social Forces*, 1955.

The usefulness of considering the self in social context has been emphasized in a number of studies. These studies often underline the fact that the self is hardly a stable, predictable entity but a variable in varying conditions. Herbert Blumer, "Attitudes and the Social Act," *Social Problems*, October, 1955, emphasizes the instability of the concept attitudes and maintains that a "Human act is not release of an already organized tendency." The actor ". . . organizes himself to act." Erving Goffman, "Alienation from Interaction," *Human Relations*, 1957, brings out the dynamic aspects of interaction. The ". . . individual must phrase his own concerns . . . to make these maximally usable by the other. . . ." He has a right to expect others ". . . to stir up their sympathies and place them at his command." S. Stansfield Sargent and Katherine Pease Beardsley, "Social Roles and Personality Traits," *The International Journal of Social Psychiatry*, Summer, 1960, support the Blumer approach by showing that college girls varied in their submissiveness and extrovertive-introvertive behavior in different social situations. Walker Percy, "The Symbolic Structure of Interpersonal Process," *Psychiatry*, February, 1961, examines the social interaction views of George H. Mead and Harry Stack Sullivan in the light of the therapist-patient relation.

The "interchange" point of view, to use a phrase of Alvin Gouldner's in a study reported below, raises the question of the energy dispositions within the organism. There has been a strong tendency to see the self as a system of demands linked closely to biology. The energy basis of "secondary" demands has been problematical. Harry Stack Sullivan made a contribution to this problem in a paper that has not had as much influence as it deserves. See "A Note on the Implications of Psychiatry, the Study of Interpersonal Relations, for Investigations in the Social Sciences," *American Journal of Sociology*, 1937. This paper is reprinted under the title "Interpersonal Processes and the Social Order" in Samuel J. Beck and Herman B. Molish (editors), *Reflexes to Intelligence* (New York: The Free Press of Glencoe, 1959).

The following studies are more general and theoretical: William J. Goode,

"A Theory of Role Strain," *American Sociological Review*, August, 1960; Dennis Wrong, "The Functional Theory of Stratification, Some Neglected Considerations," *American Sociological Review*, December, 1959; Alvin W. Gouldner, "Reciprocity and Autonomy in Functional Theory," Llewellyn Gross (editor), *Symposium in Sociological Theory* (Evanston, Ill.: Row, Peterson and Company, 1959); Charles D. Bolton, "Behavior, Experience and Relationships: A Symbolic Interactionist Point of View," *American Journal of Sociology*, July, 1958.

3 *The Uses of Social Structure*

IT HAS BEEN usual to see social structure in terms of its limitations rather than in terms of its opportunities. The sociologist has wished to establish the fact of social organization and the fact of its inertia. The studies in this section emphasize a different aspect of social structure, the kinds of services it performs for the individual enterprise. Unless we can keep this perspective in mind, we are likely to be afflicted with a serious myopia when viewing social organization.

One would not expect, perhaps, to find Sigmund Freud supporting the creative aspects of social organization, but in the following section from "Civilization and Its Discontents," Freud referred to a "pleasure" not biological in the usual sense but clearly based on one's participation in the resources of a cultural tradition:

> There is . . . one means of transferring the instinctual aims into such directions that they cannot be frustrated by the outer world. Its success is greatest when a man knows how to heighten sufficiently his capacity for obtaining pleasure from mental and intellectual work. Fate has little power against him then. This kind of satisfaction, such as the artist's joy in creation, in embodying his phantasies, or the scientist's in solving problems or discovering truth, has a special quality which we shall certainly one day be able to define metapsychologically. Until then we can only say that it seems to us "higher and finer," but compared with that of gratifying gross primitive instincts its intensity is tempered and diffused; it does not overwhelm us physically.

Man has quite a stake in his society. The articles in this section indicate a number of potentials in social structure from the view of the self.

Becker and Geer, in their article, point out how the experience of the individual in medical school tends to produce a realistic and professional idealism to replace the naïve idealism existing earlier. Clark shows how certain "mechanisms" in education bring about at least a partial reconciliation of the unsuccessful student to his change in status. These articles both show ways in which social structure aids the individual in a period of transition from one social position to another. Benjamin D. Paul, "Mental Disorder and Self-regulatory Processes in Culture: A Guatamalan Illustration," calls our attention to another kind of transition. Here the society is not shifting the individual from one position to another but faced with the problem of mental disturbance. Paul shows how the social structure studied tends at a certain point to bring effective therapeutic forces into play. In Vogt and O'Dea, "A Comparative Study of the Roles of Values in Social Action in Two Southwestern Communities," the problem is taking advantage of an opportunity to solve a community problem. The authors show how the social structure of one community made the solution possible while it prevented a solution in the other.

It is often thought that decision-making is common sense. In fact, however, individual decision requires a basic fund of facts and values and objectives that are considered within the society, to be relevant to the decision-making process. Common sense functions within a matrix of social assumptions. Davis' article, "Uncertainty in Medical Prognosis," shows how a norm in the hospital studied governs the physician's disclosure of information to parents about children who are victims of paralytic poliomyelitis. Christensen describes the different cultural norms applying to premarital sex relations in Utah, Indiana, and Denmark and shows how they are related to premarital pregnancy in the three areas. He also shows how the decisions by couples where the woman is pregnant either for marriage or for subsequent divorce are related to these different cultural norms.

The individual's search for experience cannot take place in a vacuum. It requires relations with others. These relations must be mutually intelligible if their potentialities for individual experience are to be explored. It can be readily seen that defined social situations are not simply systems of external constraint. They are also systems of potential experience with the mechanics of communication prearranged. They favor certain directions of individual development. Frequently the potential for experience that exists in one society may not exist in the same clearly defined form in another.

Klineberg's article studies the devices for communicating emotion found in Chinese literature. They are clearly different in many ways from the conventions employed in our own society. Mutuality of emotional response depends in large measure on an intelligible system of signs and symbols.

Societies establish a wide range of relationships between people with reference to authority. At first hand, one would think that the experience of being low man on the totem pole would be much the same from one society to another. Stoodley's article tends to show, however, that subjection to authority among Filipinos may not involve the elements of submissiveness and repressed hostility that are commonly associated with it.

Reina's article shows how profound, even shattering, personal experiences are defined by social structure; and the selection we have taken from Dorothy Lee's book, *Freedom and Culture*, calls our attention to the complexity of the notion of individual autonomy and reminds us that we have no monopoly of the idea. A society must have a vision of autonomy, but it must also have forms where it can be experienced. If this society should come only to praise autonomy, it may stay to bury it.

a) AIDING INDIVIDUAL TRANSITION

HOWARD S. BECKER
and BLANCHE GEER

The Fate of Idealism in Medical School

It makes some difference in a man's performance of his work whether he believes wholeheartedly in what he is doing or feels that in important respects it is a fraud, whether he feels convinced that it is a good thing or believes that it is not really of much use after all. The distinction we are making is the one people have in mind when they refer, for example, to their calling as a "noble profession" on the one hand or a "racket" on the other. In the one case they idealistically proclaim that their work is all that it claims on the surface to be; in the other they cynically concede that it is first and foremost a way of making a living and that its surface pretensions are just that and nothing more. Presumably, different modes of behavior are associated with these

Reprinted from American Sociological Review, *February, 1958, pp. 50-56, by permission of the authors and the journal.*

Revision of paper read at the annual meeting of the Midwest Sociological Society, April 5, 1957, in Des Moines, Iowa.

perspectives when wholeheartedly embraced. The cynic cuts corners with a feeling of inevitability while the idealist goes down fighting. *The Blackboard Jungle* and *Not as a Stranger* are only the most recent in a long tradition of fictional portrayals of the importance of this aspect of a man's adjustment to his work.

Professional schools often receive a major share of the blame for producing this kind of cynicism—and none more than the medical school. The idealistic young freshman changes into a tough, hardened, unfeeling doctor; or so the popular view has it. Teachers of medicine sometimes rephrase the distinction between the clinical and pre-clinical years into one between the "cynical" and "pre-cynical" years. Psychological research supports this view, presenting attitude surveys which show medical students year by year scoring lower on "idealism" and higher on "cynicism."[1] Typically, this cynicism is seen as developing in response to the shattering of ideals consequent on coming face-to-face with the realities of professional practice.

In this paper, we attempt to describe the kind of idealism that characterizes the medical freshmen and to trace both the development of cynicism and the vicissitudes of that idealism in the course of the four years of medical training. Our main themes are that though they develop cynical feelings in specific situations directly associated with their medical school experience, the medical students never lose their original idealism about the practice of medicine; that the growth of both cynicism and idealism are not simple developments, but are instead complex transformations; and that the very notions "idealism" and "cynicism" need further analysis, and must be seen as situational in their expressions rather than as stable traits possessed by individuals in greater or lesser degree. Finally, we see the greater portion of these feelings as being collective rather than individual phenomena.

Our discussion is based on a study we are now conducting at a state medical school,[2] in which we have carried on participant observation with students of all four years in all of the courses and clinical work to which they are exposed. We joined the students in their activities in school and after school and watched them at work in labs, on the hospital wards, and in the clinic. Often spending as much as a month with a small group of from five to fifteen students assigned to a particular activity, we came to know them well and were able to gather information in informal interviews and by overhearing the ordinary daily con-

1. Leonard D. Eron, "Effect of Medical Education on Medical Students," *Journal of Medical Education*, 10 (October, 1955), pp. 559-566.

2. This study is sponsored by Community Studies, Inc., of Kansas City, Missouri, and is being carried on at the University of Kansas Medical School, to whose dean, staff, and students we are indebted for their wholehearted cooperation. Professor Everett C. Hughes of the University of Chicago is director of the project.

versation of the group.[3] In the course of our observation and interviewing we have gathered much information on the subject of idealism. Of necessity, we shall have to present the very briefest statement of our findings with little or no supporting evidence.[4] The problem of idealism is, of course, many-faceted and complex and we have dealt with it in a simplified way, describing only some of its grosser features.[5]

The Freshmen

The medical students enter school with what we may think of as the idealistic notion, implicit in lay culture, that the practice of medicine is a wonderful thing and that they are going to devote their lives to service to mankind. They believe that medicine is made up of a great body of well-established facts that they will be taught from the first day on and that these facts will be of immediate practical use to them as physicians. They enter school expecting to work industriously and expecting that if they work hard enough they will be able to master this body of fact and thus become good doctors.

3. The technique of participant observation has not been fully systematized, but some approaches to this have been made. See, for example, Florence R. Kluckhohn, "The Participant Observer Technique in Small Communities," *American Journal of Sociology*, 45 (November, 1940), pp. 331-343; Arthur Vidich, "Participant Observation and the Collection and Interpretation of Data," *ibid.*, 60 (January, 1955), pp. 354-360; William Foote Whyte, "Observational Field-Work Methods," in Maria Jahoda, Morton Deutsch, and Stuart W. Cook (editors), *Research Methods in the Social Sciences*, New York: Dryden Press, 1951, II, pp. 393-514; and *Street Corner Society* (Enlarged Edition), Chicago: University of Chicago Press, 1955, pp. 279-358; Rosalie Hankey Wax, "Twelve Years Later: An Analysis of Field Experience," *American Journal of Sociology*, 63 (September, 1957), pp. 133-142; Morris S. Schwartz and Charlotte Green Schwartz, "Problems in Participant Observation," *ibid.*, 60 (January, 1955), pp. 343-353; and Howard S. Becker and Blanche Geer, "Participant Observation and Interviewing: A Comparison," *Human Organization*, 16 (Fall, 1957), pp. 28-32. The last item represents the first of a projected series of papers attempting to make explicit the operations involved in this method. For a short description of some techniques used in this study, see Howard S. Becker, "Interviewing Medical Students," *American Journal of Sociology*, 62 (September, 1956), pp. 199-201.

4. A fuller analysis and presentation of evidence is contained in Howard S. Becker, Blanche Geer, Everett C. Hughes, and Anselm Strauss, *Boys in White*, Chicago: University of Chicago Press, 1961.

5. Renee Fox has shown how complex one aspect of this whole subject is in her analysis of the way medical students at Cornell become aware of and adjust to both their own failure to master all available knowledge and the gaps in current knowledge in many fields. See her "Training for Uncertainty," in Robert K. Merton, George G. Reader, and Patricia L. Kendall, *The Student Physician: Introductory Studies in the Sociology of Medical Education*, Cambridge: Harvard University Press, 1957, pp. 207-241.

In several ways the first year of medical school does not live up to their expectations. They are disillusioned when they find they will not be near patients at all, that the first year will be just like another year of college. In fact, some feel that it is not even as good as college because their work in certain areas is not as thorough as courses in the same fields in undergraduate school. They come to think that their courses (with the exception of anatomy) are not worth much because, in the first place, the faculty (being Ph.D.'s) know nothing about the practice of medicine, and, in the second place, the subject matter itself is irrelevant, or as the students say, "ancient history."

The freshmen are further disillusioned when the faculty tells them in a variety of ways that there is more to medicine than they can possibly learn. They realize it may be impossible for them to learn all they need to know in order to practice medicine properly. Their disillusionment becomes more profound when they discover that this statement of the faculty is literally true.[6] Experience in trying to master the details of the anatomy of the extremities convinces them that they cannot do so in the time they have. Their expectation of hard work is not disappointed; they put in an eight-hour day of classes and laboratories, and study four or five hours a night and most of the weekend as well.

Some of the students, the brightest, continue to attempt to learn it all, but succeed only in getting more and more worried about their work. The majority decide that, since they can't learn it all, they must select from among all the facts presented to them those they will attempt to learn. There are two ways of making this selection. On the one hand, the student may decide on the basis of his own uninformed notions about the nature of medical practice that many facts are not important, since they relate to things which seldom come up in the actual practice of medicine; therefore, he reasons, it is useless to learn them. On the other hand, the student can decide that the important thing is to pass his examinations and, therefore, that the important facts are those which are likely to be asked on an examination; he uses this as a basis for selecting both facts to memorize and courses for intensive study. For example, the work in physiology is dismissed on both of these grounds, being considered neither relevant to the facts of medical life nor important in terms of the amount of time the faculty devotes to it and the number of examinations in the subject.

A student may use either or both of these bases of selection at the beginning of the year, before many tests have been given. But after a few tests have been taken, the student makes "what the faculty wants" the chief basis of his selection of what to learn, for he now has a better

6. Compare Fox's description of student reaction to this problem at Cornell (*op. cit.*, pp. 209-221).

idea of what this is and also has become aware that it is possible to fail examinations and that he therefore must learn the expectations of the faculty if he wishes to stay in school. The fact that one group of students, that with the highest prestige in the class, took this view early and did well on examinations was decisive in swinging the whole class around to this position. The students were equally influenced to become "test-wise" by the fact that, although they had all been in the upper range in their colleges, the class average on the first examination was frighteningly low.

In becoming test-wise, the students begin to develop systems for discovering the faculty wishes and learning them. These systems are both methods for studying their texts and short-cuts that can be taken in laboratory work. For instance, they begin to select facts for memorization by looking over the files of old examinations maintained in each of the medical fraternity houses. They share tip-offs from the lectures and offhand remarks of the faculty as to what will be on the examinations. In anatomy, they agree not to bother to dissect out subcutaneous nerves, reasoning that it is both difficult and time-consuming and the information can be secured from books with less effort. The interaction involved in the development of such systems and short-cuts helps to create a social group of a class which had previously been only an aggregation of smaller and less organized groups.

In this medical school, the students learn in this way to distinguish between the activities of the first year and their original view that everything that happens to them in medical school will be important. Thus they become cynical about the value of their activities in the first year. They feel that the real thing—learning which will help them to help mankind—has been postponed, perhaps until the second year, or perhaps even further, at which time they will be able again to act on idealistic premises. They believe that what they do in their later years in school under supervision will be about the same thing they will do, as physicians, on their own; the first year had disappointed this expectation.

There is one matter, however, about which the students are not disappointed during the first year: the so-called trauma of dealing with the cadaver. But this experience, rather than producing cynicism, reinforces the student's attachment to his idealistic view of medicine by making him feel that he is experiencing at least some of the necessary unpleasantness of the doctor's work. Such difficulties, however, do not loom as large for the student as those of solving the problem of just what the faculty wants.

On this and other points, a working consensus develops in the new consolidated group about the interpretation of their experience in medical school and its norms of conduct. This consensus, which we call *student culture,*[7] focuses their attention almost completely on their day-to-day activities in school and obscures or sidetracks their earlier idealistic preoccupations. Cynicism, griping, and minor cheating become endemic, but the cynicism is specific to the educational situation, to the first year, and to only parts of it. Thus the students keep their cynicism separate from their idealistic feelings and by postponement protect their belief that medicine is a wonderful thing, that their school is a fine one, and that they will become good doctors.

Later Years

The sophomore year does not differ greatly from the freshman year. Both the work load and anxiety over examinations probably increase. Though they begin some medical activities, as in their attendance at autopsies and particularly in their introductory course in physical diagnosis, most of what they do continues to repeat the pattern of the college science curriculum. Their attention still centers on the problem of getting through school by doing well in examinations.

During the third and fourth, or clinical years, teaching takes a new form. In place of lectures and laboratories, the students' work now consists of the study of actual patients admitted to the hospital or seen in the clinic. Each patient who enters the hospital is assigned to a student who interviews him about his illnesses, past and present, and performs a physical examination. He wrties this up for the patient's chart, and appends the diagnosis and the treatment that he would use were he allowed actually to treat the patient. During conferences with faculty physicians, often held at the patient's bedside, the student is quizzed about items of his report and called upon to defend them or to explain their significance. Most of the teaching in the clinical years is of this order.

Contact with patients brings a new set of circumstances with which the student must deal. He no longer feels the great pressure created by tests, for he is told by the faculty, and this is confirmed by his daily experience, that examinations are now less important. His problems now become those of coping with a steady stream of patients in a way that will please the staff man under whom he is working, and of handling what is sometimes a tremendous load of clinical work so as to allow

7. The concept of student culture is analyzed in some detail in Howard S. Becker and Blanche Geer, "Student Culture in Medical School," *Harvard Educational Review*, 28 (Winter, 1958), pp. 70-80.

himself time for studying diseases and treatments that interest him and for play and family life.

The students earlier have expected that once they reach the clinical years they will be able to realize their idealistic ambitions to help people and to learn those things immediately useful in aiding people who are ill. But they find themselves working to understand cases as medical problems rather than working to help the sick and memorizing the relevant available facts so that these can be produced immediately for a questioning staff man. When they make ward rounds with a faculty member they are likely to be quizzed about any of the seemingly countless facts possibly related to the condition of the patient for whom they are "caring."

Observers speak of the cynicism that overtakes the student and the lack of concern for his patients as human beings. This change does take place, but it is not produced solely by "the anxiety brought about by the presence of death and suffering."[8] The student becomes preoccupied with the technical aspects of the cases with which he deals because the faculty requires him to do so. He is questioned about so many technical details that he must spend most of his time learning them.

The frustrations created by his position in the teaching hospital further divert the student from idealistic concerns. He finds himself low man in a hierarchy based on clinical experience, so that he is allowed very little of the medical responsibility he would like to assume. Because of his lack of experience, he cannot write orders, and he receives permission to perform medical and surgical procedures (if at all) at a rate he considers far too slow. He usually must content himself with "mere" vicarious participation in the drama of danger, life, and death that he sees as the core of medical practice. The student culture accents these difficulties so that events (and especially those involving patients) are interpreted and reacted to as they push him toward or hold him back from further participation in this drama. He does not think in terms the layman might use.

As a result of the increasingly technical emphasis of his thinking the student appears cynical to the non-medical outsider, though from his own point of view he is simply seeing what is "really important." Instead of reacting with the layman's horror and sympathy for the patient to the sight of a cancerous organ that has been surgically removed, the student is more likely to regret that he was not allowed to close the incision at the completion of the operation, and to rue the

---

8. Dana L. Farnsworth, "Some Observations on the Attitudes and Motivations of the Harvard Medical Student," *Harvard Medical Alumni Bulletin,* January, 1956, p. 34.

hours that he must spend searching in the fatty flesh for the lymph nodes that will reveal how far the disease has spread. As in other lines of work, he drops lay attitudes for those more relevant to the way the event affects someone in his position.

This is not to say that the students lose their original idealism. When issues of idealism are openly raised in a situation they define as appropriate, they respond as they might have when they were freshmen. But the influence of the student culture is such that questions which might bring forth this idealism are not brought up. Students are often assigned patients for examination and follow-up whose conditions might be expected to provoke idealistic crises. Students discuss such patients, however, with reference to the problems they create for the *student*. Patients with terminal diseases who are a long time dying, and patients with chronic diseases who show little change from week to week, are more likely to be viewed as creating extra work without extra compensation in knowledge or the opportunity to practice new skills than as examples of illness which raise questions about euthanasia. Such cases require the student to spend time every day checking on progress which he feels will probably not take place and to write long "progress" notes in the patient's chart although little progress has occurred.

This apparent cynicism is a collective matter. Group activities are built around this kind of workaday perspective, constraining the students in two ways. First, they do not openly express the lay idealistic notions they may hold, for their culture does not sanction such expression; second, they are less likely to have thoughts of this deviant kind when they are engaged in group activity. The collective nature of this "cynicism" is indicated by the fact that students become more openly idealistic whenever they are removed from the influence of student culture—when they are alone with a sociologist as they near the finish of school and sense the approaching end of student life, for example, or when they are isolated from their classmates and therefore are less influenced by this culture.[9]

They still feel, as advanced students, though much less so than before, that school is irrelevant to actual medical practice. Many of their tasks, like running laboratory tests on patients newly admitted to the hospital or examining surgical specimens in the pathology laboratory, seem to them to have nothing to do with their visions of their future activity as doctors. As in their freshman year, they believe that perhaps they must obtain the knowledge they will need in spite of the school. They still conceive of medicine as a huge body of proven facts, but no longer believe that they will ever be able to master it all. They now

9. See the discussion in Howard S. Becker, "Interviewing Medical Students," *op. cit.*

say that they are going to try to apply the solution of the practicing M.D. to their own dilemma: learn a few things that they are interested in very well and know enough about other things to pass examinations while in school and, later on in practice, to know to which specialist to send difficult patients.

Their original medical idealism reasserts itself as the end of school approaches. Seniors show more interest than students in earlier years in serious ethical dilemmas of the kind they expect to face in practice. They have become aware of ethical problems laymen often see as crucial for the physician—whether it is right to keep patients with fatal diseases alive as long as possible, or what should be done if an influential patient demands an abortion—and worry about them. As they near graduation and student culture begins to break down as the soon-to-be doctors are about to go their separate ways, these questions are more and more openly discussed.

While in school, they have added to their earlier idealism a new and peculiarly professional idealism. Even though they know that few doctors live up to the standards they have been taught, they intend always to examine their patients thoroughly and to give treatment based on firm diagnosis rather than merely to relieve symptoms. This expansion and transformation of idealism appear most explicitly in their consideration of alternative careers, concerning both specialization and the kind of arrangements to be made for setting up practice. Many of their hypothetical choices aim at making it possible for them to be the kind of doctors their original idealism pictured. Many seniors consider specialty training so that they will be able to work in a limited field in which it will be more nearly possible to know all there is to know, thus avoiding the necessity of dealing in a more ignorant way with the wider range of problems general practice would present. In the same manner, they think of schemes to establish partnerships or other arrangements making it easier to avoid a work load which would prevent them from giving each patient the thorough examination and care they now see as ideal.

In other words, as school comes to an end, the cynicism specific to the school situation also comes to an end and their original and more general idealism about medicine comes to the fore again, though within a framework of more realistic alternatives. Their idealism is now more informed although no less selfless.

Discussion

We have used the words "idealism" and "cynicism" loosely in our description of the changeable state of mind of the medical student, playing on ambiguities we can now attempt to clear up. Retaining a core of common meaning, the dictionary definition, in our reference to the person's belief in the worth of his activity and the claims made for it, we have seen that this is not a generalized trait of the students we studied but rather an attitude which varies greatly, depending on the particular activity the worth of which is questioned and the situation in which the attitude is expressed.

This variability of the idealistic attitude suggests that in using such an element of personal perspective in sociological anlysis one should not treat it as homogeneous but should make a determined search for subtypes which may arise under different conditions and have differing consequences. Such subtypes presumably can be constructed along many dimensions. There might, for instance, be consistent variations in the medical students' idealism through the four years of school that are related to their social class backgrounds. We have stressed in this report the subtypes that can be constructed according to variations in the object of the idealistic attitude and variations in the audience the person has in mind when he adopts the attitude. The medical students can be viewed as both idealistic and cynical, depending on whether one has in mind their view of their school activities or the future they envision for themselves as doctors. Further, they might take one or another of these positions depending on whether their implied audience is made up of other students, their instructors, or the lay public.

A final complication arises because cynicism and idealism are not merely attributes of the actor, but are as dependent on the person doing the attributing as they are on the qualities of the individual to whom they are attributed.[10] Though the student may see his own disregard of the unique personal troubles of a particular patient as proper scientific objectivity, the layman may view this objectivity as heartless cynicism.[11]

Having made these analytic distinctions, we can now summarize the transformations of these characteristics as we have seen them occurring among medical students. Some of the students' determined idealism at the outset is reaction against the lay notion, of which they are uncomfortably aware, that doctors are money-hungry cynics; they counter this with an idealism of similar lay origin stressing the doctor's devotion to service. But this idealism soon meets a setback, as students find that it will not be relevant for awhile, since medical school has, it seems, little relation to the practice of medicine, as they see it. As it has not been refuted, but only shown to be temporarily beside the point, the students "agree" to set this idealism aside in favor of a realistic approach to the

10. See Philip Selznick's related discussion of fanaticism in *TVA and the Grass Roots*, Berkeley: University of California Press, 1953, pp. 205-213.

11. George Orwell gives the layman's side in his essay, "How the Poor Die," in *Shooting an Elephant and Other Essays*, London: Secker and Warburg, 1950, pp. 18-32.

problem of getting through school. This approach, which we have labeled as the cynicism specific to the school experience, serves as protection for the earlier grandiose feelings about medicine by postponing their exposure to reality to a distant future. As that future approaches near the end of the four years and its possible mistreatment of their ideals moves closer, the students again worry about maintaining their integrity, this time in actual medical practice. They use some of the knowledge they have gained to plan careers which, it is hoped, can best bring their ideals to realization.

We can put this in propositional form by saying that when a man's ideals are challenged by outsiders and then further strained by reality, he may salvage them by postponing their application to a future time when conditions are expected to be more propitious.

BURTON R. CLARK

The "Cooling-Out" Function in Higher Education

A major problem of democratic society is inconsistency between encouragement to achieve and the realities of limited opportunity. Democracy asks individuals to act as if social mobility were universally possible; status is to be won by individual effort, and rewards are to accrue to those who try. But democratic societies also need selective training institutions, and hierarchical work organizations permit in-

Reprinted from "The 'Cooling-Out' Function in Higher Education," by Burton R. Clark, The American Journal of Sociology *(May, 1960), pp. 569-576, by permission of The University of Chicago Press. Copyright 1960 by the University of Chicago.*

Revised and extended version of paper read at the Fifty-fourth Annual Meeting of the American Sociological Association, Chicago, September 3-5, 1959. I am indebted to Erving Goffman and Martin A. Trow for criticism and to Sheldon Messinger for extended conceptual and editorial comment.

creasingly fewer persons to succeed at ascending levels. Situations of opportunity are also situations of denial and failure. Thus democratic societies need not only to motivate achievement but also to mollify those denied it in order to sustain motivation in the face of disappointment and to deflect resentment. In the modern mass democracy, with its large-scale organization, elaborated ideologies of equal access and participation, and minimal commitment to social origin as a basis for status, the task becomes critical.

The problem of blocked opportunity has been approached sociologically through means-ends analysis. Merton and others have called attention to the phenomenon of dissociation between culturally instilled goals and institutionally provided means of realization; discrepancy between ends and means is seen as a basic social source of individual frustration and recalcitrance.[1] We shall here extend means-ends analysis in another direction, to the responses of organized groups to means-ends disparities, in particular focusing attention on ameliorative processes that lessen the strains of dissociation. We shall do so by analyzing the most prevalent type of dissociation between aspirations and avenues in American education, specifying the structure and processes that reduce the stress of structural disparity and individual denial. Certain components of American higher education perform what may be called the cooling-out function,[2] and it is to these that attention will be drawn.

The Ends-Means Disjuncture

In American higher education the aspirations of the multitude are encouraged by "open-door" admission to public-supported colleges. The means of moving upward in status and of maintaining high status now include some years in college, and a college education is a prerequisite of the better positions in business and the professions. The trend is

1. "Aberrant behavior may be regarded sociologically as a symptom of dissociation between culturally prescribed aspirations and socially structured avenues for realizing these aspirations" (Robert K. Merton, "Social Structure and Anomie," in *Social Theory and Social Structure* [rev. ed.; New York: Free Press, 1957], p. 134). See also Herbert H. Hyman, "The Value Systems of Different Classes: A Social Psychological Contribution to the Analysis of Stratification," in Reinhard Bendix and Seymour M. Lipset (eds.), *Class, Status and Power: A Reader in Social Stratification* (New York: Free Press, 1953), pp. 426-42; and the papers by Robert Dubin, Richard A. Cloward, Robert K. Merton, and Dorothy L. Meier, and Wendell Bell, in *American Sociological Review,* Vol. XXIV (April, 1959).

2. I am indebted to Erving Goffman's original statement of the cooling-out conception. See his "Cooling the Mark Out: Some Aspects of Adaptation to Failure," *Psychiatry,* XV (November, 1952), 451-63. Sheldon Messinger called the relevance of this concept to my attention.

toward an even tighter connection between higher education and higher occupations, as increased specialization and professionalization insure that more persons will need more preparation. The high-school graduate, seeing college as essential to success, will seek to enter some college, regardless of his record in high school.

A second and allied source of public interest in unlimited entry into college is the ideology of equal opportunity.[3] Strictly interpreted, equality of opportunity means selection according to ability, without regard to extraneous considerations. Popularly interpreted, however, equal opportunity in obtaining a college education is widely taken to mean unlimited access to some form of college: in California, for example, state educational authorities maintain that high-school graduates who cannot qualify for the state university or state college should still have the "opportunity of attending a publicly supported institution of higher education," this being "an essential part of the state's goal of guaranteeing equal educational opportunities to all its citizens."[4] To deny access to college is then to deny equal opportunity. Higher education should make a seat available without judgment on past performance.

Many other features of current American life encourage college-going. School officials are reluctant to establish early critical hurdles for the young, as is done in Europe. With little enforced screening in the precollege years, vocational choice and educational selection are postponed to the college years or later. In addition, the United States, a wealthy country, is readily supporting a large complex of colleges, and its expanding economy requires more specialists. Recently, a natural concern that manpower be fully utilized has encouraged the extending of college training to more and different kinds of students. Going to college is also in some segments of society the thing to do; as a last resort, it is more attractive than the army or a job. Thus ethical and practical urges together encourage the high-school graduate to believe that college is both a necessity and a right; similarly, parents and elected officials incline toward legislation and admission practices that insure entry for large numbers; and educational authorities find the need and justification for easy admission.

Even where pressures have been decisive in widening admission

---

3. Seymour Martin Lipset and Reinhard Bendix, *Social Mobility in Industrial Society* (Berkeley: University of California Press, 1959), pp. 78-101.

4. *A Study of the Need for Additional Centers of Public Higher Education in California* (Sacramento: California State Department of Education, 1957), p. 128. For somewhat similar interpretations by educators and laymen nationally see Francis J. Brown (ed.), *Approaching Equality of Opportunity in Higher Education* (Washington, D.C.: American Council on Education, 1955), and the President's Committee on Education beyond the High School, *Second Report to the President* (Washington, D.C.: Government Printing Office, 1957).

policy, however, the system of higher education has continued to be shaped partly by other interests. The practices of public colleges are influenced by the academic personnel, the organizational requirements of colleges, and external pressures other than those behind the open door. Standards of performance and graduation are maintained. A commitment to standards is encouraged by a set of values in which the status of a college, as defined by academicians and a large body of educated laymen, is closely linked to the perceived quality of faculty, student body, and curriculum. The raising of standards is supported by the faculty's desire to work with promising students and to enjoy membership in an enterprise of reputed quality—college authorities find low standards and poor students a handicap in competing with other colleges for such resources as able faculty as well as for academic status. The wish is widespread that college education be of the highest quality for the preparation of leaders in public affairs, business, and the professions. In brief, the institutional means of the students' progress toward college graduation and subsequent goals are shaped in large part by a commitment to quality embodied in college staffs, traditions, and images.

The conflict between open-door admission and performance of high quality often means a wide discrepancy between the hopes of entering students and the means of their realization. Students who pursue ends for which a college education is required but who have little academic ability gain admission into colleges only to encounter standards of performance they cannot meet. As a result, while some students of low promise are successful, for large numbers failure is inevitable and *structured*. The denial is delayed, taking place within the college instead of at the edge of the system. It requires that many colleges handle the student who intends to complete college and has been allowed to become involved but whose destiny is to fail.

Responses to Disjuncture

What is done with the student whose destiny will normally be early termination? One answer is unequivocal dismissal. This "hard" response is found in the state university that bows to pressure for broad admission but then protects standards by heavy drop-out. In the first year it weeds out many of the incompetent, who may number a third or more of the entering class.[5] The response of the college is hard in that failure is clearly defined as such. Failure is public; the student often returns home.

5. One national report showed that one out of eight entering students (12.5 per cent) in publicly controlled colleges does not remain beyond the first term or semester; one out of three (31 per cent) is out by the end of the first year; and

This abrupt change in status and in access to the means of achievement may occur simultaneously in a large college or university for hundreds, and sometimes thousands, of students after the first semester and at the end of the freshman year. The delayed denial is often viewed on the outside as heartless, a slaughter of the innocents.[6] This excites public pressure and anxiety, and apparently the practice cannot be extended indefinitely as the demand for admission to college increases.

A second answer is to sidetrack unpromising students rather than have them fail. This is the "soft" response: never to dismiss a student but to provide him with an alternative. One form of it in some state universities is the detour to an extension division or a general college, which has the advantage of appearing not very different from the main road. Sometimes "easy" fields of study, such as education, business administration, and social science, are used as alternatives to dismissal.[7] The major form of the soft response is not found in the four-year college or university, however, but in the college that specializes in handling students who will soon be leaving—typically, the two-year public junior college.

In most states where the two-year college is a part of higher education, the students likely to be caught in the means-ends disjuncture are assigned to it in large numbers. In California, where there are over sixty public two-year colleges in a diversified system that includes the state university and numerous four-year state colleges, the junior college is unselective in admissions and by law, custom, and self-conception accepts all who wish to enter.[8] It is tuition-free, local, and under local control.

---

about one out of two (46.6 per cent) leaves within the first two years. In state universities alone, about one out of four withdraws in the first year and 40 per cent in two years (Robert E. Iffert, *Retention and Withdrawal of College Students* [Washington, D.C.: Department of Health, Education, and Welfare, 1958], pp. 15-20). Students withdraw for many reasons, but scholastic aptitude is related to their staying power: "A sizeable number of students of medium ability enter college, but . . . few if any of them remain longer than two years" (*A Restudy of the Needs of California in Higher Education* [Sacramento: California State Department of Education, 1955], p. 120).

6. Robert L. Kelly, *The American Colleges and the Social Order* (New York: Macmillan Co., 1940), pp. 220-21.

7. One study has noted that on many campuses the business school serves "as a dumping ground for students who cannot make the grade in engineering or some branch of the liberal arts," this being a consequence of lower promotion standards than are found in most other branches of the university (Frank C. Pierson, *The Education of American Businessmen* [New York: McGraw-Hill Book Co., 1959], p. 63). Pierson also summarizes data on intelligence of students by field of study which indicate that education, business, and social science rank near the bottom in quality of students (*ibid.*, pp. 65-72).

8. Burton R. Clark, *The Open Door College: A Case Study* (New York: McGraw-Hill Book Co., 1960), pp. 44-45.

Most of its entering students want to try for the baccalaureate degree, transferring to a "senior" college after one or two years. About two-thirds of the students in the junior colleges of the state are in programs that permit transferring; but, of these, only about one-third actually transfer to a four-year college.[9] The remainder, or two out of three of the professed transfer students, are "latent terminal students": their announced intention and program of study entails four years of college, but in reality their work terminates in the junior college. Constituting about half of all the students in the California junior colleges, and somewhere between one-third and one-half of junior college students nationally,[10] these students cannot be ignored by the colleges. Understanding their careers is important to understanding modern higher education.

The Reorienting Process

This type of student in the junior college is handled by being moved out of a transfer major to a one- or two-year program of vocational, business, or semiprofessional training. This calls for the relinquishing of his original intention, and he is induced to accept a substitute that has lower status in both the college and society in general.

In one junior college[11] the initial move in a cooling-out process is pre-entrance testing: low scores on achievement tests lead poorly qualified students into remedial classes. Assignment to remedial work casts doubt and slows the student's movement into bona fide transfer courses. The remedial courses are, in effect, a subcollege. The student's achievement scores are made part of a counseling folder that will become increasingly significant to him. An objective record of ability and performance begins to accumulate.

A second step is a counseling interview before the beginning of the first semester, and before all subsequent semesters for returning students. "At this interview the counselor assists the student to choose the proper courses in light of his objective, his test scores, the high school record and test records from his previous schools."[12] Assistance in choosing "the proper courses" is gentle at first. Of the common case of the student who wants to be an engineer but who is not a promising candidate, a counselor said: "I never openly countermand his choice but edge him

9. *Ibid.*, p. 116.

10. Leland L. Medsker, *The Junior College: Progress and Prospect* (New York: McGraw-Hill Book Co., 1960), chap. iv.

11. San Jose City College, San Jose, Calif. For the larger study see Clark, *op. cit.*

12. San Jose Junior College, Handbook for Counselors, 1957-58, p. 2. Statements in quotation marks in the next few paragraphs are cited from this.

toward a terminal program by gradually laying out the facts of life." Counselors may become more severe later when grades provide a talking point and when the student knows that he is in trouble. In the earlier counseling the desire of the student has much weight; the counselor limits himself to giving advice and stating the probability of success. The advice is entered in the counseling record that shadows the student.

A third and major step in reorienting the latent terminal student is a special course entitled "Orientation to College," mandatory for entering students. All sections of it are taught by teacher-counselors who comprise the counseling staff, and one of its purposes is "to assist students in evaluating their own abilities, interests, and aptitudes; in assaying their vocational choices in light of this evaluation; and in making educational plans to implement their choices." A major section of it takes up vocational planning; vocational tests are given at a time when opportunities and requirements in various fields of work are discussed. The tests include the "Lee Thorpe Interest Inventory" ("given to all students for motivating a self-appraisal of vocational choice") and the "Strong Interest Inventory" ("for all who are undecided about choice or who show disparity between accomplishment and vocational choice"). Mechanical and clerical aptitude tests are taken by all. The aptitudes are directly related to the college's terminal programs, with special tests, such as a pre-engineering ability test, being given according to need. Then an "occupational paper is required of all students for their chosen occupation"; in it the student writes on the required training and education and makes a "self-appraisal of fitness."

Tests and papers are then used in class discussion and counseling interviews, in which the students themselves arrange and work with a counselor's folder and a student test profile and, in so doing, are repeatedly confronted by the accumulating evidence–the test scores, course grades, recommendations of teachers and counselors. This procedure is intended to heighten self-awareness of capacity in relation to choice and hence to strike particularly at the latent terminal student. The teacher-counselors are urged constantly to "be alert to the problem of unrealistic vocational goals" and to "help students to accept their limitations and strive for success in other worthwhile objectives that are within their grasp." The orientation class was considered a good place "to talk tough," to explain in an *impersonal* way the facts of life for the overambitious student. Talking tough to a whole group is part of a soft treatment of the individual.

Following the vocational counseling, the orientation course turns to "building an educational program," to study of the requirements for graduation of the college in transfer and terminal curriculum, and to planning of a four-semester program. The students also become acquainted with the requirements of the colleges to which they hope to transfer, here contemplating additional hurdles such as the entrance examinations of other colleges. Again, the hard facts of the road ahead are brought to bear on self-appraisal.

If he wishes, the latent terminal student may ignore the counselor's advice and the test scores. While in the counseling class, he is also in other courses, and he can wait to see what happens. Adverse counseling advice and poor tests scores may not shut off his hope of completing college; when this is the case, the deterrent will be encountered in the regular classes. Here the student is divested of expectations, lingering from high school, that he will automatically pass and, hopefully, automatically be transferred. Then, receiving low grades, he is thrown back into the counseling orbit, a fourth step in his reorientation and a move justified by his actual accomplishment. The following indicates the nature of the referral system:

> *Need for Improvement Notices* are issued by instructors to students who are doing unsatisfactory work. The carbon copy of the notice is given to the counselor who will be available for conference with the student. The responsibility lies with the student to see his counselor. However, experience shows that some counselees are unable to be sufficiently self-directive to seek aid. The counselor should, in such cases, send for the student, using the Request for Conference blank. If the student fails to respond to the Request for Conference slip, this may become a disciplinary matter and should be referred to the deans.
>
> After a conference has been held, the Need for Improvement notices are filed in the student's folder. *This may be important* in case of a complaint concerning the fairness of a final grade.[13]

This directs the student to more advice and self-assessment, as soon and as often as he has classroom difficulty. The carbon-copy routine makes it certain that, if he does not seek advice, advice will seek him. The paper work and bureaucratic procedure have the purpose of recording referral and advice in black and white, where they may later be appealed to impersonally. As put in an unpublished report of the college, the overaspiring student and the one who seems to be in the wrong program require "skillful and delicate handling. An accumulation of pertinent factual information may serve to fortify the objectivity of the student-counselor relationship." While the counselor advises delicately and patiently, but persistently, the student is confronted with the record with increasing frequency.

A fifth step, one necessary for many in the throes of discouragement, is probation: "Students [whose] grade point averages fall below 2.0 [C] in any semester will, upon recommendation by the Scholarship

13. *Ibid.*, p. 20.

Committee, be placed on probationary standing." A second failure places the student on second probation, and a third may mean that he will be advised to withdraw from the college altogether. The procedure is not designed to rid the college of a large number of students, for they may continue on probation for three consecutive semesters; its purpose is not to provide a status halfway out of the college but to "assist the student to seek an objective (major field) at a level on which he can succeed."[14] An important effect of probation is its slow killing-off of the lingering hopes of the most stubborn latent terminal students. A "transfer student" must have a C average to receive the Associate in Arts (a two-year degree) offered by the junior college, but no minimum average is set for terminal students. More important, four-year colleges require a C average or higher for the transfer student. Thus probationary status is the final blow to hopes of transferring and, indeed, even to graduating from the junior college under a transfer-student label. The point is reached where the student must permit himself to be reclassified or else drop out. In this college, 30 per cent of the students enrolled at the end of the spring semester, 1955-56, who returned the following fall were on probation; three out of four of these were transfer students in name.[15]

This sequence of procedures is a specific process of cooling-out;[16] its effect, at the best, is to let down hopes gently and unexplosively. Through it students who are failing or barely passing find their occupational and academic future being redefined. Along the way, teacher-counselors urge the latent terminal student to give up his plan of transferring and stand ready to console him in accepting a terminal curriculum. The drawn-out denial when it is effective is in place of a personal, hard "No"; instead, the student is brought to realize, finally, that it is best to ease himself out of the competition to transfer.

Cooling-Out Features

In the cooling-out process in the junior college are several features which are likely to be found in other settings where failure or denial is the effect of a structured discrepancy between ends and means, the

14. Statement taken from unpublished material.

15. San Jose Junior College, "Digest of Analysis of the Records of 468 Students Placed on Probation for the Fall Semester, 1956," September 3, 1956.

16. Goffman's original statement of the concept of cooling-out referred to how the disappointing of expectations is handled by the disappointed person and especially by those responsible for the disappointment. Although his main illustration was the confidence game, where facts and potential achievement are deliberately misrepresented to the "mark" (the victim) by operators of the game, Goffman also

responsible operatives or "coolers" cannot leave the scene or hide their identities, and the disappointment is threatening in some way to those responsible for it. At work and in training institutions this is common. The features are:

1. *Alternative Achievement.* Substitute avenues may be made to appear not too different from what is given up, particularly as to status. The person destined to be denied or who fails is invited to interpret the second effort as more appropriate to his particular talent and is made to see that it will be the less frustrating. Here one does not fail but rectifies a mistake. The substitute status reflects less unfavorably on personal capacity than does being dismissed and forced to leave the scene. The terminal student in the junior college may appear not very different from the transfer student—an "engineering aide," for example, instead of an "engineer"—and to be proceeding to something with a status of its own. Failure in college can be treated as if it did not happen; so, too, can poor performance in industry.[17]

2. *Gradual Disengagement.* By a gradual series of steps, movement to a goal may be stalled, self-assessment encouraged, and evidence produced of performance. This leads toward the available alternatives at little cost. It also keeps the person in a counseling milieu in which advice is furnished, whether actively sought or not. Compared with the original hopes, however, it is a deteriorating situation. If the individual does not give up peacefully, he will be in trouble.

3. *Objective Denial.* Reorientation is, finally, confrontation by the facts. A record of poor performance helps to detach the organization and its agents from the emotional aspects of the cooling-out work. In a sense, the overaspiring student in the junior college confronts himself, as he lives with the accumulating evidence, instead of the organization. The college offers opportunity; it is the record that forces denial. Record-keeping and other bureaucratic procedures appeal to universal criteria and reduce the influence of personal ties, and the personnel are thereby protected. Modern personnel record-keeping, in general, has the function of documenting denial.

4. *Agents of Consolation.* Counselors are available who are patient with the overambitious and who work to change their intentions. They believe in the value of the alternative careers, though of lower social status, and are practiced in consoling. In college and in other settings counseling is to reduce aspiration as well as to define and to help fulfil

---

applied the concept to failure in which those responsible act in good faith (*op. cit., passim*). "Cooling-out" is a widely useful idea when used to refer to a function that may vary in deliberateness.

17. *Ibid.*, p. 457; cf. Perrin Stryker, "How to Fire an Executive," *Fortune*, L (October, 1954), 116-17 and 178-92.

it. The teacher-counselor in the "soft" junior college is in contrast to the scholar in the "hard" college who simply gives a low grade to the failing student.

5. *Avoidance of Standards.* A cooling-out process avoids appealing to standards that are ambiguous to begin with. While a "hard" attitude toward failure generally allows a single set of criteria, a "soft" treatment assumes that many kinds of ability are valuable, each in its place. Proper classification and placement are then paramount, while standards become relative.

Importance of Concealment

For an organization and its agents one dilemma of a cooling-out role is that it must be kept reasonably away from public scrutiny and not clearly perceived or understood by prospective clientele. Should it become obvious, the organization's ability to perform it would be impaired. If high-school seniors and their families were to define the junior college as a place which diverts college-bound students, a probable consequence would be a turning-away from the junior college and increased pressure for admission to the four-year colleges and universities that are otherwise protected to some degree. This would, of course, render superfluous the part now played by the junior college in the division of labor among colleges.

The cooling-out function of the junior college is kept hidden, for one thing, as other functions are highlighted. The junior college stresses "the transfer function," "the terminal function," etc., not that of transforming transfer into terminal students; indeed, it is widely identified as principally a transfer station. The other side of cooling-out is the successful performance in junior college of students who did poorly in high school or who have overcome socioeconomic handcaps, for they are drawn into higher education rather than taken out of it. Advocates of the junior college point to this salvaging of talented manpower, otherwise lost to the community and nation. It is indeed a function of the open door to let hidden talent be uncovered.

Then, too, cooling-out itself is reinterpreted so as to appeal widely. The junior college may be viewed as a place where all high-school graduates have the opportunity to explore possible careers and find the type of education appropriate to their individual ability; in short, as a place where everyone is admitted and everyone succeeds. As described by the former president of the University of California:

> A prime virtue of the junior college, I think, is that most of its students succeed in what they set out to accomplish, and cross the finish line before they grow weary of the race. After two years in a course that they have

chosen, they can go out prepared for activities that satisfy them, instead of being branded as failures. Thus the broadest possible opportunity may be provided for the largest number to make an honest try at further education with some possibility of success and with no route to a desired goal completely barred to them.[18]

The students themselves help to keep this function concealed by wishful unawareness. Those who cannot enter other colleges but still hope to complete four years will be motivated at first not to admit the cooling-out process to consciousness. Once exposed to it, they again will be led not to acknowledge it, and so they are saved insult to their self-image.

In summary, the cooling-out process in higher education is one whereby systematic discrepancy between aspiration and avenue is covered over and stress for the individual and the system is minimized. The provision of readily available alternative achievements in itself is an important device for alleviating the stress consequent on failure and so preventing anomic and deviant behavior. The general result of cooling-out processes is that society can continue to encourage maximum effort without major disturbance from unfulfilled promises and expectations.

18. Robert Gordon Sproul, "Many Millions More," *Educational Record*, XXXIX (April, 1958), 102.

BENJAMIN D. PAUL

Mental Disorder and Self-Regulating Processes in Culture: A Guatemalan Illustration

The concept of culture, like the proverbial elephant, has been seen from many sides. To some, culture appears primarily as a pattern. To others, it is a process, a frame of perception, a precipitate of history, a mechanism for survival. These are all mutually reconcilable. The particular view depends on one's line of vision and on one's immediate purposes. From where I stand, and for purposes of this meeting, culture can be viewed as a type of "self-correcting" mechanism.

Culture, if it is in working order, lends purpose and direction to the lives of those it serves. All forms of organization, however, are achieved at some price. The costs may be widely distributed throughout the society in the form of strains built into the "typical" personality, or they can be borne disproportionately by a minority of indivduals, those typed as "deviants" by their fellows.

My concern here is with the deviant person, and more especially with a process in group behavior which first works in the direction of pushing the individual deeper into deviancy and then, in response to a behavioral signal from the deviant, reverses its direction to bring the disturbed individual back into a better state of balance with society. It is this reversible process which suggests comparison with self-regulating mechanisms, such as the thermostat on the governor of a steam engine.

Abstractly and generally considered, the conception is both simple and familiar. But its applicability to the socio-cultural sphere remains to be clarified. It is my hope that presentation of a detailed and concrete case will help to communicate the conception of self-regulating forces within culture and possibly stimulate productive comparisons. The case that follows will also raise other problems such as the relation of social role structure to individual deviance in simple societies, and the nature of the interchange between cultural and personality dynamics.

When my wife and I settled down as anthropologists in an Indian

---

Reprinted from Interrelations between the Social Environment and Psychiatric Disorders, *pp. 51-67, by permission of the publisher, Milbank Memorial Fund, and the author.*

village on Lake Atitlán in Guatemala, we made the mistake of hiring the wrong girl as household helper. She soon proved inadequate in many respects, but it was no easy matter to discharge her in view of the fact that her father was an important person whose good will we were eager to preserve. We did manage to dismiss her on some face-saving pretext, proceeding with caution before hiring another girl. After a careful inspection of the field-of-choice, we selected Maria, the central figure in this case, a person who eventually deserted our household, abandoned her own baby, and suffered a psychotic episode.

These unexpected events occurred after Maria had been working with us daily for ten weeks. During this time she had proved herself a good helper in the house, a lively and engaging companion, and a good source of information, if not always a source of good information. We came to know her as well as we knew anyone in the village, recording observations on what turned out to be a pre-morbid period in her life.

Who was Maria? She was a very attractive girl of eighteen, commanding attention even in a village renowned for its beautiful women. She was separated from her husband—her second—at the time she came to work for us and had a nine-month old baby girl. She was the daughter of a man named Manuel, who was, in some ways, an "operator." Manuel and a brother were early orphaned and raised by a kinsman who was a strict disciplinarian and taskmaster. Manuel's brother turned out to be a ne'er-do-well who was living with his seventh wife, and barely eking out a living at the time we arrived. Manuel had enjoyed better fortune. He had married strategically, thereby acquiring a house and land, and had managed to become a shaman, one of about six in the village. Shamanism can be a road to power, and though there was some question as to the legitimacy of his credentials (supernatural signs), he exerted a fair amount of influence in community councils. He was also regarded by some as a man who was lazy, and who sought to escape honest effort in a culture which extols the virtue of diligent labor in the fields. His wife's original inheritance had dwindled somewhat under his mediocre management.

Maria's mother came from one of the wealthy families with a considerable admixture of *ladino* (non-Indian) blood. She was a handsome woman of lighter-than-average complexion, a conscientious housekeeper, and a dutiful wife. But her life was punctuated by violent arguments with her husband, typically touched off by Manuel's habit of coming home drunk from a *fiesta*, and by her complaints that he was dissolving her inheritance in drinking debts. Manuel finally gave up drinking and took to smoking a pipe.

Maria was the oldest of six surviving children. Three children had died in infancy before Maria was born. According to relatives and neighbors, Maria had received much attention and affection as a baby. She was a sickly child, requiring more than ordinary care. When she was old enough to travel, her father took her on trips and to the fields as his traveling companion, a privilege commonly reserved for sons rather than daughters. But later on her father's indulgent attitude changed to one of criticism and punishment. He scolded and beat her for carrying tales ("She was always a great liar and troublemaker"), for her laziness around the house, and for getting into fights with her younger siblings.

Another girl, Juana, was born when Maria was fifteen months old. When Maria came to work for us, Juana was sixteen or seventeen years old. She was married, lived with her husband in her parents' home, and was pregnant with her first child. There was no love lost between Maria and Juana. They had a history of frequent quarrels and had even been rivals for the same beau. While Maria had more attractive features, Juana's lighter skin color carried more prestige. In marked contrast to Maria, Juana was a "good daughter," conforming to cultural expectations which distinguished sharply between the behavior prescribed for men and the behavior prescribed for women. Juana was obedient and respectful toward her parents, worked hard about the house, seldom sought to leave the house for idle purposes, and remained properly reticent in the presence of outsiders.

Some of Maria's traits suggested psychological affinity with masculine rather than with feminine standards. In a community where Maya is the native language, most of the women quickly forget what Spanish they learn as girls in grade school and feel ashamed to use the little they can remember. Men, in contrast, find Spanish useful in their commerce with the outside world. Maria not only had a fair command of Spanish but seemed to take pride in using it. She used her charms to attract men, but her attitude toward them was essentially competitive and hostile. By local standards, she was immodest and aggressive. She was disobedient and resisted authority; at home she was quarrelsome, dominating her younger siblings and engaging in arguments with her father.

Her first marriage lasted only a few months; her husband had accused her of carrying on flirtations with other men. Her second marriage, which had dissolved before we arrived, had been to a culturally marginal man of unstable character. The son of a wealthy family, he had been educated in the capital of Guatemala and had become a schoolteacher, but later lost his job because of excessive drinking. Maria quarreled with her husband and her mother-in-law, the marriage broke up, and she returned with a baby to live with her parents, having no other place to go.

Maria "happened" to be around when we needed a helper. Men and children visited our house freely from the beginning, but women and girls, deterred by fear of public disapproval, tended to keep a polite distance. Maria was one of our first female visitors. She volunteered her assistance about the house and kitchen and immediately began to help us with our Spanish. We thought the decision to hire her was ours, but in retrospect, it seems that Maria in fact selected us.

She was vivacious, gossipy, and an avid informant, but she embroidered nimbly. She was witty and a very clever mimic, but would occasionally lapse into morose silences. She seldom assumed a submissive attitude. When she was corrected in her household duties, she would respond by correcting our Spanish or by withdrawing into dignified silence.

Maria had a flair for the gruesome and the destructive. Once she helped a young man remove a chigger-like insect from his toe. This is done with a needle. She laughed and joked about sticking the needle into his eyes and all over his body. Another time she gave us an account of a celebrated murder that had occurred when she was only a few years old. With the aid of an accomplice, one man had killed another, over a woman. The culprits were apprehended and sent to the penitentiary, where the accomplice eventually died. These were the facts, and Maria presented them, but she allowed her imagination to embellish the story with a wealth of colorful and improbable details. According to her vivid version, the assassin hacked up the body, split the head open, extracted the brain, and put it in his pocket. The victim was also shot but wasn't killed until he received the fifth bullet. The accomplice did not merely die during his imprisonment, according to Maria; he was hacked to death, just as the original victim had been.

Maria worked for us part-time, and we paid her weekly. Sometimes she brought along her daughter and let her crawl about our floor. Most of the time the baby was left in the care of her mother or younger siblings. Their house was only a short distance from ours, and Maria could go home to breast-feed the baby. She seemed, in general, to be quite unconcerned about her child.

In our house, where she could escape the protective vigilance of her kinsmen, she had the rare opportunity of meeting the men who came to visit us. This enabled her to carry on conversations and surreptitiously arrange to run away and marry José, one of our informants. Like her previous husband, José was culturally marginal and was hoping to leave his native village when he could find employment in the capital. To disguise their plans, both Maria and José assured us that they wouldn't think of marrying since they were cousins and that their sustained conversations had to do with intrigues involving third parties. One evening when we left Maria alone for a moment, washing the supper dishes, she disappeared, eloping with José to his house. In Maria's village, at the present time, eloping with the boy and leaving the unsuspecting parents is the dominant form of marriage. In this case, Maria found it more convenient to use our house rather than her own as a staging area for the elopement.

Inevitably, Maria's parents learned the facts of the case by the following morning. Manuel, her father, came to our house and asked when we could give him the money he assumed we owed his daughter for the ten weeks of her employment. She apparently had told him that we had not yet begun to pay her. She had told us that her father kept her salary and that she had nothing left to buy essential clothes. In sympathy for her plight, we had presented her a blouse and other items for the Easter holidays.

Following local practices in connection with the elopement pattern, Manuel went to the village court house the day after Maria's disappearance to bring suit against her and José. He wanted to see her punished severely for having caused him anger and humiliation and especially for having abandoned her baby. This was a heartless thing to do to the baby, he contended, and it placed a heavy responsibility on his family, especially since the child was still nursing. The court imposed a fine on the couple, which José's father paid, terminating the court case but not the marriage. Maria returned to live with José and his parents. Her baby was awarded by the court to relatives of the child's real father. They claimed the baby on grounds that they had materially contributed to its support, and they claimed to be able to provide a wet-nurse, a paternal aunt who was then nursing a baby of her own.

People in the village spoke ill of Maria, not so much for eloping from her parents as for deserting her baby. There is no bottle feeding in the village, wet-nursing is regarded as a temporary expedient at best, and it is generally assumed that a baby under one year of age has a poor chance to survive if separated from its mother. Apparently feeling that the baby would be an obstacle in her new marriage, Maria made no effort to keep or regain her. Manuel remained bitter; relationships between Maria and her own family were completely ruptured.

Having alienated nearly everybody else, Maria could still count on José and his parents—but not for long. She promptly antagonized her new mother-in-law, whose name happened to be Juana, the same as the name of Maria's next younger sister. Her mother-in-law charged Maria with indolence and insubordination, and with giving orders to children of the household over whom Maria had no authority.

About a month after their marriage, Maria had a violent argument with José. He accused her of flirting with another man, and she accused him of making overtures to another girl. She reviled José and his parents. He responded by beating her. She in turn suffered a violent attack of *cólera* (rage), a culturally patterned syndrome consisting, according to local conceptions, of a swelling of the heart due to an excess of "bad blood," and consequent symptoms of gasping and suffocation. An attack of *cólera* is nearly always the product of an acrimonious quarrel. It gives the appearance of being a kind of adult temper-tantrum with screaming generally suppressed, and some of the anger directed at the self. The local culture frowns on the expression of overt hostility but nevertheless heated arguments sometimes occur, engendering secondary anxiety which can lead to *cólera*.

Later that night, after the quarrel and the attack of *cólera*, Maria lapsed into a state of unconsciousness which turned out to be the onset of a dissociated episode. Her husband tried to rouse her but could not. He summoned his father, Francisco, but he too was unsuccessful in trying to wake her. In their own words, they found her "cold and stiff as though dead for good." The Maya word *kamik* refers both to death and to unconsciousness, hence the phrase "dead for good" is a Spanish rendering to distinguish death from other losses of consciousness.

José and Francisco were frightened. Francisco shook his son and demanded, "What have you done to her?" He supposed that José might have beaten his wife to death. Francisco then called in a *ladina* (non-Indian) school mistress temporarily residing in the village. The schoolteacher tried some remedies, but without effect. Francisco next summoned one of the village shamans (native medico-magical specialists). The shaman came but was reluctant to try one of his medicines because, as he remarked, "She already looks so serious." He feared she would die, and he did not want to assume any responsibility. He remained in the house, however, and in about two hours Maria showed signs of life. She began to wail that spirits of the dead were surrounding her and were trying to take her to the realm of the dead. This heightened the fears of those present. The shaman left abruptly, saying that this was not a case for him. Ghosts are not taken lightly by people of this village; their arrival suggests that death is imminent.

Maria was in a state of fugue; she did not respond to overtures and did not recognize what was happening about her. She walked about the house talking and arguing, but only with the spirits. She told the spirits that she did not want to go along.

Realizing that she was *loca* (crazy), Francisco sent for the appropriate shaman. Of the six or seven shamans in the village, only one was qualified by his calling and by experience to deal with insanity. That person, it so happened, was Manuel, Maria's father.

Until this moment, Francisco and Manuel had not been on speaking terms owing to the elopement and the subsequent court case. But that night the breach was speedily remedied. Now in the role of a critical specialist and not in the role of an injured father, Manuel swung into action. He advised that Maria be taken immediately to the neighboring town of Atitlán, regarded as the seat of sorcery, to see a still more powerful shaman, a person who had once cured Manuel of a stubborn illness and had thus become Manuel's mentor in the shamanistic arts.

At two o'clock at night the party set out by canoe—Maria, her father, José, and José's parents. Maria resisted, but she was forcibly taken by the arm. Just before dawn they arrived in Atitlán. Manuel called on the other shaman, and they all paid a visit to the abode of the powerful and dreaded *Maximon*, the master of insanity and black magic. Candles were burned, incense was offered, and the two shamans held conversations with the mystic power, unseen in the darkness of the night.

The seance ended with the diagnosis that Maria had fallen victim to the power of malignant supernatural forces. The cause lay in a history of sinful behavior on the part of any or all of the following: Maria, her father and mother; her husband José, his father and mother. Hence, the first step in the course of treatment was to be a ritual whipping administered to all six by a senior relative. This could be done only by the aged mother of Francisco, the only living grandparent of the couple. The party returned to the village and asked the grandmother to carry out the whipping. This was to be done as a gesture and as a symbol, and not as an act of corporal punishment. Even though it involved more exorcism than exercise, the old lady refused to cooperate. Like the first shaman who had run out on the case, she feared that someone would die, and did not want to incur any blame. But many other steps were taken. Considerable time, money, and effort were expended by both sets of parents in an effort to placate the threatening spirits. Resort was made to additional shamans and new remedies. The details of the course of cure are not relevant here. The significant thing is that the onset of Maria's illness created a marked change in the pattern of interpersonal activity within her kinship circle and that Maria was aware that not she alone but a group of people were locked in battle with the threatening forces.

Within about a week, Maria had a remission. For awhile she was not as gay as she had been, but she resumed her normal round of activities and no longer suffered from hallucinations. During the six or seven additional months we continued to reside in the village, Maria lived a normal life.

What was Maria's own version of events at the time of her seizure? Several days after the onset of her symptoms, my wife interviewed Maria, visiting her in the home of her own parents. After the night she first experienced hallucinations, she was afraid to remain in the household of Francisco, her father-in-law, for fear of ghosts. "I am afraid to go out of the house," Maria told my wife. "When I go out I feel as though someone were following me. I feel that the spirits are around me." Then virtually without questioning, she gave the following account.

"Saturday night at 11:00 o'clock, I felt that I had left the house of Francisco, that I was walking around strange streets and places, accompanied by spirits of dead women who had come for me. It is absolutely true that I was dead [unconscious] for two or three hours. I didn't feel a thing. My body was completely cold, but my spirit was walking around with the dead.

"They took me to a place where a man brought out a very big book. He looked in it and asked, 'Are you Juana?' and I told him, 'No.' He asked my mother's name and my father's name and other things about me, and then he said, 'No, you are not Juana. Your name is not here, but her name is. You must return. We don't want you here yet.' It wasn't me they wanted but my mother-in-law."

It should be recalled that Maria's sister and her mother-in-law are both called Juana. It is possible that the two persons were merged in Maria's imagery; she had reportedly told another informant that the Juana in her hallucinations was her own sister rather than her husband's mother.

"It was Rosario, the dead sister of my mother-in-law, who took me there, and she was the one who was with me all the time. When I got there, I saw all the dead people whom I had known. They were all there. But the Lord told me to return, that my name was not recorded. Rosario was angry. She had wanted her sister, Juana, called in to confront her dead parents and answer to the charge of stealing all the inheritance which the parents had left. Rosario argued that I should remain, saying 'This one is at least her daughter-in-law. Let her stay.' She was angry.

"Then some of the other [here she names a number of actual women who had recently died in childbirth] wouldn't let me leave. Whenever I tried to pass by in the road, they blocked my path. They said to me, 'You must stay here and help us give milk to the babies.' There were babies all over the ground, without any clothes on, rolling around and playing on the ground. One of the dead women said she was very tired from having nursed the babies and wanted me to stay and help them because there were so many [dead] babies there, but I don't have any milk now." This last statement of Maria's was contrary to fact. According to her own mother, Maria did have milk.

"Finally I didn't want to leave; I wanted to remain there with them, but the father of Juana [José's grandfather] came along the road and beat me with a whip and threw me on the ground and told me to leave." She then recounted how she journeyed home and how her spirit traveled through distant lands for a period of four days under the guidance of Rosario's spirit.

Though she spoke of her spirit as having wandered for four days, Maria actually went to stay in her father's house after the first night of her seizure. This was the first time she had appeared in her parents' home since the evening she had eloped from our house.

But shifting residence had no immediate effect on Maria's condition. According to information that we received from José's sister, for three days "Maria talked out loud, constantly addressing the spirits, protesting that she had no milk, exclaiming that they were trying to take her. When her husband tried to calm her, she would shake off his hand or hit him." According to Maria's mother, Maria was unable to sleep but walked up and down talking to the spirits and intermittently singing and dancing.

The songs she sang were snatches of esoteric, shamanistic incantations she had overheard her father chanting at times when he had come home drunk. Shamans are not supposed to sing their songs or to recite their verses in the presence of children. The words and the tunes are powerful, and capable of bringing disaster to those who sing them without warrant. When Maria's father heard her burst into these songs during the period of her breakdown, he scolded her severely, and ordered her to desist immediately. "This is why you have gone crazy," he told her, "from singing sacred songs that you have no business with."

By the end of a week, Maria was well enough to go out for a walk with her husband. Instead of returning to her father's home, the couple again went to live with José's parents. Maria greeter her father-in-law: "How would you like two laborers who are seeking work and lodging?" To this Francisco replied, "Where are the laborers?" "Why, José and I," said Maria, "I no longer wish to stay in my own father's house." She then offered Francisco a cup of soft drink as a gesture of amity. Francisco hesitated, pointing out that Maria's father might become vexed over the couple's unannounced departure from Manuel's household, especially "since I asked him to do us the favor of curing your illness." Francisco finally consented and accepted the drink after Maria protested that there was nothing wrong with her, that if she were ill she would be in bed. At eight or nine o'clock they all went to sleep.

That same night at one o'clock Maria rose from her bed in a rage and began beating José furiously. His cries aroused his sister's husband who rushed in to investigate, but Maria knocked him to the floor and reached for an axe handle. By this time Francisco appeared in the room. As Francisco reported it, he found Maria climbing over the prostrate brother-in-law and lunging for the latter's testicles. With the aid of his son and son-in-law, Francisco managed to seize Maria and tie her with ropes.

She pleaded for mercy. "I don't want you to kill my son [or son-in-law]," Francisco replied, "So I am going to have you sent away to prison." But her pleas prevailed. She promised never again to misbehave. Thereafter indeed her disturbing symptoms lifted and she resumed her normal activities, continuing to live with José. Of course, "normal" does not preclude occasional quarrels.

How did people in the community explain Maria's strange behavior? Some said the basic fault resided with Manuel, her father—that he had performed unethical acts in the past, and that he was now being punished through his daughter. Other said the fault was Maria's directly. Still others blamed José; others said the sickness was brought on by misdeeds on the part of José's parents. Others thought it to be a combination.

What are the general implications of this case? Let me first raise, in order to dispose of them, two issues which this case does little to resolve. The first issue is this: Do the dynamics of mental disorder remain constant from culture to culture, or do they vary? An easy but equivocal answer is that the psychodynamic *process* is essentially the same, but the *content* (the specific symptoms and manifestations) differs with the cultural milieu. This partly begs the question as to what is content and what is process. In this particular case I should suppose that content refers to the nature of Maria's visual and auditory hallucinations. Perhaps the processes revealed in her behavior fall into place as those characteristic of a "castrating female." Maria was both seductive and hostile towards men; she had met with failure in her effort to escape her culturally-prescribed feminine role, and had finally resorted to a temporary retreat from reality.

The second issue I want to dispose of briefly is this: Do the roots of psychopathology lie tangled in the skein of interpersonal relations, that is, in the social process; or do they reach deeper, originating in hereditary predispositions? Again, the case is necessarily ambiguous in this regard. The data can be so interpreted as to support either view. Maria's social history is certainly an etiological factor, but whether her life experience is the ultimate cause or only the proximate cause must remain an open question. It takes a carefully devised experimental design and not just a case to probe a problem of this kind effectively.

I come now to three general implications that are somewhat more positive. The first of these has to do with the range of role-choice available in a given society. Some authorities say that middle-class women in the United States are torn between competing roles, those of mother, glamor girl, careerist, and the like. There is the wear of indecision arising from excessive latitude of choice, leading to emotional conflict and in some cases to psychopathology. This viewpoint implies that a more unitary, more well defined, feminine role would provoke less anxiety. The case of Maria makes one wonder. The society in which she lived, with its clear defination of the female role, stands as a reminder that the pinch may only be shifted to another foot. There is essentially but one allowed feminine role, the wife-mother-housekeeper role, one that is socially subordinate to the male role. The system works reasonably well for most women in the society. There is no indication that women as a group are more unhappy than men in this Guatemalan village. But in the case of a person like Maria, who was unconventional for reasons of predisposition or socialization or both, the culture provided no role alternatives, no legitimate means of escape into nondomestic activity. Maria tried desperately to evade the demands of her milieu by marrying a succession of culturally marginal men who might have had the means and the motivation to leave the village to live in a less constricting urban environment. In the United States she might have become absorbed in a professional career. In her village she could only rebel, and eventually break with reality when the battle became unbearable. As a matter of fact, Maria did eventually escape from the village. Five years later when we revisited Guatemala, we learned that she and José had moved to Guatemala City and were raising a family.

The second of my concluding points relates to the question of secondary guilt in mental patients. If emotional illness connotes personal inadequacy in the judgment of society and hence also in the self-estimation of the patient, this should arouse secondary guilt, or blaming one's self for being emotionally disturbed. This in turn might aggravate the illness in spiral fashion. If secondary guilt can be a handicap to recovery, then the culture of the Guatemalan village tends to mitigate this particular handicap and thus encourage remission or recovery. Two cultural features permit escape from a sense of secondary guilt. One is the fact that hallucinations are not culturally defined as products of fantasy. Sights and sounds of ghosts are regarded by most normal people in Maria's village not as fears and fancies but as real occurrences. It was never doubted by others that dead women actually surrounded Maria during her illness. Maria thought so at the time, and she continued to think so after recovery. In Maria's village people do not share our quip: "I'm hallucinating again."

The difference between Maria and her kinsmen was that she could see and hear the spirits that were present, while they could not see or hear them. Spirits are believed capable of making themselves selectively visible and invisible. Maria was sick in the eyes of her neighbors not because she imagined visitations, but because she was host to visitations, just as we might consider a person sick because he is host to microbes we cannot see but know to be present on the basis of our cultural information.

The other cultural circumstance that minimizes secondary guilt is the merciful ambiguity of the blameful agent in bringing on Maria's sickness. Spirits are sent for a cause (bad behavior) but who committed the transgression? Was Manuel really the intended target? Some thought he was. If so, was it because he himself had done evil things or was it because of hidden enemies who wished him ill? Both these thoughts were expressed. Was it Francisco? Was it José? Was it Maria herself? Some certainly thought so. Was the malefactor Maria's mother-in-law, Juana? Maria certainly thought so, and some agreed with her. Each judge could cast blame where he would and find cultural justification for his judgment. It is locally believed that supernatural retribution is sometimes ineffective against people with "strong" characters, and that in such cases the punishment is deflected onto more susceptible kinsmen, usually offspring. It is likely that in her own mind, Maria was only an innocent bystander who fell victim to ghostly vengeance directed at someone else in the household. Our culture, having discredited these non-rational escapes, makes it more difficult for the mental patient to avoid a sense of secondary guilt or conscious self-blame.

The last of my three general points reverts to the concept of self-regulation in the socio-cultural process. When a ribbon in a typewriter moves far enough in one direction it trips a hammer and the movement is reversed. A like process appears to have occurred in Maria's human environment. The more she tried to evade the feminine role, the more she was renounced by society. Progressively alienating her parents, her parents-in-law, and finally her husband—her last social prop—she and her society had reached a state of complete mutual rejection. At this point, quantitative saturation brought a qualitative change; unable to proceed further in the same direction, Maria suddenly and dramatically altered her mode of behavior from argument and rebellion to psychological withdrawal. This culturally available act redefined the social situation. She was no longer an active threat to society and its norms; she was now regarded by those about her as the passive target of a more sinister threat, the forces of literal death. Any kinsman might be struck when ghosts are around. Any relative might in fact be to blame. To save themselves, for purely personal reasons if for no others, her relatives had to work for Maria and with Maria to repel the invading spirits. The process of social alienation was now reversed; the ribbon was winding the other way. Community of concern and anxiety is an important form of social solidarity. Groups of relatives who had been at odds with each other—her husband's family and her own family—now came together in common action. From an attitude of scorn and avoidance, her own father switched to one of sympathy and assistance. Once shunned by society, Maria was now the center of attention. She became the center of attention in a very literal sense. It is believed that the soul of anyone who is gravely sick, whether the disease is emotional or organic, is in peril of being seized by were-animals who wait for the weakened patient to be left unguarded. It is therefore necessary for relatives and neighbors to be in constant protective attendance. Maria was under day-and-night vigilance during most of the time that she (and her kinsmen) were in deepest danger.

Maria recovered. I should like to think that the process of redefinition and reversal just described was instrumental in the remission of her symptoms. What differs in Maria's society from our own is not so much the actual process of mental disorder as the *cultural definition* of this process—belief in an external threat and in joint jeopardy. By an abrupt switch in her mode of deviance, Maria was able to trip the cultural lever that set restitutive processes in motion. Having no hospitals to hide her in, the community provided Maria with a key to re-enter their own society.

EVON Z. VOGT

and THOMAS F. O'DEA

A Comparative Study of the Role of Values in Social Action in Two Southwestern Communities

It is one of the central hypotheses of the Values Study Project that value-orientations play an important part in the shaping of social institutions and in influencing the forms of observed social action. By value-orientations are understood those views of the world, often implicitly held, which define the meaning of human life or the "life situation of man" and thereby provide the context in which day-to-day problems are solved.[1] The present article is an outgrowth of one phase of the field research carried out in western New Mexico. It presents the record of two communities composed of people with a similar cultural background and living in the same general ecological setting.

The responses of these two communities to similar problems were found to be quite different. Since the physical setting of the two villages is remarkably similar, the explanation for the differences were sought in the manner in which each group viewed the situation and the kind of social relationships and legitimate expectations which each felt appropriate in meeting situational challenges. In this sphere of value-orientations a marked difference was found. Moreover, the differences in response to situation in the two cases were found to be related to the differences between the value-orientations central to these communities.

Reprinted from American Sociological Review, *1953, pp. 645-654, by permission of the authors and the journal.*

The authors are indebted to the Rockefeller Foundation (Social Science Division) for the financial support of the research reported in this paper as part of the Comparative Study of Values in Five Cultures Project of the Laboratory of Social Relations at Harvard University. We also wish to express our appreciation to Ethel M. Albert, Wilfrid C. Bailey, Clyde Kluckhohn, Anne Parsons, and John M. Roberts for criticisms and suggestions in the preparation of the paper.

1. Clyde Kluckhohn, "Values and Value-Orientations in the Theory of Action: An Exploration in Definition and Classification," *Toward a General Theory of Action*, edited by Talcott Parsons and E. A. Shils, Cambridge: Harvard University Press, 1951, p. 410.

We do not deny the importance of situational factors. Nor do we intend to disparage the importance of historical convergence of value-orientations with concrete situations in explaining the centrality of some values as against others and in leading to the deep internalization of the values we discuss. But the importance of value-orientations as an element in understanding the situation of action is inescapably clear. All the elements of what Parsons has called the action frame of reference—the actors, the means and conditions which comprise the situation, and the value-orientations of the actors—enter into the act.[2] The primacy of any one in any individual case does not permit generalization. Yet the present study testifies to the great importance of the third element—the value-orientations—in shaping the final action which ensues.

Focus of the Inquiry

The inquiry is focused upon a comparison of the Mormon community of *Rimrock*[3] with the Texan community of *Homestead*, both having populations of approximately 250 and both located (forty miles apart) on the southern portion of the Colorado Plateau in western New Mexico. The natural environmental setting is virtually the same for the two villages: the prevailing elevations stand at 7,000 feet; the landscapes are characterized by mesa and canyon country; the flora and fauna are typical of the Upper Sonoran Life Zone with stands of pinyon, juniper, sagebrush, and blue gramma grass and some intrusions of Ponderosa pine, Douglas fir, Englemann spruce, and Gambel oak from a higher life zone; the region has a steppe climate with an average annual precipitation of 14 inches (which varies greatly from year to year) and with killing frosts occurring late in the spring and early in the autumn.[4] The single important environmental difference between the two communities is that Rimrock is located near the base of a mountain range which has elevations rising to 9,000 feet, and a storage reservoir (fed by melting snow packs from these higher elevations) has made irrigation

2. Talcott Parsons, *The Structure of Social Action*, New York: Free Press, 1949, pp. 43-86; *Essays in Sociological Theory*, New York: Free Press, 1949, pp. 32-40; *The Social System*, New York: Free Press, 1951, pp. 3-24.

3. "Rimrock" and "Homestead" are pseudonyms used to protect the anonymity of our informants.

4. For additional ecological details on the region see Evon Z. Vogt, *Navaho Veterans: A Study of Changing Values*, Peabody Museum of Harvard University, Papers, Vol. XLI, No. 1, 1951, pp. 11-12; and John Landgraf, *Land-Use in the Ramah Area of New Mexico: An Anthropological Approach to Areal Study*, Peabody Museum of Harvard University, Vol. XLII, No. 1, 1954.

agriculture possible in Rimrock, while in Homestead there is only dry-land farming. Today both villages have subsistence patterns based upon combinations of farming (mainly irrigated crops of alfalfa and wheat in Rimrock, and dry-land crops of pinto beans in Homestead) and live-stock raising (mainly Hereford beef cattle in both villages).

Rimrock was settled by Mormon missionaries in the 1870's as part of a larger project to plant settlements in the area of northern Arizona. Rimrock itself, unlike the Arizona sites, was established as a missionary outpost and the intention of the settlers was the conversion of the Indians, a task conceived in terms of the *Book of Mormon*, which defines the American Indian as "a remnant of Israel."

The early settlers were "called" by the Church, that is, they were selected and sent out by the Church authorities. The early years were exceeding difficult and only the discipline of the Church and the loyalty of the settlers to its gospel kept them at the task. Drought, crop diseases, and the breaking of the earth and rock dam which they had constructed for the storage of irrigation water added to their difficulties, as did the fact that they had merely squatted on the land and were forced to purchase it at an exorbitant price to avoid eviction. The purchase money was given by the Church authorities in Salt Lake City, who also supplied 5,000 pounds of seed wheat in another period of dearth. The original settlers were largely from northern Utah although there were also some converts from the southern states who had been involved in unsuccessful Arizona settlements a few years earlier.

As the emphasis shifted from missionary activities to farming, Rimrock developed into a not unusual Mormon village, despite its peripheral position to the rest of Mormondom. Irrigation farming was supplemented by cattle raising on the open range. In the early 1930's the Mormons began to buy range land, and Rimrock's economy shifted to a focus upon cattle raising. Today villagers own a total of 149 sections of range land and about four sections of irrigated or irrigable land devoted to gardens and some irrigated pastures in the immediate vicinity of the village. The family farm is still the basic economic unit, although partnerships formed upon a kinship basis and devoted to cattle raising have been important in raising the economic level of the village as a whole. In recent years some of the villagers—also on the basis of a kinship partnership—purchased the local trading post which is engaged in trading with the Indians as well as local village business. In addition to 12 family partnerships which own 111 sections of land, there is a village cooperative which owns 38 sections. Privately-owned commercial facilities in the village include two stores, a boarding house, two garages, a saddle and leather shop, and a small restaurant. With this economic variety there is considerable difference in the distribution of wealth.

The Church is the central core of the village and its complex hierarchical structure, including the auxiliary organizations which activate women, youth, and young children, involves a large portion of the villagers in active participation. The church structure is backed up and impenetrated by the kinship structure. Moreover, church organization and kinship not only unify Rimrock into a social unit, they also integrate it into the larger structure of the Mormon Church and relate it by affinity and consanguinity to the rest of Mormondom.

Rimrock has been less affected by secularization than most Mormon villages in Utah and is less assimilated into generalized American patterns.[5] Its relative isolation has both kept such pressures from impinging upon it with full force and enhanced its formal and informal ties with the Church, preserving many of the characteristics of a Mormon village of a generation ago.

Homestead was settled by migrants from the South Plains area of western Texas and Oklahoma in the early 1930's. The migration represented a small aspect of that vast movement of people westward to California which was popularized in Steinbeck's *Grapes of Wrath* and which was the subject of investigation by many governmental agencies in the 1930's and 1940's.[6] Instead of going on to California, these homesteaders settled in a number of semi-arid farming areas in northern and western New Mexico and proceeded to develop an economy centered around the production of pinto beans. The migration coincided with the period of national depression and was due in part to severe economic conditions on the South Plains which forced families to leave their Texas and Oklahoma communities, in part to the attraction of land available for homesteading which held out the promise of family-owned farms for families who had previously owned little or no land or who had lost their land during the depression. The land base controlled by the homesteaders comprises approximately 100 sections. Each farm unit is operated by a nuclear family; there are no partnerships. Farms now average two sections in size and are scattered as far as twenty miles from the crossroads center of the community which contains the two stores, the school, the post office, two garages, a filling station, a small restaurant, a bean warehouse, a small bar, and two church buildings. Through the years, farming technology has shifted almost completely from horse-drawn implements to mechanized equipment.

With the hazardous farming conditions (periodic droughts and early

5. Lowry Nelson, *The Mormon Village.* Salt Lake City: University of Utah Press, 1952, pp. 275-85.

6. See especially the reports of the Tolan Committee, U.S. Congress, "House Committee to Investigate the Interstate Migration of Destitute Citizens," 76th Congress, 3rd Session, Volume 6, Part 6, 1940.

killing frosts) out-migration from Homestead has been relatively high. A few of these families have gone on to California, but more of them have moved to irrigated farms in the middle Rio Grande Valley and entered an agricultural situation which in its physical environmental aspects is similar to the situation in the Mormon community of Rimrock.

The Mormon Case

In broad perspective these two villages present local variations of generalized American culture. They share the common American value-orientations which emphasize the importance of achievement and success, progress and optimism, and rational mastery over nature. In the Mormon case, these were taken over from the 19th century American milieu in western New York where the Church was founded, and reinterpreted in terms of an elaborate theological conception of the universe as a dynamic process in which God and men are active collaborators in an eternal progression to greater power through increasing mastery.[7] The present life was and is conceived as a single episode in an infinity of work and mastery. The result was the heightening for the Mormons of convictions shared with most other Americans. Moreover, this conception was closely related to the belief in the reopening of divine revelation through the agency first of Joseph Smith, the original Mormon prophet, and later through the institutionalized channels of the Mormon Church. The Mormons conceived of themselves as a covenant people especially chosen for a divine task. This task was the building of the kingdom of God on earth and in this project—attempted four times unsuccessfully before the eventual migration to the west—much of the religious and secular socialism of the early 19th century found a profound reflection. The Mormon prophet proposed the "Law of Consecration" in an attempt to reconcile private initiative with cooperative endeavor. Contention led to its abandonment in 1838 after some five years of unsuccessful experiment. Yet this withdrawal did not limit, but indeed rather enhanced, its future influence in Mormon settlement. The "Law of Consecration" was no longer interpreted as a blueprint prescribing social institutions of a definite sort, but its values lent a strong cooperative bias to much of later Mormon activity.[8] In the context of the notion of peculiarity

7. The data from Rimrock are based upon seven months' field experience in the community during 1950-51. Additional data on this community will be provided in O'Dea's forthcoming monograph on *Mormon Values: The Significance of a Religious Outlook for Social Action.*

8. The "Law of Consecration" became the basis of the Mormon pattern of cooperative activity also known as "The United Order of Enoch." Cf. Joseph A.

and reinforced by out-group antagonism and persecution, these values became deeply embedded in Mormon orientations. The preference for agriculture combined with an emphasis upon community and lay participation in church activities resulted in the formation of compact villages rather than isolated family farmsteads as the typical Mormon settlement pattern.[9]

While Rimrock and Homestead share most of the central value-orientations of general American culture, they differ significantly in the values governing social relationships. Rimrock, with a stress upon community cooperation, an ethnocentrism resulting from the notion of their own peculiarity, and a village pattern of settlement, is more like the other Mormon villages of the West than it is like Homestead.

The stress upon *community cooperation* in Rimrock contrasts markedly with the stress upon *individual independence* found in Homestead. This contrast is one of emphasis, for individual initiative is important in Rimrock, especially in family farming and cattle raising, whereas cooperative activity does occur in Homestead. In Rimrock, however, the expectations are such that one must show his fellows or at least convince himself that he has good cause for *not* committing his time and resources to community efforts while in Homestead cooperative action takes place *only* after certainty has been reached that the claims of other individuals upon one's time and resources are legitimate.

Rimrock was a cooperative venture from the start, and very early the irrigation company, a mutual non-profit corporation chartered under state law, emerged from the early water association informally developed around—and in a sense within—the Church. In all situations which transcend the capacities of individual families or family combinations, Rimrock Mormons have recourse to cooperative techniques. Let us examine four examples.

The "Tight" Land Situation. Rimrock Mormons, feeling themselves "gathered," dislike having to migrate to non-Mormon areas. However, after World War II the 32 returned veterans faced a choice between poverty and under-employment or leaving the community. This situation became the concern of the Church and was discussed in its upper lay priesthood bodies in the village. It was decided to buy land to enable the veterans to remain. The possibilities of land purchase in the area were almost nonexistent and it appeared that nothing could be done, when unexpectedly the opportunity to buy some 38 sections presented itself. At the time, the village did not have the needed 10,000 dollars for the

---

Geddes, *The United Order among the Mormons*, Salt Lake City: Deseret News Press, 1924; Edward J. Allen, *The Second United Order among the Mormons*, New York: Columbia University Press, 1936.

9. Nelson, *op. cit.*, pp. 25-54.

down payment, so the sum was borrowed from the Cooperative Security Corporation, a Church Welfare Plan agency, and the land was purchased. The patterns revealed here—community concern over a community problem, and appeal to and reception of aid from the general authorities of the Church—are typically Mormon. However, Mormon cooperation did not end here. Instead of breaking up the purchased land into plots to be individually owned and farmed, the parcel was kept as a unit, and a cooperative Rimrock Land and Cattle Company was formed. The company copied and adapted the form of the mutual irrigation company. Shares were sold in the village, each member being limited to two. A quota of cattle per share per year to be run on the land and a quota of bulls relative to cows were established. The cattle are privately owned, but the land is owned and managed cooperatively. The calves are the property of the owners of the cows. The project, which has not been limited to veterans, supplements other earnings sufficiently to keep most of the veterans in the village.

The Graveling of the Village Streets. The streets of Rimrock were in bad repair in the fall of 1950. That summer a construction company had brought much large equipment into the area to build and gravel a section of a state highway which runs through the village. Before this company left, taking its equipment with it, villagers, again acting through the Church organization, decided that the village should avail itself of the opportunity and have the town's streets graveled. This was discussed in the Sunday priesthood meeting and announced at the Sunday sacrament meeting. A meeting was called for Monday evening, and each household was asked to send a representative. The meeting was well attended, and although not every family had a member present, practically all were represented at least by proxy. There was considerable discussion, and it was finally decided to pay 800 dollars for the job which meant a 20 dollar donation from each family. The local trader paid a larger amount, and, within a few days after the meeting, the total amount was collected. Only one villager raised objections to the proceedings. Although he was a man of importance locally, he was soon silenced by a much poorer man who invoked Mormon values of progress and cooperation and pledged to give 25 dollars which was 5 dollars above the norm.

The Construction of a High School Gymnasium. In 1951 a plan for the construction of a high school gymnasium was presented to the Rimrock villagers. Funds for materials and for certain skilled labor would be provided from state school appropriations, providing that the local residents would contribute the labor for construction. The plan was discussed in a Sunday priesthood meeting in the church, and later meetings were held both in the church and in the schoolhouse. Under the leadership of the principal of the school (who is also a member of the higher priesthood), arrangements were made whereby each able-bodied man in the community would either contribute at least 50 hours of labor or 50 dollars (the latter to be used to hire outside laborers) toward the construction. The original blueprint was extended to include a row of classrooms for the high school around the large central gymnasium.

Work on the new building began in late 1951, continued through 1952, and is now (in 1953) nearing completion. The enterprise was not carried through without difficulties. A few families were sympathetic at first but failed to contribute full amounts of either labor or cash, and some were unsympathetic toward the operation from the start. The high school principal had to keep reminding the villagers about their pledges to support the enterprise. But in the end the project was successful, and it represented an important cooperative effort on the part of the majority.

The Community Dances. The Mormons have always considered dancing to be an important form of recreation—in fact a particularly Mormon form of recreation. Almost every Friday evening a dance is held in the village church house. These dances are family affairs and are opened and closed with prayer. They are part of the general Church recreation program and are paid for by what is called locally "the budget." The budget refers to the plan under which villagers pay 15 dollars per family per year to cover a large number of entertainments, all sponsored by the Church auxiliary organization for youth, the Young Men's Mutual Improvement Association, and the Young Women's Mutual Improvement Association. The budget payment admits all members of the family to such entertainments.

Observation of these dances over a six months period did not reveal any tension or fighting. Smoking and drinking are forbidden to loyal Mormons, and those who smoked did so outside and away from the building. At dances held in the local school there has been evidence of drinking, and at times fighting has resulted from the presence of non-villagers. But on the whole the Rimrock dances are peaceful family affairs.

Rimrock reveals itself responding to group problems *as a group.* The economic ethic set forth by Joseph Smith in the Law of Consecration is seen in the dual commitment to private individual initiative (family farms and family partnerships in business and agriculture) and to cooperative endeavor in larger communal problems (irrigation company, land and cattle company, graveling the streets, and construction of school gymnasium). For the Mormons, cooperation has become second nature. It has become part of the institutionalized structure of expectations, reinforced by religious conviction and social control.

The Homesteader Case

The value-stress upon individual independence of action has deep roots in the history of the homesteader group.[10] The homesteaders were part of the westward migration from the hill country of the Southern Appalachians to the Panhandle country of Texas and Oklahoma and from there to the Southwest and California. Throughout their historical experience there has been an emphasis upon a rough and ready self-reliance and individualism, the Jacksonianism of the frontier West. The move to western New Mexico from the South Plains was made predominantly by isolated nuclear families, and Homestead became a community of scattered, individually-owned farmsteads—a geographical situation and a settlement pattern which reinforced the stress upon individualism.

Let us now examine the influence of this individualistic value-orientation upon a series of situations comparable to those that were described for Rimrock.

The "Tight" Land Situation. In 1934 the Federal Security Administration, working in conjunction with the Land Use Division of the Department of Agriculture, proposed a "unit re-organization plan." This plan would have enabled the homesteaders to acquire additional tracts of land and permit them to run more livestock and hence depend less upon the more hazardous economic pursuit of dry-land pinto bean farming. It called for the use of government funds to purchase large ranches near the Homestead area which would be managed cooperatively by a board of directors selected by the community. The scheme collapsed while it was still in the planning stages, because it was clear that each family expected to acquire its own private holdings on the range and that a cooperative would not work in Homestead.

The Graveling of the Village Streets. During the winter of 1949-50 the construction company which was building the highway through Rimrock was also building a small section of highway north of Homestead. The constructon company offered to gravel the streets of Homestead center if the residents who lived in the village would cooperatively contribute enough funds for the purpose. This community plan was rejected by the homesteaders, and an alternative plan was followed. Each of the operators of several of the service institutions—including

10. The data from Homestead are based upon a year's field work in the community during 1949-50. Additional data on this community will be provided in Vogt's *Modern Homesteaders: The Life of a Twentieth Century Frontier Community*, Cambridge, Mass.: Belknap Press of Harvard University Press, 1955. See also Vogt, "Water Witching: An Interpretation of a Ritual Pattern in a Rural American Community," *Scientific Monthly, LXXV* (September, 1952).

the two stores, the bar, and the post office—independently hired the construction company truck drivers to haul a few loads of gravel to be placed in front of his own place of business, which still left the rest of the village streets a sea of mud in rainy weather.

The Construction of a High School Gymnasium. In 1950 the same plan for the construction of a new gymnasium was presented to the homesteaders as was presented to the Mormon village of Rimrock. As noted above, this plan was accepted by the community of Rimrock, and the new building is now nearing completion. But the plan was rejected by the residents of Homestead at a meeting in the summer of 1950, and there were long speeches to the effect that "I've got to look after my own farm and my own family first; I can't be up here in town building a gymnasium." Later in the summer additional funds were provided for labor; and with these funds adobe bricks were made, the foundation was dug, and construction was started—the homesteaders being willing to work on the gumnasium on a purely business basis at a dollar an hour. But as soon as the funds were exhausted, construction stopped. Today a partially completed gymnasium, and stacks of some 10,000 adobe bricks disintegrating slowly with the rains, stand as monuments to the individualism of the homesteaders.

The Community Dances. As in Rimrock the village dances in Homestead are important focal points for community activity. These affairs take place several times a year in the schoolhouse and are always well-attended. But while the dances in Rimrock are well-coordinated activities which carry through the evening, the dances in Homestead often end when tensions between rival families result in fist-fights. And there is always the expectation in Homestead that a dance (or other cooperative activity such as a picnic or rodeo) may end at any moment and the level of activity reduced to the component nuclear families which form the only solid core of social organization within the community.

The individualistic value-orientation of the homesteaders also has important functional relationships to the religious organization of the community. With the exception of two men who are professed atheists, all of the homesteaders define themselves as Christians. But denominationalism is rife, there being ten different denominations represented in the village: Baptist, Presbyterian, Methodist, Nazarene, Campbellite, Holiness, Seventh Day Adventist, Mormon, Catholic, and Present Day Disciples.

In the most general terms, this religious differentiation in Homestead can be interpreted as a function of the individualistic and factionalizing tendencies in the social system. In a culture with a value-stress upon independent individual action combined with a "freedom of religion" ideology, adhering to one's own denomination becomes an important means of expressing individualism and of focusing factional disputes around a doctrine and a concrete institutional framework. In turn, the doctrinal differences promote additional factionalizing tendencies, with the result that competing churches become the battleground for a cumulative and circularly reinforcing struggle between rival small factions within the community.[11]

To sum up, we may say that the strong commitment to an individualistic value-orientation has resulted in a social system in which interpersonal relations are strongly colored by a kind of factionalism and in which persons and groups become related to one another in a competitive, feuding relationship. The homesteaders do not live on their widely separated farms and ignore one another, as it might be possible to do. On the other hand, they do not cooperate in community affairs as closely as does a hive of bees. They interact, but a constant feuding tone permeates the economic, social, and religious structure of the community.

Relationship between the Two Communities

Although there is some trading in livestock, feed, and other crops, the most important contacts between the two communities are not economic but are social and recreational. The village baseball teams have scheduled games with one another for the past two decades, and there is almost always joint participation in the community dances and in the summer rodeos in the two communities. Despite Mormon objections to close associations with "gentiles," there is also considerable interdating between the two communities among the teen-age groups, and three intermarriages have taken place.

In general, the homesteaders envy and admire the Mormons' economic organization, their irrigated land, and more promising prospects for good crops each year. On the other hand, they regard the Mormons as cliquish and unfriendly and fail completely to understand why anyone "wants to live all bunched up the way the Mormons do." They feel that the Mormons are inbred and think they should be glad to get "new blood" from intermarriages with homesteaders. They add, "That Mormon religion is something we can't understand at all." Finally, the homesteaders say that Mormons "used to have more than one wife, and some probably still do; they dance in the church, they're against liquor,

11. This relationship between churches and factionalizing tendencies has also been observed by Bailey in his unpublished study of a community in west Texas, in the heart of the ancestral home region of the present residents of Homestead. Cf. Wilfrid C. Bailey, "A Study of a Texas Panhandle Community; A Preliminary Report on Cotton Center, Texas," Values Study Files, Harvard University.

coffee, and tobacco, and they always talk about Joseph Smith and the *Book of Mormon.*"

The Mormons consider their own way of life distinctly superior to that of the homesteaders in every way. Some will admit that the homesteaders have the virtue of being more friendly and of "mixing more with others," and their efforts in the face of farming hazards are admired, but Homestead is generally regarded as a rough and in some ways immoral community, especially because of the drinking, smoking, and fighting (particularly at dances) that takes place. They also feel that Homestead is disorganized and that the churches are not doing what they should for the community. For the past few years they have been making regular missionary trips to Homestead, but to date they have made no conversions.

Comparisons and Conclusions

In the case of Rimrock and Homestead, we are dealing with two communities which are comparable in population, in ecological setting, and which are variants of the same general culture. The two outstanding differences are: (a) irrigation versus dry-land farming and associated differences in settlement pattern, compact village versus isolated farmstead type;[12] (b) a value stress upon cooperative community action versus a stress upon individual action. The important question here involves the relationship (if any) between these two sets of variables. Is the cooperation in Rimrock directly a function of an irrigation agriculture situation with a compact village settlement pattern, the rugged individualism in Homestead, a function of a dry-land farming situation with a scattered settlement pattern? Or did these value-orientations arise out of earlier historical experience in each case, influence the types of communities which were established in western New Mexico, and later persist in the face of changed economic situations? We shall attempt to demonstrate that the second proposition is more in accord with the historical facts as we now know them.

Nelson has recently shown that the general pattern of the Mormon village is neither a direct function (in its beginnings) of the requirements of irrigation agriculture, nor of the need for protection against Indians on the frontier. Rather, the basic pattern was a social invention of the Mormons, motivated by a sense of urgent need to prepare a dwelling place for the "Savior" at "His Second Coming." The "Plat of the City of Zion" was invented by Joseph Smith, Sidney Rigdon, and Frederick G. Williams in 1833 and has formed the basis for the laying out of most

12. Cf. Nelson, *op. cit.*, p. 4.

Mormon villages, even those established in the Middle West before the Mormons migrated to Utah.[13]

It is very clear that both the compact village pattern and the cooperative social arrangements centered around the church existed before the Mormons engaged in irrigation agriculture and had a strong influence upon the development of community structure not only in Utah but in the Mormon settlements like Rimrock on the periphery of the Mormon culture area. There is no objective reason in the Rimrock ecological and cultural setting (the local Navahos and Zunis did not pose a threat to pioneer settlements in the 1880's) why the Mormons could not have set up a community which conformed more to the isolated farmstead type with a greater stress upon individualistic social relations. Once the Mormon community was established, it is clear that the cooperation required by irrigation agriculture of the Mormon type and the general organization of the church strongly reinforced the value stress upon communal social action.

It is of further significance that as the population expanded and the Rimrock Mormons shifted from irrigation agricultural pursuits to dry-land ranching in the region outside of the Rimrock valley, the earlier cooperative patterns modeled on the mutual irrigation company were applied to the solution of economic problems that are identical to those faced by the Homesteaders. Moreover, in midwestern and eastern cities to which Mormons have recently moved, church wards have purchased and cooperatively worked church welfare plan farms.

In Homestead, on the other hand, our evidence indicates that the first settlers were drawn from a westward-moving population which stressed a frontier-type of self-reliance and individualism. They were searching for a place where each man could "own his own farm and be his own boss." Each family settled on its isolated homestead claim, and there emerged from the beginning an isolated farmstead type of settlement pattern in which the nuclear family was the solidary unit. The service center which was built up later simply occupied lots that were sold to storekeepers, filling station operators, the bartender, and others, by the four families who owned the four sections which joined at a crossroads. Only two of these four family homes were located near the service center at the crossroads. The other two families continued to maintain their homes in other quarters of their sections and lived almost a mile from "town." In 1952 one of the former families built a new home located over a mile from the center of town, and commented that they had always looked forward to "getting out of town."

There is no objective reason in the Homestead ecological setting why

13. *Ibid.*, pp. 28-38.

there could not be more clustering of houses into a compact village and more community cooperation than actually exists. One would not expect those farmers whose farms are located 15 or 20 miles from the service center to live in "town" and travel out to work each day. But there is no reason why those families living within two or three miles of the village center could not live in town and work their fields from there. In typical Mormon villages a large percentage of the farms are located more than three miles from the farm homes. For example, in Rimrock over 31 per cent, in Escalante over 38 per cent, and in Ephriam over 30 per cent of the farms are located from three to eight or more miles from the center of the villages.[14]

It is clear that the homesteaders were operating with a set of individualistic property arrangements (drawn, of course, from our generalized American culture) and that their strong stress upon individualism led to a quite different utilization of these property patterns (than was the case with the Mormons) and to the establishment of a highly scattered type of community. Once Homestead was established, the individualism permitted by the scattered dry-land farming pattern, and encouraged by the emphasis upon the small nuclear family unit and upon multi-denominationalism in church affiliation reacted on and strongly reinforced the value stress upon individual independence. It is evident that the homesteaders continue to prefer this way of life, as shown by their remarks concerning the "bunched up" character of a Mormon village and the fact that a number of families have recently moved "out of town" when they built new houses.

Of further interest is the fact that when homesteader families move to irrigated farms in the middle Rio Grande Valley, the stress upon individual action tends to persist strongly. They do not readily develop cooperative patterns to deal with this new setting which is similar to the situation in the irrigated valley of the Mormons at Rimrock. Indeed, one of the principal innovations they have been promoting in one region along the Rio Grande where they are replacing Spanish-Americans on the irrigated farming land is a system of meters on irrigation ditches. These meters will measure the water flowing into each individual farmer's ditches, and effectively eliminate the need for more highly organized cooperative arrangements for distributing the available supply of water.

In conclusion, we should like to reiterate that we are strongly cognizant of situational factors. If the Rimrock Mormons had not been able to settle in a valley which was watered by melting snow packs from a nearby mountain and which provided the possibilities for the construction of storage reservoir, they certainly could not have developed an irri-

14. *Ibid.*, pp. 99 and 144, for data on Escalante and Ephriam.

gation agricultural sysem at all. In the case of Rimrock, however, the actual site of settlement was selected from among several possible sites in a larger situation. The selection was largely influenced by Mormon preconceptions of the type of village they wished to establish. In fact, Mormons chose the irrigable valleys throughout the inter-montane West. On the other hand, the physical environmental features for the development of irrigation were simply not present in the Homestead setting, and the people had no alternative to dry-land farming. There is no evidence to suggest that had they found an irrigable valley, they would have developed it along Mormon lines. In fact, the homesteaders' activities in the Rio Grande Valley suggest just the opposite. It is clear that the situational facts did not *determine* in any simple sense the contrasting community structures which emerged. Rather, the situations set certain limits, but within these limits contrasting value-orientations influenced the development of two quite different community types. It would appear that solutions to problems of community settlement pattern and the type of concrete social action which ensues are set within a value framework which importantly influences the selections made with the range of possibilities existing within an objective situation.

b) SIMPLIFYING DECISIONS

FRED DAVIS

Uncertainty in Medical Prognosis: Clinical and Functional

MEDICAL sociology is indebted to Talcott Parsons for having called attention to the important influence of uncertainty on the relationship between doctor and patient in the treatment of illness and disease.[1]

1. Talcott Parsons, *The Social System* (New York: Free Press, 1951), pp. 466-69.

This is described as a primary source of strain in the physician's role, not only because clinically it so often obscures and vitiates definitive diagnoses and prognoses, but also because in an optimistic and solution-demanding culture such as ours it poses serious and delicate problems in the communicating of the unknown and the problematic to the patient and his family. In line with this view, Renée Fox has recently made an insightful analysis of the curriculum of a medical school, showing how, both from a formal and an informal standpoint, one of its functions is to socialize the student to cope more successfully with uncertainty.[2]

Granting the self-evident plausibility of the hypothesis, sociological studies of medical practice thus far have neglected to assess empirically its scope and significance in the actual treatment of specific illnesses or diseases.[3] As a ready-made explanation of a disturbing element in the relationship between doctor and patient, the concept—uncertainty—stands in danger of being applied in a catch-all fashion whnever, for example, the sociologist notes that communication from doctor to patient is characterized by duplicity, evasion, or other forms of strain. That other factors, having relatively little to do with uncertainty, can also systematically generate strain in the relationship may unfortunately be ignored because of the disposition to subsume phenomena under pre-existent categories.

The present paper examines the scope and significance of uncertainty as evidenced in the treatment of a particular disease. Specifically, it seeks to distinguish between "real" uncertainty as a clinical and scientific phenomenon and the uses to which uncertainty—real or pretended, "functional" uncertainty—lends itself in the management of patients and their families by hospital physicians and other treatment personnel. By

---

Reprinted from "Uncertainty in Medical Prognosis: Clinical and Functional," by Fred Davis, The American Journal of Sociology, *July, 1960, pp. 41-47, by permission of The University of Chicago Press. Copyright 1960 by the University of Chicago.*

Revised version of a paper read at the annual meeting of the American Sociological Society, Chicago, September, 1959. I wish to thank Anselm Strauss, Julius A. Roth, and Stephen A. Richardson for their valuable criticisms. Acknowledgment is also due my former colleagues, Harvey A. Robinson, Joseph S. Bierman, Toba Tahl, Arthur Silverstein, and Martin Gorten, of the Polio Project, Psychiatric Institute, University of Maryland Medical School, with whom I collaborated in research. The project was aided by a grant from the National Foundation—THE AUTHOR.

2. Renée Fox, "Training for Uncertainty," in R. K. Merton, G. Reader, and P. L. Kendall (eds.), *The Student Physician* (Cambridge, Mass.: Harvard University Press, 1957), pp. 207-41.

3. Partial exception must be made for the as yet largely unpublished works of Julius A. Roth (Community Studies, Inc., Kansas City, Missouri) on treatment procedures in the tuberculosis hospital. Several of the points to be discussed here are treated from a somewhat different vantage point by Roth under such headings as "Control of Information" and "Negotiation and Bargaining between Staff and Patients."

extrapolation this distinction suggests a fourfold typology of patterns of communication from doctor to patient analysis of which highlights important sources of strain other than uncertainty.

The disease in question is paralytic poliomyelitis, and the subjects are fourteen Baltimore families, in each of which a young child had contracted the disease. These were studied longitudinally over a two-year period by an interdisciplinary team of social scientists and research physicians whose broad interest was in assessing the total impact of the experience on child and family. Except for one family that dropped out midway in the study, in each case the child with polio and his parents were interviewed at intervals from the time of the child's admission to a pediatrics ward in the acute stage of the disease to approximately a year and a half following his discharge from a convalescent hospital.

From the very first interview with the parents, held within a week or so following the child's admission to the hospital, to the fourteenth and final interview with them some two years later, the research was aimed at determining at every stage what the parents knew and understood about polio in general and their child's condition in particular and through whom and how they came to acquire such knowledge and understanding as they had on these matters. In addition to being interviewed in home and office, the parents were also observed from time to time in the hospital on visiting days—this being their only regular opportunity to discuss their child's condition with the physician-in-charge as he made his round of the ward. It might be noted here that, with few exceptions, the parents soon came to regard these encounters as especially frustrating and of little value in getting information on questions which were troubling them. Although the situation on visiting day did not permit the observers to come away with word-for-word records of what went on, their perfunctory character was sufficiently evident to substantiate the descriptions later given by the parents in interview. As one mother remarked:

> Well, they [the doctors] don't tell you anything, hardly. They don't seem to want to. I mean, you start asking questions and they say, "Well, I only have about three minutes to talk to you." And the things that you ask, they don't seem to want to answer you. So I don't ask them anything any more.

Finally, to round out coverage of the network of communication involving the parents, interviews were held with the hospital physicians, physiotherapists, and other ancillary personnel responsible for the child's treatment and care. Here a major goal was to learn what their diagnosis and prognosis were of the child's condition and on what medical considerations these were based.

By bringing together the interview and observational data gathered from these several sources, it was possible to compare and contrast, at successive stages of the disease and its treatment, what the parents knew and understood of the child's condition with what the doctors knew and understood. One must assume that the doctor's knowledge of the disease and its physical effects is more accurate, comprehensive, and profound than that of the parents. The problem, then, could be stated: How much information was communicated to the parents? How was it communicated? And what consequences did this communication have on the parents' expectations of the child's illness and prospects for recovery?[4] And, since in paralytic poliomyelitis (as in many other diseases and illnesses) uncertainty does affect the making of diagnoses and prognoses, an attempt was made to assess the scope, significance, and duration of uncertainty for the doctor. This then provided some basis for inferring the extent to which the parents' knowledge and expectations, or lack thereof, could also be attributed ultimately to uncertainty.

For purposes of simplicity, the discussion that follows is restricted to uncertainty only as it impinges on the prognosis of residual disability expected as a result of the poliomyelitic attack. This subsumes questions of such relatively great moment to child and parent as: Would he be permanently handicapped? Would he require the aid of braces and other supportive appliances? Would his handicap be so severe as to prevent him from engaging in a wide range of normal motor activities or be barely detectable?

Now the pathological course of paralytic poliomyelitis is such that, during the first weeks following onset, it is difficult in most cases for even the most skilled diagnostician to make anything like a definite prognosis of probable residual impairment and functional disability. During the acute phase of the disease and for a period thereafter, the examining physician has no practical way of directly measuring or indirectly inferring the amount of permanent damage or destruction sustained by the horn cells of the spinal cord as a result of the viral attack. (It is basically the condition of these cells, and not that of the muscles neurologically activated by them, that accounts for the paralysis.) Roughly, a one- to three-month period for spontaneous recovery of the damaged spinal cells—a highly unpredictable matter in itself—must first be allowed for before the effects of the disease are sufficiently stabilized to permit a clinically well-founded prognosis.

During this initial period of the child's hospitalization, therefore, the physician is hardly ever able to tell the parents anything definite about

4. See Fred Davis, "Definitions of Time and Recovery in Paralytic Polio Convalescence," *American Journal of Sociology*, LXI (May, 1956), 582-87.

the child's prospects of regaining lost muscular function. In view of the very real uncertainty, to attempt to do so would indeed be hazardous. To the parents' insistent questions, "How will he come out of it?" "Will he have to wear a brace?" "Will his walk be normal?" and so on, the invariable response of treatment personnel was that they did not know and that only time would tell. Thus during these first weeks the parents came to adopt a longer time perspective and more qualified outlook than they had to begin with.[5]

By about the sixth week to the third month following onset of the disease, however, the orthopedist and physiotherapist are in position to make reasonably sound prognoses of the amount and type of residual handicap. This is done on the basis of periodic muscle examinations from which the amount and rate of return of affected muscular capacity is plotted. The guiding contingencies for prognosis are:

> Muscles that have shown early and rapidly developing return of strength will probably make a full recovery. Those which have but moderate or little strength at the end of this period will probably never make complete recovery. Muscles which are completely paralyzed at the end of this period will probably always remain so. In other words, at the end of this period the spinal motor cells have or have not recovered their physiologic activity and no further change in them may be expected.[6]

By this time, therefore, the element of clinical uncertainty regarding outcome, so conspicuously present when the child is first stricken, is greatly reduced for the physician, if not altogether eliminated.[7] Was there then a commensurate gain in the parents' understanding of the child's condition after this six-week to three-month period had passed? Did they then, as did the doctors, come to view certain outcomes as highly probable and others as improbable?

On the basis of intensive and repeated interviewing of the parents over a two-year period, the answer to these questions is that, except for one case in which the muscle check pointed clearly to full recovery, the parents were neither told nor explicitly prepared by the treatment per-

5. *Ibid.*, pp. 583-85.

6. The American Orthopaedic Association, "Infantile Paralysis, or Acute Poliomyelitis: A Brief Primer of the Disease and Its Treatment," *Journal of the American Medical Association*, CXXXI (August 24, 1946), 1414.

7. As in nearly all applied fields of endeavor, medicine necessarily deals in probabilities rather than absolutes. Hence some measure of uncertainty is always present, the crucial question being the matter of degree and not the mere presence. Admittedly, no hard-and-fast lines can be drawn at the point at which uncertainty acquires therapeutic significance; but, if the concept is to have any analytical value at all, it cannot be applied to all instances of illness in which it is possible to concede the existence of some degree of uncertainty, however slight. If this were done, there would not be an instance to which it did not apply.

sonnel to expect an outcome significantly different from that which they understandably hoped for, namely, a complete and natural recovery for the child. This does not imply that the doctors issued falsely optimistic prognoses or that, through indirection and other subtleties, they sought to encourage the parents to expect more by way of recovery than was possible. Rather, what typically transpired was that the parents were kept in the dark. The doctors' answers to their questions were couched for the most part in such hedging, evasive, or unintelligibly technical terms[8] as to cause them, from many such contacts, to expect a more favorable recovery than could be justified by the facts then known. As one treatment-staff member put it, "We try not to tell them too much. It's better if they find out for themselves in a natural sort of way."

Indeed, it was disheartening to note how, for many of the parents, "the natural way" consisted of a painfully slow and prolonged dwindling of expectations for a complete and natural recovery. This is ironical when one considers that as early as two to three months following onset the doctors and physiotherapists were able to tell members of the research team with considerable confidence that one child would require bracing for an indefinite period; that another would never walk with a normal gait; that a third would require a bone-fusion operation before he would be able to hold himself erect; and so on. By contrast, the parents of these children came to know these prognoses much later, if at all. And even then their understanding of them was in most instances partial and subject to considerable distortion.

But what is of special interest here is the way in which uncertainty, a *real* factor in the early diagnosis and treatment of the paralyzed child, came more and more to serve the purely managerial ends of the treatment personnel in their interaction with parents. Long after the doctor himself was no longer in doubt about the outcome, the perpetuation of uncertainty in doctor-to-family communication, although perhaps neither premeditated nor intended, can nonetheless best be understood in terms of its functions in the treatment system. These are several, and closely connected.

Foremost is the way in which the pretense of uncertainty as to outcome serves to reduce materially the expenditure of additional time, effort, and involvement which a frank and straightforward prognosis to the family might entail. The doctor implicitly recognizes that, were he to tell the family that the child would remain crippled or otherwise impaired to some significant extent, he would easily become embroiled in much more than a simple, factual medical prognosis. Presenting so

8. Cf. Bernard Kutner, "Surgeons and Their Patients," in E. Gartly Jaco (ed.), *Patients, Physicians and Illness* (New York: Free Press, 1958), p. 390.

unwelcome a prospect is bound to meet with a strong—and, according to many of the treatment personnel, "unmanageable"—emotional reaction from parents; among other things, it so threatens basic life-values which they cherish for the child, such as physical attractiveness, vocational achievement, a good marriage, and, perhaps most of all, his being perceived and responded to in society as "normal, like everyone else." Moreover, to the extent to which the doctor feels some professional compunction to so inform the parents, the bustling, time-conscious work milieu of the hospital supports him in the convenient rationalization that, even were he to take the trouble, the family could not or would not understand what he had to tell them anyway.[9] Therefore, in hedging, being evasive, equivocating, and cutting short his contact with the parents, the doctor was able to avoid "scenes" with them and having to explain to and comfort them, tasks, at least in the hospital, often viewed as onerous and time-consuming.

Second, since the parents had been told repeatedly during the first weeks of the child's illness that the outcome was subject to great uncertainty, it was not difficult for them, once having accepted the idea, to maintain and even to exaggerate it, particularly in those cases in which the child's progress fell short of full recovery. For, equivocally, uncertainty can be ground for hope as well as despair; and when, for example, after six months of convalescence the child returned home crippled, the parents could and characteristically did interpret uncertainty to mean that he still stood a good chance of making a full and natural recovery in the indefinite future. The belief in a recuperative moratorium was held long after there was any real possibility of the child's making a full recovery, and with a number of families it had the unfortunate effect of diverting them from taking full advantage of available rehabilitation procedures and therapies. In fact, with few exceptions the parents typically mistook rehabilitation for cure, and, because little was done to correct this misapprehension, they often passively consented to a regimen prescribed for the child which they might have rejected had they known that it had nothing to do with effecting a cure.[10]

Last, it must be noted that in the art (as opposed to the science and technique) of medicine, a sociologically inescapable facet of treatment

9. *Ibid.*, p. 391. Particularly with working-class families, of which there were ten out of fourteen in the study, the propensity of doctors (and other professionals, for that matter) to resort to this paricular rationalization is accentuated accordingly. However, the barriers toward giving any parent this kind of information appeared so pervasive that the four lower-middle-class and middle-class families fared hardly any better.

10. See W. E. Moore and M. N. Tumin, "Some Social Functions of Ignorance," *American Sociological Review*, XIV (December, 1949), 787-95.

—often irrespective of how much is clinically known or unknown—is frequently that of somehow getting the patient and his family to accept, "put up with," or "make the best of" the socially and physically disadvantageous consequences of illness. Both patient and family are understandably reluctant to do this at first, if for no other reason than that it usually entails a dramatic revaluation in identity and self-conception. Not only in paralytic poliomyelitis but in numerous other chronic and long-term illnesses, such as cardiac disease, cancer, tuberculosis, mental illness, and diabetes, such is usually the case. Depending on a number of variables, not the least of which are those of personality, the cultural background of the family, and the treatment setting, a number of stratagems besides that of rendering a full and frank diagnosis and prognosis (even when clinically known) are open to the physician who must carry the family through this difficult period.[11] Whereas the evasiveness and equivocality of hospital treatment staff described here may not have been as skilled or effective a means for accomplishing this as others which come to mind, it must in fairness be recognized that there is still little agreement within medical circles on what practice should be in these circumstances. (The perennial debate on whether a patient and his family should be told that he is dying of cancer, and when and how much they should be told, is an extreme though highly relevant case in point.) And perhaps the easiest recourse of the hospital practitioner—who, organizationally, is better barricaded and further removed from the family than, for example, the neighborhood physician—is to avoid it altogether.

Clearly, then, clinical uncertainty is not responsible for all that is not communicated to the patient and his family. Other factors, interests, and circumstances intrude in the rendering of medical prognoses, with the result that what the patient is told is uncertain and problematic may often not be so at all. And, conversely, what he is made to feel is quite certain may actually be highly uncertain. As the rough fourfold schema of Figure 1 suggests, there are at least two modes of communication

Figure 1

	Certainty	*Uncertainty*
Prognosis given patient	(1) Communication	(2) Dissimulation
Prognosis not given patient	(3) Evasion	(4) Admission of uncertainty

11. Doctors are by no means the only ones who are routinely called upon to shepherd others through difficult status transitions (see Erving Goffman, "On Cooling the Mark Out," *Psychiatry*, XV [November, 1952], 451-63).

(2 and 3) that reveal a discrepancy between what the doctor knows and what he tells the patient. Before turning to these, however, we shall consider the two "pure," non-discrepant modes (1 and 4).

The first of these, "Communication" (1), refers to the common occurrence in which the physician can, in accordance with the state of medical knowledge and his own skill, make a reasonably definite prognosis of the condition requiring treatment and communicate it to the patient in terms sufficiently comprehensible to him. Though not always as uncomplicated as it sounds, this is perhaps the main kind of exchange of information between doctors and patients, particularly as regards the simple and minor ailments brought daily to the average practitioner's attention. It is also, of course, the ideal mode of communication toward which the relationship of doctor and patient universally aspires.

On the other hand, an "Admission of Uncertainty" (4), where no other prognosis is clinically justifiable, is by its nature a more difficult and unstable mode of communication, the manifestations of which will vary considerably, depending on the personal and institutional contexts of practice. Such instability derives mainly from certain mutually reinforcing interests of the two parties: the doctor, who as a matter of professional obligation seeks to narrow the range of uncertainty as far as possible, and the patient, who wishes simply and often naïvely to know what is wrong and how he can be made to feel better. These and other pressures that would prevent an open admission of uncertainty can more easily be resisted in the bureaucratized hospital setting—as, indeed, they initially were in the case of the families of the children with polio—than, for example, in neighborhood private practice. For, given the widespread intolerance of uncertainty in our culture, the hospital-anchored physician is better insulated from the prejudices, sensitivities, and economic sanctions of those he treats than is his neighborhood counterpart.[12] The latter, particularly if his practice comes mainly from word-of-mouth referrals by an established clientele, runs the potentially costly risk of driving patients elsewhere, that is, to a more "accommodating" competitor, if he states his uncertainty in too bald and unrelieved a manner. Differential economic and reputational risks of this kind in medical practice may be, incidentally, not wholly unrelated to the increasing contemporary tendency to assign the untreatable, chronic, or highly problematic condition to the relatively impersonal hospital setting, where whatever may occur redounds less decisively to the disadvantage (or credit) of any single responsible individual unless it be of the patient.

Owing in large part to a currently inadequate scientific grounding,

12. Cf. Eliot Freidson, "Client Control and Medical Practice," *American Journal of Sociology*, LXV (January, 1960), 374-82.

certain fields of medical practice, as psychiatry, permit little more than admissions of uncertainty in a very large number of cases. Yet, even here, it is to be questioned whether the office psychiatrist can as a matter of course adopt the same unyielding, non-committal, antiprognostic stance with his private, fee-paying patients as does the state-hospital psychiatrist with the severely mentally ill and their families—this despite the fact that nowadays, as with pneumonia and the common cold, the psychopathology treated in the mental hospital affords better grounds for prognosis than do the psychoneuroses and character disorders seen in the consulting room. Nonetheless, in the case of the latter, there is usually held out—after all due qualification and reservation—a vague, implied possibility that somehow "a better adjustment," "a more satisfactory utilization of personality resources," etc., may be induced.

As these remarks imply, "Dissimulation" (2)—the rendering of a prognosis which the physician knows to be unsubstantiated clinically—is the more likely if the doctor's reputation and livelihood are derived for the most part from the favorable opinions and referrals of an independent lay clientele. Sheer professional vanity may, of course, also enter in. The subtleties, ruses, and deceptions that betoken dissimulation, from the innocuous sugar-pill placebo to unwarranted major surgery, are too many and too imaginatively varied to consider here. But it is essentially this guise of medical practice that has historically been the butt of much lively ridicule and satire, as, for example, in the fumbling presumptions of Stern's Dr. Slop and the excruciating ministrations of Romains' Dr. Knock. More venial forms of the art are sometimes resorted to in order to delay until the physician has had a chance to observe how a condition develops or until protracted laboratory investigations are completed. Since so many of the undiagnosable illnesses and ailments that are brought to doctors would "take care of themselves" in any case, the judicious employment of dissimulation is perhaps not so hazardous from the therapeutic standpoint as one might at first conclude. That it often affords the patient a significant measure of psychological relief from anxiety is, in fact, cited by some in its defense, albeit with the qualification that it should not be used in cases where anything serious might be expected.

"Evasion" (3)—the failure to communicate a clinically substantiated prognosis—has already been considered at some length. As noted, this was the primary mode of communication employed by the hospital treatment staff when confronted with the queries and concerns of the parents. Little need be added here except to emphasize that the informal institutionalization of this mode is closely related to the practitioner's ability to remove himself from the many "technically secondary" (i.e., non-organic) problems and issues that often follow in the wake of serious illness in the family. The large hospital, with its complex proliferation of specialized services and personnel, is particularly conducive to it, especially if the attending physician is not the patient's own but someone assigned to him.[13]

The discussion carries no implication that physicians will, in accordance with the setting of their practice and the kinds of illnesses they treat, invariably, or even primarily, address themselves to questions of prognostic certainty and uncertainty in the manner outlined. Nor is it suggested that important shifts from one mode of communication to another do not occur at different stages of treatment of particular patients. Our aim has been rather to temper to some extent the predominantly cognitive emphasis that the issue of uncertainty has received in medical sociology, as if all that passed for uncertainty or certainty in the communication between doctor and patient were wholly a function of the current state of scientific and clinical knowledge. In demonstrating that other values and interests also influence the doctor-patient transaction, we have done little more than exemplify a familiar sociological axiom, namely, that this, too, is anchored in society, and we must perforce take account of its numerous non-rational and irrational elements.

13. See T. Burling, E. M. Lentz, and R. N. Wilson, *The Give and Take in Hospitals* (New York: G. P. Putnam's Sons, 1956), pp. 317-33. The treatment of polio is highly specialized, and in none of the fourteen cases was the hospitalized child treated by a family physician. Moreover, the very considerable costs of treatment, far beyond the means of all but the wealthy, were borne in whole or very large part by the National Foundation and not by the families themselves. This served to reduce further the claims the parents felt they could make on the doctor's time and attention.

HAROLD T. CHRISTENSEN

Cultural Relativism and Premarital Sex Norms

In noting that behavioral standards vary over time and from society to society, William Graham Sumner made the now classic statement: "The mores can make anything right." By this he meant that moral problems are interpreted differently by different societies—that questions of right and wrong are relative to the particular culture in which the behavior occurs. This theory has been labeled *cultural relativism.* It challenges the notion of absolute standards of judgment to be applied uniformly regardless of time or place.

But there has been little quantitative research to test the theory of cultural relativism, especially as applied to modern Western societies. Furthermore, the tendency has been to stop with a simple noting of attitudinal and behavioral differences, without pinning down the relativism of the *consequences* of these differences. For example, it is well known that some societies are rather restrictive and others very permissive regarding premarital sexual behavior;[1] but there is almost no information as to whether this behavior has the same or different *effects* (in terms of mental health, subsequent social behavior, or both) across these contrasting types of societies.

This paper is an attempt to illuminate further the notion of cultural relativism by applying it to differing sets of premarital sex norms. Since

---

Reprinted from American Sociological Review, *February, 1960, pp. 31-39, by permission of the author and the journal.*

Slightly revised version of a paper read at the Fourth World Congress of Sociology, sponsored by the International Sociological Association, September, 1959.

In an earlier paper prepared for the Fourth International Seminar on Family Research, held at Wageningen, Holland, two years ago, the writer presented certain preliminary data on the sex norms of the same cultures treated here and sketched in his "theory of value relevance." Since that time, more data bearing on the problem have been gathered and the analysis has been extended. The present report is a continuation of the previous one, and it is expected that still others will follow. See Harold T. Christensen, "Value Variables in Pregnancy Timing: Some Intercultural Comparisons," in Nels Anderson, editor, Studies of the Family, *Gottingen, Germany: Vanderhoeck & Ruprecht, 1958, Vol. III, pp. 29-45.*

1. See e.g., George Peter Murdock, *Social Structure,* New York: Macmillan, 1949, pp. 260-283.

premarital pregnancy can be reliably measured by use of a method known as "record linkage,"[2] whereas most other levels of sexual behavior are more elusive, the focus here is upon this phenomenon.[3] We are interested in both regularities and variations among the cultures studied, with special reference to the consequences of premarital pregnancy.

Specifically, it is hypothesized that the more permissive the culture regarding sexual matters, the greater will be the incidence of premarital pregnancy, *but the lesser will be the effects of such pregnancy as pressure either for hasty marriage or for subsequent divorce.* It is further hypothesized that certain aspects of premarital pregnancy *are not culturally relevant.*

Sex Norms in Three Cultures[4]

In order to treat culture as a variable, we have made identical observations in three widely divergent areas. The first is the state of Utah, where the Mormon Church is dominant and premarital sex norms tend to be extremely conservative, almost to the point of being puritanical. Here, religion is a motivating force in the lives of most people, and the religious interpretation of premarital sexual intercourse is that it is an extremely grievous sin. Waiting until marriage for sexual intercourse—"keeping the law of chastity"—is regarded as one of the highest of virtues.[5]

The second is the state of Indiana, which in many ways is typical of the United States as a whole. It is centrally located and heterogeneous in culture. It is approximately an average state in size, in rural-urban distribution, in population numbers and composition, and in various social

2. For descriptions of this method, see Christensen, *loc. cit.;* and Harold T. Christensen, "The Method of Record Linkage Applied to Family Data," *Marriage and Family Living*, 20 (February, 1958), pp. 38-43.

3. It is expected that the questionnaire and interview data that were collected to throw light upon other aspects of sexual behavior in these same cultures, will eventually be reported also.

4. For more detailed descriptions of these differing sex norms, see Christensen, "Value Variables . . .," *op. cit.*, pp. 30-35.

5. In this connection, it is interesting to recall Kinsey's finding to the effect that religiously devout men and women participate less in all socially disapproved forms of sexual behavior. He regarded religion as being the "most important factor in restricting premarital activity in the United States." See Alfred C. Kinsey *et al.*, *Sexual Behavior in the Human Female*, Philadelphia: Saunders, 1953, pp. 324, 686-687, and *passim.*

indices such as median income, school attendance, and marriage, birth, and divorce rates. The "chastity norm" is a part of the prevailing culture in Indiana as in most of the United States–in prescription even if less so in practice. And there are religious incentives, promoted by a variety of denominations, which give support to the sexual mores.

The third location is Denmark, which, like all of Scandinavia, has a long tradition of sexual intercourse during the engagement. This goes back three or four centuries at least, in spite of efforts by the State Lutheran Church to establish a chastity code.[6] In this connection, it is important to point out that, although most Danes have their names on the church records, they seldom attend church services. Except for a few, religion in Denmark is not a strong motivating force in the lives of the people. Croog notes the importance of understanding the *ring engagement*–which has almost the status of a formal marriage, including rights to sexual intercourse, and obligations to marry if pregnancy results–as background for interpreting sexual behavior in Denmark. He also explains how this pattern of sexual freedom is spreading to include the more informal "going steady" relationships; and how these practices are encouraged by a liberal clergy, by welfare laws which make abortion and unmarried motherhood relatively easy, and by the facility with which premarital sexual behavior can be rationalized since "everyone is doing it."[7] Svalastoga cites five recent empirical studies to support his claim that: "Coitus before marriage may now safely be considered the rule and chastity the exception in Scandinavia."[8]

Thus these three areas have widely different norms regarding premarital sexual behavior. At the one extreme is Utah, dominated by a homogeneous culture and conservative religious tradition. There, the moral condemnation of premarital sexual intercourse under all circumstances has the support of strong supernatural sanctions. At the other extreme is Denmark, with a liberal tradition in sexual matters, and a religious membership, which, though homogeneous, is only nominal. There, premarital sexual intercourse, if accompanied by love and the intent to marry, tends to be an accepted practice. Somewhere in between these two extremes lies Indiana, with norms more moderate, more variable, and yet somewhat typical of the country of which it is a part.

6. Cf. K. Robert Wikman, *Die Einleitung der Ehe*, Aabo, Finland: Acta Academiae Aaboensis, XI, 1937; and Georg Hansen, *Saedelighedsforhold Blandt Landbefolkningen i Denmark i det 18 Aarhundrede*, Copenhagen: Det Danske Forlag, 1957.

7. Sydney H. Croog, "Aspects of the Cultural Background of Premarital Pregnancy in Denmark," *Social Forces*, 30 (December, 1951), pp. 215-219.

8. Kaare Svalastoga, "The Family in Scandinavia," *Marriage and Family Living*, 16 (November, 1954), pp. 374-380; quotation from p. 337.

Incidences of Premarital Conception

For any accurate measure of premarital conception, one needs to know three quantities: abortion among the unmarried, both spontaneous and induced; illegitimacy, that is, birth outside of marriage; and the number of weddings that are preceded by pregnancy.[9]

Unfortunately, there are no available statistics to enable us to make comparisons on the relative numbers of abortions.

With regard to illegitimacy, official statistics for 1955, which are typical of recent years, show the per cent of all births occurring outside of wedlock to be 0.9 for Utah, 2.9 for Indiana, and 6.6 for Denmark.

Table 1. Selected Indices of Premarital Conception

	UNITED STATES		DENMARK	
Indices	*Utah County, Utah*	*Tippecanoe County, Indiana*	*City of Copenhagen*	*Entire Country*
I. Illegitimacy Rate*	**0.9**	**2.9**	**11.2**	**6.6**
II. Premarital conception rates†				
A. Child born within first 6 months of marriage	**9.0**	**9.7(10.0)‡**	**24.2(31.1)‡**	**32.9(34.9)‡**
B. Child born within first 9 months of marriage	**30.9**	**23.9(26.1)‡**	**30.5(39.3)‡**	**44.3(48.5)‡**

*Per cent of all births occurring outside of wedlock. Calculations based upon official reported statistics for the year 1955.

†Per cent of marital first births occurring within six and nine months of the wedding, respectively. Figures in the first three columns are from the Utah County, Tippecanoe County, and Copenhagen studies described in the paper. Fourth column figures were derived from the *Statistisk Aarbog 1956*. Copenhagen: Bianco Lunos Bogtrykkeri, 1956, Table 25, p. 35, and are for the calendar year 1955.

‡Figures in parentheses are adjusted indices, derived by using only those births which occurred during the first four years of marriage as the base for calculation. This adjustment is for the purpose of making the figures comparable in this respect with the Utah indices shown in the first column.

(See Table 1.) Thus, in these societies, illegitimacy increases with each advance in the sexual permissiveness of the culture.

Although illegitimacy rates be obtained from published statistics for whole populations, it has been necessary to conduct sample studies for measures of the premarital conceptions which end in postmarital births.[10] As a consequence, the following analysis relies heavily upon the writer's earlier record linkage studies of Utah County, Utah, and Tippecanoe

9. Strictly speaking, early birth within marriage provides the only available accurate measure of premarital conception. Some unmarried women have abortions and illegitimate birth; the term "premarital" hardly describes them. Yet, since it is likely that the majority of such women later get married, no great violence is done in using the concepts in this way. In Denmark, for example, one study has shown that by age six well over half of all children born out of wedlock are then living with their mother who has since been married—in most cases to the child's father. See "Den Familiemaessige Placering af Børn Født Uden For Aegteskab," *Statistisk Maanedsskrift*, 30 (No. 9, 1954), pp. 193-195.

10. Denmark has published nation-wide statistics on this phenomenon, but the United States has not.

County, Indiana, and his more recent parallel investigation of Copenhagen, Denmark. The Utah County data were derived by comparing marriages occurring during the years 1905-07, 1913-15, 1921-23, and 1929-31 with birth records for four years following each wedding, in order to find the date of the first birth. This process yielded 1,670 cases. The Tippecanoe County data were derived by taking marriages which occurred during the years 1919-21, 1929-31, and 1939-41, matching them with the birth records searched for five years following the wedding, and finally checking against the divorce records to discover which marriages ended in failure. The result consisted of 1,531 cases involving a first child, with 137 of these cases terminating in divorce. The Copenhagen data were derived by taking every third marriage which occurred during a single year, 1938, eliminating cases involving remarriage and those in which the wife was thirty or more years of age, and then checking both birth and divorce recordings for sixteen years following the wedding. These steps provided a sample of 1,029 cases involving a first child, with 215 ending in divorce.

These samples from three cultures are not, of course strictly comparable. They were drawn in slightly different ways and have somewhat different compositions. Nevertheless, the contrasts reported below are of sufficient magnitude to suggest at least tentative answers to the problem posed.

From Table 1, it may be observed that the same general pattern holds for this phenomenon as was previously noted for illegitimacy. The six months index, which is a sure minimum measure of premarital conception, makes the clearest comparison. It shows the lowest incidence of premarital pregnancy in Utah, a somewhat higher incidence in Indiana, but a considerably higher incidence in Denmark. The nine months index is less valuable since it includes unknown numbers of postmarital conceptions.[11] The higher rate for Utah than for Indiana may simply reflect the tendency to earlier postmarital conceptions in Utah.[12]

These findings may be viewed as validation for our earlier labelings. In these cross-cultural comparisons, behavior has been found to be consistent with attitudes; and, attitudes *plus behavior* have differentiated Utah and Denmark at opposite ends of a continuum describing premarital sex norms, with Indiana in between.

11. The normal period of uterogestation in human beings is 266 days, or slightly less than nine calendar months. Furthermore, premature births would cause a number of early postmarital conception cases to be included in this index.

12. Cf. Christensen, "Value Variables . . .," *op. cit.*, pp. 35-38. See also Figure 1 of the present paper, where Utah is shown to have proportionately more conceptions *at the time of marriage* than Indiana. Of course, some of these may actually be premarital by a day or so, but the other explanation for the Utah-Indiana differential seems more plausible to the writer.

An interesting contrast between Copenhagen and the whole of Denmark can be seen by comparing the last two columns of Table 1. Copenhagen shows higher illegitimacy rates than the national figures, but relatively low rates of premarital conception. Though interpretation of the contrast takes us beyond available data, we hazard a guess: Copenhagen, being metropolitan in character, reflects the more liberal sex culture, including a sophistication which discourages rushing into marriage just because of pregnancy; thus, it is possible that disproportionately more premaritally pregnant couples in Copenhagen either put off marriage until after the child is born or elect against it entirely. An alternative possibility is that women with an illegitimate pregnancy tend to move to Copenhagen some time before the child is born.

Associated Factors

Not only does the incidence of premarital pregnancy differ from culture to culture, as demonstrated above, but it varies among certain sub-groups within each culture. As shown in Table 2, there are strong

Table 2. Factors Associated with Premarital Conception*

Factors	PER CENT OF FIRST BIRTHS PREMARITALLY CONCEIVED Utah County, Utah	Tippecanoe County, Indiana	Copenhagen, Denmark
Wife's age at marriage			
Young group‡	14.4	13.2	29.0
Older group	7.7	5.7	15.1
Type of Ceremony§			
Civil	16.6	21.0	37.0
Religious	1.1	9.9	13.5
Husband's occupation			
Laborer	17.9	16.0	30.0
All other	8.6	7.2	18.2

*All factor differences were found to be statistically significant in all three samples.

†As used here: per cent of marital first births within the first 196 days of marriage (Utah and Indiana), or within the first 182 days of marriage (Denmark).

‡This group was defined in the Utah sample as aged 20 or under, in the Indiana sample as aged 24 or under, and in the Danish sample as aged 23 or under.

§In the Utah sample, the division is not strictly civil-religious, but rather nontemple-temple. Since the most orthodox Mormons marry in one of the temples, this group would represent the most religiously motivated of the religious marriages. But the non-temple group, though mostly civil marriages, would include *some* religious marriages—where these did not take place in a Mormon temple.

and consistent tendencies for premarital conception to be higher with young age at marriage in contrast to the older ages, with a civil wedding in contrast to the religious ceremony, and with a laboring occupation in contrast to the more skilled and professional ways of earning a living. Each of these differences was found to be in the same direction and to be statistically significant for each of the three cultures studies, which is evidence of certain cross-cultural regularities.

Perhaps youth gets into difficulties of this kind because of its lack of sophistication. Furthermore, since premarital pregnancy encourages earlier marriages than couples otherwise would undertake, marriages of this sort are certain to involve more of the younger-aged persons. The higher proportions of premarital pregnancy among those who have a civil wedding may possibly be explained by a relative lack of religious influence in the lives of these people, plus an attempt on the part of those who become pregnant to hurry the wedding and to avoid the judgment of the church or the scorn of fellow church members. The disproportionately high premarital pregnancy percentages for persons in the laboring occupations may largely be due to the greater sexual permissiveness found in the lower social classes, plus their relative lack of education. But, whatever the complete explanation, there is the strong suggestion here that broad cultural norms may be to some extent overruled by the operation of other factors.[13]

Effects upon Timing of the Wedding

The tendency to be philosophical about a premarital pregnancy when it happens, so as not to be stampeded into a marriage, seems to be much more characteristic of Denmark than of Indiana or Utah. It is suggested, perhaps, by the higher Danish illegitimacy rates.

But even stronger evidence is presented in Figure 1, which has been constructed from estimated dates of conception calculated by counting back 266 days from each date of birth. It may be noted that, whereas in the Utah and Indiana samples the modal time of conception is one lunar month after marriage, in the Danish sample it is five lunar months *before* the marriage. As a matter of fact the Danish data show many more couples conceiving about five months before the marriage than at any other time; in that culture, therefore, premarital conception coupled with subsequent delayed marriage must be considered as the norm. The Indiana curve is bimodal, with the peak for premarital conceptions at two lunar months prior to marriage—suggesting a tendency to get married as soon as possible after the second menstrual period has been missed and the doctor's positive diagnosis has been given. The Utah curve starts low and moves up regularly until the time of marriage and immediately thereafter, when it is the highest of all three.

The fact just noted is further evidence of Utah's pattern of early conception following the wedding. Of the three cultures here com-

13. Of course, these factors also have cultural content, but they—and possibly many others—seem not to be confined by the limits of an area or a society; hence the suggestion of cross-cultural regularities.

pared, Utah has not only the lowest rates of premarital conception but the highest rate of *early* postmarital conception.

Apparently, in Denmark there is little pressure to hurry marriage merely because of pregnancy.[14] In Indiana the tendency is to marry

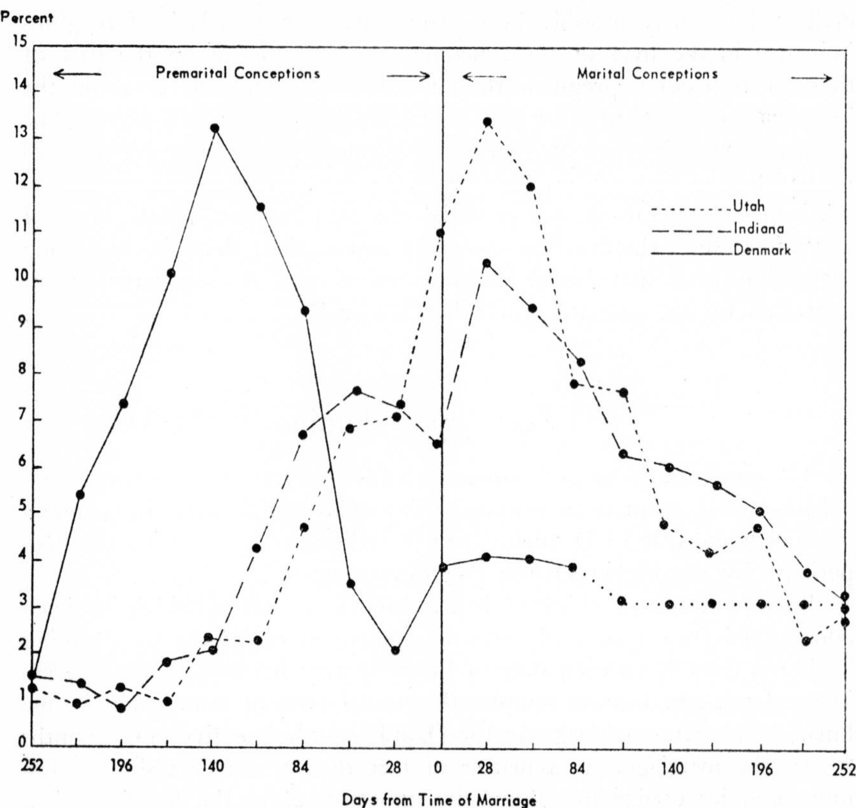

FIGURE 1. Pregnancy Inception as Related to Time of Marriage: A Cross-Cultural Comparison. Days from Time of Marriage. (Data are for births occurring during the first nineteen lunar months of marriage and are expressed as percentages.)

immediately after the pregnancy is definitely known so as to hide the fact from the public. Couples who have premarital sexual intercourse in Utah, on the other hand, seem to hurry marriage because of that fact alone, without waiting for pregnancy to force them into it (religious

14. In attempting to explain this situation to the writer, several Danish scholars have pointed to the current great housing shortage in Copenhagen—which means waiting for a place to live, thereby discouraging any rush into marriage. When reminded that the figures used here are for 1938 marriages, however, these observers were quick to admit that the argument doesn't apply, since there was little housing shortage then.

guilt is a sufficient sanction once the "law of chastity" has been broken).[15]

As Kinsey has pointed out, "The psychologic significance of any type of sexual activity very largely depends upon what the individual and his social group choose to make of it."[16] Since in Danish culture there is less stigma placed on premarital conception and on illegitimacy than in Indiana, and especially in Utah, the differences in timing pattern for the wedding once pregnancy has occurred may be explained in cultural terms.

Effects upon the Divorce Rate

This type of explanation may also apply to possible variations in divorce rate differentials of premarital pregnancy *versus* postmarital pregnancy cases. We would hypothesize that the more liberal the culture the *less* likely is premarital pregnancy to be followed by divorce. This hypothesis is tested with data from the Indiana and Danish samples.[17]

For Tippecanoe County, it has been reported earlier that the divorce rate is significantly higher for premarital than postmarital pregnancy couples.[18] For marriages occurring in Copenhagen during 1948, Holm has shown that, with age controlled, the divorce rate is not significantly different for couples bearing a child within the first nine months of marriage than for all other cases.[19] At first glance, this seems to bear out our hypothesis.

It is to be noted, however, that Holm did not compare premarital pregnancy cases with postmarital pregnancy cases, as was done for Tippecanoe County, but rather with all non-premarital pregnancy cases, including childless couples. Since those who become divorced are less likely to have children than those who do not,[20] the inclusion of child-

15. Although this latter explanation is speculative, it is plausible. Chastity is so stressed in Mormon culture that the religiously oriented offender may panic and try to ease his conscience by getting married.

16. Kinsey, *op. cit.*, p. 320.

17. Unfortunately, in our Utah sample record linkage was limited to marriage and birth data; whereas in the Indiana and Denmark samples divorce data were also included.

18. Harold T. Christensen and Hanna H. Meissner, "Studies in Child Spacing: III–Premarital Pregnancy as a Factor in Divorce," *American Sociological Review*, 18 (December, 1953), pp. 641-644.

19. Henry F. Holm, Actuary for the City of Copenhagen's Statistical Office, *Statistisk Maanedsskrift*, 33 (No. 4, 1957), Table 12, p. 117.

20. In the writer's Copenhagen sample of 1938 marriages, for example, 57.0 per cent of the childless marriages ended in divorce or separation as compared with 20.9 per cent of the fertile marriages. A primary explanation for this differential

less cases in the non-premarital pregnancy category would raise the divorce rate for that category and, in this way, would obscure the true comparison. What is needed is a comparison between divorce rates of premarital and postmarital pregnancy cases; for unless non-conceivers are excluded, it is impossible to determine the effects of conception timing.

Table 3 is designed to compare the Copenhagen and Tippecanoe

Table 3. Divorce Rate Comparison by Interval to First Birth

	COPENHAGEN, DENMARK			*TIPPECANOE COUNTY, INDIANA*		
Classification	*Number of Cases*	*Number Divorced*	*Per Cent Divorced*	*Number of Cases*	*Number Divorced*	*Per Cent Divorced*
Interval between marriage and first birth						
(1) 0-139 days (premarital pregnancy, marriage delayed)	176	60	34.1	71	14	19.7
(2) 140-265 days (premarital pregnancy, marriage hurried)	129	31	24.0	276	39	14.1
(3) 266 days—4.99 years (post-marital pregnancy)	572	111	19.4	1184	84	7.1
Percentage difference between divorce rates						
(4) Between lines 2 and 1			42.1			39.7
(5) Between lines 3 and 2			23.7*			98.6*

*No direct formula has been located for testing the statistical significance of this intersample difference between differences in proportions. However, an approximate equivalent test is to consider $p_1 - p_2 < p_3 - p_4$ (where $p_1 = 24.0$, $p_2 = 19.4$, $p_3 = 14.1$, and $p_4 = 7.1$). When the *p*-values are changed according to the arcsine transform, they have been placed on a comparable scale and the use of the normal probability table is permitted. This procedure yields a probability for a one-tailed test of .12.

Alternatively, we may approximately test $p_1/p_2 < p_3/p_4$ if we assume $p_1/p_2 - p_3/p_4$ is normally distributed, and use an approximate variance formula. Since the hypothesis is stated in terms of the greater ratio for the United States than for Denmark, a one-tailed test is permissible, yielding a probability of .038. There is no way to evaluate the assumption of a normal distribution for this test.

County samples concerning possible effects of premarital and postmarital pregnancy upon the divorce rate. As noted above, these two samples are not strictly comparable, but they are approximately so.[21] It seems probable that the following generalizations are at least tentatively justified:

---

is that many of the divorces occur relatively soon after the wedding, before the couple has decided to start a family.

21. See descriptions of the two samples, above. Calculations for Table 3 are based uniformly on cases having a first child born within five years of the wedding. Although absolute divorce rates cannot be compared across the two samples—since they would be influenced in distinctive ways by differential emigration and differential lengths of time of exposure to the divorce possibility—there seems to be no good reason why the *relative* rates by pregnancy timing cannot be compared.

(1) In both populations there is the clear tendency for the divorce rate to fall as the length of interval between marriage and first birth increases. This means that premarital pregnancy cases are more likely to end in divorce than are postmarital pregnancy cases,[22] and that those premarital pregnancy couples who delay marriage for a considerable time after the knowledge of pregnancy have the highest divorce rate of all—in Denmark as well as Indiana.

(2) The *relative* difference in divorce rate between premarital pregnancy couples who hurried marriage and those who delayed it is essentially the same for both populations. Thus, Copenhagen figures show a 42.1 per cent difference between these two rates as compared with a difference of 39.7 per cent in Tippencanoe County, an intersample difference that is not significant.

The facts that both samples show substantially higher divorce rates for couples who delay marriage after knowledge of pregnancy and that the differentials in this respect are about the same in the two cultures suggest universal tendencies for certain pregnant couples to marry under the pressure of social responsibility (for example, sympathy for the lover, consideration for the future child, or parental influence). The data also suggest that, statistically speaking, such "shot gun" marriages do not turn out well.

(3) The *relative* difference in divorce rate between postmarital pregnancy couples and the premarital couples who married soon after the discovery of pregnancy is four times greater in the Indiana sample (98.6 per cent compared with 23.7 per cent), an intersample difference that by some tests is statistically significant. (See footnote to Table 3.)

The fact that the postmarital pregnancy divorce rate is lower in both cultures is evidence that premarital pregnancy—even when associated with an early wedding—tends generally to make the marriage's survival chances less than even. This may be because some marriages take place under pressure from others and are therefore accompanied by resentment, or because in their haste to escape public scorn the couple marries without adequate preparation, or in the absence of love, or in

22. There is an interesting parallel finding from the Copenhagen data: marriages in which the wife had borne an illegitimate child previously showed a divorce rate of 45.7, as compared with 20.9 for childbearing marriages where she had not. A partial explanation, of course, may be that a selective factor is operating, which may mean that the least stable personalities are the ones most likely to become pregnant before marriage and also to be divorced later. But another possibility is that, through such things as resentment about the necessity to marry, guilt feelings, and poor preparation and unsuitable personality matching because of a hasty or pressured marriage, the premarital pregnancy may itself help to bring about divorce. In the Tippecanoe County study, the writer controlled other divorce-producing factors, through matching, and still found premarital pregnancy to be significantly associated with high divorce; see Christensen and Meissner, *loc. cit.*

the face of ill-matched personalities. But the fact that the postmarital-premarital pregnancy divorce rate differential is substantially less in Denmark, gives strong support to our hypothesis. It seems probable that in Denmark, where sexual relations outside of marriage are more or less accepted, premarital pregnancy will have less negative effect upon marriage than in Indiana, where it is expected that sexual intercourse and pregnancy be confined to marriage.

Summary and Theory

Premarital sex norms in Utah, Indiana, and Denmark stand in sharp contrast—with Utah being very conservative or restrictive, and Denmark being extremely liberal or permissive. As might be expected, therefore, premarital pregnancy rates were found to be lowest in the Utah sample and highest in the Danish sample, with the difference being considerable. Furthermore, certain consequences of premarital pregnancy were found to vary from culture to culture. Thus permissive Denmark, at the time of the study, showed the longest delay between premarital conception and the wedding, and the smallest divorce rate differential between premarital pregnancy and postmarital pregnancy cases.[23] In all three cultures the same factors were associated with premarital pregnancy: namely, young age at marriage, a civil wedding, and a laboring occupation.

In some respects our data give support to the idea of cultural relativism. It has been shown that both the rates and effects of premarital pregnancy are to a considerable extent relative to the cultures involved. The most liberal culture was found to have the most premarital pregnancy, but also the least negative effects therefrom; in Denmark there is less pressure than in the American cases either to speed up the wedding or to resort to divorce when premarital pregnancy occurs. Thus, the relationship is not simply a matter of how premarital pregnancy affects

23. As noted above, divorce rate comparison does not include the Utah sample since data were not available. It is believed, however, that the Utah divorce rate differential (between premarital and postmarital pregnancy cases) probably is the greatest of the three areas—because premarital sexual intimacy is most strongly condemned there.

This unestablished assumption can be argued by an analogy. The drinking of alcoholic beverages is also strongly condemned in Utah (and in the rest of Mormon culture). Research shows that Mormon college students have the lowest incidence of drinking among religious groups, but that, of the drinkers, Mormon students have a very high rate of alcoholism. This suggests that cultural restrictions can lower the incidence of the condemned practice, but that for those who indulge, the negative effects are apt to be extreme. Cf. Robert Strauss and Selden D. Bacon, *Drinking in College*, New Haven: Yale University Press, 1953, *passim.*

subsequent behavior, considered in a vacuum, but rather how it affects this behavior in the light of particular norms. Cultural norms represent an intervening variable.

But there are also *regularities* among the cultures studied. In all of them, pregnancy usually takes place within marriage. In all of them also, premarital pregnancy is found to be associated with young age, a civil wedding, and a laboring occupation. Finally, the Indiana-Denmark comparisons reveal a parallel phenomenon of higher divorce rates for premarital pregnancy than for postmarital pregnancy cases. These rates are especially high, and in similar magnitude within both cultures, for couples who delay marriage until just before the child is born. Forced marriage, in other words, seems to work against marital success regardless of the culture. All of this suggests the existence of certain universals which are to some extent independent of the cultural variable.

The present analysis is concerned with *inter*cultural comparisons. The next step is to see if the theory applies to the *intra*cultural level, that is, when interpersonal differences are taken into account. We hypothesize both regularity and variability at that level also, with personal values having very much the same effects as cultural norms are found to have in this report.

c) MAKING COMMUNICATION INTELLIGIBLE

OTTO KLINEBERG

Emotional Expression in Chinese Literature

The fact that the expression of the emotions is at least to some extent patterned by social factors is probably known to all psychologists. Even in our own society there is considerable evidence that this is so. When we turn to the descriptions of other cultures, instances of this patterning occur frequently. One of the most striking examples is the copious shedding of tears by the Andaman Islanders and the Maori of New Zealand when friends meet after an absence, or when two warring parties make peace. Another is the smile with which the Japanese responds to the scolding of his superior, or which accompanies his announcement of the death of his favorite son.

This paper represents part of a more extensive study of emotional expression among the Chinese, an investigation made possible by a Guggenheim Fellowship and a supplementary grant from the Social Science Research Council. Among the various techniques employed, it seemed valuable in the case of a civilization as articulate as the Chinese to examine at least a portion of the Chinese literature for the light it might throw on this problem. There is not much precedent for the reading of novels as a technique of psychological investigation, but in this case it seemed warranted at least as an introduction to more objective methods.

Before turning to the question of the kind of expression involved, a word should be said as to the related question of the amount of expression which the culture permits. There are, for example, many

Reprinted from The Journal of Abnormal and Social Psychology, *October, 1938, pp. 517-520, by permission of the author and the journal.*

admonitions—especially to the young girl—not to show emotion too readily. In *Required Studies for Women* we find such warnings as the following: "Do not show your unhappiness easily and do not smile easily"; also, "Do not let your teeth be seen when you smile," that is, your smile must be so circumspect that the teeth do not show. On the other hand, there are many occasions on which the emotion of grief has to be displayed. One piece of advice from the same volume reads, "If your father or mother is sick, do not be far from his or her bed. Do not even take off your girdle. Taste all the medicine yourself. Pray your god for his or her health. If anything unfortunate happens cry bitterly."

The alleged inscrutability of the Chinese, which as a matter of fact has been greatly exaggerated, completely breaks down in the case of grief. Not only is grief expressed, but there is an elaborate set of rules and regulations which insure that it shall be properly expressed. One of the Chinese classics is *The Book of Rites*, a considerable portion of which is devoted to the technique of the mourning ceremonial, with elaborate instructions as to just what procedure should be followed in order that the expression of the grief may be socially acceptable.

The most extreme degree of patterning of emotional expression is found on the Chinese stage, and is illustrated by the following examples from a Chinese *Treatise on Acting*. There is an occasional pattern which does conform closely to our own; for example, "taking the left sleeve with the right hand and raising it to the eyes as if to wipe the tears" is clearly an expression of sorrow. There are others, however, that are not so clear. To "draw one leg up and stand on one foot" means surprise. To "raise one hand as high as the face and fan the face with the sleeve" means anger, as does also to "blow the beard to make it fly up." Joy or satisfaction is represented by stretching "the left arm flatly to the left and the right arm to the right." To "move one hand around in front of the middle of the beard and touch your head with the fingers of the other hand" means sorrow, while to "put the middle part of the beard into the mouth with both hands and bite firmly" indicates that one has come to a decision. To "raise both hands above the head with the palms turned outwards and the fingers pointing up, let the sleeves hang down behind the hands, then walk towards the other person, shake the sleeves over, and let the hands fall" means love.

There were two long novels which were read for this study; one, *The Dream of the Red Chamber*, was read in Chinese, with considerable help from Miss Wu T'ien Min, a graduate student at Yenching University, and the other, *All Men Are Brothers*, in Pearl Buck's English translation. These represent two of the three most famous Chinese novels, the third being *The Romance of the Three Kingdoms. The*

Dream of the Red Chamber is a love story; *All Men Are Brothers* is a tale of swashbuckling adventure dealing with the so-called "bandits" who are among the most picturesque figures of Chinese legend and history. Besides these, several modern stories were also consulted.

In some cases the descriptions of emotional expression correpond closely to our own. When we read (D.R.C.), for example, that "everyone trembled with a face the color of clay," there can be little doubt that fear is meant. The same holds for the statement that "every one of his hairs stood on end, and the pimples came out on the skin all over his body" (from "Married Life Awakening the World"). Other descriptions of fear (A.M.B.) are the following: "A cold sweat broke forth on his whole body, and he trembled without ceasing"; "it was as though her two feet were nailed to the ground and she would fain have shrieked but her mouth was like a mute's"; "they stood like death with mouths ajar"; "they were so frightened that their waters and wastes burst out of them." In general, it may be said that fear is expressed in very much the same way in the Chinese literature as in our own. As far as other emotions are concerned, in the sentence, "He gnashed his teeth until they were all but ground to dust," we recognize anger; "He was listless and silent" suggests sorrow; "His face was red and he went creeping alone outside the village" clearly indicates shame. There is no doubt of the frequent similarity between Chinese and Western forms of expression.

There are also differences, however. When we read "They stretched out their tongues" (D.R.C.), most of us would not recognize this description as meaning surprise, except for the context. This phrase as an expression of surprise occurs with great frequency, and it would be easy to give many examples. The sentence "Her eyes grew round and opened wide," would probably suggest to most of us surprise or fear; to the Chinese is usually means anger. This expression, with slight variations, also occurs very often. In the form "He made his two eyes round and stared at him" (A.M.B.), it can mean nothing but anger. "He would fain have swallowed him at a gulp" (A.M.B.) implies hatred; our own "I could eat you up!" has a somewhat different significance. "He scratched his ears and cheeks" would probably suggest embarrassment to us, but in *The Dream of the Red Chamber* it means happiness. "He clapped his hands" (D.R.C.) is likely to mean worry or disappointment.

The case of anger appears to be particularly interesting. We have already noted the expressions connected with "round eyes," "eyes wide open," "staring," etc. We find in addition descriptions like these: "He laughed a great ho-ho," and "He smiled a chill smile," and "He looked at them and he smiled and cursed them" (A.M.B.). Both the laugh and the smile of anger or contempt occur in our own culture, but apparently not nearly so frequently as in China and the Chinese literature. More curious still is the phrase "He was so angry that several times he fainted from his anger" (A.M.B.). This expression occurs frequently. When I showed wonder as to why this should be, Chinese friends said that they in turn could never understand why European women fainted so frequently in the mid-Victorian literature with which they were acquainted. Certainly the delicately nurtured young women of not so long ago did faint with astonishing ease and regularity; there were even etiquette books which taught them how to faint elegantly. Such a custom is certainly no less surprising than that the Chinese should faint in anger. The conclusion seems clear that fainting, like tears, may be conditioned by social custom to appear on widely varying occasions.

Most striking of all perhaps, is the indication in the literature that people may die of anger. "His anger has risen so that he is ill of it and lies upon his bed, and his life cannot be long assured." " 'To-day am I killed by anger' . . . and when he had finished speaking he let his soul go free" (A.M.B.). This phenomenon, incidentally, mysterious though it may sound, is reported as still occurring, and I saw one patient in a hospital in Peiping whose father was said to have died of anger after losing a lawsuit. It is important to note that a death of this kind cannot be explained as due to anything like an apoplectic stroke; it does not occur suddenly as a stroke would. When someone is very angry but is forced to suppress his anger because there is nothing he can do about it, he may become ill, faint many times, and take to his bed; death may follow after the lapse of some days or weeks. The only explanation is in terms of suggestion; the belief that people die of anger when they can do nothing about it may succeed in actually bringing on the death of an impressionable person. There is the parallel case of the Polynesian native who inadvertently eats the tabooed food of the chief, remains perfectly well as long as he does not know it, but may die when he learns what he has done.

These examples indicate that, although there are many similarities between the literary descriptions of the emotions in China and in the West, there are also important differences which must be recognized if Chinese literature is to be read intelligently. When the literary pattern is such that the expression alone is described but not labeled, real misunderstandings may arise. When I first read, for instance, "They stretched out their tongues," I did not know that surprise was meant. Our own literature is of course also rich in these unlabeled expressions. We read, "His jaw dropped"; "He gnashed his teeth"; "His lip curled"; "His eyes almost popped out of his head"; "He clenched his fists," etc., and in each case we know at once what emotion is indicated. These expressions are a part of language and must be learned in order to be understood.

The question arises as to the degree to which these Chinese literary expressions are related to expression in real life. Caution must certainly be exercised in inferring from one to the other. A Chinese reader of our literature, for instance, might conclude that laughter was dangerous to Westerners, in view of the frequency with which he read the expression "I nearly died laughing." I think I may say, however, on the basis of information obtained by methods other than the reading of novels, that the Chinese patterns which I have described do appear not only in the literature but also in real life. I may add that photographs illustrating these literary expressions are judged more easily by Chinese than by American subjects.

It seems to me to be worth while to extend this literary approach to other cultures. In the writings of India, Japan, and other peoples of the Near and Far East, material must certainly be available which would further illustrate the extent and the nature of the cultural patterning of emotional expression.

d) ESTABLISHING MODES OF RELATIONSHIP

BARTLETT H. STOODLEY

Normative Attitudes of Filipino Youth Compared with German and American Youth

THE purpose of this study is to compare attitudes of Filipino youth with attitudes of German and American youth. For this purpose the writer has adapted a questionnaire developed by McGranahan and administered by him to samples of German and American youth in 1945.[1] Relevant aspects of Filipino culture are reported, the method employed in selecting the Philippine sample is indicated, and the Filipino responses are compared to those obtained by McGranahan.

Philippine Culture and Social Organization

The Philippine sample was drawn from Christian Filipinos. There are, however, two other cultural groups in the Philippines, the "pagan" group to the north, and the Moslem group to the south. The census of 1948 lists 791,000 Moslem and 353,000 pagan. Over 90 per cent of the approximately 22 million Filipinos are Christian. Roman Catholics outnumber Protestants by about thirty to one.

The dominant Christian segment of the population is itself divided

Reprinted from American Sociological Review, *October, 1957, pp. 553-561, with the permission of the author and the journal.*

1. Donald V. McGranahan, "A Comparison of Social Attitudes among American and German Youth," *Journal of Abnormal and Social Psychology*, 41 (July, 1946), pp. 245-256.

into many linguistic sub-groups. These sub-groups have certain "boundary-maintaining" qualities—distinguishing sub-cultural traits, and a sense of their differences in history and dialect. The Cebuanos, for instance, proudly distinguish themselves from the Tagalogs. In spite of sub-group identifications, however, these linguistic groups share a common culture and social organization. Some *barrios* on Luzon may be given over to rice farming on small, separated strips of land; other barrios on the island of Cebu may feature sugar-cane production on large, corporate-owned enterprises; in coastal areas, the adult males may all be fishermen or, along the banks of the Pasig, duck-raisers; but this economic diversity does not conceal common personality ranges, common child-rearing methods, common family and group organization and common cultural norms.

Basically, Philippine society has a simple, "folk" structure, with the family the dominant socializing and occupational unit. Status groups and economic classes (using these words in Weber's sense) also constitute parts of this structure. Since the acceptance of Catholicism, and the formation of a national political organization, Church and government hierarchies have come to constitute important status groupings, as have the emerging middle class of small businessmen. Filipinos attach themselves to higher status and class positions by establishing particularistic relations. The *compadre* system is highly functional in this respect. Through such relations superordinate and subordinate groupings become organized into binding systems of particularistic rights and obligations.

The Philippine family is extended to three generations in the direct line and, collaterally, to brothers and sisters, their spouses and their children. A domiciliary unit does not include all these members, however, but some selection from them. Upon marriage a young man and woman are expected to leave their respective homes and build their own nipa hut. Relatives, usually parents, grandparents and cousins, may come later and live with them. Family rights and obligations between domiciliary units are maintained by patterns of continuous visiting.

Lines of authority in the Filipino family are carefully drawn. Children owe respect and obedience to all adults, but these obligations are increased in the case of kin and maximized with reference to parents and grandparents. To parents children owe not only respect but reverence. Children also owe respect and obedience to older siblings, regardless of sex, in proportion to the degree of seniority. Obligations to siblings, and to parents and grandparents, continue throughout the life cycle, subject however to the paramount authority that parents exercise over their own children.

Punishment is prompt and severe in the Philippine family. Physical punishment by whipping is institutionalized and freely employed. Siblings with sufficient seniority may slap or pinch younger siblings. However, affectional solidarity is likewise a characteristic of the Philippine family. It is considered no reflection on marital affection that brothers and sisters often prefer the company of each other to the company of their spouses. The authority patterns tend to be "corrected" by the affectional pattern. The Filipino mother is expected to love each new child a little more than the previous child. The cultural justification for this is that the mother is progressively more and more grateful to each new child for sparing her life. This results in institutionalized favoritism. This expectation of favoring the youngest child extends, although in lesser measure, to the father and to the other children. As a result, younger children typically can manipulate their parents and older siblings and thus gain a powerful counterweight against the family's strict authority patterns.

The authority of Filipino parents is far from arbitrary license. Its exercise is subject to the appraisal of grandparents, aunts and uncles on both sides of the family. Thus its rightful exercise tends to be continuously defined by superordinates (grandparents) and peers (aunts and uncles).[2] In addition, there is some definition by subordinates (children). The authority vested in older siblings occasionally permits at least token criticism of their parents. Furthermore, since parents have strong emotional ties to their children, they tend to exercise only the authority that is institutionalized and therefore obligatory. Although authority, when exercised, is binding on children and supported by severe sanctions, it is not employed for meticulous correction of children. Children are permitted a range of unrestricted behavior that in important respects exceeds that of the American middle-class child.[3]

Method

McGranahan's study of the social attitudes of American and German youth brought out interesting differences between the two national groups and also between the Nazi and anti-Nazi elements in German youth. Although this study had some projective aspects, and has been referred to as fundamentally a projective test, the present writer takes

2. Senior aunts and uncles are not of course strictly peers. But they are considerably closer to the parents' level than grandparents. Although grandparents no longer have decisive control over parents, the persuasive sanctions they employ are strong indeed.

3. Further details on the Philippine family are available in the writer's "Some Aspects of Tagalog Family Structure," *American Anthropologist*, 59 (April, 1957), pp. 236-249.

exception to this view.[4] It is methodologically useful to distinguish two types of authoritarianism, one that is a "normal" consequence of certain cultural norms, and another that is the consequence of certain "exciting causes" in personality process.[5] The McGranahan study examines the first type. It indicates that authoritarianism is "normal" in German culture to the extent indicated by the questions and the relevant percentages. And these findings are contrasted with the democratic (by comparison) elements in American culture as indicated by answers of American youth to the same questions. The second type of authoritarianism is examined in such studies as *The Authoritarian Personality.* There the major emphasis is on extracting a syndrome indicating important structural aspects of personality. A careful distinction between these two types of democratic-authoritarian orientations could lead to a helpful understanding of their interrelations.[6]

The McGranahan questionnaire was composed of a total of thirteen questions. Four of these questions had to be discarded for the present project.[7] Nine questions remained that could be given in practically the same form in which they were given to Germans and Americans. This relatively simple device was very satisfactory to initiate the gathering of data in an area where little research of this nature has been undertaken. The use of the McGranahan questionnaire has made possible the comparison of results in the Philippines with the results obtained with German and American youth. Pretesting showed that no advantage was gained by using a dialect. English was understood by our samples, and the English words carried connotations that were sensed by the interviewees but that did not attach to words in the dialects.

McGranahan gave the questionnaire to 1,600 American high-school students between the ages of 14 and 18 in various urban communities.

4. See T. W. Adorno, E. Frenkel-Brunswik, D. Levinson, and R. N. Sanford, *The Authoritarian Personality*, New York: Harper, 1950, p. 548, where this characterization is made.

5. As Herbert H. Hyman and Paul B. Sheatsley point out, the purpose in *The Authoritarian Personality* was not to isolate anti-democratic elements in cultural norms but ". . . the quantification of anti-democratic trends at the level of personality." See "'The Authoritarian Personality'—A Methodological Critique" in *Studies in the Scope and Method of "The Authoritarian Personality,"* Richard Christie and Marie Jahoda (Editors), New York: The Free Press, 1954, p. 75.

6. This suggestion is implicit in Hyman and Sheatsley, *op. cit.*, pp. 67-68.

7. These questions were as follows: Do you think it right to make one person suffer in a medical examination if the results will benefit the whole nation? Do you believe that a criminal who refuses to give the names of his accomplices should be beaten until he confesses? Do you consider it right for a German man to marry a Pole? In your opinion are the Americans (Germans) as a people better than the Italians? the Russians? the Poles? the French? the Germans? (the Americans?)

A stratified sample of 200 was drawn from this sample to meet crtieria with reference to religion, sex and economic level in proportions that were held to be representative of urban and suburban youth in eastern and middle western U.S.A. Reports on the "American sample" refer to this sample. The German sample was 191 youths, aged 14 to 18, drawn from the town of Bad Homburg. McGranahan reported that Bad Homburg ". . . is a fairly well-to-do town." He added that "since Bad Homburg probably corresponds more closely to Oak Park, a well-to-do suburb of Chicago, than to any of the other U.S. towns or cities, the Oak Park data (163 cases) will also be used for comparison." It is clear that education was held substantially constant in these samples.

The Philippine sample is matched to the American and German samples in respect to urbanization, education, sex, and age. Economic levels are not easily comparable, but the economic levels represented in the Philippine sample reflect the same comparative status range as the American and German levels. In order to obtain the required age span and achieve this comparable economic representation, it was necessary to draw a large sample from freshmen at the University of the Philippines. The questionnaire was given early in the freshman year, however, before prolonged exposure to "college culture."[8]

The questionnaire was given to 639 freshmen at the University. This group had an occupational distribution approximating the Oak Park sample and the Bad Homburg sample. To obtain a total group comparable to the American sample, the writer gave the questionnaire to 131 seniors in the Mapa High School in Manila where the occupational distribution was considerably lower than in the University sample. These two samples were separately analyzed and found to be not significantly different with regard to any item. It is apparent from this that there is a homogeneity of response in the Philippine upper and lower occupational levels that did not obtain in the McGranahan findings with reference to Americans. The samples from the University of the Philippines and from the Mapa High School have accordingly been combined and reported as the "Philippine sample." For the reason indicated above this sample is comparable to the American, the Oak Park and the German samples. In addition, to gain indications of attitudes of a lower economic and essentially rural group, the writer gave the questionnaire to 133 seniors in the Pasig High School. Pasig is a provin-

8. By matching the McGranahan sample with reference to education an important variable is held constant. As a result, however, the Philippine data are not to be construed as necessarily representative of youth in the society as a whole, or even of urban youth. The same conclusion follows from matching the McGranahan sample with reference to economic levels. However, controlling these factors brings out the cultural variables with particular clarity.

cial town about twenty-five kilometers from Manila.[9] Some results from the Pasig sample are referred to below.

The McGranahan questionnaire set up hypothetical situations designed to test for conflict between norms supporting individual rights and norms supporting group prerogative. The resolution of this conflict by the interviewees indicated the relative power of the classes of norms.[10] Norms supporting individual rights could be heuristically termed "democratic," and norms supporting group prerogative could be similarly termed "authoritarian." As would be anticipated, the democratic norms of Americans exercised prevailing power over the authoritarian norms; and the contrary, by comparison, was characteristic of German youth. In addition, anti-Nazi and Nazi youth were significantly differentiated by the degree to which they emphasized authoritarian norms.

Filipino responses to the questions show significant differences both from the American and German responses. Two hypotheses are suggested here to explain these differences, but more evidence than is available in this paper would be required to confirm them. In the first place we suggest that the Filipino did not see a multi-dimensional situation in the questions, but a uni-dimensional one. Human rights and group prerogative were not considered to be in apposition. They were seen as part of the same "moral" order and had to be related within that order. Secondly, and this is a corollary of the first hypothesis, prerogative was not regarded as license or naked power, but as social obligation. Thus, overtones of strength and weakness, domination and submission, were muted or absent.

Authority and the Family

It is abundantly clear in the distribution of answers to the first question (Table 1) that the Filipino places great emphasis on obedience.[11] No facile decisions are open to him as in the case of the

9. The sampling unit was the section classified by school authorities into three types based on ability. Proportional random sampling of sections was employed.

10. This approach resembles the one employed by Samuel A. Stouffer in his study, "An Analysis of Conflicting Social Norms," *American Sociological Review*, 14 (December, 1949), pp. 707-717 [reprinted in Samuel A. Stouffer, *Social Research to Test Ideas*, Chapter 3. New York: The Free Press of Glencoe, Inc., 1962]. However, in the Stouffer design the interviewee was placed in a situation of role conflict, so that role norms rather than more general cultural norms were investigated.

11. In the proportions reported for the Philippine sample in the various tables, the maximum confidence interval with 95 per cent confidence limits is ±3.5 per cent.

Table 1. Answers in Percentages* to the Question, "Which of these boys in your opinion is the worse? (a) The boy who tyrannizes and beats up smaller children, (b) the boy who disobeys his superiors as his elder brother, parents, teachers, leaders, employer, etc."

Cultural Groups	*(a)*	*(b)*	*No Answer*
American sample (200)	68	29	3
Oak Park (163)	85	13	2
Bad Homburg (191)†	41	30	29
Bad Homburg anti-Nazis (55)	49	22	29
Bad Homburg Nazis (81)	30	42	28
Philippine sample (770)	41.3	56.7	2.0

*In all tables z-scores were computed for tests of significance at the .05 level. z-scores indicate significant differences at the .05 level between Philippine sample and American samples. No computations were made of the Nazi and anti-Nazi groups in view of the small Ns.

†McGranahan used two diagnostic questions to determine the Nazi and anti-Nazi groups. A third group responded inconsistently to the questions. Therefore, the Nazi and anti-Nazi subsamples do not equal the Bad Homburg sample.

American.[12] How did the Filipino look upon this treatment of the young? Pre-testing indicated that the Filipino understood the meanings of the words "tyrannizes" and "beats up" at least sufficiently to verbalize accurately. But the writer's observations indicate that there is very little of this kind of behavior in the Philippines.[13] Certainly, there is no institutionalized attitude toward "bullying" as there is in American society, and this action in the Philippines is not met therefore with specialized distaste. No significant differences were found between the answers of males and females in the Philippine sample. In the Pasig sample, however, emphasis on obedience was even greater. It may be conjectured that American attitudes toward the "bully" had some currency in the urban Philippine sample. Filipino comments on this question indicate that Filipinos did not perceive two independent evils here. They considered that the evil of tyranny was implicit in the evil of disobedience.

In the second question (Table 2) there are again two wrongs to be

Table 2. Answers in Percentages* to the Question, "Do you think it right for a boy to run away from home if his father is cruel and brutal?"

Cultural Groups	*Yes*	*No*	*No Answer*
American sample (200)	68	30	2
Oak Park (163)	80	19	1
Bad Homburg (191)	45	50	5
Bad Homburg anti-Nazis (55)	27	67	6
Bad Homburg Nazis (81)	51	48	1
Philippine sample (770)	46.5	52.4	1.1

*Philippine sample significantly different from American samples.

12. This facility is most noticeable in the Oak Park sample, of course.

13. During about one hundred hours of observation of children's play in a Philippine barrio, the writer did not find any instance of protracted or habitual bullying.

balanced, the brutality of the father and the running away from home. As would be expected, the American sample and the Oak Park sample endorsed the running away pretty heavily. The Bad Homburg Nazis, indoctrinated to resist anti-Nazi opinion within the home, endorsed the running away more than the anti-Nazis. The Philippine sample and the Bad Homburg sample are almost identical in their responses to this question. But the comments of Filipinos probably indicate a basic difference between the attitudes of Filipinos and Germans that is related to differences in family structures. We can bring this out by considering the Filipinos who thought that the bay should not run away from home.[14] Half of those answering "no" to this question added a comment. Only 20 per cent of the commenting group in any way endorsed the theory of submission to authority. A typical response of this group was, "You should not run away because your father is your father. He is responsible for your life." The rest of the commenting group had other reasons why the boy should not run away. Some thought the boy must have deserved the treatment he got. Others considered his obligation to stay home and look after his mother. Still others emphasized the bad companions he might fall in with if he left home. And about 20 per cent of the commenting group suggested that the boy should stay home and take some kind of action to help correct the behavior of the father. The father ". . . would do brutality only if he is abnormal," and the boy should ". . . tell his father about his cruelty," or he should ". . . find the root of the cruelty and remedy it."

In Table 3 the Philippine distribution is clearly related to the institu-

Table 3. Answers in Percentages* to the Question, "Do older brothers have the right to give orders to the younger brothers and obtain their obedience with force?"

Cultural Groups	*Yes*	*No*	*No Answer*
American sample (200)	9	90	1
Oak Park (163)	8	90	2
Bad Homburg (191)	23	72	5
Bad Homburg anti-Nazis (55)	22	76	2
Bad Homburg Nazis (81)	25	74	1
Philippine sample (770)	29.1	69.0	1.9

*Null hypothesis that Bad Homburg sample and Philippine sample are from similar universes cannot be rejected. Both samples are significantly different from the American samples.

tionalized allocation of authority to senior siblings. But the sensitivity of Filipinos to abuses of authority is seen in the percentages. Only 29 per cent of them answered "yes" to this question as against 69 per cent who answered "no." The comments indicated that the question sug-

14. The null hypothesis that affirmative and negative answers are evenly distributed in the sampled universe may not be rejected.

gested too much authority for older brothers. Older brothers should be "kind" and "understanding." They ". . . may use force if the younger brothers do not follow."

Authority and the State

An extreme conflict between authority and human rights is established in the fourth question (Table 4). The question assumes a situation where there is a serious breach of military duty. McGranahan gave the questionnaire to Americans and Germans in the latter months of 1945,

Table 4. Answers in Percentages* to the Question, "Make believe that a Filipino soldier, during the last war, refused to obey an order of a superior officer to shoot an innocent military prisoner. Do you think he was right in refusing to obey this order?"

Cultural Groups	*Yes*	*No*	*No Answer*
American sample (200)	68	29	3
Oak Park (163)	84	14	2
Bad Homburg sample (191)	50	44	6
Bad Homburg anti-Nazis (55)	56	35	9
Bad Homburg Nazis (81)	46	50	4
Philippine sample (770)	66.5	32.2	1.3

* Null hypothesis that American and Philippine samples are drawn from similar universes cannot be rejected. Bad Homburg sample significantly differs from Philippine and American samples.

so that military awareness was widespread in the samples. Military awareness was probably just as widespread in the Philippines when this questionnaire was given in the fall of 1954. Memories of the Japanese occupation were still fresh. The Huk "rebellion" had only been put down in 1952, and Huk bands were still scattered through the mountains and occasionally raiding isolated *barrios*. An intensive program of military training was being conducted in all schools and colleges.

Filipinos indicated by their answers to this question the difinite limits they attach to the exercise of authority. Sixty-six per cent of this sample thought that the refusal to obey the order was justified, and this was not significantly different from the percentages in the American sample, which typically rebels against authority. The Filipino recognizes but limits authority. It is noteworthy that the Pasig sample gave even larger support to the refusal to obey the order: 71 per cent supported the refusal.

In Table 5 a fairly abstract comparison of norms is indicated. The American sample preferred individual rights with a majority of 65 per cent. The Oak Park sample exceeded this with a percentage of 81. Even

Table 5. Answers in Percentages* to the Question, "In your opinion should a newspaper publish: (a) What they wish, or (b) only what is good for the country?"

Cultural Groups	*(a)*	*(b)*	*No Answer*
American sample (200)	65	33	2
Oak Park (163)	81	17	2
Bad Homburg sample (191)	51	43	6
Bad Homburg anti-Nazis (55)	64	29	7
Bad Homburg Nazis (81)	35	63	2
Philippine sample (770)	29.3	68.1	2.6

*All samples except Nazi and anti-Nazi groups, significantly different.

the German sample endorsed individual rights where military or family authority was not evident. But the Filipino, on the contrary, endorsed the theory of social obligation.[15]

But in Table 6 we see that the Filipino again carefully limits the exercise of authority even when it is employed to maintain an obligation to the group: 68 per cent of the Philippine sample considered that the punishment was excessive. It should be noted that while only 33 per cent of the American sample thought a newspaper should publish only what is good for the country, 22 per cent thought that people who unjustly criticize the government should be thrown in jail. Filipinos seem to be more sensitive to degrees of punishment, for while 68 per cent thought a newspaper should publish only what is good for the country, only 30 per cent thought that people who unjustly criticize the government should be thrown in jail. The Bad Homburg sample indicates strong support for severe sanctions, for 43 per cent thought a newspaper should publish only what is good for the country, and 36 per cent thought that people who unjustly criticize the government should be thrown in jail. Or, from another point of view, while 68 per

Table 6. Answers in Percentages* to the Question, "Should people who unjustly criticize the government of a country be thrown in jail?"

Cultural Groups	*Yes*	*No*	*No Answer*
American sample (200)	22	77	1
Oak Park (163)	21	78	1
Bad Homburg sample (191)	36	57	7
Bad Homburg anti-Nazis (55)	24	67	9
Bad Homburg Nazis (81)	46	53	1
Philippine sample (770)	30.7	68.7	0.6

*American samples significantly different from Bad Homburg sample.

15. Comments indicated very little emphasis on a theoretical individual right that should be protected and nurtured.

cent of the Philippine sample thought a newspaper should publish only what is good for the country, the same percentage (68) thought that people who unjustly criticize the government should *not* be thrown in jail.

Confidence in the Average Man

One would expect youth in a country with "democratic" norms to have confidence in the individual's responsible use of his rights. Yet in question 7 (Table 7) a majority of American youth indicated that the

Table 7. Answers in Percentages* to the Question, "Is the common Tao or the average man stupid and easily misled by propaganda?"

Cultural Groups	Yes	No	No Answer
American sample (200)	54	45	1
Offenbach sample (256)†	86	11	3
Philippine sample (770)	37.2	59.0	3.8

*All samples significantly different with reference to this question.
†McGranahan reported only the Offenbach sample here and the Friedberg sample in Table 8. We infer these questions were not given to the Bad Homburg sample. McGranahan reported, however, that responses to questions in German communities sampled were "remarkably uniform."

common man was stupid and easily led by propaganda. The German Offenbach sample gave a majority of 86 per cent to this view. In contrast only 37 per cent of the Philippine sample supported this view compared with 59 per cent who opposed it. This question is of course partly a projective question and may not tap general cultural norms. We include it here since many studies have indicated its relevance to a totalitarian personality syndrome. There is no significant difference in percentages as between males and females in the Philippine sample, or between the Philippine sample and the Pasig sample.

Although the Filipino has regard for elders and for the authority they exercise, he apparently does not think they have all the answers. The Filipino responses to question 8 (Table 8) indicate the same lack

Table 8. Answers in Percentages* to the Question, "Do you believe that the older generation of Filipinos understands the present-day problems of the Filipino youth?"

Cultural Groups	Yes	No	No Answer
American sample (200)	31	67	2
Friedberg sample (135)	53	34	13
Philippine sample (770)	31.8	62.8	5.4

*American and Philippine samples significantly different from the Friedberg sample.

of confidence in the ability of elders to solve the problems of youth that appears in the American sample. Social change is taking place in the Philippines quite as fast as it is in the United States. The same is true in Germany, but the report on the Friedberg sample indicates that parental authority in Germany carries with it an element of unquestioning acceptance. Social change is proceeding much more slowly in Pasig than in the Manila area and the responses of the Pasig sample reflect this.

Views of Great Men

The next question, "Who, in your opinion, was the greatest man in world history?" is at least partly projective in type, but it probably throws light on culturally induced attitudes. (No table is provided for this question.) Filipinos receive very little instruction in their own history. Under the Spanish they received a Spanish version of European history. Under the Americans they have received an American version of European and American history. This has resulted in a stultification of Filipino history. Young Filipinos interested in applying themselves to the history of their country have enormous difficulty in unearthing authentic documents. The Spanish, the Japanese, and the Americans have all had reason for destroying historical documents of one kind or another. It is understandable, then, that the heroes available to Filipinos for choice are much the same as the heroes available to Americans. About the only exception is the national hero and martyr, Dr. José Rizal, who was a scholar and poet of considerable stature. In answer to this question 24 per cent of the Filipino males and 9 per cent of the females mentioned Christ or God. Herodotus, Lincoln, Napoleon, and José Rizal each claimed about 5 per cent of both males and females. In terms of total choices, the Filipinos chose a higher per cent of non-political and non-military figures than either the Americans or the Germans. Three per cent of the Germans chose non-political and non-military figures in comparison with 26 per cent of the Americans and 62 per cent of the Filipinos. Again, the Filipino appears to be indicating a cultural distaste for naked power.

Conclusion

Comparisons of the results in the present study and McGranahan's indicate (a) that Filipino youth place higher emphasis on authority and obedience than American youth, (b) that they attribute less power and prerogative on the one hand and less submission on the other to structured relations of authority and obedience than German youth, (c) that they see the individual as closely identified with the group and, as a result, make less distinction between group rights and individual rights than either German or American youth.

e) ESTABLISHING CONDITIONS OF PERSONAL ENCOUNTER

RUBEN E. REINA

Two Patterns of Friendship in a Guatemalan Community

NEAR the center of the Department of Guatemala and twelve kilometers northeast of Guatemala City is located the main community of the *municipio* of Chinautla, known as Santa Cruz Chinautla.[1] The Indian population refer to this place as Pac'om and to the nearby archeological sites as *najtiminit*, or the "far-away place." The present community extends 2.5 kilometers along the bank of the river Las Vacas and is one kilometer in width. The 1950 Census shows a population of 1,672 persons, 95.8 per cent (investigator's own calculation) of whom are Indians of the Pokomam-speaking dialect.

The community is well known in most of the highland and the pied-

Reprinted from American Anthropologist, *1959, pp. 44-50, by permission of the author and the journal.*

The author wishes to acknowledge his gratitude to Cora Du Bois for reading this manuscript and for her comments. Some of the generalizations in this paper have coincided with her own views that intensity in friendship is a function of age and marital status. I also am indebted to Robbins Burling for his critical reading of the first draft of this paper.

1. The field work was conducted in the summer of 1953 and in 1955-56.

mont areas for pottery made without the potter's wheel by Indian women. The local male population resists working in the capital and has continued with the milpa activities and charcoal making. The Ladinos own three small local stores, operate the bus service to Guatemala City, and a few others have found employment in the *municipalidad.*

The Indians think of themselves as *naturales,* descending from the earlier inhabitants of najtiminit, while the Ladinos are the newcomers to Chinautla who differ culturally from that which is considered local custom. There is a third group, constituting only one per cent of the population, recognized as the *Mengalas.* They are neither Indians nor Ladinos, though they are considered *indianeros* by Ladinos because they mix socially with the Indians. The Mengala families are the old timers, who claim direct descent from Iberian families.[2]

The aim of this paper is to describe the patterns of friendship practiced by Ladinos and by Indians within their respective groups. The Ladino pattern is termed *cuello,* while Indians' social relationship is known as *camaraderia.* Since the Mengalas tend to practice the pattern of the Ladinos, they will not be discussed specifically, but it should be pointed out that they do not hesitate to follow either style according to social circumstances.

To the Ladinos, friendship has practical utility in the realm of economic and political influence; this friendship is looked upon as a mechanism beneficial from the personal viewpoint. Cuello, a favorite expression among the Ladinos, indicates that a legal matter may be accelerated, or a job for which one is not totally qualified might be secured through the personal influence of an acquaintance who is in power or knows a third party who can be influenced. The cuello complex depends upon the strength of friendship established and is often measured in terms of the number of favors dispensed to each other. It finds its main support in the nature of a convenient social relationship defined as friendship.

It follows that, for the Ladino of Chinautla, the possession of a range of friends is most favorable. Most desirable are friends among the urban Ladinos who bring prestige and of whom the local Ladino can boast loudly on social occasions, or who can be used to cause fear among others. There is the strong desire to establish ties of friendship with people of superior status and political power. Due to the socio-political instability of the last decade, the Ladinos' cuello relationships in Chinautla have fluctuated a great deal, as they discarded and added "convenient" friends from whom some economic or legal benefit can be expected.

2. The cultural position of this group will be discussed elsewhere.

However, friends under this definition can be a great problem. This became obvious when the first local Ladino, a land owner (*finquero*), became the mayor of the municipio in 1945. His Ladino acquaintances of the area, who were under his political jurisdiction, expected to have cuello to improve themselves economically, or to ameliorate punishment for themselves, or to intercede for some friend or relative. For those requesting the favor, there is no concern as to whether the person in office must transgress formal regulations. The assumption is that friendship in itself is more important than rules, and there is no law or status to prevent helping a friend in need. Friendship, in other words, means trust, favoritism, *mucha simpatía* (artificial or real as the case may be). For the Ladino mayor who was supported by a majority of Indian voters a year after the 1944 revolution, the number of petitions created a delicate situation under the new democratic political setting. All petitions could not be properly fulfilled in accordance with cuello terms, and the mayor's failure to meet these expected obligations terminated many associations. The mayor's "egotistic" characteristics became a matter for severe criticism among Ladinos, and his reputation declined rapidly thereafter. Friction, enmity, and a desire for revenge were intense among those who expectations were not met.

The Indians associate themselves under the *camarada* pattern, which differs considerably from the Ladino ideal of friendship. Indians enter into intense bonds of friendship during their days of youth. The society provides the male Indians more opportunities to show their relations publicly than it does for women, but the pattern applies to both sexes. Although camaradas are also sought during middle age, the degree of attachment and companionship appears less emotional. The following case illustrates the working aspects of the camarada complex among the young male Indians of Chinautla.

Juan and Pedro had been camaradas for a period of three years, at which time Pedro lost his mother; afterward the two young men (20 and 22 years old respectively) developed even closer bonds of friendship. Every night after work they met in some selected spot in town, went to local celebrations, danced with each other all night at festivals, and returned together to Juan's hut to sleep. On occasion, Juan would sleep in the home of Pedro who lived with his parents in another *cantón* (neighborhood). The frequent visit of Pedro to Juan's place caused some antagonism among local boys, particularly since Pedro began courting Juan's cousin. Pedro claimed that on various occasions during festivities he had protected his camarada from being beaten by the boys of his own cantón.

When they were together at festivities one would become more drunk than the other and his camarada would then protect him from getting into fights. When Pedro tangled with boys from Juan's cantón, Juan was always ready to speak up to defend him. Juan's acquaintances, by virtue of the fact that they resided in the same cantón, would then say, "Not today, let us leave Juan in peace with his camarada."

One time Pedro spoke to Juan's cousin in daylight, and the gossip circulated fast. One of the boys from the opposite cantón who was interested in the same girl announced "Yo aquél lo demuestro," implying "I will show him," and indicating more manhood on his part. When this phrase is publicly known it represents an invitation to fight. Pedro was told of the statement and said to his challenger, "You wish something bad with me?" The other answered, "Yes." Pedro then said, "If you want, let us go." They fought in seclusion and there they decided who could outdo the other. When the agreement was reached—Pedro lost the fight and the rights to go any further in the relation with the girl—they returned to let their friends know the outcome. However, Pedro and Juan continued their friendship. They were seen in the streets and at dances together, embracing each other or holding hands while sitting and drinking refreshments on Sunday mornings. One time they were seen kissing each other in a joking fashion, and in front of other boys they stated that they would like to marry each other if one were a woman. On weekends, they spent the days together here and there in the community talking, joking and hand playing. As this appeared to be deviant behavior, I questioned the local people. All agreed that it was nothing rare or strange, but was a manifestation of love (*cariño*) and real camaradería. "Everybody has a camarada and has done the same thing," was the usual response. No one remotely considered that homosexual relations could take place.

Later the two young men broke up their friendship. Juan stated that in those three years he had refrained from telling Pedro many personal secrets of his life, and he was now glad that he had because otherwise Pedro could begin to work out some sorcery (*envidia*). When I questioned Juan about the reason for breaking the friendship, he stated with great sorrow and loneliness that during the fiesta titular Pedro had become intoxicated with guaro and could no longer dance with him, so Juan began to dance with another person of his own cantón who had been seeking him as a camarada. While Juan was dancing, Pedro managed to come to the dance floor and when he found his camarada dancing with another fellow, he took this as an act of infidelity and went out angrily to find another partner. He returned with a partner and while dancing came near Juan, pushing him. Later on, while dancing, Pedro hit Juan in the face. The latter could take no more of this type of treatment from his own camarada and since the relationship had been weakening, because of Pedro's constant scenes of jealousy, he decided that this would be a good time to fight Pedro and start with a new camarada. Both were quite drunk, and they fought. Pedro went home followed by Juan and they continued fighting and insulting each other in public. Once the hangover had passed and they were told by friends of their fight, Juan became angry, and Pedro told his own father of the insults and the beating he had received. Pedro and his father went to the mayor and the following day Juan was ordered to appear in the mayor's office. Pedro's father requested that the mayor (an Indian) separate the young men officially (as a case of husband and wife) on the grounds that Juan could not be trusted as a friend and furthermore had encouraged his son to drink a great deal. Juan argued, however, that Pedro had been drinking before the friendship developed and that he had requested Pedro not to drink any more since both were members of the Saint Francis Order for laymen. Juan then said to the mayor:

> I don't want to force anybody to be my camarada, and there is no need to have separation. Pedro has no more desire (*voluntad*) to be my friend, and I don't want to force anybody to be my friend. We fought because we were drunk, and one does not know well enough what one does; but now that Pedro wishes things in this way, he can go his way and I will go mine. He is free to look for another camarada, if he is not too sad, and I will not bother him for that.

The mayor asked whether the father and son would like to make any formal charges, but both parties agreed to end the friendship without following any formalities in the court, much to the disgust of Pedro's father, whose family's dignity and reputation had been hurt.

After the separation, they would not greet each other in the street, but both avoided talking of the other in derogatory terms with a third person. However, everyone commented that they were both sad and lonesome for each other. Pedro sent a few messages to Juan to effect a reconciliation, but Juan was not interested and had begun to work out a friendship with another person of his age in order "to forget his ex-camarada."

The establishment of this new camaradería was preceded by several months of passive companionship in which a rather formal relationship prevailed before mutual emotional attachment could be noted. It was predicted that once a high intensity of friendship was attained, scenes of jealousy and frustration could be expected and the cycle would end in a state of enmity. "This happens," reasoned an Indian informant, "because there are no longer good people, and it is difficult to keep a camarada throughout life. Thus, one cannot and should not trust another person all the way." The intensity varies from case to case and not all are as extreme as this, but Indians are always ready to recount camarada experiences which ended in trauma. The explanation seems to lie in the fact that Indians seek extreme confidence (*confianza*) and this in itself endangers friendship. They demand reciprocal affection, and it is expected that the camarada will act only in a manner which will bring pleasure to his friend. Each is jealous and egotistical about his friend, a Ladino stated. He wants undivided affection, and he would prefer to lose everything rather than share a friendship with someone else. Indians do not know how to keep more than one camarada at a time.

Friendship for the Indian is a formal relationship, which he calls *puesto*, with a prescribed role and status, and it is always his firm intention to keep it. They are proud of this relationship and affectionate in it, but from a practical viewpoint have mixed feelings. A camarada is a potential enemy when the puesto is lost. A certain reserve on the part of the camaradas is therefore observed, especially in the realm of family secrets, plans, and amount earned at work. Friendship is maintained not for economic, political, or practical purposes, but only an emotional fulfillment.

The principle of the camarada complex underlies all potential relations attempted by Indians. Heretofore unknown to me in an institutionalized form, the camarada complex at first prevented my field work from running smoothly, and my relationship with informants was difficult. After several months in the field, I was obviously approached for friendship by several informants. They were talkative, paid frequent visits after work, and responded to my expectation of them as informants. A twenty-five-year-old unmarried Indian, whom I shall call Miguel, agreed to do some carpentry work. His progress with the work was rather impressive, but it soon became evident that his concentration and care were rapidly diminishing. He was given the wages he expected, but several times I noticed him carefully observing me as I engaged in friendly conversation with other potential informants. On one such occasion, when the visitor had left, Miguel took the opportunity to talk against the man and to caution me in confidential tones, saying that one had to be careful because this person was known to have frequent association with the *brujo* who had performed the ritual of the doll burial on several occasions. Death had resulted for persons represented by the doll. Because I did not heed Miguel's counsel, he became indifferent, did not come to work regularly, refused to give descriptive information (discarding the topic as of no importance), and finally did not return at all. I was later told that Miguel felt that he had tried to become a camarada and had been willing to recount the community life and its history. He felt that he knew most of the facts or knew where he could secure them, and therefore could have been a valuable assistant. For these reasons he believed that I was making a mistake in looking for other friends.

The same behavior was manifested by female Indians. María, who helped in the domestic affairs of my household, felt a lack of reciprocity in friendship after several months of work, which caused her withdrawal. Her puesto with my wife did not fulfill her expectations and although her fondness for our infant son was intense, she preferred to withdraw when she felt that another girl was stepping into her friendship with the family. More money was offered in order to keep her services, but she preferred to leave, even though it brought her actual sorrow, and let the competitor step in when her pride had been hurt. The friction between the two girls was intense afterwards. They would avoid each other, or throw scornful glances when forced to pass on the street. María did not return to visit the family and for some time avoided public encouners.

Under these social conditions, the keeping of a permanent and reliable informant was not an easy matter. The procedure was painful for both the investigator and the informant. To keep a particularly good informant, it was necessary to give him a very careful explanation of the role of the investigator and his need for maintaining contact with everyone in the community. It took a long while for the informant to become accustomed to this type of relationship, and he would often point out with disturbed feelings that he had seen "so and so" come to the house and stay all afternoon, or that he had been told some undesirable member of the community dropped in seeking a camarada puesto. At times he felt elated and happy, but on other occasions he felt hurt and distant. It took constant effort to keep him stimulated to serve as informant and, most of all, to think of this relationship in these terms while many in the community were advising him to withdraw. After several months of insecurity, he found his own puesto, became secure, and turned out to be a desirable informant who brought many acquaintances and relatives for intensive interview.

The camarada complex caused difficulty in the administration when the first Indian mayor was elected in 1947. In this case friction arose within the mayor's advisory board, which was composed of four Indian *regidores* and a *síndico*. The First Regidor was aggressively seeking to establish a camaradería with the mayor, who enjoyed great esteem among everyone in the community. This councilman was "tailing" the mayor and directly attempting to displace the other councilmen from any similar attempts. He used his power and age to curtail social interaction. Three councilmen finally were hurt, and after withdrawing they maintained only a formal and rather uncooperative business relationship with the mayor. Later, however, the intense desire and dogmatic decisions of the First Regidor endangered the mayor's role and his relationship with the national government, forcing the mayor to reject his camarada. The final stage of the camarada complex–enmity–became evident again.

There seems to be a recurrent pattern in which a close camarada relationship is followed by hostility. Conceivably, the explanation may lie in part in that those involved in the relationship are of the same sex, which prevents full emotional satisfaction; and because the great admiration of camaradas finds insufficient expression, it results in scenes of jealously and aggressive separation.

The contrast with the Ladino pattern of friendship is striking. Obviously, the camarada complex has neither an economic function nor a cuello significance. For the Indians it offers rather an emotional fulfillment and a means of assuring oneself that one will not be standing alone. Before marriage and after childhood, the camarada complex reaches high emotional intensity–at that transition in life when a Chinautleco achieves adult status but has not acquired all its emotional rewards. The strict separation of the sexes in all adult social gatherings, including dances, public rituals, and drinking occasions, reinforces the camarada complex and creates a pseudo-homosexuality. The inner emotions and sexual drives find a partial outlet in the pattern of friendship, inasmuch as it is socially approved, but the reward is temporary since the mutual admiration demands mutual perfection and exclusive attention. The friendship is soon dissolved in bitterness and disappointment.

Finally, consideration should be given to the Ladino and Indian attitudes toward friendship among each other. Ladinos find the camarada complex simply ridiculous and only possible in the context of "uncivilized" individuals. The gregarious orientation of the Ladino, his impatience, his Western European sex-role definition in free interaction across sex lines, and his utilitarian views in social relations run altogether against the Indian view and destroy any possibility of interaction at this level. The camarada complex is considered by Ladinos to be a boring kind of social interaction and too passive for the aggressive Ladino, so a cross-"race" friendship is unworkable.

f) DEFINING THE MODES OF FREEDOM

DOROTHY LEE

Individual Autonomy and Social Structure

RESPECT for individual integrity, for what we have called human dignity, has long been a tenet in American culture, and it is certainly no novel principle to anyone working in the area of interpersonal relations. However, in a heterogeneous society such as ours, and in an era of induced change and speeded tempo of living, it has been difficult to implement this tenet in the everyday details of living. We have to reconcile principles of conformity and individual initiative, group living and private freedom of choice, social regulation and personal autonomy. I believe that a study of other societies dealing with such issues in different circumstances can furnish us with insights which we can use in understanding our own situation. So I present here scattered material from a number of societies, ending with a brief sketch of the culture of the Navaho Indians, to show how the principle of personal autonomy is supported by the cultural framework.

In every society we find some organized social unit; but not everywhere does the social unit provide freedom to the individual or the opportunity for spontaneous functioning; nor do we find everywhere the value for sheer personal being of which I shall speak below. We often find a hierarchy where women or children or the uninitiated or the commoners are accorded a minority status. In some societies we find what amounts to a dictatorship; in others, the group may demand such sacrifice of individual uniqueness as to make for totalitarianism. On

From Personnel and Guidance Journal, *1956. Reprinted in Dorothy Lee,* Freedom and Culture, *Englewood Cliffs, N.J.: Prentice-Hall, Inc. (Spectrum Books), 1959, pp. 5-14.*

the other hand, in some societies we encounter a conception of individual autonomy and democratic procedures which far outstrip anything we have practiced or even have conceived of as democracy. It is only the latter kind which concerns me here.

It is often difficult for us to decide exactly how much our principle of personal autonomy involves. We find ourselves asking questions such as: to what extent can we allow a child to make his own decisions, to speak and act for himself? And: at what point do we begin to allow him to do so? For example, obviously when the mother first takes her infant to the pediatrician, she has to speak for him. Exactly when does she begin to remain silent, waiting for him to understand and answer the doctor's questions and to express his own likes and opinions and conclusions? And to what extent can she do this, using up the time of her appointment, taking up the valuable time of a busy physician?

Many of us feel that to allow a child to decide for himself and to act according to his own wish, that is, to be permissive, is to show respect for the unique being of the child. Yet for many of the societies we know, it would be presumption for any person to "allow" another to take what is essentially his prerogative—the right to decide for himself. These people do not "permit" others. When their children, as for example the children of the Wintu Indians, ask "Can I?" they are asking for information on the rules of the structure; for instance, they may be seeking clarification about a religious taboo or a social custom. They are saying in effect, "Is it permissible for me to . . . ?" and not, "Do you allow me to . . . ?" These people do not "give" freedom to their children, because it is not theirs to give. If they do not impose an external time schedule on their infants, but feed them when they are hungry, and put them to bed when they are sleepy, they are not being "permissive"; they are showing their deep-seated respect for individual worth, and their awareness of the unique tempo of the individual.

Ethnographers have presented us with many incidents, apparently commonplace and trivial, which point out for us an amazingly thoroughgoing implementation of respect for personal quality. For instance, Marian Smith tells how, when she was visiting a Sikh household in British Columbia, she noticed that a small child, asked to entertain his baby brother, merely went up to the playpen and put in a toy truck. He did not show the baby how the truck worked, how he could make the wheels go round; he gave the truck silently. This amazed the visitor, since she knew that the Sikhs were people of great empathy and warmth, and with a great love for babies. She knew, also, that the child in question had approached the baby with friendliness and affection. Yet, under similar circumstances an American child would probably have told the baby what to look for. Then she remembered the personal autonomy of the Sikh, and realized that the boy was acting consistently with the cultural values; he was furnishing the baby with the raw material for experience, and leaving him to explore and discover for himself, without any attempt to influence him. He was expressing respect, not non-involvement.

Such respect for autonomy may appear extreme to us, yet it would be taken for granted in a number of the Indian tribes in this continent. For example, an anthropology student who was observing relations between parents and children was puzzled to see a baby with hair so long that it got in his eyes and seemed to cause him discomfort, though otherwise his mother treated him with care and affection. When she finally asked why the baby's hair had been left so long, the mother answered, "He has not asked to have it cut." The baby was about eighteen months old, and could barely talk; yet the mother would not take it upon herself to act for him without his request or consent.

These instances exemplify a belief so deep that it apparently permeates behavior and decisions, and operates without question or reflection or conscious plan. It is a belief so internalized as to be regarded as almost an organic ingredient of the personality. The individual, shown absolute respect from birth and valued as sheer being for his own uniqueness, apparently learns with every experience to have this same respect and value for others; he is "trained" to be constantly sensitive to the beginnings of others.

An instance of this "training" in sensitivity comes from the culture of the Chinese. American observers had noticed that Chinese babies had learned, by the time they were about six months old, to indicate that they wanted to micturate; yet they seemed to be treated very permissively, with no attempt at toilet training. A Chinese mother explained that there actually is such "training"; only it is the mother who "trains" herself. When the baby wants to urinate, his whole body participates in the preliminary process. The Chinese mother, holding the baby in her arms, learns to be sensitive to the minute details of this process, and to hold her baby away from herself at exactly the critical moment. Eventually, the infant learns to ask to be held out. The mother neither tries to control the baby, nor does she train the infant to control himself according to imposed standards. Instead, she sensitizes herself to his rhythm, and helps him to adopt social discipline with spontaneity, starting from his unique pattern. What is interesting here is that as an end result of this, the baby is "toilet-trained" at a very early age; but it has been an experience of spontaneity for him and his autonomy has remained inviolate, because his mother has had the sensitivity and the patience to "listen" to him.

Among the Wintu Indians of California, the principle of the inviolate integrity of the individual is basic to the very morphology of the language. Many of the verbs which express coercion in our language—such as to take a baby to (the shade), or to change the baby—are formed in such a way that they express a cooperative effort instead. For example, the Wintu would say, "I *went with* the baby," instead of, "I *took* the baby." And they say, "The chief *stood with* the people," which they have to translate into English as, "The chief ruled the people." They never say, and in fact they cannot say, as we do, "I have a sister," or a "son," or "husband." Instead, they say, "I am sistered," or "I live with my sister." *To live with* is the usual way in which they express what we call possession, and they use this term for everything that they respect, so that a man will be said to live with his bow and arrows. In our society, when we try to express respect for individual uniqueness, we have to do it in so many words, and even then we have to grapple with an uncooperative language. This is why we have to resort to terms which actually defeat our ends; terms such as *permissiveness*, or phrases such as *to give freedom to the child*. In Wintu, every interpersonal reference is couched in grammar which rests on the principle of individual integrity. Yet, for this people, the emphasis on personal inviolability did not mean that the individual was isolate. There was such pervasive empathy among them that this, too, was expressed in the grammatical forms; if a boy was sick, the father used a special form of the verb phrase *to be sick*, and thus said, "I-am-sick-in-respect-of-my-son."

A corollary of the principle of individual integrity is that no personal orders can be given or taken without a violation of personal autonomy; we have been familiar with this corollary, particularly in rural areas where the farmer and his wife had "help" but not "servants." In a society such as that of Upper Burma before it was much affected by Western administration, there were no agricultural laborers nor household help at all. In the monasteries, where novices performed menial tasks, the monks did not give orders. Instead, the work was structured throughout the day; and all that the monk said to get the work done was, "Do what is lawful," reminding the novice to act according to the cultural tenet, not ordering him.

This last illustration introduces a further principle: that of structure. Many people in our society have been apprehensive of the implications of personal autonomy, because they have felt that it is apt to lead to lawlessness and chaos. Yet actually it is in connection with the highest personal autonomy that we often find the most intricately developed structure; and it is this structure that make autonomy possible in a group situation. For example, the Burmese novices could proceed without receiving orders only because the structure clearly indicated what could and could not be done and at what time of the day or month or year.

Margaret Mead and Gregory Bateson have described this combination of autonomy and structure for the Balinese. These people have an exceedingly complex calendrical system, consisting of a permutation of ten weeks of differing lengths; and this system, in combination with an intricately patterned spatial and status system, furnishes the structure according to which an individual behaves. For instance, according to the specific combination of "weeks" on which his birthday falls, and according to his status, an individual has to participate in a special way at a particular temple festival. No one imposes this tribute upon him; and no one asks for his contribution. However, because of the enormous amount of detail involved in the precision of the structure, there are officials known as reminders, who merely remind the people of the exact character of the pending festival. Each person then proceeds to act according to his peculiar position in the temporal structure, acting autonomously, finding guidance in the structure.

When the specific aspects of the structure are not clear, the people in such societies can turn to authority for clarification. And here we often find, as with the Burmese or the Navaho Indians, that the authority of the headman or the chief or the leader is in many ways like the authority of the dictionary, or of Einstein. There is no hint of coercion or command here; the people go to the leader with faith, as we go to a reference book, and the leader answers according to his greater knowledge, or clarifies an obscure point, or amplifies according to his greater experience and wisdom. He does not say: You must do this, because I order you to. Yet, he does use the *must* or its equivalent; he says, so to speak: As I see it, this is what must be done. In a sense, it is like the recipe which says: You must not open the oven door for ten minutes after you put the cake in. No housewife, preparing a cake and going to the cookbook for guidance, feels that her personal integrity is violated by this interdiction. Once she is committed to the cake-making, she finds the recipe, the structure, enabling and guiding; she finds it freeing, not restricting.

If permissiveness at times leads to lawlessness and chaos, and even to immobilization instead of the freedom to be and to act, this happens usually in those cases where "permission" goes from person to person, in a structural vacuum. It happens when the structure is by-passed through the dictatorial permissiveness of the person who takes it upon himself to allow, and by implication to forbid, another person. In the societies which were mentioned above, where we find absolute valuing of unique being, what often takes the form of permissiveness in our society exists as the freedom to be, and to find actualization; and it is found within a clearly delineated structure.

Such is the society of the Navaho Indians of Arizona and New Mexico. How long this picture will last, we cannot predict. The mineral resources of their land are now being developed, and rapid change is being introduced. What I say here draws on the autobiographies of Navaho men, as well as on recent ethnographies.

In these accounts, we find a tightly knit group, depending on mutual responsibility among all its members, a precisely structured universe, and a great respect for individual autonomy and integrity. We find people who maintain an inviolable privacy while living as a family in a one-room house, sharing work and responsibility to such an extent that even a child of six will contribute his share of mutton to the family meal. The family unit is so closely knit that, if a child of five is ill or absent, the family suffers because there is a gap in the cooperative effort; and when a man goes hunting, he can get nothing unless his wife cooperates at home by observing the necessary taboos. The well-being of a Navaho, his health and the health of all his undertakings, depend on the maintenance of harmony with nature. All being is both good and evil; and by walking carefully according to a highly structured map of procedure, within a detailed framework of "do's" and "don'ts," the Navaho can keep the proper balance of good and evil in his life, and thus find health and harmony. The rules according to which he lives originate in the structure, and come to him as guidance from the parents, not as commands.

Within this structured universe and tightly knit society, the Navaho lives in personal autonomy. Adults and children are valued for their sheer being, just because they *are*. There is no urge toward achievement; no one has to strive for success. In fact, neither is there reward for success, nor is success held out as a reward for hard work. Wealth may be the result of hard work and skill, but obviously it is also the blatant result of lack of generosity, lack of responsibility for one's relatives, perhaps even of malicious witchcraft. No good Navaho becomes and remains "wealthy" in our terms.

Hard work is valued in itself, as a personal quality which combines the ability to withstand hardship with the paramount sense of responsibility for the work of the group. Even a young child will be trained to see to it that the whole flock of sheep is safe before he takes shelter during a blizzard. This means a systematic program in developing hardihood. He is waked up at daybreak in winter, so that he may run for miles; and in summer, he runs in the hot sun of noontime. Presently, he intensifies this program by his own decision, perhaps putting sand in his moccasins to make the running more rigorous; that is, he relates himself to this discipline with spontaneity. Children learn responsibility by being given indispensable household tasks; in addition, they are given sheep of their own from the time they are about five. They are responsible for the care and welfare of these animals; thus, they acquire a further opportunity at responsible participation. Now they can take their turn at supplying the meat for the family meal, and they can contribute mutton when this is needed for ceremonials, or to entertain visitors.

Most of all, an individual has to learn to walk safely through life, maintaining his harmony with the universe. This involves learning to observe a large number of taboos and procedures, which are aspects of every act: to learn, for example, what is to be done with the left hand, which direction to have his hogan face, what is to be started in a sunwise direction, or to be taken from the east side of a tree; what to avoid touching, or saying, or looking at. All this could be seen as inhibiting, or negative, or as interfering with the individual; but to the Navaho it is guidance in the acquisition of an essential skill—the freedom to act and to be. The intricate set of regulations is like a map which affords freedom to proceed to a man lost in the jungle.

In Navaho autobiographies we often find the phrase, "I followed the advice of my parents," but rarely, "I obeyed my parents." The good Navaho does not command his child; and a mother who is aggressive toward her children, who "talks rough" to them, is strongly criticized. In teaching her children the tremendous number of taboos they have to learn for their well-being, the good Navaho mother does not say: I will punish you if you do thus-and-thus; but: Such-and-such an unpleasant thing will happen to you. The mother is guiding the child; and if the child take a wrong turn, if he breaks a taboo, he is not "guilty." He has not committed a sin against the mother and is not in need of forgiveness. He has made a mistake which he must set right.

This attitude is basic to all Navaho relatedness, so that here man is not burdened with guilt, and does not feel apologetic toward human or divine beings. He is neither grateful nor abject to his gods. As a matter of fact, he must never humble himself before them, since the process of healing, of the recovery of harmony with the universe, involves identification with the appropriate god, who would be slighted if the patient humiliated himself. This means that the Navaho has—and indeed must have—as much respect and value for himself as for others; in fact, this is the Navaho version of the principle that we have discovered so recently in our society: that we cannot accept and respect others until we learn to accept and respect ourselves.

In what I have said, I have made no distinction between adults and children, as the Navaho do not differentiate between the two in the respect they show for personal autonomy. There is no minority status for children. For example, a good Navaho will not take it upon himself to speak for another, whether for adult or child. A man, asked by a White what his wife thinks on a certain subject, is likely to answer, "I don't know, I haven't asked her." In the same way, a father, asked to sell his child's bow and arrow, will refer the request to a five-year-old boy, and abide by the child's decision not to sell, even though he knows the child is badly in need of the clothing that can be bought with the price of the toy. A woman, asked whether a certain baby could talk, said "Yes"; and when the ethnographer was puzzled by the "meaningless" sounds the baby was making, she explained that the baby could talk, but she could not understand what the baby said. All that she had the right to do was to speak for herself, to say that she could not understand. She would not presume to speak for the child, and to say—as I think we would have said—that the child was making meaningless sounds.

So the individual remains inviolate. No one coerces another among the Navaho. Traditionally, parents do not force their children to do what they unequivocally do not want to do, such as going to school or to the hospital; children are not coerced even "for their own good." As the mother of two unschooled children put it, "I listen to my children, and I have to take their word." There is no political coercion, and all leadership is traditionally incidental. A man finds himself in a position of leadership when the people seek him out because of the high degree of his inner development; because of his wisdom, his knowledge, his assumption of responsibility, his physical skill and hardihood, the wealth which he is ready to use to help his relatives. Men do not seek leadership; and White employers have found that the Navaho are reluctant to become foremen, however able they may be, and in spite of the higher pay involved. It is "fundamentally indecent" according to Clyde Kluckhohn, "for a single individual to presume to make decisions for the group," and therefore not even a leader will make decisions for others, or give orders to others.

For the Navaho mother, personal autonomy means that her child has the freedom to make his own mistakes, to suffer pain or grief or joy and learn from experience. And the child has his freedom because the mother has faith in him. This does not mean that she has high expectations of him, but that she trusts him. She knows that he is a mingling of good and evil; she knows that life is unpredictable, and that a mistake may bring disaster. But she is willing to refrain from interfering with her child as he explores, as he takes his steps in life. When the baby starts walking, the mother does not see to it that he is out of reach of the fire, and that all the sharp knives have been put away. The child gets burned a little, and the mother helps him learn from this experience that he has to be careful of fire; he has a small accident, and the mother helps him understand and deal with that particular danger. By taking a chance on her child, the mother teaches him to be ready to meet and deal with danger, instead of warning him away from danger.

This trust means that the child has freedom to move, to act, to undertake responsibility. It means that the child is given significant tasks in the household. A psychiatrist visiting a Navaho family wrote in her diary: "After supper the girl (ten years old) went to water the horses, and the boy (five years old) to take the little flock back to some older members of the family who lived in a hogan a quarter of a mile away." No mention is made here of orders given, nor of any checking on the mother's part to see that the job was done.

Coexistence of Autonomy and Limits

If the societies I have mentioned here present an enviable consistency in the expression of the principle of individual integrity, it is well to keep in mind that there may be no special virtue in this; at the time these societies were studied, they enjoyed great social homogeneity, and were relatively unchanging over time. This means that the children could learn the adult role at home by gradually sharing the life of the father or mother—as a matter of course, expecting and wanting to live the life of the parents, and to hold the same values and principles. However, the fact remains that consistency was there; that the principle was upheld by the various aspects of the culture, even by the very grammar of the language, as among the Wintu.

The practices I have presented here are not for us to copy, but rather food for thought, the basis for new insights. I have tried to show that law and limits and personal autonomy can coexist effectively, that spontaneity is not necessarily killed by group responsibility, that respect for individual integrity is not an end to be achieved by specific means, but that it can exist only if it is supported by deep conviction and by the entire way of life.

SELECTED READINGS

The readings in this section have stressed the affirmative side of the society-self relation. Although the individual is necessarily implicated in his society, it does not follow that he is always implicated to his advantage. The negative aspect of the association is stressed in the following studies, which, of course, are merely representative of an entire literature: Bingham Dai, "Personality Problems in Chinese Culture," *American Sociological Review*, October, 1941; Arnold W. Green, "Culture Normality and Personality Conflict," *American Anthropologist*, 1944; O. H. Mowrer, "Emerging Conceptions of Neurosis and Normality," in Francis L. K. Hsu (ed.), *Aspects of Culture and Personality* (New York: Abelard-Schuman, 1954).

The use of social structure to aid transition is shown in John E. Mayer, "The Self Restraint of Friends: A Mechanism in Family Transition," *Social Forces*, 1957; Erving Goffman, "Cooling the Mark Out: Some Aspects of Adaptation to Failure," *Psychiatry*, 1952.

Morris Janowitz brings out the same point with reference to military organization in *The Professional Soldier, A Social and Political Portrait*, (New York: The Free Press, 1960). "Thus, an air officer must readjust his values often with great difficulty, as his career unfolds. One of the main functions of higher education in staff and command school and war college is to assist the officer to adjust to the prestige patterns and values of higher echelons" (p. 72).

The therapeutic potential in the community is brought out in a number of studies represented by Howard E. Freeman and Ozzie G. Simmons, "Mental Patients in the Community: Family Settings and Performance Levels," *American Sociological Review*, 1958, and the same authors' "Social Class and Posthospital Performance Levels," *American Sociological Review*, 1959. See also Raymond C. Lerner, "The Therapeutic Social Club: Social Rehabilitation for Mental Patients," *International Journal of Social Psychiatry*, Summer, 1960.

Group structure serves as a basis for opinion as shown in Peter M. Blau, "Structural Effects," *American Sociological Review*, June, 1960, and may solve sticky problems of consensus as Charles K. Warriner brings out in "The Nature and Functions of Official Morality," *American Journal of Sociology*, 1958.

Thomas B. Orr, Leon H. Levy, and Sanford Rosenweig show the diffusion of signs for emotion in our own society in their study, "Judgments of Emotion from Facial Expression by College Students, Mental Retardates and Mental Hospital Patients," *Journal of Personality*, 1960. Complex culturally related emotions are described in Hu Hsien-chin, "The Chinese Concepts of Face," *American Anthropologist*, 1944.

Hsien-chin's article indicates the depth of culturally defined attitudes. The following articles sample the literature relating to this: Herbert Hyman, "The Value Systems of Different Classes: A Social Psychological Contribution to the Analysis of Stratification," in Reinhard Bendix and Seymour

Martin Lipset (eds.) *Class, Status and Power* (New York: The Free Press, 1953); Monica Lawlor, "Cultural Influences on Preferences for Designs," *Journal of Abnormal and Social Psychology*, 1955; Laura Thompson, "Logico-Aesthetic Integration in Hopi Culture," *American Anthropologist*, 1945.

Authority relationships are important to self-orientations, especially in the Western world with its complex organization. The effect of dictatorial organization on the deepest levels of the self is brought out by Bruno Bettelheim in his analysis of the German concentration camp during the last great war. See *The Informed Heart* (New York: The Free Press, 1960). Walter B. Miller analyses different types of authority in "Two Concepts of Authority," *American Anthropologist*, 1955. However, the articles by Blumer and by Sargent and Beardsley referred to in "Selected Readings" for Section Two indicated that the individual "organizes himself to act" and that he has a chameleon-like ability to put on the protective coloring of a given defined situation. Even in the extreme conditions Bettelheim describes above, the individual is sometimes able to at least reserve the right to choose his own attitude. In Manfred H. Kuhn's "Socio-cultural Determinants as Seen through the Amish," in Francis L. K. Hsu (ed.), *Aspects of Culture and Personality* (New York: Abelard-Schuman, 1954), the individual's less than total implication even in an integrated, primary group is seen in the tendency for the old to remove to Florida and enjoy conveniences seriously indicted in their own home communities.

In the field of autonomy see Dorothy Lee, *Freedom and Culture*, (Englewood Cliffs, N.J.: Prentice-Hall, Inc., 1959); Helen Merrell Lynd, *On Shame and the Search for Identity* (New York: Harcourt, Brace, and World, 1958); Erich Fromm, *Escape from Freedom* (New York: Holt, Rinehart, Winston, 1941), and *The Sane Society* (New York: Holt, Rinehart, Winston, 1955); Andraes Angyal, *Foundations for a Science of Personality* (New York: The Commonwealth Fund, 1941); Morris I. Stein and Shirley J. Heinze (eds.), *Creativity and the Individual* (New York: The Free Press, 1960).

4 *Problems of Social Nondefinition (Anomie)*

DURKHEIM'S concept of *anomie* refers to a situation where social structure is ill-defined, lacking, or not sufficiently integrated. Since we are aware of the close relation between the individual and the group structure, it is apparent that the self can be let down by failure of either the self system or the social system to operate with a minimum degree of order. Alienation and other terms are applied to the state of the individual in certain situations, but *anomie* properly applies to a *dérèglement* in the social structure. Parsons puts it well when he says that "The polar antithesis of full institutionalization is . . . *anomie*, the absence of structured complementarity of the interaction process or, what is the same thing, the complete breakdown of normative order . . ."

Cary-Lundberg has given a full description of the condition as Durkheim saw it:

> Durkheim's major concern in *Le Suicide* is with a society as a collectivity, with the state of its *ordre collectif* and of its *conscience collective*. To describe Europe's collective consciousness pre-1900, Durkheim used the term *malaise*. A sickness, not economic but moral, he said, afflicts France and the West because all previously existing *cadres* have either broken down or been worn away by time. The family unit, its members dispersed and divorced, no longer exercises its old cohesive powers. Religion, through no fault of Science, is tossed aside by men who simply will not bow to the limits it places on conduct. The gravitational pull of political parties grows ever weaker, while the mutually binding and integrating demands on workers in the old *corporations des métiers* are binding no more . . . Thus: social disorganization; discarded and discredited norms; a flat unwillingness to accept in any form a checkrein on pleasure, appetites, production or prosperity; this constellation of signs Durkheim translated into Greek. To the negative prefix *a*, he added the plural of laws, *nomous*, and turned the "no-laws" of *anomous* into French as *l'Anomie*.

Although *anomie* is a condition of the social system, it is, as we have said, bound to have significance for the selves belonging to that system. The research report of Ophelia San Juan is hardly a case of advanced *anomie*, but it calls to our minds the relation between self-orientations and the existence or nonexistence of group definitions of the situation. In this report we see that the child's sudden affliction can no longer be explained in terms of traditional causes. The society is in the process of change. Some want the doctor, some want the *herbolario;* some would give the child *pasaw*, others gall of python. There is some relief when the traditional remedy finally works, although the assembled group is additionally reassured by the testimony of the thermometer.

Nahum Z. Medalia and Otto N. Larsen give us another example of behavior that may result when events or assumed events can find no social definition. Although San Juan's report showed no hysteria, it did show a kind of free-floating uneasiness. Absence of social definition requires some kind of accommodation by the self, and sometimes the self is in no condition to take a "rational" position. Considerable irrationality is present in the data analyzed by Medalia and Larsen. They also show how belief in "an unusual physical agent" was related to other factors.

"Discarded and discredited norms," says Cary-Lundberg, tend to leave the individual adrift. Ritual obeisance to norms is not the same as passionate commitment but in our own society verbal affirmation of values is often substituted for active involvement in them. College students can be expected to see the difference, and Goldsen, Rosenberg, Williams, and Suchman indicate that they do. Inquiring minds require more from a society than pious propositions. The section of *What College Students Think* offered here illustrates this with relation to political values. The authors report that some students feel a "certain wistfulness," but find the most sensible course is to "play it cool."

Durkheim pointed out in *Suicide* that anomie may result in "irritated weariness," which can lead to suicide or homicide. Sociologists since Durkheim have examined concrete types of *anomie* and tried to predict behavior not only from such a concrete examination but also from the impact of the anomic condition on persons differently placed in the social structure. Medalia and Larsen, in the article referred to above, showed how irrational responses were related to education and other factors. A. F. Henry and J. F. Short, Jr., in *Suicide and Homicide* show that, given frustration, the choice between suicide and homicide can be significantly related to the actor's membership in high-status or low-status categories. Martin Gold in his article, "Suicide, Homicide, and the Socialization of Aggression," examines the Henry and Short hypothesis and seeks to supplement it with another.

In situations of social *anomie*, the pressure is on the individual to make maximum use of self-resources. Social *anomie* over time tends to deplete these resources. Thus, cumulative disorganization can take place. Corrective devices within the society or the self may check this process. The analysis by Theodore M. Mills in Section Two is relevant here, as are those in the next section, *Self Responses to Social Structure.*

OPHELIA SAN JUAN

Rush to Sick Child

At 12:15 noon of May 3, 1955, I found all the women scampering to the house of Irineo Gonzales. Asking Natividad Francisco Baluyot, I found out the son of Irineo was "*itinitirik ang mata.*" ("Tirik" means to put erect, as a post: when we apply the word to the eyes, we mean the black of the eyes going upwards, a motion usually followed by death, thus we usually get frantic when a sick child does so.) The baby had been having a temperature and crying continuously since morning. The father, attending the *barrio fiesta* of Barranca, Marikina, Rizal, was supposed to bring home a doctor after lunch.

All the houses in the immediate neighborhood up to the house of Simeon Santos were deprived of inhabitants in a matter of seconds. Even the clothes being washed were left without hesitation. I was about to run off too, my own curiosity pulling me. Even a small child was not to be seen left behind. I think even the dogs followed there with their masters. However, I was too hungry and hot to ignore my lunch. Believe me, I gulped everything down without chewing. Natividad and her daughter, Patring, ate in much the same hurried way I did. By the time we were through, however, the excitement had abated. Natalia returned to the house. Nati asked her what happened. They supposed the child's stomach was aching because of the hard lump there and the baby cries out whenever it's touched. The old folks, women mostly, were advising the "*arbulario*" to be called. Nobody called him, though, everybody ordering everybody to do so, but nobody moving actually. Special leaves reputedly good for stomachache, were ordered. Nobody was around to look for them, though. You have to look for them among bamboos they say, and bamboos are pretty thorny. The "arbulario"

These are the research notes of a Philippine girl who was an assistant in the editor's research. These notes have been left as submitted by Miss San Juan except that some spelling has been corrected.

(a mispronounced name for "*herbolario*" or "*erbolario*" coming from the word "herb" which he uses as drugs) was finally given up because they knew he would not come if he knew a doctor would be called later. A man was finally dispatched to fetch home the father and the doctor.

When I arrived there, the people had thinned greatly. The house was still full, though. The mother of the mother of the sick child and her other married sisters were there with their children: Roberta Avelino Baluyot, Estelita Avelino Oblipias, Dorotea Katipunan Baluyot, Remedios Francisco, Paulina Avelino, Basilia Fulgencio, Benita, etc. The children, after being certain there was nothing more to see, went down and played around the house.

The people believed the baby was "*nabalis*" or "*nausog*." "Balis" or "usog" is a half-superstition ailment—any person, hot and tired, can inflict this ailment to somebody he or she sees or talks to. They say a person who is hungry is most susceptible to catching the ailment. They also say that some people have stronger "balis" than others; that is, they either can inflict it more severely or more readily. It's purely unintentional, the infliction taking place without the person's wishing it. Whoever catches it suffers from severe stomachache, his sweat coming out cold and clammy, hands and feet getting cold. These are the usual symptoms, but they can also be absent in some cases. In severe cases, dysentery symptoms are present with fever. The pains will not subside unless the person who inflicted it puts his saliva, usually from betel nut chewing, on the sufferer's stomach. The motion of putting it is customarily that of a cross, but I think it was only from habit. The same effect, to me, will be achieved with or without the cross. The pains usually subside after one saliva-putting, but it may take several times in other cases. Some people don't believe in this; doctors certainly don't. In our place, they have a test to know whether the stomachache is from "balis" or not. The small finger would be aligned with the ring finger—right hand, that is—and if the tip of the small finger goes beyond the last knot of the ring finger, it's "balis." To ascertain who inflicted it is a trial-and-error method: several people will have to be called, all those whom the sick person saw or talked to recently. Whoever heals him is the one. If he saw a great deal of people or if all those already called cannot heal him, we use "*tawas*." The "*tawas*" is a special kind of white powder which when sprinkled on live embers with the appropriate prayers and incantations of someone who knows will take various shapes. The embers would be placed on a tin container and passed over the forehead of the sick person. The face which forms therein would be the face of the one who unintentionally inflicted the pains. We also use the "tawas" to ascertain what ghosts or whatever people from the other world like fairies, goblins, etc., are causing an undiagnosable sickness; it is also used to ascertain who is causing these creatures to inflict the ailment, maybe out of a grudge to the sick person. Also, when a person leaves a seat and another will take that seat, that other will have to tap the still warm seat and say to himself, "*Puwera, usog*" ("Out, usog"). Maybe out of habit, I myself, still do that automatically whenever I take a warm seat just left by its occupant.

Aling Meding (Remedios Francisco) had the seeds of male "*pasaw*" (a kind of wild plant, bitter like anything) upon her arrival, ground into fine powder and mixed with the mother's milk. This was given to the child. A little while later, the gall of python, dried and stored for emergencies like these in most homes with children, was ground and mixed with the mother's milk and given to the baby also.

The conversation centered around the subject of "balis" while we were waiting for Maria Santos, grandmother of the baby, whom they were suspecting to have caused the "usog." A woman remarked that anything bitter to a child who is "nababalis" will increase the pains.

"We have given several bitter doses to the baby," another answered.

For the most part, the visitors' own experiences in connection with "balis" were remembered and recounted. One of the women asked me if we also have "usog" in our place. I said yes.

Natividad Baluyot remembered how her husband just saw her, he did not even talk to her, while they were working in the shoe factory at Marikina, and she immediately felt pains in her stomach and a wall-like thickness of the abdominal muscles. They went home soon and Julio put his saliva on her stomach and she got well.

Another told the story of a man who wouldn't believe in "balis." As if by fate, he was stricken severely. He already believed after that.

When the old woman Maria arrived, she immediately took the baby. The people were loud in their assertions she was the one when the child stopped crying and slept in her arms after she had applied her betel-nut-chewed-saliva on the baby's abdomen. She was denying this. The people around laughed, as if relieved by a signal, because they had to shout at her as she was a little deaf. I could discern that the laughter, which emanated from the people in unison, was not occasioned by her deafness only, although they made it the apparent cause, but more by a feeling of an easing of the tension and apprehension for the baby. For my part, I was not relieved. I did not believe, as they all did, that the child stopped crying because he was well already. The pains might have abated a little, and as he was tired from crying, slept from exhaustion.

Nati took the temperature of the child. She said the child had no more fever. The funny part of this was when Nati gave the thermometer to me and spoke of the child's having no fever as if asking my confirmation. I never could see the mercury in a thermometer, even when I was a child, and I was placed in a tight spot. When I reached for the thermometer, I deliberately brushed my palm over the child's forehead to see if he was still hot. When I felt he had the normal temperature of a well child and I did not see any feverish flush on his cheeks, I looked at the thermometer and, without seeing any mercury mark, said his temperature was normal. The thermometer soon passed around, each one asking whoever seemed to know where the mercury is or where they can see the mark, since they did not know the white substance is called mercury. There was trouble at first before his temperature could be taken. They did not want to waken the child and so they could not open his mouth to place the thermometer in. I suggested the armpit and nobody contradicted me.

As the people thinned, only the sisters of the baby's mother remained, plus a few near neighbors. The sisters let their own children sleep and then continued their conversation.

Several other women from the other side of the barrio arrived later. They stayed in the kitchen, talking there.

NAHUM Z. MEDALIA
and OTTO N. LARSEN

Diffusion and Belief in a Collective Delusion: The Seattle Windshield Pitting Epidemic

WHILE individuals may at times lose touch with reality as their culture defines it, whole communities ordinarily do not. Yet instances are on record when this has very nearly happened: people in Mattoon, Illinois, believed for a few days in September, 1945, that a "phantom anesthetist" was prowling their town;[1] and a Martian invasion took place in the minds of many persons in the New York City area on October 30, 1938.[2] Russia's Sputniks may be expected to give rise to a wide variety of mass hallucinatory phenomena similar to those that followed our first H-bomb explosions in March, 1954. This paper analyzes one such reaction: the windshield pitting epidemic that broke out in Seattle, Washington, in the Spring of 1954.

Beginning March 23, 1954, Seattle newspapers carried intermittent reports of damage to automobile windshields in a city 80 miles to the north. Police suspected vandalism but were unable to gather proof. On the morning of April 14, newspapers reported windshield damage in a town about 65 miles from Seattle; that afternoon cars in a naval air station only 45 miles from the northern limits of the city were "peppered." On the same evening the first strike occurred in Seattle

Reprinted from American Sociological Review, *April, 1958, pp. 180-186, by permission of the authors and the journal.*

Read at the Southern Sociological Society meeting, April, 1956. The final section of this paper has been revised, following discussion by William L. Kolb. The authors are grateful to George A. Lundberg and to Harold W. Stoke, formerly Dean of the Graduate School, University of Washington, for their encouragement of the study.

1. D. M. Johnson, "The Phantom Anesthetist of Mattoon," in *Readings in Social Psychology*, edited by Guy E. Swanson, T. M. Newcomb, and Eugene H. Hartley, New York: Holt, Rinehart, Winston, 1952, pp. 208-219.

2. Hadley Cantril, "The Invasion from Mars," *ibid.*, pp. 198-207.

itself: between April 14 and 15, 242 persons telephoned the Seattle Police Department reporting damage to over 3,000 automobiles. Many of these calls came from parking lots, service stations, and so on. Most commonly, the damage reported to windshields consisted of pitting marks that grew into bubbles in the glass of about the size of a thumbnail. On the evening of the 15th, the Mayor of Seattle declared the damage was no longer a police matter and made an emergency appeal to the Governor and to President Eisenhower for help. Many persons covered their windshields with floor mats or newspaper; others simply kept their automobiles garaged. Conjecture as to cause ranged from meteoric dust to sandflea eggs hatching in the glass, but centered on possible radioactive fallout from the Eniwetok H-bomb tests conducted earlier that year. In support of this view many drivers claimed that they found tiny, metallic-looking particles about the size of a pinhead on their car windows. Newspapers also mentioned the possibility that the concern with pitting might have sprung largely from mass hysteria: people looking *at* their windshields for the first time, instead of *through* them. On April 16, calls to police dropped from 242 to 46; 10 persons called the police on the 17th, but from the 18th on no more calls were received about the subject of pitting.

Another index of the concern with windshield pitting may be seen in the rise and decline in the combined number of column inches of windshield news in the two Seattle daily newspapers during March and April. As the figures in Table 1 show, the story grew gradually, with

Table 1. Column Inches of News Concerning Windshield Phenomena in Two Seattle Daily Newspapers

Date		Column Inches
March:	23	2.0
	25	2.0
	28	2.7
	30	5.2
April:	13	14.0
	14	22.0
	15	248.0
	16	210.0
	17	109.0
	18	62.0
	19	11.0

only occasional reports, until April 13, reached a peak of interest on April 15, and became newspaper history after the 19th.

On June 10th, the University of Washington Environmental Research Laboratory, assigned by the Governor in April to investigate the pitting, issued its report.[3] This report, prepared by a chemist, stated

3. Harley H. Bovee, "Report on the 1954 Windshield Pitting Phenomenon in

that there was no evidence of pitting that could not be explained by ordinary road damage: "The number of pits increases with the age and mileage of the car." The puzzling little black particles found on many automobiles turned out under analysis to be cenospheres, formed by improper combustion of bituminous coal. According to the report, "Cenospheres are not new to Seattle. They have been observed in years past and they can be observed in cars in downtown Seattle today. They are incapable of pitting windshields by impact or otherwise." In its key passage the report concludes:

> Although there is a considerable body of testimony from reputable witnesses to the effect that windshields were pitted by some mysterious cause in the space of a few minutes or hours during the "epidemic," it has *not* been possible to substantiate a single one of these statements by scientific observation. Actually, the observed facts tend to contradict such statements.[4]

What, then, is the origin of mass delusions such as this? What is the pattern of their initial diffusion in the community? What is the process of their disappearance? How is susceptibility to belief in the delusion distributed? Which persons are most susceptible, which least, and why? The remainder of this paper will deal with these questions. Description and analysis of this case may help us to understand not only events that the common culture labels transient delusions, but also those more persistent hallucinations that take the form of outlandish conceptions of groups other than one's own, for example, to which the culture may give an accent of reality itself.

As a population basis for these inquiries, telephone subscribers in Seattle listed as private individuals were selected. The universe consisted of 179,560 names, representing telephones in approximately 84 per cent of the dwelling units located in the city as of April, 1954. Three references were made to a table of random numbers to select each person for the sample. First a page in the telephone book was drawn, then a column on the page, and finally a person in the column. By this procedure, a list of 1,000 names was compiled which constituted about one-half of one per cent of the universe. In common with many samples drawn from telephone subscription lists, the present sample was biased, compared with the Seattle population as a whole, by underrepresentation of young people, males, and of subjects with less than eleven years of schooling. This bias may simply mean that our findings concerning the collective delusion are a conservative estimate of what transpired in the total population.

---

the State of Washington," *mimeographed,* Environmental Research Laboratory, University of Washington, June 10, 1954.

4. *Ibid.,* p. 3.

The sample was interviewed by telephone between 4 and 10 P.M. on Monday, April 19, and 964 responses were obtained. Since only 4 per cent of the sample failed to answer, the possibility of systematic bias due to non-response is small. April 19th was chosen as the interview date

Table 2. A Comparison of the Characteristics of the Survey Sample and the Total Population of Seattle

Characteristic	*Total Population* (N=467,591)*	*Survey Sample (N=964)*
Sex:		
Male	50.0	45.3
Female	50.0	53.5
No response		1.2
Total per cent	100.0	100.0
Education:		
0-11 years	45.2	23.5
12 years	28.2	37.9
13 plus years	23.4	29.9
No response	3.2	8.7
Total per cent	100.0	100.0
Age:		
Below 24	33.9	5.9
25-44	32.1	52.8
45-64	23.8	26.8
Over 65	10.2	8.5
No response		6.0
Total per cent	100.0	100.0

*Source: 1950 Census of Population Bulletin P-D51.

because it was close enough to the peak of the pitting epidemic to make possible valid recollections of opinion during that period, yet far enough removed for attitudes relating to extinction of interest in the episode to assert themselves. Interviewers asked open-ended questions directed at the respondent's knowledge or experience of windshield damage; beliefs concerning the cause and duration of the epidemic; initial source of information; and protective action taken, if any.

Extent of Diffusion of Pitting News

How widely diffused was the news of windshield pitting? Interviewers found that 92.6 per cent of the 964 telephone respondents anwered "yes" to the question, "Have you heard of any unusual experience with windshields in Seattle recently?" The remainder, 7.4 per cent

(69 persons), had not heard of the windshield situation. This points to the existence in the urban community of a small core of persons who somehow remain unaware of public events despite extensive and prominent mass media coverage. Compared with the knowers, these non-knowers included fewer car owners, more females, more elderly people, and more people with relatively little education. Thus, 36 per cent of the non-knowers had no car, as against 13 per cent of the knowers; 60 per cent as against 53 per cent were females; 30 per cent as against 11 per cent were over 65 years of age, and 37 per cent of the non-knowers as compared to 22 per cent of the knowers were without a high school diploma.

Pattern of Initial Diffusion of the News

To discover how news of the pitting epidemic became diffused, interviewers asked: "How did this windshield situation in Seattle *first* come to your attention?" The answers to this question were classified into five media categories, as indicated in Table 3.

Table 3. Channel of Initial Contact with Windshield News

News Source	*Per Cent Naming Source*	
Newspapers	51	
Interpersonal	19	
Radio	18	
Television	6	
Direct experience	6	
Total per cent	100	(N=895)

The report of channel usage suggests that the early stages of the epidemic cannot be characterized as one dominated by word-of-mouth transmission as in a highly charged rumor situation. The tabulation indicates rather that the more formal instruments of mass communication had a considerable direct responsibility in bringing the pitting phenomenon to the attention of a public: three out of four of our respondents claimed they heard the news first over some channel of mass communication.

This finding of the relative role of mass media and interpersonal communication is consistent with the results of a study made a year earlier in Seattle regarding the diffusion of the news concerning the death of a prominent national political figure.[5] Contrary to the findings of the

5. Otto N. Larsen and Richard J. Hill, "Mass Media and Interpersonal Communication in the Diffusion of a News Event," *American Sociological Review*, 19 (August, 1954), pp. 426-433.

latter study, however, the present results show newspapers rather than radio to be the dominant medium as the initial source of information. What factors might have contributed to the differential prominence of radio and newspapers in the two studies? First, during the windshield event two daily newspapers were being published in the city, while at the time of the story concerning the political figure only one paper was published due to a strike involving the second paper. Perhaps of greater significance are differences in the timing and the content of the news. The windshield news was local, had built up over a longer period of time, and involved a more complex content, whereas the information about the Senator's death was a single item relayed over the radio three hours before it could appear in the first edition of the Seattle newspaper. While radio is generally considered the most adaptable and efficient mass medium for rapid coverage of the news, the windshield situation suggests that for certain kinds of information, the newspapers, without benefit of a head-start, are able to far outdistance other media in giving a public its first remembered contact with the news.

A closer look at the initial pattern of diffusion shows the role of the *newspaper* was about the same for men as for women (52 versus 51 per cent); that women were more apt than men to learn the news via the *radio* (21 versus 15 per cent) and *television* (8 versus 4 per cent); and that men claimed to have *directly observed* damage more frequently than women (8 versus 3 per cent) and also heard the news first via *interpersonal channels* more frequently than women (21 versus 17 per cent).

When these distinctions are qualified by three levels of educational attainment we find that men with college education learned the news first through newspapers to a significantly greater extent (60 per cent) than did any other educational sub-group of either sex ($P<.05$ for all comparisons);[6] that women of the lowest level of education heard the news first on television to a significantly greater extent (15 per cent) than did any other sub-group; that interpersonal communication did not vary significantly within either sex by education; and that men on the lowest educational level claimed direct experience with pitting significantly more often than any other group (12 per cent). This latter fact may reflect a more personal interest taken in cars by men than by women, either for occupational reasons or in conformance with the culture of the male sex role. We may also speculate that the activities of this latter group of persons, along with the performance of the mass media, were important in building up the early stages of the epidemic. Having heard on the morning of April 14th that a town 65 miles north had been

6. Throughout this paper "signficant" refers only to differences beyond the .05 level of confidence.

"peppered," and on that same afternoon that the naval station 45 miles from the city had been hit, men of relatively low educational attainment, particularly bus or truck drivers and parking lot or filling station attendants, may have been looking for pits on the night of April 14th. It may be hypothesized that such men were especially susceptible to belief in pitting, motivated to relay the story to others, and in a good position to do so.

Defining the Situation: Patterns of Belief

Definition of the windshield pitting situation presents a case of public response to highly contradictory news stimuli. For about three weeks prior to April 15, the police of communities north of Seattle were principally responsible for defining the situation—mainly in terms of vandalism. As police were unable to discover evidence of vandalism, however, the news emphasis changed to the theme of "mystery": *Life* magazine talked of "ghostly little pellets" in its report from a city north of Seattle on April 12; the *Seattle Times* referred to "elusive B-B snipers" on the evening of April 13. When the flood of telephone calls came to the Seattle police between the evenings of the 14th and 15th of April, the situation clearly called for redefinition. News media gave widest publicity to the redefinition supplied by the mayor of Seattle who declared, "The damage to windshields is no longer a police matter," and went on to refer to the Eniwetok H-bomb tests as a possible cause.

Concurrently newspapers began to quote physical scientists, engineers, and automobile glass "experts," as well as police, on the nature and the origin of the pitting. Content analysis of the statements made by these various defining agents shows that the physicial scientists, all from the University of Washington, gave about equal emphasis to ordinary road damage, hysteria, and to air pollution from industrial waste. Engineers, mostly from Boeing Aircraft, without exception propounded some physical cause for the unusual pitting activity; included among these were supercharged particles from the H-bomb explosion, a shifting in the earth's magnetic field, and extremely high frequency electronic waves from a giant new radio transmitter located near Seattle. Automobile experts divided their opinion between atomic ash and vandalism. The police, subsequent to April 15, gave the widest and most contradictory array of causes: atomic ash; air pollution from industrial waste; atmospheric conditions (unspecified); a chemical agent of uncertain origin; ordinary road damage; hysteria; something other than ordinary road damage; and, most frequently, vandalism.

Under these circumstances, what beliefs did our sample of telephone subscribers hold? We asked the question, "What do you think caused this?"—"this" referring to whatever the respondents said they had heard was happening to windshields. Responses yielded the following categories: *Believers*, *Undecided*, *Skeptics*, and *Refusals*, distributed as indicated in Table 4.

Table 4. Classification of Respondents by Their Definition of the Cause of the Situation*

Classification of Response	*N*	*Per Cent*
Believers: Unusual damage caused by unusual physical agent	450	50
Undecided: Had heard many explanations but, even after probing, were unwilling to suggest one most likely cause†	227	26
Skeptics: Dubious of anything other than people noting ordinary road damage	187	21
Refusals: Would not respond to or even consider this particular question	22	3
Totals	886	100

*69 non-knowers and 9 knowers for whom some background data (age, sex, etc.) are missing are not included in this table.

†Includes 33 respondents (3.7 per cent of total *N*) who gave only a "negative cause"—e.g., "not vandalism"—as explanation of pitting.

Four days after the peak presentation of the windshield news in the press, the majority of the respondents in our sample were *Believers*. That is, they were positive in their contention that there had been unusual pitting activity and that this had been caused by some unusual physical agent. The single explanation most frequently mentioned was the H-bomb. Approximately one of three (31 per cent) of the Believers attributed windshield pitting to the after-effects of thermonuclear explosions that had taken place earlier in the Pacific testing grounds. Other explanations offered by the Believers included vandalism, cosmic rays, chemicals, and meteorites.

What were the characteristics of the persons classified as Believers, Undecided, Skeptics, and Refusals? The four groups did not differ significantly in age distribution, but were distinguished by some significant differences in automobile ownership, sex, and education.

Automobile ownership was significantly higher among the "Skeptics" than in any other group: 94 per cent ownership versus 84, 84, and 85 per cent. This fact would seem to dispose of the possibility that the skepticism expressed in denying any "unusual" windshield activity might stem from the lack of possible personal involvement in the threat situation.

The sex distribution of the respondents in the four categories is reported in Table 5. Men and women were about equally apt to be "Believers" and about equally apt to refuse answers to the questions concerning cause of the pitting phenomenon. Men were significantly more skeptical than women, however, while there was a greater but

Table 5. Classification of Cause by Sex

Causal Category	Male	(Per Cent)	Female	
Believers	49		52	
Undecided	20		29	
Skeptics	28		15	
Refusals	3		4	
Total per cent	100	(N=412)	100	(N=474)

not significant proportion of women in the "Undecided" category than men.

The effects of education by sex on the presumed causes of pitting were also determined. When three levels of education (less than high school graduate, high school graduate, some college) are introduced into the analysis, there is a fairly consistent reduction of the proportion of "Undecided" and "Refusals" in both sexes, with an increase in education suggesting a greater degree of opinion structuring. There was also a consistent increase in skepticism among both sexes with an increase in education. The change was particularly marked among men, only 10.2 per cent of whom at the lowest level of education were Skeptics while 34.3 per cent of the men at the highest level of education were in this category. The corresponding range for women is from 11.5 to 16.4 per cent.

A contrasting trend develops between men and women "Believers" when education is considered. With increasing education, the proportion of male "Believers" decreases but the proportion of female "Believers" increases. Thus, 59.3 per cent of the males at the lowest level of education, 48.0 per cent at the middle level, and 40.7 per cent at the college level are "Believers." The corresponding figures for the females are 49.2, 53.3, and 54.8 per cent.

What conclusions do these trends indicate concerning susceptibility to mass illusion? The results are not entirely consistent with the findings of two widely quoted studies in mass hysteria and illusion, "The Phantom Anesthetist of Mattoon,"[7] and "The Invasion from Mars."[8] These studies relate belief in collective delusions to an individual psychological factor, suggestibility; and suggestibility in turn to low educational level. The Mattoon research draws an additional inference, that women are more suggestible than men.[9] In the present instance, we have seen that, while there was a higher proportion of "Skeptics" among men, there was no significant difference between the proportions of men

7. Johnson, *op. cit.*
8. Cantril, *op. cit.*
9. Johnson, *op. cit.*, p. 217.

and women who *believed* in the occurrence of unusual windshield pitting; moreover, in terms of "Believers," the single most "suggestible" group among our respondents consisted of men of low educational level. Finally, education appears to function quite differently for men and women insofar as their susceptibility to collective delusion is concerned. The concomitant of increasing educational level among women was a simple decrease in the number of "Undecided," with a consequent increase in the postively structured but contradictory categories of "Believer" and "Skeptic." The concomitant of increasing educational level among men, on the other hand, was a reduction in both the "Undecided" and the "Believer" categories, increasing thereby only the number of "Skeptics." These facts suggest that the operation of sex role and formal education in susceptibility to collective delusion is more complex than has been hitherto suspected.

Extinction of Interest in the Windshield Pitting Epidemic

Why did interest in the windshield pitting epidemic decline, and decline so rapidly, after the peak of the pitting news on April 15? What implications does this decline suggest for the disappearance of mass delusions generally?

Johnson, in the Mattoon study cited above, draws three conclusions about the extinction of interest in mass delusions. Referring to the mushrooming concern over the "phantom anesthetist," he writes that "such acute outbursts are necessarily self-limiting."[10] The reason given for the self-limiting nature is that "the bizarre details which captured the public imagination at the beginning of the episode became rather ridiculous when studied more leisurely." Finally, Johnson claims that the critical attitude induced by reflection increases and spreads; in consequence "it is proper to say that the wave of suggestibility in Mattoon left a wave of contrasuggestibility in its wake."[11] According to this view, extinction of interest in mass delusions is rationalistically tied to more accurate perception of reality which eventuates ultimately in a wave of contrasuggestibility.

Contrary to Johnson's conclusions, the present study suggests that "acute outbursts" of mass delusion are not necessarily self-limiting. Interest and belief in a phenomenon for which no scientific basis can be found may well persist for periods of time even in a culture presumably committed to science as the ultimate test of reality. Residents of the area north of Seattle maintained a high level of interest in the

10. *Ibid.*, p. 218.
11. *Ibid.*, p. 219.

mystery windshield pitting for almost a month before the pitting reached Seattle. Similarly, sightings of "flying saucers" are reported frequently enough to require a continuing agency for their investigation in the Air Force.[12]

Why then did concern over windshield pitting in Seattle decrease so markedly only four days after the peak outburst of interest expressed in the press and in the telephone calls to the police? The explanation does not seem to lie in a correction of the delusion by scientifically more accurate reality perception, for, as we have shown, on April 19, a majority of our respondents still believed that some physical agency had caused widespread damage to windshields in Seattle; only 21 per cent, the "Skeptics," committed themselves to the conclusion that the whole episode was based on illusion. These facts do not support the connection between interest and belief postulated by Johnson; for they show that *interest* in a mass delusion may very well decline, while *belief* in the delusion persists.

As an alternative hypothesis, we suggest that two considerations may have accounted for the precipitous decline of interest by the press and by the public in the Seattle pitting episode. The first is that the pitting became assimilated to a cause itself regarded as highly transient or episodic: the hydrogen bomb tests at Eniwetok earlier in March. In such a context it became meaningful for people to think that the pitting might have occurred in the space of a few hours or minutes on April 15 rather than over a longer period of time.

The second consideration is that the perception of windshield pitting, and the magical activities associated with this perception, succeeded in bringing to a focus and in reducing diffuse anxieties that may have served to heighten susceptibility to the delusion in the first place. The widespread association of windshield pitting with the H-bomb explosions points again to these as possible sources of the anxiety. During March and April, Seattle papers carried intermittent reports of the tests and the fall-out, hinting darkly at doom and disaster, illustrated by the following headlines:

"3 H-Bomb Victims Face Death: Doctor Reports on Fishermen."
"Witness Says: Hydrogen Test Out of Control."
"Disaster Plan Result of H-Bomb Study."
"AEC Discloses Blast Amid Mounting Concern."
"Atomic Scare Ties Up Japan Fishing Fleet."

---

12. For an account of "flying saucer" research carried on in the Air Force "Project Blue Book," see E. J. Ruppelt, *The Report on Unidentified Flying Objects,* New York: Doubleday, 1956. See also Siegfried Mandel, "The Latest on the Flying Saucer," *Saturday Review,* 39 (February 25, 1956), pp. 23 and 29.

The windshield pitting epidemic may have relieved diffuse anxieties built up by this situation in three ways. First, it focused these anxieties on a narrower area of experience, automobile windshields. Phenomena that had long passed unnoticed in the periphery of awareness—cenospheres, or small sooty particles collecting on cars; nicks and pits in windshields—now became charged with new significance. Second, the pitting epidemic may have loosened the tensions growing out of fixation on an inevitable coming blow: something was bound to happen to *us* as a result of the H-bomb tests—windshields became pitted—it's happened—now *that* threat is over. Third, the magical practices which accompanied the epidemic—for example, calling the police, appealing to the Governor and President for help, covering windshields and cleaning them—all these activities served to give people the sense that they were "doing something" about the danger that threatened.

Extinction of the windshield pitting epidemic, following this interpretation, occurred not because of a wave of contrasuggestibility, but rather because the pitting, as a new, non-institutionalized anxiety-provoking situation, was given symbolic recognition and magical control. To the extent that this type of hypothesis is supported by further research, it follows that to correct mass delusions one should not wait confidently for a wave of contrasuggestion to gather force. Nor does subsiding public concern with a delusion indicate a rejection of it in favor of reality. Reality itself will be given a magical definition so long as the anxieties that the magic symbolizes are not or cannot be dealt with through rational control.

ROSE K. GOLDSEN,
MORRIS ROSENBERG, ROBIN M. WILLIAMS, JR.,
and EDWARD A. SUCHMAN

Political Apathy, Economic Conservatism

The investigator attempting to describe the political flavor of contemporary American campuses is immediately and forcefully struck by two themes. The first is what seems to be a remarkable absence of any intense or consuming political beliefs, interests or convictions on the part of the college students. The second is extreme political and economic conservatism. Both are in marked contrast to the radicalism usually attributed to American college students in the thirties, and said to be a traditional aspect of student culture in other countries.

Political Apathy

The American college students we studied simply do not, as a group, get "worked up" about political matters. The tendency seems to be for this lack for feeling about politics to become more characteristic of the college students rather than less characteristic. For example, we had asked: "Do you ever get as worked up about something that happens in political or public affairs as you do about something that happens in your personal life?" On all the campuses we studied, students who responded "yes" to this question were

From R. K. Goldsen, M. Rosenberg, R. M. Williams, and E. A. Suchman, What College Students Think, *with permission of authors and publisher, D. Van Nostrand Co., Inc., Princeton, N.J. Copyright 1960 by D. Van Nostrand Co.*

in the minority.[1] At Cornell where we can compare responses the same students made to this question at two points in time, it turned out that a majority of the panel (54 per cent) had acknowledged in the earlier questionnaire such feelings of personal involvement in a political occurrence, but after a lapse of only two years, the comparable proportion had dwindled to 42 per cent: and this in 1952, at the height of the McCarthy era. Moreover two-thirds of those who changed at all in this regard (64 per cent) no longer, they said, ever felt "worked up" about political affairs, while only one-third indicated they had developed such feelings while at college.

It is very tempting to interpret his sort of lack of involvement and apparent disinterest in political matters as indicative principally of apathy, complacency, and unquestioning contentment with the *status quo*. Undoubtedly such an interpretation is justified in many cases. But we have found that what seems to be aloofness to political matters may sometimes be coupled with a certain realistic disenchantment with issues and causes, a sober wariness, perhaps even a certain wistfulness.

> Yes, since you ask me, I do sometimes find myself getting worked up about politics. Yes, I'm interested; and when the time comes I'll do everything that has to be done. But everything in its proper place, is my motto. No sense in getting carried away.

> When I read about peace strikes and picket lines on the campuses in the thirties, it makes me feel a little superior because the "causes" turned out to be phony. Sometimes I feel a little envious, too, because they had so much conviction that there was an easy answer. I guess today we know it's much more complicated. Anyway we play it cool.

Political Conservatism

The students' political beliefs, moreover, are decidedly conservative. Our analysis of their sober conservatism begins modestly, by examining

1. See Appendix 1 for the distribution of responses to this question at the universities polled. As this book goes to press, there seem to be some indications that this trend may be beginning to reverse itself and that perhaps college students' concern about political affairs and public issues may be reviving. For example, the Student Council at Cornell University has recognized as a legitimate campus activity (October 1960) a self-styled political party for students. The party calls itself *Action*, and declares that it is against discrimination in off-campus housing and against compulsory ROTC. A similar student political party—Slate—exists at the University of California. An Associated Press dispatch dated October 21, 1959, reported that a freshman student at the University of California engaged in a fifty-one hour hunger strike to call to the attention of the Board of Regents of the state his conscientious objection to compulsory ROTC. These sorts of occurrences have been notable for their absence from campuses during the last decade. Are they now straws in the wind?

simply their political party alignment. For although many of the students cannot vote, they customarily express sympathy and support for the political parties and the national and local candidates in an election.

At first glance, it may seem that large proportions of the students reject the traditional political parties. "Do you consider yourself a Republican, a Democrat, or an Independent in most political matters?" we asked. On the campuses we polled, 29 per cent said that they were Republicans and 26 per cent said Democrats. The greatest single proportion of responses—42 per cent—clustered in the category "Independent"; less than one per cent checked "other," and two per cent neglected to answer the question. Even at the conservative Eastern universities (Yale, Dartmouth, Wesleyan, and Cornell)—the only campuses where the "Independent ticket" did not run ahead of the major parties—still, around 40 per cent of the students declared that they were "Independent" in most political matters.

Table 1. Political Party Preference of College Students (Eleven Universities): "Do you consider yourself a Republican, a Democrat or an Independent in most political matters?"

	PERCENTAGE* WHO RESPOND					
	Republican	*Democrat*	*Independent*	*"Other"*	*No Answer*	*Total*
All students	29	26	42	1	2	(2975)
Dartmouth	47	9	42	1	1	(365)
Yale	47	14	36	1	1	(297)
Wesleyan	44	16	37	1	2	(277)
Cornell:						
Men	44	15	37	1	4	(655)
Women	35	15	46	1	3	(245)
Michigan	38	17	44	1	—	(488)
UCLA	29	32	37	1	2	(467)
Harvard	28	22	44	2	4	(453)
Wayne	17	27	53	1	2	(519)
Texas	13	42	44	1	—	(516)
North Carolina	13	41	42	2	2	(414)
Fisk	7	36	53	1	3	(134)

*Percentages are to be added horizontally.

The preponderance of students who call themselves Independent, however, does *not* mean that a substantial proportion of the students have any serious disagreement with either of the two major political parties. Our analysis of the beliefs of those who say they are independent shows that when it comes to choosing up sides on specific issues, they are middle-of-the-roaders. They tend to take a position left of the Republicans but right of the Democrats (see Table 6). If the college students call themselves politically independent it is decidedly *not* because they are hungry for some different kind of political fare. A more likely explanation is either that their allegiances are not yet fixed, or that they prefer to avoid a party label, liking to think that they consider each issue and each campaign on its own merits.

The Search for the Rebels

Even if most students have little interest in opposing the official political and social forms of American society, and even if they stand staunchly behind the existing social order, they could still be politically rebellious without necessarily espousing unorthodox political beliefs. For example, it has often been claimed that the social protest of flaming youth in the twenties, and the political and economic protest of college students in the depression years, really was a displaced rebelliousness; that only ostensibly was it directed against society and really had its roots in opposition to one's own parents as surrogates of that society. It could be that such political opposition to one's parents still exists on the campuses, simply taking the more conservative forms which are modish today for college students. Perhaps without abandoning one of the traditional political parties, the students nevertheless rebel against their parents by espousing—not an unorthodox position, but a political position which is opposed to that of their parents.

Even this rather tortured search for some kind of political rebelliousness, however, proves fruitless. Only one out of twenty-five students

Table 2. Political Affiliation of Sons Follows Political Affiliation of Fathers (Eleven Universities): "How does your father usually vote?"

Do you consider yourself, in most political matters . . .	*PERCENTAGE* WHO RESPOND:* Republican	Democrat	Independent
Total	(1025)	(1077)	(412)
Republican	65	7	12
Democrat	4	52	12
Independent	29	39	75
Other	1	1	—
No answer	1	1	—

*Omits 461 students who did not give father's usual vote.

with Republican fathers favored the Democrats, and only one out of fourteen students with Democratic fathers favored the Republicans. So strong is this tendency to echo one's father's political preference, that three-quarters of the students who had said their fathers were Independent reported that they, too, were Independent.

The present-day college student, then, is not even in political revolt against his parents. If there is any "rebelliousness" it runs the gamut from

A to B, culminating in the adoption of an "Independent" political position. And where this mild rebellion does occur, it is more likely to be in the conservative (Republican) direction.

But what about the small group of students who *did* rebel—students who supported a political party different from that of their parents? Perhaps in this group, at least, we might encounter a hard core of youthful rebels—a group of angry, or at least irritated young men who, in liberating themselves from the political traditions of their parents, have likewise declared their independence from the traditional thinking of their sociological status-groups. But no: analysis of the factors related to "rebellion" against father's vote indicates quite an opposite tendency. It turns out that students who go contrary to the political views of their fathers, are finding a way of adjusting their own political views more nearly to the accepted norms of certain sociological groups to which they feel an allegiance.

Here are a few examples which we have selected to illustrate the process. Take the matter of religious affiliation. We know that Jews and Catholics tend to vote Democratic, while Protestants tend to vote Republican. Thus, among the Republican students who came from Republican homes, only one-fifth were Jews, Catholics, or of mixed religious background. But among students who had turned *away* from their parents' Republicanism to take up the Democratic cause, roughly half were members of these minority religious groups. In the same way, among Democratic students who came from Democratic homes, about half were Protestants. Yet, those who abandoned their father's Democratic position to support the Republican party were principally Protestants (65 per cent). Have they "rebelled" against their fathers, or have they reverted to the traditional vote of their religious group, which their fathers had abandoned?

Now take the matter of economic group. We know that wealthier voters tend to prefer the Republican party, poorer ones the Democratic party. Among the Republican students who came from Republican homes, 21 per cent reported that their father's annual earnings were over $20,000. But among the students who had "rebelled" against their father's Republicanism by turning to the Democrats, only 6 per cent came from such wealthy homes. Similarly, among Democratic students who came from Democratic homes, 67 per cent reported their parents' annual earnings as less than $7,500. But among those who "rebelled" against a Democratic father by turning to the Republican party, only 56 per cent came from these lower income homes. Have they "rebelled" against their fathers, or have they reverted to the traditional vote of their economic class?

As a final example, we consider the dominant political atmosphere of the college campuses. At six of the campuses we studied, the Republican party was more popular than the Democratic; at five, the reverse situation prevailed. (See Table 1). Forty-five per cent of the students who "rebelled" against Republican fathers by turning to the Democratic party were studying at one of the heavily Democratic campuses, while only 27 per cent of those who kept up their father's Republicanism were at one of these campuses. This tendency to adopt the political views more characteristic of the campus where one is studying exists also on Democratic campuses. Again, are they rebelling against their fathers or adopting a campus norm?

Table 3. Political Affiliation of Fathers and Sons According to Religious Affiliation, Family Income, and Predominant Political Party on Campus* (Eleven Universities)

	PERCENTAGE IN EACH CATEGORY			
	Both Republican	Father Rep. Son Demo.	Both Democrat	Father Demo. Son Rep.
Total†	(664)	(45)	(565)	(75)
Religious affiliation				
Protestant	79	51	51	67
Catholic	7	9	16	17
Jewish	2	33	24	8
Mixed	9	6	4	4
Other	2	—	4	4
No answer	1	—	—	—
Father's annual income				
Under $7,500	40	56	67	56
$7,500-9,999	17	13	13	17
$10,000-19,999	20	20	12	12
$20,000 or more	21	6	5	10
No answer	2	4	3	5
Predominant political party on campus				
Heavily Republican‡	72	54	25	36
Heavily Democratic§	27	45	75	65

*See Appendix 14 for similar distributions of students who said they or their fathers were independent voters.

†Omits 496 who could not be classified on both variables.

‡This category includes Cornell, Dartmouth, Harvard, Michigan, Wesleyan, Yale, where the number of students who said they usually align themselves with the Republicans exceeded the number reporting Democratic sympathies.

§This category includes UCLA, North Carolina, Texas, Wayne, and Fisk, where the number of students preferring the Democrats exceeded the number preferring the Republican party.

This very crude analysis of something as simple as abandoning one's father's political party, sets the stage for the development of the principal theme of this section. The students are conservative, they are not rebellious, they are as little disposed to political nonconformism as they are to social nonconformism.

Economic Liberalism and Conservatism

A source of confusion in discussions of "liberalism" or "conservatism" is that at least three different components of these beliefs are often treated together. First, the economic and political elements of liberalism may be considered as if they were identical and interchangeable. While it is true that these two strands are frequently intertwined, they are nevertheless conceptually distinct. It is quite possible to hold beliefs which are politically liberal but economically conservative, even though economic laissez-faire today is a conservative philosophy while political laissez-faire is liberal. Thomas Jefferson's position—that governments have no right to restrict *either* free enterprise, *or* individual liberties—would label him today, for example, an economic conservative but a political liberal. Similarly all other combinations are possible and, in fact, do exist.[2]

At the same time, economic liberalism or conservatism may be obscured by certain strands of humanitarian beliefs which may well cut across both positions. Values of rugged individualism, and of humanitarianism, often contradictory to each other, have existed simultaneously on the American scene since the early days of the republic. Parrington has noted, for example:

> At the beginning of our national existence two rival philosophies contended for supremacy in America: the humanitarian philosophy of the French Enlightenment, based on the conception of human perfectibility and postulating as its objective an equalitarian democracy in which the political state should function as the servant to the common well-being; and the English philosophy of laissez-faire, based on the assumed universality of the acquisitive instinct and postulating a social order answering the needs of an abstract "economic man," in which the state should function in the interest of trade.[3]

Discussions of liberalism and conservatism are often further confused by defining what is basically a set of philosophical assumptions as if they were identical with one's opinion on a current issue. While given

2. The following scheme may clarify the point. It grew out of certain ideas suggested in Harold D. Lasswell, *Power and Personality* (New York, W. W. Norton and Co., 1948).

		ECONOMIC LAISSEZ FAIRE	
		Pro	Con
Political laissez faire:	Pro	Jeffersonian Democrat	Twentieth century American liberal
	Con	Reactionary	Corporate state, fascist, communist

3. Vernon L. Parrington, *Main Currents in American Thought* (New York, Harcourt, Brace & World, 1930), Book III, p. xxiii.

attitudes and opinions may well be highly correlated with liberalism or conservatism, they are bound by time and space to particular events and situations, and thus can by no means be considered defining characteristics of a philosophy. For example, at the turn of the century, a favorable attitude toward women voting might have been highly correlated with "liberalism." Today, however, for sociological and historical reasons, it is virtually irrelevant in this country.

We shall try to take up in turn each of these strands of liberalism and conservatism among the college students, focusing in this chapter[4] particularly on their economic beliefs, and reserving for a later chapter [of *What College Students Think*][4] discussion of their political beliefs and international attitudes. We shall report here as well some indications of their reactions to economic issues, and the stands they take on certain of these issues which have humanitarian overtones, relating them where possible to these basic economic assumptions.

. . . Either a Little Liberal or Else a Little Conservative

The conflicting themes of humanitarianism and rugged individualism which Parrington referred to are quite discernible in the opinions which the college students expressed. They are wholeheartedly *for* rugged individualism of a free-enterprise economic system; but many of them are nevertheless willing to abandon some aspects of a classic laissez-faire philosophy. For example, the majority (62 per cent) agree that "democracy depends fundamentally on the existence of free business enterprise." Considerably fewer, but still a majority (59 per cent), agree that "the 'welfare state' tends to destroy individual initiative." Yet only a minority (38 per cent) are willing to go so far as to declare that "government planning almost inevitably results in the loss of essential liberties and freedom"; and still fewer accept the unequivocal Jeffersonian pronouncement, "The best government is the one which governs least" (31 per cent agree).

Their attitudes towards specific economic issues indicate, moreover, that many students retreat from a strictly laissez-faire position when the issue is put in terms of preferential economic interests. Take labor unions, for example. About 40 per cent agree that "the laws governing

4. R. K. Goldsen, M. Rosenberg, R. M. Williams, and E. A. Suchman, *What College Students Think*, Princeton, N. J.: D. Van Nostrand Co., 1960, Chapter 5, pp. 97-124; Appendix, pp. 218-220.

labor unions are not strict enough." Yet, neither is student opinion ready to grant to employers the right to operate as strictly free agents. For example, at Cornell—a campus which, compared with other schools, is somewhat more conservative in its attitudes toward free enterprise, business, and labor—53 per cent of the students rejected the principle that an employer's unrestricted right to hire and fire as he sees fit ought to be viewed as "a highly important guarantee" which an ideal democracy owes to its citizens. It would certainly be an oversimplification to say that college students support the rugged individualism of a free enterprise economic system and express attitudes on given economic issues which match this basic philosophical position.

There are, too, certain economic policies with social welfare overtones which many students take for granted as essential for a benevolent democratic government. Take the matter of a minimum wage. Those who remember the discussions of whether such a guarantee by government would be desirable will certainly recall the argument: "If people are certain of a minimum wage they might lose their initiative." This argument has retained its freshness for only about a third of the students. And at Cornell in 1950, only 24 per cent rejected as unimportant or distasteful the idea that an "ideal democracy" ought to guarantee a minimum wage to every citizen. Clearly some of the traditional arguments against a minimum wage have lost their frehness (Table 4).

Table 4

	RESPONSES AT CORNELL IN 1950 (TOTAL = 2758) PERCENTAGE WHO			
	Agree	Disagree	Uncertain	No Answer
It interferes with a man's right to bargain for the price of his own labor	21	69	9	1
It requires more red tape than it's worth	10	71	19	—

Higher education, on the other hand, is still viewed as a private privilege rather than a public right, according to most of these students. Only about a third (35 per cent) agree that "college education should be free for everyone." Some of the arguments against this sort of benevolent "government paternalism" are given in Table 5. Even so, however, only 25 per cent of the Cornell students said they felt it would be unimportant or distasteful for an ideal democracy to guarantee "free college education for anyone who wants it and meets the requirements."[5]

5. Many of us in this country and in this generation may have overlooked the "welfare state" aspect of government sponsored free education, simply because it is by now so entrenched in the American way of life. But it is an example par excellence of gov-

Table 5

	RESPONSES AT ELEVEN UNIVERSITIES (TOTAL = 2975)			
	PERCENTAGE WHO			
	Agree	Disagree	Uncertain	No Answer
Educational standards would go down	56	34	9	1
It would lead to higher taxes	50	30	19	1
It would make the lower classes too dissatisfied	15	60	24	1
	RESPONSES AT CORNELL 1950 (TOTAL = 2758)			
There would not be enough executive jobs to go around	28	48	24	—
You get more out of it if you pay	24	61	14	1
The professions are overcrowded	17	58	25	—
Industry cannot absorb more trained people	11	63	25	1

Finally, how do the students react to the idea of government-guaranteed medical care? This is another aspect of welfare government which only a minority (28 per cent) were ready to accept as a highly important responsibility of a democratic government. Still, it is evident that opinion is not crystallized *against* it; for just 25 per cent said they considered such measures "of little or no importance or even undesirable" in an ideal democracy.

Table 6 gives the way the students reacted to certain well-known arguments against government-sponsored medical care.

Table 6

	RESPONSES AT CORNELL IN 1950 (TOTAL = 2758)			
	PERCENTAGE WHO			
	Agree	Disagree	Uncertain	No Answer
It would lower the quality of medical care	58	23	18	1
It would lead to higher taxes	54	25	21	—
People might learn to rely on the government for everything	53	35	12	—
More red tape than it's worth	46	32	21	1
It would perpetuate the unfit	15	60	25	—

---

ernment guaranteeing as a public right something which was formerly considered a private privilege. (See, for example, Shirley Basch, "Pains of a New Idea," *Survey Graphic*, 37, pp. 78-79, February 1948. This article shows the marked parallel between early arguments against public education, and modern arguments against socialized medicine.) At Cornell in 1950 all but 17 per cent of the students felt that this was a highly important guarantee which a democracy ought to grant to its citizens. Only two per cent rejected "free education for everyone under 16" as of little or no importance. (See Table 7.)

The general impression these distributions of opinion convey seem to be this. When it comes to expressions of economic philosophy, student opinion is on the conservative side, but covers a relatively wide range. When it comes to liberalism or conservatism in economic areas involving education and welfare, student opinion is perhaps middle-of-the-road. But when it comes to current economic issues involving business and labor, about half the students consistently express attitudes and opinions which are linked with a conservative position.

Economic liberalism or conservatism in the three senses mentioned here varies widely among the different colleges (Table 7). Fisk students are least likely to express a conservative position, whether it is a question of economic philosophy, economic issues, or education and welfare. But here is an interesting point which underlines the usefulness of distinguishing these components of liberalism-conservatism, rather than treating it as a unitary concept. Distribution of opinion on economic philosophy at Harvard resembles the Fisk profile more closely than that of any other campus, even though these Cambridge boys are decidedly more likely than, say, UCLA or Wayne to express conservative stands on current economic issues or even on educational ones.

Finally, it is clear that while philosophically conservative students are very likely to take a conservative stand on particular economic issues as well, the generalizing power of a conservative economic philosophy is substantially less when it comes to an issue with humanitarian and welfare overtones. Students who score high on a scale measuring their acceptance of the principles of economic laissez-faire differ little from those at the opposite end of that scale in the stand they take on issues with education and welfare implications.[6] But on issues involving conflicting economic interests of labor and management, their opinions and attitudes tend to match the philosophical stand they espouse (Table 8).

Party Lines

It is by now well established that supporters of the Democratic Party tend to be more inclined than Republicans to accept government intervention in economic matters.[7] This is equally true of the college students. About one out of every two students with Republican sympathies declared himself in the conservative laissez-faire camp, compared with

6. See footnote to Table 8 for an explanation of how the scale was constructed.

7. See, for example, Bernard Berelson, Paul F. Lazarsfeld, and William McPhee, *Voting* (University of Chicago Press, 1954). See also Paul F. Lazarsfeld, Bernard Berelson, and Hazel Gaudet, *The People's Choice* (New York: Columbia University Press, 1948).

Table 7. Distribution of Opinion at 11 Universities on Items Related to Economic Philosophy, Economic Issues, and Government Responsibility for Education and Welfare

	PERCENTAGE EXPRESSING CONSERVATIVE OPINIONS											
	Cross-Section All Universities	Cornell Men	Dartmouth	Fisk	Harvard	Michigan	No. Carolina	Texas	UCLA	Wayne	Wesleyan	Yale
Total =	(2975)	(655)	(365)	(134)	(453)	(488)	(414)	(516)	(467)	(519)	(277)	(297)
Economic philosophy												
Democracy depends fundamentally on the existence of free business enterprise — Agree	62	62	59	53	46	67	72	70	61	62	62	60
The "welfare state" tends to destroy individual initiative — Agree	59	60	63	32	48	69	63	60	55	56	57	64
Government planning almost inevitably results in the loss of individual liberties and freedom — Agree	38	34	30	20	23	32	34	40	30	25	25	38
The best government is the one which governs least — Agree	31	32	26	27	29	30	33	35	29	29	32	32
Economic issues												
The laws governing labor unions are not strict enough — Agree	40	52	55	22	43	54	51	45	42	40	61	55
Labor unions in this country are doing a fine job — Disagree	48	37	48	19	35	45	49	43	32	33	40	43
If people are certain of a minimum wage they might lose their initiative — Agree	35	32	38	34	23	36	51	45	27	31	34	36
The individual employer should sacrifice this right (to hire and fire without restriction) for the social welfare — Disagree		61	(Asked only at Cornell, 1950: Total 2758)									
If there is no ceiling on business profits there is a better chance to develop products at lower costs — Agree		38	(Asked only at Cornell, 1950: Total 2758)									

Free enterprise economic system considered as a deterrent to war, considered* . . .											
Highly important		41	(Asked only at Cornell, 1950: Total 2758)								
A minimum wage as a guarantee expected from an ideal democracy considered . . .											
Little or no importance		27									
Most business corporations do not give the public a true picture of how much profit they make — Disagree		29									
Education and Welfare											
College education should be free to everybody — Disagree	54	59	68	44	57	62	63	49	33	46	66
Importance attached to each measure listed, "if a government is to be considered IDEAL."†											
Free education for everyone under 16:											
High:		83	(Asked only at Cornell, 1950: Total 2758)								
Medium:		15									
Low or undesirable:		2									
Free medical care for those who cannot afford it:											
High:		28									
Medium:		47									
Low or undesirable:		25									
Free college education for everyone who wants it and meets the requirements:											
High:		25									
Medium:		47									
Low or undesirable:		28									

* See Table 6-18 for text of this question and full distribution of responses [Goldsen, *et al.*, *What College Students Think*, Princeton, N.J.: (D. Van Nostrand Co., 1960)].
† See Table 6-1 for text of this question and full distribution of responses [*Ibid.*].

roughly one out of four so-called Independents, and one out of five who supported the Democrats.

The same sorts of results appear when we consider the stands students take on economic issues linked to such a philosophy. The ones we are considering here for the purpose of illustration are attitudes toward labor unions, a minimum wage, and free college education. Among the students we studied, the results were highly consistent in showing those with Republican leanings to be more conservative than Democrats, and the "Independents" to be somewhere in between the two major parties.

Economic Status and Economic Issues

And yet, other sociological links to economic philosophy and related attitudes are quite different in the college population compared with the general population. Most community opinion studies have shown that an individual's economic position importantly influences his acceptance

Table 8. Philosophically Conservative Students Are More Likely than Others to Take a Conservative Stand on Specific Economic Issues (Eleven Universities). Position on Philosophy of Government Scale*

	PERCENTAGE GIVING INDICATED RESPONSE				
	Support Laissez Faire				*Do Not Support Laissez Faire*
	1	2	3	4	5
Total	(375)	(568)	(772)	(765)	(495)
The laws governing labor unions are not strict enough					
Agree	61	46	43	35	19
Disagree	28	34	35	40	58
?	11	20	22	25	22
If people are certain of a minimum wage they might lose their initiative					
Agree	52	49	39	27	15
Disagree	42	46	52	62	72
?	6	6	9	11	12
College education should be free to everyone					
Agree	32	32	31	38	45
Disagree	62	61	57	52	40
?	6	8	12	10	15

*This scale cumulates responses indicating agreement with the following statements:
—Democracy depends fundamentally on the existence of free business enterprise.
—The Welfare State tends to destroy individual initiative.
—Government planning almost inevitably results in the loss of essential liberties and freedom.
—The best government is the one which governs least.

Table 9. Political Party Affiliation and Philosophy of Government (Eleven Universities): "Do you consider yourself a Republican, a Democrat or an Independent in most political matters?"

	PERCENTAGE GIVING INDICATED RESPONSE		
	Republican	Independent	Democrat
Total*	(859)	(1265)	(760)
Philosophy of government scale†			
Support laissez faire	49	28	21
Intermediate	26	28	24
Do not support laissez faire	25	45	55
Laws governing labor unions are not strict enough			
Agree	55	37	29
Disagree	28	40	50
Uncertain	17	23	21
Labor unions in this country are doing a fine job			
Agree	16	30	44
Disagree	68	45	32
Uncertain	16	25	24
If people are certain of a minimum wage, they might lose their initiative			
Agree	47	33	28
Disagree	43	58	65
Uncertain	10	9	8
College education should be free to everyone			
Agree	21	37	45
Disagree	71	50	44
Uncertain	8	12	10

*Omits 91 students who mentioned other political parties or did not answer.
†For construction of this scale see footnote to Table 8.

or rejection of laissez-faire economic principles, his attitudes toward business and labor, and support for government intervention in social and economic matters. If this were as true of college students as of the general population, one would expect relatively more conservative students to have said they had come from wealthier homes; relatively fewer conservatives among those who said they had come from low income families. We find, however, that this is not necessarily the case. Conservative beliefs and attitudes were virtually as prevalent among students from each economic group. Students who had said their families were in the top income brackets were not correspondingly more likely to be in favor of a laissez-faire economic philosophy; nor were they necessarily more frequently antagonistic to government provisions for free college education. Some differences do appear between the most extreme groups, but these differences are too weak to warrant the assertion that economic position is significantly related to conservatism in these senses. (See Appendix III.)

It is not until we get down to specific questions about wages, business, and labor that we find the expected differences among wealthier and poorer students.

In other words, when it is a question of economic issues which reflect conflicting economic interests, then the student's economic background is directly linked to his attitudes and his opinions. But when it is a matter of his approach to the economic role of government in a philosophical sense, or in terms of a broadly humanitarian aim (such as education) then the power of the students' origins to determine or influence their economic liberalism or conservatism seems to become weaker than we know it to be for the general population.

If the social class origins of college students do not appear to engage quite so directly with their economic philosophy and related attitudes, this may be due in part to the greater homogeneity of our campus populations compared with a full community sample. Certainly the population of college students does not mirror the full range of economic levels in the country at large, since so few American college students come from families on the very lowest socio-economic levels. Moreover, the students are probably even more homogeneous in their feelings of class

Table 10. Father's Income Is Linked to Issues Representing Clear-Cut Economic Interests (Eleven Universities)

	PERCENTAGE GIVING INDICATED RESPONSE						
	FATHER'S ANNUAL INCOME						
	Under $3000	$3000-4999	$5000-7499	$7500-9999	$10,000-19,999	$20,000-29,999	$30,000 or More
Total*	(267)	(799)	(620)	(418)	(417)	(165)	(162)
If people are certain of a minimum wage, they might lose their initiative							
Agree	31	33	34	36	36	43	48
Disagree	60	57	57	57	55	50	42
Uncertain	9	10	9	7	9	7	10
Labor unions in this country are doing a fine job							
Agree	40	35	32	27	23	22	16
Disagree	40	40	47	51	57	56	67
Uncertain	20	25	21	22	20	22	17

*Omits 127 students who did not provide information on father's income.

identification. By the time a young man of working class origins has matriculated at a university and has committed himself to four years or more of higher education, he has undoubtedly largely taken on the values and the outlook of the future middle-class professional he aspires to be. Thus his actual economic background (in terms of his parents' dollars-and-cents income) has probably already become a minor ingredient in his economic philosophy and related attitudes. If anything, the attitudes of the class to which he relates himself at least in an anticipatory way will have his allegiance.

In addition, the humanitarian themes of American society are particularly entrenched in the culture of all college students regardless of the social class they may have started in, and even quite apart from their present class loyalties. This is probably particularly true of issues involving education.

Here, then, is a further indication of the way in which the college experience may act as a great leveler. (See also Chapter 1 [of *What College Students Think*].[8]) It can weaken the link between one's social class origins and one's sympathies for a philosophy of economic liberalism or conservatism, or one's attitudes toward economic policies of a humanitarian nature.

And yet the generalizing power of class origin by no means disappears as a result of the college experience. It becomes, so to speak, specialized. On issues that engage conflicting class interests, the student who comes initially from a relatively poorer home will tend to take a stand sympathetic to the economic interests of his family.

To put it more succinctly: you can infer a college student's economic philosophy if you know only what political party has his sympathies and what college he is attending, and further information about the economic level of his family will not substantially improve the prediction. The same clues will lead to a rather accurate inference regarding his stand on an economic issue with humanitarian overtones. If, however, you wish to infer a college student's attitude towards a current economic issue which reflects conflicting class interests, then additional information about his family's economic level will increase the accuracy of your guess.

Changes in Political Philosophy

As students move along in their college careers, they are exposed to a variety of political and ideological influences. They listen to political lectures in their classes, discuss politics and political philosophy, react to the communications of the mass media. Does the total effect of these influences, combined with the maturation process make them more liberal or more conservative?

Obviously one cannot answer this question for every place and every era. The period in which our study was conducted was characterized by a dominant atmosphere of conservatism. We found that new

8. Goldsen, *et al., op. cit.*

students entering college at this time appeared to have been enveloped in this atmosphere, and to have become increasingly conservative as they passed through college. We illustrate this process by examining how students changed their beliefs regarding a laissez-faire philosophy of government.

We begin the story by turning to the Cornell panel members, since there we can examine what happened to the opinions of each student between the first study and the second. As we compare the responses the students reported when they were underclassmen with the equivalent responses they gave us as upperclassmen, three kinds of patterns emerge which illustrate their tendency to become more, rather than less, conservative. First, as these students passed from class to class, their viewpoint, as group, seems to have become firmer. The opinions of students who were initially "on the fence" tended to crystallize as recognizably conservative opinions. Second, those who started out with a conservative stand were more likely to have maintained it. And third, those who did change their minds, tended to switch to a more conservative position.

The details are these: as freshmen and sophomores, about a third of the panel (35 per cent) reported opinions that placed them in an intermediate position on the scale we used to measure their philosophy of government.[9] By 1952, however, this proportion had declined to 26 per cent. This is a slight decline, but it indicates nevertheless that at the end of a two-year period, there were fewer "straddlers"—fewer students, that is, with ambiguous views or contradictory opinions about a liberal or conservative philosophy of government. Within the short period of time that had elapsed between these two studies, relatively more students had come to take a definite laissez-faire stand. For, among the panel members who changed their minds during these two years, the majority (55 per cent) switched to a more conservative position, while a minority (45 per cent) switched to a more liberal position.

Moreover, the conservative viewpoint on this subject was more likely to have remained unchanged, perhaps unchallenged. Roughly half of the panel members had not altered their beliefs between the two studies. Of these "stable" students, 44 per cent were initially in favor of an outright laissez-faire philosophy and retained that opinion. In contrast, 34 per cent were staunch about maintaining a contrary opinion.

These small per cent differences indicate only a possible trend, and obviously do not by themselves constitute a compelling argument. It is mainly in tracing the shiftings and balancings of opinions that the case develops convincingly. For it turns out that conservative students, regardless of whether or not they were emotionally involved or concerned in political matters, found it relatively easy to maintain their

9. See footnote to Table 8, where the construction of this scale is explained.

Table 11. Stability and Change in Position on Philosophy of Government Scale According to Degree of Involvement in Political Matters (Cornell Panel)

Later Position on Philosophy of Government Scale as Juniors and Seniors	Initial Position on Philosophy of Government Scale* as Freshmen and Sophomores: Supported Laissez Faire				Did Not Support Laissez Faire				Were in Intermediate Position			
	DEGREE OF INVOLVEMENT IN POLITICAL MATTERS†											
	Always Involved	*Became Involved*	*Became Apathetic*	*Always Apathetic*	*Always Involved*	*Became Involved*	*Became Apathetic*	*Always Apathetic*	*Always Involved*	*Became Involved*	*Became Apathetic*	*Always Apathetic*
Total	(103)	(50)	(81)	(98)	(87)	(34)	(66)	(86)	(98)	(37)	(63)	(131)
Maintained same position	61	72	58	65	75	56	58	48	34	24	29	35
Changed position on laissez faire												
Support laissez faire	—	—	—	—	6	15	10	21	39	46	46	42
Intermediate	19	18	31	22	19	30	32	31	—	—	—	—
Did not support laissez faire	19	10	10	13	—	—	—	—	27	30	25	23

*For construction of this scale, see footnote to Table 8.

†Do you ever get as worked up about something that happens in politics or public affairs as you do about something that happens in your personal life?

		Response at first interview: Yes	No
Response at second interview	Yes	Always involved	Became involved
	No	Became apathetic	Always apathetic

conservative ideology. In contrast, only the liberal student who was able to feel and to maintain some kind of emotional involvement in these matters, had an equivalent chance of maintaining his liberal outlook. The more apathetic liberal, on the other hand, had a fifty-fifty chance of becoming a conservative by the time he was a senior. It looks as if the initially conservative student may never have felt the need to question his own ideas, while the liberal student must have been sufficiently concerned to be able to defend his.

Insulating Subsystems

One reason for this may be that the involved liberal tends to hold himself aloof from the campus subsystems which possess explicitly conservative norms; for these shifts toward conservatism do not occur to the same degree throughout the diverse social groups that make up the campus social structure.

The fraternities are a case in point. They constitute a social system whose political and social norms are in general clearly conservative. Such norms, it is true, are relatively widespread throughout the Cornell campus and of course are not characteristic solely of the fraternities. But there is an important difference. The fraternities tend explicitly to socialize any members who may deviate from these conservative norms *away* from liberalism and *toward* conservatism. This is not necessarily true of the campus in general.

Here is an illustration. Let us trace what happened to the opinions of students in the panel who had started college with a generally liberal philosophy about what the role of government ought to be. Some of these liberal underclassmen joined fraternities; and if they did, about half (51 per cent) abandoned their liberal viewpoint to adopt a position closer to a strictly laissez-faire philosophy.

A few others had at first remained outside the fraternity system, joining it only as they became upperclassmen. Two-thirds of these latecomers (64 per cent) accompanied their change to fraternity membership with a parallel change to a more sympathetic attitude toward laissez-faire economics; they became more conservative.

In contrast, among the liberal students who remained unaffiliated with the fraternity system, only a small minority (23 per cent) found on the campus any reason to abandon their liberal position; the remainder (77 per cent)—by far the majority—retained their liberal viewpoint about the role of government, in spite of the fact that this was a deviant position to take on the Cornell campus. One would infer that they were able to find spheres of social circulation whose norms were not antagonistic to their liberalism, but, on the contrary, encouraged and reinforced it.

This does not imply that groups outside the fraternity system are uniformly conducive to the maintenance or development of a liberal economic philosophy. Remember, we have traced so far the opinions of only 260 students who started college with a liberal viewpoint (in this case about laissez-faire government) and this group represents only 29 per cent of all the students in the panel. Relatively more started school with conservative views (36 per cent) or with ambiguous or contradictory ideas on the subject (35 per cent). It is in tracing what happened to the opinions of the initially conservative students that it becomes clear that the Cornell campus includes many groups other than the fraternity system and even quite apart from it, which serve to reinforce conservative ideas almost to the same degree. In the fraternities these norms may be more undifferentiated, or perhaps even more explicit or intense. But they are not so widely divergent from those prevailing in other groups and other organizations on the campus.

For example, it is true that students who start out as conservatives in the fraternity system are most likely to maintain their conservatism; some 64 per cent do. But if they are independents, the proportion who continue to support laissez-faire as a philosophy of government is but

Table 12. Philosophy of Government: Liberal or Conservative Opinion as Underclassmen Compared with Opinion as Upperclassmen, Fraternity Members Compared with Unaffiliated Students (Cornell Panel)

POSITION ON PHILOSOPHY OF GOVERNMENT SCALE*	PERCENTAGE† IN EACH GROUP		
	Fraternity Members Throughout	*Initially Independent, Joined Fraternity*	*Unaffiliated Students*
Initial opinion as underclassmen			
Did not support laissez faire (Total)	(127)	(22)	(111)
As upperclassmen:			
Became more conservative	51	64	23
All others	49	36	77
Supported laissez faire (Total)	(182)	(37)	(110)
As upperclassmen:			
Remained conservative	64	70	55
All others	36	30	45
Intermediate position (Total)	(192)	(23)	(106)
As upperclassmen:			
Became conservative	45	39	34
Became liberal	24	26	27
All others	31	35	39

*See footnote to Table 8 for the construction of this scale.
†Excludes 34 panel members who could not be classified according to fraternity membership.

slightly lower (55 per cent). Even if we trace what happens to the intermediate students—those who started college with ambiguous or contradictory views on the subject—the same sorts of trends are apparent: of those who were in a fraternity 45 per cent became more conservative as they passed through college while only 24 per cent became more liberal. Yet among those who were unaffiliated with any fraternity the equivalent proportions are only slightly smaller: 34 per cent became more conservative while 27 per cent developed a more liberal philosophy of government.

In short, one could conclude that there are at least three types of spheres of circulation on the Cornell campus. There are the fraternities which reinforce conservatism in two ways; they insulate their conservative members against change and socialize their liberal members away from liberalism. There are the spheres of social circulation that attract the liberal students, encouraging their point of view, strongly reinforcing it, and insulating them against the impact of conservative norms apparent elsewhere on the campus. Finally, there is the rest of the Cornell campus, with many organizations and social subsystems, that provide spheres of social circulation whose norms are undoubtedly at least as conservative as fraternity norms. They serve to insulate their participants against liberalizing influences, but they do not necessarily socialize them away from liberalism as explicitly—or perhaps the point is, as effectively—as the fraternity system does.

There is no reason, of course, why the pattern reported here for Cornell should be assumed to have prevailed as well in the other universities which participated in the research. We are aware that other investigators have reported that college students tend to develop political and economic beliefs and attitudes that are compatible with the consensus of their own campus. Theodore Newcomb's now classic study of students at Bennington College,[10] for example, showed that students at this college in the thirties, when the climate of opinion was generally liberal, became socialized toward liberalism. A recent study of students' political beliefs at UCLA reported that liberal political beliefs and attitudes on current political issues associated with liberalism tend to be more prevalent among seniors than among underclassmen, suggesting that the college years might now be reinforcing liberalism on that campus, rather than conservatism.[11]

Yet our analysis shows that at least as far as economic philosophy is concerned, and at least during the conservative period of American

10. Theodore M. Newcomb, *Personality and Social Change* (New York: Dryden Press, 1943).

11. Hanan Selvin and Warren O. Hagstrom, *The Bulwark of Liberty* (Berkeley: University of California, January, 1959. Manuscript.)

history during which our data were gathered, liberal opinions were less prevalent among seniors. At all the universities we studied, even at such relatively liberal campuses as UCLA, the same trend seemed to occur. Had we been able to observe the development of opinion among all these students as we did at Cornell, we suspect that a similar pattern of socialization toward conservatism, particularly among fraternity men, might have been found at these schools as well.

Table 13 shows that the proportion of liberal students (those who

Table 13. Proportion of Students Who Reject Laissez-Faire Philosophy of Government Decreases from Freshman to Senior Year. Fraternity Men Compared with Independent Students* (Percentage Scoring in Two Least Conservative Positions on Philosophy of Government Scale)†

	YEAR IN COLLEGE			
	First	*Second*	*Third*	*Fourth*
Wesleyan, Cornell, Dartmouth				
Fraternity members	47 (173)	34 (238)	39 (193)	32 (171)
Independent students	49 (220)	44 (83)	48 (66)	42 (67)
Texas, North Carolina				
Fraternity members	32 (65)	32 (96)	32 (94)	27 (102)
Independent students	42 (120)	27 (103)	39 (166)	40 (130)
UCLA, Michigan				
Fraternity members	44 (58)	43 (66)	43 (116)	32 (123)
Independent students	39 (99)	51 (108)	40 (159)	50 (174)
Wayne				
Fraternity members	— (11)	— (10)	54 (45)	46 (37)
Independent students	43 (91)	52 (91)	45 (98)	54 (83)

*Excluded from this tabulation are Harvard and Yale, which do not have fraternity systems. Appendix IV shows the proportion scoring in the two most liberal positions on the philosophy of government scale at these two universities, among students in each year in college.

†For construction of this scale, see footnote to Table 8. The bases on which these per cents have been computed appear in parentheses. Excluded from consideration are fifth-year students, special students, foreign students, and other nonmatriculated students.

reject a laissez-faire philosophy of government) tends to decrease year by year among the fraternity men with the possible exception of those at Wayne; the equivalent decline among unaffiliated students is not only slighter but the pattern, year by year, shows much less regularity.

Our study suggests, therefore, that the overall impact of the college years, at least during this period of widespread conservatism in the country at large, nurtured a conservative economic philosophy, and was unsympathetic to a contrary viewpoint. In special subsystems of campus life, this tendency was strongly reinforced. The fraternities provide one such example, reminding us of an important sociological truism. In studying the development of liberalism or conservatism in a special milieu such as the college campus, it is essential to consider as relevant context not only the climate of opinion of that institution as a whole, and not only the climate of opinion in the country at large, but also the explicit norms of particular social subsystems.

Appendix I. Proportion of Positive Responses at Each University to: "Do you ever get as worked up about something that happens in politics or public affairs as you do about something that happens in your personal life?" (Eleven Universities)

	Percentage Who Say "Yes"	Total
Wayne	46	(519)
Yale	44	(297)
Wesleyan	44	(277)
Cornell Men: 1952	42	(655)
Harvard	41	(453)
Dartmouth	39	(365)
Texas	39	(516)
UCLA	38	(467)
Michigan	38	(488)
Fisk	37	(134)
North Carolina	34	(414)

Appendix II. Fathers Who Are Usually "Independent" Voters and Sons Who Are Usually "Independent" of Political Party Alignment, According to Religious Affiliation, Family Income, and Predominant Political Party on Campus (Eleven Universities)

	PERCENTAGE* IN EACH RELIGIOUS, ECONOMIC AND POLITICAL GROUP				
	Both Independent	Father Independent Son Rep.	Father Independent Son Demo.	Father Rep. Son Indep.	Father Demo. Son Indep.
Total	(308)	(51)	(50)	(302)	(419)
Religious affiliation					
Protestant	54	63	36	73	51
Catholic	11	6	12	9	15
Jewish	22	4	28	6	23
Mixed	7	25	12	8	5
Other	5	2	12	4	5
No answer	1	—	—	1	—
Father's annual income					
Under $7,500	56	53	56	48	72
$7,500-9,999	17	16	16	18	9
$10,000-19,999	15	10	18	15	10
$20,000 or more	10	20	8	15	5
No answer	3	2	2	5	3
Predominant political party on campus					
Heavily Republican†	50	48	52	54	29
Heavily Democratic‡	50	52	49	45	70

*Omits 496 who could not be classified on both "father's vote" and "own vote."

†This category includes Cornell, Dartmouth, Harvard, Michigan, Wesleyan, Yale, where the number of students who said they usually align themselves with the Republicans exceeded the number reporting Democratic sympathies.

‡This category includes UCLA, North Carolina, Texas, Wayne, and Fisk, where the number of students loyal to the Democrats exceeded the number loyal to the Republican party.

Appendix III. Philosophy of Government and Attitude toward Free College Education According to Father's Income (Eleven Universities)

	Percentage* in Each Group						
	Father's Annual Income						
	Under $3,000	$3,000-4,999	$5,000-7,499	$7,500-9,999	$10,000-19,999	$20,000-29,999	$30,000 or more
Total	(267)	(799)	(620)	(418)	(417)	(165)	(162)
Philosophy of government scale							
Support laissez faire	30	31	29	31	31	41	47
Intermediate	27	26	26	27	26	24	22
Do not support laissez faire	43	43	45	41	43	35	31
College education should be free to everyone							
Agree	46	41	33	29	32	30	39
Disagree	44	48	57	61	58	61	45
Uncertain	10	11	11	10	10	9	16

*Omits 127 students who did not provide information on father's income.
†For construction of this scale see footnote to Table 8.

Appendix IV. Philosophy of Government among Freshmen, Sophomores, Juniors, and Seniors (Harvard and Yale)*

	PERCENTAGE IN EACH ATTITUDE GROUP			
	YEAR IN COLLEGE			
	First	Second	Third	Fourth
Harvard (Total)	(120)	(110)	(111)	(109)
Support laissez faire	17	27	26	24
Intermediate	18	22	24	21
Do not support laissez faire	65	51	50	55
Yale (Total)	(86)	(70)	(75)	(65)
Support laissez faire	45	24	33	46
Intermediate	15	23	22	20
Do not support laissez faire	39	52	45	35

*For construction of this scale see footnote to Table 8.
†Fifth year students, special students, foreign students, and other non-matriculated students have been excluded from computations in the table.

c) VIOLENCE

MARTIN GOLD

Suicide, Homicide, and the Socialization of Aggression

No one has contributed more significantly to the establishment of sociology as a separate discipline than Émile Durkheim, and nowhere did he make this separation more secure than in *Suicide*. Then will an article frankly "social-psychological" in orientation, which argues from suicide-rate data, seem incongruous in a *Journal* issue dedicated to Durkheim's memory? Durkheim would not have found it so, for our approach is one he advised.

While Durkheim saw the need to emphasize the separation of sociology from other sciences, especially psychology, we do not think he intended to isolate it. In *The Rules of Sociological Method* he specifically denies that there are no links between sociology and psychology.

> We do not mean to say, of course, that the study of psychological facts is not indispensable to the sociologist. If collective life is not derived from individual life, the two are nevertheless closely related; if the latter cannot explain the former, it can at least facilitate its explanation. First, as we have shown, it is indisputable that social facts are produced by action on psychological factors. In addition, this very action is similar to that which takes place in each individual consciousness and by which are transformed the primary elements.[1]

Reprinted from "Suicide, Homicide, and the Socialization of Aggression," by Martin Gold, The American Journal of Sociology, *May, 1958, pp. 651-661, by permission of The University of Chicago Press. Copyright 1958 by the University of Chicago.*

The author wishes to thank D. R. Miller and G. E. Swanson for their aid during the research and on the manuscript. He is also grateful to J. F. Short for his helpful comments.

1. Émile Durkheim, *The Rules of Sociological Method*, trans. S. A. Solvay and J. K. Mueller, ed. G. E. G. Catlin (New York: Free Press, 1950), p. 11.

Granting the divisions among levels of generality or abstraction, each with its own reality, laws at any level of abstraction are formulated with proper regard for other levels. Just as psychological laws of perception must be consistent with what is known about neurophysiology or must bear the burden of inconsistency, so sociological laws must face up to current knowledge of psychological processes. For this reason findings at one level are clues at the other.

Our purpose is to explore the relationship between certain psychological and sociological theories and between relevant data from both disciplines which pertain to the choice of suicide or homicide as an expression of aggression. We will try to show that the choice of suicide or homicide, essentially a psychological problem, is determined in part by the individual's place in a social system. We will focus on socialization as the process by which sociological factors are translated into determinants of a psychological choice between directions of aggression.

Our research gains impetus from the work of the late Andrew F. Henry and James F. Short, reported in their book, *Suicide and Homicide*.[2] A discussion of the sociological and psychological factors leading to these two ultimate forms of aggression is only one of the several problems they discuss, but, it is the one we pursue here. This paper is not intended as a critical review of their book. Rather it is a report of research which attempts to build upon and amplify a portion of the theoretical structure they presented.

We have two specific aims: one, primarily theoretical; the other, methodological.

First, Henry's and Short's theory will be examined from a social-psychological point of view. Where they have dealt separately with psychological and sociological antecedents of suicide and homicide, we will suggest some child-rearing links which mediate between social structural variables and intrapersonal determinants of behavior. Second, we will examine the way in which Henry and Short tested their hypotheses about the choice of suicide or homicide. It seems to us that a more appropriate methodology is needed, and we will suggest a possible alternative. Finally, we will use the suggested methodology to test hypotheses generated by Henry and Short and by the theory of socialization presented here. The findings will be compared.

Theory of External Restraint

Henry and Short are interested in suicide and homicide as acts of aggression which originate in frustration. They theorize that degree of

2. A. F. Henry and J. F. Short, Jr., *Suicide and Homicide* (New York: Free Press, 1954).

external restraint distinguishes individuals who choose to commit one rather than the other. An individual is externally restrained to the degree that his alternatives of behavior are limited by others. It is postulated that, the more an individual is externally restrained, the more likely it is that he will regard others as legitimate targets for aggression. Hence, the greater the degree of external restraint upon an individual, the more likely that he will commit homicide rather than suicide.

It is assumed that individuals in higher-status categories, as indicated by four of Parsons' criteria, are less externally restrained than those in lower-status categories and are therefore more likely to prefer suicide to homicide. The criteria are achievement, possession, authority, and power. The authors specify the following high- and low-status segments of the American population:

High Status	*Low Status*
Males	Females
White	Non-white
Aged 25-34	Aged 65 or more
Army officers	Enlisted men

They hypothesize that, given frustration, members of low-status are more likely than members of high-status categories to commit homicide rather than suicide. Further, they follow Durkheim in assuming that individuals involved in more intimate social relationships are more externally restrained. Hence, married people and rural dwellers, who are more subject to external restraint, are therefore more likely to prefer homicide to suicide than single or divorced people and urbanites.

A number of Henry and Short's assumptions may be questioned. It is debatable that members of higher-status categories are less restrained externally than their lower-status counterparts. For example, the behavior appropriate for an "officer and gentleman" is in many respects more limited than that allowed an enlisted man. Drunkenness off the base, for example, is apt to earn the enlisted man mild reproof but to invoke strong penalties on an officer. Similarly, eccentricities tolerated in persons over sixty-five may result in institutionalization of a twenty-five-year-old. External restraints on behavior are exerted not only by persons but also by norms—norms which may apply more stringently to persons in higher-status positions. Rather than arguing directly from status positions, let us consider other sources of behavioral restraints, specifically, limits imposed on expressions of aggression.

What are the interpersonal events through which restraints over aggression are made manifest? What are the processes by which aggression is displaced from the restraining figures to other targets? Why the choice of the *self* as a legitimate target for aggression in the absence of any other legitimate target? In short, what are the social-psychological variables mediating between the sociological conditions and the psychological event?

The Socialization of Aggression

A body of theory exists which helps to link sociological variables with preferences for self or others as targets for aggression. A brief presentation of the theory and some supporting data will lead us to hypotheses about preferences for suicide or homicide similar to Henry and Short's.

One of the early lessons a child must learn, if he is to continue to live among others, is to control his rages. Sigmund Freud recognized the importance of hate affect as well as love in the developing personality and marked the ego's mastery of these affects as a critical point in personality development.

An individual may control his aggression in many ways. Miller and Swanson order the modes of control in their theory of defenses.[3] An impulse, like the wish to destroy, is taken as an *action-tendency* which has four components: intended act, agent or actor, target object, and affect. Control can be established by manipulation of one or several of these components.

For example, the *intention* to destroy an object may be modulated into tongue-lashing. The aggressive *agent* may be distorted, as in projection: "He wants to destroy me; I don't want to hurt him." The impulse may be displaced to another *object* such as a socially acceptable scapegoat. The *affect* may be shifted, dislike displacing hate, or it may be distorted completely through the working of a reaction formation, hate becoming love. The action-tendency as a whole may be postponed temporarily or frustrated indefinitely.

Which mode or modes of control are selected depends to a great extent on the culture in which the individual participates. Among the Sioux, for example, an infant's tantrums were a matter of pride to his parents, and he was hurt and frustrated as a child to encourage his rage. Rages were later controlled by venting them against extratribal enemies in forays which promised social rewards.[4] Among the Alorese, on the

3. D. R. Miller and G. E. Swanson, *Inner Conflict and Defense in the Child* (New York: Holt, Rinehart, Winston, 1958).

4. E. H. Erikson, "Observations on Sioux Education," *Journal of Psychology*, VII (1937), 101-56.

other hand, aggression is suppressed at an early age and later finds expression in intratribal stealing.[5]

There is evidence, too, that modes of control and expression of aggression vary among the social classes in the United States. B. Allinsmith found that the TAT protocols of lower-class adolescent boys were more apt to include direct references to and direct expressions of aggression than those of middle-class boys.[6] While lower-class boys told stories of attacking or fleeing from authority, middle-class boys either told stories devoid of hate or stories in which aggression was turned against themselves.

B. J. Beardslee aroused the anger of lower- and middle-class boys halfway through a set of story-completion projectives.[7] The middle-class boys showed the greater increase in the use of defenses against aggression from the pre- to the post-arousal story endings.

How are these differences in controls of aggression between the social classes established? Allinsmith suggests that one cause is the type of punishment meted out by parents to misbehaving children.[8] Lower-class mothers report that they or their husbands are likely to strike their children or threaten to strike them. Middle-class mothers report that their type of punishment is psychological rather than physical. Middle-class parents are more apt to say to a naughty son, "After all I've done for you . . .," or, "You ought to be *ashamed. We* don't do that sort of thing."

Allinsmith reports that type of punishment is related to boys' TAT protocols; boys who are punished physically express aggression more directly than those who are punished psychologically. She suggests that type of punishment operates in two ways to generate this relationship. First, physical punishment clearly identifies the punisher. A son can see plainly who controls the flailing arm. The relationship between parent and child is, for the moment, that of attacker and attacked. Psychological punishment creates a more subtle relationship. It is often difficult for the son to tell where his hurt feelings are coming from. Their source is more likely to seem inside him than outside. If there is to be a target for aggression then, the physically punished child, who is more likely to

5. A. Kardiner, *Psychological Frontiers of Society* (New York: Columbia University Press, 1945).

6. B. B. Allinsmith, "Parental Discipline and Children's Aggression in Two Social Classes" (unpublished Ph.D. dissertation, University of Michigan, Ann Arbor, 1954). Summarized in D. R. Miller and G. E. Swanson, "The Study of Conflict," *Nebraska Symposium on Motivation* (Lincoln, Neb.: University of Nebraska Press, 1956).

7. "The Learning of Two Mechanisms of Defense" (unpublished Ph.D. dissertation, University of Michigan, Ann Arbor, 1955). Summarized in Miller and Swanson, "The Study of Conflict," *op cit.*

8. Allinsmith, *op. cit.*

be lower-class, has an external target readily available; the psychologically punished child does not have such a ready target. If he selects one, it is likely to be himself.

Second, the type of punishment a parent administers identifies for the child the approved behavior when one is hurt or angry. The punishing parent serves as a model whom the child imitates and whose behavior instructs the moral conscience—the superego.

Why is it that lower-class parents are more likely to employ physical punishment and middle-class parents psychological punishment? McNeil has gathered data which suggest that lower-class Americans generally express themselves physically, while members of the middle class express themselves conceptually.[9] He found that lower-class adolescent boys are more spontaneous and expansive in their bodily expression of emotions in a game of statues, while their middle-class peers are more facile at the symbolic task of creating abstract drawings of emotions. He interprets these results as a reflection of the values and skills dominant in the two social classes. Lower-class boys are identifying with fathers who work with their bodies; middle-class boys are identifying with fathers who work with their heads.

Beardslee lends further support to the notion that children's behavior reflects these dominant class values.[10] She finds, as others have, that middle-class boys are apt to do better on tests of verbal intelligence than lower-class boys.

Selective factors are likely to be at work here. Since a great deal of social mobility in modern America is achieved in schools, where verbal ability is a core skill, boys who have such ability have a better chance of becoming middle-class adults. Degree of verbal facility is likely to affect modes of expression, such as the parents' expression of disapproval of the misbehavior of their children.

In an epidemiological study of psychopathology, Faris found a greater incidence of catatonia—a psychosis marked by inhibition of voluntary muscular movement—in the slum sections of cities, where manual workers are more concentrated.[11] But manic-depressive psychosis is not related to ecological areas. These findings support the statement that expression of and defenses against expression of emotion are more apt to involve the physical apparatuses in the lower class.

Several factors converge in the relationship between social class and

---

9. E. B. McNeil, "Conceptual and Motoric Expressiveness in Two Social Classes" (unpublished Ph.D. dissertation, University of Michigan, Ann Arbor, 1953). Summarized in Miller and Swanson, "The Study of Conflict," *op. cit.*

10. Beardslee, *op. cit.*

11. R. E. L. Faris, "Ecological Factors in Human Behavior," in J. McV. Hunt (ed.), *Personality and the Behavioral Disorders* (New York: Ronald Press Co., 1944), II, 736-57.

modes of aggressive expression. We have already seen how differential skills and occupations may enter into this relationship. It may also be that class ideologies concerning interpersonal relations differ. In the bureaucratic middle class, stress may be laid on "getting along" with others, for economic success rests heavily on the development of harmonious social relations. In this context direct expression of aggression becomes a disruptive force.

But, in the working class, direct aggression is not so dysfunctional. If we assume less interdependency among people and less need for harmony in social relations, the forces against expressing aggression are not so strong.

In this framework, type of punishment becomes an index to the values and skills of a category. As such, it may serve, along with social class, as a predictive variable.

Let us return now to our concern with the preference for suicide or homicide as the mode of aggressive expression. The theory presented above generates predictions similar to Henry and Short's about the kinds of people who are likely to turn aggression outward compared to those who will turn it inward. The predictions are based on the assumption that type of punishment is both an index to and a factor in shaping values concerning expression of aggression. Physical punishment leads to outward expression, while children punished psychologically should turn their aggression against themselves. The derivations below make use of the relationship found between type of punishment and social class.

Of the seven comparisons made by Henry and Short, the theory of socialization of agression makes predictions in six. There is no prediction here for the married-unmarried comparison.

Since non-whites are heavily concentrated in the working class, the theory of socialization of aggression offers the hypothesis that non-whites should show a greater preference for homicide than whites. If we accept the common assumption that army officers are recruited from the middle class and that enlisted men are more likely to be working class, especially in times of peace, we can hypothesize that army officers are more likely than enlisted men to commit suicide.

Comparing rural to urban populations, it seems safe to assume that the proportion of urban people who work in bureaucratic settings should be greater than the rural proportion. If the previous argument about the source of physical and conceptual values and modes of expression is correct, urbanites should have the greater preference for suicide.

There is evidence that in America boys are more apt to be punished physically than are girls, regardless of race or social class.[12] Therefore, females should have a greater preference for suicide than males.

12. E. Douvan and S. Withey, *A Study of Adolescent Boys* (Ann Arbor: Institute

Were we able to compare the childhood punishments administered to people now over sixty-five with the type borne by people now between twenty-five and thirty-four, we could predict to their preferred expression of aggression. Such data might be obtained by interviewing members of these two age categories or by content-analyzing the child-rearing literature their parents read. Unfortunately, data needed to test this prediction are not available. Similarly, stratified data are not available to test the prediction that middle-class people are more likely than working-class people to destroy themselves.

When we compare the hypotheses based on the socialization theory with those based on external restraint, we find that three of the four to be tested are identical. That is, both theories predict that greater preference for suicide should occur among whites, army officers, and urbanites. On the other hand, Henry and Short expect men to show a greater preference for suicide, since they are more externally restrained, while we predict women would. For women's childhood experiences are more apt than men's to be of psychological rather than physical punishment, indicative of an ideology of appropriate behavior expected from and to women.

Methodology

Before we go about testing our hypotheses, let us examine them a little more closely. We think that careful consideration of what we mean by "choice of" or "preference for" suicide or homicide suggests a more appropriate way of handling the data than Henry and Short employed.

In Part I of *Suicide and Homicide* the authors try to establish that the business cycle is a common source of frustration for all segments of the population. But they find that suicide rates do not decrease uniformly in all segments of the population in prosperous times. In addition, they report that homicide rates increase during prosperity. But, if homicidal aggression is an index of frustration, this suggests that prosperity may in part be frustrating. The authors explain that lower-status categories are relatively more deprived and frustrated by prosperity, since they gain less, relative to higher-status categories.

At this point Henry and Short state their crucial hypothesis: People in higher-status categories are more likely to prefer suicide to homicide; people in lower-status categories, homicide to suicide. If this hypothesis

for Social Research, 1955); and E. Douvan, C. Kaye, and S. Withey, *A Study of Adolescent Girls* (Ann Arbor: Institute for Social Research, 1956). I am grateful to these authors for making these data available to me.

is confirmed, then higher homicide rates during prosperity and higher suicide rates during depression are explained. Part I of their work takes this hypothesis as an important assumption.

In Part II the authors test this hypothesis. They raise the question: "Why does one person react to frustration by turning the resultant aggression against someone else, while another person reacts to frustration by turning the resultant aggression against himself?[13] They take upon themselves the responsibility of proving that members of higher-status categories are more apt to react to frustration by committing suicide and members of lower-status categories by committing homicide.

To support this, they offer absolute rates of suicide and homicide for specific years or series of years. These data show that the suicide rates presented are higher in most of the higher-status categories and that the homicide rates presented are higher in most of the lower-status categories. But it appears that Henry and Short may not really prove their point with these data.

If Henry and Short wish to demonstrate that members of higher-status categories have a greater preference for suicide than members of lower-status categories, it is not enough to demonstrate a greater suicide rate for higher-status categories. This may only indicate that they are more frustrated and hence more aggressive in general. For example, the authors' work on business cycles indicates that members of higher-status categories may at any one time be more frustrated than those in lower. If this is true, they may commit more homicide as well. Nor is it enough to demonstrate that within the higher-status category the suicide rate is higher than the homicide rate. This does tell us that higher-status citizens prefer suicide to homicide certainly, but it does not show that the preference in this category is any greater than the preference in the lower-status category where the suicide rate may also be higher than the homicide rate.

To illustrate this point, we may consider data in chapters v and vi of *Suicide and Homicide*. The writers first present evidence that the male suicide rate is higher than the female rate and so find support for their hypothesis that the higher-status category prefers aggression against self more than the lower. In chapter vii they show that the male homicide rate is also higher than the female. We might conclude from these data only that men are either more frustrated than women or more given to both these ultimate forms of violence.

In order to demonstrate a preference on the part of a population category, it is necessary to take their total amount of suicide and homicide into account. To get an index of preference for suicide over homicide, we can divide the suicide rate by the sum of suicide rate and

13. Henry and Short, *op. cit.*, p. 65.

the comparable homicide rate: (Suicide rate/Suicide rate+Homicide rate). We may call this the Suicide-Murder Ratio, or SMR.[14] Comparing the SMR of one category with the SMR of another, the larger ratio demonstrates the greater preference for suicide.

Whether or not this mode of data analysis yields results different from those obtained by Henry and Short remains to be seen. In any case, it appears to have two advantages. First, it seems a surer way to establish preference for suicide or homicide. Second, it enables us to test whether a difference in preference between categories is statistically significant. For SMR's are proportions, and, assuming an infinite population, tests of significance of differences between proportions may be applied to them.

Results

At this point we will apply the suggested methodology to the hypotheses advanced previously. We agree with Henry and Short that whites, urbanites, and army officers will demonstrate a greater preference for suicide—have a higher SMR—than non-whites, rural dwellers, and enlisted men. But, predicting to sex differences, Henry and Short think that males should have the greater preference for suicide, while the present author expects that females should.

In order to compute an SMR for a category, it is necessary to have data on the suicide rate and the homicide rate for the same population and for the same time period. It is not too difficult to get data on the number of suicides and the size of the population, so that a suicide rate can be computed. But data on homicides committed are not so easy to come by.

According to Henry and Short, "Cause of death by homicide statistics provide our most reliable comparison of homicide rates of whites and Negroes [since] the overwhelming majority of murders are committed by members of the same race as the person murdered."[15] The same type of data is used here for the racial comparison. Similarly, on the assumption that most urban murders are committed by urbanites, and most rural murders by rural dwellers, cause of death by homicide statistics are used in the rural-urban comparison also.

Table 1 presents the data comparing the preferences of white and non-whites. Supporting our predictions, it demonstrates that, in every

14. We had originally thought of calling this the Suicide-Homicide Ratio, but "SHR" is immortally Clark Hull's. Another SHR would only cause confusion.

15. Henry and Short, *op. cit.*, p. 82.

Table 1. Suicide-Murder Ratios of Whites and Non-Whites, 1930-40*

	SUICIDE RATE		HOMICIDE RATE†		SMR‡	
Year	White	Non-White	White	Non-White	White	Non-White
1930	18.0	5.9	5.9	39.5	75.3	13.0
1931	19.2	6.0	6.0	41.2	76.2	12.7
1932	19.7	6.8	5.9	40.0	77.0	14.5
1933	18.0	6.1	6.1	44.6	74.7	12.0
1934	16.6	5.9	5.7	46.5	74.4	11.3
1935	15.8	5.6	4.9	40.9	76.3	12.0
1936	15.7	5.2	4.5	41.4	77.7	11.2
1937	16.3	5.5	4.3	38.6	79.1	12.5
1938	16.4	5.5	3.8	34.9	81.1	13.6
1939	15.1	4.7	3.3	35.0	82.1	11.8
1940	15.2	5.1	3.2	34.2	82.6	13.0

*Source: United States Department of Health, Education, and Welfare, *Vital Statistics*, XXX, 467; XXXI, 485.

†Adjusted by age.

‡All differences within years between white and non-white SMR's are significant beyond .0001 (two-tailed).

year from 1930 to 1940, whites clearly chose suicide over homicide more often than did non-whites.

Table 2 presents the data on the preferences of the urban compared to the rural population, controlling on race. The prediction that urbanites have the greater preference for suicide is confirmed. Although the

Table 2. Suicide-Murder Ratios for Urban and Rural Residents, 1930, 1932, and 1933, for Whites and Non-Whites*

	Suicide Rate	Homicide Rate	SMR†
1930:			
White			
Urban	19.8	6.2	76.2
Rural	14.1	4.9	74.2
Non-white			
Urban	8.0	56.4	12.4
Rural	2.9	23.8	12.2
1932:			
White			
Urban	21.3	6.0	78.0
Rural	16.2	5.4	75.0
Non-white			
Urban	8.6	56.7	13.2
Rural	3.5	24.6	12.4
1933:			
White			
Urban	19.8	6.2	76.2
Rural	15.0	5.7	72.5
Non-white			
Urban	7.4	57.7	11.4
Rural	3.2	26.5	10.8

*Source: United States Bureau of the Census, *Mortality Statistics* for the years 1930, 1932, and 1933.

†Differences between SMR's within the white category are all significant beyond .01 (two-tailed). Differences within the non-white category are not significant (chance probability greater than .10 [two-tailed]).

differences in SMR's are not large, they are consistent over the three years we examined and within both race categories. It should be noted that presentation of the homicide rates alone would not have supported the hypothesis. According to the reasoning in *Suicide and Homicide*, the higher absolute homicide rates of the urban population would lead us to conclude that urban residents prefer homicide more than rural residents.

To compare army officers with enlisted men, it was necessary to use number of convictions for homicide as an estimate of the homicide rate, Inasmuch as not all murderers are caught, our data provide us with an approximation. Further, since the figures on convictions for homicide are low in the armed forces (no officers were convicted for this offense in the year for which data were available), data on convictions for assaults against persons are also included. So the homicide rate here is, strictly speaking, an index of "violence against others."

Table 3 reveals that army officers have a greater preference for

Table 3. Suicide-Murder Ratios of Army Officers and Enlisted Men June, 1919-June, 1920*

Category	Suicide Rate	Homicide Rate†	SMR‡
Officers	5.9	7.1	45.4
Enlisted men	5.4	22.7	19.2

*Source: "Reports of the Adjutant General, Judge Advocate General, and the Surgeon General" *Annual Report of the Secretary of War, 1920* (Washington, D.C., 1921).

†Includes assaults on persons.

‡Significance of difference in SMR's beyond .001 (two-tailed).

aggression against the self than do enlisted men. This is as predicted. Note that the data on the suicide rates alone do not reveal the true magnitude of the difference in preferences between these two categories. But, when the suicide and the homicide (assault) rates are combined in the SMR's, a large difference emerges.

To test differences between preferences of males and females for one form of aggression or another, the homicide rate is computed on the basis of convictions for homicide. Reasoning in terms of external restraint, Henry and Short expect that men will show the greater preference for suicide. The present author, taking socialization processes into account, predicts that women will show the greater preference. Table 4 presents the relevant data.

In every year, for both race categories, women are more likely to choose suicide over homicide than men are. These findings reflect a problem Henry and Short encountered. They found, consistent with their prediction, that males have higher suicide rates, but they also found, contrary to expectations, that males have higher homicide rates. It is just this type of problem which the use of SMR's avoids. Further,

Table 4. Suicide-Murder Ratios of Males and Females, White and Non-White, 1930, 1932, and 1933*

Year†	SUICIDE RATE		HOMICIDE RATE		SMR‡	
	Male	Female	Male	Female	Male	Female
1930:						
White	27.7	7.9	2.7	0.1	91.2	98.6
Non-white	9.0	2.6	8.0	1.0	52.8	71.8
1932:						
White	30.9	8.0	3.1	0.1	90.9	98.8
Non-white	10.5	2.8	21.5	2.9	32.8	49.1
1933:						
White	28.0	7.6	3.1	0.2	90.0	97.4
Non-white	9.4	2.6	22.0	2.9	29.9	47.3

*Sources: United States Department of Health, Education, and Welfare, *Vital Statistics* for the years 1930, 1932, and 1933; United States Bureau of the Census, *Prisoners in State and Federal Prisons and Reformatories* for the years 1926-36.

†Data for 1931 were incomplete.

‡All differences between male and female SMR's each year are significant beyond .001 (two-tailed).

these findings suggest that socialization practices loom as important mediating conditions between sociological categories and expressions of aggression.

But Henry and Short have still a point to make. They suggest that the female has a higher status than the male among Negroes; if this is so, they would predict that the male has the higher homicide rate. And, since Negroes are disproportionately represented in the homicide statistics, this reasoning would account for the higher male homicide rate in general. They conclude that "further research should show that the ratio of male to female homicide among Negroes is higher than the male to female homicide among whites."[16]

Table 4 supports this last hypothesis. Among the non-whites, who are predominately Negroes, there are several male murderers to one female murderer, while the ratio among whites is three to one. Even more important, a comparison of SMR's shows that there is a greater difference between the sexes in the non-white population in the preference for suicide over homicide. So Henry and Short find evidence here for their explanation of the findings.

However, the theory of socialization of aggression also explains why the difference in preference for suicide is greater between sexes among Negroes than among whites. This explanation does not seem coordinate with Henry and Short's. Our findings would be expected if the type of punishment received by boys and girls differs more among Negroes than among whites. Suppose the percentage of Negro boys who receive physical punishment is much greater than the percentage of Negro girls who receive such punishment but that the percentage of white boys who receive physical punishment is only slightly larger than the percentage of white girls who receive such punishment. Then it would

16. *Ibid.*, p. 88.

follow that Negro boys should have a much lower SMR than Negro girls, while white boys would show an SMR only slightly lower than white girls. Table 5 presents the relevant punishment data on a nationwide sample of schoolboys and girls. The subjects are aged fourteen to sixteen, and race is controlled.

Table 5 clearly validates the assumption that differences in type of

Table 5. Type of Punishment Received by Fourteen-to-Sixteen-Year-Old Males and Females, White and Negro*

	Per Cent Physical†	*Per Cent Other*	*Per Cent Never Punished*	*Per Cent Unknown*	No.
White					
Boys	8.9	85.8	3.5	1.4	649
Girls	6.2	90.0	3.2	0.5	769
Negro					
Boys	50.0	50.0	0.0	0.0	40
Girls	22.0	73.2	4.9	4.9	41

*Source: E. Douvan and S. Withey, *A Study of Adolescent Boys* (Ann Arbor: Institute for Social Research, 1955); E. Douvan, C. Kaye, and S. Withey, *A Study of Adolescent Girls* (Ann Arbor: Institute for Social Research, 1956).

†Significance of differences in percentage of physical punishment given boys and girls: white, $>$ .10; Negro, $>$ .01 (two-tailed).

punishment is greater among Negro boys and girls than among white boys and girls. Furthermore, the figures here directly parallel the SMR's in Table 4: the white children are less likely than the Negroes to be punished physically and to show the lower SMR's. There is strong evidence here, then, that the manner in which children are socialized, as indicated by the way in which they are punished, is a factor in determining a later preference for suicide or homicide.

Let us raise one more issue. Henry and Short present us with a contradiction of factors affecting homicide and suicide rates in the "central disorganized sectors of cities":

> From the general negative correlation between homicide and status position, we would expect the low status ethnic and Negro inhabitants of these areas to raise the homicide rate. From the suggested relation between homicide and strength of the relational system, we would expect the "homeless men" and "anonymous" residents of rooming houses in these areas to lower the homicide rate.[17]

This contradiction of factors becomes unimportant if socialization of aggression is recognized as a crucial mediating process between sociological categories and determinants of aggressive behavior. For, although there are ethnic and other differences within the central urban population, the overwhelming majority of these people, non-white or homeless, are in the working class. This fact suggests that certain socialization practices concerning aggression are generally present in the hub, which

17. *Ibid.*, p. 93.

would lead to a choice of homicide rather than suicide. By considering socialization as primary, we can generate this straightforward hypothesis involving comparisons of urban centers with the periphery, which a theory of external restraint could not.

Although the necessary rates were not available to compute the appropriate SMR's, data gathered by Schmid, and cited by Henry and Short,[18] support the hypothesis. They indicate that homicides are more concentrated in the hub than are suicides—quite a different picture from that presented by other areas.

Discussion

Now, Durkheim tentatively regarded the choice of anomic suicide or homicide as a purely psychological matter, unrelated to sociological variables. In *Suicide* he writes:

> Anomie, in fact, begets a state of exasperation and irritated weariness which may turn against the person himself or another according to circumstances; in the first case, we have suicide, in the second, homicide. The causes determining the direction of such over-excited forces probably depend on the agent's moral constitution. According to its greater or less resistance, it will incline one way rather than the other.[19]

Henry and Short suggest that the choice of suicide or homicide, prompted by a state of anomie, is not purely a psychological matter. While their *Suicide and Homicide* includes an insightful discussion of psychological determinants of this choice, they assert that sociological variables play an active and separate role as well,[20] that is, external restraint growing directly out of position in the social structure conditions expression of aggression.

Our own position lies somewhere between the two. We assert that, if sociological variables condition expression of aggression, it is necessary to search for the manner in which these variables are translated into those psychological determinants which lie closer to the actual individual choice. This position has led us to examine the socialization process, particularly socialization of aggression. We have cited evidence that a pivotal child-rearing variable—type of punishment—is related to position in the social structure. We have tried to show why this relationship exists: outward aggression seems to be more disturbing to the interpersonal relationships inherent to the middle class than to those of

18. *Ibid.*, p. 92.

19. Émile Durkheim, *Suicide*, trans. A. Spaulding and G. Simpson, ed. G. Simpson (New York: Free Press, 1951).

20. *Ibid.*, pp. 106-9.

the working class; outward aggression is more consistent with the role of men than of women in our society; and verbal ability is closely related to recruitment into social classes in our society and may have a good deal to do with the way parents punish children. It is a short step from these arguments to the choice of suicide or homicide.

We have pointed out that many of the relationships derived by Henry and Short from a theory of external restraint might equally well be derived from the association of particular socialization practices with social classes in America. Further, the problem of suicide and homicide rates in central portions of large cities, unresolved by the former, may be resolved by the latter.

But this does not by any means make the concept of external restraint less useful. On the contrary, if by external restraint we mean the degree to which one's behavior is controlled by an external other, the findings emphasize its value, for the theory of socialization presented and tested here also involves external restraint as a core concept. Physcial punishment operates to create a preference for homicide insofar as it represents a pattern of controls which allows expression of aggression and does not build in controls over direct expression. We have assumed that this type of punishment is consistent with a value system which manifests itself in other child-rearing practices as well.

But rather than formulate external restraints in terms of relationships between broad sociological categories, we have availed ourselves of the clues psychology has to offer, particularly, that the relationship between parent and child is the crucial one.

It is possible that our proposal here is not alternative to Henry and Short's. Perhaps it is in addition. Those researchers certainly make it clear that they would not ignore psychological factors. But our feeling is that we are dealing with a unity. We have attempted to bring a social-psychological orientation to bear on the problem in order to show how sociological and psychological factors are related in one process.

SELECTED READINGS

Nahum Z. Medalia, "Who Cries Wolf? The Reporters of Damage to Police in a Pseudo-Disaster," *Social Problems*, Winter, 1959, makes further analysis of the windshield-pitting episode. Morris Ginsberg, "Moral Bewilderment," *Social Forces*, 1956, stresses the need for social definition not merely of values as such but of the field of their application. Raymond Firth, "Suicide and Risk-Taking in Tikopia Society," *Psychiatry*, February, 1961, examines the concept of *anomie* in a cross-cultural setting. Responses resembling those reported by Medalia and Larsen are described by E. A. Schuler and V. J. Parenton, "A Recent Epidemic of Hysteria in a Louisiana High School," *Journal of Social Psychology*, 1943; also, Donald M. Johnson, "The Phantom Anesthetist of Mattoon: A Field Study of Mass Hysteria," *Journal of Abnormal and Social Psychology*, 1945. Other articles include Wendell Bell, "Anomie, Social Isolation and the Class Structure," *Sociometry*, 1957; Bruce P. Dohrenwend, "Egoism, Altruism, Anomie, and Fatalism: A Conceptual Analysis of Durkheim's Types," *American Sociological Review*, August, 1959; Dorothy L. Meier and Wendell Bell, "Anomia and Differential Access to the Achievement of Life Goals," *American Sociological Review*, April, 1959.

The classic exposition of *anomie* is found in Emile Durkheim, *Suicide: A Study in Sociology*, George Simpson (tr.) (New York: The Free Press, 1951), pp. 246-256. See also, Robert K. Merton, "Social Structure and Anomie" in *Social Theory and Social Structure* (New York: The Free Press, 1949). Lewis A. Coser and Bernard Rosenberg (eds.), *Sociological Theory: A Book of Readings* (New York: The Macmillan Company, 1957), present a clear exposition of *anomie*, with a helpful statement from Talcott Parsons, on pages 479-480.

5 *Self Responses to Social Structure*

SOCIETY AND SELF may be "twin born," but they are not mirror images of each other. The individual's interests are seldom completely defined by convention. And even in the respect that they are defined by convention, the individual is likely to view them as opportunities rather than strictures. The secret worlds of the self push and surge against the functional uniformities of social life. Reinhard Bendix and Bennett Berger pointed out that a society must even provide for deviance: ". . . Culture and society not only determine how others expect the individual to act, but also enable him to comply with, or to resist, these expectations." Paul Schilder indicates that uniformity in behavior and creativity are not sworn enemies: "Life history is a continuous process, in which the situation in the widest sense (nature, culture, family, attitude of the family, physique, disease) stays on the one side, and the person with his creative tendencies on the other side. It expresses itself in a series of creations which are again dependent upon the situation."

When we look at role performance from this perspective, we see that it normally contains a wider measure of choice and tolerance than has received general recognition in the sociological literature. An allowance for these factors can avoid what Dennis Wrong has termed "the oversocialized conception of man." The studies in this section suggest the varieties of response to social structure, indicating behaviors within the system and also those that tend to change or even defeat it.

The term conformity has often been used to describe behavior consistent with defined expectations. The connotation of this term implies personal disinclination and external compulsion. It thus fails to mark out the element of willing and rewarding inclination that may exist in the self. Robert W. Avery, in a review of Herbert Kaufman's *The Forest Ranger*, speaks to this point when he says: "Recruitment, training, and an almost Marine-like identification with the Forest Service produce rangers who want to conform in spite of distraction." This is no slavish obeisance to a stronger will; the strong will, Kaufman believes, resides in the ranger. In keeping with his theme, he leaves the reader to ponder that most elusive sociological paradox: "Why it is that men find their independence when they take as their own the goals and values of those upon whom they are manifestly dependent?" For a situation of this sort I have employed the term "acceptance." The article by Howard S. Becker, "Becoming a Marihuana User," is an example of the development of acceptance in a concrete social situation. I think the process described here can be taken as a prototype of acceptance in general. It is interesting to observe the gradual and subtle implication of the actor in the defined situation.

Robert K. Merton recently suggested the term "variance" to describe behavior that is not squarely in line with social expectation but certainly within the area of social toleration. In the study, "Public Health as a Career of Medicine: Secondary Choice within a Profession," Back, Phillips, Coker, and Donnelly call attention to the factors involved in a variant behavior pattern among certain medical students. By looking both at the structure of the situation and the characteristics of the actors, they have constructed a rounded picture of a "deviant specialty."

Ben-David, "Rules and Innovations in Medicine," describes aspects of social structure that may favor innovating behavior. Mahony shows how the chief of Moen Island, in the Truk District, was able to bring about a remarkable adaptation of traditional social structure to entirely new uses and purposes. This study is also a needed corrective for the view that simple, "mechanical" societies are incapable of rapid alteration.

At least since Merton's study, "Social Structure and Anomie," it has become commonplace that the legitimate or socially approved means of achieving goals are not equally accessible to all segments of a society. Richard A. Cloward adds piquancy and depth to the analysis of deviant behavior by showing that illegitimate means to the achievement of goals are also not equally accessible to all segments of a society. The author points out that the various criteria governing access to illegitimate means, ethnicity for instance, all ". . . pertain to criminal activity historically associated with the lower class. Most middle- or upper-class persons—even when interested in following 'lower-class' criminal careers —would no doubt have difficulty in fulfilling this ambition because of inappropriate preparation." The author applies his thesis to the understanding of innovation and "retreatism."

Conflict may exist at the social or the self level and usually the two are related. The studies presented here point to inconsistencies in the social structure. Individuals responding to inconsistent structural expectations are likely to perplex others or themselves. Kirkpatrick and Kanin, "Male Sex Aggression on a University Campus," show the behavior of a large number of young men who refused to take "no" for an answer. Although adjudged inadmissible in the dating situation by a considerable number of young women, this indomitable behavior in other contexts measures up to the highest standards for the American male.

Campbell and Pettigrew, "Racial and Moral Crisis: The Role of Little Rock Ministers," show clergymen "perplexed in the extreme" in trying to chart their personal courses. The authors evaluate the importance of "the self-reference system," "the professional reference system," and "the membership reference system" in influencing the behavior of Little Rock ministers during the crisis over school integration in 1957.

a) WITHIN SOCIAL TOLERANCE

1) Acceptance

HOWARD S. BECKER

Becoming a Marihuana User

THE use of marihuana is and has been the focus of a good deal of attention on the part of both scientists and laymen. One of the major problems students of the practice have addressed themselves to has been the identification of those individual psychological traits which differentiate marihuana users from nonusers and which are assumed to account for the use of the drug. That approach, common in the study of behavior categorized as deviant, is based on the premise that the presence of a given kind of behavior in an individual can best be explained as the

Reprinted from "Becoming a Marihuana User," by Howard S. Becker, The American Journal of Sociology, *November, 1953, pp. 235-242, by permission of The University of Chicago Press. Copyright 1953 by the University of Chicago.*

Paper read at the meetings of the Midwest Sociological Society in Omaha, Nebraska, April 25, 1953. The research on which this paper is based was done while I was a member of the staff of the Chicago Narcotics Survey, a study done by the Chicago Area Project, Inc., under a grant from the National Mental Health Institute. My thanks to Solomon Kobrin, Harold Finestone, Henry McKay, and Anselm Strauss, who read and discussed with me earlier versions of this paper.

result of some trait which predisposes or motivates him to engage in the behavior.[1]

This study is likewise concerned with accounting for the presence or absence of marihuana use in an individual's behavior. It starts, however, from a different premise: that the presence of a given kind of behavior is the result of a sequence of social experiences during which the person acquires a conception of the meaning of the behavior, and perceptions and judgments of objects and situations, all of which make the activity possible and desirable. Thus, the motivation or disposition to engage in the activity is built up in the course of learning to engage in it and does not antedate this learning process. For such a view it is not necessary to identify those "traits" which "cause" the behavior. Instead, the problem becomes one of describing the set of changes in the person's conception of the activity and of the experience it provides for him.[2]

This paper seeks to describe the sequence of changes in attitude and experience which lead to *the use of marihuana for pleasure.* Marihuana does not produce addiction, as do alcohol and the opiate drugs; there is no withdrawal sickness and no ineradicable craving for the drug.[3] The most frequent pattern of use might be termed "recreational." The drug is used occasionally for the pleasure the user finds in it, a relatively casual kind of behavior in comparison with that connected with the use of addicting drugs. The term "use for pleasure" is meant to emphasize the noncompulsive and casual character of the behavior. It is also meant to eliminate from consideration here those few cases in which marihuana is used for its prestige value only, as a symbol that one is a certain kind of person, with no pleasure at all being derived from its use.

The analysis presented here is conceived of as demonstrating the greater explanatory usefulness of the kind of theory outlined above as opposed to the predispositional theories now current. This may be seen in two ways: (1) predispositional theories cannot account for that group of users (whose existence is admitted)[4] who do not exhibit the trait or traits considered to cause the behavior and (2) such theories cannot

1. See, as examples of this approach, the following: Eli Marcovitz and Henry J. Meyers, "The Marihuana Addict in the Army," *War Medicine,* VI (December, 1944), 382-91; Herbert S. Gaskill, "Marihuana, an Intoxicant," *American Journal of Psychiatry,* CII (September, 1945), 202-4; Sol Charen and Luis Perelman, "Personality Studies of Marihuana Addicts," *American Journal of Psychiatry,* CII March, 1946), 674-82.

2. This approach stems from George Herbert Mead's discussion of objects in *Mind, Self, and Society* (Chicago: University of Chicago Press, 1934), pp. 277-80.

3. Cf. Roger Adams, "Marihuana," *Bulletin of the New York Academy of Medicine,* XVIII (November, 1942), 705-30.

4. Cf. Lawrence Kolb, "Marihuana," *Federal Probation,* II (July, 1938), 22-25; and Walter Bromberg, "Marihuana: A Psychiatric Study," *Journal of the American Medical Association,* CXIII (July 1, 1939), 11.

account for the great variability over time of a given individual's behavior with reference to the drug. The same person will at one stage be unable to use the drug for pleasure, at a later stage be able and willing to do so, and, still later, again be unable to use it in this way. These changes, difficult to explain from a predispositional or motivational theory, are readily understandable in terms of changes in the individual's conception of the drug as is the existence of "normal" users.

The study attempted to arrive at a general statement of the sequence of changes in individual attitude and experience which have always occurred when the individual has become willing and able to use marihuana for pleasure and which have not occurred or not been permanently maintained when this is not the case. This generalization is stated in universal terms in order that negative cases may be discovered and used to revise the explanatory hypothesis.[5]

Fifty interviews with marihuana users from a variety of social backgrounds and present positions in society constitute the data from which the generalization was constructed and against which it was tested.[6] The interviews focused on the history of the person's experience with the drug, seeking major changes in his attitude toward it and in his actual use of it and the reasons for these changes. The final generalization is a statement of that sequence of changes in attitude which occurred in every case known to me in which the person came to use marihuana for pleasure. Until a negative case is found, it may be considered as an explanation of all cases of marihuana use for pleasure. In addition, changes from use to nonuse are shown to be related to similar changes in conception, and in each case it is possible to explain variations in the individual's behavior in these terms.

This paper covers only a portion of the natural history of an individual's use of marihuana,[7] starting with the person having arrived at the point of willingness to try marihuana. He knows that others use it to "get high," but he does not know what this means in concrete terms. He is curious about the experience, ignorant of what it may turn out to be, and afraid that it may be more than he has bargained for. The steps outlined below, if he undergoes them all and maintains the attitudes developed in them, leave him willing and able to use the drug for pleasure when the opportunity presents itself.

5. The method used is that described by Alfred R. Lindesmith in his *Opiate Addiction* (Bloomington: Principia Press, 1947), chap. i. I would like also to acknowledge the important role Lindesmith's work played in shaping my thinking about the genesis of marihuana use.

6. Most of the interviews were done by the author. I am grateful to Solomon Kobrin and Harold Finestone for allowing me to make use of interviews done by them.

7. I hope to discuss elsewhere other stages in this natural history.

I

The novice does not ordinarily get high the first time he smokes marihuana, and several attempts are usually necessary to induce this state. One explanation of this may be that the drug is not smoked "properly," that is, in a way that insures sufficient dosage to produce real symptoms of intoxication. Most users agree that it cannot be smoked like tobacco if one is to get high:

> Take in a lot of air, you know, and . . . I don't know how to describe it, you don't smoke it like a cigarette, you draw in a lot of air and get it deep down in your system and then keep it there. Keep it there as long as you can.

Without the use of some such technique[8] the drug will produce no effects, and the user will be unable to get high:

> The trouble with people like that [who are not able to get high] is that they're just not smoking it right, that's all there is to it. Either they're not holding it down long enough, or they're getting too much air and not enough smoke, or the other way around or something like that. A lot of people just don't smoke it right, so naturally nothing's gonna happen.

If nothing happens, it is manifestly impossible for the user to develop a conception of the drug as an object which can be used for pleasure, and use will therefore not continue. The first step in the sequence of events that must occur if the person is to become a user is that he must learn to use the proper smoking technique in order that his use of the drug will produce some effects in terms of which his conception of it can change.

Such a change is, as might be expected, a result of the individual's participation in groups in which marihuana is used. In them the individual learns the proper way to smoke the drug. This may occur through direct teaching:

> I was smoking like I did an ordinary cigarette. He said, "No, don't do it like that." He said, "Suck it, you know, draw in and hold it in your lungs till you . . . for a period of time."
>
> I said, "Is there any limit of time to hold it?"
>
> He said, "No, just till you feel that you want to let it out, let it out." So I did that three or four times.

Many new users are ashamed to admit ignorance and, pretending to know already, must learn through the more indirect means of observation and imitation:

---

8. A pharmacologist notes that this ritual is in fact an extremely efficient way of getting the drug into the blood stream (R. P. Walton, *Marihuana: America's New Drug Problem* [Philadelphia: J. B. Lippincott, 1938], p. 48).

> I came on like I had turned on [smoked marihuana] many times before, you know. I didn't want to seem like a punk to this cat. See, like I didn't know the first thing about it—how to smoke it, or what was going to happen, or what. I just watched him like a hawk—I didn't take my eyes off him for a second, because I wanted to do everything just as he did it. I watched how he held it, how he smoked it, and everything. Then when he gave it to me I just came on cool, as though I knew exactly what the score was. I held it like he did and took a poke just the way he did.

No person continued marihuana use for pleasure without learning a technique that supplied sufficient dosage for the effects of the drug to appear. Only when this was learned was it possible for a conception of the drug as an object which could be used for pleasure to emerge. Without such a conception marihuana use was considered meaningless and did not continue.

II

Even after he learns the proper smoking technique, the new user may not get high and thus not form a conception of the drug as something which can be used for pleasure. A remark made by a user suggested the reason for this difficulty in getting high and pointed to the next necessary step on the road to being a user:

> I was told during an interview, "As a matter of fact, I've seen a guy who was high out of his mind and didn't know it."
>
> I expressed disbelief: "How can that be, man?"
>
> The interviewee said, "Well, it's pretty strange, I'll grant you that, but I've seen it. This guy got on with me, claiming that he'd never got high, one of those guys, and he got completely stoned. And he kept insisting that he wasn't high. So I had to prove to him that he was."

What does this mean? It suggests that being high consists of two elements: the presence of symptoms caused by marihuana use and the recognition of these symptoms and their connection by the user with his use of the drug. It is not enough, that is, that the effects be present; they alone do not automatically provide the experience of being high. The user must be able to point them out to himself and consciously connect them with his having smoked marihuana before he can have this experience. Otherwise, regardless of the actual effects produced, he considers that the drug has had no effect on him: "I figured it either had no effect on me or other people were exaggerating its effect on them, you know. I thought it was probably psychological, see." Such persons believe that the whole thing is an illusion and that the wish to be high leads the user to deceive himself into believing that something is happening when, in fact, nothing is. They do not continue marihuana use, feeling that "it does nothing" for them.

Typically, however, the novice has faith (developed from his observation of users who do get high) that the drug actually will produce some new experience and continues to experiment with it until it does. His failure to get high worries him, and he is likely to ask more experienced users or provoke comments from them about it. In such conversations he is made aware of specific details of his experience which he may not have noticed or may have noticed but failed to identify as symptoms of being high:

> I didn't get high the first time. . . . I don't think I held it in long enough. I probably let it out, you know, you're a little afraid. The second time I wasn't sure, and he [smoking companion] told me, like I asked him for some of the symptoms or something, how would I know, you know. . . . So he told me to sit on a stool. I sat on—I think I sat on a bar stool—and he said, "Let your feet hang," and then when I got down my feet were real cold, you know.
>
> And I started feeling it, you know. That was the first time. And then about a week after that, sometime pretty close to it, I really got on. That was the first time I got on a big laughing kick, you know. Then I really knew I was on.

One symptom of being high is an intense hunger. In the next case the novice becomes aware of this and gets high for the first time:

> They were just laughing the hell out of me because like I was eating so much. I just scoffed [ate] so much food, and they were just laughing at me, you know. Sometimes I'd be looking at them, you know, wondering why they're laughing, you know, not knowing what I was doing. [Well, did they tell you why they were laughing eventually?] Yeah, yeah, I come back, "Hey, man, what's happening?" Like, you know, like I'd ask, "What's happening?" and all of sudden I feel weird, you know. "Man, you're on, you know. You're on pot [high on marihuana]." I said, "No, am I?" Like I don't know what's happening.

The learning may occur in more indirect ways:

> I heard little remarks that were made by other people. Somebody said, "My legs are rubbery," and I can't remember all the remarks that were made because I was very attentively listening for all these cues for what I was supposed to feel like.

The novice, then, eager to have this feeling, picks up from other users some concrete referents of the term "high" and applies these notions to his own experience. The new concepts make it possible for him to locate these symptoms among his own sensations and to point out to himself a "something different" in his experience that he connects with drug use. It is only when he can do this that he is high. In the next case, the contrast between two successive experiences of a user makes clear the crucial importance of the awareness of the symptoms in being high and re-emphasizes the important role of interaction with other users in acquiring the concepts that make this awareness possible:

> [Did you get high the first time you turned on?] Yeah, sure. Although, come to think of it, I guess I really didn't. I mean, like that first time it was more or less of a mild drunk. I was happy, I guess, you know what I mean. But I didn't really know I was high, you know what I mean. It was only after the second time I got high that I realized I was high the first time. Then I knew that something different was happening.
>
> [How did you know that?] How did I know? If what happened to me that night would of happened to you, you would've known, believe me. We played the first tune for almost two hours—one tune! Imagine, man! We got on the stand and played this one tune, we started at nine o'clock. When we got finished I looked at my watch, it's a quarter to eleven. Almost two hours on one tune. And it didn't seem like anything.
>
> I mean, you know, it does that to you. It's like you have much more time or something. Anyway, when I saw that, man, it was too much. I knew I must really be high or something if anything like that could happen. See, and then they explained to me that that's what it did to you, you had a different sense of time and everything. So I realized that that's what it was. I knew then. Like the first time, I probably felt that way, you know, but I didn't know what's happening.

It is only when the novice becomes able to get high in this sense that he will continue to use marihuana for pleasure. In every case in which use continued, the user had acquired the necessary concepts with which to express to himself the fact that he was experiencing new sensations caused by the drug. That is, for use to continue, it is necessary not only to use the drug so as to produce effects but also to learn to perceive these effects when they occur. In this way marihuana acquires meaning for the user as an object which can be used for pleasure.

With increasing experience the user develops a greater appreciation of the drug's effects; he continues to learn to get high. He examines succeeding experiences closely, looking for new effects, making sure the old ones are still there. Out of this there grows a stable set of categories for experiencing the drug's effects whose presence enables the user to get high with ease.

The ability to perceive the drug's effects must be maintained if use is to continue; if it is lost, marihuana use ceases. Two kinds of evidence support this statement. First, people who become heavy users of alcohol, barbiturates, or opiates do not continue to smoke marihuana, largely because they lose the ability to distinguish between its effects and those of the other drugs.[9] They no longer know whether the marihuana gets them high. Second, in those few cases in which an individual uses marihuana in such quantities that he is always high, he is apt to get this same feeling that the drug has no effect on him, since the essential element of a noticeable difference between feeling high and feeling normal is missing. In such a situation, use is likely to be given up completely, but temporarily, in order that the user may once again be able to perceive the difference.

III

One more step is necessary if the used who has now learned to get high is to continue use. He must learn to enjoy the effects he has just learned to experience. Marihuana-produced sensations are not automatically or necessarily pleasurable. The taste for such experience is a socially acquired one, not different in kind from acquired tastes for oysters or dry martinis. The user feels dizzy, thirsty; his scalp tingles; he misjudges time and distances; and so on. Are these things pleasurable? He isn't sure. If he is to continue marihuana use, he must decide that they are. Otherwise, getting high, while a real enough experience, will be an unpleasant one he would rather avoid.

The effects of the drug, when first perceived, may be physically unpleasant or at least ambiguous:

> It started taking effect, and I didn't know what was happening, you know. what it was, and I was very sick. I walked around the room, walking around the room trying to get off, you know; it just scared me at first, you know. I wasn't used to that kind of feeling.

In addition, the novice's naïve interpretation of what is happening to him may further confuse and frighten him, particularly if he decides, as many do, that he is going insane:

> I felt I was insane, you know. Everything people done to me just wigged me. I couldn't hold a conversation, and my mind would be wandering, and I was always thinking, oh, I don't know, weird things, like hearing music different. . . . I get the feeling that I can't talk to anyone. I'll goof completely.

9. "Smokers have repeatedly stated that the consumption of whiskey while smoking negates the potency of the drug. They find it very difficult to get 'high' while drinking whiskey and because of that smokers will not drink while using the 'weed' " (cf. New York City Mayor's Committee on Marihuana, *The Marihuana Problem in the City of New York* [Lancaster, Pa.: Jacques Cattell Press, 1944], p. 13).

Given these typically frightening and unpleasant first experiences, the beginner will not continue use unless he learns to redefine the sensations as pleasurable:

It was offered to me, and I tried it. I'll tell you one thing. I never did enjoy it at all. I mean it was just nothing that I could enjoy. [Well, did you get high when you turned on?] Oh, yeah, I got definite feelings from it. But I didn't enjoy them. I mean I got plenty of reactions, but they were mostly reactions of fear. [You were frightened?] Yes. I didn't enjoy it. I couldn't seem to relax with it, you know. If you can't relax with a thing, you can't enjoy it, I don't think.

In other cases the first experiences were also definitely unpleasant, but the person did become a marihuana user. This occurred, however, only after a later experience enabled him to redefine the sensations as pleasurable:

[This man's first experience was extremely unpleasant, involving distortion of spatial relationships and sounds, violent thirst, and panic produced by these symptoms.] After the first time I didn't turn on for about, I'd say, ten months to a year. . . . It wasn't a moral thing; it was because I'd gotten so frightened, bein' so high. An' I didn't want to go through that again, I mean, my reaction was, "Well, if this is what they call bein' high, I don't dig [like] it." . . . So I didn't turn on for a year almost, accounta that. . . .

Well, my friends started, an' consequently I started again. But I didn't have any more, I didn't have that same initial reaction, after I started turning on again.

[In interaction with his friends he became able to find pleasure in the effects of the drug and eventually became a regular user.]

In no case will use continue without such a redefinition of the effects as enjoyable.

This redefinition occurs, typically, in interaction with more experienced users who, in a number of ways, teach the novice to find pleasure in this experience which is at first so frightening.[10] They may reassure him as to the temporary character of the unpleasant sensations and minimize their seriousness, at the same time calling attention to the more enjoyable aspects. An experienced user describes how he handles newcomers to marihuana use:

Well, they get pretty high sometimes. The average person isn't ready for that, and it is a little frightening to them sometimes. I mean, they've been high on lush [alcohol], and they get higher that way than they've ever been before, and they don't know what's happening to them. Because they think they're going to keep going up, up, up till they lose their minds or begin doing weird things or something. You have to like reassure them, explain to them that they're not really flipping or anything, that they're gonna be all

10. Charen and Perelman, *op. cit.*, p. 679.

right. You have to just talk them out of being afraid. Keep talking to them, reassuring, telling them it's all right. And come on with your own story, you know: "The same thing happened to me. You'll get to like that after awhile." Keep coming on like that; pretty soon you talk them out of being scared. And besides they see you doing it and nothing horrible is happening to you, so that gives them more confidence.

The more experienced user may also teach the novice to regulate the amount he smokes more carefully, so as to avoid any severely uncomfortable symptoms while retaining the pleasant ones. Finally, he teaches the new user that he can "get to like it after awhile." He teaches him to regard those ambiguous experiences formerly defined as unpleasant as enjoyable. The older user in the following incident is a person whose tastes have shifted in this way, and his remarks have the effect of helping others to make a similar redefinition:

> A new user had her first experience of the effects of marihuana and became frightened and hysterical. She "felt like she was half in and half out of the room" and experienced a number of alarming physical symptoms. One of the more experienced users present said, "She's dragged because she's high like that. I'd give anything to get that high myself. I haven't been that high in years."

In short, what was once frightening and distasteful becomes, after a taste for it is built up, pleasant, desired, and sought after. Enjoyment is introduced by the favorable definition of the experience that one acquires from others. Without this, use will not continue, for marihuana will not be for the user an object he can use for pleasure.

In addition to being a necessary step in becoming a user, this represents an important condition for continued use. It is quite common for experienced users suddenly to have an unpleasant or frightening experience, which they cannot define as pleasurable, either because they have used a larger amount of marihuana than usual or because it turns out to be a higher-quality marihuana than they expected. The user has sensations which go beyond any conception he has of what being high is and is in much the same situation as the novice, uncomfortable and frightened. He may blame it on an overdose and simply be more careful in the future. But he may make this the occasion for a rethinking of his attitude toward the drug and decide that it no longer can give him pleasure. When this occurs and is not followed by a redefinition of the drug as capable of producing pleasure, use will cease.

The likelihood of such a redefinition occurring depends on the degree of the individual's participation with other users. Where this participation is intensive, the individual is quickly talked out of his feeling against marihuana use. In the next case, on the other hand, the experience was very disturbing, and the aftermath of the incident cut the person's participation with other users to almost zero. Use stopped for three years and began again only when a combination of circumstances, important among which was a resumption of ties with users, made possible a redefinition of the nature of the drug:

It was too much, like I only made about four pokes, and I couldn't even get it out of my mouth, I was so high, and I got real flipped. In the basement, you know, I just couldn't stay in there anymore. My heart was pounding real hard, you know, and I was going out of my mind; I thought I was losing my mind completely. So I cut out of this basement, and this other guy, he's out of his mind, told me, "Don't, don't leave me, man. Stay here." And I couldn't.

I walked outside, and it was five below zero, and I thought I was dying, and I had my coat open; I was sweating, I was perspiring. My whole insides were all . . ., and I walked about two blocks away, and I fainted behind a bush. I don't know how long I laid there. I woke up, and I was feeling the worst, I can't describe it at all, so I made it to a bowling alley, man, and I was trying to act normal, I was trying to shoot pool, you know, trying to act real normal, and I couldn't lay and I couldn't stand up and I couldn't sit down, and I went up and laid down where some guys that spot pins lay down, and that didn't help me, and I went down to a doctor's office. I was going to go in there and tell the doctor to put me out of my misery . . . because my heart was pounding so hard, you know. . . . So then all week end I started flipping, seeing things there and going through hell, you know, all kinds of abnormal things. . . . I just quit for a long time then.

[He went to a doctor who defined the symptoms for him as those of a nervous breakdown caused by "nerves" and "worries." Although he was no longer using marihuana, he had some recurrences of the symptoms which led him to suspect that "it was all his nerves."] So I just stopped worrying, you know; so it was about thirty-six months later I started making it again. I'd just take a few pokes, you know. [He first resumed use in the company of the same user-friend with whom he had been involved in the original incident.]

A person, then, cannot begin to use marihuana for pleasure, or continue its use for pleasure, unless he learns to define its effects as enjoyable, unless is becomes and remains an object which he conceives of as capable of producing pleasure.

IV

In summary, an individual will be able to use marihuana for pleasure only when he goes through a process of learning to conceive of it as an object which can be used in this way. No one becomes a user without (1) learning to smoke the drug in a way which will produce real effects; (2) learning to recognize the effects and connect them with drug use (learning, in other words, to get high); and (3) learning to enjoy the sensations he perceives. In the course of this process he develops a disposition or motivation to use marihuana which was not and could not have been present when he began use, for it involves and depends on conceptions of the drug which could only grow out of the kind of actual experience detailed above. On completion of this process he is willing and able to use marihuana for pleasure.

He has learned, in short, to answer "Yes" to the question: "Is it fun?" The direction his further use of the drug takes depends on his being able to continue to answer "Yes" to this question and, in addition, on his being able to answer "Yes" to other questions which arise as he becomes aware of the implications of the fact that the society as a whole disapproves of the practice: "Is it expedient?" "Is it moral?"[11] Once he has acquired the ability to get enjoyment out of the drug, use will continue to be possible for him. Considerations of morality and expediency, occasioned by the reactions of society, may interfere and inhibit use, but use continues to be a possibility in terms of his conception of the drug. The act becomes impossible only when the ability to enjoy the experience of being high is lost, through a change in the user's conception of the drug occasioned by certain kinds of experience with it.

In comparing this theory with those which ascribe marihuana use to motives or predispositions rooted deep in individual behavior, the evidence makes it clear that marihuana use for pleasure can occur only when the process described above is undergone and cannot occur without it. This is apparently so without reference to the nature of the individual's personal makeup or psychic problems. Such theories assume that people have stable modes of response which predetermine the way they will act in relation to any particular situation or object and that, when they come in contact with the given object or situation, they act in the way in which their makeup predisposes them.

This analysis of the genesis of marihuana use shows that the individuals who come in contact with a given object may respond to it at first in a great variety of ways. If a stable form of new behavior toward the object is to emerge, a transformation of meanings must occur, in which the person develops a new conception of the nature of the object.[12] This happens in a series of communicative acts in which others point out new aspects of his experience to him, present him with new interpretations of events, and help him achieve a new conceptual organization of his world, without which the new behavior is not possible. Persons who do not achieve the proper kind of conceptualization are

11. Another paper will discuss the series of developments in attitude that occurs as the individual begins to take account of these matters and adjust his use to them.

12. Cf. Anselm Strauss, "The Development and Transformation of Monetary Meanings in the Child," *American Sociological Review*, XVII (June, 1952), 275-86.

unable to engage in the given behavior and turn off in the direction of some other relationship to the object or activity.

This suggests that behavior of any kind might fruitfully be studied developmentally, in terms of changes in meanings and concepts, their organization and reorganization, and the way they channel behavior, making some acts possible while excluding others.

2) Variance

KURT W. BACK,
BERNARD S. PHILLIPS, ROBERT E. COKER, JR.,
and THOMAS G. DONNELLY

Public Health as a Career in Medicine: Secondary Choice within a Profession

ONE of the striking features of contemporary society is the multitude of distinct occupations. *The Dictionary of Occupational Titles* lists almost 25,000 different occupations, and other detailed classifications reach similar numbers. This fact alone suggests the difficulty of rational occupational choices. Not only is the number of alternatives beyond the ability of the individual to assess, but many occupations are completely unfamiliar to most people. Many of the day-to-day activities and require-

Reprinted from American Sociological Review, *October, 1958, pp. 533-541, by permission of the authors and the journal.*

Based on paper presented at the annual meeting of the American Sociological Society, Washington, D.C., August, 1957. The research program reported here is supported by a grant from the National Institute of Health, U.S. Public Health Service. It was developed under the auspices of the Subcommittee on Recruitment of the Committee on

ments for success in even relatively familiar occupations are virtually unknown. The image of an occupation is primarily defined for the prospective entrant by those of its activities which are known to the general public, either directly or through media of communication. Training for occupations typically is acquired with respect to "job-families" and not for specific occupations. Vocational preparation and occupational choice are rarely made for a highly specific occupation: few people prepare themselves and make plans for becoming refrigerator repairmen, stock analysts, or public health officers; more likely they think of preparing for mechanical work, business, or medicine.

Thus, a prospective entrant into the labor force usually is unfamiliar with the many possible fields open to him and has a vague or distorted view of those occupations with which he is relatively familiar. Even when he is undergoing training, his perception of the specific fields to which his training leads him and his possible or probable satisfaction with these fields are unclear. Given this situation, it is exceedingly difficult for the individual to end up in a specific field which is "ideal" for him.

Specialization is often viewed as a functional process for an economic system. However, the functions it fulfills for the individual also should be carefully examined. By providing a series of alternatives for the person who has already chosen a general field, specialization allows him to make secondary choices which can result in closer approximation to an optimum choice. No matter how far removed the primary choice may be from an individual's own interests and abilities, there is the possibility of one or a series of secondary choices which can, at least partially, close this gap.

Most theories of vocational selection stress that it is a continuing process, developing from general, vague and unrealistic choices to specific and realistic ones, Ginzberg,[1] for example, distinguishes three periods: fantasy choices, tentative choices, and realistic choices. Caplow[2] criticizes the notion that these stages invariably occur, viewing occupational selection more as a continuous process, especially within the educational sys-

---

Professional Education of the American Public Health Association under the Chairmanship of Franklyn B. Amos, M.D. The Chairman of the Subcommittee's special study group which developed the plan for the research is John H. Venable, M.D. The original concept of the study came from the Public Health Education Branch, Division of Public Health Methods, U.S. Public Health Service, Mayhew Derryberry, Ph.D., Chief. Substantial contributions have been made to the project and to the development of this paper by Bernard G. Greenberg.

1. E. Ginzberg, S. W. Ginsburg, S. Axelrod, and J. L. Herma, *Occupational Choice, An Approach to a General Theory*, New York: Columbia University Press, 1951.

2. T. Caplow, *The Sociology of Work*, Minneapolis: University of Minnesota Press, 1954.

tem. Super[3] relates vocational choice to psychological stages in the life cycle: the life stages of growth, exploration, establishment, maintenance and decline parallel the work stages of preparatory work, initial work, trial work, stable work, and retirement; and both depend on the development and adjustment of the self-concept. Differences in the development of the self-concept may then lead to different kinds of career patterns, and some of the stages may be omitted and modified. The series of choices in the later stages of the process, it is assumed, enable the individual to hold a more realistic appraisal both of the self and of the objective situation. The possible avenues for future choices, however, are limited by previous decisions.

Since much of the interest in this field derives from vocational guidance and because subjects for study are readily available in secondary schools, initial choices of occupation have received considerably more attention than later choices within careers. This paper reports the framework and research design of a study of one example of *secondary choice*, the selection of specialties by physicians and medical students, especially specialization in public health. It includes data collected in three medical schools in the course of designing a national study.

The Case of Medicine and Public Health

Specialization in medicine is a strategic area in which to study the crystallization of occupational choice. For professions prescribe definite courses of training: pre-professional, general professional, and specialized. Hence the junctures at which decisions must be made, as well as the implications of choices for future training, are formalized. The choice of whether to specialize and in what field must be made by everybody in the profession and has definite consequences for training and work. Moreover, medicine is a highly visible professional career, the physician coming into direct contact with numerous individuals and especially with children, usually under impressive circumstances. Medicine, therefore, is a field which sharply illustrates vocational selection, adjustment of an early ideal to reality, and the formation of professional standards.

A profession like medicine involves a set of prescribed patterns. The individual medical student develops preferences among behavior patterns which correspond to a greater or lesser extent with the professional mold. One of the aims of professional training is to fit the preferences to the prescriptions. But this goal can be met only imperfectly since not all individual differences in needs and values can be molded to one pattern.

3. D. E. Super, *The Psychology of Careers*, New York: Harper Brothers, 1957.

Secondary choices, then, represent opportunities to achieve greater idiosyncratic satisfaction while still maintaining professional standing.

Different specialties represent different degrees of deviation from the general professional model. Within the medical field it seems that internal medicine, for example, corresponds more closely to the model of a physician than does psychiatry.[4]

In studying the process of secondary choice public health is distinctive in that it represents a particularly deviate specialty. Many features of the occupation of public health physicians are markedly different from the corresponding characteristics of the general field of medicine. An outstanding feature of medical training, a climax of the student's experience, is the clinical work with individual patients. While the core of the "normal" physician's activity is individual diagnosis and treatment, the public health physician, in undertaking community diagnosis and treatment, rarely handles patients on an individual basis, but spends a great amount of his time in administrative and community-relations work. His variety of diagnosis and treatment consists to a great extent, in fact, of administrative acts. Most physicians see themselves, moreover, working as individualistic entrepreneurs—as Hughes has said, the "medical model is a hangover from the outmoded one of the business world."[5] Contrastingly, public health physicians are salaried, frequently functioning either within strict civil service rules or as political appointees of elected officials.

Entering public health represents, therefore, a distinct deviation from a normal medical career from the point of view of medical students. But public health physicians must have the same general training as other prospective physicians and expose themselves to the same influences and selection procedures. Here we have a case, then, where preparation for a wider occupation comes in conflict with the choice of a special field. Analysis of this extreme situation is valuable in understanding the general problem of choice of specific occupation.

Pressures against Specialization in Public Health

The first big hurdle for the prospective physician is admission to medical school. Medical schools generally list certain science courses as a minimum requirement and claim that they do not discriminate in favor of those who were science majors as undergraduates. Nevertheless, the

4. H. L. Smith, "Psychiatry in Medicine—Intra or Interprofessional Relationships?" *American Journal of Sociology*, 63 (November, 1957), pp. 285-289.

5. E. C. Hughes, "The Making of a Physician: General Statement of Ideas and Problems," *Human Organization*, 14 (1956), pp. 21-23.

belief is widespread among pre-medical students that a great number of science courses will help admission to medical school. In a recent national survey of medical students 27 per cent of the freshmen reported that they had studied a major in college other than the one they preferred. Two-thirds of these students were influenced to do so by their pre-medical advisers, and almost half thought that this procedure would increase their chances of getting into medical school.[6] In a panel discussion of this study, an educator comments: "I understand students sometimes say that after acceptance to the medical school they can take various courses they couldn't take before because they didn't dare take them, because their advisers didn't want them to or because taking them might influence acceptance to medical school."[7] The effect of this attitude is two-fold. The pre-medical student is discouraged from studying in the humanities and social sciences and is therefore less likely to become interested in those social and cultural aspects of health and disease which are the concern of public health. On the other hand, the undergraduate student who is interested in the latter problems is less likely to take pre-medical courses and to apply to medical schools and probably, if he does so, is less likely to be admitted.

If the student entering medical school is thus unlikely to be interested in the problems of public health, his instruction in most medical schools will do little to stimulate such an interest. The subject matter which the medical student must absorb during his four years of study is considerable, to which is added his training in the art of clinical practice. Medical schools are understandably reluctant to increase the student's load with courses which seem only vaguely related to the "primary" topics. Of the eighty-three medical schools, twenty-nine have no independent departments of public health or (what is not quite the same) of preventive medicine. And even those existing courses in these fields are often short seminars with time begrudged from the major clinical or pre-clinical areas.

Medical schools, of course, teach more than the contents of the formal curriculum: they are also the place where the future physician absorbs the values of the professional group. Among other matters, he learns what kind of work different kinds of physicians do, what standards are used for evaluating different careers, and how a physician should act toward laymen. Public health tends to be seen in these surroundings as a marginal field. The limited instruction in this subject gives students little informa-

6. H. H. Gee, "The Student's View of the Admissions Process," in *The Appraisal of Applicants to Medical Schools, Journal of Medical Education,* October, 1957, Part II, pp. 140-152.

7. Norman F. Witt, "Needs for Liaison with Undergraduate Colleges," *ibid.*, p. 163. Cf. A. W. Schmidt, "Medicine and the Liberal Arts," *Journal of Medical Education,* 32 (1957), pp. 255-262.

tion about the specialty and also leaves them with the impression that public health is peripheral as a medical profession.

The place of the physician in a public health setting necessitates a good deal of give-and-take with members of other professions as well as with numerous official and non-official community agencies. The public health physician does not have the unquestioned authority physicians tend to possess in the hospital or the air of omniscience which they assume at times toward patients. On many issues concerning the relation of the physician to society, such as the organization of medical care, the public health profession generally espouses different views from those of the spokesmen of organized medicine. These are matters relatively foreign to medical training.

Finally, the informal interaction among students, with faculty members, and with physicians affiliated with the teaching hospital influences the student's future career. Informal guidance and aid by older members of the profession usually begin in medical school; influential members of the faculty can encourage students toward different careers through offering or refusing help. Oswald Hall has shown how much the success of the physician depends on the relationship which he has been able to establish with other members of the profession, and how the image which the young physician has of himself can determine his future.[8] With respect to public health, not only is little time generally given to the subject within the medical curriculum, but possibly teachers of preventive medicine are primarily oriented to the context of private practice. In any event, there are few public health role models in medical schools, and those available are inconsistent with the numerous clinical models of other fields of medicine.

The Bases for Secondary Choice

The pressures within the profession, then, against the choice of public health are very strong. Commitment to a career of medicine as the primary choice, therefore, seems almost to preclude specialization in public health (the secondary choice). Yet the latter career is selected by a minority, a fact begging explanation.

Secondary choices may function to correct discrepancies between preferred modes of activity and the professional model. Physicians who enter public health presumably have original dispositions which are

8. Oswald Hall, "The Stages of a Medical Career," *American Journal of Sociology*, 53 (March, 1948), pp. 327-333, and "Types of Medical Careers," *American Journal of Sociology*, 55 (November, 1949), pp. 243-253.

markedly inconsistent with this model. They must also be able to resist strong pressures. In the following sections data are presented which illustrate the origin and maintenance of this deviant pattern. The data are taken from the medical school setting, revealing clearly the impact of the medical model on the individual, with his unique dispositions, and the degree to which a molding process occurs.

Personality. In accordance with this formulation, we may expect differences in personality traits between physicians in public health and other physicians. Here two areas seem to be especially important: the contrast between individual preferences and organizational endeavor; and the nature of social objects of influence, that is, whether the individual feels more comfortable dealing with people as individuals or in groups. These two areas are closely related to the differences between public health and other medical specialties. The work of the physician generally is with individual patients; he is trained to assume authority and to inspire confidence in an essentially two-person situation. Correspondingly, he can work alone, or in a loose association with other physicians. The public health physician is concerned with the community as a whole; he can be most effective as a group worker. Not an individual practitioner, he must function within some organization, and, ideally, he should have traits that maximize such activity.

Comparisons were made of test scores of thirty-two students not intending to go into public health and of seven physicians who were students in a school of public health at an Eastern University. On the Edwards Personal Preference Scale, the two groups showed significant differences (five per cent level) in that the medical students had higher scores for achievement and aggression needs, the public health students for deference, abasement, and nurturance needs. On the Allport-Vernon-Lindzey Study of Values, the two groups differed significantly on four scales: the medical students scored higher on theoretical and aesthetic values, the public health students on social and religious values. As expected, the needs and values of the medical students refer to individual achievement and enjoyment, while those of the public health students relate to identification with or subordination to a larger whole. Although these groups are not strictly comparable—the public health students are older and already have professional experience—the differences are consistent with our hypothesis.

Peer Influence. Students may be exposed to differential influences within the medical school. Sociometric study can trace the influence pattern among the students and between students and faculty. Other studies of influence suggest the hypothesis that a group standard concerning the preference of specialties develops in medical school, and that students who are least frequently chosen by their peers on sociometric tests because of limited prestige or personal attraction are more likely to deviate from the group standard.

A study was made of four classes of a Southern medical school.[9] From the freshman to the senior class, students seem increasingly to move in the direction of what they conceive the group standard to be. They were asked to rank fifteen fields of medicine, first, on the basis of their own interests and, second, according to their perception of the interests of most medical students. In each of the fifteen fields the average choice of the seniors was different from that of the freshmen. The trend from the freshman to the senior year generally was in the same direction as the difference between the freshmen's perception of the interests of most medical students, and their own choices. The data upon which Table 1

Table 1. Freshman and Senior Preferences for Specialties and Freshmen's Perception of Group Preference. Direction of Difference between Freshmen and Senior Choices

Seniors (Compared with Freshman)	*More Favorable*	*Less Favorable*
Differences between perceived group choice and own choice (freshmen)		
Group choice: More favorable	5	1
Less favorable	0	7
Same	2	0

(Entries are number of specialties rated)

is based show this pattern in twelve of the specialties, if ties are eliminated. For example, freshmen give surgery an average rank of 6.8 with respect to personal interest. But their conception of how most medical students would rank surgery (the group standard) is more favorable and averages 2.5. Seniors give surgery an average rank of 5.4 in terms of personal interest, a change upward reflecting, no doubt, the more favorable group standard.[10] Public health, contrastingly, illustrates a trend in the opposite direction. This field ranks 11.5 (a low rating) in terms of personal interest among freshmen and 12.8 (an even lower rating) according to their view of how most medical students would rank this field. Seniors give it an average rank of 12.7.

Evidence of the influence of student relationships on the rank order of choices can be found in an analysis of sociometric patterns. As direct

9. The students studied numbered 253 of a school enrollment of approximately 300. All students were requested but not required to attend an assembly at which questionnaires were completed.

10. This change from freshmen to seniors, however, does not occur in gradual intermediate steps from year to year.

questions about influence of other students typically bring denials, an indirect approach was used.

If students arrive at consensus through mutual discussion and persuasion, it is likely that those who have more contacts with others would learn the generally accepted order of preference earlier than students with fewer contacts. The degree of contact was measured by three interrelated questions in a sociometric questionnaire: "Whom do you like best?" "To whom do you talk most about your future?" and, "To whom would you go for advice on a personal problem?" The four classes were divided into three approximately corresponding popularity groups: high (three or more choices), medium (one or two choices), and low (no choices). In the resulting twelve groups (three popularity groups in four classes), agreement on preferred specialties was computed by Kendall's W, the coefficient of concordance. Table 2 presents the results.

Table 2. Agreement on Preference for Specialties of Different Popularity Groups* (Coefficients of Concordance)

	High Popularity	Medium Popularity	Low Popularity
	W	W	W
Freshmen	.45	.44	.29
Sophomores	.52	.43	.36
Juniors	.40	.51	.62
Seniors	.56	.67	.54

*N of raters ranges between 12 and 35 per group. N of specialties rated is 15 in every case.

There is little difference from class to class in agreement about the highly popular group of specialties; this consensus seems to be established in the freshmen year. On the other hand, in the "low" group, the coefficient of concordance increases during the first three years. Students who have more contacts and are therefore presumably exposed to more peer-group influence reach the common standard of agreement more quickly than the isolates.

Additional evidence is provided by inspecting the relation between the average ranks of interest for specialties of each group. The average rank order correlation of interests between the high and low popularity groups converges from the freshman to the senior year. The correlation coefficient between the two groups is .72 for freshmen, increases for sophomores and juniors, and reaches .95, close to perfect agreement, for seniors. Whatever their popularity, students show very similar preferences in the senior year.

Faculty Influence. Faculty influence on student choice of field may be highly effective. Kendall and Selvin[11] suggest, for example, that low-

11. P. L. Kendall and H. C. Selvin, "Tendencies toward Specialization in Medical Training," in R. K. Merton, G. Reader, and P. L. Kendall (editors), *The Student Physician,* Cambridge: Harvard University Press, 1957. pp. 153-174.

ranking students indicating a preference for a specialized internship are discouraged by staff members from applying for one. Conversely, high-ranking students expressing interest in such specialized training seem to receive encouragement and support from the staff.

Students' choices of faculty members provide information on this influence pattern. They were asked a series of sociometric questions about members of the faculty they liked best in general, as teachers, as doctors, and as sources of advice on personal, scholastic, and career problems.[12] Half of all of the responses to these questions refer to only eight individuals of the total two hundred faculty members. But the patterns vary according to year in medical school, each class tending to concentrate on different individuals. There is a trend, moveover, away from choices of the preclinical science faculty and toward choices of the clinical faculty in succeeding classes, culminating in the senior class. Thus the clinician has the greater influence on the graduating physician.

The modal direction of this influence is indicated by inspecting the responses of the senior class. The two individuals most frequently chosen account for 50 per cent of choices on the question, "Who is the best doctor?" and 45 per cent on "Whose advice would you ask for first on which field of medicine to enter?" Responses to other questions are less concentrated, ranging from 35 per cent ("Who is the best teacher?" and "To whom would you take your scholastic problems?" to 20 per cent ("Whom do you like best?"). On all seven questions, the two faculty members most frequently named were members of the Departments of Internal Medicine, Obstetrics, or Pediatrics.

The emergent pattern, then, seems to be that a small proportion of the staff are the sociometric stars in diverse areas, that a few from among these become more influential in student selection of specialties as graduation approaches, and that these individuals, representing a limited number of clinical fields, provide medical role models for the students.

Perception and Valuation. Personality and social influences have important consequences for secondary choice. But what is it that medical students like or dislike about an occupation? What are their images of the specialized fields?

Students in the Southern medical school were asked to rate fifteen medical activities according to their appeal to them on a scale ranging from "Very Much" to "Not At All." The examples were designed so as to represent five types of activity: diagnosis, therapy, ancillary work,

12. The items were: (1) Whom do you like best? (2) Who is the best teacher? (3) To whom would you take your scolastic problems? (4) To whom would you take your personal problems? (5) Whose advice would you ask first on which field of medicine to enter? (6) To whom have you talked about your future? (7) Who is the best doctor?

supervision, and community relations.[13] The five types are shown in the context of different specialties, for example: "Determining the source of an outbreak of food poisoning" (diagnosis, public health); "Performing an appendectomy" (therapy, surgery); "Giving a talk to the Parent-Teachers Association on what the family physician wants to know when you phone him" (community relations, general practice). In this way, the relative influence of the kind of activity or the specialty itself in student preferences may be estimated.

Table 3 shows the results of the analysis of variance of these ratings.

Table 3. Preference Rating for Medical Activities Associated with Different Specialties

*(A) MEAN RATINGS**

Activities:	Specialties: Surgery	General Practice	Public Health	Total
Diagnosis	1.04	1.54	.52	1.03
Treatment	.78	.73	−.12	.46
Supervision	.50	.59	−.02	.36
Ancillary	.61	.43	−.75	−.10
Community relations	−.30	.20	−.28	−.13
Total	.53	.70	−.13	

N = 257

(B) ANALYSIS OF VARIANCE

Source:	d.f.	Sum of Squares	Mean Squares	F
Activity	4	591.241	147.81	204.†
Specialty	2	488.097	244.048	337.†
Class in school	3	3.814	1.271	1.76
Act. × Specialty	8	150.368	18.796	26.0†
Act. × Class	12	42.100	3.51	4.85†
Class × Specialty	6	6.378	1.063	1.47
Act. × Spec. × class	24	18.637	.776	1.07
"Error"	3796	2750.165	.724	

*Scores are computed on a five-point scale, ranging from +2 ("appeals very much") to −2 ("not at all").
†$P < .01$.

The main effects of both activities and type of specialty are highly significant. There is a definite order of preference for activities among students: diagnosis, therapy, supervision, ancillary work, and community relations. But each activity is definitely less liked when associated with public health than with other fields of medicine. For instance, the average rating for diagnosis in public health is only as favorable as the rating for supervision in general practice. The interaction effects, although signifi-

13. These five types of activities were based on a study by E. M. Cohart and W. R. Willard, "A Time Study Method for Public Health—The Yale Study," *Public Health Reports*, 70 (1955) pp. 570-576; and "Functional Distribution of Working Time in Five County Health Departments," *ibid.*, pp. 713-719.

cant, are very small in comparison with the two main effects (the main effects are significant even in comparison with the interaction effects). The interaction between specialty and activity is the result of certain upsets of general pattern, probably a function of the particular example used in the question, while the change of preference for activities over the years of school produced no consistent trends. Public health, therefore, is handicapped in the eyes of the students on two grounds: activities which characterize it are rated low in general and any activity is rated lower if it is connected with public health.

Another approach to perception of the specialties involved an open-ended question on what students would like most and least about working in eight fields of medicine. Table 4, which summarizes the data obtained in this way includes only the five most frequently mentioned categories for each specialty.

Table 4. Five Most Desirable and Undesirable Aspects of Fields within the Medical Profession*

	Public Health	*Dermatology*	*General Practice*	*Internal Medicine*	*Pathology*	*Psychiatry*	*Surgery*	*Teaching*
Degree to which there are close relationships with patients	U	—	D	D	U	D	U	U
Variety of activities	D,U	D, U	D, U	D, U	D, U	—	D, U	U
Hours of work	D	D	U	U	D	D	—	D
The particular kind of work involved	U	U	—	D	U	D	D	D
Problems necessitating exacting thought	D	D	D	D	D	—	—	—
Amount of certainty of effect	—	U	U	U	—	U	D	—
Availability of opportunities for helping people	D	U	D	—	—	D	D	D
Type of patients	—	U	U	U	—	U	—	—
Degree of opportunity for learning	—	—	—	D	D	D	—	D
Income	—	D	—	—	—	—	—	U
Physical aspects of the work	—	—	U†	—	U†	—	U†	
Degree of independence possible	U	—	—	—	—	—	—	U
Degree to which there are close relationships with colleagues, community people	D	—	D	—	—	—	—	—
Degree of research involved in the work	—	—	—	—	D	—	—	D, U
Consequences of failure	—	D	—	—	—	—	U	—
Abilities involved	U	—	—	—	—	U	D, U	—
Type of colleague	—	—	—	—	—	U	—	—
Emotional aspects of the work	—	—	—	—	—	U	—	—
Difficulties of attainment	—	—	—	U	—	—	—	—
Danger of contagion	—	—	—	—	U	—	—	—

*D indicates the aspect perceived as desirable, while U indicates it perceived as undesirable.

†In the case of pathology, physical inactivity constituted an undesirable aspect of the field; with respect to general practice and surgery, physical strain was perceived as undesirable.

These results indicate a fairly high degree of uniformity in the perception of the specialties. For one thing, there are very few instances in which the same field is mentioned as "liked most" and "liked least" on a given factor by different respondents.[14] Another indication of uniformity is that each specialty is accorded a relatively unique combination of factors. Although some factors are mentioned for a number of specialties, their frequencies of response usually vary.

The relationship of a given uniformity of affect to the socialization process within the medical school may be inferred from Table 5, which

Table 5. "Lack of Close Relationships with Patients" as the Factor Liked Least in Three Fields

	Freshmen	*Sophomores*	*Juniors*	*Seniors*
	%	%	%	%
Pathology	37 (78)*	45 (78)	57 (60)	59 (54)
Public health	14 (85)	29 (83)	43 (67)	41 (56)
Teaching	22 (80)	32 (77)	29 (69)	36 (53)

*Numbers in parentheses show the total number of responses in each class.

presents an example of the responses of different classes. The three fields listed are those for which "lack of close relationships with patients" appears in Table 4 as a factor which is liked least. The increasing proportion of responses, as well as the absolute degree of uniformity in perceiving the specialties, suggests the development of norms with respect to desirable and undesirable aspects of the different fields.

Commitment to Career. Our final approach concerns the whole career line. We have discussed and illustrated the hypothesis that public health is a deviant choice often resulting from incomplete socialization within the medical school. It is likely, moreover, that the selection of public health in many cases is made after leaving medical school. One study of local and state health departments, for example, reveals a typical pattern in which the physician enters this field some years after his medical schooling and after he has worked in one or more positions other than public health.[15] Among the approximately 300 students from three medical schools about whom we have information, not one gave public health as his first choice. A small percentage of these physicians, however, probably will go into the public health field. If this is the case, physicians entering public health change their career plans more frequently than those who do not.

Some supporting data for this hypothesis are to be found in a recent

14. The chief exception here is the category "variety of activities," which is perhaps a relatively inclusive and indefinite one.

15. E. M. Cohart and W. R. Willard, "Experience of Public Health Workers," *Public Health Reports*, 70 (1955), pp. 1116-1124.

study.[16] Stiles and Watson asked public health students to rate 26 factors according to their importance in choice of a profession. They rated more highly than did students in other health professions (dentistry, medicine, pharmacy, nursing) the following factors: an agreeable opportunity, close relation to the favorite occupation, influence of a teacher, environmental influence, and military experience. Although a large proportion of public health students are not physicians, the fact that all of these reasons refer to change of plans is consistent with our reasoning. Comparison of the career patterns of diplomates in preventive medicine and public health with those in internal medicine, surgery, pathology, and psychiatry, shows additional support for this hypothesis (Table 6). Examination of a sample of the listings in the *Directory of Medical Specialists*,[17] indicates that specialists in preventive medicine are more likely than others to list experience in different medical fields. Even qualification as a specialist in a different field, which implies considerable experience in this specialty and thus is infrequent, occurs among specialists in preventive medicine more often than elsewhere.

Table 6. Experience in Outside Specialties of Physicians in Different Specialties

	Preventive Medicine	Internal Medicine	Surgery	Pathology	Psychiatry
Per cent listing experience in other fields of medicine	29.0	26.4	24.0	5.6	17.5
Per cent qualified by a different board	7.0	1.6	4.0	.8	1.9
Number	(500)	(125)	(125)	(125)	(103)

These findings concerning careers, although fragmentary, point up again the marginal position of the public health physician. The physician who is less committed to a specific career and receptive to accidental influences probably will eventually select a deviant specialty.

16. W. W. Stiles and Lois C. Watson, "Motivation of Persons Electing Public Health as a Career," *American Journal of Public Health*, 45 (1955), pp. 1563-1568.

17. *Directory of Medical Specialists*, Vol. VIII. Chicago: Marquis–Who's Who, 1957.

JOSEPH BEN-DAVID

Roles and Innovations in Medicine

UNTIL approximately the middle of the last century the majority of men engaged in scientific research were not scientists in their main occupation. But contemporary research in most of the sciences has become a career, chosen like any other profession. This trend was first discernible in Germany in the second half of the last century, and it has further developed during this century, mainly in the United States and lately in Russia. In Britain and France the development was slower, but the same tendency is observable there.

The development of scientific research into a separate profession brought about a considerable acceleration in the process of discovery. Indeed, it has been one of the conditions which made it possible to turn science from an unpredictable process into a tool which can be applied to practical purposes.[1] But scientific advance has many facets: besides increased activity, measured by indexes such as discoveries, publications, or, in technology, patents, there are questions of the quality and the type of discovery.

Reprinted from "Roles and Innovations in Medicine," by Joseph Ben-David, The American Journal of Sociology, *May, 1960, pp. 557-568, by permission of The Chicago University Press.*

The first draft of this paper was written while the author was a fellow at the Center for Advanced Study in the Behavioral Sciences, Stanford, California. He wishes to express his thanks to Professors S. N. Eisenstadt, Jerusalem; M. Janowitz, Ann Arbor; E. A. Shils, Chicago; and Mr. A. Zloczover, Jerusalem, for their valuable comments, and to Mr. A. Howard, graduate student at Stanford University, for his assistance with the research.

1. The present author has summarized this in a forthcoming paper, "The Development of the Medical Sciences." About the emergence of applied science from professionalized pure science in chemistry see D. S. L. Cardwell, *The Organization of Science in England* (London, 1957), p. 184.

In the latter respects the results of professional science may not be unequivocally superior to those of amateur science. Doubts are raised by at least one plausible hypothesis often mentioned in the literature on technological inventions: that "revolutionary" inventions are usually made by outsiders, that is, by men who are not engaged in the occupation which is affected by them and are, therefore, not bound by professional custom and tradition.[2] This proposition—if it has any substance—suggests interesting implications for the development of science. According to it, professionalization, which necessarily turns scientific research into a monopoly of insiders rather than—as it used to be until well into the nineteenth century—of inspired amateurs (i.e., outsiders), may ultimately endanger its revolutionary character.

Propositions formulated in such general terms are often of limited relevance. In addition, the professionalization of science is an inevitable corollary of its development, and there seems to be much empirical evidence that the process has not, in fact, diminished the revolutionary character of science. Indeed one of the chief proponents of the proposition suggests that it is increasingly less relevant under present-day conditions.[3] Yet there is a simple and straightforward logic behind the argument, and the historical material which supports it is intuitively convincing.

The difficulty with the application of the proposition seems to be the loose definition of the outsider as well as of revolutionary innovation (or invention, or discovery). Obviously, the meaning of outsider changes with increasing differentiation of roles. The distance between the respective roles of a farmer and a medicine man in a primitive society—in terms of the knowledge which is necessary to perform them, the socialization through which the individual reaches them, and the social context within which both roles are performed—is perhaps less than the distance between the experimental physiologist and the physician who uses the results of his work.[4] It is obvious, therefore, that any useful application of the proposition has to be based on a precise definition and analysis of roles. Similarly, the term "revolutionary" innovation has to be replaced by a more specific one. We must investigate, therefore, the relationship between the definitions of the roles of people engaged in research and in practice in a certain field and the kind of innovations produced there.

---

2. S. C. Gilfillan, *The Sociology of Invention* (Chicago, 1935), pp. 88-91.

3. W. Kaempfert, "A New Patent Office for a New Age," in J. E. Thornton (ed.), *Science and the Social Order* (Washington, D.C., 1939), pp. 160-163.

4. As noted by Gilfillan, most outsiders mentioned in the literature of technical invention were, in fact, relative outsiders only, with various connections with the fields in which they eventually made their discoveries.

We propose to investigate the relationship in the field of medicine. In medicine it is relatively easy to find two distinct roles which are interrelated and mixed in various ways in various countries: the career scientists, especially in the basic medical sciences (whether trained in medicine or not), and the medical practitioners who receive considerable scientific training but are not engaged in research as an occupation. Until the middle of the last century the two roles were only rudimentarily differentiated. Science was not yet a career, and the majority of biologists, and quite a few scientists in other fields, too, were practicing doctors or at least initially chose medicine as their career, only later, as a result of exceptional achievement, to become full-time scientists. In a few countries the undifferentiated pattern has survived until quite recently, at least in some fields of medicine.

The proposition of the role of the outsider can be applied to this development as follows: The range of practical problems which force themselves upon "practitioners" is, at any moment, infinitely varied. The range of scientific problems, on the other hand, is largely confined within the theoretical boundaries of the scientific disciplines. Specialized research personnel working in autonomous and affluent scientific organizations, which can determine their policies without paying attention to practical demands, may be, therefore, the most efficient agents in promoting rapid scientific growth in a period—but only in a period—when a good idea is at hand of how to explore a series of well-defined phenomena. In such periods there is great advantage in concentrating upon those phenomena rather than dispersing resources on problems which may be unsoluble by the existing methods.

But in the long run the returns in knowledge which can be gained from the increasingly precise investigation of a limited range of problems may be diminishing. Continuous productivity can follow then only from shifting the focus of attention to new problems and developing adequate methods of investigating them. Practice in such times is an invaluable guide in locating relevant problems—rather than finding illusory ones, which happened not infrequently in the history of academic thinking—and in adapting existing methods or devising new ones. Its problems are always real, and it usually possesses a tradition which is the result of a long collective process of trial and error and which may suggest the way toward new theory and new methods.

Similar arguments can be put forward in favor of training and keeping scientists interested in a broad variety of scientific and perhaps also humanistic disciplines, as against specialization in a relatively narrow field. However, the social conditions determining the relationship between research and practice are different from those determining the degree of specialization. In this paper, therefore, we shall restrict ourselves to the exploration of the first of these two problems, namely, the effects of medical practice on research.

First, we shall investigate the relationship between scientific and practical roles in countries where the differentiation of these roles has occurred on a considerable scale to see the extent of the opportunities for practitioner research and the kind of communication between those in the two roles. Then we shall analyze the reception of a type of innovation which proved fruitful in the long run but in which there was good reason a priori to expect initial lack of interest, even hostility, among professional scientists, because it implied a fundamentally different view of illness than that scientifically accepted and because the new view was at first established by standards scientifically not quite acceptable. If our reasoning is valid—that influences coming from practice direct research to significant problems not implied in the existing scientific theory and methodology—then the influence will certainly show in this type of innovation.

The old system whereby medical practitioners conducted their own research and created organizations which contributed to the advancement of science still existed in Germany in the sixties and seventies of the last century.[5] But it had begun to decline as early as the forties. The fast development of the medical sciences created a paradoxical situation, since, in the state of knowledge at the time, the only thing one could do with good conscience was research, the accepted cures of the practicing profession having been shown to lack scientific foundation. Thus a cleavage arose between those who regarded themselves as medical scientists and those who practiced medicine. The spirit prevailing among the former is reflected in the opinion of the director of a public hospital in 1845: "Just as our precursors were more concerned with the success of their cures, so are we more concerned with our inquiries. Our purpose, therefore, is a purely scientific one. Medicine is a science, not an art."[6]

In spite of the limited use of medical science, there soon came into being a profession of medical scientists who, within a short space of time, monopolized not only the medical faculties but, as a matter of fact, the public hospitals too.[7] Thus practitioners gradually lost all access to facilities—laboratories and hospitals—necessary for research, while, owing to technical advance, facilities even for clinical research became increasingly elaborate.

---

5. P. Diepgen, *Geschichte der Medizin* (Berlin, 1955), Vol. II, No. 1, pp. 213-14, and Vol. II, No. 2, pp. 282-83.

6. Quoted by Diepgen (*ibid.*, Vol. II, No. 1, pp. 152-53).

7. Th. Billroth, *The Medical Sciences in the German Universities* (New York, 1924), p. 27; A. Flexner, *Medical Education in Europe* (New York, 1912), pp. 145-66.

This development had been paralleled by a decrease in the opportunity for meaningful communication between the two sectors of the profession. Around the middle of the century, when the monopolization of the academic and hospital facilities and positions by the scientists in the profession were already far advanced, the yearly meetings of the natural scientists and physicians—the *Naturforscherversammlungen*—still played an important role in German scientific life. Out of these assemblies arose the German medical association in the seventies, which was a much more narrowly professional affair, mainly of practitioners alone. Finally, at the turn of the century, there came into being a new association of medical practitioners, overwhelmingly absorbed in "unionist" activities designed to better the economic status of the profession.[8] The staffs of medical faculties and public hospitals were often not members of these associations at all.[9]

The introduction of the new type of scientific medical training and research in the United States took place under rather different circumstances; much of the initiative came from the professional organization of the practitioners. The decisive steps toward the establishment of proper scientific facilities were taken around 1890 when it became apparent that medical research could greatly benefit therapy (i.e., after the great bacteriological discoveries), and the innovations were designed to benefit practice as well as research. The balanced development of the up-to-date facilities in the large American research hospitals differs from the development in Germany, where there may be excellent facilities, such as a laboratory in the field of special interest of a head of a department, but where the facilities for the treatment of most patients may be, as a rule, quite modest.[10] As a result, no type of important facilities came to be monopolized by the full-time scientific professionals. Some practitioners continue teaching part time in medical schools, and, more important, an increasing number of them have access to first-class hospital and laboratory facilities.[11] Practitioners as well as full-time

8. W. Ewald, *Soziale Medizin* (Berlin, 1911), II, 403-8.

9. *Final Report of the Commission on Medical Education* (New York, 1932), p. 344.

10. A. Flexner, *Medical Education: A Comparative Study* (New York, 1925), pp. 223-26; cf. Diepgen, *op. cit.*, Vol. II, No. 2, p. 281.

11. This situation is the result of constant and often open conflict between various sectors of the profession rather than of generally accepted policies. The conflict has usually centered around full-time clinical appointments in teaching hospitals, which, had they become the general rule, might have created a situation similar to that in Germany (Flexner, *Medical Education in the United States and Canada*, p. 278; cf. M. A. Fishbein, *History of the American Medical Association* [Philadelphia, 1947], pp. 322-24; James H. Means, *Doctors, People and Government* [Boston, 1953]). On a case where the problem reached the courts see "Hospital Hassle: Who's Exploiting Whom?" *Medical Economics*, XXXIII (November, 1956), 321-62. About the actual state of affairs see the

research personnel have remained members of the same professional organization which has played an active part in the academic and research policies of the medical schools as well as in defending the material interests of doctors. Organizational unity among all the sectors of the medical profession has often been accompanied by tension, but there is no doubt that the professional organization has provided an efficient means of communication between practitioners and scientists—in both directions.[12] Activities of the organization, such as the medical conventions, have preserved the kind of symbolical significance and spectacularity for the public as well as the profession as the *Naturforscherversammlungen* had in Germany around the middle of the last century.

A further reason why the American scientific system is more open to pressures coming from practitioners or even the public at large (though the public would not ordinarily take a stand in matters concerning science) is largely due to the scientific administrator, who is usually a man who had acquired an academic standing and then left it for full-time academic administration. Administrative tasks make it imperative for him to be practical, especially in the United States, where pressure groups are powerful. On the other hand, he possesses a sufficient understanding of the nature and requirements of research and identifies himself mainly with the scientific profession. This makes it possible, at least in principle, for him to be a link between research and practice.[13] (In Germany, in spite of individual exceptions, this role has not developed. Administration and scientific leadership were kept strictly apart. There were two separate roles, the *Kurator*, an administrator appointed by the state, and the *Rektor*, elected head of the faculty for a limited period of time.)[14]

The following further differences between the United States and the German systems are presumably a result of the described conditions:

In Germany academic personnel have used their academic titles (*Professor*, *Dozent*, etc.) rather than their medical designation (*Doktor*); in the United States the last-named has usually been preferred. In the training of student physicians, the German faculties defined their task as providing an introduction into the science of medicine; most practical knowledge was supposedly acquired in practice. On the other hand,

President's Commission on the Health Needs of the Nation, *Building America's Health* (Washington, D.C., 1951), II, 202-3.

12. R. H. Shryock, *American Medical Research: Past and Present* (New York, 1947), pp. 119-20, and the sources quoted in n. 14.

13. L. Wilson, *The Academic Man* (New York, 1942), pp. 84-93; A. Flexner, *I Remember* (New York, 1940); D. Fleming, *William Welch and the Rise of Modern Medicine* (Boston, 1954), pp. 129-32.

14. A. Flexner, *Universities: American, English, German* (New York, 1930), pp. 321-24.

American medical schools—even the most research-oriented—undertake to teach the student how to practice, making considerable effort to approach eminently practical problems in a systematic fashion rather than to delimit science authoritatively from practice.[15]

Thus the definition of the roles of people engaged in medical research had undergone the following changes during the late nineteenth and early twentieth centuries. In Germany research and teaching became an entirely separate role from practice by the end of the nineteenth century. About the same time began the differentiation of research roles from practice in the United States and Britain, but in the latter the development had been limited to the basic medical sciences. This role differentiation led in Germany to the deprivation of the practitioners from all the facilities necessary for research and to a lowering of the status of the practitioners as compared with the scientists. None of these results followed the large-scale development of medical research roles in America. Finally, in Britain and even more in France, the early-nineteenth-century type practitioner-scientist had predominated until quite recently.

We have to see now whether scientists acting in these different roles displayed different attitudes to the innovations we are interested in, namely, where there is good reason to expect that interest in practice played an important role in the discovery. To repeat, the innovations involve a fundamentally different view of the investigated phenomenon—illness—from the view scientifically accepted; they are fruitful in the long run but are established in a way not quite acceptable by the standards of scientific methodology. Perhaps one could distinguish these as "fundamental marginal innovations." Two instances of these aroused a long controversy, international in scope, so that the material relating to them is sufficient to show the alignment of various positions and differences in the nature of contributions: the beginnings of bacteriology and psychoanalysis.

A great deal of what was to constitute the bacteriological view of illness had been for a long time part and parcel of the medical tradition. The idea of contagion goes back to antiquity, and so does the practice of inoculation; even the idea of *contagium animatum* had been put forward in the seventeenth century.[16] But the great advances in pathological and physiological studies of illness, from the beginning of the century, lent no scientific foundation or support to the bacteriological view. The theoretical analysis of the requirements of bacteriological research by one of the leading anatomists of the age, Jacob Henle (1840),

15. Flexner, *Medical Education in Europe*, pp. 145-66; R. K. Merton, G. G. Reader, and P. L. Kendall (eds.), *The Student Physician* (Cambridge, Mass., 1957).

16. F. H. Garrison, *An Introduction to the History of Medicine* (Philadelphia, 1929), pp. 75, 117, 253.

was regarded, as a recent historian of medicine put it, as a "rear-guard action" in defense of a traditional approach to illness which had no scientific future.[17] Nevertheless, for more than ten years before the decisive experiments of Koch finally settled the question whether or not illness can be caused by specific living agents transferred from one person to another, there was a growing interest in the problem. Striking clinical evidence had come much earlier in the work of Semmelweis, which, however, had been well-nigh forgotten. But interest in it was revived by the work of Lister and the laboratory experiments of Pasteur and other French scientists. Before the crucial experiments of Koch, however, they were open to other interpretations.[18]

At this time Germany was already leading in medical research. Indeed, the first important clinical discovery in the field of bacteriology was made in Austria, and the clarification of the methodological requirements for testing the new theory and some very pertinent research were done by German professors of medicine. Yet during all this time (roughly from the mid-forties to the mid-seventies of the last century) the majority of the academic profession in Germany stood aloof from bacteriology. They regarded it as a matter of minor importance and did their best to quench the enthusiasm of the practitioners for the discoveries of Lister—having succeeded previously in consigning the work of Semmelweis virtually to oblivion. With few exceptions (Cohn, Klebs) all incentive for research during the sixties and early seventies came from France and Britain, where science was much less professionalized, and from the German practitioners, by one of whom, indeed, the crucial experiment was made.[19]

It was no coincidence that practitioners were more interested in this line of research than scientists. The increasingly refined pathological studies proved most satisfactory in helping the latter to understand illness. The fact that they provided no means of curing illness might have been a sad conclusion for the more humane among the doctors, but one which scientists bore—and spread—with heroic resignation worthy of a profession whose destiny was the *Entzauberung* of (removing the magic from) the world. Besides, they preferred the negative views of Liebig, Hoppe-Seyler, Virchow, and other outstanding representatives of established academic disciplines, as against a new kind of theory which threatened to revive the discredited ideas of vitalism. Practitioners, on the other hand, even though they had to submit intellectually to the scientific argument, could find little satisfaction in it. They turned

17. G. Rosen, *A History of Public Health* (New York, 1958), pp. 297-99.

18. Diepgen, *op. cit.*, Vol. II, No. 2, pp. 115-25.

19. *Ibid.*, pp. 123-24; R. H. Shryock, *The Development of Modern Medicine* (New York, 1947), pp. 283-84.

eagerly, therefore, to the works of Pasteur and Lister and evinced more interest in them than in the scientifically more impeccable work of physiologists and pathologists. The crucial investigations of Koch, too, were connected with a practical problem: the causes of anthrax, which caused great damage in the district where he worked as medical officer. His experiments are considered classic examples of correct scientific method. Yet quite a few hypotheses crucial for the design of his experiments were derived not from the traditions of the scientific laboratories but from the everyday observations of the people about the climatic conditions under which the disease occurred.[20]

Problems of medical (and veterinarian and agricultural) practice thus had been important in the initiation of bacteriological research; originally, more interest was taken in it by practitioners than by professional scientists. Although only the early experiments of Koch took place entirely outside the academic framework (later he became the director of a research institute and a university professor), at least three of the most important discoveries took place under conditions marginally academic. Semmelweis was unable to establish his case by the accepted rules of the academic game and was rejected by the Austrian academic profession. Even discounting some of the legends attached to this tragic figure, it seems that he was greatly motivated by the wish to help, which was at considerable variance with the crude form of "therapeutic nihilism" prevalent at that time in Vienna, and that, in spite of his scientific capacity, he always had been "maladjusted" to the academic framework.[21]

As a chemist, Pasteur falls outside the framework of this discussion, but the importance that the solution of practical problems played in his discovery fits very well into this framework. For reasons connected with his career, he abruptly left his early work of great theoretical interest and abandoned his self-image of pure scientist for that of a helper of the human race through science. This led him to the investigation of the phenomena of fermentation and prevention of diseases out of which emerged his discoveries.[22] Lister worked in Britain, where there was no differentiation between academic medicine and medical practice. Villemin and Davaine also worked outside the academic framework. Among all the pioneers in bacteriology, only Klebs was a proper academic physician.[23] Yet, in spite of their marginal positions in relation to the circles

20. R. Dubos, *Louis Pasteur: Franc-tireur de la science* (Paris, 1955), pp. 119-22, 245-46; Diepgen, *op. cit.*, II, 115-25.

21. Garrison, *op. cit.*, p. 436. Even as late as 1861 his book activated a new campaign against him in which Virchow participated (see A. Castiglioni, *A History of Medicine* [New York, 1947], p. 726).

22. Dubos, *op. cit.*, pp. 16-17, 86-87, 362-89.

23. Garrison, *op. cit.*, pp. 575-77, 580-81, 616. Many of Koch's early co-workers—

of authoritative science, their work—and Koch's as well—grew out of the academic milieu. Semmelweis came from the Vienna clinical school; Pasteur's work is related to the Franco-German school of chemistry; Lister's work was a result of Pasteur's; and Koch's was the last link in a chain which started with Henle and included much important research as well as the clarification of methodological requirements. Finally, once the decisive beginnings were made, the further development of the discipline was most efficiently pursued by the academic machinery of Germany.

In assessing the contribution of practitioners to this field of inquiry, therefore, it seems that their importance in the early stage of bacteriological research was that they provided an alternative frame of reference (or "reference group") to the scientific one. For one whose career is the exploration of the question, "What can be known about illness?" the choice of bacteriology could not have seemed a very good risk at a time when it seemed almost impossible to investigate bacteriological problems in a methodologically satisfactory way. Besides, committing one's self to research in this field implied a conflict with the materialistic ideologies then prevailing in scientific circles.

All these considerations mattered very little if one chose as one's frame of reference medical practice rather than science. In this case the question decisive for the choice of subject was, "What can be done about illness?" and from this point of view bacteriolgical research looked more promising than either physiology or pathology. Besides, it must have been much easier for a practitioner, or for someone identifying himself with practitioners (in medicine, in industry, etc.), to disregard the professional ideologies of the scientists which would have prejudiced him against anything suspect as vitalism. Thus, while some of the important early discoveries were made by academic scientists, those who committed themselves most to the bacteriological hypotheses were mostly practitioner-scientists of the old type. The central innovator, Pasteur, it is true, was a professional academic scientist, but at a certain stage of his career he was compelled to use his scientific talent for the solution of practical problems. From this point on, he consciously adopted the new role of what might be called today "applied scientist," in which the criteria of relevance and success were different from those accepted in the academic profession. This explains, too, why the prac-

Löffler, Gaffky, Hueppe, and Flügge—were former army surgeons, as was the French pioneer of bacteriology, Villemin (Garrison, *op. cit.*, pp. 581-82, 616). The only academic group proper which supported the bacteriological approach was the botanist (Dubos, *op. cit.*, pp. 119-22). They obviously had an interest in a theory which used something from their discipline in the explanation of phenomena previously attributed to chemical factors.

titioners as a group accepted the new theories in opposition to the view of the academic profession.

All this tends to support the hypothesis that practice plays an important and systematic role in the orientation of research toward new problems. Psychoanalysis provides additional confirmatory evidence.

Before Freud started his investigations of the neuroses, he was a scholar engaged in the kind of medical research that was the usual preparation for an academic career in German and Austrian medicine.[24] The influences which turned his interests into new directions were his studies with French clinicians; later, after he had to renounce his academic plans, his association with a well-known Viennese *Hausarzt* (family practitioner), Breuer; and, finally, his own private practice.[25] There he encountered neuroses which were either unknown to or neglected by academic medicine. He approached these phenomena with the mental habits of a person trained in scientific research.

Like the great French clinicians early in the century, when he found the existing methods of treatment useless and the definitions of mental illness irrelevant to his cases, he started to make painstaking clinical observations, keeping his eyes open to things that were usually considered irrelevant and abandoning methods and theories (including, at the beginning, his own) when contradicted by evidence.[26] In this way, his attention was directed to phenomena which were all known to practicing doctors as part of the "art" or the etiquette of medicine but not systematically thought of as etiological in the causation and the therapy of illness. This is obvious in such key concepts of psychoanalytic therapy as transference and counter transference, which are descriptions of what goes on between doctor and patient in many kinds of treatment and not only in psychotherapy. And, as pointed out by Parsons, many elements of the medical etiquette have come to be used as technical tools of psychoanalysis.[27] Such things are the relationship of trust between doctor and patient (both ways), the handling of uncertainty, and the insistence on the autonomy of the patient and on his will to be cured. Even fee for service has been treated in psychoanalysis as a technical problem of therapy.[28]

---

24. On Freud's early scientific career see E. Jones, *The Life and Work of Sigmund Freud* (London, 1955), Vol. I, chaps. v-vi, x.

25. *Ibid.*, chap. xi; S. Freud, *An Autobiographical Study* (London, 1935). The most perceptive summary of these influences is Philip Rieff, *Freud: The Mind of a Moralist* (New York: Viking Press, 1959).

26. Freud, *op. cit.*, pp. 26-27, 58, 60-62, 109-10.

27. T. Parsons, *The Social System* (New York: Free Press, 1951), pp. 326-479.

28. Freud, *op. cit.*, pp. 46, 48; S. Lorand and W. A. Console, "Therapeutic Results in

This exposition may seem to emphasize unduly the method of psychoanalysis at the expense of its more controversial substantive hypotheses about sexual development. There was a great deal of non-scientific element in Freud's thinking and declarations about sex; like D. H. Lawrence in England, he regarded it as his mission to destroy all the mystery, shame, and guilt surrounding it. But such prophetic overtones were not unusual among nineteenth-century scientists, and—at least in the early writings of Freud—they are not difficult to separate from the scientific elements of his work.[29] The latter consisted of the systematic clinical description and analysis of neuroses and the search for a positive biological basis of these elusive mental phenomena. Even his emphasis on pregenital sexuality was, to a large extent, an attempt to apply the developmental concepts of embryology to the explanation of complex human behavior.[30]

If this interpretation of the beginnings of psychoanalysis is correct, it justifies quoting it as a parallel to bacteriology. Psychoanalysis, too, was a novel theory of illness containing, however, traditional elements of medical thinking and practice. As a theory it was even more suspect than bacteriology. Scientific opposition to the latter was largely to the reintroduction of elements reminiscent of vitalism while psychoanalytic concepts were frankly anthropomorphic and to some extent voluntaristic. To this extent it was justifiable to see it as something akin to prescientific medical thinking.

The methodological problems raised by psychoanalysis also looked hopeless (again, not unlike but even more than in the case of bacteriology). True, it was a striking application of rigorous clinical thinking to new phenomena; but by that time clinical methods were increasingly replaced, or supplemented by laboratory research, and no one envisaged the possibility of this kind of research in psychoanalysis, although, in the beginning at least, Freud was confident that eventually a physiological basis of his theories would be found.[31]

Few people would doubt nowadays that all these objections to psychoanalysis were correct. But the objections of Liebig and Virchow

---

Psychoanalytic Treatment without Fee" and "Discussion" of the article by W. C. M. Scott in *International Journal of Psychoanalysis,* XXXVII (1956), 59-65.

29. Cf. E. H. Erikson, *Childhood and Society* (London, n.d.), pp. 58-59. It has been correctly emphasized by Rieff *(op. cit.)* that, even in his "prophetic" role, Freud tried to behave much more like a scientist than did Virchow or Pasteur. Freud always shunned dramatic effect and popular appeal. But, of course, this might have been due partly to his greater insecurity about his status as a scientist.

30. Apart from Freud's own writings, especially the earlier ones, see Erikson, *op. cit.,* pp. 59-61; J. Bowlby, "The Child's Tie to His Mother," *International Journal of Psychoanalysis,* XXXIX (1958), 1-24.

31. Jones, *op. cit.,* chap. ii.

to Pasteur's work also proved to be correct in the long run. Yet in both instances scientific and practical progress was achieved for some time by less than perfect methodology.[32] On these grounds one feels justified in classifying psychoanalysis in the same category as bacteriology as a fundamental marginal innovation.

Let us now turn to the social structure of the process of innovation and of the reaction of academic circles to it. Important elements of the innovation came from academically less developed, more anarchic France, where there were no qualms about using the ill-understood but for many purposes useful method of hypnosis. Freud himself came from German academic medicine, but he had to renounce his academic career for practice. He was interested in research and had to abandon his scientific career because of a combination of lack of opportunity, inadequate means, and insufficient success, owing probably to a limited talent for exact research.[33] Going into practice was a comedown for him; besides, he was not attracted to the role of the healer ("Aus fruehen Jahren ist mir nichts von einem Beduerfnis, leidenden Menschen zu helfen, bekannt. . . . Ich habe auch niemals 'Doktor' gespielt").[34] Having to become a practicing doctor, therefore, threatened his self-identity. He solved this problem by turning the searchlight of research on the neuroses specific to private practice and by making scientific techniques of various elements of the traditional healing role which repelled him.

There were, then, differences in the motivation of Freud, on the one hand, and the pioneers of bacteriology, especially Pasteur, on the other hand. Freud wanted to prove that he was a scientist, though engaged in practice; Pasteur wanted to prove that he, as a scientist, could make decisive contribution to the solution of practical problems. But the social situations out of which the innovations emerged were similar. In both cases there were phenomena which presented practical problems but were not promising in the mind of the person whose aim was to find out what could be known about illness; in both cases the innovation was the result of applying systematic scientific thinking to these phenomena as well as to the traditions existing about them among those accustomed to deal with them. Finally, in both cases those whose work to some extent led up to the innovation were people in the loosely defined role of practitioner-scientist, like the French clinicians, Lister, and perhaps Breuer, while the central figures who established the innovation were professional scientists, or at least were trained for such careers, but were thrown into situations where they had to prove themselves

32. Shryock, *Modern Medicine*, p. 305; Dubos, *op. cit.*, pp. 155-56.

33. Jones, *op. cit.*, chaps. v-vi.

34. From S. Freud, "Nachwort zur Frage der Laienanalyse," *Gesammelte Schriften* (London, 1948), XIV, 290.

through the solution of practical problems. Now they had to choose their problems according to the criterion of "something to be done" rather than the accepted scientific criteria of their times.

This process whereby a person in Role A is set to achieve the aims of Role B can be described as "role hybridization." The innovation is the result of an attempt to apply the usual means in Role A to achieve the goals of Role B. Obviously, successful innovation is not the only possible outcome. The means of Role A may be irrelevant to the goals of Role B, or the relearning of Role B may be a more acceptable solution than the creating of a new combination out of the elements of the two roles. In our cases the means of the scientific role—exact observation and isolation of factors through experiment or clinical reasoning—were relevant to the practical goals to which they were applied, and the definition of the situation created a problem which could not be solved, or not satisfactorily, by learning the other role as it then existed. Pasteur was expected to prove himself through practical results as a scientist; Freud, of course, could have become a practitioner, but this would have meant an admission of defeat on his part. He was interested in science and not interested in practice; furthermore, in Austria and Germany at that time, when the status of the scientist was high, that of the practitioner relatively low, and the old role of practitioner-scientist almost extinct, to abandon the scientific career was also to lose status. Innovation, therefore, remained the only satisfactory solution.

In Austria and Germany the new theory—psychoanalysis—was not taken seriously by the academic circles and was not given any opportunity in the universities. Criticism of it was often hostile and coarse; it was censured as immoral because of its sexual theories, and the psychoanalysts were at times boycotted, especially by universities and public hospitals. Freud and his followers did their best to expose the narrow-minded prejudice, stupidity, and, in some cases, dishonesty of their most virulent opponents.[35] However, the opposition could not have been successful had psychoanalysis been recognized by at least part of the scientific public. The academic leadership of Germany did not consist of the people made ridiculous by the psychoanalysts, and, if the new theory was practically boycotted in German academic medicine, this happened with the consent of quite a few unprejudiced and brilliant people who were afraid of neither Jew (some were Jews themselves) nor, one presumes, sex. Their behavior was motivated by the fact that psychoanalysis was bad science and that their definition of science was

---

35. Jones, *op. cit.*, Vol. II, chap. iv; the official psychoanalytical view of the subject as stated by Freud was that opposition to psychoanalysis had emotional and not intellectual sources ("Die Wiederstaende gegen die Psychoanalyse," *Gesammelte Schriften,* XIV, 108).

a strictly professional one. Working where there was an organizational cleavage between practice and scientific research, they took no interest in a theory which had only practical achievements and aesthetic appeal to commend it.

In consequence, psychoanalysis was driven in Vienna—and, indeed, everywhere in Austria and Germany—very nearly into the position of a medical sect officially denounced at scientific meetings, instead of having been absorbed, transformed, and utilized to any great extent in psychological and psychiatric research and practice.[36] At least this was the case until the 1920's. It is difficult to determine to what extent the exclusion of psychoanalysis from academic science for a period of about twenty years was due to its very grave shortcomings as a science or to the fact that by that time academic science, including academic medicine, had become a much more closed system than it was at the time of the controversy over bacteriology. But the latter explanation is supported by the reception of psychoanalysis in the United States. Objections and doubts existed in American circles not less than in Germany; there were, moreover, attempts to suppress the new theory by official denunciations at scientific congresses, as in Germany, but without success. The new theories received the attention of some practitioners as well as of professors of medicine and psychology.[37]

This can be attributed partly to the fact that, from the point of view of the organization and professionalization of science, the United States at the beginning of the twentieth century was in the same stage of development as was Germany in the 1850's and 1860's. The process had just started to gather momentum. However, if only the rudimentary stage of the organization and professionalization of science had been the cause of the different reception of psychoanalysis in the United States, one would expect opinion to be divided, as it was about bacteriology in Germany: support for the theory would have come from practitioners and opposition from academic scientists. But, as a matter of fact, the cleavage of opinions was never on these lines; much of the support came from academic circles. The scientific reference group in the United States was more open than in Germany, owing apparently to the institional arrangements (as previously described), which provided a link between science and the groups interested in its application.[38]

36. Jones, *op. cit.*, pp. 107-25; Freud, *An Autobiographical Study*, pp. 87-101.

37. Jones, *op. cit.*, pp. 111-16; Shryock, *American Medical Research: Past and Present*, pp. 225-33.

38. For evidence that the relative openness of the academic system to psychoanalysis and other marginal medical trends was maintained by precisely these institutional arrangements see H. Cushing, *The Life of Sir William Osler* (Oxford, 1925), pp. 181, 221; Jones, *op. cit.*, II, 99; R. Sand, *The Advance to Social Medicine* (London, 1952), pp. 516-20, 545-49; Fleming, *op. cit.*, pp. 140-41, 144-45, 161-73. About the attitude of the

This analysis of the beginnings of bacteriology and psychoanalysis lends general support to the proposition that contact with practice may be important in reorienting research toward the investigation of new and fruitful problems. The practitioner-scientists appear as forerunners, supporters, and disciples in the history of two innovations, bacteriology and psychoanalysis, the central figures in both were "role hybrids" who were led to the innovation by an abrupt change from theoretical research to applied science. The practitioner-scientist, as well as the role hybrid, each are in a position to shift frames of reference relatively easily. But it can be assumed that those whose training and main role is that of the "scientist" will be more capable of generalizing, and more motivated to generalize, their findings and establish themselves as innovators than the practitioner-scientists.[39]

This interpretation may be relevant to the eventual investigation of patterns of discovery resulting from shifts from one scientific discipline to the other. Scientific disciplines differ from one another in the degree of their theoretical closure and methodological precision. The phenomena most similar to role hybridization would be shifts from a theoretically and methodologically more advanced discipline to one less advanced. These must be distinguished from shifts between two disciplines of the same level and from less to more advanced disciplines.

As far as the organization of science is concerned, the seemingly paradoxical conclusion is that professionalization of research does not in itself decrease the chances of innovations by outsiders. As a matter of fact, theoretically, it increases the chances, since, the more differentiated a field, the greater the likelihood of role hybridization in it. In practice, however, the differentiation of research from practice and the professionalization of science may take place in such a way as to make it difficult for scientists to engage in marginal problems without endangering their status beyond the risk taken by every innovator. Where an academic system reacts to marginal innovations, as the German system did to early bacteriology and, even more, to psychoanalysis, there is great risk in investigating problems considered irrelevant by academic authorities. It will be, therefore, relatively difficult to shift frames of reference. This is, indeed, shown in the relatively unimportant share of German academicians in establishing bacteriology as a science and in the fact

representative psychiatric circles to psychoanalysis see G. Zilboorg and G. W. Henry, *A History of Medical Psychology* (New York, 1941), pp. 500-506; J. K. Hall (ed.), *One Hundred Years of American Psychiatry* (New York, 1944), p. 305.

39. On priority in innovation as an institutionalized feature of science see R. K. Merton, "Priorities in Scientific Discovery: A Chapter in the Sociology of Science," *American Sociological Review,* XXII (1957), 635-59. According to this, it can be assumed that professional scientists are more motivated than practitioner-scientists to innovation.

that psychoanalysis developed into a movement rather than science in Austria and Germany.

If this analysis is correct, one would expect such "closed" academic systems as the German to lose efficiency because of their resistance to marginal innovations. This is, indeed, what happened to German academic medicine. On the other hand, this loss of efficiency may be temporary. Once the innovation is sufficiently established in another system, it may be taken up by the closed one and developed there rapidly, as, in fact, happened to German bacteriology.

At a later stage of the differentiation and professionalization of scientific roles mechanisms arose which mediated between the two types of activity and apparently broke down the barrier to communication found between practice and research in the last decades of the nineteenth century. The kind of professional structure which emerged in the United States made possible the differentiation of scientific roles, yet prevented a cleavage between the outlook of the academic and practicing sectors of the profession.

From this point of view medical "professionalism," which consciously aims at maintaining a balance between the development of medical sciences and practice, can be regarded as a sequel to the establishment of research as a separate institution during the nineteenth century. It is a social structure, or, rather, one of the structures, since there are certainly more than one, which represents a phase of growing integration between science and practice following the differentiation of academic research in the medical field out of the context of amateur and practitioners' research during the last century. The spread of professionalization in an increasing number of disciplines suggests that the sequence of events observed in medicine may have its parallels in other fields.

FRANK J. MAHONY

The Innovation of a Savings System in Truk

THIS is a report on an unusual savings system initiated in 1951 in the Caroline Islands. It began on Moen Island and spread rapidly throughout the Truk District.[1] The purpose of this paper is to describe the savings system: how it started, how it developed, and what were its results.

The savings system was first started by Petrus, the chief of Moen Island, a highly intelligent and the most widely respected man in the Truk District. For some time Petrus had been concerned about his people's attitudes towards money, which led to its being used in what he considered a wasteful manner. Before the savings system was begun, he tried several times to get the people of Moen Island to buy shares of stock in Truk Trading Company, the largest export and import firm in the Truk District (and at that time the only one) with total annual sales of over a million dollars. Many people did buy some stock, which has a fixed price of $25.00 per share, but after receiving an annual dividend of 10 per cent, which was considered very inadequate, most people cashed in their holdings. Somewhat later he tried to get each village of Moen Island to build up a small fund of money. This was done by setting aside a special day each week when people would work for their villages in addition to the already established island work day. This

Reprinted from American Anthropologist, *June, 1960, pp. 465-482, by permission of the author and the journal.*

The writer has been employed continuously since 1950 by the United States Trust Territory of the Pacific Islands in the position of anthropologist. In this capacity, reports on the savings system have been prepared for the administration. One of these reports was read by Saul H. Riesenberg, who made several helpful suggestions. I also wish to acknowledge the assistance provided by Sherwood L. Washburn in getting out to the field as well as the advice and encouragement during early field work of Thomas Gladwin.

1. The Truk District, located in the Eastern Caroline Islands, is an administrative unit of the Trust Territory. The Truk District consists of Truk itself, and two groups of coral atolls or islands. Truk is made up of a large circular coral reef, forming a lagoon thirty to forty miles in diameter, in which a number of small volcanic islands are situated. Of the two groups of atolls, one stretches away to the south and east of Truk for about two hundred miles and is known roughly as the Mortlock Islands. The other is scattered to the north and west of Truk for a distance of one hundred eighty miles and has come to be known as the Western Islands.

system was called *sata,* from the English word charter, and was a local adaptation of a practice introduced by the Japanese. However, the village funds never amounted to very much. Having first tried to get individuals, and later villages, to establish savings funds, and already having a large island fund to work with, it was a logical move for Petrus to try to establish savings funds for the districts of Moen Island. The innovation of these district savings funds was the beginning of the savings system.

Another reason Petrus wanted to build up savings funds for the people of Moen was to enable them to purchase shares of stock in Truk Trading Company. Petrus hoped to extend his influence over this expanding corporation. He had already used the Moen Island fund, built up through taxes, to purchase 10 per cent of Truk Trading Company stock, the maximum allowable to any one individual or group, and had encouraged individuals to buy shares. When the savings system proved successful, at Petrus' urging much of the money was used to purchase shares of stock and the people of Moen and other friends of Petrus acquired greater control of the company. Partly for this, as well as for many other reasons, Petrus was eventually elected president of Truk Trading Company, a position he still holds. Thus Petrus' stated desire to help his people was combined with his personal ambitions.

From this point of view the innovation of the savings system was only one of a number of maneuvers that Petrus carried out in his struggle to gain greater control of Truk Trading Company. The story of his fight for control is as interesting, in its own way, as are attempts to control large corporations in more advanced societies. Though he has had almost no formal education, Petrus has a keen intelligence and has always shown great shrewdness. It should not be concluded, however, that he is just another operator out for personal gain. Those who know him best know that he has always been a devoted servant of his people and that he has never compromised his sense of justice, honesty, and integrity for the sake of personal profit. He is a born leader; a man who would rather direct than be directed, and who derives great pleasure from exercising his talents for leadership. These statements may sound like platitudes but they are quite true.

Possibly searching his mind for an alternative to taxation as a means of raising money, Petrus conceived the idea of soliciting voluntary contributions to build up savings funds. He states that this idea came to him when he thought of the aboriginal practice of soliciting food and other goods from relatives and close friends. After forming this idea he announced to the people of Mwän, his own village, that he wanted to experiment with a new way of accumulating money. Mwän Village then held a meeting which was attended by officials from other parts of the island. Speeches were made, and then people sang songs, as individuals voluntarily placed a few pennies at a time on a centrally located table. Immediately Petrus observed that people were embarrassed by having to leave their places and get up in front of the rest of the group to make contributions. He therefore decided that at future meetings he would have someone go around with a bowl or plate to spare people the embarrassment of getting up in front of the group. After the few dollars collected at the meeting had been counted, Petrus consulted with the officials, and all agreed to try the system out in the various districts of Moen Island.

Before proceeding it would be well to say a word about the organization of Moen Island. Like most other inhabited islands in Truk District, Moen is organized as a municipality. Each municipality is headed by an elected chief (called magistrate in the official terminology) and he is assisted by a secretary, a treasurer, an advisory council, and other minor officials. On Moen, each district has a head and each village has a chief, a secretary, and a council. There are about fifteen villages on Moen which are grouped into five districts, about three villages to a district. (The division of the island into districts was introduced by the Japanese primarily as a means of organizing labor battalions. On most of the larger islands, however, the Trukese quickly integrated the districts into their existing political structure, making them an intermediate step between the villages and the island government.) The districts do not have much functional importance, but when the savings system was begun it was conceived of in terms of the organization into districts, and the savings meetings that were first held were called "District Meetings."

When the "District Meetings" began they seemed to be patterned after Christian church services. A typical meeting would be opened by a song and a prayer, followed by a talk from one of the island leaders who would explain the purpose of the meeting. This would be followed by oratorical speeches (*afanafan*) from other officials, urging the people to be good. Each of these speeches would be interspersed with songs sung by the assembled crowd. Alternate singing and oratory might last until noon when a short break would be taken to eat the noon meal. Women were then selected from each village in the district to take turns passing a small plate or bowl into which the assembled people would place their deposits or contributions. As the plate was passed the people would sing. Occasionally the woman who was passing the plate would break into an aboriginal dance routine or sing a few lines of a song. After each woman had had a turn, the money would be counted, while someone, usually Petrus, made the final speech. The meeting ended after an announcement had been made enumerating the total amount of money collected and a final prayer said. The pattern of the meetings appeared to be an imitation of church services; the main features being singing, sermons, and the collection of money. In addition the Bible was used as a main source of material for the speeches, and most of the songs that were sung were either Catholic or Protestant hymns. The resemblance was so close that some missionaries prevented their church members from attending the savings meetings. In private and in public, Petrus and other officials denied that there was any connection or relationship between the savings meetings and church services. They also explained that the people drew on their knowledge of the Bible and religious hymns only because there was little else they knew. Subsequently the missionaries withdrew their ban; and thereafter island officials enjoined the people to make secular speeches and sing secular songs. This resulted in a great flourish of original song writing and speech making.

As an example of the type of speeches that were made we list the topics for speeches that appeared on one of the programs for a savings meeting. Topics included: disobedience, obedience, invasion, defense, selfishness, generosity, haughtiness, humility, breaking the law, obeying the law, breaking, making, covetousness, suppressing desire, crooked, straight, hate, love, disagreement, cooperation, slothfulness, perseverance, theft and honesty. These topics were all suggested by chief Petrus. As examples of the many songs that were composed for, and sung at savings meetings, we present the following which have been freely translated from Trukese:

1

Thank you very much Anlipich and also Petrus;
Don't you have one dollar that you can give to us?

We are asking you Meipung and also Effou;
Don't you have one dollar that you can give to us?

Hey Ukochik, Erman! Why are you so quiet?
Don't you have one dollar that you can give to us?

Say, where's Elis? I don't see his face.
Doesn't he have two dollars that he can give to us?

Thank you very much Michuo, for what you have in your pocket.
That five dollars that you are going to give to us.

Well, who else is going to help advance our district?
Why there's Michi carrying three hundred dollars in his pocket!

2

Good afternoon Mr. Petrus and Justice Anlipich
And to Mr. Meipung as well as Effou.

Good afternoon chiefs, councilmen, advisory bodies and youth groups who have come from far away places
As well as strangers and all of us people, everyone.

Oh, we will bring our hearts together for our island government.
For it will be built out of love and cooperation.
With cooperation, cooperation only—joy for our island government.
With love, with love, with love, with love,
For understanding love, obedience and an unassuming manner is what we thrive on.

Wake up for the sun is rising.
Get working tools and go to our places of work and work hard.
We're lazy but we'll try to work hard.
We're stupid but we'll try hard in school.
We're sinful but we'll try hard in religion.
For our island will progress through perseverance.

Oh we will all be happy in our work.
We will work for food and work for money by cutting copra, gardening and fishing.
We will sell these things to build up our island.
And so that our company[2] will help us to progress.

Contributions that people made in these meetings were given the name *töchap* by Petrus. This word was coined by some anonymous individual and became a regular feature of Trukese slang shortly after the war. One is said to *töchap*, for example, if one bets on a poker hand without looking at the cards or knowing what they are. Or again if one manufactures drinking alcohol without the permission of island officials, which would be a violation of island regulations, one is also said to *töchap*. Thus the word denotes the doing of something brazen, illegal, or out of the ordinary. Hence, in the context of the savings system, we shall translate this word as "daring contribution." Petrus' use of this term was a conscious attempt to stimulate people and arouse their interest in savings meetings. The device worked and it was not long before the meetings themselves began to be known universally as "daring contribution meetings."

The money that was collected formed district funds. Each district fund belonged in common to the people of the district, but was kept in safekeeping by island officials and used to make loans to qualified persons. In the very beginning, a separate officials' fund was also set up so that money contributed by officials would belong to them in common. This was necessary because most officials were from outside any one district and would lose the use of their money to the district unless it were separately accounted for. Soon other groups, desiring to save

2. Truk Trading Co.

money for special purposes, requested permission of island officials to set up small funds of their own. As a result, additional funds were gradually established for the Catholics, Protestants, elders, and young men of each district.

The first of the "District Meetings" had been held early in 1951. Meetings continued to take place for the following year and a half, until a total of ten meetings had been held, two for each district of Moen. The total amount of money collected from all of these meetings for deposit in the district savings and loan funds was only a little more than one thousand dollars.

In an attempt to stimulate greater savings, and possibly to change the form of the system so that it would be less similar to a church service, Petrus decided that savings deposits would henceforth be made by sibs. (The establishment of a savings fund for each of the sibs in a district had been suggested, apparently, by the numerous requests for setting up funds for different groups. People had shown that they were not particularly interested in the district funds, but were interested in saving money for more meaningful groups.) Money collected from the sibs was to be held in the island office, which would keep records and be accountable for the amount of money saved by each sib. In practice, however, lineages actually controlled the money; for the money was collected by lineages and eventually spent by lineages. Bookkeeping chores were consequently decentralized. Island officials kept a record only of the amount deposited by each sib in a district. Each lineage of a sib, however, kept a record of the amount of its contribution to the sib's fund. Petrus made plans for other changes and discussed them in a meeting with all the village chiefs. Village chiefs then held discussions with the people, after which they reported back to island officials.

When all the changes had been discussed and agreed upon, and the first meetings held, the situation was approximately as follows. Individuals contributed money to their respective lineages. Lineages of the same sib then put their funds together. When each sib had collected the money together it was placed in an envelope and the name of the sib written on it. This money was collected long before the meeting and was called the "contents of the envelope" (*masowen futo*). Specific times were set aside in the course of the meeting for different sibs to deposit the "contents of the envelope." After the envelope was deposited a certain time was allowed for sib members to make additional contributions to their sibs by tossing coins on a table. This additional deposit was called "weighting down the envelope" (*chouchoun futo*). The idea for this distinction came from aboriginal food competitions held between different sibs or lineages. In these competitive feasts a sib usually made a large initial offering of food, *rasanap*, followed by a smaller additional offering called *chouchou,* or weighting down. "Daring contributions" remained, but this term was now applied only to those donations made to a sib by persons who were not members of that sib. In other words, any sib member who made a contribution to his own sib during the course of the meeting was "weighting down the envelope," but if an individual made a contribution to a sib other than his own, it was a "daring contribution." The feature of having a woman solicit contributions was eliminated. In its stead two tables were set up at the front of the meeting house where people were to deposit their contributions as they filed past, it apparently being felt that people had completely overcome their initial embarrassment at having to get up in front of others to make contributions. One of the tables was reserved for the "contents of the envelope" and "daring contributions," and the other table for "weighting down the envelope." To add emphasis to these changes, Petrus changed the name of the savings system from "District Meetings" to "Sib" or "Lineage Meetings" (*mwichen einang, einang* means either sib or lineage). The vast majority of people, however, continued to refer to the system as "daring contribution meetings."

In addition, an agendum was drawn up for each of these meetings showing all the important activities that were to take place. Usually the agenda were surreptitiously mimeographed in one of the Truk District administration offices, through connections established with native employees of the administration.

In an effort to assure the financial success of these new style meetings, a distribution of money was made by the Moen Island office. Moen Island's income from its labor tax, and the dividends from its stock in Truk Trading Company, were distributed to all the villages. The villages in turn distributed the money among lineages. By this means Petrus made sure that the meetings would get off to a good start.

Beginning in the summer of 1952, several meetings were held along these lines; but within a few months Petrus added more features to the already complicated arrangements. To the two tables already in use, a third table was added where coins could be placed for the purpose of "hiring songs" (*satan kön*). By placing fifty cents on this third table anyone could have any song repeated. This innovation was suggested by the practice of hiring or chartering personnel or equipment, an example of which has already been given. Petrus added this so that the length of time people continued to deposit money could be stretched out, even though a singing group had already gone through its repertory. Also, specific times were now set aside when people could make "daring contributions" to the singing. This change was suggested by a village official who simply made a logical extension of the idea of "daring contributions" to the singing. (All of these types of contributions were accounted for by island officials and equitably credited to the various sibs.) Though previously villages had alternated with each other in singing, subsequently each village sang for only a certain portion of the meeting, after which it was relieved by another village. The villages were thus brought into competition with one another and prizes were offered to the villages that did the best singing.

As these changes were made the savings system gradually lost its similarity to a church service and began to resemble a Trukese first fruits ceremony. The savings system and the first fruits eventually came to resemble one another in the following ways: The offerings are gathered by lineages and brought to the chiefs (officials). There is a good deal of singing by groups which compete against each other, and many speeches are made. Offerings are then distributed back to the lineages and, in one way or another, an exchange of offerings is effected between lineages.

When the savings system became patterned after the first fruits ceremony its popularity increased a great deal. The reasons for this popularity were many. In Truk there is a strong identification between the individual and his lineage. By depositing money with their lineages, individuals felt that they were the direct beneficiaries of their savings, a feeling they did not have when they were contributing to the more nebulous district funds. Also, by organizing the savings system in terms of lineages and sibs, the element of competition began to assume a more important role. Lineages, sibs, and districts vied with one another to see which could accumulate the greatest amount of savings.

In addition most people felt that the reorganized savings system provided a new way to make lots of money. The "daring contribution" that others made to one's own sib was regarded as a profit. Few seemed to realize that the net effect would be for these contributions to cancel each other out. People also felt that the use of sib and lineage funds to make loans at high interest rates would result in tremendous profits. Once again they did not seem to realize that, having left themselves bereft of cash by putting almost all their money in the savings system, they would consequently be the greatest borrowers, and the earnings of their savings would be balanced by the interest they paid.

As the savings system developed, people discovered that their expectations of profit were not being realized. However, enthusiasm was sustained because people saw that they were actually saving money and also because they became delighted with the general festivities. People busied themselves composing songs and practiced singing them. They dressed up to go to meetings and either made speeches or listened to them. Youths and young girls were provided with occasions to flirt with each other. In short, to a people whose round of activities consists largely of making a living during the week and going to church on Sundays, the meetings provided a golden opportunity to have a good time. For all of these reasons the savings system met with great financial success.

"Sib Meetings" far outdistanced "District Meetings" in the amount of money collected. Whereas in the ten "District Meetings" that had been held, only a little more than $1,000 was collected, the following ten "Sib Meetings" produced a total of $27,116.75, as much as $4,500 being deposited at a single meeting. Amongst a people whose per capita annual income is somewhat less than $50.00, this is a large sum of money. Anyone who could satisfy island officials that he had the ability to return the money was allowed to borrow. Interest on loans was first charged at the rate of 10 per cent per month. If a man borrowed ten dollars and at the end of a month was unable to return the money he paid one dollar interest and continued to hang on to the ten dollars. Many regarded this as a rare privilege and a great benefit. Although the interest rate was later reduced to 10 per cent per quarter, as time went on it became increasingly difficult to collect not only the interest but the principal of the loans. Consequently after the first ten "Sib Meetings," island officials decided not to make any more loans. Thereafter deposits were counted and held in the island office for a short time. Then the money was returned to the lineages and they invested it in the common stock of Truk Trading Company, or made purchases of large capital items such as motor boats, sewing machines, and so forth.

In order to delineate the prevailing spirit of the savings meetings, and to give an accurate account of what actually took place during them, we pass on to a detailed examination of a single one of these meetings. The meeting we will examine is the one that took place in the First District of Moen Island on September 5, 1953. This particular meeting is selected because, in a way, it was a high point of the savings system. The chief of Uman Island and some of his officials and friends attended this meeting to learn about the savings system so they could introduce it to their own island. Later, the savings system made its first appearance outside Moen Island when one of the villages of Uman held a savings meeting on September 18, 1953. It was entirely logical that the savings system should spread first to Uman Island because the current chief of that island was a boyhood friend of Petrus. They had attended mission school together in their youth and the chief of Uman was always strongly influenced by whatever Petrus said or did. As a result, the chief of Uman was the first to ask Petrus' permission to learn about the savings system so that he could introduce it to his own island.

At least four months prior to this meeting some preparations were already under way. New songs were composed especially for the occasion. Practice sessions were also held in each village of the district where conditions and events of the coming meeting were simulated.

Shortly after dawn of the appointed day the people of the First District assembled at the meeting house. The meeting was opened with speeches by several different officials. When the speeches were over, singing and contributions got under way. Activities went on until shortly after noon, when a break was taken to consume the midday meal. Then people reassembled at the meeting house.

The meeting was reopened in the afternoon with an announcement from Effou. He stated that they would start with "daring contributions" for the singing. Then singing and contributions began. Contributors came from inside and outside to thread their way through to the tables and deposit their offerings, a few cents at a time.[3] After depositing their coins, they then picked their way out the front door. Officials and guests made contributions by tossing coins onto the tables from their seated positions on the platform.

After about ten minutes Effou motioned for the singing to stop and announced that the Rengou Sib would deposit the "contents of the envelope" at his table. He also explained where coins should be placed for "weighting down the envelope," for "daring contributions," and for "song hirings." After this announcement, singing began and deposits poured on the tables. After about fifteen minutes, contributions stopped coming in and Effou announced that the Rengou Sib was finished and everyone would make "daring contributions" to the singing again.

At this point let us paraphrase the notes that were taken during the course of the meeting:

A quiet, sedate, young man is acting as song leader. He is making a brave effort to lead the songs but all the while people come up and stuff coins into his pockets, force coins into his mouth or stick them inside his ears. The money belongs to the song leader, it is explained to me, unless someone comes and takes it away from him before he is through directing the singing. Sure enough, other people begin to come up and take the coins away from him. After about ten minutes, "daring contributions" to the singing peters out and Effou announces that the meeting is progressing too slowly. He states that they are contributing their money in dribs and drabs and that they should make larger contributions to speed things up. He adds that it is now time for the

3. The flow of coins through a savings meeting was an interesting phenomenon in itself. People were continuously thrusting bills and large coins through windows and doorways near the tables to the money counters. As soon as officials had counted small coins they were passed around behind them in exchange for larger denominations. When people got small change, of course, they came around through the meeting and began depositing it back on the tables. There was thus a constant flow of small coins up to the tables, out the windows to the people, and back around to the tables again.

Due to the desire for small change for these meetings there was always a great demand for it just before a meeting was to be held. At these times small coins virtually disappeared from normal circulation and local merchants were forced to make change with sticks of gum.

Achaw Sib to deposit the "contents of the envelope" and so the singing and flow of donations begin again.

While all this is going on people continuously sprinkle perfume and hair oil on the heads of the singers until most of them become soaked to the skin. As some people sprinkle perfume or hair oil on the heads of others, they lift the flower leis from their heads. Effou announces that they should not take flower leis from one another because someone is liable to get mad. Nevertheless the lei stealing continues with as much abandon as before. (Exchanging leis and sprinkling oil and perfume were prominent features of aboriginal dances, long since stamped out by missionaries because of their licentiousness. Giving and taking coins from the song leader is also a reinterpretation of the practice of giving and taking food and flowers from dance leaders.) Effou soon announces that the Achaw Sib is finished and it is time for "daring contributions" to the singing again. At this moment someone substituted a glass of water for the usual hair oil libation and tossed it all over the chief of Iräs Village. Everyone laughs while the chief manages to smile through some embarrassment. Things quiet down and a few moments later Effou announces that the Rääk Sib will deposit the "contents of the envelope."

Just now a woman came and placed a beautiful flower lei on my head which she had just stolen from someone else; someone gives me another lei, and another lei, and another. Finally I take all but one and give them to the man on my right. He accepts them and redistributes them on the heads of the singers. A moment later a hand reaches out and snatches the single remaining lei from my head while tossing a coin in my lap, apparently in lieu of the usual bath with hair oil. I pick the coin up and look at it. It is a five cent piece. I show it to the man on my left. He takes it, puts it in his pocket and laughs.

Effou motions for the singing to stop and announces that the Rääk Sib has weighted down their envelope to the amount of $13.25. Then he says it is time to make "daring contributions" to the singing and so singing and donations begin again.

These activities continued through the afternoon and well into the evening. Finally at about nine o'clock, Petrus rose to talk. He made a long speech touching on many topics and punctuated by hushed silences and roaring laughter. Among things he discussed was the value of money and the virtues of saving it. He stated that too much money had been wasted on hair oil and perfume and that entirely too much flirting went along with its use. He welcomed visitors and guests, thanked them for coming, and said that the people should always be nice to them. This led to a discussion of relations between foreigners and Trukese and he pointed out that all men were really the same under the skin. When he concluded his speech, Effou rose to present the prizes for singing. When the prizes were distributed everyone clapped and Effou said the meeting was all over. Officials stood up first, then the people rose, sang out "good-by," and began to disperse to their homes.

Thus ended this meeting in the First District of Moen Island—full of gaiety and confusion but financially very successful. The amount of money deposited in the savings system during the course of this meeting totaled $2,315.36. The money was deposited in the following ways:

"Contents of the envelope," $1,666.90. This is the total amount of money collected by sibs and deposited at specified times during the meeting. Amounts varied from the $9.00 deposited by Inänifat Sib to the $191.50 deposited by Masanö Sib.

"Weighting down the envelope," $287.48. This is the total of the amount which the members of each sib added to their deposits during the course of the meeting. Inänifat Sib, for example, was credited with $1.17, while Masanö Sib was credited with $21.55.

"Daring contributions" to the sibs, $235.37. This is the amount contributed by nonmembers of sibs at times during the meeting when sib members were "weighting down the envelope." $.31 was contributed to Inänifat Sib, while $9.93 was contributed to Masanö Sib.

"Song hirings," $73.00. This money was contributed fifty cents at a time by persons who wanted to hear songs repeated. Although an accounting was kept during the meeting of the amount each village earned through "song hirings," this was later disregarded and the money credited evenly to the sibs.

"Daring contributions" to the singing, $37.61. This amount of money was donated a few cents at a time during the periods set aside in the meeting for this purpose.

In addition a special contribution of $15.00 was made by the chief of Uman and his friends in appreciation of this opportunity to learn about the savings system.

A short time later, sibs and lineages of the First District were urged to withdraw the funds deposited with island officials during this meeting and use the money to purchase stock in Truk Trading Company. In addition to purchases of common stock and other goods, a large number of people put at least part of the funds they withdrew back into the savings system at future meetings. Consequently some of the money continually circulated through the savings system. Island officials asserted, however, that this was improper. Money that had been counted once, they said, was not supposed to be counted a second time.

Afterward, at the conclusion of each savings system meeting, the people of Moen withdrew their funds from the island office. Island officials continued to be responsible for the more than $27,000 in savings that had originally been accumulated. To the date of this writing they are still attempting to recover the balance of these funds that is out on loan.

Modifications in the savings system continued to be made on Moen Island. Island officials, apparently weary of spending hours and hours in attendance at all of these meetings, reduced the scope of the regular meetings and, at the same time, expanded the practice sessions. All of the monetary features of the regular meetings were incorporated into the practice sessions. Money collected at the practice sessions was equitably divided among the various sibs and then deposited at the regular meeting only as the "contents of the envelope." All the other monetary features of the regular meeting were thus eliminated. In effect, preparations for meetings became the focus of activity, while the meetings themselves were reduced to formalities.

One odd feature, introduced into the savings system on Moen, gained great popularity and became a regular feature of savings meetings on Moen as well as on many of the other islands that eventually took over the system. This feature was started by a man of the Fourth District. He conceived the idea of calling up his sister's husband to match any contributions he made to his sib. This was not unusual because a man has great authority over his sister's husband (or sisters' husbands). A man can order (ökkunöw) his sister's husband to bring food and he can take clothing or money from him and be under no obligation to return it. In the savings system, when a man called up his sister's husband, the two entered into a kind of contest. Each time the man put down some money, his sister's husband had to match the contribution. If he was able to continue matching his brother-in-law's deposits, everyone would clap for him, but if he failed everyone would laugh because he had been shamed. This feature was soon extended to other individuals and groups. When a person would get up and say, "hiring of so and so," or "daring contribution for so and so," the person or group whose name was called was required to make a deposit. When the feature was extended to other persons and groups, they no longer had to match the amount but just make a contribution.[4] It was this particular form of the feature that became most popular. At a savings meeting on Udot, for example, a man of sib *x* called for contributions from all the men of his sib, all the men in his father's sib, all the officials, and all the spouses of the women of sib *x*, i.e., his sisters' husbands among others. As one man of this last group made his deposit he said jokingly, "I'm through marrying sib *x* women." A sib *x* woman then answered this amusing challenge by making a deposit and saying, "daring contribution for all the spouses of sib *x* women that their faces may go to sleep," i.e., that they may neither look at another woman nor see what their own wives were doing. Later, cowboy movies added their influence to this feature when certain officials on Moen arranged to have themselves "shot." In

4. When this took place my attendance at savings meetings began to turn into a rather expensive research project as I was frequently called upon to make contributions. Attendance at meetings of the First District of Moen was less expensive since I participated as a "member" of one of the sibs and consequently shared in the proceeds.

accordance with pre-arranged signals, an individual would get up during a meeting, cock his finger at an official and shout "pow." The official then rose and called out the names of the groups that should make deposits. Still later, at some meetings, people just went around "shooting" each other and anyone who was "shot" was required to make a contribution.

Meanwhile, starting in 1953, the savings system began to spread to other islands and institutions. As already mentioned it made its first appearance outside Moen Island on September 18, 1953, when a savings meeting was held in one of the villages of Uman Island. At first a small group of people objected to the savings system on Uman and boycotted earlier meetings. When meetings proved successful, however, objections practically vanished and almost everyone participated.

Here is how one individual described this first meeting:

> We got together in a meeting on September 18. The reason for the meeting was the first fruits. We made the first fruits for our village chief. And that's the time we invited the island officials to come too. That's when we started to collect that money. . . . The meeting started with praying and then speeches were made about the reason for the meeting. The purpose was the "first preserved breadfruit." Then we started to collect money for the village. We collected the money by hearths *(fanang)*. A bowl was put on the table for each hearth. Then anyone who was able to, put a "daring contribution" in the bowl. If anyone wasn't able to contribute money, that was all right. We collected $150. That money was for the village. . . . We lent the money to Raymond and he is going to pay us back with interest.

It is significant that when the savings system first appeared on another island it was combined with a first fruit ceremony and money was collected by hearths. Hearths, it should be noted, are earth ovens over which small houses are built. Each lineage usually has a particular named hearth where first fruits are prepared. In the savings meetings on Uman the hearths symbolized lineages.

After this, savings meetings were no longer combined with first fruits ceremonies on Uman, although money for the villages continued to be collected by hearths. Meetings continued to be held on Uman and many changes took place. For example, the name of the savings system was changed, an esoteric name being adopted from a word used in aboriginal chants. One addition, introduced by the island secretary who was very familiar with Japanese customs, was the holding of a lottery. Prizes were offered and tickets sold during meetings. Love songs, accompanied by guitars, were also frequently substituted for group singing. And, after experimenting for a while in loaning its funds, Uman began to follow Moen's example in purchasing Truk Trading Company stock.

About a month later, on October 15, 1953, the savings system was tried out on Pwene, one of the municipalities of Tol Island in the Truk Lagoon. It was introduced there by the secretary, who had also been a close friend of Petrus ever since they had shared adjacent beds during their confinement in a Japanese hospital. He was the third person to request permission of Petrus to hold savings meetings. On Pwene, savings meetings closely imitated the pattern established on Moen, although there was a good deal of confusion at first due to lack of understanding. The only major variations were that savings meetings were held by villages and each lineage in a village cared for its own funds. (This slight change was made on most islands because the system developed on Moen—of collecting money by village-oriented lineages but depositing it by district-oriented sibs—was rather awkward.) Officials did not take funds into their safe keeping but kept a record of the amount saved by each lineage, requesting the lineages to inform them if they spent the money or if they added more to their savings. The chief told the people that, although he wanted them to buy shares of stock in Truk Trading Company, they were free to use the funds in any way they wished.

After the savings system had been tried out on Uman and Pwene, it began to spread all over the Truk District. Up to this point people had been hesitating to adopt the system for fear of displeasing Petrus and the people of Moen. The adoption of the savings system by islands other than Moen was a signal that it was all right to go ahead. There is no doubt that many islands were eager to adopt the system. Reports of the tremendous savings accumulated on Moen spread far and wide and were a subject of conversation everywhere in the Truk District, as well as in many places throughout the Caroline and Marshall Islands. Consequently, during the following month, savings meetings were held on five different, widely scattered islands. These were Nomwin in the Western group, Udot and Eot in the Truk Lagoon, and Nama and Losap in the Mortlock group. Only Nomwin and Udot sent representatives to Petrus to request instruction in the savings system and permission to hold meetings on their islands. On the rest of these islands the savings system was introduced by persons who had become familiar with it through long periods of residence on Moen. And, with the exception of Nama, all these islands used the funds for the purchase of Truk Trading Company stock.

The five islands that held savings meetings in late October and early November, 1953, copied the general pattern of the savings system that had been developed on Moen, although each island introduced its own modifications. Of these five islands, Nama made the most changes. The chief of Nama had learned about the savings system from some of his people who had been living on Moen and was anxious to try it out. The native pastor of Nama made a speech in church vigorously objecting to the savings system on the grounds that boys and girls would be wearing flower leis and mingling too closely with one another. The chief, who was antipathetic to the pastor to begin with, decided to go ahead with savings meetings anyway and preparations were begun.

There are only three sibs on Nama, which are divided into thirteen, fourteen, and eleven lineages respectively. It was decided that each of these lineages would present precisely ten dollars as the "contents of the envelope." Each sib was allotted a different portion of the meeting when its lineages would present their envelopes. As on Moen, three tables were set up in the meeting house. However, their functions were quite different. One table was reserved for the sib chief who collected the "contents of the envelope" from the heads of his sib's constituent lineages and "weighting down the envelope" from all members of the sib. The second table was reserved as a place where the children of the men of the sib (*öfökur*) could deposit their contributions to the sib. The third table was reserved as a place where the people at large could make their contributions to the sib.

The function of the tables was changed due to a misunderstanding and confusion between the types of deposits put on the tables and the feature of soliciting contributions by calling out the names of different groups. The chief of Nama also imposed his own acquisitive thinking on the original uncertainty in finally deciding how the tables should be used. The chief gave a good indication of his feelings when asked how he felt about the savings system. "You can really raise money in this kind of business," he said. (Here he used the Japanese word for business.) "People are ashamed," he continued, "not to get up and make contributions. The children of the men of a sib are ashamed because their fathers give them coconut trees and other things and if they don't make contributions to their father's sib, it's just like they don't love them."

From the thirty-eight lineages on Nama, $380 was collected. This, together with about $40.00 in other contributions, made a total of about $420. The people of Nama used these funds to start a wholesale store on Moen Island, a project they had been planning for some time. The Nama store, which later became chartered as the Nama Trading Company, with headquarters on Moen Island, did a thriving business in competition with the Truk Trading Company.

In 1954 the savings system began to spread through the Mortlocks. Its development there was strongly encouraged by the chief of Lukunor. For some years past, the chief of Lukunor had been petitioning the administration for assistance in starting a company that would compete with Truk Trading Company. Like the chief of Nama, he saw that the savings system might provide a means to raise funds for this company.

He started the savings system on Lukunor and encouraged its development elsewhere in the Mortlocks. As a result, many of these islands used savings system funds to purchase shares of stock from the initial offering of the Mortlock Trading Company. Consequently the savings system was partly responsible, not only for the purchase of large blocks of stock in Truk Trading Company, but also for raising capital for the formation of two new companies which grew and prospered in competition with Truk Trading Company. Today these three firms are the only legitimate outfits doing an importing and wholesale business in the Truk District.

On Lukunor the savings system was considerably simplified. Three tables were set up in the meeting, one for each of the three villages of Lukunor. Each table was presided over by the village secretary who recorded the name of each individual and the amount of his "daring contribution." Since these "daring contributions" were going for the purchase of stock in the Mortlock Trading Company, it was desired that a record be kept of the amount of stock each person was to be entitled to. Each village formed a singing group and each group alternated in singing as "daring contributions" were made. Songs could be hired at the rate of 25 cents for each song. Money collected by each village through "song hirings" went into village funds and was used to buy food for village feasts. The savings system on nearby islands, such as Oneop and Moch, was very similar to this in as much as representatives of the chief of Lukunor were frequently in attendance. It would appear that on these islands the savings system was not patterned on the basis of any analogy but was dominated by the strictly instrumental purpose of raising money for the Mortlock Trading Company. It was these islands, too, that held savings system meetings during administrative field trips, primarily, it seemed, to relieve visiting administrative personnel of their pocket money.

Meanwhile the savings system was continuing to spread out elsewhere. In January of 1954 it was adopted by one of the political factions of Fefan Island. For some time Fefan had been divided into two factions. one of which was numerically superior and had been able to control the chieftainship through a series of elections over the years. The chief, a highly acculturated half caste, was indifferent to the savings system at first. However, when the hostile faction decided they wanted to try it, he opposed it. The hostile faction went ahead anyway. They got permission from Petrus, but adopted the system from nearby Uman Island where two or three of their leaders had close friends. Consequently they followed Uman in changing the name of the system, in collecting money by hearths, and in holding a lottery during savings meetings.

The system continued to be adopted by other islands and by mid-1955 savings system meetings had been or were being held on twelve of the fifteen municipalities of Truk, on ten of the eleven Mortlock municipalities, but on only two of the thirteen Western municipalities. The reason the savings system did not spread to the Western group may be because these islands are much less acculturated. Consequently, these people are somewhat apathetic about the uses of money and savings system did not have much appeal to them. The people of the Mortlocks tried to get the Western Islands interested in forming a new company (what eventually became the Mortlock Trading Company) but their efforts were met largely with indifference.

Of the three municipalities that the savings system did not spread to on Truk, two, Parem and Sis, are tiny islands which are split by two fiercely antagonistic political factions. On one of these islands the chieftainship had shifted back and forth between the two factions in a series of elections that had been decided by a majority of only one, two, or three votes. Fefan, though divided into factions, had been able to hold savings meetings because it is a larger island and the factions were divided geographically as well as politically.

Pata, one of the municipalities of Tol Island, was the third area in Truk Lagoon where the savings system did not take hold. This municipality was ruled by a chief who was a lay pastor of his church and who held a high position in its inner councils. He was opposed to the savings system on semi-religious grounds. He believed that the savings system provided a situation where an invidious comparison was made between those who had money and those who had little or none. Consequently, he was strongly opposed to the system and never allowed meetings to be held in his municipality.[5]

Financially the savings system was a great success. This success dated from the time it became somewhat analogous to a first fruits ceremony. The accumulation of large sums of money in the savings system paralleled the accumulation of large amounts of food in first fruits ceremonies. Ordinarily the Trukese gather and prepare only enough food for two or three days. However, for the first fruits ceremony, or for food competitions that are occasionally held between sibs and lineages, enormous amounts of food may be prepared.

In this connection a good case might be made showing that the Trukese tend to have the same attitudes for money that they have for food. Although in part they treat money much as Westerners do, and

5. More recently, the chief opposed the importation of beer into his municipality, but this proved to be his demise. He lost the following election and an ordinance was passed allowing the importation of beer into the municipality.

I have no satisfactory explanation for the failure of Satawan Island in the Mortlocks to hold savings meetings. However, at meetings of the chiefs of the Mortlock municipalities, savings meetings were held, and the chief of Satawan participated along with the rest.

though in part their attitudes are ambivalent, in part also they seem to regard money with the same attitudes and values that they have for food. Consequently they appear to treat money, not so much as capital or as a medium of exchange, but as an item of consumption–something that must be used up before it goes bad. Indeed, Japanese yen and postal savings became worthless after the war, an eventuality that would reinforce such attitudes. If this is correct it would explain a great deal about the savings system. It would help explain how the basic innovation occurred to Petrus, i.e., the solicitation of money rather than food. It would help to explain why the savings system later became analogous to a first fruits ceremony. It would also help explain why certain practices associated with food, such as "weighting down" at food competitions or giving and taking of food from dance leaders, were linked with money in the context of the savings system. It might even explain, for instance, why Moen Island officials stated that when savings system funds had been counted once, they were not supposed to be counted a second time. Viewed from this perspective the savings system takes on new meaning.[6]

Money accumulated in the savings system was used to establish funds from which loans were made. On many islands people also used these funds for the purchase of the common stock of Truk Trading Company. (Indeed, after the savings system became popular, the company, which had always had a surplus of stock in its treasury, completely sold out its supply of common stock and has lately been considering a secondary issue.) Savings system funds also provided some of the capital to help start two other companies which are now competing with Truk Trading Company. The savings system also enabled people to buy relatively expensive capital goods they ordinarily might have been unable to purchase. With funds accumulated through the savings system in 1955, for instance, the people of the First District of Moen Island were able to buy four jeeps, five skiffs, two outboard motors, a large number of sewing machines, and a great quantity of cement, lumber, and other building materials for the construction of more substantial homes. If the savings system had not come into being, much of the money that was used for these purposes would have been squandered in small amounts on a host of inconsequential items. By means of this rather unusual savings system, then, the Trukese people were able to save their money and to convert these savings into different forms of capital.

6. The prior existence of Truk Trading Co. does not tend to invalidate this hypothesis or the generalization that the Trukese are ordinarily unable to save money. Encouraged by the American administration, the company was originally begun through the initiative of an American, who is its present manager, with capital funds that were largely provided by a small group of highly acculturated Trukese half castes.

At present enthusiasm for the savings system has waned. Part of the reason for this is that some of the objectives of the savings system have been accomplished, and further, that the people's attention has been diverted to other matters. Municipal governments are being completely reorganized prior to receiving municipal charters. Also, in 1957, a Truk District Congress was formed and given a charter by the High Commissioner. Island leaders, preoccupied with these political affairs, were unable to devote their attention to the savings system.

The savings system also declined because its novelty wore off and people began to be bored with it and lose interest. By 1957, when most other islands were no longer having meetings, the people of Moen indicated to an agreeable officialdom that they would just as soon discontinue the system.[7] Since then, sporadic savings system meetings have been held by schools and charitable organizations, but the chances are that before long these too will cease. Thus the savings system is dying out and probably will not be revived.[8]

7. It was at about this time that the Trukese first discovered bingo. This game captured the Trukese fancy and in a short time almost every retail store was running a bingo game nightly and offering its merchandise as prizes. Two years later, in 1959, legislation was passed allowing the importation of beer into the Truk District and its consumption in municipalities on the basis of local option. As a result, the Trukese are today devoting a good deal of their surplus time and money to bingo and beer.

8. Several people have suggested a possible relationship between the savings system and millenarian movements. Jack Fischer, who attended some of the meetings, has noted, in personal correspondence, the following similarities: (1) irrational and exaggerated hopes as to benefits in the near future; (2) an air of excitement in the meetings; (3) the apparent embarrassment of Petrus at the meeting Fischer attended; (4) rapid spread and decline; and (5) disillusionment with economic development and the gap between American and Trukese standards of living.

I do not think that the savings system was enough like a millenarian movement to warrant its classification as such and I would offer the following comments: (1) Petrus is not a typical millenarian leader (Fischer grants this but adds that the people may have tried to fit him into this role); (2) the savings system was begun in a routine manner without reference to any kind of supernatural experience; (3) in its origin, and throughout its development and spread, the savings system was completely under the control of the administration, sponsored by democratically elected officials of each island so that, in effect, it was simply one other aspect of routine island government administration; (4) there were no "nativistic" or "revivalistic" aspects to the meetings; those aboriginal behavior patterns that cropped up in the meetings were survivals which were making their appearance in other social contexts as well; and (5) the savings system was quite pragmatically oriented towards goals which were obtainable and which, in many cases, were actually attained; no semi-miraculous events were expected and there was no feeling that the savings system would solve all financial problems.

c) OUTSIDE SOCIAL TOLERANCE

1) Deviance

RICHARD A. CLOWARD

Illegitimate Means, Anomie, and Deviant Behavior

THIS paper[1] represents an attempt to consolidate two major sociological traditions of thought about the problem of deviant behavior. The first, exemplified by the work of Emile Durkheim and Robert K. Merton, may be called the anomie tradition.[2] The second, illustrated principally by the studies of Clifford R. Shaw, Henry D. McKay, and Edwin H. Sutherland, may be called the "cultural transmission" and "differential association" tradition.[3] Despite some reciprocal borrowing of ideas, these intellectual traditions developed more or less independently. By seeking to consolidate them, a more adequate theory of deviant behavior may be constructed.

Reprinted from American Sociological Review, *April, 1959, pp. 164-176, by permission of the author and the journal.*

1. This paper is based on research conducted in a penal setting. For a more detailed statement see Richard A. Cloward and Lloyd E. Ohlin, *Delinquency and Opportunity*, New York: Free Press, 1960.

2. See especially Emile Durkheim, *Suicide*, translated by J. A. Spaulding and George Simpson, New York: Free Press, 1951; and Robert K. Merton, *Social Theory and Social Structure*, New York: Free Press, 1957, Chapters 4 and 5.

3. See especially the following: Clifford R. Shaw, *The Jack-Roller*, Chicago: The University of Chicago Press, 1930; Clifford R. Shaw, *The Natural History of a Delinquent Career*, Chicago: The University of Chicago Press, 1931; Clifford R. Shaw *et al.*, *Delinquency Areas*, Chicago: The University of Chicago Press, 1940; Clifford R. Shaw and Henry D. McKay, *Juvenile Delinquency and Urban Areas*, Chicago: The University of Chicago Press, 1942; Edwin H. Sutherland, editor, *The Professional Thief*, Chicago: The University of Chicago Press, 1937; Edwin H. Sutherland, *Principles of Criminology*, 4th edition, Philadelphia: Lippincott, 1947; Edwin H. Sutherland, *White Collar Crime*, New York: Dryden, 1949.

Differentials in Availability of Legitimate Means: The Theory of Anomie

The theory of anomie has undergone two major phases of development. Durkheim first used the concept to explain deviant behavior. He focused on the way in which various social conditions lead to "overweening ambition," and how, in turn, unlimited aspirations ultimately produce a breakdown in regulatory norms. Robert K. Merton has systematized and extended the theory, directing attention to patterns of disjunction between culturally prescribed goals and socially organized access to them by *legitimate* means. In this paper, a third phase is outlined. An additional variable is incorporated in the developing scheme of anomie, namely, the concept of *differentials in access to success-goals by illegitimate means.*[4]

Phase I: Unlimited Aspirations and the Breakdown of Regulatory Norms. In Durkheim's work, a basic distinction is made between "physical needs" and "moral needs." The importance of this distinction was heightened for Durkheim because he viewed physical needs as being regulated automatically by features of man's organic structure. Nothing in the organic structure, however, is capable of regulating social desires; as Durkheim put it, man's "capacity for feeling is in itself an insatiable and bottomless abyss."[5] If man is to function without "friction," "the passions must first be limited. . . . But since the individual has no way of limiting them, this must be done by some force exterior to him." Durkheim viewed the collective order as the external regulating force which defined and ordered the goals to which men should orient their behavior. If the collective order is disrupted or disturbed, however, men's aspirations may then rise, exceeding all possibilities of fulfillment. Under these conditions, "de-regulation or anomy" ensues: "At the very moment when traditional rules have lost their authority, the richer prize offered these appetites stimulates them and makes them more exigent and impatient of control. The state of de-regulation or anomy is thus further heightened by passions being less disciplined precisely when they need

4. "Illegitimate means" are those proscribed by the mores. The concept therefore includes "illegal means" as a special case but is not coterminous with illegal behavior, which refers only to the violation of legal norms. In several parts of this paper, I refer to particular forms of deviant behavior which entail violation of the law and there use the more restricted term, "illegal means." But the more general concept of illegitimate means is needed to cover the wider gamut of deviant behavior and to relate the theories under review here to the evolving theory of "legitimacy" in sociology.

5. All of the excerpts in this section are from Durkheim, *op. cit.*, pp. 247-257.

more disciplining." Finally, pressures toward deviant behavior were said to develop when man's aspirations no longer matched the possibilities of fulfillment.

Durkheim therefore turned to the question of *when* the regulatory functions of the collective order break down. Several such states were identified, including sudden depression, sudden prosperity, and rapid technological change. His object was to show how, under these conditions, men are led to aspire to goals extremely difficult if not impossible to attain. As Durkheim saw it, sudden depression results in deviant behavior because

> Something like a declassification occurs which suddenly casts certain individuals into a lower state than their previous one. Then they must reduce their requirements, restrain their needs, learn greater self-control. . . . But society cannot adjust them instantaneously to this new life and teach them to practice the increased self-repression to which they are unaccustomed. So they are not adjusted to the condition forced on them, and its very prospect is intolerable; hence the suffering which detaches them from a reduced existence even before they have made trial of it.

Prosperity, according to Durkheim, could have much the same effect as depression, particularly if upward changes in economic conditions are abrupt. The very abruptness of these changes presumably heightens aspirations beyond possibility of fulfillment, and this too puts a strain on the regulatory apparatus of the society.

According to Durkheim, "the sphere of trade and industry . . . is actually in a chronic state [of anomie]." Rapid technological developments and the existence of vast, unexploited markets excite the imagination with the seemingly limitless possibilities for the accumulation of wealth. As Durkheim said of the producer of goods, "now that he may assume to have almost the entire world as his customer, how could passions accept their former confinement in the face of such limitless prospects?" Continuing, Durkheim states that "such is the source of excitement predominating in this part of society. . . . Here the state of crisis and anomie [are] constant and, so to speak, normal. From top to bottom of the ladder, greed is aroused without knowing where to find ultimate foothold. Nothing can calm it, since its goal is far beyond all it can attain."

In developing the theory, Durkheim characterized goals in the industrial society, and specified the way in which unlimited aspirations are induced. He spoke of "dispositions . . . so inbred that society has grown to accept them and is accustomed to think them normal," and he portrayed these "inbred dispositions": "It is everlastingly repeated that it is man's nature to be eternally dissatisfied, constantly to advance, without relief or rest, toward an indefinite goal. The longing for infinity is daily represented as a mark of moral distinction. . . ." And it was precisely these pressures to strive for "infinite" or "receding" goals, in Durkheim's view, that generate a breakdown in regulatory norms, for "when there is no other aim but to outstrip constantly the point arrived at, how painful to be thrown back!"

Phase II: Disjunction between Cultural Goals and Socially Structured Opportunity. Durkheim's description of the emergence of "overweening ambition" and the subsequent breakdown of regulatory norms constitutes one of the links between his work and the later development of the theory by Robert K. Merton. In his classic essay, "Social Structure and Anomie," Merton suggests that goals and norms may vary independently of each other, and that this sometimes leads to malintegrated states. In his view, two polar types of disjunction may occur: "There may develop a very heavy, at times a virtually exclusive, stress upon the value of particular goals, involving comparatively little concern with the institutionally prescribed means of striving toward these goals. . . . This constitutes one type of malintegrated culture."[6] On the other hand, "A second polar type is found where activities originally conceived as instrumental are transmuted into self-contained practices, lacking further objectives. . . . Sheer conformity becomes a central value." Merton notes that "between these extreme types are societies which maintain a rough balance between emphases upon cultural goals and institutionalized practices, and these constitute the integrated and relatively stable, though changing societies."

Having identified patterns of disjunction between goals and norms, Merton is enabled to define anomie more precisely: "Anomie [may be] conceived as a breakdown in the cultural structure, occurring particularly when there is an acute disjunction between cultural norms and goals and the socially structured capacities of members of the group to act in accord with them."

Of the two kinds of malintegrated societies, Merton is primarily interested in the one in which "there is an exceptionally strong emphasis upon specific goals without a corresponding emphasis upon institutional procedures." He states that attenuation between goals and norms, leading to anomie or "normlessness," comes about because men in such societies internalize an emphasis on common success-goals under conditions of varying access to them. The essence of this hypothesis is captured in the following excerpt:

It is only when a system of cultural values extols, virtually above all else, certain *common* success-goals for the population at large while the social

6. For this excerpt and those which follow immediately, see Merton, *op. cit.*, pp. 131-194.

structure rigorously restricts or completely closes access to approved modes of reaching these goals *for a considerable part of the same population,* that deviant behavior ensues on a large scale.

The focus, in short, is on the way in which the social structure puts a strain upon the cultural structure. Here one may point to diverse structural differentials in access to culturally approved goals by legitimate means, for example, differentials of age, sex, ethnic status, and social class. Pressures for anomie or normlessness vary from one social position to another, depending on the nature of these differentials.

In summary, Merton extends the theory of anomie in two principal ways. He explicitly identifies types of anomic or malintegrated societies by focusing upon the relationship between cultural goals and norms. And, by directing attention to patterned differentials in the access to success-goals by legitimate means, he shows how the social structure exerts a strain upon the cultural structure, leading in turn to anomie or normlessness.

Phase III: The Concept of Illegitimate Means. Once processes generating differentials in pressures are identified, there is then the question of how these pressures are resolved, or how men respond to them. In this connection, Merton enumerates five basic categories of behavior or role adaptations which are likely to emerge: conformity, innovation, ritualism, retreatism, and rebellion. These adaptations differ depending on the individual's acceptance or rejection of cultural goals, and depending on his adherence to or violation of institutional norms. Furthermore, Merton sees the distribution of these adaptations principally as the consequence of two variables: the relative extent of pressure, and values, particularly "internalized prohibitions," governing the use of various illegitimate means.

It is a familiar sociological idea that values serve to order the choices of deviant (as well as conforming) adaptations which develop under conditions of stress. Comparative studies of ethnic groups, for example, have shown that some tend to engage in distinctive forms of deviance; thus Jews exhibit low rates of alcoholism and alcoholic psychoses.[7] Various investigators have suggested that the emphasis on rationality, fear of expressing aggression, and other alleged components of the "Jewish" value system constrain modes of deviance which involve "loss

7. See, e.g., Seldon D. Bacon, "Social Settings Conducive to Alcoholism—A Sociological Approach to a Medical Problem," *Journal of the American Medical Association,* 16 (May, 1957), pp. 177-181; Robert F. Bales, "Cultural Differences in Rates of Alcoholism," *Quarterly Journal of Studies on Alcohol,* 16 (March, 1946), pp. 480-499; Jerome H. Skolnick, "A Study of the Relation of Ethnic Background to Arrests for Inebriety," *Quarterly Journal of Studies on Alcohol,* 15 (December, 1954), pp. 451-474.

of control" over behavior.[8] In contrast, the Irish show a much higher rate of alcoholic deviance because, it has been argued, their cultural emphasis on masculinity encourages the excessive use of alcohol under conditions of strain.[9]

Merton suggests that differing rates of ritualistic and innovating behavior in the middle and lower classes result from differential emphases in socialization. The "rule-oriented" accent in middle-class socialization presumably disposes persons to handle stress by engaging in ritualistic rather than innovating behavior. The lower-class person, contrastingly, having internalized less stringent norms, can violate conventions with less guilt and anxiety.[10] Values, in other words, exercise a canalizing influence, limiting the choice of deviant adaptations for persons variously distributed throughout the social system.

Apart from both socially patterned pressures, which give rise to deviance, and from values, which determine choices of adaptations, a further variable should be taken into account: namely, *differentials in availability of illegitimate means*. For example, the notion that innovating behavior may result from unfulfilled aspirations and imperfect socialization with respect to conventional norms implies that illegitimate means are freely available—as if the individual, having decided that "you can't make it legitimately," then simply turns to illegitimate means which are readily at hand whatever his position in the social structure. However, these means may not be available. As noted above, the anomie theory assumes that conventional means are differentially distributed, that some individuals, because of their social position, enjoy certain advantages which are denied to others. Note, for example, variations in the degree to which members of various classes are fully exposed to and thus acquire the values, education, and skills which facilitate upward mobility. It should not be startling, therefore, to find similar variations in the availability of illegitimate means.

Several sociologists have alluded to such variations without explicitly incorporating this variable in a theory of deviant behavior. Sutherland, for example, writes that "an inclination to steal is not a sufficient explanation of the genesis of the professional thief."[11] Moreover, "the person must be appreciated by the professional thieves. He must be appraised as having an adequate equipment of wits, front, talking-ability, honesty, reliability, nerve and determination." In short, "a person can

8. See Isidor T. Thorner, "Ascetic Protestantism and Alcoholism," *Psychiatry*, 16 (May, 1953), pp. 167-176; and Nathan Glazer, "Why Jews Stay Sober," *Commentary*, 13 (February, 1952), pp. 181-186.

9. See Bales, *op. cit.*

10. Merton, *op. cit.*, p. 151.

11. For this excerpt and those which follow immediately, see Sutherland, *The Professional Thief*, pp. 211-213.

be a professional thief only if he is recognized and received as such by other professional thieves." But recognition is not freely accorded:

> Selection and tutelage are the two necessary elements in the process of acquiring recognition as a professional thief. . . . A person cannot acquire recognition as a professional thief until he has had tutelage in professional theft, *and tutelage is given only to a few persons selected from the total population.*

Furthermore, the aspirant is judged by high standards of performance, for only "a very small percentage of those who start on this process ever reach the stage of professional theft." The burden of these remarks—dealing with the processes of selection, induction, and assumption of full status in the criminal group—is that motivations or pressures toward deviance do not fully account for deviant behavior. The "self-made" thief—lacking knowledge of the ways of securing immunity from prosecution and similar techniques of defense—"would quickly land in prison." Sutherland is in effect pointing to differentials in access to the role of professional thief. Although the criteria of selection are not altogether clear from his analysis, definite evaluative standards do appear to exist; depending on their content, certain categories of individuals would be placed at a disadvantage and others would be favored.

The availability of illegitimate means, then, is controlled by various criteria in the same manner that has long been ascribed to conventional means. Both systems of opportunity are (1) limited, rather than infinitely available, and (2) differentially available depending on the location of persons in the social structure.

When we employ the term "means," whether legitimate or illegitimate, at least two things are implied: first, that there are appropriate learning environments for the acquisition of the values and skills associated with the performance of a particular role; and second, that the individual has opportunities to discharge the role once he has been prepared. The term subsumes, therefore, both *learning structures* and *opportunity structures.*

A case in point is recruitment and preparation for careers in the rackets. There are fertile criminal learning environments for the young in neighborhoods where the rackets flourish as stable, indigenous institutions. Because these environments afford integration of offenders of different ages, the young are exposed to "differential associations" which facilitate the acquisition of criminal values and skills. Yet preparation for the role may not insure that the individual will ever discharge it. For one thing, more youngsters may be recruited into these patterns of differential association than can possibly be absorbed, following their "training," by the adult criminal structure. There may be a surplus of contenders for these elite positions, leading in turn to the necessity for criteria and mechanisms of selection. Hence a certain proportion of those who aspire may not be permitted to engage in the behavior for which they have been prepared.

This illustration is similar in every respect, save for the route followed, to the case of those who seek careers in the sphere of legitimate business. Here, again, is the initial problem of securing access to appropriate learning environments, such as colleges and post-graduate school of business. Having acquired the values and skills needed for a business career, graduates then face the problem of whether or not they can successfully discharge the roles for which they have been prepared. Formal training itself is not sufficient for occupational success, for many forces intervene to determine who shall succeed and fail in the competitive world of business and industry—as throughout the entire conventional occupational structure.

This distinction between learning structures and opportunity structures was suggested some years ago by Sutherland. In 1944, he circulated an unpublished paper which briefly discusses the proposition that "criminal behavior is partially a function of opportunities to commit specific classes of crimes, such as embezzlement, bank burglary, or illicit heterosexual intercourse."[12] He did not, however, take up the problem of differentials in opportunity as a concept to be systematically incorporated in a theory of deviant behavior. Instead, he held that "opportunity" is a necessary but not sufficient explanation of the commission of criminal acts, "since some persons who have opportunities to embezzle, become intoxicated, engage in illicit heterosexual intercourse or to commit other crimes do not do so." He also noted that the differential association theory did not constitute a full explanation of criminal activity, for, notwithstanding differential association, "it is axiomatic that persons who commit a specific crime must have the opportunity to commit that crime." He therefore concluded that

> While opportunity may be partially a function of association with criminal patterns and of the specialized techniques thus acquired, *it is not determined entirely in that manner*, and consequently differential association is not the sufficient cause of criminal behavior. [emphasis not in original]

In Sutherland's statements, two meanings are attributed to the term "opportunity." As suggested above, it may be useful to separate these for analytical purposes. In the first sense, Sutherland appears to be saying that opportunity consists in part of learning structures. The principal

12. For this excerpt and those which follow immediately, see Albert Cohen, Alfred Lindesmith, and Karl Schuessler, editors, *The Sutherland Papers*, Bloomington: Indiana University Press, 1956, pp. 31-35.

components of his theory of differential association are that "criminal behavior is learned," and, furthermore, that "criminal behavior is learned in interaction with other persons in a process of communication." But he also uses the term to describe situations conducive to carrying out criminal roles. Thus, for Sutherland, the commission of a criminal act would seem to depend upon the existence of two conditions: differential associations favoring the acquisition of criminal values and skills, and conditions encouraging participation in criminal activity.

This distinction heightens the importance of identifying and questioning the common assumption that illegitimate means are freely available. We can now ask (1) whether there are socially structured differentials in access to illegitimate learning environments, and (2) whether there are differentials limiting the fulfillment of illegitimate roles. If differentials exist and can be identified, we may then inquire about their consequences for the behavior of persons in different parts of the social structure. Before pursuing this question, however, we turn to a fuller discussion of the theoretical tradition established by Shaw, McKay, and Sutherland.

Differentials in Availability of Illegitimate Means: The Subculture Tradition

The concept of differentials in availability of illegitimate means is implicit in one of the major streams of American criminological theory. In this tradition, attention is focused on the processes by which persons are recruited into criminal learning environments and ultimately inducted into criminal roles. The problems here are to account for the acquisition of criminal roles and to describe the social organization of criminal activities. When the theoretical propositions contained in this tradition are reanalyzed, it becomes clear that one underlying conception is that of variations in access to success-goals by illegitimate means. Furthermore, this implicit concept may be shown to be one of the bases upon which the tradition was constructed.

In their studies of the ecology of deviant behavior in the urban environment, Shaw and McKay found that delinquency and crime tended to be confined to delimited areas and, furthermore, that such behavior persisted despite demographic changes in these areas. Hence they came to speak of "criminal tradition," of the "cultural transmission" of criminal values.[13] As a result of their observations of slum life, they concluded that *particular importance must be assigned to the integration of different age-levels of offenders.* Thus:

Stealing in the neighborhood was a common practice among the children and approved by the parents. Whenever the boys got together they talked about robbing and made more plans for stealing. I hardly knew any boys who did not go robbing. The little fellows went in for petty stealing, breaking into freight cars, and stealing junk. The older guys did big jobs like stick-up, burglary, and stealing autos. The little fellows admired the "big shots" and longed for the day when they could get into the big racket. Fellows who had "done time" were the big shots and looked up to and gave the little fellow tips on how to get by and pull off big jobs.[14]

In other words, access to criminal roles depends upon stable associations with others from whom the necessary values and skills may be learned. Shaw and McKay were describing deviant learning structures—that is, alternative routes by which people seek access to the goals which society holds to be worthwhile. They might also have pointed out that, in areas where such learning structures are unavailable, it is probably difficult for many individuals to secure access to stable criminal careers, even though motivated to do so.[15]

The concept of illegitimate means and the socially structured conditions of access to them were not explicitly recognized in the work of Shaw and McKay because, probably, they were disposed to view slum areas as "disorganized." Although they consistently referred to illegitimate activities as being organized, they nevertheless often depicted high-rate delinquency areas as disorganized because the values transmitted were criminal rather than conventional. Hence their work includes statements which we now perceive to be internally inconsistent, such as the following:

This community situation [in which Sidney was reared] was not only disorganized and thus ineffective as a unit of control, but it was characterized by a high rate of juvenile delinquency and adult crime, not to mention the widespread political corruption which had long existed in the area. Various

13. See especially *Delinquency Areas*, Chapter 16.

14. Shaw, *The Jack-Roller*, p. 54.

15. We are referring here, and throughout the paper, to stable criminal roles to which persons may orient themselves on a career basis, as in the case of racketeers, professional thieves, and the like. The point is that access to stable roles depends in the first instance upon the availability of learning structures. As Frank Tannenbaum says, "it must be insisted on that unless there were older criminals in the neighborhood who provided a moral judgement in favor of the delinquent and to whom the delinquents could look for commendation, the careers of the younger ones could not develop at all." *Crime and the Community*, New York: Ginn, 1938, p. 60.

forms of stealing and many organized delinquent and criminal gangs were prevalent in the area. These groups exercised a powerful influence and tended to create a community spirit which not only tolerated but actually fostered delinquent and criminal practices.[16]

Sutherland was among the first to perceive that the concept of social disorganization tended to obscure the stable patterns of interaction among carriers of criminal values. Like Shaw and McKay, he had been influenced by the observation that lower-class areas were organized in terms of both conventional and criminal values, but he was also impressed that these alternative value systems were supported by patterned systems of social relations. He expressly recognized that crime, far from being a random, unorganized activity, was typically an intricate and stable system of human arrangements. He therefore rejected the concept of "social disorganization" and substituted the concept of "differential group organization."

The third concept, social disorganization, was borrowed from Shaw and McKay. I had used it but had not been satisfied with it because the organization of the delinquent group, which is often very complex, is social disorganization only from an ethical or some other particularistic point of view. At the suggestion of Albert K. Cohen, this concept has been changed to differential group organization, with organization for criminal activities on one side and organization against criminal activities on the other.[17]

Having freed observation of the urban slum from conventional evaluations, Sutherland was able to focus more clearly on the way in which its social structure constitutes a "learning environment" for the acquisition of deviant values and skills. In the development of the theory of "differential association" and "differential group organization," he came close to stating explicitly the concept of differentials in access to illegitimate means. But Sutherland was essentially interested in learning processes, and thus he did not ask how such access varies in different parts of the social structure, nor did he inquire about the consequences for behavior of variations in the accessibility of these means.[18]

---

16. Shaw, *The Natural History of a Delinquent Career*, p. 229.

17. Cohen, Lindesmith, and Schuessler, *op. cit.*, p. 21.

18. It is interesting to note that the concept of differentials in access to *legitimate* means did not attain explicit recognition in Sutherland's work, nor in the work of many others in the "subculture" tradition. This attests to the independent development of the two traditions being discussed. Thus the ninth proposition in the differential association theory is stated as follows:

"*(9) Through criminal behavior is an expression of general needs and values, it is not explained by those general needs and values since non-criminal behavior is an expression of the same needs and values.* Thieves generally steal in order to secure money, but likewise honest laborers work in order to secure money. The attempts

Of course, it is perfectly true that "striving for status," the "money motive" and similar modes of socially approved goal-oriented behavior do not as such account for both deviant and conformist behavior. But if goal-oriented behavior occurs under conditions of socially structured obstacles to fulfillment by legitimate means, the resulting pressures might then lead to deviance. In other words, Sutherland appears to assume that the distribution of access to success-goals by legitimate means is uniform rather than variable, irrespective of location in the social structure. See his *Principles of Criminology*, 4th edition, pp. 7-8.

William F. Whyte, in his classic study of an urban slum, advanced the empirical description of the structure and organization of illegitimate means a step beyond that of Sutherland. Like Sutherland, Whyte rejected the earlier view of the slum as disorganized:

> It is customary for the sociologist to study the slum district in terms of "social disorganization" and to neglect to see that an area such as Cornerville has a complex and well-established organization of its own. . . . I found that in every group there was a hierarchical structure of social relations binding the individuals to one another and that the groups were also related hierarchically to one another. Where the group was formally organized into a political club, this was immediately apparent, but for informal groups it was no less true.[19]

Whyte's contribution to our understanding of the organization of illegitimate means in the slum consists primarily in showing that individuals who participate in stable illicit enterprise do not constitute a separate or isolated segment of the community. Rather, these persons are closely integrated with the occupants of conventional roles. In describing the relationship between racketeers and politicians, for example, he notes that

> The rackets and political organizations extend from the bottom to the top of Cornerville society, mesh with one another, and integrate a large part of the life of the district. They provide a general framework for the understanding of the actions of both "little guys" and "big shots."[20]

Whyte's view of the slum differs somewhat from that conveyed by the term "differential group organization." He does not emphasize the idea that the slum is composed of two different systems, conventional and deviant, but rather the way in which the occupants of these various

---

by many scholars to explain criminal behavior by general drives and values, such as the happiness principle, striving for social status, the money motive, or frustration, have been and must continue to be futile since they explain lawful behavior as completely as they explain criminal behavior."

19. William F. Whyte, *Street Corner Society*, (original edition, 1943). Chicago: The University of Chicago Press, 1955, p. viii.

20. *Ibid.*, p. xviii.

roles are integrated in a single, stable structure which organizes and patterns the life of the community.

The description of the organization of illegitimate means in slums is further developed by Solomon Kobrin in his article, "The Conflict of Values in Delinquency Areas."[21] Kobrin suggests that urban slum areas vary in the degree to which the carriers of deviant and conventional values are integrated with one another. Hence he points the way to the development of a "typology of delinquency areas based on variations in the relationship between these two systems," depicting the "polar types" on such a continuum. The first type resembles the integrated areas described in preceding paragraphs. Here, claims Kobrin, there is not merely structural integration between carriers of the two value systems, but reciprocal participation by each in the value system of the other. Thus:

> Leaders of [illegal] enterprises frequently maintain membership in such conventional institutions of their local communities as churches, fraternal and mutual benefit societies and political parties. . . . Within this framework the influence of each of the two value systems is reciprocal, the leaders of illegal enterprise participating in the primary orientation of the conventional elements in the population, and the latter, through their participation in a local power structure sustained in large part by illicit activity, participating perforce in the alternate, criminal value system.

Kobrin also notes that in some urban slums there is a tendency for the relationships between carriers of deviant and convential values to break down. Such areas constitute the second polar type. Because of disorganizing forces such as "drastic change in the class, ethnic, or racial characteristics of its population," Kobrin suggests that "the bearers of the conventional culture and its value system are without the customary institutional machinery and therefore in effect partially demobilized with reference to the diffusion of their value system." At the same time, the criminal "value system remains implicit" since this type of area is "characterized principally by the absence of systematic and organized adult activity in violation of the law, despite the fact that many adults in these areas commit violations." Since both value systems remain implicit, the possibilities for effective integration are precluded.

The importance of these observations may be seen if we ask how accessibility of illegal means varies with the relative integration of conventional and criminal values from one type of area to another. In this connection, Kobrin points out that the "integrated" area apparently constitutes a "training ground" for the acquisition of criminal values and skills.

21. *American Sociological Review*, 16 (October, 1951), pp. 657-658, which includes the excerpts which follow immediately.

The stable position of illicit enterprise in the adult society of the community is reflected in the character of delinquent conduct on the part of children. While delinquency in all high rate areas is intrinsically disorderly in that it is unrelated to official programs for the education of the young, in the [integrated community] boys may more or less realistically recognize the potentialities for personal progress in local society through access to delinquency. In a general way, therefore, delinquent activity in these areas constitutes a training ground for the acquisition of skill in the use of violence, concealment of offense, evasion of detection and arrest, and the purchase of immunity from punishment. Those who come to excel in these respects are frequently noted and valued by adult leaders in the rackets who are confronted, as are the leaders of all income-producing enterprises, with problems of the recruitment of competent personnel.

With respect to the contrasting or "unintegrated area," Kobrin makes no mention of the extent to which learning structures and opportunities for criminal careers are available. Yet his portrayal of such areas as lacking in the articulation of either conventional or criminal values suggests that the appropriate learning structures—principally the integration of offenders of different age levels—are not available. Furthermore, his depiction of adult violative activity as "unorganized" suggests that the illegal opportunity structure is severely limited. Even if youngsters were able to secure adequate preparation for criminal roles, the problem would appear to be that the social structure of such neighborhoods provides few opportunities for stable, criminal careers. For Kobrin's analysis—as well as those of Whyte and others before him—leads to the conclusion that illegal opportunity structures tend to emerge in lower-class areas only when stable patterns of accommodation and integration arise between the carriers of conventional and deviant values. Where these values remain unorganized and implicit, or where their carriers are in open conflict, opportunities for stable criminal role performance are more or less limited.[22]

Other factors may be cited which affect access to criminal roles. For example, there is a good deal of anecdotal evidence which reveals that access to the upper echelons of organized racketeering is controlled, at

---

22. The excellent work by Albert K. Cohen has been omitted from this discussion because it is dealt with in a second article, "Types of Delinquent Subcultures," prepared jointly with Lloyd E. Ohlin (mimeographed, December, 1958, New York School of Social Work, Columbia University). It may be noted that although Cohen does not explicitly affirm continuity with either the Durkheim-Merton or the Shaw-McKay-Sutherland traditions, we believe that he clearly belongs in the former. He does not deal with what appears to be the essence of the Shaw-McKay-Sutherland tradition, namely, the crucial social functions performed by the integration of offenders of differing age-levels and the integration of adult carriers of criminal and conventional values. Rather, he is concerned primarily with the way in which discrepancies between status aspirations and possibilities for achievement generate pressures for delinquent behavior. The latter notion is a central feature in the anomie tradition.

least in part, by ethnicity. Some ethnic groups are found disproportionately in the upper ranks and others disproportionately in the lower. From an historical perspective, as Bell has shown, this realm has been successively dominated by Irish, East-European Jews, and more recently, by Italians.[23] Various other ethnic groups have been virtually excluded or at least relegated to lower-echelon positions. Despite the fact that many rackets (especially "policy") have flourished in predominantly Negro neighborhoods, there have been but one or two Negroes who have been known to rise to the top in syndicated crime. As in the conventional world, Negroes are relegated to the more menial tasks. Moreover, access to elite positions in the rackets may be governed in part by kinship criteria, for various accounts of the blood relations among top racketeers indicate that nepotism is the general rule.[24] It has also been noted that kinship criteria sometimes govern access to stable criminal roles, as in the case of the pickpocket.[25] And there are, of course, deep-rooted sex differentials in access to illegal means. Although women are often employed in criminal vocations—for example, thievery, confidence games, and extortion—and must be employed in others—such as prostitution—nevertheless females are excluded from many criminal activities.[26]

Of the various criteria governing access to illegitimate means, class differentials may be among the most important. The differentials noted in the preceding paragraph—age, sex, ethnicity, kinship, and the like—all pertain to criminal activity historically associated with the lower class. Most middle- or upper-class persons—even when interested in following "lower-class" criminal careers—would no doubt have difficulty in fulfilling this ambition because of inappropriate preparation. The prerequisite attitudes and skills are more easily acquired if the individual is a member of the lower class; most middle- and upper-class persons could not easily unlearn their own class culture in order to learn a new one. By the same token, access to many "white collar" criminal roles is closed to lower-class persons. Some occupations afford abundant opportunities to engage in illegitimate activity; other offer virtually none. The businessman, for example, not only has at his disposal the means to do

23. Daniel Bell, "Crime as an American Way of Life," *The Antioch Review* (Summer, 1953), pp. 131-154.

24. For a discussion of kinship relationships among top racketeers, see Stanley Frank, "The Rap Gangsters Fear Most," *The Saturday Evening Post* (August 9, 1958), pp. 26ff. This article is based on a review of the files of the United States Immigration and Naturalization Service.

25. See David W. Maurer, *Whiz Mob: A Correlation of the Technical Argot of Pickpockets with Their Behavior Pattern*, Publication of the American Dialect Society, No. 24, 1955.

26. For a discussion of racial, nationality, and sex differentials governing access to a stable criminal role, see *ibid.*, Chapter 6.

so, but, as some studies have shown, he is under persistent pressure to employ illegitimate means, if only to maintain a competitive advantage in the market place. But for those in many other occupations, white collar modes of criminal activity are simply not an alternative.[27]

Some Implications of a Consolidated Approach to Deviant Behavior

It is now possible to consolidate the two sociological traditions described above. Our analysis makes it clear that these traditions are oriented to different aspects of the same problem: differentials in access to opportunity. One tradition focuses on legitimate opportunity, the other on illegitimate. By incorporating the concept of differentials in access to *illegitimate* means, the theory of anomie may be extended to include seemingly unrelated studies and theories of deviant behavior which form a part of the literature of American criminology. In this final section, we try to show how a consolidated approach might advance the understanding of both rates and types of deviant conduct. The discussion centers on the conditions of access to *both* systems of means, legitimate and illegitimate.

The Distribution of Criminal Behavior. One problem which has plagued the criminologist is the absence of adequate data on social differentials in criminal activity. Many have held that the highest crime rates are to be found in the lower social strata. Others have suggested that rates in the middle and upper classes may be much higher than is ordinarily thought. The question of the social distribution of crime remains problematic.

In the absence of adequate data, the theorist has sometimes attacked this problem by assessing the extent of pressures toward normative departures in various parts of the social structure. For example, Merton remarks that his "primary aim is to discover how some social structures exert a definite pressure upon certain persons in the society to engage

27. Training in conventional, specialized occupational skills is often a prerequisite for the commission of white collar crimes, since the individual must have these skills in hand before he can secure a position entailing "trust." As Cressey says, "it may be observed that persons trained to carry on the routine duties of a position of trust have at the same time been trained in whatever skills are necessary for the violation of that position, and the technical skill necessary to trust violation is simply the technical skill necessary to holding the position in the first place." (Donald R. Cressey, *Other People's Money*, New York: Free Press, 1953, pp. 81-82.) Thus skills required in certain crimes need not be learned in association with criminals; they can be acquired through conventional learning.

in non-conforming rather than conforming conduct."[28] Having identified structural features which might be expected to generate deviance, Merton suggests the presence of a correlation between "pressures toward deviation" and "rate of deviance."

> But whatever the differential rates of deviant behavior in the several social strata, and we know from many sources that the official crime statistics uniformly showing higher rates in the lower strata are far from complete or reliable, *it appears from our analysis that the greater pressures toward deviation are exerted upon the lower strata.* . . . Of those located in the lower reaches of the social structure, the culture makes incompatible demands. On the one hand they are asked to orient their behavior toward the prospect of large wealth . . . and on the other, they are largely denied effective opportunities to do so institutionally. *The consequence of this structural inconsistency is a high rate of deviant behavior.*[29]

Because of the paucity and unreliability of existing criminal statistics, there is as yet no way of knowing whether or not Merton's hypothesis is correct. Until comparative studies of crime rates are available the hypothesized correlation cannot be tested.

From a theoretical perspective, however, questions may be raised about this correlation. Would we expect, to raise the principal query, the correlation to be fixed or to vary depending on the distribution of access to illegitimate means? The three possibilities are (1) that access is distributed uniformly throughout the class structure, (2) that access varies inversely with class position, and (3) that access varies directly with class position. Specification of these possibilities permits a more precise statement of the conditions under which crime rates would be expected to vary.

If access to illegitimate means is *uniformly distributed* throughout the class structure, then the proposed correlation would probably hold—higher rates of innovating behavior would be expected in the lower class than elsewhere. Lower-class persons apparently experience greater pressures toward deviance and are less restrained by internalized prohibitions from employing illegitimate means. Assuming uniform access to such means, it would therefore be reasonable to predict higher rates of innovating behavior in the lower social strata.

If access to illegitimate means varies *inversely* with class position, then the correlation would not only hold, but might even be strengthened. For pressures toward deviance, including socialization that does not altogether discourage the use of illegitimate means, would coincide with the availability of such means.

Finally, if access varies *directly* with class position, comparative rates

28. *Merton, op. cit.*, p. 132.

29. *Ibid.*, pp. 144-145.

of illegitimate activity become difficult to forecast. The higher the class position, the less the pressure to employ illegitimate means; furthermore, internalized prohibitions are apparently more effective in higher positions. If, at the same time, opportunities to use illegitimate methods are more abundant, then these factors would be in opposition. Until the precise effects of these several variables can be more adequately measured, rates cannot be safely forecast.

The concept of differentials in availability of illegitimate means may also help to clarify questions about varying crime rates among ethnic, age, religious, and sex groups, and other social divisions. This concept, then, can be systematically employed in the effort to further our understanding of the distribution of illegitimate behavior in the social structure.

Modes of Adaptation: The Case of Retreatism. By taking into account the conditions of access to legitimate *and* illegitimate means, we can further specify the circumstances under which various modes of deviant behavior arise. This may be illustrated by the case of retreatism.[30]

As defined by Merton, retreatist adaptations include such categories of behavior as alcoholism, drug addiction, and psychotic withdrawal. These adaptations entail "escape" from the frustrations of unfulfilled aspirations by withdrawal from conventional social relationships. The processes leading to retreatism are described by Merton as follows:

> [Retreatism] arises from continued failure to near the goal by legitimate measures and from an inability to use the illegitimate route because of internalized prohibitions, *this process occurring while the supreme value of the success-goal has not yet been renounced.* The conflict is resolved by abandoning *both* precipitating elements, the goals and means. The escape is complete, the conflict is eliminated and the individual is asocialized.[31]

In this view, a crucial element encouraging retreatism is internalized constraint concerning the use of illegitimate means. But this element need not be present. Merton apparently assumed that such prohibitions are essential because, in their absence, the logic of his scheme would compel him to predict that innovating behavior would result. But the assumption that the individual uninhibited in the use of illegitimate means becomes an innovator presupposes that successful innovation is only a matter of motivation. Once the concept of differentials in access to illegitimate means is introduced, however, it becomes clear that re-

30. Retreatist behavior is but one of many types of deviant adaptations which might be re-analyzed in terms of this consolidated theoretical approach. In subsequent papers, being prepared jointly with Lloyd E. Ohlin, other cases of deviant behavior—e.g., collective disturbances in prisons and subcultural adaptations among juvenile delinquents—will be examined. In this connection, see footnote 22.

31. Merton, *op. cit.*, pp. 153-154.

treatism is possible even in the absence of internalized prohibitions. For we may now ask how individuals respond when they fail in the use of *both* legitimate and illegitimate means. If illegitimate means are unavailable, if efforts at innovation fail, then retreatist adaptations may still be the consequence, and the "escape" mechanisms chosen by the defeated individual may perhaps be all the more deviant because of his "double failure."

This does not mean that retreatist adaptations cannot arise precisely as Merton suggests: namely, that the conversion from conformity to retreatism takes place in one step, without intervening adaptations. But this is only one route to retreatism. The conversion may at times entail intervening stages and intervening adaptations, particularly of an innovating type. This possibility helps to account for the fact that certain categories of individuals cited as retreatists—for example, hobos—often show extensive histories of arrests and convictions for various illegal acts. It also helps to explain retreatist adaptations among individuals who have not necessarily internalized strong restraints on the use of illegitimate means. In short, retreatist adaptations may arise with considerable frequency among those who are failures in both worlds, conventional and illegitimate alike.[32]

Future research on retreatist behavior might well examine the interval between conformity and retreatism. To what extent does the individual entertain the possibility of resorting to illegitimate means, and to what extent does he actually seek to mobilize such means? If the individual turns to innovating devices, the question of whether or not he becomes a retreatist may then depend upon the relative accessibility of illegitimate means. For although the frustrated conformist seeks a solution to status discontent by adopting such methods, there is the further problem of whether or not he possesses appropriate skills and has opportunities for their use. We suggest therefore that data be gathered on preliminary responses to status discontent—and on the individual's perceptions of the efficacy of employing illegitimate means, the content of his skills, and the objective situation of illegitimate opportunity available to him.

Respecification of the processes leading to retreatism may also help to resolve difficulties entailed in ascertaining rates of retreatism in differ-

32. The processes of "double failure" being specified here may be of value in re-analyzing the correlation between alcoholism and petty crime. Investigation of the *careers* of petty criminals who are alcoholic may reveal that after being actively oriented toward stable criminal careers they then lost out in the competitive struggle. See, e.g., Irwin Deutscher, "The Petty Offender: A Sociological Alien," *The Journal of Criminal Law, Criminology and Police Science,* 44 (January-February, 1954), pp. 592-595; Albert D. Ullman *et al.*, "Some Social Characteristics of Misdemeanants," *The Journal of Criminal Law, Criminology and Police Science,* 48 (May-June, 1957), pp. 44-53.

ent parts of the social structure. Although Merton does not indicate explicitly where this adaptation might be expected to arise, he specifies some of the social conditions which encourage high rates of retreatism. Thus the latter is apt to mark the behavior of downwardly mobile persons, who experience a sudden breakdown in established social relations, and such individuals as the retired, who have lost major social roles.[33]

The long-standing difficulties in forecasting differential rates of retreatism may perhaps be attributed to the assumption that retreatists have fully internalized values prohibiting the use of illegitimate means. That this prohibition especially characterizes socialization in the middle and upper classes probably calls for the prediction that retreatism occurs primarily in those classes—and that the hobohemias, "drug cultures," and the ranks of the alcoholics are populated primarily by individuals from the upper reaches of society. It would appear from various accounts of hobohemia and skid row, however, that many of these persons are the products of slum life, and, furthermore, that their behavior is not necessarily controlled by values which preclude resort to illegitimate means. But once it is recognized that retreatism may arise in response to limitations on both systems of means, the difficulty of locating this adaptation is lessened, if not resolved. Thus retreatist behavior may vary with the particular process by which it is generated. The process described by Merton may be somewhat more characteristic of higher positions in the social structure where rule-oriented socialization is typical, while in the lower strata retreatism may tend more often to be the consequence of unsuccessful attempts at innovation.

Summary

This paper attempts to identify and to define the concept of differential opportunity structures. It has been suggested that this concept helps to extend the developing theory of social structure and anomie. Furthermore, by linking propositions regarding the accessibility of *both* legitimate and illegitimate opportunity structures, a basis is provided for consolidating various major traditions of sociological thought on nonconformity. The concept of differential systems of opportunity and of variations in access to them, it is hoped, will suggest new possibilities for research on the relationship between social structure and deviant behavior.

33. Merton, *op. cit.*, pp. 188-189.

CLIFFORD KIRKPATRICK
and EUGENE KANIN

Male Sex Aggression on a University Campus

A PERSON-TO-PERSON relationship that is characterized by exploitation and shared stigma provides the conceptual framework for this research. In abstract ideal-typical terms, member B of an AB pair is urged by member A to participate in behavior desired by A but prohibited by primary group and institutional controls. B may develop ambivalent resistance but yield to a point where stigma would be involved with disclosure. With B's apparent reluctance to seek guidance from the primary group or to appeal to institutional protection, the exploitative advantage of A is increased, leading to further overtures. B's involvement and participation further increase stigmatization and isolation from primary group or institutional protection. Illustrations might include incest, homosexuality, sex aggression against children, violence between family members, illegally selling drugs, and procurer-prostitute relationships.

This type of person-to-person relationship was explored by an investigation of sexual aggressiveness in dating-courtship relationships on a university campus. The study was prompted by some case material reporting instances of violent male aggression with reluctance on the part of the offended girls to invoke protection and punishment.

An eight page mimeographed schedule was distributed to the females in twenty-two varied university classes, the male members being dismissed. In general cooperation was excellent. Only two girls refused to fill out the schedules. However, the 291 female students whose usable schedules were completely analyzed cannot be regarded as a representative sample from a defined student universe. The responding group was

---

Reprinted from American Sociological Review, *February, 1957, pp. 52-58, by permission of the authors and the journal.*

Acknowledgment is made of assistance from the Graduate School Research Fund of Indiana University. Appreciation must also be expressed to Sandra Rubinstein for helpful suggestions.

biased in favor of underclassmen, the quota index for freshmen being 131.5 (100 equals proportionate representation), for sophomores 181.3, juniors 85.6, and seniors 49.7. Sorority girls were overrepresented as shown by a quota index of 173.7.

The questionnaire distinguished five degrees of erotic aggressiveness, namely attempts at "necking," "petting" above the waist, "petting" below the waist, sex intercourse, and attempts at sex intercourse with violence or threats of violence. The reporting of offensiveness by the respondents implied no confession that they were willing participants at any level of erotic behavior. Undoubtedly male behavior often became offensive after willing participation at milder levels of erotic intimacy. In the interest of gaining full cooperation the questionnaire was carefully devised to avoid probing the sex conduct of the female respondents. Instead the basic data were focused on the non-incriminating reports of being "offended" by intimacy level, frequency, and number of men. The girls could have been extremely prudish or could have been offended at the means rather than the erotic goals pursued by the offenders.

Erotic Offensiveness

Of the 291 responding girls 55.7 per cent reported themselves offended at least once during the academic year at some level of erotic intimacy. The experiences of being offended were not altogether associated with trivial situations as shown by the fact that 20.9 per cent were offended by forceful attempts at intercourse and 6.2 per cent by "aggressively forceful attempts at sex intercourse in the course of which menacing threats or coercive infliction of physical pain were employed." There is no reason to think that offended girls had merely a single unpleasant experience with one partner. The 162 offended girls reported 1022 offensive episodes. While for some girls offensive experience was no doubt trivial, considerable mention was made of fear and guilt reactions.

A seasonal variation may exist in the reported offensive behavior of male students. Since the schedules covered the period only from September 15, 1954, to May 15, 1955, the full record of exposure during September and May is not available. If the number of episodes for September and May are extrapolated by doubling the episodes reported for half month periods, then a U shaped curve can be drawn from the data indicating a higher prevalence in fall and spring.

A 3×3 table yielding a Chi square significant at the .05 level suggests that episodes of lesser offensiveness are concentrated in the fall and the more offensive episodes in the spring. The excess of mildly offensive episodes in the fall may have been due to imperfect communication between members of newly formed pairs. The concentration of episodes more seriously offensive in the spring may have been due to involvement in continuing affairs in which offensive behavior reflected frustration of sex tensions and perhaps assumed exploitability of the female because of her emotional involvement.

Characteristics of Offended Girls

The offended girls reported themselves younger than did the non-offended. The mean age of the offended girls was 18.8 and the corresponding mean age of the 129 non-offended girls was 19.0 (C.R.=2.5). A 2×3 table relating victims and non-victims to three age categories yielded a Chi square $.02 > P > .01$. The number of semesters of college work is closely related to age. The mean semester standing of the 162 offended girls was 3.6 while that of the 129 non-offended girls was 4.1 (C.R.=2.0). The difference could be due either to prudishness of younger students or to their assumed exploitability.

Frequency of dating is a personal characteristic which might be associated with differential proneness to be offended in the course of dating-courtship behavior. In response to a question concerning total number of dates in April, 1955, the mean figure given by the offended was 11.6 in contrast to 10.3 for non-offended girls (C.R.=1.3). The *eta* between number of dates per month (April) and total number of episodes reported by offended girls was only .24. Thus it would seem that dating frequency is an exposure variable which need not be taken seriously into account in interpreting other findings. Dating frequency in relation to maximum level of offensiveness reported by the offended girls yielded an insignificant Chi square ($.70 > P > .50$).

Girls with lower group status characteristics rendering them more exploitable would seem more likely to report themselves offended. A 2×2 table distributing sorority and non-sorority girls as offended or non-offended, however, showed sorority girls in slight excess among the offended ($.30 > P > .20$).

It might still be argued that of the offended girls the sorority members, less exploitable as compared with non-sorority girls, would experience offensiveness at milder maximum levels. A 2×5 table, including the five intimacy levels at which maximum offensiveness occurred, showed such a trend but yielded a Chi square without statistical significance ($.30 > P > .20$).

The non-significant findings concerning sorority status do not take into account the number of episodes at various levels of offensiveness.

In Table 1 it is shown more clearly that the offensive experience of sorority girls is relatively concentrated at the milder levels of offensiveness.[1]

Table 1. Offensive Episodes Experienced by Sorority and Non-Sorority Girls by Levels of Erotic Intimacy

	Sorority	Non-Sorority	Total
Necking and petting above the waist	333	415	748
Petting below the waist	55	136	191
Attempted intercourse and attempted intercourse with violence	28	55	83
Total	416	606	1022

$x^2 = 17.35$; *d.f.* $= 2$; $P < .001$

The implications of sorority status in the present context are not clear. It may be that high group status makes such girls offended easily even at mild levels of aggression or it may be that greater dating frequency means exposure to offensiveness at a mild level. The dating frequency of sorority girls who were offended was 12.4 as compared to 9.5 for offended non-sorority girls (C.R.=3.6). It can be said that the *savoir faire* attributed to sorority girls did not prevent them from getting into situations reported as offensive.

Respondents were asked, "Do you consider yourself religious?" In spite of theoretically greater intolerance of male aggression, girls answering "yes" seem less likely to report offensive experience (Chi square at $.10 > P > .05$ level).

The relative academic class standing of offended and offenders was obtained from the schedules. Of the 388 offenders known only as reported by offended girls, 358 were students with known class standing. Of these students 9.5 per cent offended girls one or two years more advanced than themselves, 34.1 per cent offended girls of the same class standing, 43.6 per cent offended girls one class below, and 12.8 per cent offended girls three or four years lower in class standing. The mean difference in class standing in favor of the offenders was 1.2 with a sigma of .05. The evidence shows that offenders tend to be of higher academic class than the offended respondents, but exploitation is not proven since the normal class discrepancies for pairs dating without erotic offensiveness are not known.

Some limited evidence is available concerning relative socio-economic standing of the offended girls and the men whom they described as offenders. Of the 388 offenders, 68.1 per cent were reported as of the same "socio-economic status" as their offended partners, 13.9 per cent

1. Levels of aggression are telescoped in order to satisfy requirements for Chi square.

were reported as lower, and 18.0 per cent reported as of higher status. Ratings of relative socio-economic status probably are lacking in reliability and validity. Offenders could be down-graded because they were offensive or up-graded to soothe a latent guilt feeling at having been involved with offensive behavior.

The proportion of fraternity men among the offenders is high implying a quota index of 205.8 with reference to the proportion of fraternity men in the male student body. It is possible, however, that fraternity men date more, without being more aggressive per date, than non-fraternity men. A table distributing the female offended and the male offenders by organizational (fraternity-sorority) status shows a rather clear pattern of homogamy rather than supporting a theory that men are especially predatory toward non-sorority girls. It does seem clear that open communication and *savoir faire* attributed to sorority girls and fraternity men does not prevent experiences reported as offensive. There seem to be misunderstandings even among the "Greeks."

Data are available in Table 2 concerning relationship involvement

Table 2. Relationship Involvement and Erotic Intimacy Level at Which Offensiveness Occurs, by Episodes

	NECKING AND PETTING ABOVE THE WAIST		*PETTING BELOW THE WAIST*		*ATTEMPTED INTERCOURSE AND ATTEMPTED INTERCOURSE WITH VIOLENCE*		*Total*
	N	*Per Cent*	*N*	*Per Cent*	*N*	*Per Cent*	
Ride home, first date, occasional date	411	55.0	60	31.4	25	30.1	496 (48.5%)
Regular or steady date	295	39.4	104	54.5	43	51.8	442 (43.3%)
Pinned, engaged	42	5.6	27	14.1	15	18.1	84 (8.2%)
Totals	748	100.0	191	100.0	83	100.0	1022 (100.0%)

$x^2 = 57.26$; *d.f.* $= 4$; $P < .001$; $C = .230$.

and erotic intimacy level at which offensiveness occurs. Table 2, which includes column percentages, suggests that there is a significant association of offensiveness at a mild level of erotic intimacy with a non-involved pairing and offensiveness at a serious level with "pinned" or engagement relationships. It could be plausibly argued that offensive experience at a mild level of intimacy and involvement is due to misunderstanding while experiences at a more serious level and with greater relationship involvement are due to male exploitation of feminine involvement.

The experience of being offended might be further related to selectivity in formation and disruption of courtship relationships. Offended girls may express their dissatisfaction with a promptness depending upon involvement and the aggressiveness of offending males. A ratio E/M may be defined as number of episodes at a certain level of erotic intimacy divided by the number of men offensively aggressive at that level. The tolerance ratios E/M of Table 3 represent frequency of repeated offensiveness by the same man at a given level. A ratio of 2.00 would mean

Table 3. Number of Men, Episodes, and Tolerance Ratio for Five Levels of Erotic Intimacy

Levels of Aggression	*Men*	*Episodes*	E/M
Necking	231	367	1.58
Petting above the waist	177	381	2.15
Petting below the waist	92	191	2.07
Attempted intercourse	48	73	1.52
Attempted intercourse with violence	10	10	1.00
Man-level total	558*	1022	
Number of men	388		

*Multiple count due to some men active more than once at same or different levels.

that on the average each offending man was guilty of two offensive episodes at a given level. A ratio of 1.00 means that no man was permitted a repetition of his offensive conduct at a particular level. Presumably the ratios vary according to successful prevention of aggression and with termination of relationships which led to offensive behavior.

It is interesting to note that at the milder level of necking, about half the men repeated their offensive behavior. For others the situation was defined after the first offense or the relationship terminated. Since it has been shown in Table 2 that offensiveness at the necking level was associated with casual dating, it is probable that dating relationships without emotional involvement were selectively broken, thus curtailing offensive behavior. It is interesting to note a higher tolerance ratio at the next two levels of erotic intimacy, meaning that on the average offensive behavior was repeated about twice. The probable explanation is greater emotional involvement of the girls in more meaningful relationships with corresponding exploitability. At the fourth level the tolerance ratio drops to 1.52 suggesting that in spite of emotional involvement the aggression went beyond whatever tolerance was furthered by emotional involvement. Given violence and threats of violence no repetition was permitted, even though seven out of the ten such episodes involved girls in regular-dating, "pinned," or engaged relationships. Whether these seven episodes led to selective termination or redefinition of courtship relationships is unknown.

Emotional Effects, Reactions and Hypothetical Reactions

The offended respondents were asked to define their emotional reaction to offensive episodes by adjectives such as anger, guilt, and fear. While the terminology varied, it proved easy to group responses in the four categories of Table 4. Table 4 indicates that guilt feelings may vary

Table 4. Emotional Reactions of Offended Respondents by Level of Erotic Intimacy

	NECKING AND PETTING ABOVE THE WAIST		PETTING BELOW THE WAIST		ATTEMPTED INTERCOURSE AND ATTEMPTED INTERCOURSE WITH VIOLENCE		Total
	N	Per Cent	N	Per Cent	N	Per Cent	
Anger	138	48.4	45	42.0	27	35.0	210 (44.78%)
Guilt	53	18.6	28	26.2	16	20.8	97 (20.68%)
Fear	42	14.7	25	23.4	29	37.7	96 (20.47%)
Disgust, disillusionment or confusion	52	18.3	9	8.4	5	6.5	66 (14.07%)
Totals	285	100.0	107	100.0	77	100.0	469 (100.0%)

$x^2 = 30.03$; *d.f.* = 6; P < .001.

with involvement and degree of aggression. The stress upon guilt is at a maximum at the intermediate level, probably associated with emotional involvement on the part of the girls and possibly provocation. Guilt feelings seem to be somewhat relieved by more extreme male aggressiveness for which girls could disclaim responsibility. It is probable that, within limits, involvement furthers guilt feelings, shared stigma, and corresponding exploitability.

The offended respondents were also asked with the aid of an 8 item checklist what they did about offensive episodes and had opportunity to make responses in their own words. The replies were readily grouped into the five categories of Table 5. Table 5 shows the limited reliance upon authority. The percentage of girls reporting offensive episodes to authorities was insignificant in spite of the claims of a counseling service. "Discussion and warnings" within the companion group, such as a sorority, was less common at the more extreme levels of erotic intimacy while secrecy became the more common policy.

Evidence is available from both offended and non-offended respondents concerning comparative hypothetical reactions. The offended were asked "What would you now do?" presumably after reflection upon offensive experience. In every case non-offended respondents volunteered answers to this hypothetical question in spite of their own lack of offensive experiences. The responses could be readily grouped within the eleven categories shown in Table 6, five of which could be grouped under the heading "Appeals to Authority." Especially striking is the greater emphasis of the offended upon personal interaction with the aggressor

Table 5. Answers of Respondents to the Question "What Did You Do?"

	NECKING AND PETTING ABOVE THE WAIST		PETTING BELOW THE WAIST		ATTEMPTED INTERCOURSE AND ATTEMPTED INTERCOURSE WITH VIOLENCE		Totals	CRITICAL RATIOS—COLUMNS 1 AND 3
	N	Per Cent	N	Per Cent	N	Per Cent		
Selective avoidance	126	36.95	21	25.30	21	30.88	168 (34.15%)	
Discussion and warning re age group	115	33.73	17	20.48	11	16.18	143 (29.06%)	3.4
Secrecy	66	19.35	38	45.78	33	48.53	137 (27.85%)	4.5
Discussion with aggressor	11	3.23	3	3.62	3	4.41	17 (3.46%)	
Report to authority	23	6.74	4	4.82	0		27 (5.48%)	
Totals	341	100.0	83	100.00	68	100.00	492 (100.0%)	

Table 6. Comparative Hypothetical Adjustive Reactions of Offended and Non-offended Respondents

	OFFENDED		NON-OFFENDED		CRITICAL RATIOS—OFFENDED VS. NON-OFFENDED
	N	Per Cent	N	Per Cent	
Discussion with aggressor: reason and rebuke	157	37.92	109	16.42	8.1
Deterrence or avoidance: physical and verbal	135	32.61	187	28.16	
Selective avoidance	76	18.36	169	25.45	3.2
Vague or cynical	24	5.80	31	4.67	
Discussion and warning re age group	13	3.14	47	7.08	2.7
Secrecy	6	1.45	17	2.56	
APPEALS TO AUTHORITY					
Report to parents	2	0.48	26	3.92	
Report to academic authority	1	0.24	39	5.87	
Report to civic authority	0		18	2.71	
Report to clergy	0		2	0.30	
"Report it" and "Report it to authorities'	0		19	2.86	
Total appeals to authority		0.72		15.66	
Totals	414	100.00	664	100.00	

in terms of reason and rebuke.[2] While appeals to authority were generally unfavored, girls reporting offensive experiences were especially disinclined to favor this type of adjustive reaction. There is some support for our ideal-typical formulation that exploitation and stigma lead to withdrawal from institutional protection with ultimate increased dependence upon the pair relationship.

In terms of possibly altered selective perception it might be expected that offended girls would give higher estimates of the prevalence of offensive behavior than would non-offended girls. The offended girls estimate that the average college girl experiences 4.2 offensive episodes in the course of a college year. The corresponding mean estimate made by non-offended respondents was only 2.7 (C.R.=4.9).

Summary

There is evidence on one campus suggesting that in courtship relationships there is a progressive pattern of exploitation, involvement, ambivalent resistance, awareness of shared stigma, and reduced reliance upon institutional controls with corresponding stress on control within the dyadic relationship.

One possible educational implication of this study is that college girls should be trained in *informed* self-reliance. Extreme offensive experience associated with stigma seems to reduce reliance upon parents, peer groups and certainly upon formal agencies of control and guidance. However, to avoid cumulative personal exploitation and exploitation of other victims because of secrecy, parents, peer groups, and formal agencies should operate so as to avoid stigmatization. The self-reliant girl, really in need of help and judiciously aware of that need, should not be made to fear a confusion of punitive and advisory functions.

2. It may seem strange that in Table 6 "secrecy" and "discussion and warning re age group" are infrequently mentioned as adjustive reactions as compared with their prominence in the checkings of Table 5. The answer probably lies in the fact that the data of Table 5 were largely derived from a checklist rather than from volunteered statements as in the case of Table 6. Respondents given an open ended question as to what they would *do* would naturally neglect the passive reaction of secrecy.

ERNEST Q. CAMPBELL
and THOMAS F. PETTIGREW

Racial and Moral Crisis: The Role of the Little Rock Ministers

THIS paper[1] analyzes the conduct of the ministers in established denominations in Little Rock, Arkansas, during the crisis over the admission of Negro students to the Central High School in the fall of 1957. How do ministers behave in racial crisis, caught between integrationist and segregationist forces?

One might expect that Little Rock's clergymen would favor school integration. All the major national Protestant bodies have adopted forceful declarations commending the Supreme Court's desegregation decision of 1954 and urging their members to comply with it. And southern pastors have voted in favor of these statements at their church conferences—and sometimes have even issued similar pronouncements to their own congregations.[2] But the southern man of God faces serious congregational opposition if he attempts to express his integrationist beliefs publicly in the local community. The vast majority of southern whites—even those living in the Middle South—are definitely against racial desegregation.[3]

---

1. This study was supported by a grant from the Laboratory of Social Relations, Harvard University. The authors wish to express their gratitude to Professor Samuel A. Stouffer for his suggestions. Two brief popular accounts of aspects of this study have appeared previously: "Men of God in Racial Crisis," *Christian Century*, LXXV (June 4, 1958), 663-65, and "Vignettes from Little Rock," *Christianity and Crisis,* XVIII (September 29, 1958), 128-36.

2. For example, local ministerial groups issued such statements in New Orleans, Louisiana; Richmond, Virginia; Dallas and Houston, Texas; and Atlanta, Macon, and Columbus, Georgia. For a review of national church statements see "Protestantism Speaks on Justice and Integration," *Christian Century*, LXXV (February 5, 1958), 164-66.

3. A 1956 National Opinion Research Center poll indicated that only one in every seven white southerners approves school integration (H. H. Hyman and P. B.

The purpose of this study is to determine how the ministers of established denominations in Little Rock behaved in the conflict. In analyzing their behavior, we treat self-expectations as an independent variable. This is contrary to the usual course, in which the actor is important analytically only because he is caught between contradictory *external* expectations. The standard model of role conflict treats ego as forced to decide between the incompatible norms of groups that can impose sanctions for non-conformity. This model—which is essentially what Lazarsfeld means by cross-pressures—skirts the issue of whether ego imposes expectations on itself and punishes deviations. Pressure and sanction are external to the actor. Hence the typical model tends to be ahistorical in the sense that a finite number of cross-pressuring groups are used to predict the actor's behavior. It is assumed that the actor cannot have developed from periods of prior socialization any normative expectations for his behavior which would have an independent existence.[4] This additional variable—the actor's expectations of himself—is especially meaningful in the analysis.

Though it is a city of approximately 125,000, Little Rock has much of the atmosphere and easy communication of a small town. It is located in almost the geometric center of the state, and physically and culturally it borders on both the Deep South-like delta country to the east and south and the Mountain South-like hill country to the west and north. Thus Little Rock is not a city of the Deep South. Its public transportation had been successfully integrated in 1956, and its voters, as late as March, 1957, had elected two men to the school board who supported the board's plan for token integration of Central High School. And yet Little Rock

---

Sheatsley, "Attitudes toward Desegregation," *Scientific American*, CXCV [December, 1956], 35-39). A 1956 survey by the American Institute of Public Opinion showed that in the Middle South—including Arkansas—only one in five whites approved of school integration (M. M. Tumin, *Segregation and Desegregation* [New York: Anti-Defamation League of B'nai B'rith, 1957], p. 109).

4. By showing that the actor may have a predisposition toward either a particularistic or a universalistic "solution" to role conflicts in instances where the particularistic-universalistic dimension is relevant, Stouffer and Toby link the study of personality to that of role obligations in a way rarely done (Samuel A. Stouffer and Jackson Toby, "Role Conflict and Personality," *American Journal of Sociology*, LVI [March, 1951], 395-406 [reprinted in Samuel A. Stouffer, *Social Research to Test Ideas*, Chapter 3, New York: The Free Press of Glencoe, 1962]). This study, however, treats the personal predisposition as a determinant of conflict resolution rather than a factor in conflict development. Much the same is true of Gross's analysis (Neal Gross, Ward S. Mason, and Alexander McEachern, *Explorations in Role Analysis: Studies of the School Superintendency Role* [New York: John Wiley & Sons, 1958], esp. chaps. xv, xvi, and xvii).

is a southern city, with southern traditions of race relations. These patterns became of world-wide interest after Governor Faubus called out the National Guard to prevent desegregation and thereby set off the most publicized and the most critical chain of events in the integration process to date.

Only two ministers devoted their sermons to the impending change on the Sunday before the fateful opening of school in September, 1957. Both warmly approved of the step and hoped for its success. Other ministers alluded to it in prayer or comment. It was commonly believed that a majority of the leading denominations' clergy favored the school board's "gradual" plan. This impression seemed confirmed when immediately after Governor Faubus had surrounded Central High with troops fifteen of the city's most prominent ministers issued a protest in, according to the local *Arkansas Gazette*, "the strongest language permissible to men of God."

When Negro students appeared at the high school for the first time, they were escorted by four white Protestant ministers and a number of prominent Negro leaders. Two of the four whites are local clergymen, one being the president of the biracial ministerial association, the other, president of the local Human Relations Council. Many of the more influential ministers of the city had been asked the night before to join this escort. Some demurred; others said they would try to come. Only two appeared.

On September 23, the day of the rioting near Central High School, several leaders of the ministerial association personally urged immediate counteraction on the mayor and the chief of police. Later, support was solicited from selected ministers in the state to issue a declaration of Christian principle, but dissension over the statement prevented its publication. Indeed, *no* systematic attempts were made by the clergy to appeal to the conscience of the community. Such statements as individual ministers did express were usually—though not always—appeals for "law and order" rather than a Christian defense of the principle of desegregation.

Several weeks after the rioting, plans for a community-wide prayer service began to develop. Care was taken to present this service in as neutral terms as possible. Compromise and reconciliation were stressed: never was it described as organized prayers for integration. And indorsements came from both sides of the controversy—from President Eisenhower and from Governor Faubus. As one of the sponsors put it: "Good Christians can honestly disagree on the question of segregation or integration. But we can all join together in prayers for guidance, that peace may return to our city." The services in the cooperating churches were held on Columbus Day, October 12. All the leading churches participated, with only the working-class sects conspicuously missing. The services varied widely from informal prayers to elaborate programs, and attendances varied widely, too, and totaled perhaps six thousand.

These "prayers for peace" may best be viewed as a ritualistic termination of any attempts by the clergy to direct the course of events in the racial crisis. The prayers had met the national demand for ministerial action and the ministers' own need to act; and they had completed the whole unpleasant business. Despite sporadic efforts by a small number to undertake more effective steps, the ministers lapsed into a general silence that continued throughout the school year.

We began our work in Little Rock in the week after the peace prayers. Following a series of background interviews and a careful analysis of ministerial action as recorded in the press, twenty-nine detailed interviews with ministers were held.[5] Twenty-seven of them are Protestants and two are Jewish; the Roman Catholics did not cooperate.

This sample was not selected randomly; the so-called "snowball technique" was used in order to include the most influential church leaders. This involves asking each interviewee to name the members of the Little Rock clergy that he considers to be "the most influential." The first interview was made with an announced leader of the peace prayers, and interviewing was continued with all the men mentioned as influential until no new names were suggested. We added a number of ministers who were not named but who had taken strongly liberal positions during the crisis. Thus our sample is most heavily weighted with the pastors of the larger churches with the greatest prestige and the pastors of smaller churches who had assumed active roles in the conflict. These two groups, we anticipated, would have to contend with the greatest amount of incompatibility in role.

Most of the interviews were held in the church offices. Rapport, which was generally excellent, was partly secured by the authors' identification with southern educational institutions. A detailed summary, as nearly as possible a verbatim account, was placed on Audograph recording equipment shortly after the completion of each interview. Information in three broad areas was sought, and to this end a series of open-ended questions was developed. A series of questions was aimed at determining whether the respondent was a segregationist or an integrationist. A segregationist here is defined as one who prefers racial barriers as presently constituted; an integrationist is one to whom the removal of

5. Thirteen additional interviews were held with the sect leaders of an openly prosegregation prayer service. None of these were members of the ministerial association or were in personal contact with any ministers of the established denominations. A detailed report on them will be published.

legal and artificial barriers to racial contact is morally preferable to the present system.[6]

Each interviewee was asked to give a complete account of what he had done and said in both his parish and in the community at large regarding the racial crisis. If he had not been active or vocal, we probed him for the reason and to learn if he had felt guilty over his failure to state the moral imperatives.

A final set of questions dealt with the pastor's perception of his congregation's reaction to whatever stand he had taken. If pressure had been applied on him by his parishioners, we probed him to learn exactly what pressure had been used and how.

The Segregationist

Only five of the twenty-nine clergymen we interviewed were segregationists by our definition. None was avidly so, and, unlike segregationist ministers of the sects, none depended on "chapter-and-verse Scripture" to defend his stand. All men in their late fifties or sixties, they did not think that the crisis was a religious matter. One of them was a supervising administrator in a denominational hierarchy. Although all five were affiliated with prominent denominations, they were not among the leaders of the local ministerial body.

These five men have not been publicly active in defending segregation.[7] Each was opposed to violence, and none showed evidence of internal discomfort or conflict. All five cooperated with the neutrally toned prayers for peace. As one of them commented, "You certainly can't go wrong by praying. Praying can't hurt you on anything."

The Inactive Integrationist

Inactive integrationists had done enough—or believed they had done enough—to acquaint their congregations with their sympathy with racial tolerance and integration, but during the crucial weeks of the crisis they were generally silent. These, representing as they do all major denominations, varied considerably as to age and size of church served. Included among them were virtually all the ministers of high prestige, many of

6. Using the interview, three judges, the two authors and a graduate assistant, independently rated each respondent as either a segregationist or an integrationist. Agreement between the three raters was complete for twenty-seven of the twenty-nine cases.

7. Again, this is in contrast to the sect segregationists. One sect minister is president and another is the chaplain of the local Citizens' Council.

whom had signed the protest against Governor Faubus at the start of the crisis and later were advocates of the peace prayer services. Some had spoken out in favor of "law and order" and in criticism of violence. They had not, however, defended the continued attendance of the Negro students in the high school, and they had not challenged their members to defend educational desegregation as a Christian obligation. They were publicly viewed as integrationists only because they had supported "law and order" and had not defended segregation.

Altogether, the inactive integrationists comprise sixteen out of the twenty-nine of our sample. Because it was not a random sample, we cannot draw inferences regarding the division of the total ministerial community or of ministers of established denominations into integrationist and segregationist camps. However, since the sample underrepresents the uninfluential minister who had not been in the public eye during the crisis, we may conclude that a large majority of Little Rock's men of God did not encourage their members to define the issue as religious, nor did they initiate actions or participate in programs aimed at integration.

The Active Integrationist

Eight of our respondents can be designated as active integrationists because they continued to defend integration in principle and to insist that support of racial integration is nothing less than a Christian imperative. They were, on the whole, young men who have headed their small churches for only a few years. Most were disturbed that the churches of the city were segregated; some have urged their churches to admit Negroes.

Most of the active integrationists had serious difficulty with their members because of their activities, evidence of which was lowered Sunday-morning attendance, requests for transfer, diminished giving, personal snubs and insults, and rumors of sentiment for their dismissal. One had concluded that his usefulness to his congregation had ended and accordingly had requested to be transferred. By the end of 1958, several others had been removed from their pulpits.

One thing all twenty-nine of the sample had in common was a segregationist congregation.[8] Without exception, they believed that the majority of their members were strong opponents of racial integration. The highest estimate given by any integrationist of the proportion of his congregation which supported his views was 40 per cent; the median estimate for segregation was 75 per cent. Only three interviewees thought

8. Our study of a modest sample of church members bore out the ministers' estimates of predominantly pro-segregation sentiment in their congregations.

that a majority of their members would "accept" a strong public defense of integration by their minister.

Personal integrity, alone, would lead the liberal Little Rock minister to defend integration and condemn those who support segregation. However, the minister is obligated to consider the expectations of his church membership, especially inasmuch as the members' reactions bear upon his own effectiveness.

When an individual is responsible to a public, we distinguish three systems as relevant to his behavior: the self-reference system (SRS), the professional reference system (PRS), and the membership reference system (MRS). The SRS consists of the actor's demands, expectations, and images regarding himself. It may be thought of as what the actor would do in the absence of sanctions from external sources. We have already seen that typically the SRS would support racial integration.[9] The PRS consists of several sources mutually related to his occupational role yet independent of his congregation: national and regional church bodies, the local ecclesiastical hierarchy, if any, the local ministerial association, personal contacts and friendships with fellow ministers, and, probably, an image of "my church." Finally, the MRS consists simply of the minister's congregation. We have already seen that it favored segregation or at least ministerial neutrality.

The net effect of three reference systems seems to favor the cause of integration. Were they equal in strength, and were there no contrary forces internal to any of them, this conclusion is obvious. The minister would then feel committed to support the official national policy of his denomination; his knowledge that fellow ministers were similarly committed would support him, and the local hierarchy would encourage him to make this decision and reassure him should his congregation threaten disaffection. These external influences would reinforce his own values, resulting in forthright action in stating and urging the Christian imperatives. However, internal inconsistencies in the PRS and the SRS restrain what on first examination appears to be an influence toward the defense of integration.

The Professional Reference System

Two overriding characteristics of the PRS minimize its liberalizing influence. First, most of its components cannot or do not impose sanc-

9. Although groups make demands, impose sanctions, and significantly affect the actors' self-expectations and self-sanctions, nevertheless, we treat the self-reference system as an independent variable in role conflict. This system seems especially significant where personal action is contrary to the pressure of known and significant groups.

tions for non-conformity to their expectations. Second, those parts of the PRS that can impose sanctions also impose other demands on the minister, inconsistent with the defense of racial integration before members who, in large part, believe in racial separation and whose beliefs are profoundly emotional.

The Inability to Impose Sanctions

The national and regional associations that serve as the official "voice of the church" are not organized to confer effective rewards or punishments on individual ministers. Especially is this true in the case of failure to espouse national racial policy or to act decisively in the presence of racial tension. This is even more true of the local ministerial association; it does not presume to censure or praise its members. Conversely, the local church hierarchy is an immediate source of sanctions. It has the responsibility of recommending or assigning parishes, and of assisting the pastor in expanding the program of his church.

The probability and the nature of sanctions from fellow ministers among whom one has personal contacts and friends are somewhat more difficult to specify. However, it does not appear likely that he is subject to sanctions if he does not conform to their expectations by liberal behavior on racial matters. Should he indorse and actively support segregationist and violent elements, this would be another matter. If he is silent or guarded, however, it is not likely to subject him to sanction. The active integrationists in Little Rock expressed disappointment at the inaction of their associates while at the same time suggesting possible mitigating circumstances. There is no evidence that personal or professional ties had been damaged.

Among the various components of the PRS, then, only the local ecclesiastica, which does not exist for some, and, to a considerably lesser extent, fellow ministers, are conceivable sources influencing the minister's decision to be silent, restrained, or forthright.

Conflicting Expectations and Mitigated Pressures

The role of the minister as community reformer is not as institutionalized (i.e., it does not have as significant a built-in system of rewards and punishments) as are certain other roles associated with the ministry. The minister is responsible for the over-all conduct of the affairs of the church and is judged successful or unsuccessful according to how they prosper. He must encourage cooperative endeavor, reconciling differences, and bring people together. Vigor and high morale of the membership are reflected in increased financial support and a growing membership, and his fellow ministers and his church superiors are keenly sensitive to these evidences of his effectiveness. His goal, elusive though it may be, is maximum support from all members of an ever growing congregation.

The church hierarchy keeps records. It hears reports and rumors. It does not like to see divided congregations, alienated ministers, reduced membership, or decreased contributions. Responsible as it is for the destiny of the denomination in a given territory, it compares its changing fortunes with those of rival churches. In assigning ministers to parishes, it rewards some with prominent pulpits and punishes others with posts of low prestige or little promise. However exalted the moral virtue the minister expounds, the hierarchy does not wish him to damn his listeners to hell—unless somehow he gets them back in time to attend service next Sunday. Promotions for him are determined far less by the number of times he defends unpopular causes, however virtuous their merit, than by the state of the physical plant and the state of the coffer.

Now it is especially commendable if the minister can defend the cause and state the imperative with such tact or imprint that cleavages are not opened or loyalties alienated. If, however, the moral imperative and church cohesion are mutually incompatible, there is little doubt that the church superiors favor the latter. One administrator told two of his ministers, "It's o.k. to be liberal, boys: just don't stick your neck out." Indeed, ecclesiastical officials advised younger ministers, systematically, to "go slow," reminding them of the possibility of permanent damage to the church through rash action.

Under these circumstances pressure from the national church to take an advanced position on racial matters loses much of its force. The minister is rewarded *only* if his efforts do not endanger the membership of the church: "Don't lose your congregation." Similarly, the prospect of an unfavorable response from his congregation protects him from the (possibly liberal) church hierarchy; he need only point to what happened to Pastor X, who did not heed the rumblings in his congregation. The higher officials, themselves keenly aware of local values and customs, will understand. And his fellow ministers, too, are, after all, in the same boat. They give him sympathy, not censure, if he says, "My hands are tied." An informal rationale develops that reassures the pastor: "These things take time," "You can't change people overnight," "You can't talk to people when they won't listen." There is strong sympathy for the forthright pastor who is in real trouble, but he is looked on as an object lesson. Thus the ministers reinforce each other in inaction, despite their common antipathy to segregation.

The Self-Reference System

We still must reckon with the demands the minister imposes upon himself. It is obvious that the actor has the power of self-sanction, through guilt. A threatening sense of unworthiness, of inadequacy in God's sight, cannot be taken lightly. Similarly, to grant one's self the biblical commendation "Well done" is a significant reward. We have said that the self is an influence favoring action in support of desegregation. Can the inactive integrationist, then, either avoid or control the sense of guilt?

Our data are not entirely appropriate to the question. Nevertheless, four circumstances—all of which permit of generalization to other cases—appear at least partially to prevent the sense of guilt. These include major characteristics of the ministerial role, several ministerial values and "working propositions," certain techniques for communicating without explicit commitment, and the gratifying reactions of extreme opposition forces.

The Role Structure

The church, as an institutional structure, sets criteria by which the minister may assess his management of the religious enterprise; it does *not* offer criteria by which to evaluate his stand on controversial issues.[10] This encourages, even compels, the minister to base his self-image, hence his sense of worth or unworth, on his success in managing his church. Thus, if church members do not share his goals, three types of institutionalized responsibilities restrain him in reform.

In the first place, the minister is required to be a cohesive force, to "maintain a fellowship in peace, harmony, and Christian love," rather than to promote dissension. Thus some ministers prayed during the Columbus Day services that members "carry no opinion to the point of disrupting the Christian fellowship."

Second, he is expected to show a progressive increase in the membership of his church. Pro-integration activity, lacking mass support, is likely to drive members to other churches.

10. Blizzard does not find a "community reformer" or "social critic" role in the ministry (see Samuel W. Blizzard, "The Minister's Dilemma," *Christian Century*, LXXIII [April 25, 1956], 508-10).

Finally, his task is to encourage maximum annual giving and to plan for the improvement and expansion of the plant. It is hardly surprising that several inactive integrationists who were engaged in vital fund-raising campaigns shrank from action that might endanger their success.

Working Propositions

The minister makes certain assumptions about his work that reduce the likelihood of guilt when he does not defend moral convictions that his members reject. He is, first, a devotee of education, by which he means the gradual growth and development of spiritual assets—in contrast to his counterpart of an earlier period, who was more likely to believe in sudden change through conversion. He also believes that communication with the sinner must be preserved at all costs ("You can't teach those you can't reach") and for long enough to effect gradual change in attitude and behavior. A crisis, when feelings run high, is not the time to risk alienating those one wishes to change. For example, Pastor X acted decisively but, in so doing, damaged or lost his pastorate: "Look at him; he can't do any good now."

Communication Techniques

The minister may avoid committing himself unequivocally.[11] Some use the "every man a priest" technique, for example, the stating of his own opinion while expressing tolerance for contradictory ones and reminding his listeners that their access to God's truth is equal with his. Others use the "deeper issues" approach; generalities such as the brotherhood of man, brotherly love, humility, and universal justice are discussed without specific reference to the race issue, in the hope that the listener may make the association himself. Still another course is to remind listeners that "God is watching," that the question of race has religious significance and therefore they should "act like Christians." There is also the method of deriding the avowed segregationists without supporting their opposites. The "exaggerated southerner" technique, which may be supplementary to any of the others, involves a heavy southern drawl and, where possible, reference to an aristocratic line of planter descent.

11. For a full description and illustration of such techniques as used in Little Rock see our *Christians in Racial Crisis: A Study of Little Rock's Ministers* (Washington, D.C.: Public Affairs Press, 1959).

These techniques do not demand belief in integration as a Christian imperative. Further, except for the "every man a priest" technique, they do not commit the speaker to integrationist goals as religious values; the listener may make applications as he chooses. The speaker, on the other hand, can assure himself that the connections are there to be made; he supplies, as it were, a do-it-yourself moral kit.

Reaction of the Opposition

The ministerial body in Little Rock, except for pastors to dissident fundamentalist sects, is defined by agitated segregationists as a bunch of "race-mixers" and "nigger-lovers." For example, the charge was made that the peace prayers were intended to "further integration under a hypocritical veneer of prayer" and that the sect pastors sponsored prayers for segregation "to show that not all of the city's ministers believe in mixing the races." Indeed, ministers of major denominations were charged with having "race on the mind" so that they were straying from, even rejecting, the biblical standard to further their un-Christian goals.

The effect of opposition by segregation extremists was to convince certain inactive integrationists that indeed they *had* been courageous and forthright. The minister, having actually appropriated the opposition's evaluation of his behavior, reversing its affective tone found the reassurance he needed that his personal convictions had been adequately and forcefully expressed.

Were the force of the membership reference system not what it is, the professional reference system and the self-reference system would supply support to integration that was not limited to "law and order" appeals and the denunciation of violence. However, since "Don't lose your congregation" is itself a strong professional and personal demand, the force of the PRS is neutralized, and the pressure from the SRS becomes confused and conflicting. Inaction is a typical response to conflicting pressures within both the internal and the external system.

It is not surprising, then, that most Little Rock ministers have been far less active and vocal in the racial crisis than the policies of their national church bodies and their sense of identification with them, as well as their own value systems, would lead one to expect. Rather, what is surprising is that a small number continued to express vigorously the moral imperative as they saw it, in the face of congregational disaffection, threatened reprisal, and the lukewarm support or quiet discouragement of their superiors and peers.

SELECTED READINGS

The factors involved in an acceptance situation are complex, as Becker's study shows. A study by Leonard Berkowitz is relevant in this connection: "Group Norms among Bomber Crews: Patterns of Perceived Crew Attitudes, 'Actual' Crew Attitudes, and Crew Liking Related to Aircrew Effectiveness in Far Eastern Combat," *Sociometry*, 1956. W. G. Head, "Adaptive Sociology," *British Journal of Sociology*, March, 1961, insists that proper role performance involves the protection and maintenance of one's private rights. For this purpose he says that a certain "safeguard distance" is necessary. Paul Tillich, "Conformity," *Social Research*, 1957, indicates that compliance to group ways does not produce conformity unless the "individual form" is "subdued by the collective form." An excellent description of acceptance is available in Robert Bunker, *Other Men's Skies* (Bloomington, Ind.: Indiana University Press, 1956), especially "Young Men of the Pueblo," pp., 121-158. See also Herbert Kaufman, *The Forest Ranger: A Study in Administrative Behavior* (Baltimore: Johns Hopkins Press, 1960).

Fred Vogt, "The American Indian in Transition: Reformation and Status Innovation," *American Journal of Sociology*, January, 1957, describes inventions in social structure; diffusion of invention is shown by James Coleman, Elihu Katz, and Herbert Menzel, "The Diffusion of Innovation among Physicians," *Sociometry*, 1957. Innovation is usually considered to result from some kind of challenge to the individual or the society, but Morris Janowitz, *The Professional Soldier* (New York: The Free Press, 1960), Chapter 8, indicates that entrance into the "nucleus of the elite," in the officer corps, is open ". . . to persons with unconventional careers." As an instance of the institutionalization of innovation, this has prime importance.

Cloward's thesis with reference to "illegitimate means," is expanded in Richard A. Cloward and Lloyd E. Ohlin, *Delinquency and Opportunity* (New York: The Free Press, 1960). A comprehensive examination of nonconforming behavior and the literature connected with it is found in Marshall B. Clinard, *Sociology of Deviant Behavior* (New York: Holt, Rinehart, Winston, 1957). Albert K. Cohen, *Delinquent Boys: The Culture of the Gang* (New York: The Free Press, 1955), has had wide influence. With reference to this book see John I. Kitsuse and David C. Diettrick, "Delinquent Boys: A Critique," *American Sociological Review*, April, 1959.

Studies with emphasis on the intrapsychic aspects of conflict are: Bingham Dai, "Obsessive-Compulsive Disorder in Chinese Culture," *Social Problems*, 1957; G. M. Gilbert, "Sex Differences in Mental Health," *International Journal of Social Psychiatry*, Winter, 1959.

6 *Social Aspects of Self Structure*

IN THIS SECTION some of the relations between society and certain important "structural" dimensions of the self are examined. These dimensions are also problematical at the present time.

We may take adjustment operationally as indicating general ability of the individual to live in a tolerable association with his society. Adjustment should be read here not as a goal, or *summum bonum,* but as a state often leading to a productive or creative social-self relationship. This word, like the others in this section, is elusive and must be evaluated in terms of the concrete data which are taken to indicate adjustment or nonadjustment.

Burchinal, Hawkes, and Gardner, "Adjustment Characteristics of Rural and Urban Children," show evidence that if rural living used to be a natural resource for personality stability, this resource is being exhausted. The battery of studies examined by the authors suggest that the rural way of life is less and less a sociological reality. This fact poses an important challenge to a society when we consider the importance of Cooley's "primary group" in the formation of viable personalities.

In this context Litwak's paper, the second of two papers on the extended family, appears as a response to the challenge mentioned above. He considers that a "modified extended family" may aid rather than restrict the kind of geographic mobility that has been considered part and parcel of industrial and urban living.

The industrial revolution was a problem in Comte's time, and it has not ceased to be a problem in our time. Inkeles in his study, "Industrial Man: The Relation of Status to Experience, Perception, and Value," shows that important attitudes, viewed in a number of societies, are correlated with position or status in the industrial system. To the extent brought out by the evidence and cautiously examined by the author, modern man is responding to the influences of his work situation. Thus, while he is undoubtedly still "national man," he is becoming more and more "industrial man."

The degree to which aspiration and achievement orientation have been ingrained in the American middle class has long been a focus of study. A classic study in this area is Max Weber, *The Protestant Ethic and the Spirit of Capitalism,* which indicated a religious source as a contributing cause of Western economic motivation. A number of recent studies have examined this thesis in terms of contemporary American society. Mack, Murphy, and Yellin, in "The Protestant Ethic, Level of Aspiration, and Social Mobility: An Empirical Test," found no significant differences in social mobility patterns between samples of Protestants and Catholics, and they conclude that ". . . whatever influence these two religious subcultures have upon their adherents in our society, so far as the Weberian thesis is concerned, is overridden by the general ethos."

Studies have tended to support the proposition that aspiration characterized the American middle class more than the lower class. LaMar T. Empey puts this question in a rather different way, however. Although "absolute" occupational aspirations of the "upper classes" have been found to be higher than those of the lower classes, the author points out that when relative starting positions are taken into account lower-class individuals prefer and anticipate significantly higher status than their fathers. This study suggests, as the author points out, that lower-class youth have not limited their occupational aspirations to the class horizon.

Dynes, Clarke, and Dinitz, in "Levels of Occupational Aspiration: Some Aspects of Family Experience as a Variable," throw some interesting light on aspiration. They show that "Unsatisfactory interpersonal relationships in the family of orientation were significantly related to high aspirational levels. . . ."

Martin and Westie, looking for the tolerant personality, needed 429 respondents to find 41 persons "qualified for the Tolerant category." Their study confirms many of the findings in T. W. Adorno, *et al.*, *The Authoritarian Personality*, and also calls attention to the presence in our society of ". . . Happy Bigots whose prejudices are born, not so much of personal psychological difficulties, but rather of the fact that their community and various groups inculcate . . . and approve of their prejudices. . . ." In such circumstances the tolerant person may be a deviant ". . . and a legitimate subject for analysis in terms of abnormal psychology." Orville G. Brim, in "Attitude Content-Intensity and Probability Expectations," presents a sophisticated experimental design concerned with attitudes, their directional aspect, and the strength with which they are held. He offers explanations for the U-shaped curve that relates them: "Individual differences in both intensity and extremity of responses to attitude and expectancy questions are considered to be the result of individual differences in need for security." Brim's article, although its conclusions are applied to the experimental situation, indicates a relation between the "need for security" and a "tolerance of ambiguity" that is disquieting in a world where we need a maximum tolerance of insecurity and also a maximum tolerance of ambiguity. Seymour Martin

Lipset, in "Working-Class Authoritarianism" examines ". . . the myth of the liberating power of the proletariat . . ." a phrase he quotes from Ignazio Silone. "Both evidence and theory," he says, "suggest . . . that the lower strata are relatively more authoritarian, that . . . they will be more attracted to an extremist movement than to a moderate and democratic one, and that, once recruited, they will not be alienated by its lack of democracy. . . ."

a) ADJUSTMENT

LEE G. BURCHINAL, GLENN R. HAWKES,
and BRUCE GARDNER

Adjustment Characteristics of Rural and Urban Children

SOCIOLOGISTS and other students of human group behavior have long employed various constructs or classificatory devices to help understand and predict human behavior. These constructs or guides have included racial, ethnic, and social class membership, primary or secondary group memberships, the church-sect dichotomy, and the many variants of the folk-urban or sacred-secular dichotomies. These con-

Reprinted from American Sociological Review, *February, 1957, pp. 81-87, by permission of the authors and the journal.*

Published as Journal Paper No. J-2984 of the Iowa Agricultural Experiment Station, Ames, Iowa, Project No. 1171, Home Economics Research. Acknowledgment is due Leone Kell of the Kansas Agricultural Experiment Station, Ruth Hoeflin of the Ohio Agricultural Experiment Station, and Helen Dawe of the Wisconsin Agricultural Experiment Station for their collaboration in this regional research project.

structs have been employed because they have had and perhaps some of them still have important predictive values. One of the traditional dichotomies used by American sociologists has been the rural-urban classification of persons and their social-psychological characteristics.

Burgess and Cottrell[1] and Schroeder[2] found that married persons who came from a rural or small town background tended to have somewhat better chances of happiness in marriage than couples who came from an urban background. This relationship, however, was not found by Terman and Oden[3] or by Locke.[4] Mangus found very clear evidence that the average level of personality adjustment was significantly higher among the farm children than among the urban children in Miami County, Ohio.[5] On the basis of the findings reported by Mangus, a rural-urban classification of children still has utility for predicting group personality differences. But if we assume that the rural areas of America are being urbanized in the social-psychological sense, we should expect to find little or no difference in various social-psychological characteristics of rural and urban children and youth.

The purpose of this paper is to test further the usefulness of the rural-urban or the farm, rural-nonfarm, and urban classification of children in regard to their levels of personality adjustment. Data gathered from three separate studies are presented to test the hypothesis that there are no significant differences among farm, rural-nonfarm, and urban children in their levels of personality adjustment. Personality adjustment is defined and measured in terms of standardized tests used for pre-adolescent children.

The Miami County Study

Mangus' findings were based on 1229 third and sixth grade children living in Miami County, Ohio, during the spring of 1946. Of these children, 371 lived on farms, 573 lived in rural-nonfarm homes, and 285

1. E. W. Burgess and L. S. Cottrell, *Predicting Success or Failure in Marriage*, New York: Prentice-Hall, 1939, p. 376.

2. C. W. Schroeder, "Divorce in a City of 100,000 Population," Ph.D. Thesis, University of Chicago, 1938, p. 98.

3. L. M. Terman, and M. H. Oden, *The Gifted Child Grows Up*, Stanford: Stanford University Press, 1947, p. 747.

4. H. J. Locke, *Predicting Adjustment in Marriage*, New York: Holt, Rinehart, Winston, 1951, p. 338.

5. A. R. Mangus, "Personality Adjustment of Rural and Urban Children," *American Sociological Review*, 13 (October, 1948), pp. 566-575. See also A. R. Mangus, and J. R. Seeley, "Mental Health Needs in a Rural and Semi-rural Area," Mimeo. Bull. No. 195, Ohio State University, 1947.

lived in a city of 17,000 persons. The California test of personality, elementary series, was administered to these children.[6] Other indices of the children's personality patterns were also obtained, but these are not discussed here since no comparable data were obtained in the studies reported in this paper.

Mangus found no significant differences between the self and social adjustment mean scores of farm and rural-nonfarm children. When he compared the self and social adjustment mean scores of farm children with the same scores for the urban children, he found significant differences favoring the farm children. Rural nonfarm children also had significantly higher mean scores on the two California test scores than the city children.

In addition to testing mean differences on the two scores of the California test, Mangus also compared the mean scores of the three groups of children on the twelve subtests of the California test. (See footnote 6 for descriptions of the subtests.) The farm children differed favorably and significantly from city children in every component of self adjustment except one, and on this subtest–sense of personal freedom–the farm children were "on par with their city cousins." In three of the six components of the social adjustment score, the farm children were also superior to the urban children. Farm and rural-nonfarm children showed significant superiority in social skills, on the average they were better adjusted to the school situation, and as a group they were establishing better community relations than the urban children included in the survey. No significant differences were found among the three groups of children on the other three dimensions of the social adjustment section of the test.

On the basis of these findings, there can be no quarrel with Mangus' summary:

> It appears conclusive that in Miami County in the spring of 1946, farm children as a group had achieved a somewhat higher level of personal and social adjustment than urban children living in a small city included in the study.[7]

6. The California test is divided into two major sections so that it yields scores relating to "self or personal adjustment" and "social adjustment." Each of the sections of the test also yields six subscores. Subtests combined under the concept of personal adjustment give scores designed to provide estimates of the child's self-reliance, his feelings of personal worth, his feelings of belonging, his sense of personal freedom, his social withdrawing tendencies, and of his nervous symptoms. Subtest scores combined under the social adjustment score include measures of the child's attitudes toward social standards, his social skills, his freedom from anti-social tendencies, his family, school and community relationships.

7. Mangus, *op. cit.*, pp. 567-568.

Mangus was careful, however, not to claim any generality for the results obtained in Miami County. Data from three later studies are discussed below and compared with the findings reported by Mangus.

Hamilton County Study

Research workers from Iowa State College administered the California Test of Personality primary series, 1942 edition, to 642 children in Hamilton County, Iowa, during March, 1950. One of the purposes of this survey was to determine if any significant differences existed between the personal or self and social adjustment scores of samples of urban and rural children in that county. Children in the first four grades of Webster City, population 7,600 in 1950, constituted the urban sample and children in the first four grades of rural one-room schools within the Webster City trading area comprised the rural sample of children. There were 485 children in the former category and 157 in the latter. The self and social adjustment mean scores made by the two groups of children are shown in Table 1.

Table 1. Self, Social, and Total Adjustment Mean Scores, Rural and Urban Children, Grades 1-4, Hamilton County, Iowa, 1950

		SELF-ADJUSTMENT		SOCIAL ADJUSTMENT		TOTAL ADJUSTMENT	
Residence	Number	Mean	SD	Mean	SD	Mean	SD
Urban	485	35.12	6.23	40.56	5.46	75.68	10.32
Rural	157	34.26	6.86	41.31	4.89	75.57	10.50

These data indicated that the differences between personality adjustment scores of the farm and city children studied were negligible. For the self adjustment scores, the mean difference of .86 in favor of the urban children was not significant (t=1.46, .10<P<.20). The rural children scored .75 points higher on the average than the urban children on the social adjustment half of the California test, but this difference was also nonsignificant (t=1.53, .10<P<.20). The total mean score difference of .11 likewise failed to show a significant difference between the two groups of children (t=.12, P>.50).

These results support the null hypothesis stated earlier in this paper. For the two samples of children, one from a small city in central Iowa and the other from rural areas surrounding that city, it was not possible to detect any significant differences in levels of self or social adjustment as measured by the older edition of the California test.

The Marshalltown Study

The study reported in this section comes closer to a replication of Mangus' study than the Webster City study or the four-state investigation reported later. In March, 1956, 130 fifth grade children in three schools in Marshalltown, Iowa, completed the California Test of Personality, elementary series, 1953 edition. The data from Marshalltown, however, are based on only 74 children. Answer sheets for children who were judged by their teachers to be "slow" or poor readers and children who came from rural communities by bus to Marshalltown schools were not included in the analysis. While no sampling plan was used in selecting fifth grade classes in the Marshalltown elementary schools, the four fifth grade classes tested made up a fairly representative sample of children in that grade level. Marshalltown had a 1950 population of approximately 20,000.

For the purpose of comparing the scores made by the Marshalltown sample of Iowa children, 55 fifth and sixth graders from a rural school in a county adjoining Marshalltown were also given the same form and edition of the California test. This school was located in a community of approximately 400 persons. Mean scores for these two groups of children on the two major subscores and total scores of the California test are listed in Table 2.

Table 2. Personal, Social, and Total Adjustment Mean Scores, Marshalltown and Rural Story County, Fifth and Sixth Grade Children, Iowa, 1956

		SELF-ADJUSTMENT		*SOCIAL ADJUSTMENT*		*TOTAL ADJUSTMENT*	
Residence	*Number*	*Mean*	*SD*	*Mean*	*SD*	*Mean*	*SD*
Urban	74	53.80	11.05	57.34	9.11	111.14	18.99
Rural*	55	51.24	9.37	54.89	9.61	106.31	17.79

*Includes some rural-nonfarm children as well as farm children.

The urban children's personal, social, and total adjustment mean scores were higher than the combined farm and rural-nonfarm children's mean scores. When the mean differences were tested statistically, however, none of the differences was significant: for the difference of 2.56 points on the personal adjustment score $t = 1.38$; for the 2.45 mean difference on the social adjustment score, $t = 1.47$; for the mean difference of 4.83 points on the total scores, $t = 1.46$; and for all tests, $.10 < P < .20$.

While the rural and urban children tested in this investigation constitute a fairly small sample, the results agree with those found in the

Hamilton County study. Additional support is lent to the hypothesis that no significant differences existed between the personality adjustment characteristics of rural and urban children.

Although there were no significant differences between the two groups of children on the personal, social, and total adjustment scores, it is possible that some significant and perhaps important differences might be observed between the two groups on the twelve subscores that make up the California test. The means, standard deviations, and t values for the urban and rural children on the twelve subtests are shown in Table 3. Surprisingly, the urban children scored higher than the rural

Table 3. Mean Adjustment Scores, Marshalltown and Rural Story County, Fifth and Sixth Grade Children, Iowa, 1956

	URBAN (N = 74)		RURAL (N = 55)			
Personal Adjustment	*Mean*	*SD*	*Mean*	*SD*	*Mean Difference*	*t Value*
Self-reliance	8.15	1.81	7.73	1.68	.42	1.34
Personal worth	9.24	2.20	8.60	2.45	.64	1.56
Personal freedom	9.92	2.34	9.33	1.91	.59	1.53
Sense of belonging	10.08	1.77	10.07	1.77	.01	.03
Withdrawing tendencies	8.03	3.12	7.27	2.87	.76	1.42
Nervous symptoms	8.37	3.06	8.24	2.49	.13	.26
Social adjustment						
Social standards	10.57	1.43	10.54	1.56	.03	.11
Social skills	9.08	1.92	8.80	2.13	.28	.78
Anti-social tendencies	8.51	2.68	7.89	2.51	.62	1.33
Family relations	9.93	2.17	9.45	2.41	.48	1.18
School relations	9.55	2.17	8.71	2.66	.84	1.99*
Community relations	9.81	1.67	9.67	1.44	.14	.50

*This was the only value that was significant, $P = .05$.

children on all twelve components of the California test, but for the samples used in this investigation, only one of the differences was reliable. The mean difference of .84 on the school relations subtest had a t value equal to 1.99, which just reached the 5 per cent level of significance. If a larger sample had been used, it is possible that some of the other differences noted might have been significant. In their present form, however, the subtest data, based on fairly small samples, offer with the one exception further substantiation for the hypothesis that rural and urban children do not significantly differ in their personality adjustment characteristics.

A Four-State Investigation

During the 1954-55 school year, data relating to personality development of children were gathered from 256 children and their families in Iowa, Ohio, Kansas, and Wisconsin. Within each of the four states, two strata of population, rural areas and cities in the 2,500 to 10,000 range, were defined. Eight sample points, defined as elementary school districts and divided between the two strata in each state on the basis of the relative sizes of the strata, were drawn for each state sample by a probability method.[8] Eight children, whose parents were living together and who had at least one sibling, were randomly selected from the fifth grade class or classes at each of the sampling points.

The sample of 256 children completed the Rogers test of personality adjustment.[9] Four subscores–feelings of personal inferiority, social maladjustment, family relationships, and day dreaming–are derived from the Rogers test. These four subscores are also combined into a total score. The personality inferiority score measures roughly the extent to which a child thinks himself to be physically or mentally inadequate–duller, weaker, less good looking, or less capable than his peers. The social maladjustment score is a measure of the extent to which a child is unhappy in his group contacts, poor at making friends, poor in social skills. The family relations score indicates the degree of conflict and maladjustment a child has in his relations with his parents and siblings, such as jealousies, antagonisms, feelings of being rejected, and over dependence. The extent to which a child indulges in fantasies and unrealistic thinking is indicated by the day dreaming score. Rogers considered the total score as a measure of the seriousness of the child's maladjustment.

The children comprising the total sample were classified as farm, rural-nonfarm, and urban according to their present place of residence.[10]

8. For more detailed descriptions of the sample design, see G. R. Hawkes, L. G. Burchinal, Bruce Gardner, "Marital Satisfaction, Personality Characteristics, and Parental Acceptance of Children," *Journal of Counseling Psychology*, 3 (Fall, 1956), p. 217; Lee Burchinal, Glenn Hawkes, and Bruce Gardner, "The Relationship between Parental Acceptance and Adjustment of Children," *Child Development*, in press; also see Lee Burchinal, "The Relations of Parental Acceptance to Adjustment of Children," Unpublished Ph.D. dissertation, Ohio State University, 1956. A description of the family background characteristics of the children may be found in Glenn R. Hawkes, Lee G. Burchinal, Bruce Gardner, and Blaine M. Porter, "Parents' Acceptance of Their Children," *Journal of Home Economics*, 48 (March, 1956), pp. 196-197.

9. C. Rogers, *Measuring Personality Adjustment in Children Nine to Thirteen Years of Age*, New York: Teachers College, Columbia University, 1931. For a more detailed description of the subscores see esp. pp. 28-32. A discussion of the Rogers test may also be found in H. H. Remmers and N. L. Gage, *Educational Measurement and Evaluation*, New York: Harpers, 1943, pp. 354-356.

In the present study reliability coefficients based on 51 children retested at a one-week interval ranged from .67 to .77. Rogers reported reliability coefficients for a group of 43 children tested after one month ranging from .65 to .72. These reliabilities appear adequate for group use of this type of test.

10. The data from the four state samples were combined into one total sample

The means and standard deviations for each group of children on the five Rogers scores are shown in Table 4.

It is evident from an inspection of the means listed in Table 4 that, except for the day dreaming scores, probably no significant differences existed among the farm, rural-nonfarm, and urban children. Nevertheless, analysis of variance ratios were determined for each of the five sets

Table 4. Means on the Rogers Test, Samples of Rural and Urban Fifth Grade Children, Iowa, Ohio, Kansas, and Wisconsin, 1954-1955

		PERSONAL INFERIORITY		SOCIAL MALADJUSTMENT		FAMILY RELATIONS		DAY DREAMING		TOTAL SCORE	
Residence	*Number*	*Mean*	*SD*	*Mean*	*SD*	*Mean*	*SD*	*Mean*	*SD*	*Mean*	*SD*
Farm	77	11.62	4.59	14.44	4.26	8.54	3.95	2.08	2.19	36.70	7.99
Rural-nonfarm	131	11.69	4.60	15.01	4.66	9.19	3.98	3.34	2.66	39.07	8.16
Urban	48	11.40	4.42	14.77	4.08	8.94	3.19	4.06	2.25	39.19	8.39

of means. For brevity, the analysis of variance tables have been omitted. The F ratio values were as follows: for personality inferiority, $F_{(2,253)} = .07$, $P > .05$; for social maladjustment, $F_{(2,253)} = .40$, $P > .05$; for family relations, $F_{(2,253)} = .68$, $P > .05$; for day dreaming, $F_{(2,253)} = 10.99$, $P < .01$; and total scores, $F_{(2,253)} = 2.31$, $P > .05$. Farm, rural-nonfarm, and urban children did not differ as groups in their responses to four of the five Rogers test scores. They did show significant mean differences in regard to the day dreaming scores. Since the day dreaming means were significantly different, t tests were calculated for the differences between the groups.

Higher score on the Rogers test is indicative of maladjustment for the characteristic being measured. Higher day dreaming scores signify responses that indicate an avoidance of reality by the child, such as wishing he were younger, or not wanting to grow up, desiring to be alone, or preferring make-believe friends and situations over real life people and things.

The farm children showed the least degree of day dreaming ($M = 2.08$), the rural-nonfarm children an intermediate degree ($M = 3.34$),

after analysis of variance indicated that state mean differences were nonsignificant. It should be noted that unweighted sample point data were employed in these analyses and that each state sample was assumed to be a simple random sample. Statistical studies of the data showed that unweighted data provided unbiased estimates and that it was reasonable to assume that each state sample could be treated as if it were a simple random sample. For details, see Burchinal, *op. cit.*, Appendix A, "Calculation of Weighted Statistics," and, Appendix B, "The Significance of the Differences among the Parents' and the Children's Mean Scores"; or see Burchinal, *et al.*, *op. cit.*

and the urban children the most active fantasy life ($M = 4.06$). The mean difference of 1.26 points between the farm and rural-nonfarm children was significant ($t = 3.52$, $P < .001$). The difference between the farm and urban children was also significant ($t = 4.86$, $P < .001$), but the rural-nonfarm and urban mean difference was not significant ($t = 1.67$, $.05 < P < .10$). A number of "ex post facto" explanations might be offered for the differences in fantasy involvement indicated by the several groups of children studied. It is possible that the farm children who live closer to the natural cycles of the seasons and of life and death, who have responsibilities and jobs about the farm, and who perhaps spend less of their play time in groups or gangs, would be expected to exhibit less fantasy involvement. Rural-nonfarm and urban children may have fewer jobs about their homes and spend more of their time in social play, in which case the child's natural use of fantasy might be abetted.

Except for the intriguing differences in the degrees of children's day dreaming involvement, the results of the analysis of Rogers adjustment scores made by farm, rural-nonfarm, and children from small cities again support the hypothesis of this study.

Discussion

Data derived from three original studies reported in this article provided opportunities for 23 comparisons of mean personality scores for rural and urban or farm, rural-nonfarm, and urban children. Only one of the tests failed to support the hypothesis that there were no significant differences in the levels of personality adjustment of children from these three strata. None of the other studies reported here is precisely a replication of the study reported by Mangus. His data were based on a larger number of children, 1229 divided into three strata by place of residence, while the data for the other three studies are based on smaller samples: 642 in Hamilton County, 129 in Marshalltown and Story County, and 256 children drawn from four states. Mangus compared farm and rural-nonfarm children with children from a city of approximately 17,000. The Hamilton County study permitted comparisons between rural children in very small schools and children from a city of 7,600. No differences were found between the Hamilton County rural and urban children, but Webster City, Iowa, is a much smaller city than the city cited by Mangus. Marshalltown, Iowa, with a 1950 population of approximately 20,000 corresponds more closely to the city included by Mangus in his study. The comparative rural group of children for the Marshalltown children, however, included both farm and rural-nonfarm children. The combination of the latter two groups might not be objectionable since Mangus found few differences between the farm and rural-nonfarm children in his study. Different editions of the California test were used in these two studies, but essentially the same measuring qualities were present in both forms. In this study, the rural-urban differences were nonsignificant, but there was a suggestion that given larger samples of rural children and urban children from larger cities, reliable differences favoring the urban children might be found. Finally, the four-state sample of children permitted testing for differences in personality adjustment scores for farm, rural-nonfarm, and small city children. The bulk of the data again suggested that measurable personality differences did not exist among these groups of children.

What order can be established for the results of these four studies?

First, it must be recognized that present paper and pencil personality tests are, at best, only gross indicators of the level of personality integration or mental health of children. It has been assumed, however, that the tests used in these studies are at least reasonably valid measures.

Second, as already indicated, the data for these four studies were drawn from different parts of the country and involved sampling of different strata of population. Studies of social class, regional, and ethnic differences among segments of the American population, have made sociologists reluctant to generalize their findings beyond the limits of the samples employed in their studies. What was found true for rural and urban differences in southwestern Ohio failed to appear in a study of an approximately similar age group of children taken ten years later from central Iowa. In fact, there was a suggestion of a reverse set of findings. Data from four midwestern states also failed to support the Ohio findings.

Some clarification of these varying results might be achieved if a brief personality theory note is interjected. Personality is a bio-social product, a more or less organized set of systems of attitudes and behavior patterns developed by the individual on the basis of his original endowments and the interaction of this maturing organism with his social environment. The rural-urban dichotomy has been used as a broad classification for describing what have been assumed to be different learning environments for children and youth. But as the levels of living, educational opportunities, sizes of families, and the impact of mass media continue to become equalized for rural and urban families, the rural-urban dichotomy should become less and less useful for assessing personality differences of children from these strata of our population. If this is true, then the following inferences should be upheld by empirical data:

1. No significant differences in measurable personality characteristics

should be expected between farm and rural-nonfarm children. The family and other social learning environments of these two groups of children should be fairly similar. The four studies discussed in this paper all support this inference.

2. Assuming a trend toward urbanization of small towns and rural areas, one should expect to find no significant differences in personality characteristics of farm and rural-nonfarm children and children from smaller cities. The Hamilton County and the four-state investigation support this supposition.

3. If any rural-urban differences in children's personality characteristics still exist, the differences should be expected to be found between rural children and children coming from larger urban areas. We might also expect to find differences between personality characteristics of children living in small towns and large cities if we assume the varying environments provide sufficiently different learning experiences or operate causally upon family child-rearing practices. Mangus' data support the position that rural children enjoy a relatively more favorable environment for healthy personality development than urban children. Data from the Marshalltown study, however, do not support this view. Adequate data could be obtained to answer this question only if properly controlled samples of children from rural areas, small towns, medium sized and larger cities were given one or several personality measures. However, in view of the lack of such data, one can only reiterate the caution expressed by Mangus in not generalizing findings beyond the samples upon which they were based. If the present trend of social change continues to flow outward from urban areas, the results of the Marshalltown study might be taken as indicative of the increasing similarity of rural and urban children and youth.

EUGENE LITWAK

Geographic Mobility and Extended Family Cohesion

THIS is the second of two companion papers, both of which seek to demonstrate that *modified* extended family relations are consistent with democratic industrial society.[1] These papers, then, attempt to modify Parsons' hypothesis that the isolated nuclear family is the only type which is functional for such a society.[2] Because Parsons so clearly relates his hypothesis to a more general theory of class and business organization there is considerable value in keeping his point of view in the forefront of discussion, for its modification under such circumstances provides rich intellectual dividends.

Parsons assumes only one kind of extended family relational pattern, the "classical" type exemplified in the Polish and Irish peasant families.[3] There is some evidence, however, for the existence of a modified[4] extended family that is theoretically more relevant and empirically more predictive than either of the two alternatives posed by Parsons' hypothesis—the isolated nuclear family and the classical extended family.[5]

Reprinted from American Sociological Review, *June, 1960, pp. 385-394, by permission of the author and the journal.*

The author wishes to express his thanks to Glenn H. Beyer, Director of the Cornell Housing Research Center for permitting use of the data in this study, and to Paul F. Lazarsfeld, Arthur R. Cohen, and Bernard Barber for their helpful comments, although they are not necessarily in agreement with the author's point of view.

1. The first paper is Eugene Litwak, "Occupational Mobility and Extended Family Cohesion," *American Sociological Review,* 25 (February, 1960), pp. 9-21.

2. Talcott Parsons, "The Social Structure of the Family," in Ruth N. Ashen, editor, *The Family: Its Function and Destiny,* New York: Harper, 1949, pp. 191-192.

3. These families were marked by geographical propinquity, occupational integration, strict authority of extended family over nuclear family, and stress on extended rather than nuclear family relations.

4. The modified extended family differs from past extended families in that it does not require geographical propinquity, occupational nepotism, or integration, and there are no strict authority relations, but equalitarian ones. Family relations differ from those of the isolated nuclear family in that significant aid is provided to nuclear families, although this aid has to do with standard of living (housing, illness, leisure pursuits) rather than occupational appointments or promotions.

5. The counter hypothesis advanced in this paper is a modification of Parsons' position in that it accepts his analysis that the classical extended family is disfunc-

The present inquiry supplements the earlier paper by demonstrating that modified extended family relations can be maintained despite differential geographical mobility. The first part of this paper examines the assumptions underlying Parsons' point of view as well as the modification suggested herein. In the second part empirical evidence is presented to show that extended family identification can be maintained despite geographical mobility.

Geographical Mobility and Extended Family Anomy

There are at least three arguments which support the view that extended family relations are not consistent with geographical mobility: (1) individuals who are strongly attached to their extended families will be reluctant to move even if better jobs are available elsewhere; (2) it is unlikely that identification with extended family will be retained where only one nuclear family moves while the rest of the extended family remains behind; and (3) it is financially more difficult to move a large family and locate jobs for many individuals simultaneously.

The first and third of these propositions suggest that individuals with extended family ties are unlikely to move. The second proposition suggests that if they do move individuals are unlikely to retain their extended family identification with those who remain behind. These arguments can be buttressed by the more general analysis of Homans, who points out that contact is one of the four major prerequisites for primary group cohesion.[6] Since these are familiar arguments they need not be elaborated.

Geographical Mobility and Extended Family Cohesion

In this analysis, major attention is given to propositions which are contrary to those stated above, namely, the following: (1) individuals who are part of a modified extended family grouping are in a better position to move because the latter legitimizes such moves, and as a consequence provides economic, social, and psychological support; (2) extended family relations can be maintained over great geographical distances because modern advances in communication techniques have minimized the socially disruptive effects of geographic distance; and

---

tional for contemporary society, but it rejects his view that the isolated nuclear family is the only theoretically meaningful alternative.

6. George C. Homans, *The Human Group*, New York: Harcourt, Brace, and World, 1950, p. 36.

(3) financial difficulties of moving extended families in a bureaucratic industrialized society are minimized because family coalescence takes place when the family is at its peak earning capacity and when it is least likely to disrupt the industrial organization.

1. *Modified extended families aid geographical mobility.* Implicit in the argument that extended family relations lead to a reluctance to move is the view that extended families cannot legitimize geographical mobility. If it can be demonstrated that in current society the contrary is the case, then it can also be shown that such families have far greater facilities than the isolated nuclear family for encouraging spatial movement.

Past instances of legitimation of such movement by the extended family help to clarify the point. In situations of economic or political catastrophe (the Irish potato famine or the Russian pogroms), the extended family encouraged mobility. Given this type of situation, the extended family had at least two advantages over the isolated nuclear family. First, its greater numbers permitted easier accumulation of capital to finance the trip of any given nuclear family. This led to a push and pull kind of migration, with the migrant sending money to help those who had remained behind. Secondly, because of its close ties and size the extended family had superior lines of communication. Thus the migrant became a communication outpost for those who remained behind, providing information on jobs, housing, local social customs, and language. Those who had migrated earlier also could aid the newcomer at the most difficult point of migration.[7]

In a mature industrial society there is great institutional pressure on the extended family to legitimate differential geographical mobility among its nuclear family members. This pressure derives from the fact that the extended family can never fully control the economic destiny of its nuclear sub-parts. Although the extended family provides important aid, the major source of economic support for the nuclear family must come from its own occupational success, which is based much more on merit than nepotism. As a consequence, if the extended family wants to see its member nuclear families become successful, it must accept one of the chief prerequisites to occupational success–geographical mobility.[8]

7. Of the large literature on this point, see e.g., Walter Firey, *Land Use in Central Boston,* Cambridge: Harvard University Press, 1947, pp. 184-186.

8. C. Wright Mills, C. Senior, and R. K. Goldsen in the *Puerto Rican Journey,* New York: Harper, 1950, p. 51, provide some indirect evidence on legitimation when they point out that the Puerto Rican migrant rarely moves out of a sense of economic necessity but because of a desire for economic betterment. They also show that these migrants rely on extended family communications before migrating (pp. 53-55). These facts illustrate that for the lowest income strata of migrants there has been a legitimation of geographical mobility for maximizing goals. This would

In other words, it is postulated that a semi-independent relation links the nuclear family to the extended family. Because the extended family cannot offer a complete guarantee of occupational success it legitimates the moves of nuclear family members. On the other hand, receiving as it does significant aid in achieving many of its goals, the nuclear family retains its extended family connections despite geographical distance.

2. *Extended family identification is retained despite breaks in face-to-face contact.* There are two reasons why extended families can provide important supplements to nuclear family goal achievement despite geographical distance and therefore two reasons why extended family identification can be maintained despite breaks in face-to-face contact.[9] As noted above, the rapid development of techniques of communication has made it relatively easy for family members to keep contact despite great distances. Nor does distance, in a money economy, prevent or seriously hinder such aids to family members as help in times of illness, emergency loans or gifts, home purchase, and the like—all at long range.

3. *Geographical coalescence takes place at peaks of earning power.* Although the extended family encourages mobility when it is occupationally rewarding, it does not do so when such moves no longer bring rewards. Given the character of large-scale organizations, there are regular occasions when geographical mobility is not linked to occupational rewards, for example, when the individual is at the peak of his career. The career in the large organization is one in which the individual moves up until he reaches a position from which he can no longer advance; here he remains until he retires. Careers of bureaucrats are rarely downward. Two aspects of this situation are particularly important in the present context: (1) once a person has advanced as far as he can occupationally his working efficiency is no longer tied to geographic moves; and (2) it is at this point that the nuclear family is in the best economic position to support moves of extended family. At this period of his life, the careerist can seek a position near his extended family if he can find a job which matches his present one. Or he can encourage retired parents to settle near him. In short, it is suggested that when the extended family does coalesce it does not lead to undue financial strain

seem to be doubly true of the middle-class migrant since he is economically better off to start with.

9. In addition to these assumptions, two more general ones should be made. First, it is assumed (in counter-distinction to W. F. Ogburn, for example, in "The Changing Functions of the Family," *Selected Studies in Marriage and the Family*, New York: Holt, Rinehart, Winston, 1953, pp. 74-75) that extended families have not lost their functions. See Litwak, *op. cit.* Secondly, it is assumed that extensive family activity does not lead to occupational nepotism *(ibid.)*; but Parsons' hypothesis states that extended family structures will collapse, or nepotism will destroy the industrial order.

(trying to locate jobs for many people simultaneously), nor is it likely to mean an irrational distribution of labor since it involves either retired people or job exchanges between people on the same occupational level.

Findings

In order to test alternative propositions about the relationship between family structure and geographical mobility, data from a survey of 920 white married women living in the Buffalo, New York, urban area were analyzed. The sample is biased in the direction of white, younger, middle-class, native-born individuals and as such is not representative of the total population.[10] However, the bias is a useful one since this is the very group which should most likely illustrate Parsons' hypothesis.[11] If it can be shown that his hypothesis does not hold for this group, then it is unlikely to hold for any division of the society.

1. *Mobility reduces extended family face-to-face contact.* The common basis for the opposing views—that geographical mobility is or is not antithetical to extended family relations—should be made explicit so that it is not mistaken for the main issue. Both positions are in agreement that geographical mobility generally reduces extended family face-to-face contact. Of the respondents in this study, 52 per cent with relatives living in the city received one or more family visits a week. In contrast, only four per cent of those with no such nearby relatives received visits this frequently.

2. *Breaks in face-to-face contact do not reduce extended family identification.* Central to the argument advanced in this paper is the view that geographical distance between relatives does not necessarily lead to a loss of extended family identification. In order to measure family orientation, all individuals were asked to respond to the following state-

10. The field study was conducted in the Buffalo area between June and October, 1952. For details of the study and the sampling, see Glenn H. Beyer, Thomas W. Mackesey, and James E. Montgomery, *Houses Are for People: A Study of Home Buyer Motivations*, Ithaca: Cornell University Housing Research Center, 1955. Some special features of the sample should be noted here. The sample cannot be considered to be a random one. Being a study designed to investigate housing, five or six different sampling procedures based on neighborhood and housing design were used. The varied nature of the sample complicates the problem of the appropriate statistical test. Therefore the argument must rest heavily on its theoretical plausibility and its consistency with other relevant studies. However, if the assumptions of a random area sample are made, and the sign and Wilcoxon signed-ranks tests are used, then all major findings are significant at the .05 level and beyond. The signs for these tests were always taken from the most complex table in which the given variables appeared.

11. Parsons, *op. cit.*, pp. 180-181.

ments: (1) "Generally I like the whole family to spend evenings together." (2) "I want a house where family members can spend time together." (3) "I want a location which would make it easy for relatives to get together." (4) "I want a house with enough room for our parents to feel free to move in." These items formed a Guttman scale pattern.[12] Individuals who answered items 3 or 4 positively[13] were considered to be oriented toward the extended family. Those who answered items 1 or 2, but not 3 or 4, positively were considered to be nuclear family oriented. Those who answered none[14] of the questions positively were classified as non-family oriented.

In order to measure the effects of distance between relatives on family identification, all respondents were divided into two categories, those who had relatives living in town and those who did not. The data presented in Table 1 indicate that geographical distance does not mean a loss of identity. Those who are geographically distant from their relatives are as likely as those who live nearby to retain their extended family identification (22 and 20 per cent, respectively).

Table 1 very likely underestimates the relationship between mobility and extended family identification, since there may have been many individuals who either moved to the community because their relatives

Table 1. Geographical Distance Does Not Lead to a Loss of Extended Family Identification

	Percentage Extended Family Oriented	Percentage Nuclear Family Oriented	Percentage Non-Family Oriented	Total
Relatives living in town	20	52	28	100 (648)*
Relatives living out of town	22	58	20	100 (272)

*In this and the following tables the figures in parentheses indicate the population base for a given percentage. For tests of significance in these tables, see Footnote 10.

---

12. Although these items were dichotomized to form a Guttman scale pattern, it is not argued that they meet all of the requirements for such a scale. See Eugene Litwak, *Primary Group Instruments of Social Control in Industrial Society: The Extended Family and the Neighborhood*, unpublished Ph.D. thesis, Columbia University, 1958, pp. 43-47.

13. The fact that only four per cent of the population answered item 4 positively means that item 3 defines extended family orientation for most of the population. In this connection, no assumption is made that this operational definition exhausts the meaning of extended family orientation; it is only assumed that it will correlate highly with any other measures of extended family orientation.

14. Because some people may have interpreted "family" to mean only extended family it is possible that in this non-family oriented group there are some people who are nuclear family oriented. This plus the fact that the items were dichotomized to maximize their scaling properties suggests that little reliance should be placed on the absolute percentage of people exhibiting each value position but only on their differential distribution in various groups.

lived there or encouraged relatives to come later. In such cases family identification would have been maintained initially despite geographical distance. To deal with this question, all respondents again were divided, this time between those who spent their first 20 years in the city under study and those who were raised elsewhere. If the latter are considered to be migrants, it can be seen from Table 2 that the migrants (23 per cent) are more likely than the non-migrants (18 per cent) to be identified with their extended families.

Table 2. Migrants Are Not Less Extended Family Identified than Non-Migrants

	Percentage Extended Family Oriented	Percentage Nuclear Family Oriented	Percentage Non-Family Oriented	Total
Spent major part of first 20 years in city	18	51	31	100 (504)
Spent major part of first 20 years out of the city	23	56	21	100 (416)

3. *Close identification with extended family does not prevent nuclear families from moving away.* Are people who are close to their extended families likely to leave them in order to advance themselves occupationally? To measure the likelihood of persons moving from the community for occupational reasons, the respondents were asked the following question: "Is there a good chance that your husband might take a job out of town?" Those who answered "yes" were classified as potential migrants. To test the likelihood of leaving their relatives, only respondents with relatives in town were examined. It can be seen from Table 3 that those individuals more closely identified with the extended family also were more likely to leave the city and presumably their nearby relatives (23 and 14 per cent, respectively). The same point can be made for the general population if the figures from Tables 1 and 2 are calculated to show how likely family oriented persons are to be migrants. Table 4

Table 3. Strong Identification with Relatives Does Not Prevent People from Taking Jobs Elsewhere

	Among Those with Relatives in the City the Percentage Saying Good Chance Husband Will Take Job Out of Town
Extended family orientation	23 (128)
Nuclear family orientation	18 (336)
Non-family orientation	14 (184)

Table 4. People Identified with Extended Family Are as Likely or More Likely to Be Migrants than Others

	Percentage Raised Out of Town	Percentage Having No Relatives in the City
Extended family oriented	51 (187)	32 (187)
Nuclear family oriented	47 (493)	31 (493)
Non-family oriented	37 (240)	23(240)

presents results which are consistent with Table 3. People are likely to move, then, even when they are strongly identified with their families, and once having moved away from them, they are likely to retain their family identity.

4. *Bureaucratic career and extended family mobility.* The analysis is thus far consistent with the view that in modern bureaucratic society extended family relations can retain their viability despite differential rates of geographic mobility. To be fully consistent, however, it should be shown that extended family movement is related to career development in the way anticipated by the foregoing discussion. For it was pointed out that it is only when the individual is on the upswing of his career that mobility will be encouraged, while it will be discouraged when he reaches the peak.

In order to measure career stages individuals were asked: "Within the next ten years, do you expect the head of the household will be making: a. a great deal more than now; b. somewhat more than now; c. same as now; d. other, e.g., retired, don't know, etc." Those who said that they expected to earn "a great deal more" income were assumed to be on the upswing of their careers, those who named "somewhat more" were assumed to be fast approaching the peak, while all others were assumed to have reached the peak or plateau of their careers.[15] Table 5 confirms

Table 5. Those on the Upswing of Their Career Are Likely to Be Migrants

	Within the Next Ten Years	Percentage without Relatives Living in the City
Upswing of career	Expect to make a great deal more than now	39 (183)
Medium point	Expect to make somewhat more than now	29 (603)
Peak of career or plateau	Expect to make the same or somewhat less than now	16 (134)

15. Since 95 per cent of the sample subjects were 45 or younger, and since the study was conducted during a period of great prosperity, virtually no one said he expected to earn less than now.

the view that bureaucratic development is congenial to family movement when people are upwardly mobile: 39 per cent of those on the upswing were migrants, while only 16 per cent of those who had reached their career plateaus were migrants.

Two additional bits of evidence supplement this point. First, if the hypothesis advanced in this paper is correct, the individuals who are both extended family oriented and rising in their careers should be most mobile because they have the advantage of aid from their extended families. Comparatively speaking, extended family identity should not lead to mobility when individuals have reached the career plateau. Table 6 suggests that this is the case. When individuals are moving ahead occupationally, those who are psychologically close to their families are much more mobile than those who dissociate themselves from their families (47 and 22 per cent, respectively, are mobile). In contrast, among people at the career peak, the extended family oriented are no more mobile than the non-family oriented (12 and 11 per cent, respectively).

Table 6. Extended Family Identification Is Likely to Encourage Geographical Mobility When Individuals Are on the Upswing of Their Careers

		PERCENTAGE HAVING NO RELATIVES IN THE CITY		
	Within the Next Ten Years	*Extended Family Oriented*	*Nuclear Family Oriented*	*Non-Family Oriented*
Upswing of career	Expect to make a great deal more than now	47 (49)*	40 (107)	22 (27)
Medium point of career	Expect to make somewhat more than now	30 (112)	31 (322)	27 (169)
Peak or plateau of career	Expect to make the same or less than now	12 (26)	22 (63)	11 (45)

*This cell reads as follows: 47 per cent of the 49 people who are extended family oriented and who expect to make a great deal more in the future have no relatives in the city.

The second bit of evidence which supports the view that extended family aid encourages mobility on the upswing of the career and discourages it otherwise involves the direction of the move. Individuals who have reached the career plateau *might possibly* still move if such moves meant bringing them closer to their extended family. To investigate this possibility, respondents were asked: "Compared to your last house is your present house closer, the same, or farther away from your family?" Table 7 shows that where individuals are climbing the ladder they are as likely, if not more likely, to move away from their relatives when they are identified with their extended families as when they are not (53 per cent as compared to 37 and 48 per cent). However, where individuals have reached the occupational plateau, those who are identified

Table 7. Extended Family Identification Is Likely to Encourage Moves* Away from the Extended Family When People Are on the Upswing of Their Careers

	PERCENTAGE WHOSE LAST MOVE CARRIED THEM FARTHER FROM THEIR FAMILIES		
	Extended Family Oriented	Nuclear Family Oriented	Non-Family Oriented
Expect to make a great deal more in 10 years	53 (49)†	37 (67)	48 (27)
Expect to make somewhat more	52 (112)	56 (322)	59 (169)
Expect to make the same or less	38 (26)	62 (63)	53 (45)

*Those with relatives in the city were classified together with those without relatives, since the same statistical pattern occurred in each case.

†This figure reads 53 per cent of 49 people who were extended family oriented and who expected to earn a great deal more in the next ten years moved farther away from their families.

with their extended families are less likely to move away from them (38 per cent as compared to 62 and 53 per cent).

In short, the evidence presented here indicates that the career strongly influences the extent and the direction of geographical mobility in a manner consistent with the view that extended family relations are viable in contemporary bureaucratic society.

5. *Bureaucratic and non-bureaucratic careers.* This index of career, however, does not necessarily imply a *bureaucratic* career. Earlier discussions often assume that careers take place in a bureaucratic context. Therefore, the findings of this study should be further differentiated in terms of bureaucratic and non-bureaucratic occupations. In order to isolate the non-bureaucratic career, working-class persons whose fathers were also from a working-class occupational group were segregated from the rest of the population. Non-manual middle-class and upper-class individuals are more likely to follow bureaucratic careers, involving standard promotional steps associated with geographical mobility.[16]

---

16. On the basis of the U.S. Census's occupational categories, the husband and the husband's father were classified into: (1) professional, technical, and kindred, and managers, officials, and proprietors; (2) clerical and kindred workers, and sales workers; or (3) all others except farmers or farm help. Husbands' and husbands' fathers' occupations were cross classified to provide four occupational categories: (1) upper-class husbands whose parents were upper-class; (2) husbands whose parents were from a higher occupational group; (3) husbands whose parents were from a lower occupational group; (4) working-class husbands whose parents were working-class. Two groups were eliminated: all individuals of farm background; and middle-class individuals of middle-class parentage (excluded because of the small number of cases). The stationary upper-class group is considered to approximate most closely the bureaucratic occupations while the stationary manual groups are assumed to be the polar opposite. Here "upper-class" does not refer to an old-line "aristocracy" but to a professional-managerial occupational grouping. By definition, all people in administrative positions in large-scale organizations and professionals are included in the upper-class or upwardly mobile occupational groups. There remains the question of whether or not they constitute a sufficiently

In contrast, these features do not necessarily mark occupational advancement among manual workers. In this group occupational success may mean the achievement of plant seniority or the opening of a small business.[17] In such cases success is negatively related to future geographic mobility. As a consequence, a manual worker who envisions an upswing in his career may encourage family members to settle nearby because future success is closely linked to present location. Thus, it is expected that occupational advance has far different meanings for members of the working class and for the middle- and upper-class persons.

In Table 8 it can be seen that the only instances of upswings in

Table 8. Only Among Upper- and Middle-Class Bureaucratic Occupations Do Career Lines Play a Role

		PERCENTAGE HAVING NO RELATIVES IN THE CITY			
	Within the Next Ten Years	*Stationary Upper-Class**	*Upwardly Mobile*	*Downwardly Mobile*	*Stationary Manual Workers*
Upswing of career	Expect to make a great deal more than now	43 (76)†	39 (72)	40 (25)	10 (10)
Medium point of career	Expect to make somewhat more than now	42 (146)	39 (183)	26 (99)	11 (176)
Peak or plateau of career	Expect to make the same or less than now	23 (26)	13 (32)	28 (18)	12 (58)

*For a definition of occupational classification, see footnote 16.

†This cell should read as follows: 43 per cent of the 76 people who were stationary upper-class and who had high expectations of future economic improvement had no relatives in the city.

careers leading to geographic mobility occur among members of the upper class (43 per cent of those who are on the upswing have no relatives in the community compared to 23 per cent of those who have achieved a plateau). For members of the stationary working class, occupational advancement is least likely, comparatively speaking, to result in geographical mobility (10 per cent of those on the upswing and 12 per cent of those on the plateau have relatives in the city).

Table 8 more than any other should indicate the limitations of the present hypothesis. The latter cannot claim to explain any major fea-

large number within the overall classification to give a distinct direction. Gold and Slater in a study based upon a random sample of the Detroit area point out that in the one category roughly similar in age and occupation to the "upper-class" in this investigation, 74 per cent of the individuals were members of a bureaucratic organization. Martin Gold and Carol Slater, "Office, Factory, Store—and Family: A Study of Integration Setting," *American Sociological Review*, 23 (February, 1958), pp. 66, 69.

17. See, e.g., Seymour Martin Lipset and Reinhard Bendix, "Social Mobility and Occupational Career Patterns," in Bendix and Lipset, editors, *Class, Status and Power*, New York: Free Press, 1953, pp. 457-459.

tures of current American society but only the behavior of members of that group which is often thought to be prototypical of future American society—those belonging to bureaucratic occupations. It is assumed here that future societies will in fact become increasingly bureaucratized. Since Parsons' analysis is largely concerned with this same group,[18] it is maintained that this study provides evidence contrary to his hypothesis.

6. *The extended family and emotional, social, and economic aid.* Extended families have a unique function in providing aid to those who are moving. This is based partly on the fact that family membership is defined in terms of blood ties and therefore is least pervious to changes in social contact, and partly on the fact that the individual receives his earliest and crucial socialization with people who eventually become extended family members. The individual might find voluntary associations of lesser help than family aid because new personal contacts must be established when one moves, and old contacts tend to have no continuing meaning when geographical contact is broken. Aid from neighbors has somewhat the same character. This point emerges clearly when newcomers to a neighborhood are compared with long-term residents in terms of the average amount of social participation in various areas of life. Table 9 shows that family contacts are as likely, if not more likely, to occur among newcomers than among long-term residents. In contrast, neighborhood and club affiliations are likely to increase the

Table 9. The Extended Family Meets the Needs of Recent Movers*

	Percentage Receiving Frequent Family Visits†	Percentage Belonging to More Than One Club‡	Percentage Knowing Five or More Neighbors§	Total Population
		RESPONDENTS HAVING NO RELATIVES IN THE CITY		
Newcomers	22	25	38	110
Long-term residents	16	51	63	166
Difference	08	−26	−25	
		RESPONDENTS HAVING RELATIVES IN THE CITY		
Newcomers	54	44	41	163
Long-term residents	49	43	60	485
Difference	05	01	−19	

*The respondents were divided between the newcomers or those people who had lived in their houses nine months or less and the long-term residents or all others.

†When no relatives in the city a frequent visit is defined as one or more family visits a month—either invited or non-invited. When relatives live in the city a frequent visit is defined as one or more family visits a week.

‡This is the closest approximation to the average number of clubs to which the population belonged.

§This is the closest approximation to the average number of neighbors the respondents knew well enough to call on.

18. Parsons, *op. cit.*, pp. 180-181.

longer individuals live in the neighborhood.[19] This suggests the unique function of the extended family during the moving crisis.

Secondary Evidence

The evidence presented above consistently documents the position that extended family relations are not antithetical to geographical mobility in bureaucratic industralized society. In fact, at times such relationships actually encourage mobility. The limits of the sample, however, place severe restrictions on the general application of these data. It is of some importance, therefore, to seek in other researches supportive evidence for extended family viability.

First, as a necessary but not sufficient condition, it should be shown that extended family relations are fairly extensive in American society today. In recent years, four studies that provide data on extended family visiting have been carried out, respectively, in Los Angeles, Detroit, San Francisco, and Buffalo. Three of these indicate that close to 50 per cent of the residents made one or more such visits a week. And three of the four investigations, on the basis of comparisons of family, neighbors, friends, and voluntary associations, conclude that the family relationships were either the most frequent or the most vital. These findings, as limited as they are, strongly suggest that extended family relations are extensive.[20]

What is of even greater interest is that these studies indicate that middle-class white persons share this viability with others and that these relations are highly important ones. Thus Sussman, in a study of middle-class white Protestant families, shows that 80 per cent of the family relationships studied involved giving aid, and in 70 per cent of the cases respondents felt that the recipients would suffer loss of status if the aid were not continued. Morever, this aid had much more to do with standard of living than with locating jobs or helping people to advance in them through nepotism.[21] This investigation was supplemented by a

19. The striking differences between respondents with relatives living in the city and those without nearby relatives, shown in Table 9, are discussed in an unpublished paper, Eugene Litwak, "Voluntary Associations and Primary Group Development in Industrial Society."

20. Morris Alexrod, "Urban Structure and Social Participation," *American Sociological Review*, 21 (February, 1956), pp. 13-18; Wendell Bell and Marion D. Boat, "Urban Neighborhoods and Informal Social Relations," *American Journal of Sociology*, 62 (January, 1957), pp. 391-398; Scott Greer, "Urbanism Reconsidered," *American Sociological Review*, 21 (February, 1956), p. 22; Litwak, *Primary Group Instruments . . . , op. cit.*, p. 82.

21. Marvin B. Sussman, "The Help Pattern in Middle Class Family," *American Sociological Review*, 18 (February, 1953), pp. 22-28 *passim.*

study by Bell and Boat which indicates that 76 per cent of the low income and 84 per cent of the high income subjects could count on extended family aid in cases of illness lasting a month or longer; they also report that 90 per cent of the respondents indicated that at least one member of the extended family was a close friend.[22] Studies on working class families,[23] Puerto Rican families,[24] Negro families,[25] and Italian families[26] indicate that extended family relations in these cases are viable and warm.

Although these relations are of a far different character from the middle-class family contacts discussed in this paper,[27] the studies of working-class and ethnic groups do provide insight into the extension and warmth of extended family relations in all strata of contemporary society. They do not by themselves refute Parsons' formulation because he assumes that extended family relations are declining, not that they have disappeared. However, they buttress the alternative hypothesis advanced here since they do suggest a basic prerequisite of that hypothesis, namely, that extended family relations are viable in contemporary urban society.

Conclusions

It is argued, then, that these relations can retain their social significance under industrial bureaucratic pressures for geographical mobility. Evidence has been presented that is inconsistent with Parsons' hypothesis. Two theoretical points support this contrary view: first, that the extended family relationship which does not demand geographical propinquity (not examined by Parsons) is a significant form of social behavior; second, that theoretically the most efficient organization combines the ability of large-scale bureaucracy to handle uniform situations with the primary group's ability to deal with idiosyncratic situations. These two theoretical points suggest that there is both a need and a capacity for extended families to exist in modern society.

The data presented here (and in the earlier companion paper) dem-

22. Bell and Boat, *op. cit.*, p. 396.

23. Michael Young and Peter Willmott, *Family and Kinship in East London*, London: Routledge and Kegan Paul, 1957, pp. 159-166.

24. Mills, Senior, and Goldsen, *op. cit.*, pp. 115, 117.

25. E. Franklin Frazier, "The Impact of Urban Civilization upon Negro Family Life," P. K. Hatt and A. J. Reiss, Jr., editors, *Cities and Societies: The Revised Reader in Urban Sociology*, New York: Free Press, 1957, pp. 495-496.

26. Firey, *op. cit.*, pp. 184-186.

27. Cf. Litwak, "Occupational Mobility and Extended Family Cohesion," *op. cit.*

onstrate that persons separated from their families retained their extended family orientation; those with close family identification were as likely, if not more likely, to leave their family for occupational reasons; those on the upswing of their careers were apt to move away from their families and to receive family support; those on the career plateau were not likely to move or to move toward their family; that considerations of this kind hold only for bureaucratic occupations; and that the modified extended family seems to be uniquely suited to provide succor during periods of movement. These findings suggest interesting questions for future research. With respect to the family system, there is a need to isolate the mechanisms by which the nuclear family retains its semi-independence while receiving aid from the extended family.[28] It is also important to specify in greater detail the limits of the modified extended family organization in terms of time (does it extend over two or three generations?) and social distance (is it limited, for example, to parents and married children or siblings?). Concerning the occupational system, it is important to identify the type of bureaucratic structure which permits the family to be linked with occupations without affecting productivity.[29] For the analysis of class structure, the question arises as to how likely it is that extended family relations become significant factors blurring class identification without reducing occupational mobility.

28. Cf. Eugene Litwak, "The Use of Extended Family Groups in the Achievement of Social Goals: Some Policy Implications," *Social Problems*.

29. Cf. Litwak, "Occupational Mobility and Extended Family Cohesion," *op. cit.;* and *Primary Group Instruments . . .* , *op. cit.*, pp. 6-30.

ALEX INKELES

Industrial Man: The Relation of Status to Experience, Perception, and Value

EVER larger segments of the world's population are living and will come to live in what is now commonly called "industrial society." The standard complex of institutions—most notably the factory—associated with this system daily becomes more widely diffused into a variety of traditional and even "primitive" cultural contexts. These institutions rather rigorously prescribe a set of norms, with regard to such matters as dress, time, order, and authority, which must be conformed to, at least during the time that individuals are engaged in their industrial and related occupations. This aspect of the diffusion of the industrial order is easily recognized.

It is less evident that the distinctive roles of the industrial system also foster typical patterns of perception, opinions, beliefs, and values which are not institutionally prescribed but arise spontaneously as new sub-

Reprinted from "Industrial Man: The Relation of Status to Experience, Perception, and Value," by Alex Inkeles, The American Journal of Sociology, *July, 1960, pp. 1-31, by permission of The University of Chicago Press. Copyright 1960 by the University of Chicago.*

This a revised and somewhat abridged version of a report prepared for the Conference on Political Modernization which met in June, 1959, under the auspices of the Committee on Comparative Politics of the Social Science Research Council. I am particularly indebted to the Committee's chairman, Professor Gabriel Almond, for support and encouragement. The data were assembled with the aid of a grant from the Ford Foundation, supplemented by the Russian Research Center at Harvard. Dr. Elmo C. Wilson generously made available special tabulations from studies undertaken by International Research Associates, Inc. Jay Greenfield rendered creative research assistance.—THE AUTHOR

cultures in response to the institutional conditions provided by the typically differentiated role-structure of modern industrial society. This paper reports an exploratory comparative study of the influence of these standard environments on attitudes, which yielded considerable evidence that the process is effective and pervasive.

In this investigation I take the institutioinal pattern or setting as given and the repsonses to it, particularly those not explicitly required by the institutional forms, as the dependent variable. The individual and groups of individuals, not institutions, are the central concern, and we study variation not in formal institutional arrangements but in individual and collective social perception and action. Only one institutional complex is considered here, namely, that which characterizes the modern large-scale, bureaucratic industrial system. What is not given, namely the response to it, will be sought in a number of different realms but in each case will be measured through reported experiences and expressed attitudes and values.

The underlying theory is very simple. It is assumed that people have experiences, develop attitudes, and form values in response to the forces or pressures which their environment creates. By "environment" we mean, particularly, networks of interpersonal relations and the patterns of reward and punishment one normally experiences in them. They include not only access to facilities and items of consumption, necessary and conspicuous, but also such intangibles as prestige, the comforts of security, respectful treatment, calculability in the actions of significant others, and so on. The theory holds that, within broad limits, the same situational pressures, the same framework for living, will be experienced as similar and will generate the same or similar response by people from different countries. This is, of course, not a denial of individual variation, of personality as a determinant of perception, cognition, or affect. Neither is it meant to deny the effect of traditional cultural ways on behavior. These will mute the independent effect of the industrial institutional environment, but it is assumed that they cannot eliminate it. Rather, its force is sufficiently great to assert itself clearly despite the countervailing influence of personal idiosyncrasy and traditional cultural ways of thinking and feeling. Insofar as industrialization, urbanization, and the development of large-scale bureaucratic structures and their usual accompaniments create a standard environment with standard institutional pressures for particular groups, to that degree should they produce relatively standard patterns of experience, attitude, and value—standard, not uniform, pressures. The situation of worker and manager may be relatively standard in the factory, wherever it is located, but relative to each other these positions are by no means uniform.

The test of the assumption is very simple. It is made by comparing the perceptions, attitudes, and values of those in comparable positions in the typical hierarchies of modern society, in particular the occupational, educational, and socioeconomic. If the "foreign" (read: "industrial"), externally introduced institutional environment plays no role, there should be no pattern or similarity in the response of incumbents of a given type of position from country to country. If there is such a pattern—if, for example, workers are everywhere less "happy" or "optimistic," or more insistent on obedience in children, than are engineers—this can come only from the similarity of their situation in the hierarchical setting of occupation, income, or education, since on the basis of their nationality or culture alone they should obviously differ.

To discern this influence of the industrial environment is, of course, not the same as determining either its extent or its intensity. The pressure generated by the institutional setting of industrialism may affect only a narrow range of experience and attitude—possibly only that relating to work experience. It may exert only a moderate influence, producing only a small part of the variance, the main part being accounted for by other factors, such as traditional cultural orientations. These are important problems for further elucidation. For now, we restrict ourselves to a statement of the main proposition—*that men's environment, as expressed in the institutional patterns they adopt or have introduced to them, shapes their experience, and through this their perceptions, attitudes and values, in standardized ways which are manifest from country to country, despite the countervailing randomizing influence of traditional cultural patterns.* I trust it will be understood without great elaboration that this proposition is stated so unequivocally only to facilitate clear exposition. The hypothesis is tentative, a guide to the exploration which this paper reports and not a dictum or an empirically established fact. We are equally interested in proof and disproof and must expect to find both supporting, negating, and ambiguous evidence.

I can hardly claim novelty for the proposition. The idea that the institutions in which men live shape their character and their views is old indeed. So is the more refined notion that a man's distinctive standing and role within the social structure will influence not only his perspective on the world but his wishes, beliefs, and values as well. Probably very few will argue that any people can indefinitely, or even for very long, utilize the material and institutional forms of industrial society without also absorbing some of its culture. At the same time, very few will argue that the industrial system is indeed so standardized or its influence so compelling as to permit no variation in the culture of those who share it. The obvious task of serious investigation, therefore, is to determine with some degree of precision where and how far the institutions of industrial society impose or foster the development of new subcultures wherever they are introduced and in what realms of life and to what degree traditional patterns maintain a relative independence of or immunity to the influence of the industrial institutional system.

There are two main avenues open to us. The first would be to designate certain attitudes or values as indexes of the industrial "subculture" and then to test the degree of association between these indexes and the level of industrialization in various countries. This is essentally the path taken by Davis and Lipset in their comparative studies. Both used the percentage of males engaged in non-agricultural pursuits, and the per capita consumption of energy, as indexes of industrialization. For his dependent variable, Davis studied the degree of urbanization; Lipset, the extent and stability of democratic political processes.[1] If we were to follow this path, our dependent variable would be the proportion of the population in each country holding a certain belief or sharing a particular value presumed to be fostered by the industrial milieu—for example, the belief that most human problems can ultimately be solved by technological advances.

There are several reasons for not adopting this procedure. Indexes of industrialization tend to generalize to the population, as a whole, characteristics which may in fact be intensely developed in only one segment. An outstanding example would be the Soviet Union, which is highly and intensely industrialized, but in which about half the population is engaged in agriculture. In such cases a nationwide index of the industrial subculture might be low, not because the industrialized segment of the population failed to show the expected characteristic, but because so large a part of the population was not integrated into the industrial structure. Our theory applies only to those segments of the population whose life conditions are standardized through industrial or other large-scale bureaucratic organizations.

Another reason for not adopting this method is that the average level of response for a nation may so heavily reflect traditional cultural orientations, or recent events, as to mask the independent influence of the industrial environment. To control this would require matching countries sharing the same traditional culture but varying in degree of industrialization. On the face of it, many would deny the possibility of meaningfully accomplishing this, even if the pool of countries available for matching were much larger than it is.

The most compelling reason for not relying on a single national

1. Kingsley Davis and Hilda H. Golden, "Urbanization and the Development of Pre-Industrial Areas," in Paul K. Hatt and Albert J. Reiss, Jr. (eds.), *Cities and Society* (rev. ed.; New York: Free Press, 1957), pp. 120-140; Seymour M. Lipset, "Some Social Requisites of Democracy: Economic Development and Political Legitimacy," *American Political Science Review,* LIII (March, 1959), 69-105.

average as an index of the industrial subculture, however, lies in the nature of the theory being tested. The idea that the industrial institutional order carries with it a distinctive industrial culture does not necessarily mean that the culture is the same for all who live in industrial society. This commonly made assumption can be quite misleading. We should, rather, expect that, in accord with the differences among positions in the modern occupational hierarchy, the different occupational groups will have differentiated attitudes and values. What is likely to be common to industrial societies, therefore, is not a single idea or a set of commonly held ideas but a particular *structure* of experience, attitude, and value which takes its form from the occupational structure.

Our expectation, that the distinctive feature of the industrial culture is a structure of response characteristic of the occupational hierarchy as a whole, also accounts for our not adopting the simple alternative of studying just one distinctive group, such as factory workers. From country to country the proportion of factory workers giving a particular answer might be quite different, yet in each country the workers might stand in a fixed relation to the other strata. This regularity would not be evident at all if we studied only one typical occupational group in different societies. We therefore take as our unit of analysis not a national average or a score for a particular group but the structure of response in some status hierarchy representing the entire nation or, at least, its industrialized segment.

We will speak of the existence of a structure of response when the proportion in each stratum (occupation, prestige, income, or educational group) reporting certain experiences or holding particular views rises or falls more or less regularly as we ascend or descend the hierarchy. We will speak of a cross-national *pattern,* with which we are most concerned, when the structure of response is more or less the same as we move from country to country—that is, when the direction and, to some degree, the magnitude of the changes in proportion are similar in different national populations.

We assume that the industrial order fixes the situation of different groups relative to each other in a more or less invariant fashion. We also assume that occupational groups, as units, respond distinctively to their occupational environment and the world outside it according to their situation and the characteristic pressures it generates. Insofar as these assumptions are correct, we should expect to find a cross-national pattern of response on many issues directly and indirectly related to the typical pattern of experience in the roles common in industrial society. The similarity in the structure of response as we move from country to country may exist, even though the average response varies widely from one nation to another. The typical response of any population may be strongly shaped by its traditional culture, and that of any particular group in some country may be influenced by a unique local situation. But, by focusing on the occupational hierarchy as a whole, country by country, we at once control both the effect of traditional culture at the national level and the special circumstances affecting one or another occupational group at the "local" level.

To test these assumptions, we should, ideally, have data gathered for this specific purpose. Our samples should come from a variety of countries selected to represent diverse cultural traditions, and the sample from each country should be restricted to those holding strictly comparable positions in each respective society's industrial sector. The questionnaires would be carefully translated to insure comparability of meaning. But what is actually available is very far from meeting the optimum requirements. I have had to rely on already completed studies drawn from a file of the reports of various national survey agencies,[2] the one major international compilation edited by Hadley Cantril,[3] the few, more systematic, comparative studies such as those undertaken by UNESCO[4] and International Research Associates, Inc. (INRA),[5] and sundry other scattered sources. None of these studies was designed for the purpose for which we wish to use them. The selection of countries is highly variable. The sample subgroups are frequently not equivalent from country to country, and it has been necessary to use other criteria of stratification than occupational status, which is most relevant to our theory. The questions used in different countries are often only very approximate equivalents. Under the circumstances, failure to find the expected patterns would be somewhat inconclusive as a test of our hypothesis. On the other hand, the presence of so many potentially randomizing influences in the data means that the emergence of the expected pattern, even if weakly manifested, may be taken as highly suggestive of the probable predictive power of the theory.

2. Particularly useful were the Italian agency *Doxa Bolletino* published in Milan (hereinafter cited as "*Doxa*"), the releases of the Netherlands Institute of Public Opinion in Amsterdam (hereinafter cited as "NIPO"), and the bulletins of the Australian Gallup Polls of Melbourne (hereinafter cited as "AGP").

3. Hadley W. Cantril (ed.), *Public Opinion, 1935-1946* (Princeton, N.J.: Princeton University Press, 1951).

4. William Buchanan and Hadley Cantril, *How Nations See Each Other* (Urbana: University of Illinois Press, 1953).

5. During 1958 they undertook a substantial number of comparative surveys, released through the *New York Herald Tribune.* Additional tabulations were made available through the courtesy and cooperation of Dr. Elmo Wilson. Although the Gallup affiliates in various countries often ask the same question at more or less the same time, detailed consolidated results suitable for comparative study are generally not available. Some reconstruction is possible from the bulletins released by the individual affiliates.

The Realm of Work

If our theory holds at all, it should be most effective in ordering information in the realm in which it has most direct and immediate applicability, namely, within the industrial enterprise. Wherever the factory or the large-scale organization exists, there will be a clearly stratified hierarchy of authority and of technical competence. A hierarchy of income, prestige, and other rewards will also be found following the main lines of the hierarchy of authority and technical competence. There is, naturally, a great deal of variation, but the general pattern is seldom departed from in fundamentals.

Our problem, then, is this: In what ways and to what extent does this objective hierarchy, this standardization of external conditions of work and pay, shape the attitudes and feelings of the incumbents of the commonly differentiated positions? We may begin with the simplest and perhaps most obvious of examples—that relating to job satisfaction, or the sense of pleasure or gratification a man finds in his work. Since those in certain positions, such as managers and engineers, are almost always better paid, given more security, granted more respect, and perhaps also allowed more freedom and autonomy, we may reasonably expect that they will more often express satisfaction.

As Table 1 reveals, this expectation is indeed borne out. We have in hand fairly good data on job satisfaction in six countries, covering a fair range of situations. There is a definite and unmistakable structure in the responses manifested from country to country. Those standing at the top are, as a rule, more satisfied than those in the lower positions. Indeed, in every country the proportion who report job satisfaction decreases quite regularly as we descend the steps of the standard occupational hierarchy. Even the departures from the strict step pattern appear to be the same, at least in those countries where the data permit a comparison. Thus, in each of the three countries for which we have the more refined data (United States, U.S.S.R., Germany), the skilled manual workers are slightly more often found among the satisfied than are the rank-and-file white-collar workers. This presumably reflects the fact that, generally, the pay and often the prestige accorded the skilled worker exceeds that of ordinary white-collar personnel.

There are, of course, some other departures from the standard pattern which could not be so easily explained. Note, for example, that in Germany the group with the smallest proportion satisfied are the unskilled workers, whereas the farm laborers are twice as often satisfied men. The latter are disgruntled only as often as the semiskilled workers. By contrast, in the Soviet group the situation is reversed. The man least often satisfied is the peasant.

Table 1. National Comparisons of Job Satisfaction, by Occupation (Percentage Satisfied*)

U.S.S.R.		*U.S.*		*Germany*		*Italy*		*Sweden*		*Norway*	
		Large business	100								
		Small business	91					Upper Class	84	Upper class	93
Administrative, professional	77	Professional	82	Professional	75						
Semiprofessional	70			Upper white collar	65						
White collar	60	White collar	82	Civil servants	51			Middle class	72	Middle class	88
				Lower white collar	33						
Skilled worker	62	Skilled manual	84	Skilled worker	47	Skilled worker	68				
Semiskilled	45	Semiskilled	76	Semiskilled	21	Artisan	62	Working class	69	Working class	83
Unskilled	23	Unskilled	72	Unskilled	11	Unskilled	57				
Peasant	12			Farm labor	23	Farm labor	43				

**U.S.S.R.*—percentage answering "Yes" to: "Did you like the job you held in 1940?" (Soviet-refugee data, Russian Research Center, Harvard University). *U.S.*—percentage answering "Yes" to: "Are you satisfied or dissatisfied with your present job?" (Richard Centers, "Motivational Aspects of Occupational Stratification," *Journal of Social Psychology*, XXVII [1948], 100). *Germany*—percentage who would choose present occupation in response to: "If you were again 15 years old and could start again, would you choose your present occupation or another one?" (from German poll data, courtesy of S. M. Lipset). *Italy*—those "satisfied" or "fairly satisfied" with work *(Doxa Bolletino)*. *Sweden and Norway*—percentage giving "satisfied" in response to question: "Are you satisfied with your present occupation, or do you think that something else would suit you better?" (Hadley W. Cantril [ed.], *Public Opinion, 1935-1946* [Princeton, N. J.: Princeton University Press, 1951], p. 535).

Such variations, or departures from a standard, point to quite important differentiation in the relative positions of particular occupational groups in different countries. Consequently, our method, far from covering up or glossing over the differences between countries, can serve as a definite pointer for locating precisely what is distinctive in the situation of a particular group in a given country.

The data on job satisfaction illustrate well the appropriateness of the model of analysis sketched in the preceding section. Although all the countries are advanced, well-to-do representatives of the West European complex of industrial nations, the *average* level of satisfaction in each is markedly different. For example, in the United States the national average would clearly be over 80 per cent satisfied, whereas in Germany it would be closer to 40 per cent. Similarly, if only one particular occupational group, such as the semiskilled workers, were considered, one would be led to conclude that their shared status by no means produced a shared or standard effect, regardless of nationality. On the contrary, the proportion satisfied among the semiskilled ranges from 21 per cent in Germany to 76 per cent in the United States. Yet, as we have seen in Table 1, there *is* a definite, unmistakable, and obviously quite meaningful pattern in the experience of job satisfaction which is uniform from country to country. But that, to repeat, emerges only when the unit of analysis is the occupational hierarchy as a whole and when attention is on the pattern of response within it rather than on the data, country by country or group by group.

It may seem obvious that, in all the countries for which we have data, job satisfaction is structured, with those higher in the hierarchy of occupations more often satisfied. Of course, those who are not ready to take a close look at the obvious have little need for science. Certainly it is less pejorative to say the example is striking rather than obvious. In any event, it is not presented first as definitive proof of the theory but rather because it so clearly illustrates the mode of analysis to be used later in assessing reactions which are not so "obviously" derivable from the external conditions of the individual's situation at work.

A more serious criticism is that we unduly stress the regularity in the pattern across national lines while slighting the impressive differences in the absolute proportion satisfied in the several countries. Choice of emphasis is largely a consequence of one's purpose; the concern here is to discover regularity in human social behavior in response to standard stimulus conditions, something which seems rather more difficult to find than examples of diversity. This is not to say that for some purposes the location and analysis of differences is not more important. For example, if you wished to predict whether unskilled workers in Europe were more likely to vote communist, or for whatever was the legal party of the far left, it would be quite important to know that, compared to unskilled workers in the United States, they are seldom satisfied on the job.

But, even here, it is only when you have the comparative data that you are alerted to take special notice of the German or Italian workers' response. Furthermore, the signal does not rest mainly on comparing German and American *workers*. The striking nature of the German response is evident only when we realize that German professionals and businessmen were satisfied about as often as were their American counterparts, whereas this is *not* true of workers. If Germans in all occupational groups characteristically reported job satisfaction less often than their opposite numbers in other countries, we would have to assume that some economic or cultural factor common to all Germans, or something peculiar or distinctive in the question put to them, accounted for the difference. Indeed, if we found such homogeneity *within* nations existing simultaneously with substantial differences among nations in the response to questions which, on theoretical grounds, we expected to show the predicted step pattern, that would constitute evidence refuting our hypothesis.

Finally, in assessing average or typical responses from country to country, we should keep in mind the possibility that these differences may be not so much a reflection of real differences in sentiments as an artifact of technique. We must take account of the marked effect produced by changes in question wording, differences in meaning introduced through translation, and variations in the conventions used for reporting answers to a question. In many of the comparisons made in this paper the questions used were only approximate equivalents. Thus, to assess job satisfaction, we might for one country have the question, "Do you like your job?"; for another, "Do you enjoy your work?"; and for a third, "Would you take the same job again if you started over?" Each may legitimately be taken as a measure of job satisfaction. Yet, if asked of a single population in one country, they would probably yield quite different proportions of "satisfied" workers. Nevertheless, the underlying structure of response would undoubtedly be similar for all three measures, with each showing the professional managerial groups most satisfied, the workers and farm laborers least so. This is not a purely hypothetical example. It can clearly be demonstrated on the basis of data available for the United States, the U.S.S.R., and other countries. Even in more systematic international polls the translation of the questions often gives them special meanings which influence the level of response in different countries. In addition, different conventions used in asking the questions and reporting the answers further influence the picture. In one case the alternatives offered may be only "I like my job" or "I don't like my job." But another study may include a third alternative, such as "I like it somewhat." These variations can obviously have a marked effect on the absolute proportion considered "satisfied" in one or another country.

If job satisfaction is a response to the "objective" factors which characterize the job as a whole, it should also respond to variations in the individual factors which make up the job complex. One of the most obvious determinants of job satisfaction, therefore, should be the salary or wage it carries. Data for the United States and the Soviet Union suggest a very direct connection. The higher the job in the hierarchy of power and prestige, the more often will the incumbents be satisfied with their pay. This is in good part, though not exclusively, because the pay is generally greater for jobs high in the hierarchy. Yet pay alone is not sufficient to account for reported job satisfaction. If it were, the step pattern shown in Table 1 should be fairly uniform for all the countries. In fact, it is not.

In both the Soviet Union and Germany, as against the United States, there are sharp breaks or discontinuities. For example, the proportion satisfied falls off precipitously between the skilled and semiskilled. There is another sharp drop in going from semiskilled to the unskilled, and again in going from semiskilled to the peasants. An initial exploration suggests the cause is not a difference in the structure of the wage scales, which are relatively similar in these countries. It seems instead to have to do with the "absolute" meaning of the very low pay received by those at the bottom in Germany and the U.S.S.R. as against the standard of living possible to the unskilled American worker even when he *is* at the bottom. In addition, differences in the absolute levels of prestige and self-respect which those at the bottom can command also seem to play a role.

Values about Jobs. It may be obvious that position in the occupational hierarchy, because it determines income and psychic reward, should influence the sense of job satisfaction. But what about *values?* Should the things people want from jobs also be so determined? We might reasonably make any one of three assumptions. Since values are presumably what is "shared" in any culture, we might expect that in each country everyone would want pretty much the same qualities in a job, with more or less the same intensity. On the other hand, if we assume that what people want is determined by what their life situation induces them to desire, we will expect systematic variation in the values reflected in job evaluations made by those at different levels of the occupational hierarchy. A third possibility would be that what men will want in a job will be determined by the kinds of men they are, that is, by their personality or training.

These three theories are not necessarily totally independent of each other, and only a full-scale analysis with data of good quality could settle the issue by revealing the relative weight of the factors and their interrelations. The scattered data in hand suggest that there are definitely some common values about the occupational realm shared not only within particular countries but in all modern, large-scale, more or less industrial societies, without much differentiation within the population by occupational group. Inkeles and Rossi located and analyzed the relative standing of lists of occupations in six industrial countries.[6] To an extraordinary degree the occupations were ranked in the same order. More important for us, they found very little variation in the evaluation of these occupations from one subgroup of the population to another. In other words, whether a worker or a professor does the rating, both place the doctor, lawyer, and engineer very near the top of the list, the ordinary worker about two-thirds of the way down, and the shoe-shine boy or garbage man at the bottom. This seems to be true for all countries, although there are some interesting variations which cannot be gone into here.

In the light of these findings, are we not forced to restate the theory with which we started? The evaluation of occupations seems not to be influenced by differential situational pressures. At least the rater's own position in the occupational structure seems to make no fundamental difference in how he evaluates the standing or prestige of occupations. It might be objected that, after all, a man's standing in the community is a pretty "objective" thing. Anyone can see how much respect a doctor gets from everyone else. The fact that people agree on his standing is therefore "natural." But even so this requires that we reformulate our theory to say that a rater's own position or situation can be expected to influence only his *subjective* judgments—those statements in which he reports what *he* feels, or what he wants or likes. This is, however, a very confining assumption and more conservative than is strictly necessary. For we will see that certain estimates made by people about situations which are as "objective" and "external" as the standing of an occupation *are* influenced by the position of the observer, just as the experiments of Solomon Asch have shown that interpersonal situations can have a marked effect on the reported perception of such objective physical facts as the length of a line. But it may be that situationally determined perceptions of "objective" facts are not common and partake of a special nature. For the present, then, let us make the more conservative assump-

6. A. Inkeles and P. Rossi, "National Comparisons of Occupational Prestige," *American Journal of Sociology*, LXI (1956), 329-39. These values may also be shared in countries not so highly industrialized but already incorporated into or influenced by currents of modernization (see E. Tiryakian, "The Prestige Evaluation of Occupations in an Underdeveloped Country: The Philippines," *American Journal of Sociology*, LXIII [1958], 390-99).

tion that only intrinsically "subjective" reactions will be shaped by one's position in the social structure.

The qualities a man desires in his job certainly may be regarded as personal and subjective choices. Such desires may be assumed to reflect deeper values. Do those in different positions in the occupational hierarchy then wish for different qualities in a job? The relevant question has been asked in a number of countries, but I have located appropriate cross-tabulations for only two. The results suggest that there are some patterns which hold up across national lines. But there is also substantial variation, an absence of pattern, with regard to certain classes and dimensions, which obviously reflects very important differences in the general state of affairs within the two countries and in the relative position of certain special groups within each.

We may begin with the more regular patterns (Table 2). In both

Table 2. Quality Most Desired in a Work Situation, in Percentages by Country and Occupation

	PREFERENCES OF SAMPLE OF SOVIET REFUGEES*				
Occupation	*Adequate Pay*	*Interesting Work*	*Free of Fear*	*All Others*	N
Intelligentsia	8	62	6	24	95
White collar	23	31	13	33	62
Skilled workers	22	27	15	36	33
Ordinary workers	48	20	13	19	56
Peasants	57	9	17	17	35
	PREFERENCES OF SAMPLE IN UNITED STATES†				
	High Pay	*Interesting Work‡*	*Security*	*Independence*	*Other*
Large business	6	52	2	7	33
Professional	3	50	3	12	32
Small business	6	41	5	22	26
White collar	7	42	12	17	22
Skilled manual	4	36	13	22	25
Semiskilled	6	20	26	24	24
Unskilled	8	19	29	15	29
Farm tenant and laborer	12	21	20	18	29

*Based on coding of qualitative personal interviews from the Harvard Project on th Soviet Social System.

†Based on R. Centers, "Motivational Aspects of Occupational Stratification," *Journal of Social Psychology*, XXVIII (November, 1948), 187-218, Table 11.

‡Includes: "A very interesting job" and "A job where you could express your feelings, ideas, talent, or skill."

the United States and the Soviet refugee sample, those who hold jobs of higher status are much more likely to be concerned about having a job which is "interesting," stimulating, challenging, permits self-expression, and so on. The proportion of professionals desiring this quality, as against the proportion of unskilled workers citing it, produces a ratio of about 3:1 in both countries.

But the role of large income is quite different in the two countries. In the United States it is a factor in the "free choice" of a *job* for only 3 to 8 per cent, and there is no step pattern. In the Soviet Union, by contrast, the responses are highly patterned. Large earnings are the primary consideration for 57 per cent of the peasants and only 8 per cent of the intelligentsia. This may be striking evidence that in the United States, at least in 1948 and perhaps beyond, pay was no longer so desperately problematical an issue for the working class as it was in many other countries. Americans seem sure that if they have work their pay will be decently adequate. Additional evidence for this conclusion lies in the fact that, when Americans cited their reasons for being dissatisfied with a job, low pay accounted for only one-fifth of the complaints and was actually cited more often by white-collar than manual workers, whereas in the Soviet sample more than two-thirds of the dissatisfied workers and peasants cited low pay as the reason for their dissatisfaction and did so much more often than ordinary white-collar workers.

Our impression—that workers are generally concerned to increase their pay, while those more highly placed care more about interesting work[7]—must be tempered by the consideration of security. As between still more pay or still more interesting work, it seems that those higher in the scale will vote for increased interest, the worker for more pay. But what about security, or certainty, *as against* more pay linked to uncertainty? A number of questions asked in different countries bear on this issue. They all suggest that workers, more often than the middle classes, will choose certainty of income, or security, over more money with less security.

Thus in the Soviet-American comparison (Table 2) it is evident that security is much more a concern for the American workers than it is for professional-administrative people. Unskilled workers cited security as the basis for choosing a job in 29 per cent of the cases as against 2 per cent among those in more favored occupations. The Soviet data are not strictly comparable, since, in that context, security meant mainly freedom from fear of the secret police. Even so, it is striking that the intelligentsia, which experienced by far the highest rate of political

7. In the Netherlands (NIPO, Ballot 118, November, 1948) the question was asked: "Could you tell me for what purpose you work?" A break by socioeconomic standing revealed little patterning. "For family and children" was the chief reason given by all groups, and "money" next. The relative importance of money as against family and children was actually greatest among the well-to-do. Whether this is mainly a result of the difference in the question, or is evidence that there is no pattern here which can be expected cross-nationally, cannot be said on the basis of present evidence.

arrest, nevertheless cited freedom from fear as the quality "most desired" in a job only one-half as often as did the ordinary workers.

In Australia, people were asked to choose between a straight raise or an incentive award. Among employers, 76 per cent chose the riskier incentive award, but only about 50 per cent of the workers did so.[8] The issue of security is only indirectly raised here. But in a number of cases the choice between more money and less security, or the reverse, has been put more directly, although the results are unfortunately not always reported with a class break.[9] In three out of four cases where this break is available, the choice of security over earnings is more often favored by workers than by those higher in the occupational or income hierarchy. The question has been asked in the United States a number of times in slightly different form. In 1940 the choice was between "a steady job earning just enough to get by on, with no prospect for advancement," as against "a job that pays a high wage, but with a 50/50 chance of getting promoted or fired." Forty-five per cent of factory labor as against a mere 8 per cent of executives chose the low-income-high-security alternative.[10] On another form of the question, 64 per cent of professionals and executives were willing to risk all their savings on a promising venture, whereas only 40 per cent of unemployed workers inclined to this course as against sticking to "a good steady job."[11]

These results are congruent with those from the Soviet Union. Here the alternatives offered were: "A job that pays fairly well and is secure, but offers little opportunity for advancement," as against: "A job that pays less well and is not secure, but offers good opportunities for advancement." In the Soviet-refugee sample, among men under 40, the proportion preferring advancement over security falls from 50 per cent in the intelligentsia to about 23 per cent among workers and peasants. The ratio of preference for security over advancement is about 4:5 in the intelligentsia, but the preference for security increases to 3:1 among workers.

The evidence seems strong that, when offered the incentive of pro-

8. Reported in *Doxa,* IV, No. 23-24 (December, 1950). The size of the plant in which the worker is employed seems to play a role here. In smaller plants (fifty or fewer employees) 56 per cent chose the incentive pay, but in larger plants only 45 per cent would take the risk. Size of plant seems an important factor in shaping the workers' perception and attitudes, and we should give it more systematic treatment in future studies. S. M. Lipset and Juan Linz, in their unpublished study, "The Social Bases of Political Diversity in Western Democracies," have noted several German studies which reveal that the larger the factory, the more radical will be the workers in it.

9. In Denmark, NIPO, Ballot of April 11, 1943, for example.

10. Cantril (ed.), *op. cit.,* p. 530.

11. *Public Opinion Quarterly,* XIV (Spring, 1950), 182.

motion or success at the risk of security, those in high-status occupations are willing to take risks which are shunned by the manual classes, who favor security above all else. But we are brought up short by the fact that in both Britain and Australia the same occupational differentiation is not noted in response to a seemingly similar question: "Which is more important in a job—as high wages as possible or security with lower wages?" In the British sample security was chosen over high wages by at least 2:1 *in all groups.* Indeed, the preference for security was strongest among salaried clerical and professional executive groups.[12] For Australia we do not have the exact percentage but are told "all occupational groups have similar ideas" in overwhelmingly preferring security to the better-paying but presumably insecure job.[13]

The conflict between these results and those reported for the U.S. and U.S.S.R. may be less glaring than appears at first glance. It should be observed that in both the American and Soviet studies there was an added element not present in the British and Australian question, namely, the prospect of promotion or "advancement." It may be that our initial formulation was either too sweeping or too imprecise. Perhaps we should have said that, where there is a prospect of advancement, a promise of special success, then those in the occupations of higher status will more readily take risks, but, where security is balanced against high earnings alone, they will act like most others in preferring security. Formulated thus, our expectation is more congruent with relevant psychological theory treating "need achievement" as a risk-taking propensity[14] and with the evidence that it is much more common among those higher in the occupational hierarchy.[15]

This formulation is also more in line with our earlier finding that in judging the qualities of a job those in the positions of higher status were not particularly preoccupied with high earnings. Fortunately, we have a partial test of the soundness of our shift in emphasis, since an American sample was also asked a question similar to the one used in

12. Cantril (ed.), *op. cit.*, p. 1016.

13. AGP, Nos. 579-89 (March-April, 1949). This issue also reports that at that time Gallup asked the same question in a number of the other countries, but the results are not reported with class breaks. The proportion of the total samples choosing the steady job is so high in Canada (85 per cent), Holland (79 per cent), and Sweden (71 per cent) that we must assume that in those countries as well the steady job was the overwhelming favorite in all groups.

14. See J. W. Atkinson, "Motivational Determinants of Risk-Taking Behavior," *Psychological Review*, LXIV (1957), 359-72.

15. This is suggested by a number of the studies in J. W. Atkinson (ed.), *Motives in Fantasy, Action, and Society* (Princeton, N.J.: D. Van Nostrand Co., 1958). Definitive evidence based on a national sample has been collected by the Survey Research Center at the University of Michigan in a study, directed by Gerald Gurin and Joseph Veroff, to be published soon.

Britain and Australia.[16] Under this condition, *with no mention of advancement*, the response was markedly different from that reported above. Although there was still some structured occupational differentiation, it was very slight compared to that observed when the hope of advancement was one of the conditions. With the question in this form the overwhelming majority of Americans at all occupational levels chose the secure job, as had their opposite numbers in Britain and Australia.

That seemingly so slight a difference in wording a question can produce so marked a difference in the structure of response must give us real pause about this whole enterprise. It warns against interpreting all the scattered and limited findings we have and demonstrates the great importance of doing carefully designed, focused, informed, special studies of our own as soon as possible. But it should not discourage us. It does not cast serious doubt upon the basic theory. In the case just discussed, for example, we did not refute the general proposition that the higher status groups respond in a different way than those of lower status when confronted with certain alternative choices in the job realm. But we did see the necessity for refinement in delineating precisely what has special appeal to these groups and wherein they share values in common. The theory therefore becomes less global, less "omnipredictive," but, in the long run, more interesting and more suggestive for future work.

To sum up our findings in the realm of work: We see striking confirmation of the differential effect of the job situation on the perception of one's experience in it. The evidence is powerful and unmistakable that satisfaction with one's job is differentially experienced by those in the several standard occupational positions. From country to country, we observe a clear positive correlation between the over-all status of occupations and the experience of satisfaction in them. This seems to hold, as well, for the relation between satisfaction and the components of the job, such as the pay, but the evidence is thinner here. We may expect that the relationship will hold for other components, such as the prestige of the job and the autonomy or independence it affords. Job situation appears also to pattern many values germane to the occupational realm, such as the qualities most desired in a job and the image of a good or bad boss.[17]

At the same time, we note that there are certain attitudes which posi-

16. It was worded as follows: "Some people prefer a job which pays very well even though it may not be so secure (permanent). Other people prefer a steady job even though it may not pay so much. Which would you, yourself, prefer—the steady job or the better-paying one?" (*Public Opinion Quarterly*, XIII [Fall, 1949], 553).

17. For lack of space the relevant evidence with regard to images of the good and bad boss has not been presented.

tion in the occupational hierarchy does not seem to influence. For example, all occupational groups agree on the relative ranking of the status or desirability of different jobs. And they seem to agree in favoring job security at less pay over a better-paying but less secure job. Yet in the latter realm we discover an interesting fact. When we add the special ingredient of a promise of success, promotion or advancement, we trigger a special propensity to risk-taking in those in more esteemed occupations, whereas those in the manual classes remain unmoved and stick to security. This alerts us to the importance of precision and refinement in seeking the exact nature of the values and beliefs which differentiate the social groups on the basis of position in the occupational hierarchy, as against those which they share in common with all of their nationality or all who participate in modern society.

On Happiness

Granted that happiness is a very elusive thing, we may yet make so bold as to study it and to do so through so crude a device as a public-opinion poll. Of course we should not naïvely accept what a man says when we ask him, "Are you happy?" But neither is it reasonable to assume that whatever he says means the opposite. That would be all too regular and a sure key to the truth. Some men will be truly cheerful but suspect our purpose; fear of the "evil eye," or a trait of personality, may lead them to deny publicly their true feeling. If everyone answered the question in a random and, in that sense, meaningless way, we would expect by chance that 50 per cent in any population would say "Yes," 50 per cent "No," and that no control variable such as age, sex, or income would reveal anything but this 50/50 division.

Common sense tells us that some groups produce more people who feel they are happy than do others, and with reason. Those about to commit suicide tell their friends, doctors, or diaries that they are miserable; those who are about to get divorced are likely to report their marriage is unhappy. Admittedly, where there are pressures which make people disguise their true feelings, their more or less public report of how they feel will certainly reduce the clarity of the relationship between the objective situation and their true inner feeling. If, despite this built-in and essentially uncontrollable distortion, we still find strong and meaningful connections between a man's situation and what he says about his happiness, then we must assume that the "real" connection is, if anything, not weaker but stronger than the one which emerges in our data.

Both direct and indirect questions have been used in an effort to assess individual happiness. An identical direct question was put to people in the U.S., England, France, and Canada during 1946. By contrast to the Anglo-Saxon trio, the French emerge as dour indeed: in the other countries a third or more were "very happy," but in France only 8 per cent. Forty per cent of the French said they were "not very happy," as against a maximum of 10 per cent elsewhere.[18] Much the same question was asked in 1949 by at least six of the Gallup affiliates, with similar results. Only 11 per cent of the French were "very happy," as against a range of from 26 per cent in Norway to 52 per cent in Australia.[19] Unfortunately, we do not have cross-tabulations by stratification variables for either of these two studies, but comparable data from Italy and Britain leave little doubt that, when these are made, we will find in each society that such happiness as anyone cares to admit will be found oftenest among those in the more advantaged strata of society.

In the British study men were asked: "In the last twenty-four hours, have you had a hearty laugh?" Women were asked whether they had had a "good cry," an effort being made to disarm them by prefacing the question with the statement: "Many doctors say it is good to give vent to your feelings by crying once in a while." Although the questions do not deal directly with happiness, they very probably measure much the same thing. The proportion who had laughed in the last twenty-four hours decreased, and the proportion who had cried increased, as one descended the socioeconomic scale (Table 3). The differentiation was

Table 3. Laughing and Crying in England by Class and Sex*

Economic Class	*Percentage Who Laughed in Last 24 Hours (Men Only)*	*Percentage Who Cried in Last 24 Hours (Women Only)*
Well-to-do	47	12
Average	50	11
Below average	41	16
Poor	26	27

*Reported in *Doxa Bolletino*, Vol. V, No. 6 (April, 1956).

sharp, however, only in the case of the very poor, who had laughed only half as often and had cried twice as often as did those in the middle and upper economic classes.

I have asked many people, including several large audiences, to predict the outcome of this poll. The great majority invariably expected

18. Cantril (ed.), *op. cit.*, p. 281.

19. AGP, Nos. 569-78 (February-March, 1949). The other countries were Holland (43 per cent), the United States (43 per cent), and the United Kingdom (39 per cent).

the working class to laugh more often. They express surprise at the findings and generally question me closely as to the time and country involved.[20] On learning the study was done in England, they invariably offer an *ad hoc* explanation, based on assumptions about the character of English society, and regularly volunteer the opinion that certainly in Italy the results would be different. Unfortunately the same question seems not to have been asked in sunny Italy. But its smiling workers and singing peasants have been asked two other questions which should serve our purpose. The first was simple and straightforward: "Just now do you feel happy or unhappy?" The second was more complex: "Could you summarize in a few words the state (or balance) of your life today?" The respondents were then offered a choice of six sentences suggesting various combinations and degrees of pain and joy ranging from "Life has given me only joys and satisfactions," to "Life has given me only pain and disillusionment."

The results are fairly unambiguous but, as is so often true of such data, by no means completely so. For example, on the first "test" the lowest proportion of happy people is found among one of the more favored groups—the managers (*dirigente*), a category which seems to include free professionals. On the other hand, this group is quite "normal" on the second test, reporting life to be full of pain and disillusionment less often than any other group. Leaving aside such complications, however, we may conclude that on the whole, in Italy no less than in Britain, happiness is much more commonly reported by the advantaged strata of society, while sadness and despair are more standard in the manual and depressed classes. Of course, the well-to-do have no monopoly on happiness, nor does a majority of the working class report itself miserable. In all classes the central tendency is toward some mixture of happiness and pain. But at the extremes the general pattern we have found elsewhere is manifested here as well. As we ascend the occupational ladder, the proportion who are "very" or "fairly" happy rises from 29 per cent among farm laborers and ordinary workers to 47 per cent among employers.[21] Similarly, at the other extreme, workers report themselves as unhappy two-and-a-half times as often as do the employers and managers. Among the manual classes the ratio of the happy to

20. These audiences were generally composed of faculty and students, supplemented by people in the college or university community who attend lectures "open to the public"—safely characterized as solidly middle class. Despite their high average level of education, they seemed to harbor a stereotype of the working class which in important respects is strikingly analogous to that held by southern whites about the poor, irresponsible, but "happy" Negro.

21. There is, however, not much to choose between the lowest categories who are clustered around the 30 per cent level (cf. *Doxa*, No. 12 [April, 1948]).

the unhappy is as low as 1:1, whereas in the more advantaged groups it is almost 5:1.

Much the same pattern is shown in the second test. The life of much pain and little joy is claimed by about 50 per cent of workers and farm laborers, by as few as 23 per cent of the managers and professionals, and by about one-third of employers and farm owners (Table 4).

Table 4. Balance of Joy and Pain in Life in Italy, in Percentages by Occupation*

Occupation	*More Pain than Joy†*	*More Joy than Pain‡*	*A Balance of Joy and Pain§*	*No Answer*
Employer	32	20	45	3
Manager	23	23	56	..
Farm owner and operator	33	20	46	1
White collar	28	15	55	2
Artisan	36	12	51	1
Worker	48	11	41	..
Farm laborer	51	11	38	1

**Doxa Bolletina*, No. 12 (April, 1948).
†Includes the response: "Life has given *only* pains and disillusion."
‡Includes: "Life has given me *only* joys and satisfactions."
§Includes: "Many pains but also many joys" and "Few pains and few joys." Among workers and farm laborers and employees the choice of "few joys" predominated markedly; among managers, the reverse; and by the remainder the two alternatives were equally chosen.

To assess happiness in a number of countries simultaneously we must, unfortunately, use a question which can at best be taken as only a rough approximation of those dealing directly with happiness, namely, one inquiring about "satisfaction." What happiness is may be somewhat ambiguous, but we are generally clear that it deals with an *emotional* state. "Satisfaction" is a much more ambiguous term, and, when not further specified, it can mean satisfaction with one's financial situation, social or political advancement, family life, or any one of a number of things. Furthermore, "happiness" may be translated fairly well from one language to another, but "satisfaction" changes its meaning. In addition, in the available comparative study the question on satisfaction came immediately after one on security, and this probably led people more often to respond in terms of financial criteria rather than of general satisfaction in life. Consequently, to check the reasonableness of using the question on satisfaction in life as an index of happiness, I compared the results (for Italy) of two different polls, one asking directly about happiness (described above), the other using the question on satisfaction from the available cross-national study. The structure of the answers was very similar (Table 5). On both questions, business and farm owners and managers reported themselves either dissatisfied or unhappy only half as often as did manual and farm workers, with clerks and artisans

Table 5. Comparison of Italian Results on Questions of "Happiness" and "Satisfaction with Situation" (Per Cent)

Occupation	"Dissatisfied" with Present Situation*	Occupation	"Unhappy" at This Moment†
Business owners	31	Employers	10
Salaried managers	35	Managers	10
Farm owners	32	Farm owners	10
Artisans	43	Artisans	16
Clerks	55	Employees	14
Manual workers	64	Workers	26
Farm workers	63	Farm laborers	20

*From William Buchanan and Hadley Cantril, *How Nations See Each Other* (Urbana: University of Illinois Press, 1953), p. 176. The question was the same as that reported in Table 6 for nine countries including Italy.
†From *Doxa Bolletino*, No. 12 (April, 1948).

falling in between. The correlation was not perfect, but there was quite close association.

Allowing, then, for many necessary reservations, let us look at the responses to the question, "How satisfied are you with the way you are getting on now?" which was asked simultaneously in nine countries. The results (Table 6) are certainly less sharp and clear-cut than those ob-

Table 6. Percentage Dissatisfied with How They Are "Getting On" by Country and Occupation*

	OCCUPATION						
Country	Owners	Managers	Profes-sionals	White Collar	Artisans	Workers	Farm Labor
Australia	11	18	15	22	31	17	17
Britain	41	21	14	36	40	36	26
France	38	29	55	56	56	67	63
Germany	46	39	50	35	37	48	52
Italy	31	35	46	55	43	64	63
Mexico	58	57	50	55	67	65	75
Netherlands	26	15	22	23	37	43	41
Norway	7	4	2	11	12	11	22
United States	20	22	26	24	28	31	39

*Adapted from data in Appendix D of William Buchanan and Hadley Cantril, *How Nations See Each Other* (Urbana: University of Illinois Press, 1953), pp. 125-216.

tained for job satisfaction. There are numerous irregularities and ambiguities. For example, Germany produces not our familiar step pattern but a U-shaped curve, and Australia yields, if anything, an inverted U. These cases suggest what the table as a whole hints, namely, that the question is ambiguous and people respond to it in terms of different criteria. Nevertheless, there seems to be an underlying cross-national pattern. The higher non-manual positions hold at least rank 1 (lowest proportion dissatisfied), 2, or 3 in seven of nine countries, whereas the workers held so high a rank in no country and the farm laborers in one. The occupations were originally listed in a rough approximation of their standing in the hierarchy of power and rewards. It is interesting, therefore, that when we sum the rank orders for each occupation we emerge with a regular progression which follows the original ordering. Except for the owners, whose score of 27 is strongly affected by their extremely deviant response in Britain, there is a steady increase from managers (20), through professionals (24), white collar (33), artisans and skilled workers (45), and workers (50), to farm labor (53). That a comparable cross-national pattern emerges when either socioeconomic status or education is used as the independent variable strengthens our conviction that the underlying structure is real. The fact that the relationship holds more firmly when occupation or economic status rather than education are the independent variables suggests that, as we anticipated, the answers more strongly reflect satisfaction with economic than with spiritual welfare.

Whatever their weakness as a guide to the cross-national pattern we seek, these data also point to the usefulness of our procedure for identifying groups with special problems or distinctive responses to more general problems. It is striking, for example, that in Britain the owners formed the group whose members were *most* often dissatisfied with the way they were "getting on." But this was 1948, when they were threatened by the highest level reached by the wave of nationalization sentiment in England, and so the result is not surprising.

Some of the difficulty raised by the question on "satisfaction with getting on" could be avoided if the respondent were asked to disregard his financial condition. An international poll meeting this requirement is, unfortunately, not at hand. We should, however, examine an International Research Associate study in which the wording of the question and its location in the questionnaire may have somewhat reduced the role of economic referents. The question was: "Do you feel that you have gotten as far ahead as you should at this stage of your life, or are you dissatisfied with the progress you have made so far?" Here again, unfortunately, the question would probably be understood by many to mean mainly economic or material "getting ahead" or "progress." This assumption is greatly strengthened by the fact that the responses are more regular and the differences sharper when socioeconomic status rather than occupation is used (Table 7). Using socioeconomic status to classify the respondents, we find the step structure present in eight of eleven cases, markedly so in four. There is no instance in which the result is the complete reverse of our expectation, but in three countries the group classified as "middle" has the lowest proportion satisfied. Using occupation as the independent variable, we again have four strong cases and a fifth which is up to standard, but now six fail to qualify. In

Table 7. Percentage Satisfied with Progress in Life, by Country and Status*

	OCCUPATION			SOCIOECONOMIC GROUP		
Country	Executive, Professional	White Collar	Wage Earner	Upper	Middle	Lower
Australia	70	64	66	73	70	65
Austria	61	60	47	64	59	60
Belgium	37	36	21	43	41	34
Brazil†	74	60	63	81	71	54
Britain	79	66	70	73	68	71
Denmark	77	78	68	81	75	64
Germany	73	71	68	73	72	65
Japan	52	42	33	50	40	13
Netherlands	61	57	59	67	58	66
Norway	89	79	70	87	71	60
Sweden	71	58	67	80	67	60

*Tabulations from a study conducted by International Research Associates.
† Rio de Janeiro and São Paulo only.

five of these instances the difficulty arises again from the fact that a higher proportion of the middle level of white-collar workers are dissatisfied than is the case among workers. If we compare the executive-professional and worker groups alone, the pattern is clear-cut in all eleven cases.[22]

In sum, no very "pure" measure of feelings of happiness or of spiritual or psychic (as against material) well-being, applied cross-nationally and fully reported, is at hand. Taking the available evidence together, however, we cannot entertain any other hypothesis but that the feeling of happiness or of psychic well-being is unevenly distributed in most, perhaps all, countries. Those who are economically well off, those with more education or whose jobs require more training and skill, more often report themselves happy, joyous, laughing, free of sorrow, satisfied with life's progress. Even though the pattern is weak or ambiguous in some cases, there has not been a single case of a *reversal* of the pattern, that is, a case where measures of happiness are inversely related to measures of status, in studies involving fifteen different countries—at least six of which were studied on two different occasions, through the use of somewhat different questions. There is, then, good reason to challenge the image of the "carefree but happy poor." As one angry man wrote to me, after he had read a news report of a speech I had made reporting the relation of laughter to social status: "And what the hell do you think the poor have to laugh about, anyway?"

Plausible as this contention may be on the surface, it is obviously not

22. A twelfth case, France, was a strong instance of the expected relationship. Since socioeconomic status classifications were not available for France, it was excluded from Table 7 to make both parts strictly comparable.

the end but only the beginning of a study. If those who are better placed and more fortunate more often report they are happy, can we test the validity of this report by such other measures as their rates of suicide, homicide, and mental illness?[23] If the proportion satisfied rises with income, will better-paid workers in any country be happier than those less well paid at the same occupational level? Will raising the incomes of all increase the happiness of all, or does it require an unequal gain to bring happiness to some? What of the man who is well educated but poorly paid, or rich but poorly educated? Some questions of this kind can be answered by further cross-tabulation of the original IBM cards, which it is hoped will be possible at a later date.[24] Some will require new cross-national studies clearly focused on these issues.

The Mastery-Optimism Complex

Those lower in the occupational hierarchy bring certain important personal characteristics or propensities to their typical "assignments" in life, which tendencies are reinforced by conditions of their characteristic setting. Their education is limited, they generally will not have benefited from travel, and they confront most of the challenges of the outside world with minimum training or skill. Their home environment, particularly the example of the father, will probably have taught blind obedience to authority, if not as a virtue, at least as necessity.[25] Even before he goes to work, the factory will have been described to the working-class boy: its great power, its vast size, the impersonality of its processes, and the mystery of the forces which move within it. On arriving at the plant, the young worker will find many of his images and expectations confirmed. Personnel clerks will treat him as something to be fitted into impersonal categories. If there is a doctor who passes on his fitness, the worker may well sense that he is treated as an object assessed, not as a person examined. The foreman will probably be a tough

23. Suicide rates rise with socioeconomic status, but their absolute frequency is quite low in all groups. Homicides, many times more common than suicide, and psychopathic illness, which is incomparably more frequent, are both markedly commoner in the lower classes. Insofar as these rates, when combined, provide an index of misery, the pattern observed would be congruent with that already described.

24. The Roper Center for Public Opinion Research at Williams College plans to collect the IBM cards from studies conducted since World War II in some twenty countries. If this objective is achieved, it will open exceptional opportunities for comparative research.

25. But not necessarily respect. Indeed, the experience of the harsh and peremptory demands for obedience experienced by those at lower status levels more often breeds surface conformity and, beneath that, a smoldering hatred or disrespect for authority, except when so strong as to compel or win blind allegiance.

character who makes it clear who is boss, what is expected, what happens to those who step out of line. All the force and power that the lowly employee sees around him will appear to be under the control of people distant and not highly visible who are controlled by others more distant, more powerful, and still more invisible. The other workers, if not initially suspicious, perhaps will immediately begin a briefing on how to stay out of trouble, replete with accounts of unpleasant things which happened to people who could not stay out of trouble, and other tales which make evident the workers' helplessness. If he is too energetic, the new worker will soon be taught by the others, by force if necessary, to restrict his output, to "play it safe," and to be cautious.

These forces conspire to impress upon the worker a particular view of himself and his relation to the world of work and beyond. His image of the world is, as a result, likely to be that of a place of great complexity whose workings are not too easily comprehended by the common man. He has rights, but he needs friends who are more powerful or knowledgeable, who can explain things, tell him where to go, or help him by putting in a good word in the right place, like a key in a special lock which opens closed doors. For his own part, he feels he should stick to his job, not ask too many questions, and stay out of trouble. Part of staying out of trouble involves keeping one's workmates assured of one's sense of solidarity with them; group loyalty must be placed above personal ambition and self-aggrandizement. But the requirement to conform to orders from above and, at the same time, to pressures from one's equals encourages his impression of other people as unreliable, untrustworthy, and out to do for themselves first. The one thing a man can really count on are his own sensations, and this fosters a certain hedonism: "Eat, drink, (fornicate) and be merry." These impulses, can, however, be gratified only sporadically because of one's dependency, insecurity, and liability to punishment by powers which do not favor too many riotous good times.

A comparable profile for someone at the other end of the occupational hierarchy would presumably be quite different, if not always polar. It is this relative polarization, and the steady gradations as we move from one extreme to the other, which cause the step pattern of experiences and reactions which we have observed and on the basis of which we could generate a host of specific propositions and predictions. For nine-tenths of the propositions there would be no data with which to test them. It will be more economical, therefore, to assemble all the seemingly relevant comparative materials available and to select the topics for investigation in accord with them. We have good comparative data on feelings of personal competence, on images of human nature and its malleability, and on several questions which may be taken as alternative measures of optimism.

Personal Competence. Lacking skills, education, and training, directed by people who have more power than he has and who exercise it effectively over him, the member of the lower classes may be expected less often than others to have self-confidence, that is, a favorable assessment of his competence and capacity. This feeling could presumably be tapped by a single general question. More specific questions, separately testing self-confidence about technical or managerial ability in, say, hospitals, courts, or schools, would presumably produce sharper differentiation. At the same time, there might be some areas where those of lower status typically felt more competent or at least less in conflict. For example, the staff at the University of Michigan Survey Research Center reports in an informal communication that their data suggest middle-class men are more often insecure in their performance as husbands than are lower-class men.

Asked point-blank: "Are you troubled with feelings that you can't do things as well as others can?"—most people in most countries said "No." But the proportion who said they were troubled by feelings of inadequacy rose as high as 59 per cent (in the lower class in Brazil); the question is clearly worth examining. The only break available is by socio-economic status.[26] It provides some, but only modest, corroboration of our expectation. Of twelve countries reporting, the expected pattern is clear-cut and moderately strong only in Denmark and Brazil. In the latter the proportion who feel less competent rises from 43 per cent in the upper class, to 52 per cent in the middle class, and then to 59 per cent in the lower class. But these cases are offset by Australia, which clearly reverses the predicted direction. Even if we adopt the crude standard of qualifying all countries in which the lower class had the highest proportion troubled by feelings of inadequacy, only seven of the twelve countries qualify.

This is hardly impressive support for our theory. One reason for this outcome may be the ambiguity of the referent "others." The theory predicts mainly that those in the lower strata will feel less competent than "others" who are *above* them. But many answering the question undoubtedly took as their referent "others" on the same level. Insofar as this was the case, it would obviously reduce the differentiation between classes. The results may also have been influenced by ambiguity as to the types of competence the questioner had in mind. There are, of course, some areas where lower-class people may generally feel quite

26. Table not shown. I am indebted to Dr. Elmo Wilson and the International Research Associates for the data.

competent, or at least not disposed to question their own competence. If they had such areas in mind, they would be less likely to say "Yes" to the question.

We may then say that there is some slight evidence that groups of lower status tend in many countries to be the least often assured about their own general competence. Very rarely are they the group with the most pervasive feeling of adequacy. But the issue is not simple, and the response depends upon the area of life. Our main gain here, then, is perhaps increased awareness of the complexity or subtlety of the issue.

Child-Rearing Values. Not only is the horizon restricted for the individual of lower status, himself; he also tends to insure his self-perpetuation by restricting the horizon of his children and others who share his disadvantaged status. Less well equipped with education and experience than those in more favored positions, he learns that a little bit of security is a good thing and that it is wiser to choose what is certain than to strive for the perhaps unattainable. Consequently, we may expect him to be much less likely than persons of middle or upper status to urge a young man to strive for an occupation with high status which may not be easily obtained, and much more likely to urge the young man to go after a well-paid, secure job at the working-class level. This is true not only in everyday practice but holds even under the stimulus of a white-collar interviewer who saves the interviewee further embarrassment by offering him conditions free of the objective restrictions he may know actually exist. In one International Research Associates poll in nine countries, the question was put: "If an *intelligent young man who seemed suited for almost any line of work* asked your advice, what occupation would you be most likely to recommend for him?" (Italics supplied.) Rather consistently from country to country, people of lower socioeconomic status choose the modest goal of "skilled labor" for such a boy much more often than do the more advantaged classes (Table 8). Very similar results were obtained with comparable questions in the United States, in Italy, and with Soviet refugees.

We might again say that this is obvious. It is, furthermore, objective and realistic to advise the working-class boy to set his job sights low. But should we assume that a father's occupational position influences his values in child-rearing only in regard to the "objective" realm of job choices? The influence of the father's life situation may be expected to flow over into other areas; ambition itself may be affected. And not only ambition, but a number of other values which guide child-rearing may well fall into class-determined patterns.

An International Research Associates study inquired which value is the most important to teach to children and offered as choices: "To be ambitious and get ahead"; "To obey parents"; "To enjoy themselves";

Table 8. Occupations Recommended to Young Men in Percentages by Country and Occupation*

Country and Occupation Recommended	RESPONDENT'S OCCUPATION: Executive, Professional	White Collar	Wage Earner
Australia:			
Engineering, science	24	26	20
Skilled labor	10	11	28
Belgium:			
Engineering, science	43	52	28
Skilled labor	8	11	33
Britain:			
Engineering, science	54	50	48
Skilled labor	7	6	9
Denmark:			
Engineering, science	8	15	8
Skilled labor	7	7	17
France:			
Engineering, science	20	30	19
Skilled labor	8	5	11
Japan:			
Engineering, science	24	22	26
Skilled labor	1	—	2
Netherlands:			
Engineering, science	33	39	22
Skilled labor	7	5	13
Norway:			
Engineering, science	11	17	19
Skilled labor	15	18	16
Sweden:			
Engineering, science	12	19	15
Skilled labor	8	8	15

*Adapted from data made available by International Research Associates through the courtesy of Dr. Elmo Wilson.

"To place their trust in God"; and "To be decent and honest." Since in our Soviet-refugee study we had already investigated very similar values and had found patterns broadly congruent with the theory underlying the thinking in this report,[27] I undertook to predict the outcome of the INRA inquiry. The main assumption, following from general theory and supported by the earlier study, was that traditional, restrictive, cautious, conventional values are much stronger among manual workers, whereas the belief in effort, striving, energetic mastery, and the sacrifice necessary to those ends is much stronger in the middle class. On the basis of this fundamental assumption. I predicted for the INRA study that ambition would be more stressed by the middle class, obedience to parents by the working class. A secondary prediction was that the values

27. Alex Inkeles, "Social Change and Social Character: The Role of Parental Mediation," *Journal of Social Issues,* XI, No. 2 (1955), 12-23.

focused on personal qualities produced by careful training, such as decency and honesty, would be more stressed by the middle classes. Although predicting emphasis on religion was obviously complicated, I assumed that trust in God, taken as an *external* source of authority and power, would be stronger among manual workers. Finally, I anticipated that stress on enjoyment would be more evident in the working class, presumably as compensation for past and present frustrations and anticipated future deprivations.

These predictions are generally, but not consistently, borne out by the data (Table 9). The working class does have the lowest proportion

Table 9. Values in Child-Rearing, in Percentages by Country and Socioeconomic Status*

Country and Child-Rearing Values	SOCIOECONOMIC STATUS Upper	Middle	Lower
Australia:			
Ambition	5	3	8
Obedience to parents	13	17	23
Enjoyment	—	—	1
Trust in God	26	33	25
Decency; honesty	60	51	45
Don't know	5	4	3
No. of respondents	94	313	367
Australia:			
Ambition	17	14	11
Obedience to parents	21	21	27
Enjoyment	8	10	8
Trust in God	13	13	14
Decency; honesty	53	51	50
Don't know	2	2	1
No. of respondents	273	581	161
Brazil:†			
Ambition	9	9	6
Obedience to parents	13	21	23
Enjoyment	2	1	1
Trust in God	22	26	37
Decency; honesty	55	41	34
Don't know	2	2	1
No. of respondents	188	292	320
Britain:			
Ambition	7	14	7
Obedience to parents	8	10	17
Enjoyment	1	2	—
Trust in God	26	21	20
Decency; honesty	60	53	52
Don't know	3	1	4
No. of respondents	175	170	152
Denmark:			
Ambition	11	13	9
Obedience to parents	14	18	15

*Data provided by International Research Associates, from a release of March 13, 1958.
† Rio de Janeiro and São Paulo only.

Table 9. (Continued)

Country and Child-Rearing Values	SOCIOECONOMIC STATUS Upper	Middle	Lower
Enjoyment	2	1	3
Trust in God	16	9	10
Decency; honesty	54	56	61
Don't know	3	3	2
No. of respondents	167	390	129
Germany:			
Ambition	16	17	12
Obedience to parents	24	21	22
Enjoyment	—	1	2
Trust in God	17	10	11
Decency; honesty	61	62	61
Don't know	2	2	2
No. of respondents	120	595	270
Italy:			
Ambition	22	13	17
Obedience to parents	22	21	31
Enjoyment	5	2	5
Trust in God	29	31	31
Decency; honesty	53	56	45
Don't know	2	2	2
No. of respondents	148	435	712
Japan:			
Ambition	20	24	22
Obedience to parents	6	9	19
Enjoyment	4	3	1
Trust in God	4	4	6
Decency; honesty	64	58	46
Don't know	2	2	6
No. of respondents	368	422	69
Netherlands:			
Ambition	8	4	3
Obedience to parents	4	9	12
Enjoyment	1	2	2
Trust in God	40	41	37
Decency; honesty	46	48	50
Don't know	4	2	2
No. of respondents	214	147	142
Norway:			
Ambition	23	13	11
Obedience to parents	8	15	11
Enjoyment	1	—	—
Trust in God	11	17	26
Decency; honesty	51	50	46
Don't know	6	5	6
No. of respondents	142	519	72
Sweden:			
Ambition:	12	16	18
Obedience to parents	15	24	38
Enjoyment	3	3	12
Trust in God	12	9	26
Decency; honesty	76	72	59
Don't know	2	1	1
No. of respondents	156	307	91

stressing ambition in six of eleven countries and is tied in a seventh, a position held only twice each by the middle and upper socioeconomic groups. Only three countries show the usual step pattern, however, and there are two clear-cut reversals to offset them. The absence of pattern is largely a result of the tendency, perhaps not surprising, of the middle class to exceed the upper classes in stressing ambition in rearing children.

Our prediction with regard to emphasis on obedience is more firmly supported. The lower class has the highest proportion stressing it in eight of eleven cases, and it took no less than second place in the remaining three countries. In six the expected step pattern is clearly manifested, and there are no reversals.

Among the second-line predictions, the estimate with regard to decency and honesty was relatively correct. In seven of eleven countries, the higher the socioeconomic status, the greater the proportion emphasizing it. In an eighth case the lower class behaves as expected, but the middle class is out of line. In addition to one unpatterned case, however, there are two clear reversals. The prediction with regard to trust in God was not confirmed: the lower class did most often have the highest proportion, but it also was most often in last place; in general, there was almost a complete lack of pattern from country to country. We may note, finally, that not much can be said about the theme of enjoying one's self, since it was mentioned by only 1 or 2 per cent in most countries.

In general, the class patterning in which we are interested manifests itself again, but the patterns are not strong. In most cases only a few percentage points separated one class from the other. In values in child-rearing, cultural forces—particularly those deriving from ethnic and religious membership—play a powerful role and may, indeed, be the prime movers. Yet the fact that in this initial and unrefined procedure we can see a definite patterning of values that fit the expectations derived from our general theory is encouraging and recommends us to further and fuller exploration.

Changing Human Nature. His conception of the nature of human nature reveals much of a man's overt ideology, but questions which delve deep are unfortunately not at hand. However, in nine countries national samples were asked whether they thought their compatriots' "national characteristics" were due to the way they were brought up or were born in them and, also, whether "human nature" can be changed.

Our theory leads us to predict that the more advantaged classes will more often hold upbringing rather than heredity to determine national characteristics and will more often express belief in the malleability of human nature. This outcome is not assumed to be merely a function of intelligence and knowledge. Indeed, when people are grouped by education rather than by socioeconomic level, the strength of the association between social position and the belief that national characteristics are a product of training becomes much smaller and the patterning more confused and ambiguous. Rather, it follows from differences in training and life situation; those in the professional and managerial classes will more often have grown up in an environment that stressed training and character development, and in their work they will have learned the importance of mastering and transforming things by disciplined will and effort. By contrast, those in the working and peasant classes will have grown up in an atmosphere of more conventional beliefs and will have been taught to see important events as largely independent of the individual's will or effort. The manual worker enjoys less opportunity to assess the evident variability of behavior in different situations, and his life at work will foster the impression of an unchanging life order. When it is changed "from above," he will be less able to assess the shifting pressures and forces at work and therefore is more likely to see change as a product of some powerful person's fixed character.

We must allow for certain forces which will, however, operate to push the results in the opposite direction. In the upper, and particularly the aristocratic upper, classes, obvious forces enforce the notion that character is inborn and immutable, the finest of these inborn character types of course being concentrated in the aristocratic classes. This sentiment, often quickly adopted by the *nouveaux riches*, might act sharply to decrease the proportion among the well-to-do, taken as a whole, who believe character to be mainly a product of training and hence subject to change.

Of nine national samples, seven fell into the step pattern in assessing the origins of national characteristics; the proportion who stated that these characteristics result from the way people are brought up rose with each step up the socioeconomic ladder. Three of the seven are, however, not clear-cut because the highest or "wealthy" group either does not show a higher proportion believing in training or even shows a much lower proportion than does the group average in socioeconomic status. This relates to the point about the aristocratic conception of upper-class status discussed above. In two countries there is no definite pattern, but there are no clear-cut reversals. The belief that human nature can be changed is similarly patterned by social class membership. Of nine countries, the step pattern is found in six; the proportion who believe human nature can be changed again rises as one ascends the socioeconomic scale (Table 10). But again the pattern is marred by the tendency of the wealthy to stress training less often than does the aver-

Table 10. Percentage Who Believe in the Possibility of Change in Human Nature, by Country and Class*

Socioeconomic Status†	Australia	Britain	France	Germany	Italy	Mexico	Netherlands	Norway	U.S.
Wealthy	54	55	70	50	31	59	42	57	54
Average	45	46	63	58	37	37	50	58	50
Below average	42	38	61	51	31	38	43	57	49
Very poor	39	30	50	40	35	26	38	51	50

*From data by country in Appendix D of William Buchanan and Hadley Cantril, *How Nations See Each Other* (Urbana: University of Illinois Press, 1953), pp. 125-216.

†Judgment of interviewer.

age income group. This was true in four of the seven cases of patterning. Italy, Norway, and the United States show no pattern. Again, there are no reversals.

This outcome definitely supports our hypothesis, even allowing for the fact that the supporting evidence is somewhat weak in the case of estimates of the origins of national characteristics. For example, in one of the clearest manifestations of the structured response, in Germany the proportion who stress training rises by only five per cent or so on each step up the socioeconomic ladder, with 21 per cent of the very poor at one extreme and 36 per cent of the wealthy at the other. Bigger ranges are present in opinions about changing human nature, the difference between the wealthy and the very poor being as many as 33 percentage points. On both questions the pattern is, furthermore, blurred by the tendency of the wealthy to entertain the belief in the immutability of human nature and the inborn character of national traits. We must particularly regret, therefore, that the responses were not cross-tabulated by occupation.

Optimism and Control of the Atom. Views about the possibility of changing human nature have been treated here as evidence of a belief in the importance of character training and in the possibility of man's control and mastery over himself. Belief in the possibility of changing human nature can also be interpreted as expressing a certain optimism about *social* man and his future progress and a faith in the meaningfulness of efforts to master one's physical and social environment. The superior intellectual equipment which the more advantaged bring to situations, their advanced training and actual experience, encourage and support them in developing and maintaining optimism. To them the world is less a mysterious and threatening place. It presents obstacles, but those are assumed to be controllable by forces at man's disposal so long as he applies skill, motivation, and good will. Evidence for the more frequent occurrence of optimism in the advantaged classes is not ample, but a number of very suggestive items come to hand which support the assumption.

The sources of atomic energy present so great a potential threat to man that they often induce visions of the total destruction of civilization and even human existence. But atomic energy also holds the possibility of great benefits. Casual reading of newspapers led us to assume that fears about the destructive misuse of atomic energy have a particularly strong hold on the better-educated segments of modern society. But our theory also leads us to believe that the same people—because of their greater faith in man's ability to change, adopt, transform, and control natural and social forces—should more often hold the belief that *ultimately* the beneficial effects of atomic energy will predominate. For Australia and the United States there are class data by education, on responses to the question: "In the long run do you think atomic energy will do more harm than good, or more good than harm?"[28] In both countries the differentiation by education is extremely sharp, and in both cases the differences are in the expected direction, that is, there is greater optimism as one ascends the educational ladder (Table 11).

Table 11. Estimates of Long-Run Effects of Atomic Energy, in Percentages by Country and Education

Education	More Good than Harm	More Harm than Good	Can't Say or Don't Know
United States*			
University	69	20	11
Secondary	55	30	15
Primary	40	40	20
Australia†			
Higher	61	18	21
Middle	47	25	28
Lower	31	23	46

*_Doxa Bolletino_, Vol. II, No. 22 (November, 1948).
†Australian Gallup Polls of Melbourne, _Bulletin_, Nos. 645-61 (January-February, 1950).

These striking indications of the greater frequency with which optimism, based on mastery of natural and social forces, is found among the better-educated are further supported, although less dramatically, by the results of a question on war and peace. In the UNESCO study the question was put as follows: "Do you believe that it will be possible for all countries to live together at peace with each other?" Certainly this strains optimism more than does the question on atomic energy. Even so, in four of nine countries the step pattern was clearly manifested, and in no case was the proportion giving the more optimistic answer less among those with university training than among those with only primary schooling (Table 12).

28. The question was apparently also asked in 1950 in other countries with Gallup affiliates, but I do not have the results cross-tabulated by any stratification variable.

Table 12. Belief in Possibility of Peace, in Percentages by Country and Education*

Country	EDUCATIONAL LEVEL Primary	Secondary	University
Australia	41	40	53
Britain	45	50	52
France	47	48	54
Germany†	59	53	59
Italy	30	31	30
Mexico	16	19	33
Netherlands	41	52	45
Norway	54	57	62
United States	49	47	57

*Positive responses to the question: "Do you believe that it will be possible for all countries to live together at peace with each other?" Taken from data in William Buchanan and Hadley Cantril, *How Nations See Each Other* (Urbana: University of Illinois Press, 1953), Appendix D.

†British Zone only.

Economic Optimism. It may be argued on common-sense grounds that optimism is obviously more to be expected from the well-to-do—after all, they have more to be optimistic about. In this view optimism is just an alternative formulation for happiness, to be explained on the same grounds. This might seem to be in accord with the theory that one's situation shapes one's perspective. But it is only superficially in accord with the more explicit formulation just developed, that those who are better educated and trained, and hold more responsible positions, will be more optimistic *specifically about those situations where the possibility of man's mastery of himself or his environment is involved.* This is not the same thing as saying they will be generally and indiscriminately more optimistic, even where definite or precise objective assessments are involved. A judgment about the possibility that man can develop the institutional prerequisites to peace is by no means the same thing as a judgment as to whether there will be a war in the next few years. Fundamental optimism about man's capacity to organize and solve his problems could well lead one to believe that *in the long run* man will develop the means for preserving peace, even while realism prompts the prediction that there may be a war in the next few years. When an estimate of the probability of war *within a fixed time period* was requested, the well-to-do were less optimistic or, to put it better for our purposes, more "realistic," in virtually all of the studies which reported class breaks.

Thus in Great Britain in October, 1946, the proportion who felt there would be a war in the next twenty-five years rose steadily from 30 per cent among the very poor to 44 per cent among those above the middle class. Numerous other studies in Britain in this period yielded similar findings, as did also a poll in Sweden in April, 1945, and in France on

January 16, 1946.[29] It is interesting that Buchanan and Cantril also noted, but may have misunderstood, the apparent disagreement of the national totals which affirmed the possibility of peace in their study and the proportions which, in surveys made by others in the same countries and in the same year, were reported as expecting another big war in the next ten years. This disagreement led Buchanan and Cantril to feel that responses to these questions lack "validity." They may, but our analysis suggests that, if the responses are not highly correlated, it is because the questions often tap quite different dimensions of opinion, even though their wording is superficially comparable. Optimism about man's *ultimate* capacity to master his own nature and his social forms should not be confused with optimism about the immediate chances of war.

Neither should optimism about man's potential for mastering himself and his environment be mistakenly assumed to be the simple equivalent of optimism about general economic development and personal economic prospects. We have a substantial number of studies reporting optimism about the national economy or about individual or personal economic prospects. There is no pattern from country to country, or at least no *consistent* pattern, in the responses to such questions as: "How soon do you expect a peace standard of living after the signing of a new peace treaty?" "Do you expect to be better off next year?" "Will there be a depression in the next two years?" Sometimes there is no structure of opinion at all; sometimes the higher classes are more optimistic, in other cases the lower classes. Often in one country a particular group is outstanding in its pessimism, but this is not true for the same group in other countries.[30] This has led us to conclude that specifically *economic* optimism is mainly determined by the unique economic conditions in a nation as a whole or by the distinctive prospects of certain groups in particular countries at different times. The economic optimism of particular groups is apparently not predictable either from their general position as wealthy or poor or by some common characteristic of their situation which prevails across national boundaries.

This is strikingly evident in the UNESCO study, in which the same question on economic expectations was asked in a number of countries in the same year: "When the war ended did you expect you would be

29. See Cantril (ed.), *op. cit.*, pp. 785-88. Comparable questions were asked in Australia and the Netherlands, but class breaks were not reported (AGP, Nos. 579-89 [March-April, 1949]; Ballots 141, 145, 148 [April, May, July, 1949]). There are many technical problems raised by such questions, and the results remain ambiguous (see Buchanan and Cantril, *op. cit.*, p. 62).

30. See AGP, Nos. 529-36 (July, 1948); NIPO, Ballot 129 (February, 1949), question 7B; and studies in the U. S., Great Britain, and Hungary reported in Cantril (ed.), *op. cit.*, pp. 63 (question 29), 66 (question 48 and 50), 141 (question 19), and 147 (question 6).

getting along better, worse, or about the same, as you actually are getting along at the present time?" The question did not explicitly call for an assessment of economic prospects, but, from its context and the response pattern, it evidently was generally taken to apply to economic welfare. It also suffers from the defect of asking people how they had felt some years *earlier*, "when the war ended." This would be a rather indefinite time, not the same in all countries. These considerations must limit our confidence in the distinctive relevance of the answers to the issue discussed above. Such ambiguity in a question typically "washes out" patterns which might otherwise be observed. Allowing for it, there is virtually no steady association, country by country, between occupation and the percentage who at the end of the war (presumably 1945) expected to be getting along better than they actually were in 1948 (Table 13). For example, in Italy, the Netherlands, and the United States,

Table 13. Expectations of Personal Economic Betterment, in Percentages by Country and Occupation*

	OCCUPATION							
Country	*Business Owners*	*Farm Owners*	*Salaried Managers*	*Profes-sionals*	*Clerical Workers*	*Artisans*	*Manual Workers*	*Farm Laborers*
Australia	49	66	52	39	49	55	53	42
Britain	61	57	49	48	60	60	56	74
France	67	80	79	89	79	81	81	80
Germany†	49	37	45	47	44	39	50	42
Italy	38	37	29	21	37	37	52	54
Mexico	35	14	52	41	34	43	37	38
Netherlands	30	58	53	44	52	56	66	64
Norway	39	36	48	28	58	58	52	57
United States	29	30	38	37	45	49	36	22

* Persons who at the end of World War II *expected* to be getting along better than they now actually are. From data in Appendix D of William Buchanan and Hadley Cantril, *How Nations See Each Other* (Urbana: University of Illinois Press, 1953), pp. 125-216.

†British Zone only.

business owners yielded more or less the lowest proportions indicating that they had thought at the end of the war that things would turn out better than they seemed to have done by 1948. But in Britain, Germany, and France, the opposite was the case; business owners were outstanding in the proportion who reported that at the end of the war they had been too optimistic—in 1948 they were not getting on as well as they had earlier anticipated. A comparable lack of agreement is shown at other levels, and consequently there is no pattern in the responses by occupation from country to country.

This lack of pattern contrasts very sharply with the findings from a different question on economic prospects put to the same samples, namely, that on job security (Table 14). In this case, the structure of response, by occupation, was very similar from country to country and

Table 14. Job Security Compared to Average, in Percentages by Country and Occupation

Country	OCCUPATION Business Owners	Farm Owners	Salaried Managers	Profes-sionals	Clerical Workers	Artisans	Manual Workers	Farm Laborers
Australia	60	53	70	79	57	50	48	33
Britain	47	43	52	56	31	30	32	29
France	24	27	43	28	20	16	10	11
Germany†	29	28	26	24	28	42	20	12
Italy	39	22	18	34	31	18	15	6
Mexico	59	100	74	80	62	50	46	38
Netherlands	48	20	51	51	36	19	11	7
Norway	4	18	48	24	21	14	29	9
United States	53	42	47	65	37	37	28	22

*From data by country in Appendix D of William Buchanan and Hadley Cantril, *How Nations See Each Other* (Urbana: University of Illinois Press, 1953), pp. 125-216.
†British Zone only.

is particularly clear-cut in the four occupational groups at the bottom of the hierarchy. In seven of the nine countries farm laborers consistently had the lowest proportion, rank 8, reporting job security, and, in the remaining two countries, rank 7. By contrast, on the preceding question on expectations of economic outcome farm laborers held rank 8 only once, rank 7 once, and were actually in the first rank twice (see Table 13). The sum of differences between the average rank and the attained rank for each occupational group in all countries was two or three times larger for most occupational groups when economic welfare rather than job security was assessed.

We may then conclude that the degree of job security remains a fairly fixed quality or attribute of jobs *relative to each other* in the industrial hierarchy. Estimates of job security, therefore, yield a comparable structure of responses from country to country, rather than being variable in the manner of more general estimates of economic prospects. Even if economic security in a country decreases, it will probably drop for all or most groups, thus insuring that the cross-national pattern will be maintained. Within limits this will probably be true even when the decrease in security hits one stratum, such as workers, harder than others. To some degree the security pattern is built into the nature of large-scale industrial organization. It therefore produces a similar pattern from country to country.[31] The prospects for economic improvement

31. Perhaps an exception should be made for communist or socialist countries, but I think not. At least in the Soviet Union, if there is reorganization in industry the professional personnel are, I believe, actually more assured of continuing employment than are the ordinary workers. Of course, the communist countries have experienced chronic labor shortages while attempting rapid industrialization, and this has tended to eliminate insecurity about unemployment at all levels, except where political circumstances excluded a man from the right to work.

for any group, especially relative to others, are by no means "structurally given" to anything like the same degree. Nothing in the nature of large-scale economic organization dictates what progress any stratum, relative to other strata, may or should make in the next year or the year after.

At first glance the fact that position on the socioeconomic ladder does not make possible prediction of the pattern of economic optimism from country to country may seem to impugn our original general theory. But the theory does not predict that the well-off will be uniformly optimistic about economic affairs. It states, rather, that the opinions and attitudes of men in all countries will be similarly shaped or patterned to the degree that they face similar objective conditions or situations, and are located in comparable positions in networks of power, influence, and interpersonal relations. Insofar as economic conditions held varying promise of good or bad outcomes for particular economic strata in the individual nations, to that degree we would expect to find the local expressions of economic optimism more or less distinctive. Such lack of pattern is exactly what we do find. But the variation observed is probably not random. We would, however, take ourselves far afield if we endeavored to discover the rational or objective basis for each variation in response, group by group and country by country.

There are many other areas into which we might look—politics, religion, recreation, family life.[32] But the purpose of this study is to open a discussion, not to settle an issue. The following statements seem justified by our experience:

There is substantial evidence, over a wide attitudinal and experiential range, that perceptions, opinions, and values are systematically ordered in modern societies. The proportion of people who give a particular response increases or decreases fairly regularly as we move up or down the typical status ladders of occupation, income, education, and prestige. These patterns emerge not only in realms which are obviously closely related to status pressures but also in areas seemingly far removed. In every country the average or typical response may be distinctive, but the same order or structure is manifested within *each*, even though they vary widely in their economic and political development and have unique cultural histories. This similarity in the patterning of response seems best explained by assuming that, in significant degree, perceptions, attitudes and values are shaped by the networks of interpersonal relations in which individuals are enmeshed and particularly by rewards and punishments.

It follows that a careful study of the specific external situation of the major subgroups in any country would enable one to deduce the dis-

32. The previously cited work in progress by S. M. Lipset and Juan Linz parallels this analysis in its application to political belief and action.

tinctive internal life—the perceptions, attitudes, and values—of those groups relative to each other. This makes the very large assumption, however, that one is equipped with a great battery of subtheories which specify the probable psychological outcome of a very wide range of diverse external situations, taken alone and in numerous combinations. With or without the requisite battery of subtheories, this is, in effect, what historians, anthropologists, and sociologists frequently attempt to do when they analyze life in some one nation or culture. However, the uniqueness of the external situation studied in each case, and the *ad hoc* nature of the theory used, make it difficult to test and refine theory and on this basis to accumulate firm empirical knowledge.

The cross-national or comparative approach permits concentration on a few widely present situational forces and facilitates the systematic testing and validation of theory. This paper's concentration on modern industrial society should not be understood, however, as suggesting it to be the only realm in which the theory sketched here is applicable. On the contrary, we expect that, whenever any set of nations places major social strata in a structure highly comparable from society to society, a cross-national attitudinal pattern similar to the one we observed will also be found. Theoretically, a parallel analysis could be made for the various strata of medieval European societies, of the traditional monarchies of the eighteenth century, or of the underdeveloped nations of the early twentieth century. In fact, any such effort would probably founder, either because we could not secure adequate information on the specific distribution of attitudes or because we could not satisfy the requirement that the situation of the subgroups, and the hierarchies in which they were organized, be strictly comparable from one society to the next.

The choice of industrial society as a field of investigation is therefore not based solely on grounds of methodological expediency or political interest. It is the only setting which relatively unambiguously satisfies the conditions to which the theory has critical relevance. Modern society, most notably in the factory system, and secondarily in large-scale bureaucratic organizations in business, government, and other fields, is more or less unique in the extent to which it produces standardized contexts of experience. These are exportable, and are sought after to a degree which far exceeds the exportability of most other culture complexes. And to an extent far beyond what is true of other complexes, these resist being reformulated, changed, or adapted to suit the larger sociocultural environment into which they bluntly intrude or are invited or accepted.

The patterns of reaction we have observed are to be expected, however, only insofar as the hierarchies in the different countries are equivalent, not merely in the positions recognized, but also in the conditions of existence they provide for the incumbents of those statuses. Departures from the standard pattern (as distinguished from differences in the average response for any country) must in all cases be assumed to arise from empirically discoverable variations in the conditions of existence, by status. It follows, therefore, that, to the degree a nation's social structure approximates the model of a full-scale primary industrial society, to that degree will it more clearly show the differentiated structure of response we have delineated, and do so over a wider range of topics, problems, or areas of experience. There are, of course, many theoretical and methodological difficulties in developing a model of industrial society, which we cannot go into here. Suffice it to say that England before World War I, the United States between World Wars I and II, the Soviet Union and Western Germany after World War II all can be shown to have approximated the model in important respects. My anticipation is that all the currently developed nations and all those on the verge of developing will at some point approximate the model and will at that point show most clearly the patterns we have described.

This brings us to the often cited tendencies toward homogenization of experience in the most advanced industrial countries, notably the United States. If one general theory is valid, then to the extent that the conditions of life, the network of interpersonal relations in which people work, the patterns of reward and punishment, come to be more and more alike regardless of status and situs, to that degree should their perceptions, attitudes, and values become similar. In other words, the typical step pattern we observed would become less and less evident and might eventually disappear altogether. Furthermore, to the degree that similar conditions came to prevail in other countries, the same process of homogenization could be expected to manifest itself there as well. Indeed, although it seems far off and far-fetched, it could very well be that we will, in the future, come to have a fairly uniform world culture, in which not only nations but groups within nations will have lost their distinctive subcultures. In important respects—exclusive of such elements as language—most people might come to share a uniform, homogeneous culture as citizens of the world. This culture might make them, at least as group members, more or less indistinguishable in perceptual tendency, opinion, and belief not only from their fellow citizens in the same nation and their occupational peers in other nations but from all men everywhere.[33]

33. For a forceful—indeed extreme—argument of this position, including an exposition of the forces working to bring it about, see Roderick Seidenberg, *Posthistoric Man: An Inquiry* (Boston: Beacon Press, 1957).

Such speculation of course goes far beyond what our data can at present support even remotely. The data are, furthermore, by no means unambiguous. The questions put in different countries, for one thing, are not comparable. But it is highly improbable that ambiguity in the stimulus would generate agreement in the response pattern. On the contrary, the likelihood is vastly greater that any consistent pattern really there would be muted or muffled by questions which put, in effect, a randomly varying stimulus to respondents in the different countries. There is also the substantial problem that *within* any country a question in the same language may have quite different meaning for people with markedly dissimilar education. We obviously need to develop methods which insure that our questions, *as understood* by respondents of different countries and classes, are more strictly equivalent. We have methods which can satisfy this requirement in substantial degree. They are moderately costly, and require time, but the advantage of using them in scientific, as contrasted with the commercial, studies is great enough to warrant the cost.

Another difficulty arises with regard to the criteria to be used in determining when opinions are structured in any country and patterned across national boundaries. The usual statistical tests are not automatically applicable. In any event, for purposes of this exploratory study I have adopted a liberal and flexible definition. But in later, more systematic studies we must be prepared to specify our criteria more precisely and to apply them more rigorously.

A more imposing challenge to our findings is that in a great many items the variation in the average or typical response for different countries is so great as to dwarf into insignificance the similarity in pattern from nation to nation. The occupational or other hierarchy, in other words, often explains only a small part of the variance, at least as compared to dimensions like nationality, citizenship, or ethnicity. We should, perhaps, be pleased to have discovered *any* regularity in human behavior which persists across national boundaries, even if it is only "minor." It is also possible that often the seemingly great size of these differences among nations is more spurious than real and arises mainly from the fact that the questions used are not really comparable stimuli for the various respondents. The differences may, however, be very real indeed. If they are, then we will still have to choose between alternative explanations—the distinctive cultural tradition of a nation, on the one hand, and its level and style of economic and political development, on the other. Undoubtedly both factors exert major influence, and often they will be so intertwined as to make it impossible to assign separate weights to them. But careful selection of the countries to be studied—perhaps even matching countries with similar traditions but different economic or political development, and vice versa—would yield interesting results. It will be particularly important to seek to discover those realms of perceptions, opinion, and value which seem most influenced by the industrial social order, as against those which are relatively more tightly integrated in an autonomous pattern of traditional culture and hence more immune, or at least resistant, to change even in the presence of the standard industrial environment.

One last reservation is the claim that these data are subject to quite different explanations than those here offered. For example, the pattern can be explained as arising mainly from educational differences—not an alternative explanation, but really an integral part of my argument. The theory stresses that people are ordered in modern society in hierarchies of power, responsibility, prestige, income, and education. The amount of education a man receives is part of the structure of rewards. It also is a major element in determining his occupational status. As such it can be seen as merely an integral, although alternative, *index* of his *situation* rather than as an independent and alternative *explanation* of his *behavior*. But, quite apart from this, the theory holds that situational presures exert an influence independent of the education of the incumbents of the position. To test this assumption and to discover how great is the independent influence of education, we would, of course, need to compare the responses of people with comparable education who occupied systematically different positions, and vice versa.

We obviously need more and better research on the important problem this initial exploration has barely opened up. It is to be doubted, however, that merely by collecting more data of the type now in hand we can settle many of the issues. But through carefully designed studies, building on the experience of this exploration and sharply focused on some of the issues raised by it, we may expect to make substantial progress. We would hope to insure comparability in the meaning of the questions from country to country and from class to class. Instability and unreliability in the findings could further be greatly reduced by the use of scales to measure important universes of attitudes, in place of the single question which has been the standard in the past. Rather than gathering scattered bits and snippets of information from numerous different samples, we should aim to secure a rich set of responses from the *same* set of respondents in each country, thus providing the basis for studying patterns of interrelation among sets of perceptions, opinions and values. To aid in resolving some of the difficult problems of interpreting the findings we have so far accumulated, the countries studied should represent a wide range of stages and forms of economic development and cultural type. And the samples drawn from each should be not the bare minimum representative sample but, rather, carefully stratified and, where necessary, extensively overrepresented to provide subsamples large enough to permit complex internal comparisons. With sufficient resources we could reasonably hope to make substantial strides toward developing a respectable social psychology of industrial society.

c) ASPIRATIONS

RAYMOND W. MACK, RAYMOND J. MURPHY, and SEYMOUR YELLIN

The Protestant Ethic, Level of Aspiration, and Social Mobility: An Empirical Test

FEW debate Weber's theory that rationalized capitalism and spiritual Protestantism are ideologically compatible.[1] The thesis lends itself to the historical method, whereby one can see Protestantism as the precursor of the rise of capitalism, or to comparative analysis, wherein one cites the correlation between the capitalistic character of a society's economic order and that society's acceptance in its religious institutions

Reprinted from American Sociological Review, *June, 1956, pp. 295-300, by permission of the authors and the journal.*

Paper read at the annual meeting of the American Sociological Society, 1955.

1. Max Weber, *The Protestant Ethic and the Spirit of Capitalism* [translated by Talcott Parsons], New York: Charles Scribner's Sons, 1930.

of the tenets of the Protestant Reformation. Weber asserted that the emancipating and rationalizing effect of the Protestant Reformation made possible the rise of rational capitalism. The Catholic ethic propounded a culturally established emphasis upon other-worldliness; the rationale for the performance of earthly tasks was other-worldly: reparation for sins and purification through humility. Luther and Calvin sanctified work; they made virtues of industry, thrift, and self-denial. Wesley preached that the fruits of labor were the signs of salvation. The culmination of the Protestant Reformation, then, was to give divine sanction to the drive to excel.[2]

We can accept the evidence of a historical relationship between Protestantism and the *rise* of capitalism, but we cannot assume the existence of any relationship between the Protestant and Catholic ethics and role performance in contemporary American society. Sebastian de Grazia has subsumed the extremes of these two belief systems under the labels "Activist Directive" and "Quietist Directive," positing them as two poles of an ideal-type continuum.[3] He uses the term "directive" to denote mores which have been internalized in early childhood and thus exert unusually powerful influences upon behavior. The theoretical question which remains unanswered because of a lack of data is whether the Catholic and Protestant faiths in contemporary American society exert a potent enough influence on behavior to be accurately designated "directives." Collins, Dalton, and Roy suggest that significant differences occur in the role behavior of Catholics and Protestants in an industrial setting, but their sample is small and their conclusions are tentative.[4] Clearly, more evidence is needed. Intuitively a good argument can be made for the idea that the "American Dream," the mobility ethic, is so strong in our culture that it will override in influence sub-cultural religious dogma. That is, a child socialized in contemporary American society will be less conditioned by either the Catholic other-worldly salvation, "quietist directive," or the Protestant salvation through works, "activist directive," as such than by the positive value which our society places upon upward mobility striving.

This we propose to test empirically in the form of the null hypothesis: No significant differences will be found either in social mobility patterns or in aspiration level between samples of Protestant and Catholic Americans in several occupations. The mobility patterns will provide

2. A detailed analysis of the material here cursorily treated can be found in Adriano Tilger, *Work: What It Has Meant to Man through the Ages* (New York: Harcourt, Brace, and World, 1930).

3. Sebastian de Grazia, *The Political Community*, Chicago: University of Chicago Press, 1948, p. 59.

4. Orvis Collins, Melville Dalton, and Donald Roy, "Restriction of Output and Social Cleavage in Industry," *Applied Anthropology*, 5 (Summer, 1946), pp. 1-31.

data on role performance; the expressed level of aspiration will supplement these with evidence of intent, thus offsetting a possible difference between the two categories in life chances.

Methodology

The data analyzed here were gathered as part of a larger study of occupational role behavior and patterns of social mobility in three white-collar occupations. The sample in this larger study consists of 2,205 white males in three occupational statuses: salesmen, engineers, and bank officials and clerks. The sample is confined to white males so that analysis will not be confounded by variations accounted for by differences in race and sex. Two main considerations entered into the selection of these particular occupations: (1) They are all white-collar jobs, thus holding constant the manual–non-manual dimension, and (2) they are widely distributed on a hypothesized determinate-indeterminate continuum of occupational roles.

The theory of role determinateness which these data were gathered to test postulates statuses ranged along a continuum according to how well-defined are the rights and duties of the status and how rigid the expectations of the role. One polar type we call the determinate occupational status which has elaborately prescribed requirements for entry. The rights as well as the duties of the person occupying the status are firmly established and well known to both the actor and those with whom he interacts in his occupational role. The expectations of role behavior in such a status are narrow in range and relatively definite. An indeterminate occupational status is the opposite ideal type, characterized by less stringent requirements for entry into the occupation and shifting with both time and locale. Neither the rights nor the duties of the person occupying the status are firmly established, and the expectations of role behavior are wide in range and relatively indefinite. Engineers were selected for this research as determinate, salesmen as indeterminate, and bankers as occupying an intermediate position on the continuum.[5]

The total salesman sub-sample consists of 1,389 persons, either employed as salesmen, or applying for the position of salesman (if the applicant has had previous sales experience among his last three jobs). These individuals are distributed in a cluster sample of twenty-six companies in eleven industries. The industries correspond to the following Census Bureau classifications: *Manufacturing:* furniture and fixtures,

5. For a more complete discussion of the theory see Raymond W. Mack, "Occupational Determinateness: A Problem and Hypotheses in Role Theory," *Social Forces*, 35, 1956-1957, p. 20.

machinery, except electrical, meat products, other food industries, paper and allied products, printing, publishing, and allied industries, petroleum and coal products; *Wholesale and Retail Trade:* wholesale trade, motor vehicles and accessories retailing; *Finance, Insurance, and Real Estate; Business and Repair Services.* Salesmen are defined as persons who are outside salesmen or company representatives, thus excluding persons categorized under a broader definition of sales work, such as store clerks, door-to-door canvassers, and newsboys.

The sub-sample of engineers consists of 515 individuals of eleven engineering specialties (aeronautical, agricultural, ceramic, chemical, civil, electrical, hydraulic, industrial, mechanical, mining, and metallurgical) in fifty-nine companies. The criteria for inclusion were: (1) presently holding an engineering position, or (2) of those applying for engineering positions, either having an engineering degree or having filled an engineering position among the last three jobs.

The total for the third sub-sample, bankers, consists of 301 middle-management officials and clerks from twelve banks. Again, the criteria for inclusion were: (1) current employment in this occupational status, or (2) of those applying for a banking position, banking experience among the last three jobs.

Each person in the sample has filled out a personal history of the variety often required of employees and applicants by employers for company files. The personal history is a four-page printed form used as a projective technique by a firm of consultants to industry.[6] The questionnaire was administered at work, either by an associate of the consultant firm (a Ph.D. in Psychology) or by the personnel manager after he had completed the firm's course in administration of the personal history. It was always given to individuals, never group administered. The form contains such information as the subject's age, marital status, number of dependents, education, membership in voluntary associations, level of aspiration, the occupation of his father, and an employment history. The employment history includes types of occupations held, length of employment period at each, type of company and industry in which employed, and income. Since the total sample was not selected randomly, the degree to which it is representative of its universe in the national labor force can be estimated by inference only. First, in relation to gross size, the three occupational sub-samples are proportionate to their corresponding categories in the labor force (see Table 1). Secondly, despite the lack of random selection procedures, there does not appear to

6. The questionnaire form, and a discussion of its validity, can be found in Gilmore J. Spencer and Richard Worthington, "Validity of a Projective Technique in Predicting Sales Effectiveness," *Personnel Psychology*, 5 (Summer, 1952), pp. 125-144.

Table 1. Comparison of Sample with Universe

Occupation	Census	Sample	Percentage Which Sample Is of Census
Salesman	1,214,094	1,389	.1144
Engineers	446,954	515	.1152
Bankers	265,123	301	.1135

Source: Bureau of the Census, U.S. *Census of Population: 1950, Vol. II, Characteristics of the Population,* Part I, U.S. Summary. Washington, D.C.: Government Printing Office, 1953, Chapter C.

be any impelling reason to suspect the presence of systematic bias. Economically, the companies contributing to the sub-samples of salesmen and engineers represent a wide variety of production and distribution lines. Geographically, the firms in all three sub-samples are distributed throughout the country. Not only are all regions represented, but the companies themselves range in size from three-person firms to some of the largest corporations in the industries sampled, and are located in cities with populations varying from a few thousand to several million. Finally, no selective factors were operative within the companies with regard to employees filling out the questionnaire.

Social Mobility and Religious Affiliation

The sample in each of the three occupations for the present analysis is about one-half the size of the total *N* for that occupation in the larger study. Religious affiliation information is available only for a sharply reduced portion of the total sample for two reasons: (1) A number of individuals did not fill in this response item, and (2) FEPC legislation resulted in the removal of the religious item from the questionnaire in 1951. The possible bias arising out of a potential selectivity of respondents in favor of those with strong religious convictions is, of course, unknown. The direction of the bias is in favor of those having relatively strong feelings about their religion, the more indifferent being excluded from the analysis. The effect of the bias, therefore, would be to stack the deck against the null hypothesis; significant behavioral differences should appear more readily among those with firm religious convictions than among the disinterested. The religious affiliation of respondents who filled out the form after the question had been deleted has been inferred wherever possible from voluntary association memberships which were reported in response to other items; e.g., Masons were coded as Protestants, Knights of Columbus as Catholics. Since the number of Jews was too small to permit tests of statistical significance, they were excluded from the analysis.

Four measures of social mobility were utilized: (1) change from father to son in stratum as defined in the Census occupational category of subject;[7] (2) change during employment history in stratum as defined in the Census occupational category of subject; (3) change from father to son in status as defined in the Warner occupational category;[8] and (4) change during employment history in status as defined in the Warner occupational category. The four mobility measures will be referred to hereafter as father-son stratum, career stratum, father-son status, and career status, respectively.

The data allow, in the case of stratum mobility, for a fifteen point scale ranging from seven strata downwardly mobile (from professional to unskilled labor) to seven strata upwardly mobile with non-mobile as a midpoint. A thirteen point scale can be constructed for status mobility. For the present analysis, however, the *N* becomes far too small for such an elaborate treatment if any controls are implemented. Our research to date indicates that both age and occupation are significantly related to mobility;[9] it seemed, therefore, far more desirable to control for these two variables than to run religious affiliation against a multi-point mobility scale. Mobility, then, like religious affiliation, was dichotomized. Bifurcation of either the stratum or status mobility scales poses a question: do the non-mobile persons belong with the upwardly or the downwardly mobile? From the point of view of the Protestant ethic, one might frame an argument for either alternative, depending upon whether he chose a Calvinist or a Wesleyan emphasis. We decided that it made better sense in the present context to combine non-mobile persons with the downwardly mobile and to contrast this category with the upwardly mobile. Occupational success and achievement represent cultural imperatives in American society.[10] The extent of the rise above the social level of the parents or above the point of entry into the labor force is often taken as a measure of the individual's adherence to the dominant value

7. U.S. Bureau of the Census, *1950 Census of Population, Classified Index of Occupations and Industries*, Washington: Government Printing Office, 1950.

8. W. Lloyd Warner, Marchia Meeker, and Kenneth Eells, *Social Class in America*, Chicago: Science Research Associates, 1949, pp. 140-141.

9. Raymond W. Mack, "Toward a Theory of Occupational Choice: The Stability Factor," paper read at the annual meeting of the American Sociological Society, 1954; Raymond J. Murphy, "Mobility and Occupational Role: A Comparative Analysis" (unpublished Ph.D. dissertation, Department of Sociology, Northwestern University, 1955); Seymour Yellin, "Social Mobility and Familism" (unpublished Ph.D. dissertation, Department of Sociology, Northwestern University, 1955).

10. For an excellent discussion of this point, see Robert K. Merton, *Social Theory and Social Structure*, New York: Free Press, 1949, pp. 129-133.

system with its emphasis upon competitive effort. It therefore seemed appropriate (particularly in view of the white collar, middle-class character of the sample) to separate the upwardly mobile from those who have not been so.

The hypothesis that no significant differences in social mobility patterns would be found between Protestants and Catholics was tested by four cell Chi-square analysis. For each of the four mobility types, Chi-squares were computed within occupational sub-samples, and each occupational sub-sample was divided into those under 35 years of age and those 35 and over. These age categories are called the "Trial Work Period" and the "Stable Work Period" by Miller and Form; they comprise two distinct segments in the career patterns of the respondents, according to these researchers.[11]

The first computation, then, was run on the relationship between religious affiliation and father-son stratum mobility for salesmen under 35, the next for salesmen 35 and over, the next for bankers under 35, and so on until we moved to the next mobility type, career stratum. When this analysis was completed for two age groups within each of three occupations within each of four mobility types, 24 Chi-squares had been computed to test the association between social mobility and religious affiliation. As can be seen in Table 2, only three of these reached even the .05 level of significance, and one of those disappeared when Yates' correction was applied. A pattern of significance can hardly be suggested by two Chi-squares in a set of twenty-four, and these two are not even for the same mobility measure or the same occupation.

Among the men in these three white-collar occupations there is apparently no relationship between being Catholic or Protestant and being upwardly or downwardly mobile either from the occupational status or stratum of one's father or from one's own previous status or stratum in the labor force.

Aspiration and Religious Affiliation

It is conceivable that the Protestant ethic might be operative as a value system without producing statistically significant results in performance. For instance, differences in life chances between the social categories being analyzed might obscure its results. Thus at first blush, we should expect an exaggeration rather than a disappearance of mobility differences between Protestants and Catholics in contemporary

11. Delbert C. Miller and William H. Form, *Industrial Sociology*, New York: Harper and Brothers, 1951, pp. 700-717.

United States, since it is generally conceded that Protestants have higher status and suffer less discrimination in the job market. However, it must be remembered that the mathematics of the situation could trick us here:

Table 2. Association between Religious Affiliation and Social Mobility,* within Occupation by Age Category

Mobility Measure	Occupation	Age	N	Sum Chi-square	P
Father-son stratum	Salesmen	–35	387	2.13	.20
	Salesmen	35+	182	3.05	.10
	Bankers	–35	72	3.01	.10
	Bankers	35+	80	4.00†	.05
	Engineers	–35	91	1.35	.30
	Engineers	35+	113	0.07	.80
Career stratum	Salesmen	–35	355	1.14	.30
	Salesmen	35+	206	0.97	.80
	Bankers	–35	44	0.05	.90
	Bankers	35+	63	0.93	.50
	Engineers	–35	90	2.27	.20
	Engineers	35+	94	0.01	.95
Father-son status	Salesmen	–35	414	1.22	.30
	Salesmen	35+	189	3.92†	.05
	Bankers	–35	82	2.88	.10
	Bankers	35+	71	3.46	.10
	Engineers	–35	121	2.16	.20
	Engineers	35+	92	0.58	.90
Career status	Salesmen	–35	379	2.52	.20
	Salesmen	35+	214	0.08	.80
	Bankers	–35	47	1.39	.30
	Bankers	35+	64	0.02	.90
	Engineers	–35	98	3.25	.10
	Engineers	35+	97	0.20	.70

*All Chi-squares in this table are with one degree of freedom: Religious Affiliation has been dichotomized as "Protestant" and "Catholic"; Mobility as "Upward" and "Non and Downward."

†Yates correction has been applied.

a man born into the top stratum of the Census occupational categories has seven occupational strata available for the downward father-son stratum mobility, but he cannot possibly be upwardly mobile by this measure. Similarly, a person who enters the labor force in a job ranked seventh on the Warner scale has six categories into which he can move up, but none into which he can move down.

Secondly, if we accept the dicta of those who tell us that the American class structure is becoming more rigid,[12] we must admit that the subcultures of Protestantism and Catholicism might engender different

12. J. O. Hertzler, "Some Tendencies toward a Closed Class System in the United States," *Social Forces,* 30 (March, 1952), pp. 313-323.

value systems without producing different rates of mobility, simply because mobility was not available to the striver. To guard against the possible error of concluding that Catholic and Protestant Americans share a value system, where actually they might only share a social structure which does not allow them to implement the differences in their beliefs, we turned to an analysis of data on aspiration.

Chi-squares were calculated on the relationship between religious affiliation and two other variables: income goal and job orientation. The former was coded from a questionnaire item which asked the respondent, "Regardless of your present salary, what income do you need to enable you to live as you would *like* to live? (This relates to type of housing and general living conditions you may desire ultimately; and your response will not be construed as dissatisfaction with your present salary.)" Answers were dichotomized as "Under $10,000" and "$10,000 and over." The job orientation variable was taken from the final item on the personal history, an open-ended question which asked, "What are your plans for the future?" These were classified for the present analysis either as "Occupational Mobility" ("I want to become Sales Manager," "To work my way up in the company," "A more responsible position," and so on) or as "Non Occupation Oriented" ("Buy a place in the country and retire," "Have two more children," "See more of the United States," and so on). As in the mobility computations, both occupational and age controls were instituted.

The results of these twelve Chi-square calculations are presented in Table 3. Not one reaches the .05 level of significance. No relationship

Table 3. Association between Religious Affiliation and Occupational Aspiration* within Occupation by Age Category

Aspiration Measure	Occupation	Age	N	Sum Chi-square	P
Income goal	Salesmen	–35	412	1.34	.30
	Salesmen	35+	205	0.34	.70
	Bankers	–35	77	0.05	.90
	Bankers	35+	73	0.32	.70
	Engineers	–35	127	0.02	.90
	Engineers	35+	88	2.79	.10
Job orientation	Salesmen	–35	704	0.004	.95
	Salesmen	35+	324	0.54	.50
	Bankers	–35	134	0.35	.70
	Bankers	35+	109	0.56	.50
	Engineers	–35	264	0.27	.70
	Engineers	35+	155	0.44	.70

*All Chi-squares in this table are with one degree of freedom: Religious Affiliation has been dichotomized as "Protestant" and "Catholic"; Aspiration as "Under $10,000" and "$10,000 and over" in the case of Income Goal, "Occupational Mobility" and "Other" in the case of Job Orientation.

is indicated between religious affiliation and either income goal or work-oriented plans for the future.

Conclusions

We are unable to reject our null hypothesis. This analysis seems to indicate that whatever influence these two religious sub-cultures have upon their adherents in our society, so far as the Weberian thesis is concerned, is overriden by the general ethos.

This interpretation, however, should be accompanied by one major reservation springing from the nature of the sample. All three occupations investigated are white collar in character and of relatively high status. This should make no difference if we adopt the position that there is a culturally defined success drive shared by persons at all levels of our social structure. Such a position implies the existence of a mobility ethic external to specific occupations. However, Hyman finds inferential evidence that the desire for upward mobility varies with social class level and occupational category.[13] Stress toward upward movement may, then, represent an internal component of some occupational roles. If motivation toward upward mobility is partly a function of occupational role expectations, persons in different occupations will show different attitudes toward mobility which are derived from an internalization of their work roles.

Since all three of the occupations in this sample are middle-class categories, we must entertain the idea that the Catholics in those occupations may be thought of as internalizing the mobility ethic in their occupational roles—in other words, as already participating in the Protestant ethic.

A test of the above reservation must await research on a sample which cuts across stratum lines. Meanwhile, we must conclude that there is no evidence in these data that the Protestant ethic is participated in any less by Catholics than by Protestants in contemporary United States.

13. Herbert H. Hyman, "The Value Systems of Different Classes: A Social Psychological Contribution to the Analysis of Stratification," in Reinhard Bendix and Seymour Lipset (editors), *Class, Status and Power: A Reader in Social Stratification,* New York: Free Press, 1953, pp. 426-442.

LaMAR T. EMPEY

Social Class and Occupational Aspiration: A Comparison of Absolute and Relative Measurement

Is the American tradition of wanting to get ahead shared by the lower classes? One group of investigators holds that it is not.[1] Hollingshead, for example, says that lower-class youngsters ". . . have limited their horizons to the class horizon, and in the process they have unconsciously placed themselves in such a position that they will occupy the same levels as their parents."[2] Another group takes the opposite point of view. Its members suggest, either explicitly or implicitly, that the lower classes have internalized this tradition.[3]

Reprinted from American Sociological Review, *December, 1956, pp. 703-709, by permission of the author and the journal.*

This paper reports one phase of a project (No. 1141) on the educational and occupational planning of high school seniors conducted by the Department of Rural Sociology at the State College of Washington. This writer is indebted to W. L. Slocum and the members of the department for their help.

1. H. H. Hyman, "The Value Systems of Different Classes, in *Class, Status and Power,* edited by R. Bendix and S. M. Lipset, New York: The Free Press, 1953; W. A. Davis, "Socialization and Adolescent Personality," in the *Forty-third Yearbook of the National Society for the Study of Education,* University of Chicago, 1944, Chap. 5; W. A. Davis; "American Status Systems and the Socialization of the Child," *American Sociological Review,* 6 (June, 1941), pp. 345-346; A. B. Hollingshead, *Elmtown's Youth,* New York: John Wiley and Sons, Inc., 1949, pp. 282-287; W. A. Davis, and R. J. Havighurst, *Father of the Man,* Boston: Houghton-Mifflin Co., 1947, p. 144.

2. Hollingshead, *op. cit.,* p. 285.

3. R. E. Merton, "Social Structure and Anomie," *Social Theory and Social Structure,* New York: The Free Press, 1949, Chap. 4; J. W. Bennett and M. Tumin, *Social Life,* New York: A. A. Knopf, 1948, pp. 490, 587; R. Cattel, "The Cultural Functions of Social Stratification," *Journal of Social Psychology,* 21 (February, 1945), pp. 3-23, 25-55; E. Chinoy, "The Tradition of Opportunity and the Aspirations of Automobile Workers," *American Journal of Sociology,* 57 (March, 1952), p. 453; R. Centers, "Attitude and Belief in Relation to Occupational Stratification," *Journal of Social Psychology,* 27 (May, 1948), pp. 159-186; P. E. Davidson and H. D. Anderson, *Occupational Mobility in an American Community,* Palo Alto: Stanford University Press, 1937, p. 17; A. W. Kornhauser, "Analysis of 'Class' Structure in Contemporary American Society," in *Industrial Conflict: A Psycho-*

Previous investigations on this subject have dealt largely with occupational aspiration in absolute terms; that is, a monolithic definition of occupational success has been imposed upon the occupational hierarchy, and the aspirations of lower-class people have been compared with those of upper-class people. Almost without exception, the *absolute* occupational aspirations of the upper classes have been found to be "higher" in the economic structure than those of the lower class.[4] Because the lower classes are less inclined to aspire to professional and managerial occupations, such findings have supported the idea that they do not desire to "get ahead." But there is reason to believe that relative positions should be taken into account, that is, some attention should be paid to the class level from which the individual begins in deciding whether or not he desires to get ahead.

Mills[5] and Form[6] cite evidence which suggests that the prestige hierarchy of occupations is not viewed with the same perspective by different social strata. Other studies indicate that the lower classes do not define achievement solely in terms of a professional or managerial job, but that a skilled job, or the ownership of a small business, also represents progress.[7] Finally, in individualistic terms, the social-psychological literature on levels of aspiration suggests two important points: (1) that ". . . the feeling of success and failure does not depend upon an absolute level of achievement" but upon a variety of factors,[8] and (2) that the lower classes may be more strongly motivated to achieve (relatively speaking) than are those on strata above them.[9]

Gould theorizes that one's concept of the future is an expression of

---

logical Interpretation, Yearbook of the Society for the Psychological Study of Social Issues, edited by G. W. Hartmann and T. Newcomb, Chap. 11, p. 260.

4. Hyman, *op. cit.*, p. 432; Hollingshead, *op. cit.*, pp. 285-286; and R. Centers, "Motivational Aspects of Occupational Stratification," *Journal of Social Psychology*, 28 (November, 1948), pp. 187-217.

5. C. W. Mills, "The Middle Classes in Middle-sized Cities," *American Sociological Review*, 11 (October, 1946), pp. 525-526.

6. W. H. Form, "Toward an Occupational Social Psychology," *Journal of Social Psychology*, 24 (August, 1946), p. 97.

7. E. Ginzberg and associates, *Occupational Choice*, New York: Columbia University Press, 1951, p. 152; S. M. Lipset and R. Bendix, "Social Mobility and Occupational Career Patterns, II: Social Mobility," in *Class, Status and Power*, *op. cit.*, p. 462; Chinoy, *op. cit.*, p. 453; and Centers, "Motivational Aspects of Occupational Stratification," *op. cit.*, pp. 200-201.

8. K. Lewin and associates, "Level of Aspiration," in *Personality and the Behavior Disorders*, edited by J. McV. Hunt, New York: Ronald Press, 1944, I, Chap. 10, esp. pp. 340-345, 374-375.

9. R. Gould, "Some Sociological Determinants of Goal Strivings," *Journal of Social Psychology*, 13 (May, 1941), pp. 461-473.

one's status in the present. "The more unsatisfactory the present is conceived to be the more urgent the desire (need) to depart from it 'in the future,' and the greater the psychological distance between *now* and the situation-to-be."[10] Therefore, she says, the lower class is imbued with a "deep all-pervading" need (which the upper class does not have and the middle class only to a lesser degree) to leave the present.

But there is some question as to whether or not this psychological need of the lower class is ever actually manifest. Gould and others suggest that, despite their need to escape the present, reality compels lower-class individuals to reduce their aspirations because they are not able to accept the risk of becoming less poor.[11] In actuality, there may be a large discrepancy between the occupations they would *prefer* to enter and the ones they think they can *actually* enter. Reality aspirations may be limited after all to the class horizon.

The present paper is devoted to further study on this matter. It is based on the responses of male high school seniors to a questionnaire dealing with their occupational plans and aspirations. An effort is made to obtain a more accurate picture of occupational aspiration by measuring it both by an *absolute* and a *relative* standard: when an *absolute* standard is used, the aspirations of lower-class seniors are compared with those of upper-class seniors; when a *relative* standard is used, each senior's occupational choice is compared with that of his father. Thus, not only the actual occupation which an individual chooses but the status level from which he comes is considered in deciding whether or not he desires to get ahead. Furthermore, the analysis seeks to determine whether or not lower-class individuals seem inclined to reduce their aspirations when a comparison is made between their *preferred* occupations and the ones they *actually anticipate* entering.

The following hypotheses are examined:

1. The *absolute* occupational status aspirations of male high school seniors from the middle and upper classes are significantly higher than those of seniors from the lower classes.

2. The *relative* occupational status aspirations of lower-class seniors indicate that they *prefer* and *anticipate* having significantly higher occupational statuses than their fathers.

3. Seniors from lower strata are more inclined than those from middle and upper strata to reduce their occupational aspirations significantly when faced with the necessity of choosing between their *preferred* and *anticipated* occupations.

10. *Ibid.*, p. 468.

11. *Ibid.*, pp. 468ff; Hyman *op. cit.*, pp. 433-434; and Lewin *et al.*, *op. cit.*, pp. 344-345.

The Sample

This study is based on a probability sample of approximately one-tenth of all male seniors who were in public high schools in the state of Washington during the spring semester of 1954.[12] The population from which the sample was drawn did not include boys of high school senior age who dropped out of school before they reached the 12th grade. Any generalization to be made from the data, therefore, must make allowance for this selectiveness.[13]

Method

The occupational status of the father is used as the principal criterion for defining the social-class levels of the seniors in the study. Occupational status is measured by means of an occupational prestige scale. This scale was formed by combining the Hatt-North[14] and Smith[15] occupational prestige scales.[16] The upper and lower extremes of the scale are shown in Table 1 for illustrative purposes.

---

12. The sample is a stratified, two-stage cluster sample in which the high school, and not the student, is the primary sampling unit. In all, data were obtained from thirty-five high schools (clusters). Where tests of significance are used, non-parameter techniques are applied. The cluster-type sample makes the use of normal curve statistics prohibitively expensive and also causes a severe attrition of cases when each cluster is divided into ten occupational strata for analysis. For a complete discussion of the selection of the sample and of the calculation of sampling variance, see my unpublished Ph.D. dissertation, *Relationship of Social Class and Family Authority Patterns to Occupational Choice of Washington High School Seniors*, Department of Sociology, State College of Washington, 1955, Chap. II.

13. Reliable estimates of the number of adolescents in Washington who drop out of school before the 12th grade are rare. The 1950 census reported that 43.1 per cent of the males, ages 20-24, had not finished the 12th grade. Schmid, *et al.*, estimate that during the period between 1925 and 1951, approximately 39 per cent of the total school-age population dropped out of school between the 1st and 12th grades. (See, C. F. Schmid, *et al.*, *Enrollment Forecasts State of Washington*, Washington State Census Board, 1954.) Neither estimate accounts for population migrations.

14. P. K. Hatt and C. C. North, "Jobs and Occupations: A Popular Evaluation," in *Class, Status and Power*, *op. cit.*, pp. 411-426.

15. M. Smith, "An Empirical Scale of Prestige of Occupations," *American Sociological Review*, 8 (April, 1943), pp. 185-192.

16. When the occupations common to both scales were placed in rank order, a rank order correlation of .97 was obtained between them. This provided the justification for combining the two scales. The new scale ranks occupations from 1 to 100. The Smith scale already used this system; it was necessary to convert Hatt-North rankings to percentiles in order to make them comparable. The common

Table 1. Upper and Lower Extremes of Combined Occupational Scale

Occupation	Hatt-North Rank (Percentile)	Smith Rank (Midpoint of Interval)	Interpolated Rank	New Scale Position
Upper extreme				
U. S. Supreme Court Justice	99.4	99.5	99.5	1
U. S. Diplomat in Foreign Service	95.5	98.5	97	2
Governor of State	97.8	95.5	96.6	3
U. S. Cabinet member	95.5	97.5	96.5	4.5
U. S. Senator		96.5	96.5	4.5
Physician	97.6	91.5	94.6	6
College President or Chancellor		94.5	94.5	7
Mayor of large city	93.9	92.5	93.2	8
College professor	91.7		91.7	10
Lower extreme				
Bartender	5.5		5.5	140.5
Unskilled worker, odd jobs		4.5	4.5—	142
Share cropper—owns no livestock or equipment and does not manage farm	3.9		3.9	143
Scrub woman		3.5	3.5	144
Garbage collector	2.8	2.5	2.6	145
Street sweeper	1.7		1.7	146
Unskilled migratory worker		1.5	1.5	147
Shoe shiner	.5		.5	148.5
Professional prostitute		.5	.5	148.5

The new scale does not justify any minute measurements of difference among occupations with respect to prestige. In order to make a basis for comparison, it was divided into groups of occupations each of which represent 10 per cent of the total. Each of these groups, or deciles, was assigned a number; the lowest decile received the value 1; the highest, 10. Thus, the occupational status hierarchy was divided into ten different strata. Comparisons with respect to social class and occupational aspiration are made in terms of these ten objective strata.

Measurement of Aspiration by an Absolute Standard

The data lend strong support to the hypothesis that the *absolute* occupational status aspirations of high school seniors from the middle and

base was necessary to interpolate differences in the ranking of occupations which were common to both scales so as to assign them to their new scale position, and also to find the approximate scale value for occupations which were not common to both. A complete copy of the scale may be obtained from the author.

upper classes are significantly higher than those of seniors from the lower classes. Table 2 indicates that, with little exception, there is a direct relationship between present social level and future occupational aspiration for both preferred and anticipated occupations.[17] The higher seniors were on the social ladder, the higher their *absolute* aspirations tended to be.

Table 2. Average Preferred and Anticipated Occupational Aspiration Levels of Seniors from Different Social Strata

		PREFERRED		ANTICIPATED	
	Father's Status	N	Level of Aspiration*	N	Level of Aspiration*
(High)	10	6	7.83	6	7.83
	9	12	7.92	8	8.36
	8	52	7.63	42	7.26
	7	57	7.26	41	7.32
	6	174	6.61	132	6.45
	5	97	6.87	69	6.46
	4	184	6.47	129	5.99
	3	115	6.25	87	5.70
	2	56	6.07	45	5.69
(Low)	1	11	5.36	6	4.50
All strata		764	6.65	565	6.32

*Differences among strata were significant, Preferred: $x^2 = 50.375$; 9 d.f.; $P < .01$; $\bar{C} = .29$. Anticipated: $x^2 = 62.951$; 9 d.f.; $P < .01$; $\bar{C} = .38$.

Relative Measurement of Aspiration

The data also lend strong support to the second hypothesis. Figures 1 and 2 show that when a *relative* standard is used almost all seniors from the lower strata *prefer* and *anticipate* having significantly higher occupational statuses than their fathers. The Net Per Cent column in these figures, obtained by subtracting the percentage of seniors in each social stratum who had negative aspiration scores from those who had positive

17. Fewer seniors responded to the question on their anticipated occupations than they did to the one on their preferred occupations. However, a chi square value obtained by comparing the distribution of preferred occupations for all those who stated a preferred occupation with a distribution of preferred occupations for all those who stated both preferred and anticipated occupations did not approach significance. Consequently, there did not appear to be a selective factor associated with those who failed to state an anticipated occupation. There are additional grounds for believing that most of those who failed to respond did so because their anticipated occupations were the same as their preferred.

Stratum of Father	PERCENTAGE OF STUDENTS WHOSE ANTICIPATED OCCUPATIONAL STATUS IS: Higher than father's	The same as father's	Not as high as father's	Net Per Cent
10		17	83	- 83.3
9	12	38	50	- 37.5
8	21	38	41	- 19.0
7	46	32	22	+ 24.5
6	43	38	19	+ 24.3
5	66	12	22	+ 44.8
4	66	26	8	+ 58.9
3	78	13	9	+ 69.0
2	91	9		+ 91.1
1	83	17		+ 83.3

FIGURE 1. Preferred Occupational Mobility of Seniors from Each Stratum.

scores, indicates clearly that most seniors on the lower levels display an intense desire for upward occupational mobility.

Table 3 shows that seniors on the lower seven occupational strata had positive aspiration scores; and that, where tests could be run, seniors on the lower six occupational strata aspired to occupational status levels

Table 3. Average Preferred and Anticipated Aspiration Scores of Seniors from Different Social Strata

Father's Status	PREFERRED* Aspiration Score	PREFERRED* Level of Significance‡	ANTICIPATED† Aspiration Score	ANTICIPATED† Level of Significance‡
(High) 10	−2.17	....	−2.17	....
9	−1.08	P=.25	−0.63	....
8	−0.37	P>.25	−0.74	P=.25
7	+0.26	P=.10	+0.32	P=.10
6	+0.61	P<.01	+0.45	P<.01
5	+1.87	P<.01	+1.46	P<.01
4	+2.47	P<.01	+1.99	P<.01
3	+3.25	P<.01	+2.70	P<.01
2	+4.07	P<.01	+3.69	P<.01
(Low) 1	+4.36	....	+3.50	....
All strata	+1.78	P<.01	+1.42	P<.01

*Correlation between present level and future aspiration: −.60.
†Correlation between present level and future aspiration: −.55.
‡Levels of significance were determined by means of the "Sign" test. It is based on the binomial and permits us to compare the total number of positive diffrences with the total number of negative differences. In those cases where differences are zero, they are excluded and sample size is reduced. Largely, due to a small *n* and attrition due to exclusion of cases, degrees of significance were not obtained for the strata shown. (See Wilfred Dixon and Frank Massey, Jr., *Introduction to Statistical Analysis*, New York: McGraw-Hill Book Co., 1951, Chap. 17.)

Stratum of Father	Higher than father's	The same as father's	Not as high as father's	Net Per Cent
	PERCENTAGE OF STUDENTS WHOSE PREFERRED OCCUPATIONAL STATUS IS:			
10		17	83	- 83.3
9	8	42	50	- 41.7
8	31	33	36	- 5.8
7	47	28	25	+ 22.8
6	50	32	18	+ 31.8
5	74	15	11	+ 62.8
4	77	20	3	+ 74.0
3	87	11	2	+ 85.1
2	100			+100.0
1	100			+100.0

FIGURE 2. Anticipated Occupational Mobility of Seniors from Each Stratum.

which were significantly higher than those of their fathers. The strong tendency for lower-strata seniors to aspire upward resulted in a negative correlation of −.60 between the sons' preferred occupational statuses and their fathers' present statuses, and of −.55 between sons' anticipated statuses and fathers' present statuses. However, a word of caution must be interjected. The meaurements demonstrated in the tables and figures are subject to the error inherent in the type of measurement where a prestige scale is used. An individual at the bottom of the status ladder can go no lower in his aspirations, and a person at the top can go no higher. Such a limitation may partially explain the extremes observed throughout the paper. Nevertheless, even if the upper and lower two strata were eliminated from the analysis, the same picture would remain; the lower the status level, the greater the expressed desire for higher occupational status.

Supplementary information derived from Likert-type questions also lends strong support to these findings. Lower-class seniors were significantly more inclined than upper-class seniors to want a job that had a higher social standing in the community than the one their father had,[18] to rate their family income as insufficient for family needs,[19] to think it important that they have a better income than their fathers,[20] and to be dissatisfied with their fathers' occupations as the one for them.[21] In

18. $X^2=66.925$; 3 d.f.; $P<.01$; $\overline{C}=.48$.
19. $X^2=71.534$; 6 d.f.; $P<.01$; $\overline{C}=.33$.
20. $X^2=19.535$; 6 d.f.; $P<.01$; $\overline{C}=.20$.
21. $X^2=44.788$; 9 d.f.; $P<.01$; $\overline{C}=.27$.

consequence, these overall findings provide little support for the idea that lower-class seniors have limited their aspirations to their present class horizon.[22]

Reality and Aspiration Estimates

It was hypothesized that seniors from the lower classes are more inclined than those from middle and upper strata to reduce their occupational aspirations significantly when faced with the necessity of choosing between their *preferred* and *anticipated* occupations. The data lend very little support to this hypothesis. Table 4 indicates that: (1) seniors from most strata anticipated having occupations somewhat lower than their preferred ones; and (2) while seniors on the lower half of the status hierarchy tended to have larger revisions downward than those from the upper half, seniors from two middle strata (4 and 5) had revisions downward which were, or tended to be, statistically significant. Average "reality scores" (distance between preferred and anticipated occupations) and chi square values, obtained by comparing the distributions of preferred and anticipated occupations for goodness of fit for each stratum, are presented in Table 4.

Table 4. Reality Estimate of Seniors as Measured by the Distance between Their Average Preferred and Anticipated Occupational Levels

Father's Status	*N*	*Average Reality Score*	*d.f.*	*Needed x^2 Value for Sig. at 1 Per Cent Level*	*Obtained x^2 Value**
(High) 10	6	—0.001	3	11.341	2.112
9	12	+0.46			
8	52	—0.37	4	13.277	5.048
7	57	+0.06	5	15.086	1.082
6	174	—0.16	6	16.812	4.516
5	97	—0.41	5	15.086	15.035
4	184	—0.48	7	18.475	20.300
3	115	—0.55	6	16.812	9.128
2	56	—0.38	5	15.086	6.383
(Low) 1	11	—0.85			
All strata	764	—0.35	9	21.666	3.3361

*It is possible that, with another test, the revisions downward for stratum 1 might have been significant but, because the *n* was so small, it was necessary to combine it with stratum 2 for this analysis. The same was done for strata 9 and 10. In analyzing the distributions for each stratum, aspirations to strata 1-3 and 9-10 were combined in most cases because relatively few seniors aspired to these levels.

22. These findings corroborate those of Straus who used similar techniques on a statewide sample of Wisconsin students. See M. A. Straus, "Selected Factors in Occupational Choice of Wisconsin High School Seniors," unpublished master's thesis, Department of Sociology, University of Wisconsin, 1949.

Other data tend to confirm these findings. In response to the question: "What are the chances that you will enter your preferred occupation?" lower-class seniors were only slightly more inclined to think that their chances of entering their preferred occupations were less than those of seniors on strata above them.[23]

These findings lend but slight support to the idea that reality causes lower-strata seniors to reduce their occupational aspirations more than others when forced to choose between the occupations they *prefer* and the ones they *anticipate* entering. It may be, of course, that lower-strata seniors had revised their estimates downward before they stated their *preferred* occupations. Hence, when it came to stating their anticipated occupations, they had little downward revising to do. If this were the case, lower-strata seniors still *anticipated* entering occupations which would provide them with a substantial increase in occupational status over that enjoyed by their fathers.

Conclusion

The data of the study support the following hypotheses: (1) that the *absolute* occupational status aspirations of male high school seniors from the middle and upper classes are significantly higher than those of seniors from the lower classes; and (2) that the *relative* occupational status aspirations of lower-class seniors indicate that they *prefer* and *anticipate* having significantly higher occupational statuses than their fathers. The data do not support the hypothesis that seniors from lower strata are more inclined than those from middle and upper strata to reduce their occupational aspirations significantly when faced with the necessity of choosing between their *preferred* and *anticipated* occupations.

Thus, these findings do not support two important schools of thought on the occupational aspirations of lower-class youth: (1) that lower-class youth have limited their occupational aspirations to the class horizon; or (2) that lower-class youth have the same lofty occupational aspirations as those from upper strata. Instead, they show that, while the lower-class youngsters aspired to get ahead, they aspired to occupations at different status levels than those from higher strata. Their aspirations were perhaps the result of conditioning on particular socioeconomic levels. Consequently, it would seem that any attempt to impose a monolithic definition of occupational success and aspiration upon all

23. Differences among the strata were not significant, but they tended to approach significance. They could have occurred by chance approximately 11 times out of 100.

social strata would require the projection of the definition of one stratum upon all strata. Therefore, measurement of aspiration for comparative purposes would likely be most accurate if it took relativities into account.

RUSSELL R. DYNES, ALFRED C. CLARKE,
and SIMON DINITZ

Levels of Occupational Aspiration: Some Aspects of Family Experience as a Variable

A RECURRING theme in the stratification literature emphasizes the widespread acceptance of the "success" imperative in American society. Upward social mobility is not only a possibility but something to be actively sought. Although the rewards of mobility are consistently stressed, some individuals show a greater desire to achieve these rewards, while others seem more "content" with their current status and expectations. What accounts for this differential emphasis upon success? Why do some people consider it more important to "get ahead" than others? Within a given socio-economic group, what social-psychological factors differentiate individuals with high aspirations from those who have lower aspirational levels?

Much of the psychoanalytic literature has suggested that unsatisfactory interpersonal relations in early childhood produce insecurity which is translated into neurotic striving for power, recognition and success. Adler and Horney, among others, have suggested that the quest for power is frequently used as a compensatory means of attaining reassurance against the anxieties produced by unhappy childhood experi-

---

Reprinted from American Sociological Review, *April, 1956, pp. 212-215, by permission of the authors and the journal.*

ences.[1] Some sociologists have also commented on the plausibility of these relationships. Ellis, for example, studying career women, found that those who had achieved upward social mobility showed a history of greater difficulty in their early interpersonal relations than did those who were non-mobile.[2] While the personality consequences of upward social mobility have been the major focus of previous research in this area,[3] there has been surprisingly little empirical attention directed toward understanding differential levels of aspiration. Does it follow, as much of the psychoanalytic literature asserts, that individuals with high aspirations are characterized by greater difficulty in their interpersonal relations within the family of orientation than those with lower aspirations?

Research Design

Investigation of this relationship required the selection of an appropriate measure of aspiration and some index of parent-child interaction. Although aspirations have been measured in varied ways, it was felt that an occupational referent represented one of the best single measures. The scale selected was developed by Reissman and was concerned with the willingness of individuals to forego certain satisfactions in order to achieve occupational advancement.[4] In this scale, eleven considerations were specified that might prevent a person from advancing in rank and salary in their occupation.[5] Among these considerations were: leaving one's family for some time, endangering one's health, moving about the country, keeping quiet about political views, etc. Each consideration was evaluated in terms of three alternatives: (1) whether it might stop

1. See, for example, Karen Horney, *The Neurotic Personality of Our Time,* New York: Norton and Company, 1937, pp. 162-187.

2. Evelyn Ellis, "Social Psychological Correlates of Upward Social Mobility among Unmarried Career Women," *American Sociological Review,* 17 (October, 1952), pp. 558-563.

3. See, for example, A. B. Hollingshead, R. Ellis, and E. Kirby, "Social Mobility and Mental Illness," *American Sociological Review,* 19 (October, 1954), pp. 577-584.

4. Leonard Reissman, "Level of Aspiration and Social Class," *American Sociological Review,* 18 (June, 1953), pp. 233-242.

5. These considerations were ranked according to the frequency they were taken into account by the sample population in the original study and were weighted from 1 to 11. For example, a person who said that moving around the country would prevent him from making an occupational advancement received a score of 10. Conversely, if the item was not a consideration, it was scored zero. By summating the weighted responses to each of the eleven items it was possible to receive scores ranging from zero to 66.

the individual from making a change; (2) whether it might be a serious consideration but would not stop him; (3) whether it would not matter at all. Only the first alternative was scored.[6] The logic behind the scoring was that persons who would permit these considerations to stop them from making a change were expressing lower levels of aspiration than those who would disregard these factors in order to attain higher occupational status.

Since this scale had previously been used simply to differentiate gross categories and had not been employed to measure individual differences, the sample was divided into "high" and "low" aspirers, similar to the division employed by Reissman. Operationally, respondents who received scores from zero to 19 were defined as "high" aspirers and those who scored 20 or more comprised the "low" aspirers.

A second instrument was constructed concerning affectional patterns in the family of orientation. Questions relating to the respondent's relations with their parents included: degree of attachment, amount of conflict, frequency of confiding in parents, feelings of rejection, parental favoritism, and fear of punishment from parents. Items were also included concerning sibling rivalry, childhood happiness, and coercion by parents through disapproval and unfavorable comparisons. It should be noted that all of these dimensions required the respondent's definition of his relationships. No claim is made that this definition was necessarily in close correspondence with the objective situation. Even if the definitions were not objectively true to others, they were, of course, subjectively true to the respondent. The concern here was with the respondent's interpretation of the situation.

The aspiration scale and index of parent-child interaction were employed in questionnaire form[7] and were administered to 350 university students enrolled in introductory and advanced sociology classes. Since the aspirational scale was phrased in terms of occupational advancement, the women in the sample expressed their aspiration in terms of advice they might give their husbands.[8] Using both objective indices of father's occupation and a self-rating on class position, the sample population showed only slight variations in socio-economic background. Over 55 per cent of the sample came from professional and managerial backgrounds. Only 8 per cent of the sample placed themselves in the upper

6. This method of scoring was slightly different from the method used by Reissman in the original study.

7. All questionnaires were answered anonymously. Other dimensions, covered by the questionnaire but not included in this report, involved the relations between aspiration and religious ideology and the relation between aspiration and favorableness of attitude to marriage.

8. There were 153 males and 197 females in the total sample.

class, and no one identified with the lower class, while 70 per cent identified with the upper-middle class and 22 per cent with the lower-middle.

The Findings

Evidence obtained in this research essentially supports the relationship between unsatisfactory interpersonal relations in the family of orientation and high aspirational levels. The "high" aspirers stated that they had experienced feelings of rejection more frequently than did those in the "lower" group. As may be seen in Table 1, 42 per cent of the "high" aspirers indicated that they had experienced feelings of not being wanted by their fathers, while only 24 per cent of those in the "low" group had experienced similar feelings. When the data were classified according to the individuals' feelings of rejection by the mother, the percentages for the "high" and "low" groups were 34 and 20, respectively.

Table 1. Feelings of Not Being Wanted by Parents in Relation to Level of Aspiration, in Percentages

Feelings of Not Being Wanted by Parents	LEVEL OF ASPIRATION High	Low
Father*	(N=117)	(N=223)
Some	41.9	24.7
None	58.1	75.3
Mother†	(N=122)	(N=223)
Some	34.4	20.2
None	65.6	79.8

* Data concerning father, $x^2 = 10.7$; d.f. $= 1$; $P < .002$.
† Data concerning mother, $x^2 = 8.43$; d.f. $= 1$; $P < .01$.

Similarly, the data regarding parental favoritism toward a son or daughter revealed significant differences in the same direction. Table 2

Table 2. Favoritism Shown by Parents in Relation to Level of Aspiration, in Percentages

Favoritism Shown by Parents	LEVEL OF ASPIRATION High	Low
Father*	(N=95)	(N=188)
Yes	45.3	30.9
No	54.7	69.1
Mother†	(N=95)	(N=188)
Yes	41.1	25.0
No	58.9	75.0

* Data concerning father, $x^2 = 5.56$; d.f. $= 1$; $P < .02$.
† Data concerning mother, $x^2 = 7.46$; d.f. $= 1$; $P < .01$.

shows the result of this analysis. "High" aspirers defined their parents as showing more favoritism toward some child in the family than did the "low" aspirers. Furthermore, a significantly greater proportion of the "high" than the "low" aspirational groups indicated less attachment to their parents and had experienced a lesser degree of happiness during their childhood. (See Tables 3 and 4.) In addition, the "high" aspirers

Table 3. Degree of Parental Attachment in Relation to Level of Aspiration, in Percentages

Degree of Attachment to Parents	LEVEL OF ASPIRATION High	Low
Father	(N=110)	(N=222)
Much	33.6	50.9
Little	66.4	49.1
Mother	(N=123)	(N=223)
Much	52.8	66.8
Little	47.2	33.2

Data concerning father, $x^2 = 7.87$; d.f. $= 1$; $P < .01$.
Data concerning mother, $x^2 = 6.58$; d.f. $= 1$; $P < .01$.

confided less frequently in their fathers ($P < .05$) and were more fearful of punishment from them ($P < .05$).

This pattern of difference was even more pronounced when the data were further classified according to sex, ethnic origin, or religion.[9] This

Table 4. Happiness of Childhood in Relation to Level of Aspiration, in Percentages

Happiness of Childhood	LEVEL OF ASPIRATION High (N = 122)	Low (N = 224)
Happy	72.9	81.1
Average	27.1	18.9

$x^2 = 4.04$; d.f. $= 1$; $P < .05$.

finding would add some support to the observations which many have made that aspirational levels are closely associated with the person's position in the social structure. It should be noted, however, that the sample, on which this report is based, was relatively homogeneous in that it comprised a predominately urban, middle-western, Protestant, middle-class, college population.

The "high" and "low" aspirers did not differ significantly in the degree of conflict with their siblings. Neither did they differ in the fre-

9. The details of these relationships will be discussed in Alfred C. Clarke, Simon Dinitz, and Russell R. Dynes, "Levels of Aspiration and Family Affection: Religious Preference as a Variable," *Ohio Journal of Science,* 59 (March, 1959), p. 103.

quency with which they had confided in their mothers, nor in the amount of conflict with their fathers.

Since it is often assumed that aspiration is a by-product of the overt pressures of parental projection, it is interesting to note that there were no significant differences between the groups in their feelings that their parents compared them unfavorably with their siblings or peer group concerning accomplishments in school and athletics. In addition, the "high" and "low" aspirers did not differ in their estimations of the degree of disappointment their parents might have if their children did not live up to parental expectations. This negative evidence suggested that differences in aspiration are more closely related to subtle interpersonal factors than to overt parental pressures.

Summary

This study concerning the relationship between aspirational level and interpersonal experiences tends to support some of the current assumptions in the psychoanalytic literature. *Unsatisfactory interpersonal relationships in the family of orientation were significantly related to high aspirational levels and satisfactory relationships were related to lower aspirational levels.*

Since increasing attention is being given to the development of "happy" and socially well-adjusted persons by some of our institutions and social agencies, the question arises whether modifications will occur in the future to the success orientation of American society. It may well be that the increasing emphasis on personal happiness, rather than upon personal achievement, will serve to augment the growing quest for security.

Appendix: Items on Which Tables Are Based

Table 1

How frequently have you felt that you were not wanted by your *father?*

(1) Very often (2) Frequently (3) Some (4) Rarely (5) Never.

How frequently have you felt that you were not wanted by your *mother?*

(1) Very often (2) Frequently (3) Some (4) Rarely (5) Never.

In Table 1, response categories 1, 2, 3, and 4 were included in "Some," and category 5 was referred to as "None."

Table 2

During your childhood, who do you think was your father's favorite?
(1) Older brother (2) Younger brother (3) Older sister (4) Younger sister (5) Am only child (6) Yourself (7) No favorite.

During your childhood, who do you think was your mother's favorite?
(1) Older brother (2) Younger brother (3) Older sister (4) Younger sister (5) Am only child (6) Yourself (7) No favorite.

In Table 2, response categories 1, 2, 3, 4, and 6 were included in "Favoritism Shown by Parents–Yes" and category 7 was referred to as "Favoritism Shown by Parents–No." In some cases the respondents defined themselves as the favorite child. These cases were included since they were consistent with the purpose of the table, depicting a family "atmosphere" in which differential treatment of children was perceived. Cases involving only children were, of course, excluded.

Table 3

Amount of attachment between you and your *father?*
(1) Extremely close (2) Very close (3) Considerable (4) Somewhat (5) A little (6) None at all.

Amount of attachment between you and your *mother?*
(1) Extremely close (2) Very close (3) Considerable (4) Somewhat (5) A little (6) None at all.

In Table 3, response categories 1 and 2 were included in "Much" and categories 3, 4, 5, and 6 were referred to as "Little."

Table 4

How would you rate your childhood?
(1) Very happy (2) Happy (3) Average (4) Unhappy (5) Very unhappy.

In Table 4, response categories 1 and 2 were included in "Happy" and categories 3, 4, and 5 were referred to as "Average."

JAMES G. MARTIN
and FRANK R. WESTIE

The Tolerant Personality

ANALYSIS of the relation of intergroup prejudice and tolerance toward outgroups to syndromes of personality characteristics has been plagued by various methodological difficulties. Prominent among these are the problem of systematically and objectively defining categories of "tolerant" and "prejudiced" subjects. Edward Shils has observed, for example, that in *The Authoritarian Personality*,[1] "For the most part 'democrats' are distinguished from 'anti-democrats' through their rejection of a considerable series of illiberal opinions which are the stock in trade of the xenophobic fundamentalist. . . ."[2] In other words, classification of a person as "anti-democratic" is determined by his endorsement of propositions which, in effect, are the articles of faith of the bigot. Those who do not endorse such items are residually defined as "democratic." This procedure, however, could result in the inclusion of respondents who might be far from tolerant in the sense of having a neutral or disinterested attitude towards some group, particularly in view of the widespread normative approval of various forms of group prejudice.

Reprinted from American Sociological Review, *August, 1959, pp. 521-528, by permission of the authors and the journal.*

Financial support by the Indiana University Foundation and Social Science Research Council is gratefully acknowledged. Thanks are due Margaret L. Westie for revising the manuscript.

1. T. W. Adorno, *et al., The Authoritarian Personality*, New York: Harpers, 1950.

2. Edward A. Shils, "Authoritarianism: 'Right' and 'Left,'" in Richard Christie and Marie Jahoda, editors, *Studies in the Scope and Method of "The Authoritarian Personality,"* New York: Free Press, 1954, p. 29.

The concept of group prejudice and the methodology of tolerance-prejudice measurement require a "zero point" of group preference or rejection. An instrument is needed that encompasses the entire range of hypothetical tolerance-prejudice, including a midpoint indicating an absence of either positive or negative prejudice. Such a device would permit valid and consistent classification of subjects for the purpose of personality comparisons, according to scale positions established *prior* to interviewing.

This study attempts to determine the distinguishing personal and social characteristics of persons who are operationally defined as tolerant. Instruments employed in most previous investigations of the problem have been inadequate as yardsticks for the assessment of tolerance, and random sampling of subjects has occurred only with respect to a limited population, namely, college students. The study, therefore, also explores the degree to which many of the findings of previous research on prejudice and personality are valid when different techniques of scaling and sampling are invoked.

The Study Design

Prejudice toward Negroes was measured by means of the Summated Differences Scales.[3] These scales yield scores which, rather than ranging from "prejudice" to "less prejudice," range from extremely negative prejudice to neutrality (as indicated by a zero point) to extremely positive prejudice. Thus assessment of the subjects' attitudes relative to the point of neutrality between "anti-Negro" and "pro-Negro" permitted establishment of two statistical categories of subjects: a "Tolerant" category that embraced those whose scores were only slightly on either side of the zero point, and a "Prejudiced" category that encompassed those who were extremely hostile towards Negroes.

The Summated Differences Scales used in this study consisted of "Residential" and "Position" sub-scales. The Residential scale is designed to establish the degree of residential distance the subject insists upon maintaining between himself and persons of varying racial and occupational membership. The Position scale assesses the degree to which the subject is willing to have persons of various racial and occupational membership occupy positions of power and prestige in the community. These scales require the subject to respond with one of five

3. For a full description of this device see: Frank R. Westie, "A Technique for the Measurement of Race Attitudes," *American Sociological Review*, 18 (February, 1953), pp. 73-78.

alternatives to various items of the social distance type. The 192 scale items call for responses to Negroes in a variety of occupations and to Whites in these *same* occupations. Whites as well as Negroes were included in the items; the tolerance-prejudice score is a function of the *difference* in response to persons of the same occupation but of different racial designation. Thus prejudice towards Whites is measured at the same time as prejudice towards Negroes, or stated otherwise, the scoring provides scale positions for those subjects who are positively prejudiced in favor of Negroes as well as for those who are negatively prejudiced. By the same token, if the subject makes no racial distinction in his response to an item such as, "I would be willing to have a *Negro Lawyer* live next door to me," and is equally willing (or unwilling, as the case may be) to have a *White Lawyer* "live next door to me," the subject would have a Summated Differences score of zero for the pair of items. If the sum of the differences between his responses to each half of all 96 pairs of items used in this research is also zero, then his total tolerance-prejudice score is zero.

The total possible range of scores was —432 to +432. Persons whose scores fell between —70 and +70 were defined as "Tolerant."[4] Moreover, the additional requirement was invoked that those in the Tolerant category be willing to have at least two of the Negro-in-occupation types "live in his neighborhood." The minimal score requirement for inclusion in the prejudiced category was +175, and was based upon previous application of the scale in Indianapolis. The mean score of the tolerants was +31, while for the prejudiced it was +249.

The universe from which the sample was selected consisted of white adults (21 years of age or older) residing within the city limits of Indianapolis in blocks containing no Negro residents. In the Indianapolis population, as perhaps in most or all American cities, there are rela-

4. Of the many terms that have been used to describe persons at the "favorable" end of the continuum of intergroup attitudes, we have chosen the term "tolerant" as the least ambiguous and the easiest to define operationally. The people in our tolerant category are clustered on both sides of the zero point, rather than exactly on it (which would indeed make them "unprejudiced"). Some are slightly more favorable towards Whites than towards Negroes, others are slightly more favorable towards Negroes than towards Whites, while a few are actually *on* the zero point. All, however, manifest a high degree of tolerance from the standpoint of their willingness to have Negroes live near them and to have them occupy positions of power and prestige in the community.

We realize that knowledge of a person's tolerance with respect to Negroes provides us with imperfect knowledge concerning his generalized tolerance towards outgroups. In the interest of specificity and rigor in separating the two contrasting types, it was necessary to forego the inclusion of other outgroups, although the Summated Differences Scales permit the inclusion of a variety of group-objects in the items.

tively few persons who qualify as tolerant in their attitudes towards racial out-groups. This posed a serious sampling problem. It was estimated, on the basis of previous research in Indianapolis, that in order to obtain a minimum *N* of 50 tolerant persons, it would be necessary to interview a preliminary sample of approximately 500 cases. But lengthy interviewing of such a large number of persons would have been prohibitive. Consequently, the following procedure was employed: All city blocks in Indianapolis, except those in which there were Negro residents, were numbered and a sample of 100 blocks was drawn through the use of tables of random numbers. Every second household on these blocks was visited and the individual respondent was asked to complete a short prejudice scale designed specifically to serve as an initial screening device. This scale, constructed according to the internal consistency method, proved to be quite discriminating in spite of its brevity. Persons who on this scale showed little or no prejudice towards Negroes and persons who displayed very strong prejudice were asked to complete the extended questionnaire which contained the Summated Differences tolerance-prejudice scale. The subject's score on this lengthy battery of items determined whether or not he would be included in the final two categories of "Tolerant" and "Prejudiced."

From the 429 initial respondents who completed the prognostic scale, 41 persons were found who, on the subsequently administered Summated Differences scales, qualified for the Tolerant category. Also, 59 subjects with conspicuously high prejudice scores were selected for purposes of comparison, and they constituted the Prejudiced category.[5]

Findings

The tolerant and prejudiced subjects were compared with respect to 25 personal and social characteristics. These variables were selected in terms of their sociological and psychological theoretical relevance regarding the nature of prejudice and tolerance and the relationship between prejudice-tolerance and personality factors. The influence of

5. A total of 668 households were visited. Of these, 168 were "not at homes" (so classified after a minimum of two unsuccessful call-backs) and 71 refused to complete the short prejudice scale. Of the 429 persons who completed the short scale, 212 persons appeared sufficiently extreme in their attitudes to justify administration of the lengthy Summated Differences Scales and the variety of other scales and items dealing with personal characteristics. Of these 212 cases, 12 refused to fill out the longer form, and 48 failed to return the questionnaire (where they were left to be picked up later). Of the 152 who filled out the lengthy form, 13 handed it in incomplete. There were 39 subjects who failed to qualify as sufficiently tolerant or prejudiced even after completing the full questionnaire.

previous research in this area, particularly as reported in *The Authoritarian Personality*, is readily apparent.

A number of scales were constructed by the technique of internal consistency to assess the various personal and social characteristics hypothesized to be related to tolerance. These findings are summarized graphically in Figure 1, and the statistical data on the significant variables are presented in Table 1. Intercorrelations of scale scores are presented in Tables 2 and 3.

Scores on the Nationalism Scale. Tolerant subjects were significantly less nationalistic, which suggests that a negative prejudice towards Negroes is an expression of a more basic ethnocentric orientation. Evidently the tolerant person is not a "social reductionist": he does not have a strong penchant for rigidly inclusive-exclusive reference groups. Sample scale item: "The worst danger to real Americanism during the last 50 years has come from foreign ideas and agitators."[6] (The level of significance of the difference between the tolerant and prejudiced on this variable is $P < .001$.)

Scores on the Intolerance of Ambiguity Scale. The tolerant category is significantly less "intolerant of ambiguity."[7] Tolerant people appeared able and willing to perceive gradation, variation, and relativity, whereas the prejudiced persons seemed to have a need for absolute dichotomies. Unambiguous solutions are demanded for problems by the prejudiced even where no such solutions appear possible. Rigid, categorical thinking is functionally necessary for stereotyping, prejudgment, and sharp ingroup-outgroup distinctions. On the other hand, the tolerant person seems inclined to recognize that each individual, regardless of group assignment, is unique. Sample scale item: "There are two kinds of women; the pure and the bad." (Level of significance: $P < .001$.)

Scores on the Superstition Scale. The mean score of the tolerants is significantly lower, which invites the inference that they are inclined to prefer the logical and the rational, while the prejudiced persons subscribed to statements indicating a tendency to accept bizarre, mystical, and superstitious definitions of reality. The relationship here might seem tautological in that in many instances the myths that support prejudice take the form of superstitions. Moreover, terms such as "race" and "blood" have mystical appeal. Sample scale item: "Some fortune tellers can actually predict a person's future by studying the lines of his hands." (Level of significance: $P < .001$.)

6. Complete copies of the scales can be secured from J. G. Martin, Northern Illinois University, DeKalb, Illinois.

7. Cf. Else Frenkel-Brunswik, "Intolerance of Ambiguity as Emotional and Perceptual Personality Variable," *Journal of Personality*, 18 (September, 1949), pp. 108-143.

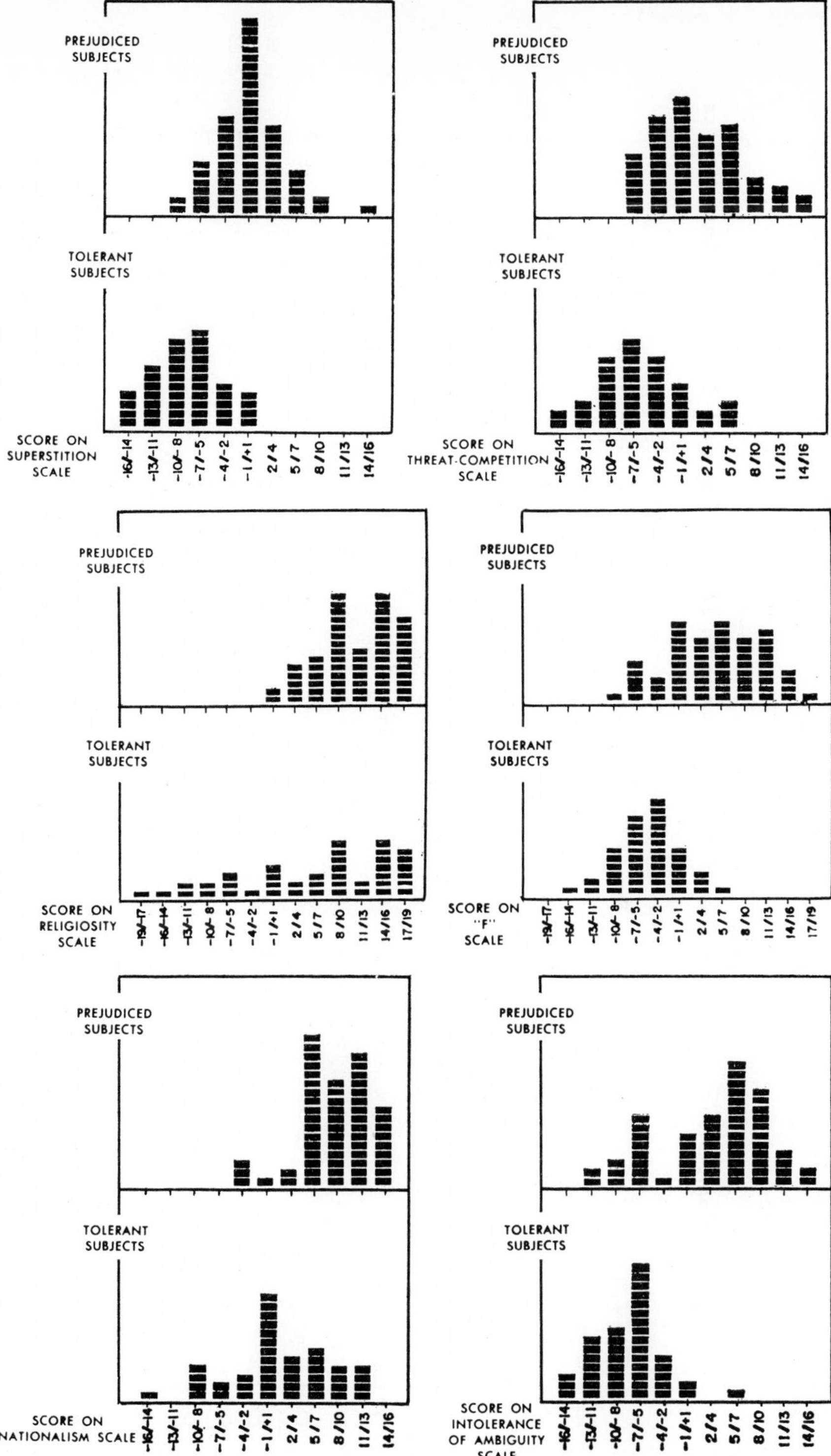

FIGURE 1. Comparative Attitude Scale. Scores of Tolerant and Prejudiced Persons.

Table 1. Comparison of Tolerant and Prejudiced Persons on Selected Personal and Social Characteristics

	TOLERANTS (N = 41)				PREJUDICED (N = 59)							
Characteristic	*Range*	$\bar{X}$	*S.D.*	*S.E.* $\bar{X}$	*Range*	$\bar{X}$	*S.D.*	*S.E.* $\bar{X}$	*S.E. Diff.*	*Ob. Diff.*	*C.R.*	*Prob.*
Nationalism	—16 to +13	+1.02	6.48	1.03	+16 to — 4	+ 9.06	3.12	.40	1.10	8.04	7.30	<.001
Intolerance of ambiguity	—15 to + 5	—7.41	4.07	.64	+16 to —12	+ 3.79	6.33	.83	1.04	11.20	10.77	<.001
Superstition pseudo-science	—15 to — 1	—7.85	4.20	.66	+15 to —10	— .19	4.33	.57	.87	7.67	8.81	<.001
Threat-competition orientation	—15 to + 6	—4.68	5.28	.84	+14 to — 7	+ 1.86	5.30	.70	1.10	6.54	5.95	<.001
"F" Scale	—15 to + 5	—4.39	4.15	.85	+18 to — 8	+ 5.07	6.25	.82	1.18	9.45	8.01	<.001
Religiosity	—18 to +18	+5.46	10.11	1.60	+18 to — 1	+11.35	4.98	1.02	1.90	5.89	3.10	<.005
Child rearing attitudes	— 5 to + 4	— .93	2.53	.40	+ 6 to — 5	+ 1.39	2.34	.31	.05	2.32	46.40	<.001
Distrust of politicians item	— 2 to + 2	— .51	1.04	.16	+ 2 to — 2	+ .24	1.08	.14	.22	.75	3.41	<.001
Opinion of mother item	— 2 to + 2	+ .90	.96	.15	+ 2 to — 2	+ 1.29	.84	.17	.22	.39	1.77	<.05
Interest in politics item	— 2 to + 2	— .48	1.17	.19	+ 2 to — 2	+ .16	1.13	.15	.24	.64	2.66	<.01
Occupational status	1 to 5	2.94	1.06	.18	2 to 6	4.33	1.36	.23	.28	1.39	4.96	<.001
Amount of education	7 to 20	14.76	2.92	.46	3 to 19	11.65	3.10	.42	.62	3.11	5.02	<.001

Scores on the Threat-Competition Scale. The mean score of the tolerant category is significantly lower on this scale, revealing a capacity for compassion, sympathy, and trust, whereas the response pattern of the prejudiced demonstrates a suspicious, competitive, "jungle" *weltanschauung.* Tolerant people, the findings indicate, are likely to stress mutual assistance and to give others the benefit of the doubt in making judgments about them. Sample scale item: "If a person doesn't look out for himself, nobody else will." (Level of significance: $P < .001$.)

Scores on the "F" Scale. The nine most efficient items from the "F" scale used in *The Authoritarian Personality* study discriminate significantly between the two categories of subjects. Sample scale item: "What the youth needs most is strict discipline, rugged determination, and the will to fight for family and country." (Level of significance: $P < .001$.)

Scores on the Religiosity Scale. The significantly lower mean score of the tolerant category indicates that the tolerant person tends to reject the fundamentalistic, doctrinaire, and conservative outlook in favor of a more humanistic orientation.[8] This religiosity scale, it should be noted, is essentially a religious conservatism scale, stressing dogma and supernaturalism. Although these results point to the conclusion that there are certain differences in the emotional-intellectual quality of the religious orientation of the two categories of subjects, no significant relationship was found between tolerance and prejudice and frequency of church attendance, praying, Bible reading, and percentage of income contributed to one's religious group. Sample scale item: "Someday Christ will return." (Level of significance: $P < .005$.)

Scores on the Child Rearing Attitudes Scale. The tolerant and the extremely prejudiced person were strikingly different in their child rearing attitudes. Tolerants were inclined to reject authoritarian practices stressing strict obedience, harsh discipline, and physical punishment. The strongly prejudiced person endorsed items suggesting a positive view toward force, retribution, conflict, and distrust. He expressed a strong preference for "obedience and respect" in children.[9] Sample scale item: "Obedience is the most important thing a child should learn." (Level of significance: $P < .001$.)

Responses of Miscellaneous Items and Background Questions. The differential frequency between tolerant and prejudiced subjects is *not* statistically significant for the following characteristics: parental rela-

8. Readers may be interested in S. M. Lipset's discussion of this point within a different context. See his "Democracy and Working-Class Authoritarianism," pp. 482-501, *American Sociological Review,* 24 (August, 1959). [See Chapter 40 of this book.]

9. Political implications of child rearing practices and related matters are discussed by Robert E. Lane in "Fathers and Sons: Foundations of Political Belief," *American Sociological Review,* 24 (August, 1959), see esp. pp. 506-509.

tions, evaluation of the father, disciplinary atmosphere of the family of orientation, frequency of punishment as child, childhood economic security, attitude towards pessimists, "Menace" choice, and self image choice. Individuals in the prejudiced category, however, expressed a more venerative attitude towards their mothers ($P < .05$), while the tolerants were less distrustful of politicians ($P < .001$) and more interested in politics ($P < .01$).

The distribution of tolerant and prejudiced subjects by religious affiliation show no significant deviation from chance. The tolerants are slightly over-represented in the "other," "Catholic," and "none" response cells, as are the prejudiced in the "Protestant" cell. There were no Jewish respondents found in the final sample.

A significantly larger proportion of females are in the prejudiced category ($P < .005$, according to Chi square analysis). Aside from the implicit reference to Negro males in the tolerance-prejudice scale items—which may or may not be offset by a similar male occupational reference for whites—this finding remains something of an enigma.

Although the two groups did not differ significantly in generational, occupational or educational mobility, the distribution of responses suggests that *downward* mobility is associated with prejudice. Tolerant subjects show a significantly higher mean occupational status and educational status ($P < .001$, for both). The modal income was the same for both categories, 4000 dollars. This result is noteworthy when one considers that the tolerants enjoyed higher educational and occupational status and expressed less economic insecurity. One surmises that tolerant people are less likely to see themselves as "economically deprived," even where there is a basis for such a view.[10]

Discussion. This research lends confidence to the basic proposition that tolerant persons differ from prejudiced persons in many personal and social respects, and that these discriminating characteristics are sufficiently numerous, pervasive, and fundamental to justify reference to tolerant and prejudiced personality syndromes. Understanding of the finer details of the functional interrelationships among these various characteristics in particular personalities would require clinical study of tolerants, defined and selected at least as carefully as those studied in the present research.

With respect to the characteristics of the prejudiced personality, our findings strongly suggest that many of the insights gained by the authors of *The Authoritarian Personality*, despite the shortcomings of their scaling methods, possess a considerable degree of validity and, despite

10. Again, reference to Lipset's "Democracy and Working-Class Authoritarianism" (*passim*), *op. cit.*, is in order.

the sampling shortcomings, probably apply to populations beyond those they studied, at least within comparable regions and sub-cultures.

However, because studies of personality and prejudice have led to many misunderstandings concerning the nature of both personality "types" and of prejudice, several qualifications should be made explicit. Of course, not every person who "tolerates" outgroups is tolerant of ambiguity, non-nationalistic, gentle in his treatment of children, and so on. The configurations as embodied in actual people are far from perfect matches of the ideal type. This is readily apparent from examination of Tables 2 and 3, which present correlations of each of the scales with

Table 2. Correlation Matrix of Scale Scores of Tolerant Subjects (N = 41)

Scale	*1*	*2*	*3*	*4*	*5*	*6*	*7*
1. Nationalism	X	.22	.39*	.01	.28	.41*	.10
2. Intolerance of ambiguity		X	.37*	—.01	.34*	.32*	.48*
3. Supersition—pseudo-science			X	.24	.40*	.31*	.36*
4. Threat-competition				X	.17	—.08	.28
5. "F"					X	.56*	.62*
6. Religiosity						X	.48*
7. Child rearing							X

*Significantly different from zero at the .05 level.

each of the others. Although in many instances the intercorrelations are substantial, in other cases the correlations do not qualify as significantly different from zero at the .05 level. But there is a degree of probability, however moderate, that the person who "tolerates" outgroups will also be generally tolerant of ambiguity, non-nationalistic, and so forth. Thus, as in the case of parole prediction devices, the predictive utility of such descriptions is much greater when applied to social groups and categories than when applied to individuals.

Perhaps the most important reason why real life embodiments of these configurations are so imperfect lies in the fact that prejudice

Table 3. Correlation Matrix of Scale Scores of Prejudiced Subjects (N = 59)

Scale	*1*	*2*	*3*	*4*	*5*	*6*	*7*
1. Nationalism	X	.32*	.32*	.22	.28*	.12	.19
2. Intolerance of ambiguity		X	.54*	.62*	.72*	.13	.29*
3. Superstition—pseudo-science			X	.52*	.58*	.02	.14
4. Threat-competition				X	.70*	—.08	.30*
5. "F"					X	.14	.28*
6. Religiosity						X	.22
7. Child rearing							X

*Significantly different from zero at the .05 level.

towards outgroups is part of the normative order of American society. Moreover, the degree to which rejection of particular outgroups is approved varies from one sub-culture to another and from region to region. Not only the community at large but the immediate groups to which the person belongs provide him with definitions of ingroups and outgroups and the "correct" feelings and behaviors in relation to their members. Under such circumstances, we find in our midst many Happy Bigots whose prejudices are born, not so much of personal psychological difficulties, but rather of the fact that their community and various groups inculcate, expect, and approve of their prejudices; personality factors probably serve primarily to predispose and to intensify or abate normative expectations. In such situations, the tolerant person may well be the deviant and a legitimate subject for analysis in terms of abnormal psychology. He may be tolerant because tolerance is deviation, and deviation may be a functionally very important retaliatory mechanism in his personality organization. On the other hand, a person with a considerable "fund of aggression" may be tolerant towards outgroups because his ingroups inculcate and expect tolerance, and although he may be tempted to engage in scapegoating, the negative sanctions may be foreboding. Finally, a person may be tolerant because he has no unusual psychological need to be prejudiced, has been exposed to the broad normative influences in the larger society favorable to tolerance, and does not find the negative sanctions of more local forces a sufficient deterrent to tolerance.[11]

11. Although he does not develop extensively the "personality" aspects of these diverse possibilities, their institutional and cultural correlates are suggestively discussed by Robert K. Merton in "Discrimination and the American Creed," in R. M. MacIver, editor, *Discrimination and National Welfare*, New York: Harper, 1949, Chapter 11.

ORVILLE G. BRIM, JR.

Attitude Content-Intensity and Probability Expectations

RESEARCH on attitudes during the past ten years has made a distinction between two aspects of attitudes called content and intensity. Content refers to the directional aspect of attitudes, while intensity refers to the strength or conviction with which they are held. For example, in attitudes of enlisted men toward their officers content refers to like or dislike of officers, while intensity refers to how strongly the respondent feels this like or dislike.

The relationship between these two aspects of attitudes is a U-shaped curve. When we correlate respondents' positions with regard to content and intensity, we find that persons who are neutral on content, who neither like nor dislike their officers in the example above, are also those persons who are low on intensity. When persons have extreme positions on content, expressing extreme liking or dislike for their officers, they also have the higher intensity scores.

A large number of studies of attitudes have demonstratd this U-shaped relationship between content and intensity. Katz,[1] Cantril,[2] Eysenck and Crown[3] have discussed attitude intensity. Guttman[4] has

---

Reprinted from American Sociological Review, *January, 1955, pp. 68-76, by permission of the author and the journal.*

Paper was presented at the meeting of the Midwest Sociological Society in Madison, Wisconsin, April 16, 1954. The report is part of the project "Personality and Cultural Factors in Probability Expectations," of the Group Behavior Laboratory of the University of Wisconsin. The project is supported in part by funds granted by the University Research Committee of the University of Wisconsin.

The author wishes to acknowledge the helpful discussion and criticism of this research by Professors Robert Campbell, J. C. Gilchrist, and Roy Francis.

1. Daniel Katz, "The Measurement of Intensity," in Hadley Cantril, *Gauging Public Opinion*, Princeton, N.J.: Princeton University Press, 1944.

2. Hadley Cantril, "The Intensity of an Attitude," *Journal of Abnormal and Social Psychology*, 41 (1946), pp. 129-135.

3. H. S. Eysenck and S. Crown, "National Stereotypes: An Experimental and Methodological Study," *International Journal of Opinion and Attitude Research*, 2 (1948), pp. 26-39.

4. Louis Guttman, "The Principal Components of Scale Analysis," in Samuel Stouffer *et al.*, *Measurement and Prediction*, Princeton, N.J.: Princeton University Press, 1950.

presented a mathematical model for the principal components of his scale analysis, and it is generally accepted that the second component has found its empirical referent in the intensity aspect of attitudes. Suchman[5] has developed the use of the intensity curve in determining the zero-point in content scales of attitudes, and at present there is widespread use of this procedure in attitude research.

Surprisingly little explanation, however, has been offered for the content-intensity relationship, in spite of this interest. The purpose of this paper is to analyze the content-intensity relationship. We turned our attention in this direction because of the research findings to be described, in which the same U-shaped curve appeared in a different type of data.

Probability Expectations and Confidence Levels

We report research here which is part of a general investigation of the probability determinants of behavior. One particular concern has been with the influence of individual and cultural factors on probability expectations of action outcomes. In an effort to capture individual differences[6] in need for security which affect expectations we have developed a simple test, consisting of 32 statements of the following form about everyday events. "The chances that an American citizen will believe in God are about – in 100." The subject fills in a probability value for the statement.

The construction of the 32 statements involved the following steps. Three sets of 32 cards were made up. One set contained 32 probability values ranging by a three-step interval from 1 to 46, and from 54 to 99. A second set contained cards designating general areas of activity—education, recreation, politics, economics, religion, health, family, and transportation and communication, with four cards for each of the eight areas. The third set contained cards indicating whether a statement should be positive or negative in regard to its conformity to generally accepted American values. The cards were selected randomly, three at a time, one from each deck, and a statement constructed which met the particular combination of criteria. The method used only statements for which the probability values were debatable or not well known, but which probably had values close to the ones specified on the cards.

5. Edward A. Suchman, "The Intensity Component in Attitude and Opinion Research," in Samuel Stouffer *et al.*, *op. cit.*

6. Discussed in a later section of the paper.

The 32 statements comprising the test are the following:[7]

(1) The chances that an adult American male will earn at least $4000 a year are about ——— in 100.

(2) . . . a student entering law school will quit before getting his law degree. . . .

(3) . . . frequent thumbsucking during childhood will make the teeth stick out (cause buck teeth). . . .

(4) . . . the President of the United States will be a man without a college education. . . .

(5) . . . a major league baseball team will win the pennant if it is in first place July 4th. . . .

(6) . . . a sexual pervert will have a low intelligence (IQ 80 or less). . . .

(7) . . . a high school graduate will go on to a freshman year in college. . . .

(8) . . . a couple getting married this year will later have divorce. . . .

(9) . . . an American male now at the age of 40 will live beyond the age of 55. . . .

(10) . . . an American family will live in a place without a telephone. . . .

(11) . . . an American family will own its own home. . . .

(12) . . . the telephone number you call will be busy. . . .

(13) . . . an American citizen will believe in God. . . .

---

7. Since the original publication of this paper a subsequent study has shown that (a) the reliability of the test on an odd-even split, corrected by the Spearman-Brown formula, is 0.81 based on an N of 50 Ss; (b) the plot of over 500 test returns appears normally distributed although no tests of normality have been made; (c) more than 200 test returns show no relationship between scores and standard socio-economic variables; (d) a sample of 100 test returns shows no relationship (r equals −0.07) with intelligence. (See Orville G. Brim, Jr., and David B. Hoff, "Individual and Situational Differences in Desire for Certainty," *Journal of Abnormal and Social Psychology*, 54 [March, 1957], pp. 225-229.) The foregoing study used college students. The findings are strongly substantiated in another series of studies on different populations: Orville G. Brim, Jr., David C. Glass, David E. Lavin, and Norman Goodman, *Personality and Decision Processes: Studies in the Social Psychology of Thinking*, Stanford, Calif.: Stanford University Press, 1962.

(14) . . . a varsity football player in an American university will be subsidized (given money for his football ability). . . .

(15) . . . an American city of over 50,000 people will have a chapter of the League of Women Voters. . . .

(16) . . . the governor of a state will be elected for a second term in office. . . .

(17) . . . a son will go into the same kind of work as his father. . . .

(18) . . . a man 70 years old will need financial help from someone to support himself. . . .

(19) . . . spanking a child will make him tell the truth next time. . . .

(20) . . . an American-born baby will get a poor and inadequate diet during his first year of life. . . .

(21) . . . an adult male will stay home instead of going to church on Sunday. . . .

(22) . . . a sixth grade teacher in the public schools will be a man. . . .

(23) . . . a child whose parents are divorced will be neurotic. . . .

(24) . . . in the United States that a girl will be married before the age of 17. . . .

(25) . . . a world's champion boxer comes from a poor family. . . .

(26) . . . an American citizen will be bilingual (speak two languages). . . .

(27) . . . a five card deal will have two cards of the same kind (one pair). . . .

(28) . . . a man with a broken neck will die. . . .

(29) . . . a crime in the United States will be solved (someone arrested and convicted for it). . . .

(30) . . . the number of auto accidents in a year will be higher than for the year just before. . . .

(31) . . . a small business (for examples, gas station, motel), will fail within 2 years after starting. . . .

(32) . . . the person one marries will have the same religion. . . .

In addition to assigning values for each statement, the subject indicates his certainty for each probability estimate by rating the estimate on the following five-point scale:

Very Sure		Partly Sure		Not Sure At All
1	2	3	4	5

Let us call the probability value assigned to the statement P_1, or the primary estimate, and use P_2 to refer to the amount of certainty the subject indicates for the P_1 estimate. P_2 is therefore the subjective confidence level which a person has for his probability estimate given in the statement. We point out that P_2 is a probability estimate also which, though crudely measured, refers to the probability that the first probability estimate, P_1, is correct.[8]

The relevant research finding is the empirical relationship between P_1 and P_2 estimates. An analysis of test returns from 101 college students shows the relationship given in Table 1. The P_1 values are grouped according to the column headings. The row gives the mean P_2 value, where 1 equals "Very Sure" and 5 equals "Not Sure at All," for each of the columns or P_1 categories. One can easily see the U-shaped curve of the P_2 mean values. The P_2 values, representing the amount of confidence in the P_1 estimate, rise toward the "Very Sure" level as the P_1 estimates move toward the extremes of 0 and 100. This result has been duplicated in another sample of 93 respondents, and in two more smaller samples of 20 respondents each.

Table 1. P_1-P_2 Relationship

	P_1 VALUES (GROUPED)										
	0-4	5-14	15-24	25-34	35-44	45-55	56-65	66-75	76-85	86-95	96-100
Sum P_2 values	340	1250	1050	966	842	1501	707	1028	704	633	121
N of responses	179	437	349	306	263	483	228	352	263	279	80
Mean P_2	1.90	2.86	3.01	3.16	3.20	3.11	3.10	2.92	2.68	2.27	1.51

One will note that the P_2 value of 3.20, which represents the least amount of certainty, occurs in the 35-44 category rather than the 45-55 category as we would expect. We attribute this fact to sampling fluctuation. One will also note that this lowest mean P_2 value of 3.20 does not

8. For a related analysis see the discussion of "belief" and "strength of belief" in C. West Churchman and Russell L. Ackoff, "Definitional Models for Belief, Opinion, and Attitude," *International Journal of Opinion and Attitude Research*, 2 (1948), pp. 151-168.

reach the lowest level of certainty, which would be represented by a mean value of 5. The greatest average uncertainty admitted by the respondents still leaves them "Partly Sure." This finding corresponds to the finding in attitude research that the zero-point or bottom of the intensity curve never actually reaches the lowest possible level.

The general rule in describing the curve is that the more extreme the probability value which a subject assigns to a statement, the more certain the subject is that this value is correct. One may now sensibly ask: Why should this relationship occur? Since our own results seem so closely related to the results of attitude research we have tried to develop an explanation which accounts for both sets of data.

We take up first, in the analysis which follows, the problem of the U-shaped curve itself, and second, the effect upon the curve of individual differences in response.

The P_1-P_2 (Content-Intensity) Relationship

When a respondent is asked to estimate the chances of some event occurring, the estimate is based on his knowledge about the event in question. Precise knowledge of the event fixes the response at some particular point along the P_1 dimension; less than precise knowledge simply sets limits within which the response may range. When the response is free to fluctuate within limits set by knowledge, then the desires of the respondent about the event in question may also influence the response. Motivation biases the response in the direction desired by the respondent, as many studies[9] have shown.

What determines the reponse, however, when the respondent is asked to estimate the chances of an event about which he knows little or nothing, and in which he has little or no interest? The answer to this question provides the explanation of the U-shaped curve. We propose that the characteristic human response to events of this nature, about which one knows and cares little, is to throw them toward the middle, or in this case the 50 per cent, range. This is an application of the old idea that events become "equiprobable through ignorance." It seems to us that this idea will be increasingly useful in the future in the interpretation of decision and judging processes. For example, research on

9. D. M. MacGregor, "The Major Determinants of the Prediction of Social Events," *Journal of Abnormal and Social Psychology*, 33 (1938), pp. 179-204; Lee J. Cronbach and Betty Mae Davis, "Belief and Desire in Wartime," *Journal of Abnormal and Social Psychology*, 39 (1944), pp. 446-458; Rose W. Marks, "The Effect of Probability, Desirability, and 'Privilege' on the Stated Expectations of Children," *Journal of Personality*, 19 (1951), pp. 332-351.

social classes in America shows the largest percentage of people claim midde-class standing. Probably some portion of these middle-class responses can be explained by the fact that class standing in America is ambiguous, and that the middle-class response simply indicates the respondent's ignorance about his rank position.[10]

The idea of equiprobability through ignorance is used here as a descriptive principle which accounts for our data. It is of interest to recognize that the best estimate an individual can make for an event about which he knows nothing is a 50 per cent estimate, because this estimate results in the maximum reduction of predictive errors when the event is completely unknown. If the individual knows a little more about the event, for example that the chances are a little better than 50 per cent, then his best estimate would be around 60 per cent and his confidence would rise slightly. If he narrowed the range of possibilities still further through knowledge that the chances are a little above 60 per cent, then his best estimate would be around 70 per cent and his confidence rises still more.

The equiprobable through ignorance principle applies to the U-shaped curve in this way. One asks individuals to respond to a series of items about which they have varying information. Items about which they have sound information, or at least believe that they do,[11] are those items on which they are "Very Sure" they are right. The P_1 estimate is fixed by the knowledge, and the P_2 estimate is "Very Sure." Responses to such items could range from 0 to 100 on the P_1 dimension, and the relationship to the P_2 responses would give a straight line, not a curve. This is discussed further below. The other items, on which they do not have adequate information, that is, on which they are "Partly Sure" or "Not Sure at All," are thrown toward the middle or 50 per cent range.

10. Richard Centers, *The Psychology of Social Classes*, Princeton, N.J.: Princeton University Press, 1949, Chapter III. Natalie Rogoff, "Social Stratification in France and in the United States," *American Journal of Sociology*, LIX (1953), pp. 347-357.

11. One must recognize that the information which the respondent uses as a basis for his estimate need not be valid information in a scientific sense. He may believe that 100 per cent of a minority group have some characteristic, and be completely certain of this, whereas in fact the probability of this characteristic occurring is quite different from his estimate. We refer to such a person as prejudiced, but it is his prejudiced expectation which determines his response, and not scientific knowledge. To suggest that individuals make extreme estimates for events about which science knows nothing and that this refutes the equiprobability principle is to miss this point. What determines the probability expectation is the information available to the person stating the expectation, and not the information possessed by others. Each individual has his personal fund of certitude and ignorance, which may or may not correspond to scientific knowledge.

This piles up in the P_1 50 per cent range responses to items for which the respondent has a low level of certainty, that is, items for which the P_2 response is unsure. When the means of the P_2 estimates are then calculated, certainty progressively declines as one moves from the extremes toward the 50 per cent range, thus giving the typical U-shaped relationship.

We consider now the conditions under which the U-shaped curve would *not* appear. Questions put to an individual may range from questions of "fact" to questions of "opinion." The term "fact" here refers to those instances in which the respondent knows the probability of an event with high exactitude, and is highly certain that this probability is correct. The term "opinion" refers to those instances in which the probability of an event is not well-known, and the respondent is not sure of his estimate. Fact and opinion thus represent the extremes of high and low exactitude and confidence between which the P_1 and P_2 probability expectations may vary.

When one asks questions of fact of a respondent, the P_1 or content response ranges from 0 to 100, depending on the item, but the P_2 intensity response is fixed at a very high certainty level. Simple examples would be (1) an estimate of the sun rising tomorrow, in which P_1 would be 100 per cent, and P_2 "Very Sure"; and (2) an estimate of heads occurring on a coin toss, in which P_1 would be 50 per cent, and P_2 again "Very Sure." In situations such as these there is no ignorance, and therefore no need to throw items toward the middle. It should be clear that responses to a sample of such *factual* items would produce a straight line relationship with P_2 at its highest value in each case, rather than a curved relationship.

In contrast to this, as one uses items involving great ignorance the curve should progressively deepen until it firmly touches the bottom or "Not Sure at All" level. Beyond this, if *all* items were items of great ignorance, the arms of the curve should disappear and all responses should fail in the 50 per cent, "Not Sure at All" range. At about this point a subject would probably refuse to respond and accuse the investigator of asking stupid questions.

The fact that we find the curvilinear relationship in our data shows that the respondents feel that they know something about some of the items, and very little about others; that the items range, in other words, somewhere between the extremes of fact and opinion as the respondent sees them.

It remains for us now to apply the equiprobable through ignorance principle to attitude data. In order to do this we must first relate attitudes to a broader expectancy theory. We consider attitudes to be feelings based on probability expectations which have the following characteristic: attitudes are feelings based on probability expectations about the instrumental or end value of certain states of affairs in terms of individual satisfaction.

An example will help to clarify this approach. Let us say that we have asked the following attitude question:

"In general, what do you think of color television?"

It is very good
It is fairly good
It is not so good
It is not good at all
Undecided

We propose that for a question such as this a person who makes the response "It is very good," does so because he believes it highly probable that color television is of value to him, e.g. he will enjoy watching the programs. The question essentially asks the respondent to decide whether the probability that color television will be satisfying to him is very high, fairly high, fairly low, or very low. If he estimates that color television has a high probability of being satisfying, then the associated affective response or attitude is that it is very good. If he estimates the probability of satisfaction to be low, then the associated attitude is that the plan is not so good.

When the intensity question which follows asks "How strongly do you feel about this?" it essentially asks the respondent to indicate how sure he is that he is right. This makes the response the equivalent of the P_2 or certainty estimate. It is noteworthy that both Katz and Suchman report that when in their research the intensity question was stated as "How sure are you of your answer?" the responses to this phrasing yielded the same results as did responses to the phrasing in terms of strength of feeling.

The content-intensity curve is therefore accounted for in the following way. Among a series of items presented to the respondent there are some for which he has sound knowledge that the event will be good or bad. The P_1 responses to such items are set from 0 to 100, and the P_2 response is "Very Sure." The associated attitudinal content response is "Very Good," etc., depending on the estimate of value, and the intensity response is "Very Strong," or "Very Sure." For the items in the series about which the respondent has little or no knowledge, that is, little or no information about whether the event is good or bad for him, then the equiprobability principle is operative. The event may be either good or bad, the respondent throws the expectation toward the 50 per cent range, and the associated content response is "Undecided" or "Indifferent." At the same time the P_2 response is low on certainty and the associated intensity response is "Not Strongly at All," or "Not Sure at All." These are items for which the respondent has no attitude because he has no basis for judging whether the event is good or bad for him. In a series of items there would pile up at the 50 per cent, not sure at all range (the indifferent, low intensity range) those items about which the respondent was ignorant. The result would be the content-intensity curve found in attitude data.

This ideal curve does not always occur. We find in many studies that the "zero point," or point of lowest intensity, occurs in some position other than "indifferent" along the content dimension. For example, Suchman[12] reports the results of a question on soldiers' attitudes towards the Army point system, in which the possible responses were those given in the television example above. The relationship between these responses and their intensity is a straight line slope with the zero or low intensity point somewhere beyond the "Not good at all" content response. The implication is that we have only half of the content-intensity curve—the favorable half—and that none of the respondents had sufficient dislike of the plan to turn the curve up at the other end. How does our analysis account for this type of result?

Let us assume that among the respondents there are some who think it 60 per cent probable that the plan will be satisfying, e.g. get them home soon from overseas, that some think it 70 per cent probable, others 80, 90, and 100. There are no respondents who think that the chances of satisfaction from the plan are less than 50 per cent. In this case, as intensity of response declines as the probability expectation ranges from 100 to 50 per cent, the result would be the straight line slope found in the data. There is no upturn of the line because no respondent has an expectation below 50 per cent.

We must now ask why, if this is the case, some of the respondents say the plan is "Not good at all" when the expected chances of satisfaction are better than 50 per cent. We would expect responses only in the "Partly good" and "Very good" categories. In answer to this we must recognize that the attitude responses are verbal statements of the desirability of the stated event. The desirability is based upon the expected probability of satisfaction from the event. The attitude question essentially asks the respondent, "How do you like your chances of satisfaction?" Now, under what conditions would a respondent say that an event which has a probability of around 60 per cent of bringing satisfaction is nevertheless "Not good at all"? The answer is: When the

12. Edward A. Suchman, *op. cit.*, p. 234.

motivation involved is very high. If motivation is high, as it certainly is with regard to getting out of the Army, then an expectation of 60 per cent is really not very good at all. The respondent demands a much higher level of certainty of satisfaction before he is willing to say that the plan is good.

In the contrary case, where motivation is low, we would expect that the zero point would occur somewhere in the favorable side of the curve, because respondents begin to refer to the event as favorable before the probability of satisfaction reaches the 50 per cent point. Suchman[13] gives an example of this type of curve in regard to soldiers' attitudes toward the WAC. We propose that soldiers' concern over the WAC is much less than their concern over getting out of military service, and that this curve is expected for this reason.

We now see that what the zero or low intensity point really marks off are those persons who think the probability of satisfaction is above 50 per cent from those who think it is below this value. We would propose this as a general principle: that the zero point always occurs at the 50 per cent value. However, when instead of probability expectations themselves the affective attitude responses (verbal statements of desirability of risk) are correlated with intensity of response, we would predict that the zero point would occur in the "favorable" and "unfavorable" range under conditions of low and high motivation respectively.

The use of the zero point to divide people favorable and unfavorable to the event, regardless of their verbal evaluation of the event, appears now as a dubious practice. The zero point divides respondents into two groups, those above and below a 50 per cent probability expectation. To then assume that all persons who expect the chances of satisfaction to be better than 50 per cent therefore "like" the event is gratuitous. Certainly they "like" the event better than those below the 50 per cent cutting point. But whether they like it in the sense that they would vote for it, fight for it, defend it, or otherwise support it in preference to some alternative, depends on their feeling about the risk level itself, which in turn depends on their motivation. This is a problem which is not answered by the use of the zero-point alone.

The U-shaped curve consistently appears in attitude data. This simply indicates that the expectations underlying the affectual responses are not all fixed by knowledge. One would predict that if one asked for attitudes which were based on factual expectations alone then there would be no content-intensity curve at all. It may be hard to imagine an attitude of "Undecided" about which one was certain or felt strongly, but such would be the case if the respondent had full and certain knowl-

13. *Ibid.*, p. 254.

edge that some state of affairs was a mixed blessing, half good for him and half bad. It is true, of course, that such cases would be unusual because the individual is motivated to make a decision one way or another, and it is the rare person who is able to suspend judgment on events which affect his own satisfaction. However, these responses in spite of their rarity should not be considered simply as "errors," as they often are in attitude research.

In sum, we believe that content responses to attitude questions are based on a class of P_1 expectations which refer to probabilities about the satisfaction to be gained from various states of affairs; and that "strength of feeling" is the equivalent of a P_2 estimate that the first expectation is correct. In these terms, the U-shaped curve relating content and intensity in attitude data is explained in the same way as the P_1-P_2 relationship; namely, as the result of the human tendency to make events equiprobable through ignorance.

Individual Differences in Responses

Analysis of attitude data has shown differences between individuals in what Suchman calls "generalized intensity" of response. Some individuals have a greater tendency to respond "intensely" to attitude items than do others. Some data presented by Suchman[14] illustrate this point. Suchman broke a large sample into three groups of about 600 respondents each, on the basis of the average intensity of their responses to a sample of content questions from eleven different universes of content. The groups are respectively high, middle, and low on average intensity. The U-shaped relationship between intensity and content is maintained, in spite of such individual differences. In the comparison of the three different groups the curves had the same zero point and almost identical shape. The difference was that the overall curves were at separate levels of intensity, so to speak.

The finding has been explained before by reference to "verbal habits"; that is, some individuals have the habit of using words or responding to words such as "Very Strong," and other individuals do not. We would say instead that the individual differences in intensity of response are not simply verbal habits, but are the effects of different degrees of motivation to escape from uncertainty.

Let us assume that all human beings have a need for security or certainty. In the effort to achieve certainty there is a tendency to deny the ambiguity of a situation by claiming that one really knows what the

14. *Ibid.*, pp. 253-261.

outcome of the situation will be. We assume further that individuals differ in this need for security, which expresses itself in individual differences in "tolerance of ambiguity." We developed our test to measure these individual differences. Responses to the test items are scored in the following manner. One takes the distance of each P_1 estimate from its nearest end point, 0 or 100 per cent, and multiplies this value by its associated P_2 value, 1 for "Very Sure," through 5 for "Not Sure at All." The products are summed and averaged for the 32 items of the test. By this procedure, the higher the score the less the individual need for security, and the greater the tolerance of ambiguity.

The test and its scoring is based on the following assumptions. Along the P_1 dimension, the more extreme the estimates of probabilities toward 0 or 100, the less ambiguous the situation becomes. Situations become true or false, things happen or do not happen, the world becomes black and white, with no grays. Along the P_2 dimension, ignorance or ambiguity diminishes as the subject raises the P_2 estimate from "Not Sure at All" toward "Very Sure." These two probability estimates together define the extent of ignorance or ambiguity in the situation. Ambiguity is not removed when the P_1 estimate is close to either 0 or 100, but the P_2 estimate remains at the "Not Sure at All" level; for example, when a subject states that probably 99 out of 100 Americans believe in God, but then states that he is not sure of this at all. Neither is ambiguity removed if the P_2 estimate rises to complete certainty, but the P_1 estimate remains around 50 per cent, as in the case of predicting heads on a coin toss. The amount of ambiguity is a function of both probability estimates. Individuals in ambiguous situations therefore have a two-fold pressure upon them. One is to push the P_1 expectations toward either extreme; the other is to raise the P_2 expectations toward the "Very Sure" level.

Our explanation of individual differences in "generalized intensity" in response to attitude items is that people high on intensity have a greater need for security, and so respond with greater conviction. In considering differences in intensity, however, one is considering only the P_2 or certainty expectations in our terms. On the basis of our interpretation it follows that an individual high on intensity must also make more frequent responses at the extremes of the P_1 or content dimension, because only in this way can he actually remove the ambiguity.

This proposition is supported by two sets of data, one from attitude research and the other from probability expectations research. Additional study of Suchman's data[15] shows that the three groups of high, middle, and low generalized intensity have respectively 25, 14, and 9 per cent

15. *Ibid.*, pp. 260-262.

of their total responses in the four extreme positions (two at either end of the scale). A chi square test comparing the three groups on the frequency of these extreme responses and the frequency of all other (middle) responses shows the probability of the difference to be less than .001. The second source of support comes from our own data. We have found that scores on the need for security test correlate significantly with the extremity of response on some standardized attitude tests.[16] However, scores based on either P_1 or P_2 expectations alone do not show as large or significant relationships to responses on the other attitude tests as do scores computed from both expectations in the manner described above. This supports our position that both P_1 and P_2 estimates are influenced by the pressure to reduce uncertainty, and that the best measure is one which combines the two.

Individual differences in security need are therefore expressed not only in the height or level of intensity of the curve, but also in the distribution of responses along the curve. Persons with high security need would have both a higher intensity level and more responses at the extreme. The greater frequency of extreme responses occurs in the following way. We have said that according to the principle of events being equiprobable through ignorance, responses to uncertain items are thrown toward the 50 per cent range. However, to make such a response is to admit one's ignorance. A strong need for security should therefore result in more items being left out along the arms of the curve where higher certainty is achieved. In contrast, respondents with a weaker need for security admit more ignorance and place more items in the 50 per cent range.

Summary

The relationship between probability estimates of occurrence of events and the certainty of these estimates shows the typical U-shaped curve found in the content-intensity relationship in attitude data. An explanation in terms of an equiprobable through ignorance principle is given for both the attitude and probability expectation data. Individual differences in both intensity and extremity of responses to attitude and expectancy questions are considered to be the result of individual differ-

16. Orville G. Brim, Jr., and David B. Hoff, *op. cit.* Since these data were originally reported, it has been recognized generally that the characteristic of "extreme response set" in test taking, previously noted in analyses of tests performance (e.g., Lee J. Cronbach, "Response Sets and Test Validity," *Educational and Psychological Measurement*, 11 [1951] 16-22), probably is caused by a motivational characteristic much like that described here.

ences in need for security. A stronger need results in proportionately more items being responded to with greater intensity and extremity as the individual seeks to avoid the middle range of response in which he admits his ignorance.

SEYMOUR MARTIN LIPSET

Working-Class Authoritarianism

THE gradual realization that extremist and intolerant movements in modern society are more likely to be based on the lower classes than on the middle and upper classes has posed a tragic dilemma for those intellectuals of the democratic left who once believed the proletariat necessarily to be a force for liberty, racial equality, and social progress. The Socialist Italian novelist Ignazio Silone has asserted that

> The myth of the liberating power of the proletariat has dissolved along with that other myth of progress. The recent examples of the Nazi labor unions, like those of Salazar and Peron . . . have at last convinced of this even those who were reluctant to admit it on the sole grounds of the totalitarian degeneration of Communism.[1]

Dramatic demonstrations of this point have been given recently by the southern workers' support of White Citizens' Councils and segrega-

---

An early version of this chapter was written for a conference on "The Future of Liberty" sponsored by the Congress for Cultural Freedom in Milan, Italy, in September, 1955.

1. "The Choice of Comrades," *Encounter*, 3 (December, 1954), p. 25. Arnold A. Rogow writing in the Socialist magazine *Dissent* even suggests that "the liberal and radical approach has always lacked a popular base, that in essence, the liberal tradition has been a confined minority, perhaps elitist, tradition." "The Revolt against Social Equality," *Dissent,* 4 (1957), p. 370.

tion in the United States and by the active participation of many British workers in the 1958 race riots in England. A "Short Talk with a Fascist Beast" (an eighteen-year-old casual laborer who took part in the beating of Negroes in London), which appeared in the left socialist *New Statesman*, portrays graphically the ideological syndrome which sometimes culminates in such behavior. "Len's" perspective is offered in detail as a prelude to an analytical survey of the authoritarian elements of the lower-class situation in modern society.

> "That's why I'm with the Fascists," he says. "They're against the blacks. That Salmon, he's a Communist. The Labour Party is Communist too. Like the unions." His mother and father, he says, are strict Labour supporters. Is he against the Labour Party? "Nah, I'm for them. They're for y'know—us. I'm for the unions too." Even though they were dominated by Communists? "Sure," he says. "I like the Communist Party. It's powerful, like." How can he be for the Communists when the fascists hate them?
>
> Len says, "Well, y'know, I'm for the fascists when they're against the nigs. But the fascists is really for the rich people y'know, like the Tories. All for the guv'nors, people like that. But the Communists are very powerful." I told him the Communist Party of Britain was quite small.
>
> "But," he says, "they got Russia behind them." His voice was full of marvel. "I admire Russia. Y'know, the people. They're peaceful. They're strong. When they say they'll do a thing, they do it. Not like us. Makes you think: they got a weapon over there can wipe us all out, with one wave of a general's arm. Destroy us completely and totally. Honest, those Russians. When they say they'll do a thing, they do it. Like in Hungary, I pity those people, the Hungarians. But did you see the Russians went in and stopped them. Tanks. Not like us in Cyprus. Our soldiers get shot in the back and what do we do? The Communists is for the small man."[2]

Such strikingly visible demonstrations of working-class ethnic prejudice and support for totalitarian political movements have been paralleled in studies of public opinion, religion, family patterns, and personality structure. Many of these studies suggest that the lower-class way of life produces individuals with rigid and intolerant approaches to politics.

At first glance the facts of political history may seem to contradict this. Since their beginnings in the nineteenth century, workers' organizations and parties have been a major force in extending political democracy, and in waging progressive political and economic battles. Before 1914, the classic division between the working-class left parties and the economically privileged right was not based solely upon such issues as redistribution of income, status, and educational opportunities, but also rested upon civil liberties and international policy. The workers, judged by the policies of their parties, were often the backbone of the fight

2. Clancy Sigal in the *New Statesman*, October 4, 1958, p. 440.

for greater political democracy, religious freedom, minority rights, and international peace, while the parties backed by the conservative middle and upper classes in much of Europe tended to favor more extremist political forms, to resist the extension of the suffrage, to back the established church, and to support jingoistic foreign policies.

Events since 1914 have gradually eroded these patterns. In some nations working-class groups have proved to be the most nationalistic sector of the population. In some they have been in the forefront of the struggle against equal rights for minority groups, and have sought to limit immigration or to impose racial standards in countries with open immigration. The conclusion of the anti-fascist era and the emergence of the cold war have shown that the struggle for freedom is not a simple variant of the economic class struggle. The threat to freedom posed by the Communist movement is as great as that once posed by Fascism and Nazism, and Communism, in all countries where it is strong, is supported mainly by the lower levels of the working class, or the rural population.[3] No other party has been as thoroughly and completely the party of the working class and the poor. Socialist parties, past and present, secured much more support from the middle classes than the Communists have.

Some socialists and liberals have suggestted that this proves nothing about authoritarian tendencies in the working class, since the Communist party often masquerades as a party seeking to fulfill the classic Western-democratic ideals of liberty, equality, and fraternity. They argue that most Communist supporters, particularly the less educated, are deceived into thinking that the Communists are simply more militant and efficient socialists. I would suggest, however, the alternative hypothesis that, rather than being a source of strain, the intransigent and intolerant aspects of Communist ideology attract members from that large stratum with low incomes, low-status occupations, and low education, which in modern industrial societies has meant largely, though not exclusively, the working class.

The social situation of the lower strata, particularly in poorer countries with low levels of education, predisposes them to view politics as black and white, good and evil. Consequently, other things being equal, they should be more likely than other strata to prefer extremist movements which suggest easy and quick solutions to social problems and have a rigid outlook.

---

3. The sources of variation in Communist strength from country to country have already been discussed in Chap. II [S. M. Lipset, *Political Man* (New York: Doubleday & Co., 1960)] in relation to the level and speed of economic development.

The "authoritarianism" of any social stratum or class is highly relative, of course, and often modified by organizational commitments to democracy and by individual cross-pressures. The lower class in any given country may be more authoritarian than the upper classes, but on an "absolute" scale all the classes in that country may be less authoritarian than any class in another country. In a country like Britain, where norms of tolerance are well developed and widespread in every social stratum, even the lowest class may be less authoritarian and more "sophisticated" than the most highly educated stratum in an underdeveloped country, where immediate problems and crises impinge on every class and short-term solutions may be sought by all groups.[4]

Commitments to democratic procedures and ideals by the principal organizations to which low-status individuals belong may also influence these individuals' actual political behavior more than their underlying personal values, no matter how authoritarian.[5] A working class which has developed an early (prior to the Communists) loyalty to democratic political and trade-union movements which have successfully fought for social and economic rights will not easily change its allegiance.

Commitments to other values or institutions by individuals (cross-pressures) may also override the most established predispositions. For example, a French, Italian, or German Catholic worker who is strongly anticapitalist may still vote for a relatively conservative party in France, Italy, or Germany, because his ties to Catholicism are stronger than his resentments about his class status; a worker strongly inclined toward authoritarian ideas may defend democratic institutions against fascist attack because of his links to anti-fascist working-class parties and unions. Conversely, those who are not inclined toward extremist politics may back an extremist party because of certain aspects of its program and political role. Many persons supported the Communists in 1936 and 1943 as an anti-fascist internationalist party.

4. See Richard Hoggart, *The Uses of Literacy* (London: Chatto and Windus, 1957), pp. 78-79 and 146-48, for a discussion of the acceptance of norms of tolerance by the British working class. E. T. Prothro and Levon Melikian, in "The California Public Opinion Scale in an Authoritarian Culture," *Public Opinion Quarterly*, 17 (1953), pp. 353-63, have shown, in a study of 130 students at the American University in Lebanon, that they exhibited the same association between authoritarianism and economic radicalism as is found among workers in America. A survey in 1951-52 of 1,800 Puerto Rican adults, representative of the entire rural population, found that 84 per cent were "somewhat authoritarian," as compared to 46 per cent for a comparable U.S. population. See Henry Wells, "Ideology and Leadership in Puerto Rican Politics," *American Political Science Review*, 49 (1955), pp. 22-40.

5. The southern Democrats were the most staunch opponents of McCarthy and his tactics, not because of any deep opposition to undemocratic methods, but rather because of an organizational commitment to the Democratic party.

The specific propensity of given social strata to support either extremist or democratic political parties, then, cannot be predicted from a knowledge of their psychological predispositions or from attitudes inferred from survey data.[6] Both evidence and theory suggest, however, that the lower strata are relatively more authoritarian, that (again, other things being equal) they will be more attracted to an extremist movement than to a moderate and democratic one, and that, once recruited, they will not be alienated by its lack of democracy, while more educated or sophisticated supporters will tend to drop away.[7]

Democracy and the Lower Classes

The poorer strata everywhere are more liberal or leftist on economic issues; they favor more welfare state measures, higher wages, graduated income taxes, support of trade-unions, and so forth. But when liberalism is defined in noneconomic terms—as support of civil liberties, internationalism, etc.—the correlation is reversed. The more well-to-do are more liberal, the poorer are more intolerant.[8]

Public opinion data from a number of countries indicate that the lower classes are much less committed to democracy as a political system than are the urban middle and upper classes. In Germany, for example, a study conducted by the UNESCO Institute at Cologne in 1953 asked a systematic sample of 3,000 Germans: "Do you think that it would better if there were one party, several parties, or no party?" The results analyzed according to occupational status indicate that the lower strata of the working class and the rural population were less likely to support a multi-party system (a reasonable index of democratic

---

6. For a detailed discussion of the fallacy of attempting to suggest that political behavior is a necessary function of political attitudes or psychological traits, see Nathan Glazer and S. M. Lipset, "The Polls on Communism and Conformity," in Daniel Bell, ed., *The New American Right* (New York: Criterion Books, 1955), pp. 141-66.

7. The term "extremist" is used to refer to movements, parties, and ideologies. "Authoritarian" refers to the attitudes and predispositions of individuals (or of groups, where a statistical aggregate of *individual* attitudes, and not group characteristics as such, are of concern). The term "authoritarian" has too many associations with studies of attitudes to be safely used to refer also to types of social organizations.

8. See two articles by G. H. Smith, "Liberalism and Level of Information," *Journal of Educational Psychology*, 39 (1948), pp. 65-82; and "The Relation of 'Enlightenment' to Liberal-Conservative Opinions," *Journal of Social Psychology*, 28 (1948), pp. 3-17.

attitudes in Westernized countries) than the middle and upper strata. (See Table 1.)

Table 1. Responses of Different German Occupational Groups to Preferred Party System in Percentages* (Male Only)

Occupational Group	Several Parties	One Party	No Party	No Opinion	Total Number of Persons
Civil servants	88	6	3	3	111
Upper white-collar	77	13	2	8	58
Free professionals	69	13	8	10	38
Skilled workers	65	22	5	8	277
Artisans	64	16	9	11	124
Lower white-collar	62	19	7	12	221
Businessmen (small)	60	15	12	13	156
Farmers	56	22	6	16	241
Semiskilled workers	49	28	7	16	301
Unskilled workers	40	27	11	22	172

*Computed from IBM cards supplied to author by the UNESCO Institute at Cologne.

Comparable results were obtained in 1958 when a similar question was asked of national or regional samples in Austria, Japan, Brazil, Canada, Mexico, West Germany, the Netherlands, Belgium, Italy, and France. Although the proportion favoring a multi-party system varied from country to country, the lower classes within each nation were least likely to favor it.[9]

Surveys in Japan, Great Britain, and the United States designed to secure general reactions to problems of civil liberties, or the rights of various minorities, have produced similar results. In Japan, the workers and the rural population were more authoritarian and less concerned with civil liberties than the middle and upper classes.[10]

In England, the psychologist H. J. Eysenck found comparable differences between people who were "tough-minded" and those who were "tender-minded" in their general social outlook. The first group tended to be intolerant of deviations from the standard moral or religious codes, to be anti-Negro, anti-Semitic, and xenophobic, while the "tender-

9. Based on as yet unpublished data in the files of the World Poll, an organization established by International Research Associates which sponsors comparable surveys in a number of countries. The question asked in this survey was: "Suppose there was a political party here which corresponds to your own opinions—one you would more or less consider 'your' party. Would you wish this to be the only party in our country with no other parties besides, or would you be against such a one-party system?" Similar correlations were found between low status and belief in the value of a strong leader.

10. See Kotaro Kido and Masataka Sugi, "A Report of Research on Social Stratification and Mobility in Tokyo" (III), *Japanese Sociological Review,* 4 (1954), pp. 74-100; and National Public Opinion Institute of Japan, Report No. 26, *A Survey Concerning the Protection of Civil Liberties* (Tokyo, 1951).

minded" were tolerant of deviation, unprejudiced, and internationalist.[11] Summing up his findings, based on attitude scales given to supporters of different British parties, Eysenck reported that "middle-class Conservatives are more tender-minded than working-class Conseratives; middle-class Liberals are more tender-minded than working-class Liberals; middle-class Socialists are more tender-minded than working-class Socialists; and even middle-class Communists are more tender-minded than working-class Communists.[12]

The evidence from various American studies is also clear and consistent—the lower strata are the least tolerant.[13] In the most systematic of these, based on a national sample of nearly 5,000 Americans, Samuel A. Stouffer divided his respondents into three categories, "less tolerant, in-between, and more tolerant," by using a scale based on responses to questions about such civil liberties as the right of free speech for Communists, critics of religion, or advocates of nationalization of industry, and the like. As the data presented in Table 2 demonstrate, tolerance

Table 2. Proportion of Male Respondents Who Are "More Tolerant" with Respect to Civil Liberties Issues*

Professional and semiprofessional	66%	(159)
Proprietors, managers, and officials	51	(223)
Clerical and sales	49	(200)
Manual workers	30	(685)
Farmers or farm workers	20	(202)

*Samuel A. Stouffer, *Communism, Conformity, and Civil Liberties* (New York: Doubleday & Co., 1955), p. 139. The figures for manual and farm workers were calculated from IBM cards kindly supplied by Professor Stouffer.

increases with moves up the social ladder. Only 30 per cent of those in manual occupations are in the "most tolerant" category, as contrasted

11. See H. J. Eysenck, *The Psychology of Politics* (London: Routledge and Kegan Paul, 1954), p. 127.

12. *Ibid.*, p. 137: for a critique of the methodology of this study which raises serious questions about its procedures see Richard Christie, "Eysenck's Treatment of the Personality of Communists," *Psychological Bulletin*, 53 (1956), pp. 411-30.

13. See Arnold W. Rose, *Studies in Reduction of Prejudice* (Chicago: American Council on Race Relations, 1948), for a review of the literature bearing on this point prior to 1948. Several studies have shown the key importance of education and the independent effect of economic status, both basic components of low status. See Daniel J. Levinson and R. Nevitt Sanford, "A Scale for the Measurement of Anti-Semitism," *Journal of Psychology*, 17 (1944), pp. 339-70, and H. H. Harlan, "Some Factors Affecting Attitudes toward Jews," *American Sociological Review*, 7 (1942), pp. 816-27, for data on attitudes toward one ethnic group. See also James G. Martin and Frank R. Westie, "The Tolerant Personality," *American Sociological Review*, 24 (1959), pp. 521-28 [reprinted in this book]. For a digest of recent research in the field of race relations in the U.S.A., see Melvin M. Tumin, *Segregation and Desegregation* (New York: Anti-Defamation League of B'nai B'rith, 1957).

with 66 per cent of the professionals, and 51 per cent of the proprietors, managers, and officials. As in Germany and Japan, farmers are low in tolerance.

The findings of public opinion surveys in thirteen different countries that the lower strata are less committed to democratic norms than the middle classes are reaffirmed by the research of more psychologically oriented investigators, who have studied the social correlates of the "authoritarian personality."[14] Many studies in this area, summarized recently, show a consistent association between authoritarianism and lower-class status.[15] One survey of 460 Los Angeles adults reported that "the working class contains a higher proportion of authoritarians than either the middle or the upper class," and that among workers, those who explicitly identified themselves as "working class" rather than "middle class" were more authoritarian.[16]

Recent research further suggests the possibility of a *negative* correlation between authoritarianism and neuroticism within the lower classes. In general, those who deviate from the standards of their group are more likely to be neurotic than those who conform, so if we assume that authoritarian traits are more or less standard among low-status people, then the more liberal members of this group should also be the more neurotic.[17] As two psychologists, Anthony Davids and Charles Eriksen, point out, where the "standard of reference on authoritarianism is quite high," people may be well adjusted *and* authoritarian.[18] And the fact that this is often the case in lower-class groups fits the hypothesis that authoritarian attitudes are "normal" and expected in such groups.[19]

---

14. See Theodore Adorno, *et al.*, *The Authoritarian Personality* (New York: Harper & Bros., 1950). This, the original study, has less consistent results on this point than the many follow-up studies. The authors themselves (p. 178) point to the inadequacy of their sample.

15. Richard Christie and Peggy Cook, "A Guide to Published Literature Relating to the Authoritarian Personality," *Journal of Psychology*, 45 (1958), pp. 171-99.

16. W. J. McKinnon and R. Centers, "Authoritarianism and Urban Stratification," *American Journal of Sociology*, 61 (1956), p. 618.

17. Too much of contemporary psychological knowledge in this area has been gained from populations most convenient for the academic investigator to reach—university students. It is often forgotten that personality and attitude syndromes may be far different for this highly select group than for other segments of the total population.

18. See Anthony Davids and Charles W. Eriksen, "Some Social and Cultural Factors Determining Relations between Authoritarianism and Measures of Neuroticism," *Journal of Consulting Psychology*, 21 (1957), pp. 155-59. This article contains many references to the relevant literature.

19. The greater compatibility of the demands of Communist party membership and working-class background as indicated by Almond's finding that twice as many

Extremist Religions and the Lower Classes

Many observers have called attention to a connection between low social status and fundamentalist or chiliastic religion. This suggests that extremist religion is a product of the same social forces that sustain authoritarian political attitude. The liberal Protestant churches, on the other hand, have been predominantly middle class in membership. In the United States, this has created a dilemma for the liberal Protestant clergy, who have tended to be liberal in their politics as well as their religion and, hence, have often wanted to spread their social and religious gospel among the lower strata. But they have found that these classes want ministers who will preach of hell-fire and salvation rather than modern Protestant theology.[20]

In the early period of the Socialist movement, Engels observed that early Christianity and the revolutionary workers' movement had "notable points of resemblance," particularly in their millennial appeals and lower-class base.[21] Recently, Elmer Clark, a student of small sects in contemporary America, has noted that such sects, like early Christianity, "originate mainly among the religiously neglected poor." He writes that

> [When] the revolts of the poor have been tinged with religion, which was nearly always the case until recent times, millennial ideas have appeared, and . . . these notions are prominent in most of the small sects which follow the evangelical tradition. Premillenarianism is essentially a defense mechanism of the disinherited; despairing of obtaining substantial blessings through social processes, they turn on the world which has withheld its benefits and look to its destruction in a cosmic cataclysm which will exalt them and cast down the rich and powerful.[22]

---

of the middle-class party members as of the working-class group in his sample of Communists had neurotic problems hints again at the normality and congruence of extremist politics with a working-class background. Gabriel Almond, *The Appeals of Communism* (Princeton: Princeton University Press, 1954), pp. 245-46.

20. See Liston Pope, *Millhands and Preachers* (New Haven: Yale University Press, 1942), pp. 105-16.

21. See Friedrich Engels, "On the Early History of Christianity," in K. Marx and F. Engels, *On Religion* (Moscow: Foreign Languages Publishing House, 1957), pp. 312-20.

22. Elmer T. Clark, *The Small Sects in America* (New York: Abingdon Press, 1949), pp. 16, 218-19. According to Bryan Wilson, "insecurity, differential status, anxiety, cultural neglect, prompt a need for readjustment which sects may, for some, provide. The maladjusted may be communities, or occupational groups, or dispersed individuals in similar marginal positions." See "An Analysis of Sect Development," *American Sociological Review*, 24 (1959), p. 8, and the same author's *Minority Religious Movements in Modern Britain* (London: Heinemann, 1960).

Ernst Troeltsch, the major historian of sectarian religion, has characterized the psychological appeal of fundamentalist religious sects in a way that might as appropriately be applied to extremist politics:

> It is the lower classes which do the really creative work, forming communities on a genuine religious basis. They alone unite imagination and simplicity of feeling with a nonreflective habit of mind, a primitive energy, and an urgent sense of need. On such a foundation alone is it possible to build up an unconditional authoritative faith in a Divine Revelation with simplicity of surrender and unshaken certainty. Only within a fellowship of this kind is there room for those who have a sense of spiritual need, and who have not acquired the habit of intellectual reasoning, which always regards everything from a relative point of view.[23]

Jehovah's Witnesses, whose membership in the United States runs into the hundreds of thousands, is an excellent example of a rapidly growing sect which "continues to attract, as in the past, the underprivileged strata."[24] The Witnesses' principal teaching is that the Kingdom of Heaven is at hand: "The end of the age is near. Armageddon is just around the corner, when the wicked will be destroyed, and the theocracy, or rule of God, will be set up upon the earth."[25] And like the Communists, their organization is "hierarchical and highly authoritarian. There is little democratic participation in the management or in the formation of policies of the movement as a whole."[26]

Direct connections between the social roots of political and of religious extremism have been observed in a number of countries. In Czarist Russia, the young Trotsky recognized the relationship and successfully recruited the first working-class members of the South Russian Workers' Union (a revolutionary Marxist organization of the late 1890s) from adherents to religious sects.[27] In Holland and Sweden, recent studies show that the Communists are strongest in regions which were once centers of fundamentalist religious revivalism. In Finland, Com-

23. Ernst Troeltsch, *The Social Teaching of the Christian Churches* (London: George Allen and Unwin, 1930), Vol. 1, p. 44.

24. See Charles S. Braden, *These Also Believe: A Study of Modern American Cults and Minority Religious Movement* (New York: Macmillan, 1949), p. 384.

25. *Ibid.*, p. 370.

26. *Ibid.*, p. 363. It may be suggested that, as in authoritarian political movements, the intolerant character of most of the sects is an attractive feature and not a source of strain for their lower-class members. Although no systematic evidence is available, this assumption would help account for the lack of tolerance for factionalism within these sects, and for the endless schisms, with the new groups as intolerant as the old, since the splits usually occur over the issue of *whose* intolerant views and methods shall prevail.

27. See Isaac Deutscher, *The Prophet Armed, Trotsky, 1879-1921* (London: Oxford University Press, 1954), pp. 30-31.

munism and revivalist Christianity often are strong in the same areas. In the poor eastern parts of Finland, the Communists have been very careful not to offend people's religious feelings. It is reported that many Communist meetings actually begin with religious hymns.[28]

This is not to imply that religious sects supported by lower-class elements necessarily or usually become centers of political protest. In fact, such sects often drain off the discontent and frustration which would otherwise flow into channels of political extremism. The point here is that rigid fundamentalism and dogmatism are linked to the same underlying characteristics, attitudes, and predispositions which find another outlet in allegiance to extremist political movements.

In his excellent study of the sources of Swedish Communism, Sven Rydenfelt analyzed the differences between two socially and economically comparable northern counties of Sweden—Vasterbotten and Norrbotten—in an attempt to explain the relatively low Communist vote in the former (2 per cent) and the much larger one in the latter (21 per cent). The Liberal party, which in Sweden gives much more support than any other party to religious extremism, was strong in Vasterbotten (30 per cent) and weak in Norrbotten (9 per cent). Since the total extremist vote in both was almost identical—30 and 32 per cent—he concluded that a general predisposition toward radicalism existed in both counties, containing some of the poorest, most socially isolated, and rootless groups in Sweden, but that its expression differed, taking a religious form in one county, and a Communist in the other: "The Communists and the religious radicals, as for instance, the Pentecostal sects, seem to be competing for the allegiance of the same groups."[29]

The Social Situation of the Lower Classes

A number of elements contribute to authoritarian predispositions in lower-class individuals. Low education, low participation in political or voluntary organizations of any type, little reading, isolated occupations, economic insecurity, and authoritarian family patterns are some of the most important. These elements are interrelated, but they are by no means identical.

28. See Sven Rydenfelt, *Kommunismen i Sverige. En Samhallsvetenskaplig Studie.* (Kund: Gleerupska Universitetsbokhandeln, 1954), pp. 296, 336-37; Wiardi Beckman Institute, *Verkiezingen in Nederland* (Amsterdam, 1951, mimeographed), pp. 15, 93-94; Jaako Novsiainen, *Kommunism Kuopion lää nissa* (Helsinki: Joensuu, 1956).

29. See W. Phillips Davison's extensive review of Sven Rydenfelt, *op. cit.*, which appeared in the *Public Opinion Quarterly*, 18 (1954-55), pp. 375-88. Quote is on p. 382.

There is consistent evidence that degree of formal education, itself closely correlated with social and economic status, is also highly correlated with undemocratic attitudes. Data from the American sociologist Samuel Stouffer's study of attitudes toward civil liberties in America and from the UNESCO Research Institute's survey of German opinion on a multi-party system (Tables 3 and 4) reveal this clearly.

Table 3. The Relationship between Occupation, Education, and Political Tolerance in the United States, 1955*

	PERCENTAGE IN THE TWO "MOST TOLERANT" CATEGORIES BY OCCUPATION			
Education	*Low Manual*	*High Manual*	*Low White Collar*	*High White Collar*
Grade school	13 (228)	21 (178)	23 (47)	26 (100)
Some high school	32 (99)	33 (124)	29 (56)	46 (68)
High school grad	40 (64)	48 (127)	47 (102)	56 (108)
Some college	— (14)	64 (36)	64 (80)	65 (37)
College grad	— (3)	— (11)	74 (147)	83 (21)

*Computed from IBM cards kindly supplied by Samuel A. Stouffer from his study, *Communism, Conformity, and Civil Liberties* (New York: Doubleday & Co., 1955).

These tables indicate that although higher occupational status within each educational level seems to make for greater tolerance, the increases in tolerance associated with higher educational level are greater than those related to higher occupational level, other factors being constant.[30] Inferior education and low occupational position are of course closely

Table 4. The Relationship between Occupation, Education, and Support of a Democratic Party System in Germany, 1953*

	PER CENT FAVORING THE EXISTENCE OF SEVERAL PARTIES BY EDUCATIONAL LEVEL	
Occupation	*Elementary School*	*High School or Higher*
Farm laborers	29 (59)	—
Manual workers	43 (1439)	52 (29)
Farmers	43 (381)	67 (9)
Lower white collar	50 (273)	68 (107)
Self-employed business	53 (365)	65 (75)
Upper white collar	58 (86)	69 (58)
Officials (govt.)	59 (158)	78 (99)
Professions	56 (18)	68 (38)

*Same source as Table 1.

30. A study based on a national sample of Americans reported that education made no difference in the extent of authoritarian responses on an "authoritarian personality" scale among workers, but that higher educational attainment reduced such responses among the middle class. The well-educated upper-middle class were least "authoritarian." Morris Janowitz and Dwaine Marvick, "Authoritarianism and Political Behavior," *Public Opinion Quarterly,* 17 (1953), pp. 195-96.

connected, and both are part of the complex making up low status, which is associated with a lack of tolerance.[31]

Low-status groups are also less apt to participate in formal organizations, read fewer magazines and books regularly, possess less information on public affairs, vote less, and, in general, take less interest in politics.[32] The available evidence suggests that each of these attributes is related to attitudes toward democracy. The 1953 UNESCO analysis of German data found that, at every occupational level, those who belonged to voluntary associations were more likely to favor a multi-party system than a one-party one.[33] American findings, too, indicate that authoritarians "do not join many community groups" as compared with non-authoritarians.[34] And it has been discovered that people poorly informed on public issues are more likely to be both *more liberal* on economic issues and *less liberal* on noneconomic ones.[35] Nonvoters and those less interested in political matters are much more intolerant and xenophobic than those who vote and have political interests.[36]

The "hard core" of "chronic know-nothings" comes disproportionately from the less literate, lower socioeconomic groups, according to a study by two American social psychologists, Herbert Hyman and Paul Sheatsley. These people are not only uninformed, but "harder to reach, no matter what the level or nature of the information." Here is another hint of the complex character of the relationship between education, liberalism, and status. Noneconomic liberalism is not a simple matter of acquiring education and information; it is at least in part a basic attitude which is actively discouraged by the social situation of

31. The independent effect of education even when other social factors are least favorable has special long-range significance in view of the rising educational level of the population. Kornhauser and his associates found that auto workers with an eighth-grade education were more authoritarian than those with more education. See A. Kornhauser, A. L. Sheppard, and A. J. Mayer, *When Labor Votes* (New York: University Books, 1956), for further data on variations in authoritarianism *within* a working-class sample.

32. The research showing the social factors such as education, status and income (themselves components of an over-all class or status index) associated with political participation is summarized in Chap. VI of S. M. Lipset, *Political Man, op. cit.*

33. Data computed for this study.

34. F. H. Sanford, *Authoritarianism and Leadership* (Philadelphia: Stevenson Brothers, 1950), p. 168. See also Mirra Komarovsky, "The Voluntary Associations of Urban Dwellers," *American Sociological Review*, 11 (1946), p. 688.

35. G. H. Smith, *op. cit.*, p. 71.

36. G. M. Connelly and H. H. Field, "The Non-Voter, Who He Is, and What He Thinks," *Public Opinion Quarterly*, 8 (1944), p. 179; Samuel A. Stouffer, *Communism, Conformity, and Civil Liberties* (New York: Doubleday & Co., 1955), and F. H. Sanford, *op. cit.*, p. 168. M. Janowitz and D. Marvick, *op. cit.*, p. 200.

lower-status persons.[37] As Genevieve Knupfer, an American psychiatrist, has pointed out in her revealing "Portrait of the Underdog,"

> Economic underprivilege is psychological underprivilege: habits of submission; little access to sources of information, lack of verbal facility . . . appear to produce a lack of self-confidence which increases the unwillingness of the low-status person to participate in many phases of our predominantly middle-class culture. . . .[38]

These characteristics also reflect the extent to which the lower strata are *isolated* from the activities, controversies, and organizations of democratic society—an isolation which prevents them from acquiring the sophisticated and complex view of the political structure which makes understandable and necessary the norms of tolerance.

In this connection it is instructive to examine once again, as extreme cases, those occupations which are most isolated, in every sense, from contact with the world outside their own group. Manual workers in "isolated occupations" which require them to live in one-industry towns or areas—miners, maritime workers, forestry workers, fishermen, and sheepshearers—exhibit high rates of Communist support in most countries.[39]

Similarly, as all public opinion surveys show, the rural population,

---

37. See Herbert Hyman and Paul B. Sheatsley, "Some Reasons Why Information Campaigns Fail," *Public Opinion Quarterly*, 11 (1947), p. 413. A recent survey of material on voluntary association memberships is contained in Charles L. Wright and Herbert Hyman, "Voluntary Association Memberships of American Adults: Evidence from National Sample Surveys," *American Sociological Review*, 23 (1958), pp. 284-94.

38. Genevieve Knupfer, "Portrait of the Underdog," *Public Opinion Quarterly*, 11 (1947), p. 114.

39. The greatest amount of comparative material is available on the miners. For Britain, see Herbert G. Nicholas, *British General Election of 1950* (London: Macmillan, 1951), pp. 318, 342, 361. For the United States, see Paul F. Brissenden, *The IWW: A Study of American Syndicalism* (New York: Columbia University Press, 1920), p. 74, and Harold F. Gosnell, *Grass Roots Politics* (Washington, D.C.: American Council on Public Affairs, 1942), pp. 31-32. For France see François Goguel, "Geographie des élections sociales de 1950-51," *Revue française de science politique*, 3 (1953), pp. 246-71. For Germany, see Ossip K. Flechtheim, *Die Kommunistische Partei Deutschlands in der Weimarer Republik* (Offenbach am Main: Bollwerk-Verlag Karl Drott, 1948), p. 211. Data are also available for Australia, Scandinavia, Spain, and Chile.

Isolation has also been linked with the differential propensity to strike of different industries. Violent strikes having the character of a mass grievance against society as a whole occur most often in isolated industries, and probably have their origins in the same social situations as those which produce extremism. See Clark Kerr and Abraham Siegel, "The Interindustry Propensity to Strike: An International Comparison," in *Industrial Conflict*, eds., A. Kornhauser, R. Dubin, and A. M. Ross (New York: McGraw-Hill Book Co., 1954), pp. 189-212.

both farmers and laborers, tends to oppose civil liberties and multi-party systems more than any other occupational group. Election surveys indicate that farm owners have been among the strongest supporters of fascist parties, while farm workers, poor farmers, and share-croppers have given even stronger backing to the Communists than has the rest of labor in countries like Italy, France, and India.[40]

The same social conditions are associated with middle-class authoritarianism. The groups which have been most prone to support fascist and other middle-class extremist ideologies have been, in addition to farmers and peasants, the small businessmen of the smaller provincial communities–groups which are also isolated from "cosmopolitan" culture and are far lower than any other non-manual-labor group in educational attainment.[41]

A second and no less important factor predisposing the lower classes toward authoritarianism is a relative lack of economic and psychological security. The lower one goes on the socioeconomic ladder, the greater economic uncertainty one finds. White-collar workers, even those who are not paid more than skilled manual workers, are less likely to suffer the tensions created by fear of loss of income. Studies of marital instability indicate that this is related to lower income and income insecurity. Such insecurity will of course affect the individual's politics and attitudes.[42] High states of tension require immediate alleviation, and this is

---

40. According to Carl Friedrich, agricultural groups are more emotionally nationalistic and potentially authoritarian politically because of the fact that they are more isolated from meeting people who are different than are urban dwellers. See "The Agricultural Basis of Emotional Nationalism," *Public Opinion Quarterly*, 1 (1937), pp. 50-51. See also Rudolf Heberle, *From Democracy to Nazism: A Regional Case Study on Political Parties in Germany* (Baton Rouge, Louisiana: Louisiana State University Press, 1945), pp. 32ff., for a discussion of the appeal of Nazism to the German rural population, and K. Kido and M. Sugi, *op. cit.*, for similar survey findings in Japan.

41. Statistical data indicate that German and Austrian Nazism, French Poujadism, and American McCarthyism have all drawn their heaviest nonrural support from the small businessmen of provincial small communities, particularly those with little education. See Chap. V [S. M. Lipset, *Political Man, op. cit.*].

42. In addition to the insecurity which is normally attendant upon lower-class existence, special conditions which uproot people from a stable community life and upset the social supports of their traditional values make them receptive to extremist chiliastic ideologies which help to redefine their world. I have already discussed some of the evidence linking the *discontinuities* and rootlessness flowing from rapid industrialization and urbanization on the politics of workers in different countries in Chap. II [*ibid.*]. Rydenfelt in his study of Swedish Communism suggests that "rootlessness" is a characteristic of individuals and occupations with high Communist voting records. See W. Phillips Davison, *op. cit.*, p. 378. Engels also called attention in the 1890s to the fact that chiliastic religions and social movements, including the revolutionary socialist one, attracted all the deviants or those

frequently found in the venting of hostility against a scapegoat and the search for a short-term solution by support of extremist groups. Research indicates that the unemployed are less tolerant toward minorities than the employed, and more likely to be Communists if they are workers, or fascists if they are middle class. Industries which have a high rate of Communists in their ranks also have high economic instability.

The lower classes' insecurities and tensions which flow from economic instability are reinforced by their particular patterns of family life. There is a great deal of direct frustration and aggression in the day-to-day lives of members of the lower classes, both children and adults. A comprehensive review of the many studies of child-rearing patterns in the United States completed in the past twenty-five years reports that their "most consistent finding" is the

> . . . more frequent use of physical punishment by working-class parents. The middle class, in contrast, resorts to reasoning, isolation, and . . . "love-oriented" techniques of discipline. . . . Such parents are more likely to overlook offenses, and when they do punish they are less likely to ridicule or inflict physical pain.[43]

A further link between such child-rearing practices and adult hostility and authoritarianism is suggested by the finding of two investigations in Boston and Detroit that physical punishments for aggression,

---

without a place in society: "all the elements which had been set free, i.e., at a loose end, by the dissolution of the old world came one after the other into the orbit of [early] Christianity . . . [as today] all throng to the working-class parties in all countries." F. Engels, *op. cit.*, pp. 319-20. See also G. Almond, *op. cit.*, p. 236 and Hadley Cantril, *The Psychology of Social Movements* (New York: John Wiley & Sons, 1941), Chaps. 8 and 9.

43. See Urie Bronfenbrenner, "Socialization and Social Class through Time and Space," in E. E. Maccoby, T. M. Newcomb, and E. L. Hartley, eds., *Readings in Social Psychology* (New York: Holt, Rinehart, Winston, 1958), p. 419. The sociologist Allison Davis has summarized in a similar vein research findings relating to intra-family relations in different classes: "The lower classes not uncommonly teach their children and adolescents to strike out with fists or knife and to be certain to hit first. Both girls and boys at adolescence may curse their father to his face or even attack him with fists, sticks, or axes in free-for-all family encounters. Husbands and wives sometimes stage pitched battles in the home, wives have their husbands arrested, and husbands try to break in or burn down their own homes when locked out. Such fights with fists or weapons, and the whipping of wives occur sooner or later in many lower-class families. They may not appear today, nor tomorrow, but they *will* appear if the observer remains long enough to see them." Allison Davis, "Socialization and Adolescent Personality," in Guy E. Swanson, *et al.*, eds., *Readings in Social Psychology* (New York: Holt, Rinehart, Winston, 1954), p. 528. (Emphasis in original.)

characteristic of the working class, tend to increase rather than decrease aggressive behavior.[44]

Lower-Class Perspectives

Acceptance of the norms of democracy requires a high level of sophistication and ego security. The less sophisticated and stable an individual, the more likely he is to favor a simplified view of politics, to fail to understand the rationale underlying tolerance of those with whom he disagrees, and to find difficulty in grasping or tolerating a gradualist image of political change.

Several studies focusing on various aspects of working-class life and culture have emphasized different components of an unsophisticated perspective. Greater suggestibility, absence of a sense of past and future (lack of a prolonged time perspective), inability to take a complex view, greater difficulty in abstracting from concrete experience, and lack of imagination (inner "reworking" of experience), each has been singled out by numerous students of quite different problems as characteristic of low status. All of these qualities are part of the complex psychological basis of authoritarianism.

The psychologist Hadley Cantril considered suggestibility to be a major psychological explanation for participation in extremist movements.[45] The two conditions for suggestibility are both typical of low-status persons: either the lack of an adequate frame of reference or general perspective, or a fixed, rigid one. A poorly developed frame of reference reflects a limited education, a paucity of the rich associations on a general level which provide a basis for evaluating experience. A fixed or rigid one—in a sense the opposite side of the same coin—reflects the tendency to elevate whatever general principles are learned to absolutes which even experience may fail to qualify and correct.

The stimulating book by the British journalist Richard Hoggart, *The Uses of Literacy*, makes the same point in another way. Low-status persons without rich and flexible perspectives are likely to lack a developed sense of the past *and* the future.

Their education is unlikely to have left them with any historical panorama

44. Some hint of the complex of psychological factors underlying lower-class authoritarianism is given in one study which reports a relationship between overt hostility and authoritarianism. See Saul M. Siegel, "The Relationship of Hostility to Authoritarianism," *Journal of Abnormal and Social Psychology*, 52 (1956), pp. 368-72.

45. See Hadley Cantril, *op. cit.*, p. 65.

or with any idea of a continuing tradition. . . . A great many people, though they may possess a considerable amount of disconnected information, have little idea of an historical or ideological pattern or process. . . . With little intellectual or cultural furniture, with little training in the testing of opposing views against reason and existing judgments, judgments are usually made according to the promptings of those group apothegms which come first to mind. . . . Similarly, there can be little real sense of the future. . . . Such a mind is, I think, particularly accessible to the temptation to live in a constant present.[46]

This concern with the present leads to a concentration on daily activities, without much inner reflection, imaginative planning of one's future, or abstract thinking unrelated to one's daily activities. One of the few studies of lower-class children which used projective techniques found that

> These young people are making an adjustment which is orientated toward the outside world rather than one which rests on a developing acquaintance with their own impulses and the handling of these impulses by fantasy and introspection. . . . They do not have a rich inner life, indeed their imaginative activity is meagre and limited. . . . When faced with a new situation, the subjects tend to react rapidly, and they do not alter their original impressions of the situation which is seen as a crude whole with little intellectual discrimination of components.[47]

Working-class life as a whole emphasizes the concrete and immediate. As Hoggart puts it,

> If we want to capture something of the essence of working-class life . . . we must say that it is the "dense and concrete" life, a life whose main stress is on the intimate, the sensory, the detailed and the personal. This would no doubt be true of working-class groups anywhere in the world.[48]

46. Richard Hoggart, *op. cit.*, pp. 158-59.

47. B. M. Spinley, *The Deprived and the Privileged* (London: Routledge and Kegan Paul, 1953), pp. 115-16. These conclusions were based on Rorschach tests given to 60 slum-area children. The last point is related to that made by another British scholar, that working-class people are not as likely as those with middle-class backgrounds to perceive the *structure* of an object, which involves thought on a more abstract level of relationships, but have an action-oriented reaction to the *content* of an object. For more discussion of this point, see B. Bernstein, "Some Sociological Determinants of Perception," *The British Journal of Sociology*, 9 (1958), pp. 160 ff.

48. Richard Hoggart, *op. cit.*, p. 88. This kind of life, like other social characteristics of human beings, has different consequences for different areas of society and social existence. It may be argued, though I personally doubt it, that this capacity to establish personal relationships, to live in the present, may be more "healthy" (in a strictly medical, mental-health sense) than a middle-class concern with status distinctions, one's own personal impact on one's life situation, and a preoccupation with the uncertain future. But on the political level of consequences,

Hoggart sees the concreteness of working-class perceptions as the main difference between them and middle-class people, who more easily meet abstract and general questions. The sharp British working-class distinction between "Us" and "Them," he notes, is

> . . . part of a more general characteristic of the outlook of most working-class people. To come to terms with the world of "Them" involves, in the end, all kinds of political and social questions, and leads eventually beyond politics and social philosophy to metaphysics. The question of how we face "Them" (whoever "They" are) is, at last, the question of how we stand in relation to anything not visibly and intimately part of our local universe. The working-class splitting of the world into "Us" and "Them" is on this side a symptom of their difficulty in meeting abstract or general questions.[49]

Hoggart is careful to emphasize that probably most persons in *any* social class are uninterested in general ideas, but still "training in the handling of ideas or in analysis" is far more characteristic of the demands of middle-class parents and occupations.[50]

A recent analysis by the British sociologist Basil Bernstein of how differences in ways of perceiving and thinking in the different classes lead to variations in social mobility also underlines the manner in which different family patterns affect authoritarianism. The middle-class parent stresses

> . . . an awareness of the importance between means and long-term ends, cognitively and affectually regarded . . . [and has] the ability to adopt appropriate measures to implement the attainment of distant ends by a purposeful means-end chain. . . . The child in the middle classes and associative levels grows up in an environment which is finely and extensively controlled; the space, time and social relationships are explicitly regulated within and outside the family group.[51]

The situation in the working-class family is quite different:

> The working-class family structure is less formally organized than the middle-class in relation to the development of the child. Although the authority within the family is explicit, the values which it expresses do not give rise to the carefully ordered universe spatially and temporally of the middle-class child. The exercise of authority will not be related to a stable system of rewards and punishments but may often appear arbitrary. The specific character of long-term goals tends to be replaced by more general

---

the problem of concern here, this same action-oriented, nonintellectualistic aspect of working-class life seems to prevent the realities of long-term social and economic trends from entering working-class consciousness, simply because such reality can enter only through the medium of abstractions and generalizations.

49. *Ibid.*, p. 86.

50. *Loc. cit.*

51. B. Bernstein, *op. cit.*, pp. 161, 165.

notions of the future, in which chance, a friend or a relative plays a greater part than the rigorous working out of connections. Thus present, or near-present, activities have greater value than the relation of the present activity to the attainment of a distant goal. The system of expectancies, or the time-span of anticipation, is shortened and this creates different sets of preferences, goals, and dissatisfactions. The environment limits the perception of the developing child of and in time. Present gratifications or present deprivations become absolute gratifications or absolute deprivations, for there exists no developed time continuum upon which present activity can be ranged. Relative to the middle-classes, the postponement of present pleasure for future gratifications will be found difficult. By implication *a more volatile patterning of affectual and expressive behavior will be found in the working-classes.*[52]

This emphasis on the immediately perceivable and concern with the personal and concrete is part and parcel of the short time perspective and the inability to perceive the complex possibilities and consequences of actions which often result in a general readiness to support extremist political and religious movements, and a generally lower level of liberalism on noneconomic questions.[53]

Even within extremist movements these differences in the perceptions and perspectives of working-class as against middle-class persons affect their experiences, readiness to join a "cause," and reasons for defecting. The American political scientist Gabriel Almond's study of 221 ex-Communists in four countries provides data on this point. He distinguishes between the "exoteric" (simple, for mass consumption) and "esoteric" (complex, for the inner circle) doctrines of the party. In contrast to middle-class members "relatively few working-class respondents had been exposed to the esoteric doctrine of the party before joining, and . . . they tended to remain unindoctrinated while in the party."[54] The middle-class recruits

> . . . tended to come to the party with more complex value patterns and expectations which were more likely to obstruct assimilation into the party. . . . The working-class member, on the other hand, is relatively untroubled by

52. *Ibid.*, p. 168 (my emphasis).

53. This hypothesis has suggestive implications for a theory of trade-union democracy, and possible strains within trade-union organizational life. Working-class union members may not be at all as concerned with dictatorial union leadership as are middle-class critics who assume that the rank and file would actively form factions, and critically evaluate union policies if not constrained by a monolithic structure imposed by the top leadership. On the other hand, the more educated, articulate staff members (on a union newspaper, for example) may want to include more literate and complex discussions of issues facing the union but feel constrained by the need to present simple, easily understood propagandistic slogans for rank-and-file consumption. The "house organ" type of union newspaper may not be due entirely to internal political necessities.

54. G. Almond, *op. cit.*, p. 244.

doctrinal apparatus, less exposed to the media of communication, and his inagination and logical powers are relatively undeveloped.[55]

One aspect of the lower classes' lack of sophistication and education is their anti-intellectualism (a phenomenon Engels long ago noted as a problem faced by working-class movements). While the complex esoteric ideology of Communism may have been one of the principal features attracting middle-class people to it, the fundamental anti-intellectualism which it shares with other extremist movements has been a source of strain for the "genuine" intellectuals within it. Thus it has been the working-class rank and file which has been least disturbed by Communism's ideological shifts, and least likely to defect.[56] Their commitment, once established, cannot usually be shaken by a sudden realization that the party, after all, does not conform to liberal and humanistic values.

This helps to explain why socialist parties have been led by a high proportion of intellectuals, in spite of an original ideological emphasis on maintaining a working-class orientation, while the Communists have alienated their intellectual leaders and are led preponderantly by those with working-class occupations.[57] Almond's study concluded that

> . . . while the party is open to all comers, working-class party members have better prospects of success in the party than middle-class recruits. This is probably due both to party policy, which has always manifested greater confidence in the reliability of working-class recruits, and to the difficulties of assimilation into the party generally experienced by middle-class party members.[58]

Making of an Authoritarian

To sum up, the lower-class individual is likely to have been exposed to punishment, lack of love, and a general atmosphere of tension and

55. *Ibid.*, p. 177.

56. *Ibid.*, pp. 313 ff., 392.

57. For French data from 1936 to 1956 see Mattei Dogan. "Les Candidats et les élus," in L'Association Française de science politique, *Les Elections du 2 janvier* (Paris: Librairie Armand Colin, 1956), p. 462, and Dogan, "L'origine sociale du personnel parlementaire français," in *Parties politiques et classes sociales en France*, edited by Maurice Duverger (Paris: Librairie Armand Colin, 1955), pp. 291-329. For a comparison of German Social Democratic and Communist parliamentary leadership before Hitler see Viktor Engelhardt, "Die Zusammensatzung des Reichstage nach Alter, Beruf, und Religionsbekenntnis," *Die Arbeit*, 8 (1931), p. 34.

58. G. Almond, *op. cit.*, p. 190. This statement was supported by analysis of the biographies of 123 Central Committee leaders of the Party in three countries, as well as by interviews with 221 ex-Communists (both leaders and rank-and-file members) in four countries, France, Italy, Great Britain, and the United States.

aggression since early childhood—all experiences which tend to produce deep-rooted hostilities expressed by ethnic prejudice, political authoritarianism, and chiliastic transvaluational religion. His educational attainment is less than that of men with higher socioeconomic status, and his association as a child with others of similar background not only fails to stimulate his intellectual interests but also creates an atmosphere which prevents his educational experience from increasing his general social sophistication and his understanding of different groups and ideas. Leaving school relatively early, he is surrounded on the job by others with a similarly restricted cultural, educational, and family background. Little external influence impinges on his limited environment. From early childhood, he has sought immediate gratifications, rather than engaged in activities which might have long-term rewards. The logic of both his adult employment and his family situation reinforces this limited time perspective. As the sociologist C. C. North has put it, isolation from heterogeneous environments, characteristic of low status, operates to "limit the source of information, to retard the development of efficiency in judgment and reasoning abilities, and to confine the attention to more trivial interests in life."[59]

All of these characteristics produce a tendency to view politics and personal relationships in black-and-white terms, a desire for immediate action, an impatience with talk and discussion, a lack of interest in organizations which have a long-range perspective, and a readiness to follow leaders who offer a demonological interpretation of the evil forces (either religious or political) which are conspiring against him.[60]

It is interesting that Lenin saw the character of the lower classes, and the tasks of those who would lead them, in somewhat these terms. He specified as the chief task of the Communist parties the leadership of the broad masses, who are "slumbering, apathetic, hidebound, inert, and dormant." These masses, said Lenin, must be aligned for the "final and decisive battle" (a term reminiscent of Armageddon) by the party which alone can present an uncompromising and unified view of the world, and an immediate program for drastic change. In contrast to "effective" Communist leadership, Lenin pointed to the democratic parties and their leadership as "vacillating, wavering, unstable" elements—

59. C. C. North, *Social Differentiation* (Chapel Hill: University of North Carolina Press, 1926), p. 247.

60. Most of these characteristics have been mentioned by child psychologists as typical of adolescent attitudes and perspectives. Werner Cohn, in an article on Jehovah's Witnesses, considers youth movements as a prototype of all such "proletarian" movements. Both "adolescence fixation and anomie are causal conditions" of their development (p. 297), and all such organizations have an "aura of social estrangement" (p. 282). See Werner Cohn, "Jehovah's Witnesses as a Proletarian Movement," *The American Scholar*, 24 (1955), pp. 281-99.

a characterization that is probably valid for any political group lacking ultimate certainty in its program and willing to grant legitimacy to opposition groups.[61]

The political outcome of these predispositions, however, is not determined by the multiplicity of factors involved. Isolation, a punishing childhood, economic and occupational insecurities, and a lack of sophistication are conducive to withdrawal, or even apathy, and to strong mobolization of hostility. The same underlying factors which predispose individuals toward support of extremist movements under certain conditions may result in total withdrawal from political activity and concern under other conditions. In "normal" periods, apathy is most frequent among such individuals, but they can be activated by a crisis, especially if it is accompanied by strong millennial appeals.[62]

Extremism as an Alternative: A Test of a Hypothesis

The proposition that the lack of a rich, complex frame of reference is the vital variable which connects low status and a predisposition toward extremism does not necessarily suggest that the lower strata will be authoritarian; it implies that, other things being equal, they will choose the least complex alternative. Thus in situations in which extremism represents the more complex rather than the less complex form of politics, low status should be associated with *opposition* to such movements and parties.

---

61. The quotes from Lenin are in his *Left Wing Communism: An Infantile Disorder* (New York: International Publishers, 1940), pp. 74-75. Lenin's point, made in another context, in his pamphlet, *What Is to Be Done?* that workers left to themselves would never develop socialist or class consciousness, and that they would remain on the level of economic "day to day" consciousness, unless an organized group of revolutionary intellectuals brought them a broader vision, is similar to the generalizations presented here concerning the inherent limited time perspective of the lower strata.

62. Various American studies indicate that those lower-class individuals who are nonvoters, and who have little political interest, tend to reject the democratic norms of tolerance. See Samuel A. Stouffer, *op. cit.*, and G. M. Connelly and H. H. Field, *op. cit.*, p. 182. Studies of the behavior of the unemployed in countries in which extremist movements were weak, such as the United States and Britain, indicate that apathy was their characteristic political response. See E. W. Bakke, *Citizens without Work* (New Haven: Yale University Press, 1940), pp. 46-70. On the other hand, German data suggest a high correlation between working-class unemployment and support of Communists, and middle-class unemployment and support of Nazis. In France, Italy, and Finland today, those who have been unemployed tend to back the large Communist parties of those countries. See Chap. VII and Erik Allardt, *Social Struktur och Politisk Aktivitet* (Helsingfors: Söderstrom Förlagsaktiebolag, 1956), pp. 84-85.

This is in fact the case wherever the Communist party is a small party competing against a large reformist party, as in England, the United States, Sweden, Norway, and other countries. Where the party is small and weak, it cannot hold out the promise of immediate changes in the situation of the most deprived. Rather, such small extremist parties usually present the fairly complex intellectual argument that in the long run they will be strengthened by tendencies inherent in the social and economic system.[63] For the poorer worker, support of the Swedish Social Democrats, the British Labour party, or the American New Deal is a simpler and more easily understood way of securing redress of grievances or improvement of social conditions than supporting an electorally insignificant Communist party.

The available evidence from Denmark, Norway, Sweden, Canada, Brazil, and Great Britain supports this point. In these countries, where the Communist party is small and a Labor or Socialist party is much larger, Communist support is stronger among the better paid and more skilled workers than it is among the less skilled and poorer strata.[64] In Italy, France, and Finland, where the Communists are the largest party on the left, the lower the income level of workers, the higher their Communist vote.[65] A comparison of the differences in the relative in-

63. Recent research on the early sources of support for the Nazi party challenges the hypothesis that it was the apathetic who came to its support prior to 1930, when it still represented a complex, long-range alternative. A negative rank-order correlation was found between the per cent increase in the Nazi vote and the increase in the proportion voting in the German election districts between 1928 and 1930. Only after it had become a relatively large party did it recruit the previously apathetic, who now could see its immediate potential. For a report of this research, see Chapter V [S. M. Lipset, *Political Man, op. cit.*].

64. For Denmark, see E. Hogh, *Vaelgeradfaerdi Danmark* (Ph.D. thesis, Sociology Institute, University of Copenhagen, 1959), Tables 6 and 9. For Norway, see Allen Barton, *Sociological and Psychological Implications of Economic Planning in Norway* (Ph.D. thesis, Department of Sociology, Columbia University, 1957); and several surveys of voting behavior in Norway conducted by Norwegian poll organizations including the 1949 FAKTA Survey, and the February 1954 and April 1956, NGI Survey, the results of which are as yet unpublished. Data from the files of the Canadian Gallup Poll for 1945, 1949, and 1953 indicate that the Labor-Progressive (Communist) party drew more support from the skilled than the unskilled sections of the working class. For Brazil, see A. Simao, "O voto operario en São Paulo," *Revista Brasilieras estudos politicos*, 1 (1956), p. 130-41.

65. For a table giving precise statistics for Italy and France, see Chap. VII [S. M. Lipset, *Political Man, op. cit.*]. See also Hadley Cantril, *The Politics of Despair* (New York: Basic Books, 1958), pp. 3-10. In pre-Hitler Germany, where the Communists were a large party, they also secured their electoral strength much more from the less skilled sections of the workers than from the more skilled. See Samuel Pratt, *The Social Basis of Nazism and Communism in Urban Germany* (M.A. thesis, Department of Sociology, Michigan State College, 1948), pp. 156 ff.

An as yet unpublished study by Dr. Pertti Pesonen, of the Institute of Political

come position of workers who vote Social Democratic and those who back the Communists in two neighboring Scandinavian countries of Finland and Sweden shows these alternative patterns clearly (Table 5).

Table 5. The Income Composition of the Working-Class Support of the Social Democratic and Communist Parties in Finland and Sweden*

FINLAND-1956			SWEDEN-1946		
Income Class in Markkaa	*Social Democrats*	*Commu-nists*	*Income Class in Kroner*	*Social Democrats*	*Commu-nists*
Under 100	8%	13%	Under 2,000	14%	8
100-400	49	50	2,001-4,000	40	38
400-600	22	29	4,001-6,000	32	30
600+	21	8	6,001+	14	24
(N)	(173)	(119)		(5176)	(907)

*The Finnish data were secured from a special run made for this study by the Finnish Gallup Poll. The Swedish statistics were recomputed from data presented in Elis Hastad, *et al.*, eds., "Gallup" och den *Svenska Valjarkaren* (Uppsala: Hugo Gebers Forlag, 1950), pp. 175-76. Both studies include rural and urban workers.

In Finland, where the Communists are very strong, their support is drawn disproportionately from the poorer workers, while in Sweden, where the Communists are a minor party, they have considerably more success with the better paid and more skilled workers than they do with the unskilled and lowly paid.[66]

This holds true in all countries for which data exist.[67] One other

Science of the University of Helsinki, of voting in the industrial city of Tampere reports that the Communist voters were more well to do than the Social Democrats. On the other hand, Communists were much more likely to have experienced unemployment during the past year (21 per cent) or in their entire work history (46 per cent) than Social Democrats (10 per cent and 23 per cent). This study suggests that the experience of recent unemployment in the family is the most important determinant of a Communist vote in Tampere.

66. Or to present the same data in another way, in Finland, 41 per cent of all workers earning less than 100 markkaa a month vote Communist, as compared with only 12 per cent among those earning over 600 markkaa. In Sweden, 7 per cent of the workers earning less than 2,000 kroner a year vote Communist, as compared with 25 per cent among those earning over 8,000.

67. It may be noted, parenthetically, that where the Socialist party is small and/or new, it also represents a complex alternative, and attracts more middle-class support proportionately than when it is a well-established mass party which can offer immediate reforms. On the other hand, when a small transvaluational group does *not* offer an intellectually complex alternative, it should draw disproportionate support from the lower strata. Such groups are the sectarian religions whose millennial appeals have no developed rationale. Some extremely slight evidence on this point in a political contest is available from a recent Norwegian poll which shows the composition of the support for various parties. Only eleven persons supporting the Christian party, a party which appeals to the more fundamentalist Lutherans who are comparable to those discussed earlier in Sweden, were included in the total sample, but 82 per cent of these came from lower-income groups (less than 10,000

country, India, offers even better evidence. In India, the Communists are a major party, constituting the government or the major opposition (with 25 per cent or more of the votes) in two states, Kerala and Andhra. While they have substantial strength in some other states, they are much weaker in the rest of India. If the proposition is valid that Communist appeal should be substantially for the lower and uneducated strata where the Party is powerful, and for the relatively higher and better educated ones where it is weak, the characteristics of Party voters should vary greatly in different parts of India, and this is in fact precisely what Table 6 shows.[68]

Table 6. Communist and Socialist Preferences in India, by Class and Education*

	COMMUNIST PARTY PREFERENCES IN		Preferences for Socialist Parties in All-India
	Kerala and Andhra	Rest of India	
Class			
Middle	7%	27%	23%
Lower-middle	19	30	36
Working	74	43	41
Education			
Illiterate	52%	43%	31%
Under-matric.	39	37	43
Matric. plus	9	20	26
(N)	(113)	(68)	(88)

*These figures have been computed from tables presented in the *Indian Institute of Public Opinion, Monthly Public Opinion Surveys*, Vol. 2, Nos. 4, 5, 6, 7 (Combined Issue), New Delhi, January-April, 1957, pp. 9-14. This was a pre-election poll, not a report of the actual voting results. The total sample was 2,868 persons. The Socialist party and the Praja-Socialist party figures are combined here, since they share essentially the same moderate program. The support given to them in Andhra and Kerala was too small to be presented separately.

Where the Indian Communist party is small, its support, like that of the two small moderate socialist parties, comes from relatively well-to-do and better educated strata. The picture shifts sharply in Kerala and Andhra, where the Communists are strong. The middle class provides only 7 per cent of Communist support there, with the working class

kroner per year). In comparison, 57 per cent of the 264 Labor Party supporters, and 39 per cent of the 21 Communist supporters earned less than 10,000 kroner. Thus the small Communist party as the most complex transvaluational alternative drew its backing from relatively high strata, while the fundamentalist Christians had the economically poorest social base of any party in the country. See the February 1954 NGI Survey, issued in December 1956 in preliminary mimeographed form.

68. These data were located after the hypothesis was formulated, and thus can be considered an independent replication.

supplying 74 per cent.[69] Educational differences among party supporters show a similar pattern.

Historical Patterns and Democratic Action

Despite the profoundly antidemocratic tendencies in lower-class groups, workers' political organizations and movements in the more industrialized democratic countries have supported *both* economic and political liberalism.[70] Workers' organizations, trade-unions and political

69. The hypothesis presented here does not attempt to explain the growth of small parties. Adaptations to major crisis situations, particularly depressions and wars, are probably the key factors initially increasing the support for a small "complex" party. For an analysis of the change in electoral support of a Socialist party as it moved up to major party status see S. M. Lipset, *Agrarian Socialism* (Berkeley: University of California Press, 1950), esp. pp. 159-78.

70. There have been many exceptions to this. The Australian Labor party has been the foremost supporter of a "white Australia." Similarly, in the United States until the advent of the ideological New Deal in the 1930s, the lower-class-based Democratic party has always been the more anti-Negro of the two parties. The American labor movement has opposed nonwhite immigration, and much of it maintains barriers against Negro members.

When the American Socialist party was a mass movement before World War I, its largest circulation newspapers, such as the Milwaukee *Social Democratic Herald* and the *Appeal to Reason* opposed racial integration. The latter stated explicitly, "Socialism will separate the races." See David A. Shannon, *The Socialist Party of America* (New York: Macmillan, 1955), pp. 49-52. Even the Marxist Socialist movement of Western Europe was not immune to the virus of anti-Semitism. Thus, before World War I there were a number of anti-Semitic incidents in which Socialists were involved, some avowedly anti-Semitic leaders connected with different socialist parties, and strong resistance to committing the socialist organizations to opposition to anti-Semitism. See E. Silberner, "The Anti-Semitic Tradition in Modern Socialism," *Scripta Hierosolymitana,* III (1956), pp. 378-96. In an article on the recent British race riots, Michael Rumney points out the working-class base of the anti-Negro sentiment and goes so far as to predict that "the Labour party will become the enemy of the Negro as time goes on." He reports that "while the Conservative party has been able to stand behind the police and take any means it feels necessary to preserve the peace, the Labour party has been strangely silent. If it speaks it will either antagonize the men who riot against West Indians, or forfeit its claim to being the party of equal rights." See "Left Mythology and British Race Riots," *The New Leader* (September 22, 1958), pp. 10-11.

British Gallup Poll surveys document these judgments. Thus in a survey completed in July 1959, the poll asked whether Jews "have more or less power than they should really have," and found, when respondents were compared according to party choice, that the anti-Semitic response of "more power" was given by 38 per cent of the Labor voters, 30 per cent of the Tories, and 27 per cent of the Liberals. Seven per cent of the Laborites, 8 per cent of the Conservatives, and 9

parties played a major role in extending political democracy in the nineteenth and early twentieth centuries. However, these struggles for political freedom by the workers, like those of the middle class before them, took place in the context of a fight for economic rights.[71] Freedom of organization and of speech, together with universal suffrage, were necessary weapons in the battle for a better standard of living, social security, shorter hours, and the like. The upper classes resisted the extension of political freedom as part of their defense of economic and social privilege.

Few groups in history have ever voluntarily espoused civil liberties and freedom for those who advocate measures they consider despicable or dangerous. Religious freedom emerged in the Western world only because the contending powers each found themselves unable to destroy the other without destroying the entire society, and because in the course of the struggle itself many men lost faith and interest in religion, and consequently the desire to suppress dissent. Similarly, universal suffrage and freedom of organization and opposition developed in many countries either as concessions to the established strength of the lower classes, or as means of controlling them—a tactic advocated and used by such sophisticated conservatives as Disraeli and Bismarck.

Once in existence, however, and although originating in a conflict

---

per cent of the Liberals thought that Jews have too little power. The same organization has reported a 1958 survey in which fewer Laborites and lower class people said that they would vote for a Jew if their party nominated one than did upper class and Conservative voters. But in all fairness it must also be noted that almost every Jew in the House of Commons represents the Labor party, and that almost all of the approximately two dozen Jews represent overwhelmingly non-Jewish constituencies.

71. Actually there are some striking similarities between the behavior of various middle-class strata when they constituted the lower strata within a predominantly aristocratic and feudal society, and the working class in newly industrialized societies who have not yet won a place in society. The affinities of both for religious and economic "radicalism," in the same sense, are striking. Calvin's doctrine of predestination, as Tawney points out, performed the same function for the eighteenth-century *bourgeoisie* as did Marx's theory of the inevitability of socialism for the proletariat in the nineteenth. Both "set their virtue at their best in sharp antithesis with the vices of the established order at its worst, taught them to feel that they were a chosen people, made them conscious of their great destiny in the Providential and resolute to realize it." The Communist party, as did the Puritans, insists on "personal responsibility, discipline and asceticism," and although the historical contents differ, they may have the same sociological roots: in isolated, status-deprived occupational groups. See R. H. Tawney, *Religion and the Rise of Capitalism* (New York: Penguin Books, 1947), pp. 9, 99. For a similar point see Donald G. MacRae, "The Bolshevik Ideology," *The Cambridge Journal*, 3 (1950), pp. 164-77.

of interests, democratic norms became part of the institutional system. Thus the Western labor and socialist movement has incorporated these values into its general ideology. But the fact that the movement's ideology is democratic does not mean that its supporters actually understand the implications. The evidence seems to indicate that understanding of and adherence to these norms are highest among leaders and lowest among followers. The general opinions or predispositions of the rank and file are relatively unimportant in predicting behavior as long as the organization to which they are loyal continues to act democratically. In spite of the workers' greater authoritarian propensity, their organizations which are anti-Communist still function as better defenders and carriers of democratic values than parties based on the middle class. In Germany, the United States, Great Britain, and Japan, individuals who support the democratic left party are more likely to support civil liberties and democratic values than people *within* each occupatonal stratum who back the conservative parties. Organized social democracy not only defends civil liberties but influences its supporters in the same direction.[72]

Conservatism is especially vulnerable in a political democracy since, as Abraham Lincoln said, there are always more poor people than well-to-do ones, and promises to redistribute wealth are difficult to rebut. Consequently, conservatives have traditionally feared a thoroughgoing political democracy and have endeavored in most countries—by restricting the franchise or by manipulating the governmental structure through second chambers or overrepresentation of rural districts and small towns (traditional conservative strongholds)—to prevent a popular majority from controlling the government. The ideology of conservatism has frequently been based on elitist values which reject the idea that there is wisdom in the voice of the electorate. Other values often defended by conservatives, like militarism or nationalism, probably also have an attraction for individuals with authoritarian predispositions.[73]

72. A striking case in point occurred in Australia in 1950. During a period of much agitation about the dangers of the Communist party, a Gallup Poll survey reported that 80 per cent of the electorate favored outlawing the Communists. Shortly after this survey, the Conservative government submitted a proposal to outlaw the party to referendum. During the referendum electoral campaign, the Labor party and the trade-unions came out vigorously against the proposal. Considerable shifting took place after this, to the point that the measure to outlaw the Communists was actually defeated by a small majority, and Catholic workers who had overwhelmingly favored the outlaw measure when first questioned by the Gallup Poll eventually followed the advice of their party and unions and voted against it. See Leicester Webb, *Communism and Democracy in Australia: A Survey of the 1951 Referendum* (New York: Frederick A. Praeger, 1955).

73. A study of the 1952 elections in the United States revealed that at every

It would be a mistake to conclude from the data presented here that the authoritarian predispositions of the lower classes necessarily constitute a threat to a democratic social system; nor should similar conclusions be drawn about the antidemocratic aspects of conservatism. Whether or not a given class supports restrictions on freedom depends on a wide constellation of factors of which those discussed here are only a part.

The instability of the democratic process in general and the strength of the Communists in particular, as we have seen are closely related to national levels of economic development, including national levels of educational attainment. The Communists represent a mass movement in the poorer countries of Europe and elsewhere, but are weak where economic development and educational attainment are high. The lower classes of the less developed countries are poorer, more insecure, less educated, and relatively more underprivileged in terms of possession of status symbols than are the lower strata of the more well-to-do nations. In the more developed, stable democracies of Western Europe, North America, and Australasia the lower classes are "in the society" as well as "of it"—that is, their isolation from the rest of the culture is much less than the social isolation of the poorer groups in other countries, who are cut off by abysmally low incomes and very low educational levels, if not by widespread illiteracy. This incorporation of the workers into the body politic in the industrialized Western world has reduced their authoritarian tendencies greatly, although in the United States, for example, McCarthy demonstrated that an irresponsible demagogue who combines a nationalist and antielitist appeal can still secure considerable support from the less educated.[74]

---

educational level (grammar school, high school, and college) individuals who scored high on an "authoritarian personality" scale were much more likely to vote for Eisenhower rather than Stevenson. Robert Lane, "Political Personality and Electoral Choice," *American Political Science Review*, 49 (1955), pp. 173-90. In Britain, a study of working-class anti-Semitism found that the small group of Conservatives in the sample were much more anti-Semitic than the Liberals and the Laborites. See James H. Robb, *Working-Class Anti-Semite* (London: Tavistock Publications, 1954), pp. 93-94.

74. "The history of the masses, however, has been a history of the most consistently anti-intellectual force in society . . . It was the American lower classes, not the upper, who gave their overwhelming support to the attacks in recent years on civil liberties. It is among the working people that one finds dominant those sects and churches most hostile to the free spirit." Lewis S. Feuer, Introduction to *Marx and Engels, Basic Writings on Politics and Philosophy* (New York: Doubleday Anchor Books, 1959), pp. xv-xvi. And in another wealthy country, white South Africa, Herbert Tingsten points out that "industrialization and commercialization . . . have formed that social class now constituting the stronghold of Boer nationalism: workers, shop assistants, clerks, lower grades of civil servants. Here, as in the

While the evidence as to the effects of rising national standards of living and education permits us to be hopeful about working-class politics and behavior in those countries in which extremism is weak, it does suggest pessimistic conclusions with regard to the less economically developed, unstable democracies. Where an extremist party has secured the support of the lower classes—often by stressing equality and economic security at the expense of liberty—it is problematic whether this support can be taken away from it by democratic methods. The Communists, in particular, combine the two types of a chiliastic view of the world. Whether democratic working-class parties, able to demonstrate convincingly their ability to defend economic and class interest, can be built up in the less stable democracies is a moot question. But the threat to democracy does not come solely from the lower strata. And in the next chapter [*The Political Man*] we will turn from working-class authoritarianism to an examination of the different varieties of fascism, which is usually identified with the middle class.

SELECTED READINGS

Indication of convergences in the adjustment of rural and urban children, referred to by Burchinal, Hawkes, and Gardner, is found in A. R. Mangus, "Personality Adjustment of Rural and Urban Children," *American Sociological Review,* 1948; G. R. Hawkes, L. G. Burchinal, and Bruce Gardner, "Marital Satisfaction, Personality Characteristics, and Parental Acceptance of Children," *Journal of Counseling Psychology,* 1956. Eugene Litwak has conducted a one-man blitz against the necessity of the nuclear family: see his "Occupational Mobility and Extended Family Cohesion," *American Sociological Review,* February, 1960; also, "Primary Group Instruments for Social Control in Industrial Society: The Extended Family and the Neighborhood," unpublished Ph.D. thesis, Columbia University, 1958.

Peter Blau, "Structural Effects," *American Sociological Review,* 1960, shows how the group acts as a resource for the formation of individual opinion. The Inkeles article indicates a deeper level of personal orientation. For a

---

United States, these 'poor whites'—more correctly, whites threatened by poverty—are the leading guardians of prejudice and white supremacy." *The Problem of South Africa* (London: Victor Gollancz, Ltd., 1955), p. 23.

related study see Reinhard Bendix, "Industrialization, Ideologies, and Social Structure," *American Sociological Review*, October, 1959.

For other studies dealing with the social aspects of aspirations see Bernard C. Rosen, "The Achievement Syndrome: A Psychocultural Dimension of Social Stratification," *American Sociological Review*, 1956; William H. Sewell, Archie O. Haller, and Murray A. Straus, "Social Status and Educational and Occupational Aspiration," *American Sociological Review*, 1957; Alan B. Wilson, "Residential Segregation of Social Classes and Aspirations of High School Students," *American Sociological Review*, December, 1959.

There is, of course, a large literature dealing with "authoritarianism." Those cited here emphasize the social aspect of this phenomenon: Don Stewart and Thomas Hoult, "A Social-Psychological Theory of the Authoritarian Personality," *American Journal of Sociology*, November, 1959; Robert E. Lane, "Fathers and Sons: Foundations of Political Belief," *American Sociological Review*, August, 1959; and Fred B. Silberstein and Melvin Seeman, "Social Mobility and Prejudice," *American Journal of Sociology*, November, 1959.

7 *Self-Feedback Process*

SOCIAL STRUCTURE, in the degree to which it is crystallized, communicates to a prospective actor a system of favored behavior. But this has no automatic efficacy with the actor; it is rather an element in his decision-making processes. But we must understand this term in a much wider sense than is usually intended. This decision making may be conscious or unconscious, compulsive or volitional, emotional or cognitive, simple or complex; nevertheless, the concrete self participates in the response to the communicated expectation and in that sense makes a decision about action. The decision-making behavior of individuals rises to a point of social visibility when the behavior departs in some respect from the normally expected. Except in limiting cases, the self reacts to the perception of a norm of conduct. In this sense there is always feedback; but feedback that is variant or deviant, that is, feedback approaching or exceeding the limits of social tolerance, may point to important social change. Much of this kind of feedback has idiosyncratic causes, and thus is not likely to produce a trend in behavior; but if a general condition—in society or self—sets up a press in the direction of variant or deviant behavior, a pattern or trend of important feedback may be observed.

The initiative of the self may be employed in a number of ways. Individuals may associate and organize for expressive or rational ends, and in this case self-responses produce a social movement that gradually becomes a concrete social structure. Theodore Abel, "The Pattern of a Successful Political Movement," presents shrewd ". . . preliminary considerations of a general nature about social movements." Sheldon L. Messinger's study of the Townsend Movement gives concrete examples of many of Abel's propositions.

Individuals with a grudge against the system may not "gang up" to change it. They may alter their way of life, slip out from under the horizons and perspectives that have served before, and try on new behaviors. If this becomes general in a significant segment of the society, we may have a change in social structure without the mediation of a social movement. Martha Sturm White, "Social Class, Child Rearing Practices, and Child Behavior," finds that there are few social class differences between the middle and the working class on "oral behavior and feeding regimen." The author, properly cautious in interpreting her findings, suggests that "The available evidence is consistent with the notion that a change in child-rearing practices has taken place . . . ." Russell Middleton and Snell Putney, "Dominance in Decisions in the Family: Race and Class Differences," find something similar going on. On the basis of the literature they expected to find American Negro families more matriarchal than white families and working-class white families more patriarchal than middle-class white families. From their own data Middleton and Putney conclude: "Contrary to the literature, our data suggest that all these groups are predominantly equalitarian." Both of these studies require confirmation, but both of them point to the probability of large-scale social change in American society.

All societies have some kind of institutional encouragement for expressive and creative behavior. The individual completes and fulfills his expressive and creative potential through a meaningful encounter with these forms. Thus, feedback, itself, does not reinstate the virtuous savage but calls attention to the complexity of the society-self relation. Nathan A. Scott, Jr., "The Broken Center: A Definition of the Crisis in Values in Modern Literature," expresses his thesis concretely when he says,

> For the lesson of Joyce's career teaches us that, though the artist cannot by fiat produce adequate surrogates for traditions of faith and culture no longer available to him, he can, in attempting to do so, dramatize with especial vividness the fact of the mythical vacuum in the modern period.

THEODORE ABEL

The Pattern of a Successful Political Movement

"Is FASCISM possible in America?," "Does Communism have a chance?," "How can the movement for Birth-control Legislation be made more effective?"

In current discussions of national affairs we frequently encounter questions like these. They demand predictions about social movements and ask for guidance in the execution of plans of change. "Social Movements," being modes of collective or pluralistic behavior, fall in the province of sociology, and the sociologist ought to be equipped to furnish a reply to questions about them.

However, prediction and guidance with regard to social movements, presuppose a generalized knowledge of the subject. We have to know the common and distinct features of social movements, and the factors or conditions significant in determining their development. We must be able to view a given situation, with its unique constellation of factors as the instance of a type; we must appraise it in terms of a general pattern, if we want to express any valid judgment about it. For the type or pattern, when constructed on the basis of intensive studies of individual cases by the method of analytical induction[1] gives us the clues to what is relevant and significant. It tells us what we have to look for in studying a particular situation, and in weighing it in relation to certain questions we may be asked about it.

In short, in order to make valid statements about a particular movement, an adequate *theory* of social movements is necessary.

Reprinted from American Sociological Review, *1937, pp. 347-352, by permission of the author and the journal.*

1. For a discussion of the method of analytical induction, cf. Znaniecki, *The Method of Sociology,* New York, 1934, chap. vi.

As yet we have no such theory. In fact, only few attempts have been made at a typological analysis of social movements.[2] They constitute a neglected field of sociological inquiry, and in most text books of sociology, or social psychology we look in vain for any reference to them.

It is the aim of this paper to present a few preliminary considerations of a general nature about social movements. Our remarks on the pattern of social movements shall be limited to a discussion of the significant factors that account for the persistence, growth, and successful termination of a political movement. The propositions set forth here are derived from an intensive study of the Hitler Movement in Germany, made by the author on the basis of six hundred life stories of members of the National Socialist Party.[3]

What is a social movement? As a mode of pluralistic behavior, it belongs to the general class of social phenomena which includes mob actions, booms, crazes, panics, revolutions, and so forth. As a sub-class, a social movement is circumscribed by pluralistic behavior functioning as an organized mass-effort directed toward a change of established folkways or institutions. A social movement may be said to exist wherever a group of individuals, operating within a community, aims to win the support of that community for the establishment of some innovation in the ways and means of promoting a common interest. The innovation or change may be a new or untried mode of procedure, or the restoration of a mode applied in the past. In either case the intention that underlies the attempted change arises from the experience of the inadequacy of a given procedure, and the belief in the adequacy of the proposed change.

A collective effort may be properly called a social movement only if it operates within the medium of a community. An attempt, for example, to change the by-laws of some association is not a social movement, since such action, as a rule, does not bear upon a community interest. The most significant social movements are those which take place on a national scale, and affect political religious and moral folkways and institutions.

From the definition of a social movement just given, it follows that a movement is, on the one hand, directed *against* something which it endeavors to combat and eliminate, and on the other hand, favors something, i.e., it is directed *toward* some goal which it is striving to realize. These two opposite but complementary intentions we call respectively the *Issue* and the *Ideology* of a movement.

---

2. Jerome Davis, *Contemporary Social Movements*, New York, 1930.

3. The points discussed in this paper is more fully developed in a book by the author, entitled *The Hitler Movement, an Interpretation Based upon 600 Autobiographies*, New York: Prentice-Hall, 1938.

What is the basis of an issue or an ideology? About behavior in general we know that the intention to act against or for something results from a problem-experience induced by some event impinging upon some value or values that the individual holds. An impinging event is always some action that brings about the modification of existing arrangements through the activities of human beings. The reaction of an individual to an event depends on how he feels or thinks it will affect his social position, possessions, intentions, relations with others—anything that is an integral part of his life organization, and thus is a value which he is set to protect, defend, and promote. The event obtains its meaning, is named or defined by the individual according to the way in which he experiences it in terms of his values.

In view of this we may say that underlying the issue of movement is the experience of a *threat* to certain values, while at the basis of an ideology lies the experience of an opportunity to *promote* certain values.

We may now ask what are the significant aspects of an ideology or issue that determine the success of a social movement. Concerning the issue, the following special conditions, favorable to concerted action, must be present, in order that a movement may materialize and maintain itself.

1. The experience of events as a threat to values must be common to many individuals. This presupposes that events will be operative over a wide area, and the values affected will be prevalent in that area.

2. A strong emotional reaction of dissatisfaction and opposition is required to sustain a movement. Assuming a rank-order of values, the strength of the reaction may be said to be directly proportional to the place which the affected values occupy in the individual's hierarchy of values.

3. No movement can occur unless *personal* values are involved, such as social status, income, and so forth. This was the case in the Hitler movement, insofar as it grew out of the dissatisfaction and opposition induced by such events as the revolution of 1918, the inflation, the economic insecurity of the white-collar class, unemployment,—all of which affected directly the personal welfare of many individuals. But for a movement to materialize, a threat or impairment of personal values must be linked to the experience of a threat or impairment of *social* values. These are values *shared* by members of the same group or community, such as traditions, group prestige, group symbols, and possessions. In terms of such values events in Germany, as for example the establishment of a republican regime, the Versailles treaty, the occupation of the Ruhr were experienced as threats. The linking of social with personal values is important not only because it enables the individual to rationalize his negative reaction, justifying a selfish reason by a group

purpose, but also because it facilitates concerted action, and makes possible the fanaticism which in most cases is necessary to keep a movement alive.

4. When different events are experienced as affecting personal and social values the dissatisfaction and opposition resulting therefrom must be capable of being focussed upon some object that can be regarded as the *common source* of the disturbing events. For example, in the case of the Hitler movement, such object was the Republican regime (more specifically the groups and individuals that enacted and supported it), the "System," as it was called, which was made responsible for all the troubles that confronted the individuals and the nation.

An adequate issue is the groundwork upon which enterprising individuals may organize some collective action. But if such action is to become a genuine social movement, there must be not only concerted opposition, but also collective striving for the realization of some plan, or scheme of betterment. Without an ideology, as we called such plans, pluralistic behavior will at best be a revolt.

An adequate ideology is one which, first of all appeals to some ideal. In the case of the Hitler Movement in Germany this ideal was the realization of a *Gemeinschaft*, i.e., a primary group relationship, uniting all Germans and in which everyone puts the common interest before self.[4]

Secondly, an adequate ideology expresses the ideal in terms of current glow words, i.e., ideas that carry a strong and prevalent emotional tone. In the Hitler Movement such words were: nationalism, socialism, racial superiority,[5] and so forth, all capable of being reinterpreted in terms of *Gemeinschaft* as the unifying concept.

Thirdly, an ideology, in order to function as the basis of a successful movement, must link up the goal with the issue. This can best be accomplished by setting forth a plan in which the items are the opposite of that which is regarded as the cause of the problem-experiences. For example, in Germany it was dictatorship vs. parliamentarianism, *Gleichschaltung* vs. liberalism, a policy of the strong hand in dealing with the Allies vs. a policy of concession and compromise, etc.

---

4. F. Tönnies' classical treatise on "*Gemeinschaft und Gesellschaft*," Berlin, 1887, and subsequent editions, has contributed to the receptivity of this ideal!

5. Anti-Semitism was an important propaganda device of the Hitler Movement, which appealed to sentiments and beliefs that were inculcated during 1870-1890, when the first wave of organized anti-Semitism since the emancipation of the Jews swept Germany under the leadership of Stoeker, Ahlward, and others. In the ideology, however, anti-Semitism is incident to the idea of "community of blood," as the basis of the *Gemeinschaft* that was to be realized, and in consequence of which the exclusion of all "non-Germans" was advocated.

Fourthly, an ideology must be propounded by a *charismatic* leader—to use Max Weber's terminology[6]—one who can induce in his followers an identification with the ideology as a cause worth fighting and dying for.

In dealing with the issue and ideology of a movement, we are considering only one group of significant factors which have to be present in order to make a movement successful. However, issue and ideology are, in a sense, only *structural* elements of a movement. The *dynamic* elements are the activities of individuals who on the basis of an issue and an ideology engage in propaganda and organization for the purpose of winning the support of the community, and in the quest for power. These individuals are banded together into what we may call the *promotion group* of the movement. The National-Socialist-German-Workmen's Party was such a promotion group. From the point of view of the causal analysis of a movement, the issue and ideology may be regarded as the basic conditions, or the potential factors which might induce individuals to action in a certain direction. For the initiation, growth and successful termination of the action, however, the activities of a promotion group and its leaders are primarily responsible. Applied to the Hitler Movement, for example, this means that it is wrong to account for its success in terms of unemployment, Versailles treaty, and similar causes. On the basis of these factors many other promotion groups attempted to organize a movement and obtain control of the government, such as the *Stahlhelm*, the Communists, and others. Primarily responsible for the success of the Hitler Movement was the way in which the promotion group presented the issue, made the ideology attractive, and manipulated the technique of propaganda and organization.

It is necessary, therefore, to consider a second group of factors, those relating to the activities of the promotion group of a movement, if we want to complete a pattern of the significant and relevant elements of a social movement.

It is more difficult to generalize on the promotion aspect of a movement than on its issue and ideology. The difficulty is due in part to the scarcity of comparable data. To a large extent, it is due, however, to the fact that the activities of a promotion group involve matters of strategy and tactics, which are to a considerable degree dependent upon the *particular* situation in which the group operates. This question awaits further investigation.

For the time being, we can generalize with a certain degree of confidence on the *tasks* which confront a promotion group, and which it must solve if a strong and successful movement is to materialize.

---

6. M. Weber, *Wirtschaft und Gemeinschaft*, 1922, p. 124.

A promotion group must first of all hold the *attention* of the community. In the case of the Hitler Movement this task was accomplished by maintaining a persistent barrage of propaganda through meetings, the press, pamphlets and posters, displays of symbols, ostentatious demonstrations, like parades and party congresses and participation in affairs affecting the community, as in the case of the Young Plan.

Secondly, it must *justify* its claim for leadership. This task the Hitler group achieved by keeping the issue alive, continuously stirring up prevalent dissatisfaction and opposition, and skilfully linking dissatisfactions with its ideology. Acceptance of the ideology was sought for by appeal to traditions and to prevailing sentiments, for example, to sentiments for "discipline and order," for unity, and for the abolition of classes.

Thirdly, a promotion group must win the *confidence* of the masses, by maneuvering itself into a position of ascendancy over competing groups, and by successfully combating its opponents. Thus, in the case of the Hitler Movement, the National Socialist Party succeeded in absorbing the members of most other groups with a nationalistic ideology, by pursuing a policy of "no compromise and no alliance." These members, as well as the large number of voters who supported the movement eventually, were won over in many cases by the shows of strength and successful defiance of the radical leftist groups, particularly the communists. This the promotion group accomplished by direct invasion of the "strongholds of the enemy," and readiness to "fight it out" if necessary.

A fourth task is the development of an adequate organization not merely for the carrying out of the propaganda, and for the struggle with competing and opposing groups, but also in preparation for the taking over of power.

These tasks require adequate leadership. What determines adequate leadership is a question we cannot answer here. We can emphasize only this point: the success of a promotional group depends to a considerable extent on its having a charismatic leader, who functions as a glorified symbol of the movement and can command the unquestioned obedience and devotion of his followers. For allegiance to a leader, the inspiration of his charisma, is primarily responsible for the winning and holding of active participants, who not only carry on the propaganda and struggle, which frequently requires neglect of personal interests, but who possess the peculiar fanaticism that enables an individual to be steadfast in the face of abuse and persecution. The fact that the Hitler Movement had a charismatic leader was, therefore, an important factor in its success.

The propositions advanced in this paper require further testing and elucidation. They indicate the direction in which a theory of social movements should be developed. As we advance our knowledge by further studies, and particularly, as we succeed in developing indices that will test the presence or absence of *significant* factors in *particular* situations, we shall be able as sociologists to perform the important function of predicting and guiding social movements, in a better fashion than we can at present.

SHELDON L. MESSINGER

Organizational Transformation: A Case Study of a Declining Social Movement

It is generally recognized that the organized arms of value-oriented social movements[1] may remain intact long after the movements themselves have lost general impetus. While it is to be expected that these structures will adapt to their changed circumstances, little attention has as yet been given to either the process or product of this adaptation. This paper reports a study of certain organizational consequences of the decline of the Townsend Movement.

Reprinted from American Sociological Review, 1955, pp. 3-10, by permission of the author and the journal.

Revised version of paper read at the annual meeting of the American Sociological Society, September, 1954. Acknowledgment is gratefully made to the Institute of Industrial Relations, University of California, Berkeley, for financial assistance in carrying out the research during the early months of 1953; to Mr. P. Leonard Jacobs and Mr. Leonard Symes, for suggestions regarding the ordering and interpretation of the data; and to Mr. John C. Cuneo, California State Organizer, Townsend Plan, Inc., for the cooperation which he and his staff extended to the writer.

1. "Value-oriented social movements" is a phrasing suggested to the writer by Ralph H. Turner. It refers to social movements fundamentally oriented toward rendering some change in the social structure and of sufficient force to develop organization.

The Townsend Mission and the End of Recruitment

While the old age pension movement seems to be gaining impetus in the United States, the Townsend Movement has all but vanished. To understand this seeming paradox it is necessary to examine the Townsend mission. This has been, and continues to be, not simply national pensions for the aged, but national pensions for the aged *as a mechanism for alleviating or preventing economic dislocation.* The mission is a blending of issues born of the 1930s, and the continued identification of Townsendites with it aids in understanding the movement's decline and the nature of its remaining structure.

Two sorts of data support this characterization of the Townsend mission, as well as the continued identification of the Organization with it.

First, the Townsend Plan,[2] major subject of most Townsend pronouncements, has maintained features directly linking pensions to economic reconstruction. Its provision requiring that the pension be spent within thirty days is intended to provide jobs by keeping money in circulation. Its stipulation that prospective recipients must cease work to become eligible is designed to combat "technological unemployment."[3] These are the key to Townsend claims that theirs is not "just another pension plan." Further, leaders justify changes in other features of the Plan as occasioned by the aim of economic reconstruction. For example, the famous "200 dollars a month," from the first a legislative impediment, was formally discarded in all forms in 1943. Informally it is still mentioned as "essential to the Plan" in the sense that at least this much is requisite to "keep the economy going." Other changeable features, justified in all their forms as necessary to economic reconstruction, include the means of financing and designation of those to receive the pension.

Second, the Organization aside from the Plan has continued to link the pension and depression issues. In 1936, a year after passage of national social security legislation, the Organization changed its name from "Old

2. That version which received the widest publicity may be found in the pamphlet *Old Age Revolving Pensions, A National Plan . . . Proposed by Dr. F. E. Townsend,* Long Beach, California: Old Age Revolving Pensions, Ltd., 1934. For a more recent version see *Townsend National Weekly,* August 1, 1953. (These and other pamphlets, letters, and newspapers cited here may be found in the Townsend Archives, Library, University of California, Los Angeles.)

3. See, e.g., *Do You Really Know the Townsend Plan?,* n.d.: Townsend Press., n.d., a pamphlet published during World War II and still circulated.

Age Revolving Pensions, Ltd." to "Townsend National Recovery Plan, Inc.," emphasizing that its mission was far from complete. Not until 1948 did the less anachronous "Townsend Plan, Inc." become the organizational style. The *Townsend National Weekly*, official newspaper of the Organization, has become since 1941 a veritable compendium of "signs" pointing to "impending" economic disaster. Throughout World War II and the post-war boom, Townsendites continued to circulate tracts stressing that their Organization aimed at "a program to bring about full industrial production for the Nation . . . [and] make jobs for the jobless."[4]

While such aims may again gain currency, it is suggested that under the changed conditions following the end of the depression the Townsend mission was deprived of relevance. Continued identification with this mission has constituted a serious block to Townsend membership maintenance and to the recruitment of new Townsendites. Combined with the short life-expectancies of old Townsendites, this has meant a rapid depletion of the Organization's ranks (see Table 1).[5] In this situa-

Table 1. National and California Townsend Membership Decline, 1936-1951*

	National Membership	*Per Cent Drop*	*California Membership*	*Per Cent Drop*
1936	2,250,000		330,000	
1951	56,656	97.5	6,839	97.9

*Sources: National and California membership figures for 1936 from U. S. House of Representatives, Select Committee Investigating Old Age Pension Organizations pursuant to H. Res. 443, *Hearings*, 74th Cong., 2nd Sess., Washington, D. C.: 1936 (hereafter: *Hearings: H. Res. 443*), pp. 41-42, 208. National membership for 1951 from Holtzman, *loc. cit.* California membership figure for 1951 compiled from records in the Townsend Archives.

4. *Why I Am for the Townsend Plan*, Cleveland, Ohio: Townsend Press, n.d.

5. Since the age-sex composition of the Townsend membership is not available, it is not possible to gauge with any accuracy the loss of membership due to death and that due to dropping out. However, the large yearly membership declines following 1939 (when yearly figures first became available) indicate that major losses came from dropouts. See Abraham Holtzman, "The Townsend Movement: A Study in Old Age Pressure Politics," unpublished doctoral dissertation, Harvard University, Cambridge, Mass., 1952, p. 267, for yearly Townsend membership figures 1939-1951.

The long-run personnel problem is, of course, effective recruitment. The considered opinion of Townsend leaders and members is that remaining Townsendites are all "oldtimers." In personal contacts with over one hundred California Townsendites, the writer found no variation in this conjecture and met only one person who had joined the Organization since 1948. The growth of such structures as George McLain's California Institute of Social Welfare, since 1941 the major old age pressure-group on the California scene, is an additional indication of what has happened to Townsend recruitment. Of McLain's 60-70,000 members in 1953, less than one per cent had ever belonged to the Townsend Organization. (According to a questionnaire administered by the Institute of Industrial Relations, University of California, Berkeley.)

tion, other "single-minded" old age groups, working to modify existing state aid legislation, have developed to absorb the membership which might earlier have gone to the Townsendites. It is in this context that the Townsend Organization has been transformed.

Organizational Transformation

The Tendency to Deflection. Townsend leaders have attempted to cope with the challenge to their social base. In the process, they have been constrained to direct action in ways deflecting the Organization from its central mission.

The first indication of this tendency came in early 1940 when California Townsendites were urged to aid in qualifying an initiative readjusting state aid legislation.[6] While the campaign was brief and the initiative was not qualified, the event is noteworthy since before this time national leaders had actively campaigned against any proposal at the state level.[7] Further, they had always carefully disassociated themselves from state "aid" proposals. The "pension," on a national level and not involving indigence requirements, was the proper Townsend goal.

Leadership purposes in supporting this proposal are not far to seek. Urging his lieutenants to support the measure, the California leader said: "Even if we should fail [to qualify it], it is believed we can secure enough publicity and good will to justify the effort. We think we can enlist many to join our ranks as a result of this campaign."[8]

In 1943, California Townsendites entered a full-blown campaign for state old age pensions.[9] The nature of this measure permitted it to be presented by both national[10] and state leaders as a "first step" toward the national Townsend Plan. Thus, while only a state-wide proposal with a dollar demand geared to existing state aid legislation (60 dollars

6. The text of the proposal is given in full in *Townsend National Weekly*, California Edition, April 13, 1940. Its major aim was to block state recovery measures directed at old age aid recipients. For evidence that the tendency to deflection, detailed here only for the California case, was general throughout the Organization see Holtzman, *op. cit.*, p. 512 ff.

7. See Holtzman, *op. cit.*, p. 510 ff.

8. Letter from John C. Cuneo, National Representative [for California], Townsend National Recovery Plan, Inc. (hereafter: TNRP, Inc.), to Members of the [California] State Advisory Board, Modesto, California: n.d. (mim.).

9. The proposal may be found in State of California, Secretary of State, *Proposed Amendments to Constitution, General Election, 1944* (hereafter: *Proposed Amendments: 1944*), Sacramento, California: State Printing Office, 1944, p. 11.

10. Holtzman (*op. cit.*, p. 516) reports that national headquarters contributed over 69,000 dollars to the California campaign. Further, speakers were provided and the *Townsend National Weekly* covered the campaign in detail.

was asked), both the "compulsory spending" and "cease work" features of the national Plan were intact. Further, indigence requirements were absent, meaning effectively the end of a state "aid" program and the institution of "pensions" if the measure passed.[11]

The initiative was qualified and placed before the voters in November 1944. It was defeated by over a million votes.[12]

By 1947 membership was at a new low, recruitment at a dead halt, and George McLain's old age pressure-group successfully competing for the allegiance of the California aged. Aware of the challenge, the California leader proposed a new local effort to national headquarters by saying:

> [Even] Dr. Townsend [who is generally opposed to local efforts] has consistently said that "we *must* put on an initiative in California . . . even if we know we will fail before we start. . . ." [This] for the reason that GM [George McLain] has announced that he, too, is going to sponsor a constitutional amendment proposing practically the same objectives. . . . If we fail to present . . . [a local] program, it is only natural that a large number of our own members will be inclined to support him in his efforts. . . . Many people have lost hope and interest in any national program becoming a reality in the near future.[13]

By no stretch of the imagination could the new measure proposed by state leaders be identified as a "little Townsend Plan."[14] First, unlike the 1943-1944 proposal, it was specifically drawn within the framework of existing state legislation for old age assistance and indigence requirements were present.[15] Second, both the all-important "compulsory spending" and "cease work" provisions of the Plan were absent. Town-

---

11. In George McLain's opinion it also meant the end of grants-in-aid under Federal Social Security Legislation, as he took pains to point out in his "Argument Against Initiative Proposition No. 11," *Proposed Amendments: 1944,* p. 12. He added: "The proposed law would pension rich and poor alike, thereby lessening the value of the dollar in the hands of the needy—an unjust and vicious proposal." Compare this with later Townsendite handling of McLain issues, below.

12. State of California, Secretary of State, *Statement of Vote, General Election, 1944,* Sacramento, California State Printing Office, 1944, p. 29.

13. Letter from John C. Cuneo, California State Organizer, TNRP, Inc. to Robert C. Townsend (son of Dr. F. E. Townsend and *de facto* head of the Organization), Treasurer, TNRP, Inc., Modesto, California: August 14, 1947.

14. The initiative, which may be found in the Townsend Archives, proposed raising state aid to 75 dollars per month, reduction of recipients age to 60 years, and institution of a one per cent "gross income tax" to finance the measure.

15. It is clear from the *Minutes* of [the Townsend California] State Council Meeting at Los Angeles, California, July 26 to 27, 1947, p. 2, that California strategists felt a lesson of the 1943-1944 campaign to have been that the closer to existing legislation, the more chance of success.

send propaganda could no longer claim that their measure would effect any significant change in the economic structure.[16]

National leaders at first opposed making a new localized proposal on the grounds that another defeat would do the Movement's national position no good.[17] In August 1947, conceding to California's pressures, they suggested that campaign funds should be raised *outside* the Organization.[18] As late as October 1947, in the midst of efforts to raise money in California for the promotion of the initiative, national leaders carried out two mass meetings in the state to collect funds for national headquarters over the unanswered objections of the California leader.[19]

By June 1948 it was clear that Townsendites had not qualified their initiative, but that McLain had qualified his. State leaders remained as silent as possible in the face of this proposal with "practically the same objectives" and tried to refocus membership attention on national issues.[20]

The passage of McLain's constitutional amendment at the polls was quickly followed by a move for repeal. When the repeal initiative qualified, California Townsend leaders faced a serious dilemma. They could not support repeal, for the advantages brought to the aged by McLain's amendment were patent—e.g., a raise in monthly grant, the end of "relative's responsibility." Nor could they fight repeal, lest an issue now entirely identified with McLain absorb all their membership's attention and funds. To meet the situation, California leaders tried to straddle the fence by proposing measures to the legislature to supplant McLain's.[21]

16. About this time, Townsend state leaders began to talk about instituting the "fundamental principles" of the Plan. This euphemism has since spread to the national level. In the 1947-1948 campaign the "gross income tax" was offered as "the fundamental principle."

17. Letter from Robert C. Townsend, Treasurer, TNRP, Inc. to John C. Cuneo, California State Organizer, TNRP, Inc., Cleveland, Ohio: July 17, 1947.

18. Letter from Robert C. Townsend, Treasurer, TNRP, Inc. to John C. Cuneo, California State Organizer, TNRP, Inc., Cleveland, Ohio: August 14, 1947.

19. It should be noted that during the October national call the California leader advised members to raise money for *it* outside the Organization! See *California Club Bulletin*, Modesto, California: September 6, 1947.

20. Of particular interest in this connection is the *California Club Bulletin*, Modesto, California: June 10, 1948, immediately following notification of the failure of the initiative to qualify for the ballot. State leaders also indirectly recommended a "no" vote on the McLain intiative through an issue-endorsing group of which they were members. See *News Letter* of the California Legislative Conference, San Francisco, California: n.d. Probably sent October 1948.

21. At least this was their declared intent; it is not clear whether action was taken. The California leader was driven to state his intentions by "the continued statements by Geo. H. McLain . . . inferring that Townsend Plan leaders and I in particular, are uniting with 'reactionary groups' to try to repeal [the McLain amendment] . . . *THE TRUTH IS* your leaders are on the job doing everything possible to see that the major

National leadership, on the other hand, insisted that the Townsend Organization stay clear of the battle, on the belated grounds that it was for national, not state, pensions. In July 1949, with a repeal measure on the ballot, the California leader wrote the following to national headquarters:

> We [California leaders] thought that [some anti-repeal statement] was necessary as many of our members are supporting McLain financially and attending his meetings, to do what they can to hold the gains they have received. . . . [Now, in view of your position] . . . it seems all we can do is drift; let McLain get the money and our members and let things take their course and keep trying to focus attention of the Washington, D.C. work.[22]

As late as 1953, the crisis continued. Too weak to promote state legislation directly, state leadership fluctuated between "preserving gains" made by others, "preventing setbacks," all within the framework of state aid legislation, and focusing attention on national issues. But now, for state leaders, the national issue, above all, is simply success. Late in 1952 the California leader wrote:

> I realize that we have always felt that it was necessary to stick to our "full program," but if the Republicans will not now accept it "in full," it seems to me that we should try to take the lead with a bill *they will accept* and get something during the next session. . . . I feel that if we don't do something along this line, we can expect McLain to capitalize on the situation and we will lose more and more of our few supporters.[23]

What we have seen here is a tendency to deflection from central aims on the part of Townsend leaders. At the national level, this tendency has been largely checked through a clearer appreciation of the "drift of things" by national leaders themselves. For this drift could only eventuate in the break-up of the national Organization. At the state level, leaders have tended to exchange identity for security in their search for a viable mission. But here, the pressure from national leadership, plus the successful capturing of vital issues by competing groups,[24]

---

gains made . . . *ARE PRESERVED.*" *Intra-organizational Bulletin*, Modesto, California: January 22, 1949.

22. Letter from John C. Cuneo, California State Organizer, Townsend Plan, Inc. (hereafter: TP, Inc.) to Robert C. Townsend, Treasurer, TP, Inc., Modesto, California: July 28, 1949.

23. Letter from John C. Cuneo, California State Organizer, TP, Inc. to Robert C. Townsend, Treasurer, TP, Inc., Modesto California: November 8, 1952.

24. This should be taken to include the identification of the Townsend Organization with its traditional mission (*i.e.*, national pensions for economic reconstruction) by relevant publics. It is not a simple matter to escape an identity long and actively sought. Such escape is even more difficult when competing leaderships continually remind potential members of past failures.

have served to hold state leaders within the Organization and to the Townsend mission.

The Tendency to Salesmanship. Loss of mass support has brought increasing financial difficulty to the Townsend Organization.[25] Adaptation to this circumstance has transformed Townsend leader-follower relations in such a way as to make recruit interest in the Townsend mission increasingly problematical.

Aside from advertising in the *Townsend National Weekly*,[26] early Townsend income came largely from the small contributions of individual members. Propaganda materials were sold in large quantities, and royalties accrued from such items as Townsend auto-stickers, buttons, and license-plate holders. It is to be noted that all of these devices *assume commitment on the part of contributors* to the Townsend Organization and its mission.

By 1939, however, members were being urged to purchase *consumable* items bearing the Townsend name. This year saw a Townsend candy bar, then "Townsend Old Fashioned Horehound Drops." In 1940, a Townsend coffee was announced. A little later a "Townsend Club Toilet Soap" and a "Townsend Club Granulated Soap" appeared. In all of these enterprises the organization merely lent its name; funds, if received, accrued from royalties. The change from auto-stickers, etc., was small but significant because purchase of these new items did not assume commitment to the Organization or its Plan. Townsendites were urged to ask for these items at their usual shopping places, thus, to encourage store owners to stock them. The Organization had yet to become a distributor itself. This was to come.[27]

Beginning in 1943, a series of health foods was offered to members. Of these, "Dr. Townsend's Vitamins and Minerals" soon became the major item. At first distributed only from national headquarters, by 1951 state offices had become distribution points, and Club members were selling pills on commission. In this year, the pills provided one-fifth of the total national income. Intra-organizational communications of all kinds reveal in this period a striking shift from programmatic matters to concern with promoting this product. Perhaps even more significant for the long run, advertising of the pills has come to leave the Organization and its Plan unmentioned. The most elaborate piece yet prepared

25. See Holtzman, *op. cit.*, pp. 313-18, 549-50, for 1934-1951 income figures.

26. While income from this source was large in the early days of the Organization, it also seems that in those days this revenue went into the pockets of Dr. Townsend and the "co-founder" of the Organization, Robert E. Clements. See *Hearings: H. Res. 443, passim.*, on this point. Such revenues are, of course, dependent on mass circulation, and presently the newspaper carries little advertising.

27. Mention of these early items may be found in *California Club Bulletins* for 1939-1940. Apparently none were successful; they are gone without a trace in 1953.

(1953) is simply titled "Vitamins and Minerals by Francis E. Townsend, M.D." Its message is entirely one of "health" and "price." Headquarters for the pills is identified as "Dr. Townsend's Vitamins and Minerals" rather than the earlier "Townsend Plan, Inc." Besides this, national radio advertising has been considered, and discussions of this matter have placed promotion of the Plan aside.

This type of money-raising activity is to be clearly differentiated from that of earlier days. Townsend leaders have come to purvey items whose purchase assumes no commitment to the Townsend mission. The pills, especially, are amenable for presentation to others, *once to be seen as potential Townsendites*, without invoking any discussion of the Organization and its aims.

The transformation of leadership activities from the presentation of a program to the purveying of products can be traced in the present approach to recruitment as well. In May 1952, discussing a proposal to offer a 50 per cent commission to members who brought in new recruits, Dr. Townsend said:

> We have innumerable people in our clubs who can be taught to sell. Let's push them into learning by making it necessary to do so if they wish to remain members of a club. After they have learned *what* to do, I believe they will continue to do—with a fifty per cent bait as inducement.[28]

In October of the same year, national headquarters distributed a "training manual" designed to "double the readership of *Townsend National Weekly* and the membership of each Townsend club."[29] The striking quality of this "manual" is that it makes clear that Townsend leaders *no longer even seek active support at large.* The issue has become simply support in itself. Members are told:

> Many big business organizations give their salesmen sales manuals written from long experience in the technique of winning friends to a product. We've done the same for you. . . . Whether you're building a model boat or being a BUSY BEE, tools and technique are the secret of success.[30]

How to extract the "cost" in manageable installments is outlined; little is said about the urgency or value of the mission at hand. The total impression received is that the best salesman is he who receives money with the least pain to the customer. And this is no doubt correct. For Townsend leaders no longer seek "converts" so much as "customers."

---

28. Letter from Dr. F. E. Townsend, President, TP, Inc. to Mildred Atwood, Secretary to John C. Cuneo, Los Angeles, California: May 19, 1952.

29. *The Busy Bee Program*, n.p.: n.d. The "program" was part of a contest with prizes for those enlisting the most new members and readers.

30. *Ibid.*

The Tendency to "Pure" Recreation. Membership activity at the level of the Clubs[31] provides a final example of the transformation of the Townsend Organization.

Townsend Club "business meetings" are remarkably similar in both form and content. Similarity of form has been encouraged by the various *Townsend Club Manuals*, each containing a procedural outline, plus local leadership unpracticed in organizational ways. Whatever variation is found in content is largely accounted for by the make-up of the Club membership. Clubs with a preponderance of highly religious members substitute "sings" for card playing. Aside from formalities, Club meetings are given to discussions of plans for social activities such as are discussed below. The usual meeting is attended by less than fifteen persons, lasts a half an hour, and is adjourned. But no one leaves. More likely than not, five or ten more people enter. Card tables are set up, and what seems to the writer to be the "real" business of the evening begins: recreation. This latter may last for several hours.[32]

This pattern may even be formalized. Examination of Club minutes often revealed that at some time in the past a motion had carried to limit the "business meeting" to an hour or less. Not all members agree that this is the proper order of things. Almost every Club has its "vocal Townsendite," a member always ready to take the floor and present the Organizational mission. Precisely toward these members such motions had been directed. The "vocal Townsendite," once perhaps a Club president, had become an outcast in his own Club. If in any executive role, he can ordinarily be found on the membership committee—a position nobody seemed to want, for obvious reasons. And even here he may remain under fire: many members feel that the membership committees misrepresent Club aims by "selling the Plan too hard," *i.e.*, presenting its realization as imminent ("even now").

Not only are membership social activities built right into Club meetings, but some Clubs have additional "pot-luck nights" or "weekly dances" specifically designed to attract non-members. These activities

31. The Clubs, established early in the history of the Organization, have always played an important role for Townsend leaders as nuclei for education, recruitment, and fund-raising. From 1100 Clubs in California in 1936, only 123 were left in 1952. They have shown a steady decrease in average membership, as well as numbers, since 1939 (the first year for which yearly records are available). E.g., in 1939 there were 91.3 members per California Club; in 1952, 45.0. (These figures are derived from records in the Townsend Archives.)

32. At one large Los Angeles Club, far along in the transformation process described here, the meeting at 11 A.M. finds less than ten persons present. By 1 P.M., when card playing begins, there are ordinarily *over 50* persons present. A check indicated that less than one-third of these had ever been members of the Townsend Organization.

would seem to furnish ideal occasions for recruitment and the distribution of Townsend propaganda. The evidence in hand suggests that once they did, but no more. Several Club leaders informed the writer that propagandizing would only lower participation, thus reduce sorely needed funds. As public interest in the Plan has flagged, there has been a related change in the nature of Townsend social activities. They have become from the viewpoint of Townsend Club leaders purely fund-raising devices. In turn these activities have become, from the viewpoint of nonmember participants, purely social.

The "vocal Townsendite" may object to this. In one Los Angeles Club a member insisted that the *Townsend National Weekly* be sold at social events and recruiting attempts made. This same member, then Club president, was the occasion of so much dissension in Club ranks that he was not reelected—which is unusual in Club histories. The next (and 1953) president, while mildly unhappy that many who attend Club social functions "don't know what we stand for," seems more distressed by any falling-off of attendance at these affairs. Further, he regards social groups (*e.g.*, public park dance clubs) as his "most serious competition," not the McLain Organization.

This phenomenon is not far different from that of the Townsend pills. The object of these affairs, as with the pills, is to raise money. This is best done, now, on a "business" basis. The business at hand, in this instance is providing recreation. And to this business local Townsend leaders apply themselves.

Summary and Conclusions: The Process and Product of Adaptation to Decline

In the ascendant phases, when social forces press for reconstruction and changes are still in the offing, the concern of leaders and members of social movements alike is with those things that must be done to translate discontent into effective and concerted action. An evident condition of this orientation is discontent itself. In turn, this discontent must be supplied or renewed by social forces which, it must be believed, can be ameliorated by banding together. These provide the dynamic of value-oriented social movements, as well as the characteristic missions with which their organized arms become identified.

When the movements themselves lose impetus through a shift in the constellation of social forces, their organized arms are deprived of conditions necessary to sustain them in their original form. But organizations are not necessarily dissolved by the abatement of the forces initially conjoining to produce them. They may gain a certain degree of autonomy from their bases and continue to exist. We will expect, however, that the abatement of the particular constellation of social forces giving rise to the movement will have important consequences for the remaining structure. The most general of these is, perhaps, increasing lack of public concern for the organizational mission. This is reflected in the ending of public discussion of the issues which the organization represents or, perhaps better put, with these issues in the frame of reference that they are placed by organizational representatives. Within the organization, the abatement of social forces spells dropping membership and, more serious in the long run, the end of effective recruitment. This latter may be reinforced by the development of alternative organizational structures competing for the same potential membership. The end of recruitment is quickly transformed into financial difficulty. Where the organization has been geared to financial support from its own adherents, this last consequence will be especially crucial.

The organized arms of declining social movements will tend to adapt to these changed conditions in characteristic ways. We can broadly describe this adaptation by asserting that the dominating orientation of leaders and members shifts *from the implementation of the values the organization is taken to represent* (by leaders, members, and public alike), *to maintaining the organizational structure as such,* even at the loss of the organization's central mission.[33] To this end, leaders will be constrained to direct action toward new issues or in new ways which will attentuate the organization's identification with the particular set of aims held to be central to it. In this process, the locus of issue-selection will tend to move outside the organization, to alternative leaderships who highlighted the growing irrelevance to most of the traditional central mission. Presumably, a new mission may be found.[34] Where this is not the case, leaders will be forced to search out new means of financing as the traditional mode of appeal falls on fewer and deafer ears. In this process, members, and especially potential members, will cease to be regarded as "converts" and will come to be seen as "customers." Finally, membership activities, initiated in a context of declining public interest

33. We do not mean to indicate that leaders do not at all times perform maintenance functions. The crucial issues are what they must do, under changed conditions, to accomplish this and the explicitness with which the function is carried out.

34. This seems unlikely. It would seem to involve, as a minimum, a shift in the organization's core membership, highly identified with the central mission; as well as a shift in perspective that most leaderships seem unable to make. Further, the identification of the organization with its traditional mission by prospective members is almost assured by the actions of alternative leaders competing for this same social base.

to support a faltering organization, will work to turn what were once the incidental rewards of participation into its only meaning. This last, by altering the basis for whatever recruitment may take place, would seem to insure that the organization, if it continues to exist, will be changed from a value-implementing agency to a recreation facility. In sum, the organizational character will stand transformed.

b) CHANGE IN SOCIAL STRUCTURE

MARTHA STURM WHITE

Social Class, Child Rearing Practices, and Child Behavior

SEVERAL recent studies have raised interesting questions about the relation of social class position to child-rearing practices. In particular there have been some challenges to the study reported on by Ericson and by Davis and Havighurst.[1] This study, carried out in Chicago in the

Reprinted from American Sociological Review, *December, 1957, pp. 704-712, with the permission of the author and the journal.*

This investigation was supported by research grants, MH 208 (C2) and M-836 (MH 1), from the National Institute of Mental Health of the National Institutes of Health, Public Health Service. The data were gathered under the direction of Frances Orr at Stanford University. The author was principal investigator for the latter grant.

1. Martha C. Ericson, "Social Status and Child Rearing Practices," in T. M. Newcomb and Eugene L. Hartley (eds.), *Readings in Social Psychology*, New York: Holt, Rinehart, Winston, pp. 494-501; A. Davis and R. J. Havighurst, "Social Class and Color Differences in Child Rearing," *American Sociological Review*, 11 (December, 1946), pp. 698-710. See also Robert J. Havighurst and Allison Davis, "A Comparison of the

early 1940's, found the middle class to be generally more severe in weaning and toilet training, and to restrict and put more demands upon the child. Later studies[2] have found several differences, primarily in the direction of more permissiveness by middle class mothers than the Chicago study described.

What are the causes of these differences? Are the samples not comparable? Are there regional differences? Or have mothers in different social class positions changed their child-rearing practices during the intervening decade? The study reported here pertains to these questions. During the first half of 1953, a group of mothers and their children were interviewed on two occasions in a study on the effects of sibling birth. An approximately equal number of middle- and working-class families were included, so that it was possible to test several social class hypotheses.

The two hypotheses reported on in this article are: (1) child-rearing practices have changed since the earlier studies were made; (2) these changes are a result of the different reference groups used by the middle- and working-class mothers.

Comments on the changing fashions in child rearing are common in popular literature, particularly comments on the increase in permissiveness, and it is possible that these remarks are a reflection of changes in practice. It is of course difficult to demonstrate a change when knowledge of prior conditions is scanty. Davis and Havighurst, for example, stress the fact that theirs is not a representative sample. However, it has frequently been taken as representative of child training practices of the time,[3] and since we have no contrary knowledge, it will be accepted as such here. The method of testing is to compare the child training practices found in California in 1953 with those of Chicago in 1943 and of Boston in 1951-52.

How or why changes take place is another question. One possibility, tested here, is that the middle class is most responsive to new ideas in

---

Chicago and Harvard Studies of Social Class Differences in Child Rearing," *American Sociological Review,* 20 (August, 1955), pp. 438-442.

2. Ethelyn Henry Klatskin, "Shifts in Child Care Practices in Three Social Classes under an Infant Care Program of Flexible Methodology," *The American Journal of Orthopsychiatry,* 22 (January, 1952), pp. 52-61; Eleanor E. Maccoby and Patricia K. Gibbs and the Staff of the Laboratory of Human Development, Harvard University, "Methods of Child Rearing in Two Social Classes," in *Readings in Child Development* edited by W. E. Martin and Celia Burns Stendler, New York: Harcourt, Brace and World, 1954; Robert R. Sears, Eleanor E. Maccoby and Harry Levin, *Patterns of Child Rearing,* New York: Row Peterson & Co., 1957.

3. As in John W. M. Whiting and Irvin L. Child, *Child Training and Personality,* New Haven: Yale University Press, 1953, pp. 66-67.

the environment, particularly those transmitted by experts and through mass media. To use Riesman's term, they are "other directed," i.e., they tend to rely on other people (outside of the family) in their environment, and on certain kinds of authority figures.[4] Although both classes rely on mass media, the middle class is more discriminating.

Other studies have established that expert ideas on child rearing have changed from decade to decade.[5] It seems conceivable that if middle-class parents are responsive to certain sources of opinion, such as experts and other people, they also might be more apt to change their practices. On this basis, we would expect the middle class to have changed their practices since the 1943 study.

Method

The Sample. The sample consisted of 74 mothers and 74 children. All of the mothers had only one child, and the child was between 2½ and 5½ years of age. These ages were chosen so that the children would be able to talk, and would be mainly under the influence of the family rather than the school. Additional requirements were that the parents be living together and be native-born.

The data were gathered during the first half of 1953 in California in the South San Francisco Peninsula area, which does not include San Francisco itself, but a string of suburban and industrial communities stretching from San Mateo to San Jose. Approximately 15 families each came from Palo Alto, Menlo Park, and San Jose, and the remainder from adjacent towns. Although the study was conducted from Stanford University, only a few families had any connection with the university.

The larger study on stress caused by the arrival of a second child in the family[6] of which this was a part required 50 of the mothers to be expecting a second child at the time of the first interview, and the remaining 24 control families (who were not expecting a baby) to be matched on a group basis by occupation of father, neighborhood, age and sex of child. Due to the difficulties of getting such a sample that could also be interviewed over a six month interval, referrals were secured

4. David Riesman, *The Lonely Crowd*, New Haven: Yale University Press, 1950, pp. 19-23, 36-55.

5. See Martha Wolfenstein, "The Emergence of Fun Morality," in *The Journal of Social Issues*, 7 (No. 4, 1951), pp. 15-25; C. B. Stendler, "Sixty Years of Child Training Practices," *Journal of Pediatrics*, 36 (January, 1950), pp. 122-134.

6. Frances Orr, "The Reactions of Young Children to the Birth of a Sibling" (in preparation as a Genetic Psychology Monograph). More extensive information on the sample and method of obtaining it can be found here.

in a variety of ways. They came from neighbors or friends of families already in the study, from Public Health Nurses, personnel managers in industry, from maternal prenatal exercise classes, from physicians and nursery school teachers, and from school district surveys. Only 14 women, or less than 6 per cent of the total 245 contacted, were uninterested or were unwilling to be interviewed. The remainder of those not used proved to be ineligible or had moved.

The Interview. The interviewing was done in the home by two experienced psychologists. While one talked to the mother for a period of between one-and-a-half and three hours, the other "interviewed" the child in his room or in the kitchen by means of doll play, Draw-A-Man tests, and other standard situations. Standard questions were used in the mother interview with follow-up probes. Many of the questions asked were identical with those of the Boston study.[7] The replies of the mother were taken down as nearly verbatim as possible.

The Measures

Social Class. The occupation of the father in the family was rated on a Warner scale with an inter-rater reliability coefficient of .93.[8] A comparison of the occupation status of the two groups may be seen in Table 1. Groups were designated as middle or working class on the basis of an index of occupation and income. Occupation was given a weight of two, income one. The resulting distribution was divided into nine socio-economic status levels; from 1 to 4 was designated middle class and from 5 to 9, working class. Thus 36 of the families were classified as middle class, 38 as working class.

This system of class placement has the advantage of making the data comparable to the Boston study, and seems a fair approximation to the Chicago data. It also rather accurately divides the group into white-collar and blue-collar occupations. Such a gross, dichotomous classification was used tentatively, but it proved to be meaningful, not unduly distorting the underlying structure, and seemed appropriate to the size of the sample and the statistical measures used.

Mother Behavior Variables. The answers to the interview questions were coded using when possible the same codes as the Boston study. Reliabilities were computed on all, and only items on which satisfactory reliabilities (.72 or above) were found were used. No reliability rating

7. Copies of the interview and codes used in the Boston study were made available by Robert S. Sears.

8. W. Lloyd Warner, Marcia Meeker, Kenneth Eells, *Social Class in America*, Chicago: Science Research Associates, Inc., 1949, pp. 140-141.

Table 1. Socio-economic Characteristics of the Sample

	CLASS	
	Middle	*Working*
Father's occupation (Warner)		
1	15 (42%)	0
2	14 (39%)	1 (3%)
3	7 (19%)	4 (10%)
4	0	10 (26%)
5	0	17 (45%)
6 & 7	0	6 (16%)
Father's education		
Grade school	0	3
7-12 grades	2	19
Some college	34	16
Mother's education		
Grade school	0	1
7-12 grades	7	26
College or technical training	29	11
Occupation of father's father		
Middle (1-3)	26	4
Working (4-7)	10	34
Occupation of mother's father		
Middle (1-3)	22	13
Working (4-7)	14	25
Social class by self-placement		
Middle	32	13
Intermediate	1	4
Working	3	20
"None"		1
Salary		
$5000 or over	32	11
Under $5000	4	27
Age of mother		
28 or under	14	21
Over 28	22	17

was possible for personality ratings of mother and child since only one person conducted each interview; consequently these ratings were used as a supplement to the parent behavior data.

Statistical Analysis. Although other investigators have used the *t* test for comparison, preliminary study indicated that the variances were not homogeneous on several items, so that chi-square seemed more appropriate for these data. Four-fold tables were used and comparisons made of the number of middle- and working-class families above and below the median of the variable in question. The break was made at the point that most nearly divided the total group evenly. In some cases a "yes" or "no" classification was more appropriate than the median. In other cases the meaning of the scale was better served by a three-fold classification, the highs, the moderates, and the lows. In these cases such a comparison was first made. This often resulted in low cell frequencies, and the median comparison was substituted when it did no violence to the relationship as indicated by the three-fold break. The two-tailed test was used and a correction for continuity was employed, since many authorities consider it mandatory for four-fold tables, regardless of cell frequencies.[9]

Results

The comparison of middle and working class on oral behavior and feeding regimen are presented in Table 2. On the whole there are few social class differences. There are no significant differences in use of breast feeding, duration of breast feeding, age when weaning is completed, extent to which demand feeding is practiced, or severity of feeding problems. There is a very slight tendency for middle-class children to have been weaned either younger or older than lower-class children (but no difference in average age of weaning), and for middle-class infant oral regimen (an overall measure scored by a rater) to have been less severe. As in the Chicago and Boston studies, middle-class mothers report significantly more thumb-sucking. However, working-class mothers report significantly more nailbiting, or biting and chewing activity.

Table 2. Social Class Differences on Oral and Feeding Variables

	Middle No. *Total*	*Working* No. *Total*
Number of children ever breast-fed*	25/36	24/38
Breast-fed one month or less	9/36	12/38
Weaned before 9 months†	7/32	2/36
Weaned after 12 months	18/32	19/36
Weaned after 18 months‡	13/32	8/36
Self demand or child set schedule*	23/36	21/38
Some feeding problems*	12/36	17/38
Severe oral regimen	11/24	23/34
Report of child thumbsucking§	23/36	14/38
Report of child nailbiting¶	6/36	16/38
Miscellaneous oral activity	8/36	7/38
Child has or has had comfort object (blanket, etc.)	24/36	23/38

* Indicates question identical with that used in Boston study.
† $x^2 = 2.92$.
‡ $x^2 = 2.07$.
§ $x^2 = 4.62$, $p < .05$.
¶ $x^2 = 4.84$, $p < .05$.

9. For example, Don Lewis and C. J. Burke, "The Use and Misuse of the Chi-Square Test," *Psychological Bulletin*, 46 (November, 1949), pp. 433-489; Frederick Mosteller and Robert R. Bush, "Selected Quantitative Techniques," p. 314 in *Handbook of Social Psychology*, edited by Gardner Lindzey, Reading, Mass.: Addison-Wesley, 1954.

In toilet training (Table 3), no difference was found in age at which bowel training was begun, but working-class mothers were significantly more severe in toilet training.

Table 3. Social Class and Toilet Training

	Middle No. Total	Working No. Total
Below median age at which bowel training begun*	18/35	21/38
Severity of toilet training* below median†	23/36	14/38

*Indicates question identical with that used in Boston study.
†$x^2 = 4.62$, $p < .05$.

As seen in Table 4, there were no significant differences in dependency—how much the child wanted to be near mother, wanted attention, objected to separation, or was judged dependent.

Table 4. Social Class and Dependency

	Middle No. Total	Working No. Total
Dependence of child (from mother's report)*		
Lows	16/36	20/38
How much mother keeps track of child*		
Lows	12/36	13/38
Amount of attention child wants*		
Lows	20/34	17/35
Objects to separation*		
Lows	14/36	18/38
Rater's judgment of amount of dependency (based on mother's report)*		
Lows	15/36	12/38

*Indicates question identical with that used in Boston study.

When we asked the mothers about obedience training (Table 5), one rather interesting significant difference was found. If the child did not

Table 5. Social Class and Obedience

	Middle No. Total	Working No. Total
Who is stricter with child*		
Father	16/36	14/38
Mother	10/36	10/38
Does mother carry through demands or occasionally drop the subject*		
Occasionally drops subject †	23/36	12/37
Strictness in requiring obedience*		
Lows	22/34	18/35

*Indicates question identical with that used in Boston study.
†$x^2 = 6.36$, $p < .02$.

do what was asked, middle-class mothers were significantly more inclined to drop the subject occasionally. However, there was no difference when they were asked if they expected immediate obedience. More mothers in both groups say the father is more strict than they, but there is no class difference.

In an area that might be described as mother's responsiveness to the child, Table 6, there was one significant difference—middle-class mothers

Table 6. Social Class and Mother's Responsiveness to Child

	Middle No. Total	Working No. Total
Tendency to pick up baby when he cried†		
Lows	16/36	27/38
Amount of fun taking care of baby		
Lows	23/36	22/38
Warmth or demonstrativeness of mother*		
Lows	22/35	18/37

*Indicates question identical with that used in Boston study.
†$x^2 = 4.58$, $p < .05$.

were more responsive to their baby's crying. They did not differ in amount of fun taking care of the baby, in the amount of demonstrativeness shown, or in how much they kept track of the child.

Several of the questions were directed at the topic of aggression. Table 7 shows that there were no differences in parents' report of

Table 7. Social Class and Aggression

	Middle No. Total	Working No. Total
Parent demands for aggression against other children*		
Lows	17/35	24/37
Extent parent encouraged child to fight back*		
Lows	9/28	12/32
Amount of fighting with other children		
Lows†	17/32	10/32
Amount of aggression within the home*		
Lows	11/36	12/38
Permissiveness for aggression against parents*		
Lows ‡	8/36	24/37
Severity of punishment for aggression against parents*		
Lows	21/34	16/34

*Indicates question identical with that used in Boston study.
†$x^2 = 2.50$, $p < .20$.
‡$x^2 = 12.22$, $p < .001$.

amount of aggression in the home, in their demands for aggression against other children, or in how much the child was encouraged to fight back. One highly significant difference was in permissiveness towards aggression against parents. Middle-class women were consistently above the median in feeling that expression of aggression should be allowed. There are some tendencies for the working-class children to be more severely punished for aggression against the parent, and to be reported as fighting more with other children.

Did these differences in training methods result in any differences among the children? Practically no class differences were found in tests (such as ability to delay gratification, Draw-A-Man), personality ratings, or aggression in doll play.[10]

Although there was no class difference on source of ideas about child rearing, the most frequently named source was the mother herself—her own ideas, her common sense, her trial and error. There was no class difference between mothers mentioning reading newspapers or magazines, but there was a significant difference if they mentioned a specific book by an expert (e.g., Spock or Gesell) rather than newspaper or magazine articles. Middle-class mothers mention the expert books more. They also mentioned other people or friends significantly more often as a source of ideas. There were slightly more middle-class women who got ideas from child-rearing authorities such as doctors or nursery in-

Table 8. Social Class and Sources of Ideas about Child-Rearing

	Middle N = 35	*Working* N = 36	x^2	p
Expert book (e.g. Spock, Gesell)	15	6	4.30	< .03*
"Reading" (newspapers, magazines)	12	13		
Authorities (physicians, nursery teachers)	8	3	1.82	< .10*
Class in child rearing	11	6	1.26	< .10*
Friends, "other people in the neighborhood"	16	8	3.02	< .05*
Own ideas, "just common sense"	25	22		
Learn from the child	3	2		
Husband	5	5		
Relatives	4	6		
Own childhood				
Positive feeling	6	9		
			2.34	< .20
Negative or mixed feelings	9	3		
Total	114	83		

*One-tail tests, since direction of differences was predicted.

structors, and from parent education classes with other mothers. Although similar numbers of working- and middle-class mothers mention their own childhoods as sources of ideas, middle-class mothers more

10. One of the most interesting differences was found on the second visit, four months later, when the children were rated on their change in psychological health. They could be rated as better, same, or worse. The middle-class children were most frequently rated better or same, while the working-class children were worse or same. The difference was highly significant.

often mention practices used by their parents which they would modify or reject. Many more sources of ideas were mentioned by the middle-class mothers.

A number of questions in the interview were designed to extract explanatory concepts, as indicators of the mothers' frames of reference, goals, and personalities. They will not be developed in this paper, but some of the raw class differences are of interest.

When mothers were asked what kind of person they wanted their child to be, they tended to answer in terms of five general categories—they wanted him to be happy, well-adjusted, a nice or good person, independent, or liked. There were class differences on two of these. More middle-class mothers said well adjusted, and more working-class mothers said a nice or good child. There were no differences in the degree to which the mothers saw themselves as similar to others in strictness, whether they perceived themselves as similar to their own parents in strictness or in sympathetic understanding, the aspects of parenthood they found most and least enjoyable, or in their own self descriptions, except that working-class women more often spontaneously mentioned that they were neat.

The mothers were also rated by the interviewer on a number of personality variables. Middle-class mothers were significantly more secure, independent, and dominant. There was a tendency for them to be more controlled, but no differences in ratings of potential anxiety, hostility, ability to express affect, aggression, constriction, ability to accept dependency, or ability to accept aggression.

Discussion

These results may be compared to those found in Chicago and in Boston (see Table 9). The main topics which all three studies had in common are feeding and toilet training.

In general the results are more in accord with those obtained in 1951-52 in Boston than those of 1943 in Chicago. Of five variables on which the Chicago study found class differences, we found no difference. Of fourteen variables also used in the Boston study, we found essentially the same results on eleven, and slightly different results on three. Considering the small sample size, and the conservatism of the statistical test, this is remarkable agreement. In addition, the over-all picture of the middle class as more permissive and less demanding of the child is in general agreement with the Boston study, rather than with the Chicago data.

The relevant question is, of course, whether these differences indicate changes in child-rearing over the decade, or whether they are artifacts

Table 9. Extent of Agreement between the Three Studies of Social Class Differences

California Social Class Findings	AGREEMENT WITH FINDINGS Chicago 1943	Boston 1951-52
1. No class difference in per cent ever breast fed	Agree	Agree
2. No class difference in median duration of breast feeding (Calif. sample: Middle—2.5 mon.; Working—1.5 mon.)	Agree	Agree
3. No difference in median age at completion of weaning (Calif. sample: Middle—13.9 mon.; Working—12.8 mon.)	Disagree	Agree
4. No difference in number of children bottle or breast fed after 12 months	Disagree	
5. No difference in per cent of infants fed when hungry	Disagree	
6. No difference in strictness of scheduling of feeding		Agree
7. Middle class reported more thumbsucking	Agree	
8. No difference in age at which bowel training begun	Disagree	Agree
9. Working class more severe in toilet training	Agree	Agree
10. No difference in demonstrativeness of affection		Agree
11. No difference in which parent is stricter with child		Agree
12. No difference in strictness in requiring obedience		Agree
13. No difference in how much mother keeps track of child		Disagree
14. Middle-class mothers report more permissiveness for aggression against parents		Agree
15. No difference in how much parent encourages child to fight back if attacked		Agree
16. No difference in permission for aggression against other children (Question may not be comparable for Chicago)	Disagree	Disagree
17. No difference in severity of punishment for aggression against parents (Slight difference in same direction as Boston study, but not significant)		Disagree

of the methods and samples used. Havinghurst and Davis have suggested that the differences may be due to sample differences, such as ethnic or religious differences, occupational classification, or regional characteristics of the country. In regard to ethnic and religious differences, the California sample had more native-born grandparents than either the Boston or Chicago studies, and there are probably as many or more Catholics as in the Boston study[11] and fewer Jewish families. We cannot say that ethnic and religious differences are not responsible for the Chicago-Boston differences, but the fact that our sample seems to be different from the Boston sample in having more native-born grandparents, more Catholics, and fewer Jews—and yet yields fairly similar results—makes less plausible any explanation depending upon these factors.

The occupational composition of the samples is not so similar as might be desired; the Boston sample contains fewer families from the lowest socio-economic levels than does the Chicago study, and there are still fewer in the California sample. Comparability of the working-class

11. Contrary to Havighurst and Davis, *op. cit.* (1955), p. 439, Maccoby reports in a personal communication that the Boston sample does contain Catholic children, since many do not start in parochial schools until the first grade.

samples is, therefore, questionable, but the middle-class samples in the three studies seem to be reasonably comparable, and it is here that some of the greatest differences in findings occur. Regional differences seem a less likely explanation because similar practices to those in Massachusetts were found in California within a two-year period.

Still another possibility is that our sample might contain so many women with upward mobile aspirations, even though objectively classified as working class, that class differences might be obliterated. If so, this would account for lack of agreement with the Chicago data. We were able to check this hypothesis since our sample was asked the class they thought of themselves as belonging to—upper, lower, working, or middle. By comparing those who subjectively identify themselves as middle and working, we have one possible method of eliminating upward-mobile members of the working class from that group. There are some differences when this comparison, rather than the objective classification, is used, but the trend is still the same. In some cases, class differences are heightened.

One possible source of bias remains: both the Boston and California samples contain largely suburban respondents, families who prefer to live in residential areas and surrounding smaller towns rather than a metropolitan city. This may well be a point of difference from the Chicago sample.

This still leaves open the hypothesis that changes in child-rearing have taken place, and that differences in reference sources of the two social classes account for the differences in practices. As had been predicted, the reference sources for the two classes are different. The middle-class mothers refer to more sources and to specific experts such as Spock; they are attentive to what friends and other mothers do. The working-class mothers are more diffuse in approach; they "read" but no one author in particular; they seem to dip less into the larger cultural mainstream than into their own inclinations and upbringing.

Several problems present themselves before the difference in reference groups can be accepted as the cause of the differences in child-rearing. The first is that this is only a partial test of the reference group hypothesis. Comparative or standard setting reference groups have been studied rather than those with a normative function.[12] It may be that the latter are more relevant.

Secondly, although the causal relationship is plausible, it has not actually been demonstrated. It is not impossible that some other factor is responsible for the use of certain child-rearing practices and choice

12. Harold H. Kelly, "Two Functions of Reference Groups," in *Readings in Social Psychology*, edited by Guy E. Swanson, T. M. Newcomb, and Eugene H. Hartley, New York: Holt, Rinehart, Winston, 1952, pp. 410-414.

of reference sources. Some such factors, primarily personality variables, are suggested by the data. These are being tested and will be reported on later.

Verification of the reference group hypothesis would still not constitute evidence that a real change in practice from 1943 to 1953 had taken place.[13] Actually, this can never be demonstrated unless additional data from these years are available. If social class behavior does indeed change over time, future studies should be expected to be *unable* to replicate these results. If similar results are obtained after a ten year period, this would be evidence against the hypothesis. If both the change and reference source hypotheses are true, then future practices of the suburban middle class should be in accord with what is being said then (or a few years earlier) in the child-rearing literature and sources of the time. These sources, incidentally, may also change.

The fact that no differences were found in the children themselves is of some interest. It may be that the measures used were insensitive. However, some of the same measures were useful and sensitive in the part of the study dealing with reaction to the birth of a sibling. It may well be that it takes longer than three or five years for class differences in the socializing process to make their mark. Perhaps it is because the majority of items reported here represent the mothers' *perceptions* of what they and the child do, and may not necessarily be descriptive of their true behavior. If the latter is so, it should be remembered that class differences in perception are an aspect of behavior worthy of study.

Summary

Thirty-six middle-class and 38 working-class mothers were interviewed in 1953 about their child-rearing practices. Significant differences

13. Indirect supporting evidence comes from a study of Evelyn Millis Duvall, "Conceptions of Parenthood," *American Journal of Sociology*, 52 (November, 1946), pp. 193-203. She found two styles of child-rearing which she called *traditional*, characterized by respect and obedience, and *developmental*, characterized by emphasis on growth and development. The traditional way of thinking was more characteristic of mothers who had a child five years or older, and the developmental of those who had a child under five years. She explained this in terms of the experience of the mother—those more experienced were more strict and less flexible. However, in the light of our change hypothesis, the difference might be explained by when the mother raised the children. Those with younger children might have been more influenced by newer ideas of the 1940's while the mothers with older children might have absorbed ideas current in the late 1930's.

A study which failed to find expected changes is reported by Charles E. Ramsey and Lowry Nelson, "Change in Values and Attitudes toward the Family," *American Sociological Review*, 21 (October, 1956), pp. 605-609.

were found in the following: middle-class mothers were less severe in toilet training, permitted more aggression against the parents, were more responsive to the baby's crying, less often carried through when they told a child to do something, reported more thumbsucking and less nail-biting. The middle-class mothers more often mentioned experts, other mothers, and friends as their sources of ideas on child-rearing. The data show far more agreement with the Boston study of 1951-52 than with the Chicago study of a decade earlier.

The available evidence is consistent with the notion that a change in child-rearing practices has taken place, and that this change is due to the different reference groups used by the two classes. However, the casual connection of the latter relationship awaits further verification.

RUSSELL MIDDLETON
and SNELL PUTNEY

Dominance in Decisions in the Family: Race and Class Differences

THE locus of power within the family is an important variable in family structure, an indication of which is dominance in making decisions. Idiosyncratic factors affect dominance in any individual couple, but among a group of families cultural or subcultural influences establish typical patterns. Thus, for example, it is reported that in Navaho culture the wife generally dominates in decisions, whereas among the Mormons it is the husband.[1]

Reprinted from "Dominance in Decisions in the Family: Race and Class Differences," by Russell Middleton and Snell Putney, The American Journal of Sociology, *May, 1960, pp. 605-609, by permission of The University of Chicago Press.*

Financial support for this study was provided by the Florida State University Research Council. We are indebted to Robert H. Smith, of Florida A & M University, who served as consultant and aided greatly in the collection of the data.

1. Fred L. Strodtbeck, "Husband-Wife Interaction over Revealed Differences," *American Sociological Review,* XVI (August, 1951), 468-73.

The making of decisions in a family may be conceptualized along a continuum from the matriarchal, through the equalitarian, to the patriarchal. The question of where the typical American family would be located on it has been the subject of considerable speculation but of comparatively little systematic research. Particularly lacking is research explicitly relating to differences in marital dominance among the subcultures in American society, for example, racial and social class groupings. The available literature—much of it impressionistic—suggests that the American Negro family tends to be matriarchal because of the important economic role of the wife and the family instability, traditional since slavery times.[2] White families, on the other hand, have a patriarchal tradition deriving from Europe. There is some evidence within both racial groups that the middle-class families have shifted to equalitarianism and that the working-class families remain closer to tradition.[3]

On the basis of the literature, then, we would expect to find that families of professionals, whether white or Negro, would reflect their middle-class orientation by being generally equalitarian in decisions. Workers, somewhat more removed from middle-class values, might be expected to remain closer to their traditions—matriarchal among Negro workers and patriarchal among white workers.

This paper reports a research project designed to determine whether or not these groups differ in dominance in family decisions, as predicted from the literature. College professors were selected to represent the professional middle class, and skilled workers to represent the working class.

We chose to observe dominance in the making of decisions rather than to rely upon self-appraisals. For both practical and theoretical reasons minor decisions of daily life, rather than crises, were selected for study.[4] In order to observe dominance in the making of minor decisions,

---

2. Maurice Davie, *Negroes in American Society* (New York: McGraw-Hill Book Co., 1949), pp. 207-9; St. Clair Drake and Horace R. Cayton, *Black Metropolis* (New York: Harcourt, Brace & World, 1945), pp. 582-83; E. Franklin Frazier, *The Negro Family in the United States* (Chicago: University of Chicago Press, 1939), pp. 125-45, 438-40; Charles S. Johnson, *Growing Up in the Black Belt* (Washington, D. C.: American Council on Education, 1941), pp. 59, 80; Charles E. King, "The Negro Maternal Family: A Product of an Economic and a Culture System," *Social Forces*, XXIV (October, 1945), 100-104; Hortense Powdermaker, *After Freedom* (New York: Viking Press, 1939), pp. 145-46; and Frances J. Woods, *Cultural Values of American Ethnic Groups* (New York: Harper & Bros., 1956), pp. 242-45.

3. Frazier, *op. cit.*, p. 439.

4. Many of the questions on which the subjects reached joint decisions were related to major problems. For example, "If you were buying a house, would you prefer to buy a small new house or a larger but older house costing the same amount?"

a modification of the technique used by Strodtbeck was developed.[5] A questionnaire seeking opinions on subjects of common family interest was filled out by each husband and wife individually. Included were questions such as the following: "Should toilet-training for a child begin before he is one year old?" "Should a couple that is getting married ask their friends for silver as wedding gifts or practical things, such as towels, sheets, and dishes?" "When friends come over to your house in the evening would you prefer to watch television or just sit and talk?" "If it becomes necessary to speak to your neighbors about their child's behavior, is it better for the husband or the wife to do it?" The questionnaire included fifteen questions in each of four areas: child care, purchases and living standards, recreation, and role attitudes; the items were selected following a pretest to determine those most likely to elicit disagreement.

After husband and wife had filled out the questionnaire individually, they were requested to fill it out a second time jointly, giving opinions "as a family." The number of disagreements on the individual questionnaires was then tabulated, and the proportion of the disagreements which were resolved in favor of the position originally taken by the husband was computed. This proportion was taken as a measure of position along the continuum between matriarchy and patriarchy.

In Strodtbeck's original technique there was some possibility that the partner with the most information would appear dominant regardless of the usual pattern of interaction.[6] In order to avoid this danger, all our questions concerned judgments of value or preference rather than matters of fact on which one partner might have more information.

Forty couples served as subjects for the study, ten from each of the following: white college professors, Negro college professors, white skilled workers, and Negro skilled workers. The subjects were brought together in homogeneous groups to promote a relaxed atmosphere and sense of anonymity. Each couple was paid a small sum.

The selection of subjects began with construction of four mailing lists, as far as possible random selections from the universes defined by the study. Final selection of subjects was made from those who responded to the mailed invitation. All subjects selected were American-born, had

---

However, deciding what their joint answer to this question will be in the experiment, as opposed to real life, is a minor decision comparable to many daily decisions.

5. Strodtbeck, *op. cit.*

6. Strodtbeck's subjects were instructed to pick which of three families with whom they were acquainted was most ambitious, had the happiest children, etc. The danger is that one partner may be less well acquainted with the other couple and hence may defer to the other partner's greater knowledge even though he is ordinarily dominant.

at least one child, had been married at least two years, were between the ages of twenty-five and forty-nine in the case of males and twenty and forty-four in the case of females, and were residents of the same small southern city. In addition, the groups were matched on mean years of marriage, mean age of husband, and mean age of wife. The matching was designed to control variables independent of race and class (Table 1).[7] The only statistically significant difference among the samples is between the mean ages of husbands for white professors and Negro skilled workers.[8]

Table 1. Characteristics of the Sample

Sample Group	Mean Years of Marriage	Mean Age of Husband	Mean Age of Wife
White professors	9.5	37.0	32.0
White workers	9.2	35.3	29.2
Negro professors	9.3	34.7	30.2
Negro workers	9.6	33.0	30.1
All couples	9.4	35.0	30.4
No. of couples	40.0	40.0	40.0

Statistical significance of the differences in dominance among the four groups was tested with the Mann-Whitney *U* Test.[9] The procedure involves ranking the couples along the continuum of dominance and testing the null hypothesis that the two groups being compared have the same distribution.

Racial and Occupational Differences

Contrary to the expectation that the racial and occupational groups would occupy different points along the continuum from matriarchy to patriarchy, no differences significant at the .05 level were discovered

7. Other characteristics such as number of children, employment of wife, and education were not matched, since these variables are not independent of socioeconomic position.

8. Although the resulting samples suffer the disadvantages of self-selection and partial matching, they may be assumed to be considerably more representative than the samples used in typical small-group research.

9. The *t* test was not used, since it cannot be justified with a measuring instrument which yields only ordinal measurement. The Mann-Whitney *U* Test is approximately as powerful for moderate or larger samples, with the advantage of being nonparametric and appropriate for use with ordinal measurement (see Sidney Siegel, *Nonparametric Statistics for the Behavioral Sciences* [New York: McGraw-Hill Book Co., 1956], pp. 116-27).

among the four samples, or between all whites compared to all Negroes, or between all professors compared to all skilled workers (Table 2). Although the probability of B error cannot be computed, a relatively powerful statistical test was used on the small differences observed, and

Table 2. Dominance in Decisions by Race and Occupation

Percentage of Decisions Won by Husbands	PERCENTAGE OF COUPLES White Professors	White Workers	Negro Professors	Negro Workers	Total
0- 32 (matriarchal)	20	20	....	20	15
33- 67 (equalitarian)	60	70	90	80	75
68-100 (patriarchal)	20	10	10	....	10
Total	100	100	100	100	100
No. of couples	10	10	10	10	40

it is probably safe to conclude that the null hypothesis should be accepted. Thus we find no evidence that whites and Negroes, professors and skilled workers, differ as to which spouse dominates in the making of daily decisions. Contrary to the literature, our data suggest that all these groups are predominantly equalitarian. In view of this, it would be interesting to conduct further investigations with lower-lower class whites and Negroes to see whether they deviated from the predominant equalitarian pattern.

The pattern of equalitarianism is essentially unchanged when the disagreements are broken down into the four areas of the questionnaire (Table 3). The proportion of disagreements won by the husband was

Table 3. Percentage of Disputed Decisions Won by Husband, by Race, Occupation, and Problem

Problem Area	White Professors	White Workers	Negro Professors	Negro Workers	Total
Child care	35.6	48.1	56.6	48.8	47.7
Purchases and living standards	64.1	53.8	41.0	46.0	50.9
Recreation	58.6	40.0	54.7	57.1	53.8
Role attitudes	47.4	38.1	58.7	54.5	49.7
Total	50.3	45.6	53.4	51.4	50.4
No. of decisions	151	160	191	175	677

not greater than .64 or less than .36 in any area or for any group. Only one of these differences is significant at the .05 level: the tendency of the families of white professors to be more patriarchal in making decisions concerning purchases and living standards than the families of Negro professors.[10] Thus, although over-all differences were lacking, there is

10. The difference between all whites and all Negroes was also significant at the .05 level in this area, but, since the difference between the white and Negro skilled

some evidence of specific differences. This gives some support to the original hypothesis of racial differences, although the difference was observed in only one area and between white and Negro professionals rather than white and Negro workers. But this lone significant difference should be interpreted with caution. Of the twenty-four tests of significance computed, at least one could have been expected to reach significance and the .05 level by pure chance. Nevertheless, the differences are larger when the data are broken down into separate areas. Therefore there is a greater possibility of B error in accepting the null hypothesis that dominance in the four samples does not differ in specific areas. Further research might be made on the hypothesis that, although, in general, there may be no differences in dominance among white and Negro professors and skilled workers, differences may exist between them in specific areas. The present study, however, does not support the hypothesis that differences exist.

The Working Wife

Previous research has suggested that the employment of the wife increases her importance in family decisions.[11] Our data permit a comparison of the relative dominance in decisions of working and non-working wives among the forty couples,[12] 65 per cent of the wives were employed outside the home, and 35 per cent were not (Table 4). The difference in dominance between working wives and non-working wives

workers was small, this result may be attributed to the difference between the two groups of professors rather than the racial differnces.

11. Robert O. Blood, Jr., and Robert L. Hamblin, "The Effect of the Wife's Employment on the Family Power Structure," *Social Forces*, XXXVI (May, 1958), 347-52; David M. Heer, "Dominance and the Working Wife," *Social Forces* XXXVI (May, 1958), 341-47.

12. The four samples were not matched on proportion of working wives. Had they been, atypical groups would have been selected. Employment of the wife, our sample lists indicated, is simply a characteristic of the families of Negro professors—at least in the Deep South. It would have been very difficult to generalize to this group from a sample which had been selected to match the much lower rate of wife employment among the white professors. Thus generalization of the findings was facilitated by leaving employment of wives uncontrolled. The assessment of the relative importance of variables such as a race and the employment of the wife in determining patterns of dominance was, however, more difficult. It is entirely possible that subcultural differences between the races might introduce a predisposition toward matriarchy, for example, which was canceled out by a predisposition toward patriarchy related to the employment of wives. Our samples were too small to permit partialing in an effort to investigate such possibilities. But the intent of the study was to investigate whether or not the subcultural groups, as they actually are, differed in dominance, and the sample was designed toward this end.

Table 4. Dominance in Decisions by Employment of Wife

Percentage of Decisions Won by Husband	PERCENTAGE OF COUPLES Wife Employed	Wife Not Employed	Total
0- 32 (matriarchal)	7.7	28.6	15.0
33- 67 (equalitarian)	76.9	71.4	75.0
68-100 (patriarchal)	15.4	....	10.0
Total	100.0	100.0	100.0
No. of couples	26	14	40

is significant well beyond the .05 level, but in a surprising direction: families in which the wife works are significantly *more* patriarchal in decisions than those in which the wife does not work in direct contradiction to findings of previous studies.

If the data are again broken down into the four areas in which questions were asked, the working wives are found to be significantly less dominant, at the .05 level, in three of the four—child-rearing, recreation, and role attitudes. They do not differ significantly from the non-working wives in decisions about purchases and living standards, where a difference might be expected, since the working wife contributes to the family income. In the other three areas the working wives are less dominant than the non-working wives.

Since the difference between families with working wives and those with non-working wives was clearly significant when other differences were not, it is unlikely that this is a spurious result arising from other differences between the groups. However, it is difficult to interpret. It is worth noting that previous studies were based on the subjects' statements rather than observation of their behavior. Perhaps we have here another example of people saying one thing and doing another.

A possible interpretation of our findings would be that husbands whose wives do not work tend to leave minor family decisions largely to the wife. Husbands of working wives, on the other hand, almost necessarily participate to a much greater degree in home life and might, therefore, be expected to play a greater role in minor family decisions. Further research might investigate the validity of this post factum interpretation.

NATHAN A. SCOTT, JR.

The Broken Center: A Definition of the Crisis of Values in Modern Literature

Things fall apart; the centre cannot hold;
Mere anarchy is loosed upon the world
....
The best lack all conviction, while the worst
Are full of passionate intensity.

—WILLIAM BUTLER YEATS, "The Second Coming."[1]

We need a theme? then let that be our theme:
that we, poor grovellers between faith and doubt,
the sun and north star lost, and compass out,
the heart's weak engine all but stopped, the time
timeless in this chaos of our wills—
that we must ask a theme, something to think,
something to say, between dawn and dark,
something to hold to, something to love.

—CONRAD AIKEN, *Time in the Rock.*[2]

ONE of the characters in the dialogue on which Richard Chase has based his recent brilliant book *The Democratic Vista* gives me a kind of text for this essay when he remarks: ". . . it seems that the greatest

Reprinted from Symbolism in Religion and Literature *(1960), pp. 178-202, by permission of the author, the editor, Rollo May, and the publisher, George Braziller, Inc.*

1. William Butler Yeats, "The Second Coming," from *The Collected Poems of W. B. Yeats,* copyright 1924 by The Macmillan Company (New York) and used with their permission and that of Macmillan & Co. Ltd. (London). Copyright 1952 by Bertha Georgie Yeats.

2. Conrad Aiken, *Time in the Rock* (New York: Charles Scribner's Sons, 1936), p. 2. Copyright 1936 by Conrad Aiken.

writers of the first half of the twentieth century lived in a high, tense world of strenuous and difficult metaphysics, moral doctrine, political ideology, and religious feeling."[3] The young man who says this is a graduate student of literature who, together with his wife and two children, is spending a late summer weekend on the Massachusetts coast in the home of a professor at his university, and it is to his senior friend that he offers this observation. He is perhaps being characteristic of his generation when he argues that "it is no longer possible to share" the intellectual and spiritual preoccupations of the great heroes of the modern tradition, of people like Eliot and Joyce and Pound. But though this may be a foreclosure that is too narrow and too premature, he does, nevertheless, identify accurately what is the most important distinguishing feature of the great classic tradition of modern letters, for that is most certainly a tradition that posits "a high, tense world of strenuous and difficult metaphysics . . . and religious feeling."

When we think, for example, of Mann and Lawrence and Kafka and Faulkner, it becomes immediately apparent that these are writers not all of whom are easily to be sheltered under the same umbrella; their methods of practicing the arts of fiction and the various gestures they make toward reality all represent the amazing differentiation of attitude and language that is a chief hallmark of literary art in our period. But, despite this multifariousness of creative technique and of fundamental point of view, they are writers whom we feel impelled to regard as constituting in some sense a genuine community and a unitary tradition. And this is a view that we take because these are writers whose own most emphatic insistence has been upon the fact of their being unsustained by any vital and helpful traditions; the community they form has been rooted, in other words, in their common awareness of their isolation. Nor has their isolation been primarily an affair of the artist's tenuous position in the polity of modern society. That position, to be sure, has been something uncertain and problematic, and the artist's social marginality has at times undoubtedly greatly added to his unease. But what for him has most fundamentally given to life the aspect of crisis has been that recession of faith and that erosion of the religious terrain announced by Nietzsche in the nineteenth century, and, in our own time, by Sartre.

In such an age, when all is in doubt and when, as Yeats says, "Things fall apart" and "the centre cannot hold"—in such an age, the philosopher may not be utterly crippled, if he is willing to have his vocation confined to the analysis of nothing more than the structure of sentences; and the social critic can always be kept busy in notating the tics and the

3. Richard Chase, *The Democratic Vista: A Dialogue on Life and Letters in Contemporary America* (New York: Doubleday, 1958), p. 16.

spasms that are the signs of our distress. And in similar reduced ways the other custodians of the cultural life may in some manner continue to function when overtaken by a late bad time. But when the traditional premises regarding the radical significance of things have collapsed and when there is no longer any robust common faith to orient the imaginative faculties of men with respect to the ultimate mysteries of existence—when, in other words, the basic presuppositions of a culture have become just yawning question marks, then the literary artist is thrust upon a most desolate frontier indeed. For, though he is sometimes spoken of as presiding over an act of *communication*, this is a vulgar version of his role that could pass muster only in an age of television and of what is called "the mass-audience." The writer may, to be sure, take his stand before a microphone and speak to a crowd in whose fate he is not at all implicated; and, when he does this, it may be that he plays a part in something that might be called a process of *communication*. Yet, when this is his position, surely it is impossible for anything to be "shared, in a new and illuminating intensity of awareness."[4] Indeed, as Allen Tate has reminded us, the very concept of literature as *Communication* may well, in its current connotation, betoken a tragic victory of modern secularism over the human spirit.

> Our unexamined theory of literature as communication could not have appeared in an age in which communion was still possible for any appreciable majority of persons. The word communication presupposes the victory of the secularized society of means without ends. The poet, on the one hand, shouts to the public, on the other (some distance away), not the rediscovery of the common experience, but a certain pitch of sound to which the well-conditioned adrenals of humanity obligingly respond.[5]

No, Tate says, the language of *communication* may be the language of radio and television, but it is not the language which the artist seeks sensitively to supervise, for that is the language not of communication but of *communion:* it is a language into which an effort has been made to put a deep and authentic knowledge of what is involved in the life together of free men; so it is a language that invites us to re-enter what Martin Buber calls "the world of *I* and *Thou*."

Which is, of course, to say that the language of imaginative literature is not the ethically and spiritually neutral jargon of any science: it is, rather, a language which, if it is to do its proper work, needs to be heavily weighted with the beliefs, the sentiments and valuations that are the deep source in the culture of its "hum and buzz of implication"[6] and that bind the people together with ties that separate them from the

4. Allen Tate, *The Forlorn Demon* (Chicago: Henry Regnery Co., 1953), p. 13.

5. *Ibid.*, p. 12.

6. Lionel Trilling, *The Liberal Imagination* (New York: Viking Press, 1950), p. 206.

peoples of other cultures. Only when the artist's language bears this kind of freight can it be something more than a vehicle of communication: only then can it become an instrument of communion and what all art is ultimately intended to be—namely, a servant of love.

But now we are brought back to that desolate frontier on which I have said the modern writer has found himself, for what has made his position as an artist so insecure has been precisely the very great difficulty he has had in making contact with any significant body of belief that, having vital authority in our period, might furnish his imagination with the premises of its functioning and facilitate the transaction between himself and his reader. "In the profoundest human sense," said Kenneth Burke in one of his early books, "one communicates in a *weighted* vocabulary in which the weightings are shared by [one's] group as a whole."[7] But it is just at this point that modern culture has represented great privation. There is, in fact, little of anything at all of profound significance that is widely shared by modern men. The dominant dispensation has been of a scientific character, but Max Planck tells us that "there is scarcely [even] a scientific axiom that is not now-a-days denied by somebody."[8] And, outside the realm of our scientific culture, the resistant pressure offered to the relativizing tendencies of our time has been negligible indeed.

In his important book *Diagnosis of Our Time*,[9] Karl Mannheim proposes the interesting and cogent hypothesis that the despiritualization of modern life is best understood in terms of the gradual evaporation in our period of authentic "paradigmatic experience" and of those great "primordial images or archetypes" which, being formed out of this kind of experience, have directed the human enterprise in the most genuinely creative moments of cultural history. By "paradigmatic experience" Dr. Mannheim means those "basic experiences which carry more weight than others, and which are unforgettable in comparison with others that are merely passing sensations." Without experiences of this kind, he says,

> ". . . no consistent conduct, no character formation and no real human coexistence and co-operation are possible. Without them our universe of discourse loses its articulation, conduct falls to pieces, and only disconnected bits of successful behaviour patterns and fragments of adjustment to an ever-changing environment remain."

And his contention is that "paradigmatic experience," in so far as it yields some conviction as to what is radically significant, does also, in

7. Herbert Muller, *Modern Fiction* (New York: Funk and Wagnalls, 1937), p. 10.

8. Harry Slochower, *No Voice Is Wholly Lost* (New York: Creative Age Press, Inc., 1945), p. vii.

9. Karl Mannheim, *Diagnosis of Our Time* (New York: Oxford University Press, 1944), p. 146-148.

effect, create a kind of "ontological hierarchy," in accordance with which we say, " 'This is bad, this is good, this is better.' " But, of course, the whole drive of the positivistically oriented secularism of modern culture has been towards such "a neutralization of that ontological hierarchy in the world of experience" as encourages the belief that "one experience is as important as any other" and that the question of right or wrong merely concerns the most efficient environmental adjustments. So the result has been the evaporation of those "primordial images" which objectify a people's faith and provide the moral imagination with its basic premises. And when there are no "paradigmatic experiences," then nothing is any longer revealed as having decisive importance, and men are ruled by a kind of "kaleidoscopic concept of life" which, in giving an equal significance to everything, does, in effect, attribute radical significance to nothing at all. In such an age, the individual is condemned to the awful prison of his own individuality, since nothing means the same thing to any broad segment of people—and the primary fact about the human community is disclosed as being the complete collapse of anything resembling genuine community.

This is a fact which has been dramatized by much recent social criticism in its notation of the astonishing lack of drama in modern society. The life of the average megalopolitan today is ungraced by any rituals which strengthen the ties of sympathy and fellow-feeling. Nor is the civic scene complicated and enlivened by any round of celebrations and festivities comparable to the religious liturgies or the secular rites that figured so largely in the common life of earlier times. In the great cities of our day we are cave dwellers, scurrying about the urban wilderness from one vast compound to another, like "bits of paper, whirled by the cold wind";[10] and, like the members of Captain Ahab's crew, we are, as Melville says, "nearly all Islanders," none "acknowledging the common continent of men, but each *Isolato* living on a separate continent of his own."

This, then, is the intractable and unpromising reality that confronts the modern writer. Burke says that it is the artist's task to supervise a *weighted* language whose weightings are shared by the commonalty. But it has been the fate of the modern artist to live in a time when the commonalty, as anything more than a statistical assemblage of unrelated atoms, is something to be remembered only by the historical imagination. And this is why the problem of understanding modern literature so largely involves the problem of understanding the stratagems that become inevitable for the artist when history commits him to the practice of his vocation in such a vacuum.

10. T. S. Eliot, "Burnt Norton," *Four Quartets* (New York: Harcourt, Brace, and World, 1943). p. 6.

What the modern artist has needed to find are "systems of reference, acceptable to the experience of our time, by means of which he [could] give order and unity to his work."[11] This is, indeed, what the artist has always needed, and, when the circumstances of his culture have afforded a good soil for art to grow in, the ethos of his community has provided him with coordinating analogies and key metaphors and with myths and symbols which, in flowing out of the funded memories and experience of his people, could well serve him as instruments for the full evocation of the human communion. Surely it is no merely willful or sentimental nostalgia that leads us, when we roam back through the tradition, to account in these terms for the greatness of the achievement of Sophocles and Dante, of Shakespeare and Racine, or, on a far less exalted level, of, say, Madame de Lafayette or Jane Austen. In these older writers we feel a kind of freedom and a kind of security of reference that strike us as being a consequence of their having had the good fortune to live in cultures which, having a vital unity, could liberally provide those "primordial images" and "archetypes" which centralize and order the poetic imagination. These older writers were the lucky ones, for they did not have to invent ways of construing experience; they were lucky because the writer who has to expend energy on philosophical and theological enterprises before he can get his literary project under way will have squandered reserves of imaginative power that, in more favorable circumstances, would be used up in the practice of his art. And when one thinks, say, of Jane Austen in relation to the woman of our own time who wrote such a book as *Nightwood*, we cannot help but feel that the older writer was also lucky because, in receiving her ultimate terms of reference from her culture, she was relieved of any uncertainty about how to establish contact with her readers and was, therefore, enabled to make the kinds of assumptions that facilitate the poetic transaction.

This is precisely the kind of luck, however, that the writer in the modern period has not enjoyed. Inheriting no traditional and widely accepted frame of values from his culture, before his art could be steadied by some executive principle of valuation, it has been necessary for the artist to try to construct some viable system of belief for himself, by means of an effort of personal vision. He has had to be, in a sense, his own priest, his own guide, his own Virgil. He has been condemned by the cultural circumstances of his time to draw from within himself everything that forms and orders his art. The deep waters in which he

11. Stanley R. Hopper, "The Problem of Moral Isolation in Contemporary Literature." In *Spiritual Problems in Contemporary Literature*, ed. Stanley R. Hopper (New York: Harper & Brothers, 1952), p. 153.

has swum have been those of his own individual mind, and he has had to plunge deep in his search for the principles by which the anarchy of experience might be controlled and given a shape and a significance. Thus we might say that the reigning law of the modern movement in the arts has been that of the *principium individuationis*.

Indeed, all the great literature of the modern period might be said to be a literature of metaphysical isolation, for the modern artist—and this is perhaps the fundamental truth about him—has experienced a great loneliness, the kind of loneliness that is known by the soul when it has to undertake, unaided by ministries either of Church or of culture, the adventure of discovering the fundamental principles of meaning. Unquestionably, this accounts for the obscurity of so many great modern texts—of Rimbaud's *Une Saison en Enfer*, of Rilke's *Duino Elegies*, Joyce's *Finnegans Wake*, or Malcolm Lowry's *Under the Volcano*. Amidst the confusion in values of his age, the artist is attempting to invent for himself a system of attitudes and beliefs that will give meaning to his world. And it is this idiosyncrasy, this extreme individuality, of modern poetic vision that has often made our finest literature so difficult to penetrate. What has been most distinctive of the great heroes of the modern tradition is, as Stephen Spender says, that they assumed the task "of re-experiencing everything as though it had never been experienced before, and then expressing it not in terms with which traditions and education have made us familiar but in new ones minted out"[12] of their separate sensibilities. In a time when

So various
And multifoliate are our breeds of faith
That we could furnish a herbarium
With the American specimens alone[13]

the writer felt himself to be without a common background of reference which could orient and bring into a profound rapport his own imaginative faculties and those of his readers. So he has turned inward, pursuing a system of values or beliefs in the world of his own subjectivity. Thus, as Spender says,

> It becomes increasingly more difficult for the reader to understand the significance of the writer's symbols and language, without his having experienced the process of the writer's experiencing. . . . Hence a vast literature explaining texts and the circumstances of each writer's life has grown up around the modern movement.

12. Stephen Spender, *The Creative Element* (London: Hamish Hamilton, 1953), p. 176-177.

13. From *Essay on Rime*, by Karl Shapiro, p. 63. Copyright 1945 by Karl Shapiro. Reprinted by permission of Random House, Inc.

And this is a development that has tended to institutionalize the originally unique experimentations of the great pioneers and to make them, indeed, a staple of the new academic tradition—as is indicated, for example, by the notification we are given on the jacket of William York Tindall's book on Joyce that, as the publisher says, Tindall "is a member of the James Joyce Society, and has made the pilgrimage to Dublin."[14] Yet this is precisely what Joyce's work demands—membership in scholarly societies devoted to its study and foundation-sponsored tours to Dublin in search of scraps of information that may assist us in unraveling the bafflements of his incredibly complex art. For this writer "is in himself a culture and a country with myths and dialects derived from other ones."[15] And the necessity we confront, when we tackle a book like *Finnegans Wake,* is one of trying to make some sense of a vast chaotic array of notes toward what its author heroically strove to make the great modern novel.

Indeed, the Joycean experiment, however stillborn it may in part have been, does at least, in a way, succeed in stating the significant questions and in drawing attention to a fundamental dilemma of the artist in our period. For the lesson of Joyce's career teaches us that, though the artist cannot by fiat produce adequate surrogates for traditions of faith and culture no longer available to him, he can, in attempting to do so, dramatize with especial vividness the fact of the mythical vacuum in the modern period. And that is what Joyce succeeded in doing. As T. S. Eliot put the issue in his famous review of *Ulysses* in 1923:

> In using the myth, in manipulating a continuous parallel between contemporaneity and antiquity, Joyce is pursuing a method which others must pursue after him. . . . It is simply a way of controlling or ordering, of giving a shape and a significance to the immense panorama of futility and anarchy which is contemporary history.[16]

And it is the radicalism of his effort to find this shape and this significance that makes him the great exemplar of the literary artist in the modern age; he gives the age away, by which I mean that he puts us in mind of how much "the greatest writers of the first half of the twentieth century lived in a high, tense world of strenuous and difficult metaphysics . . . and religious feeling." And though they may seem to be "the more austerely religious in that [they have not often been] prejudiced

14. William York Tindall, *James Joyce* (New York: Charles Scribner's Sons, 1950).

15. Spender, *op. cit.*

16. T. E. Eliot, "Ulysses, Order and Myth." In *Critiques and Essays on Modern Fiction,* ed. John W. Aldridge (New York: Ronald Press, 1952), p. 426.

by religious belief"[17] of an orthdox sort, we should not, even so, allow their heterodoxy to obscure the authenticity of their researches into the human condition and the immense courage with which they have steered their lonely, separate courses through the spiritual void of our time.

Now it is precisely the kind of extreme self-reliance in the quest for "first principles" that I have been positing as the inescapable necessity facing the modern writer; it is precisely this that makes evident his descendance from the great Romantics of the last century. And it also makes evident the fact that the literature of the age of Joyce and Kafka is essentially a late development of the Romantic movement. Here, we must not be misled by the vigorous anti-Romanticism that informs so much of twentieth-century literature. It is true, of course, that men like Valéry, Eliot, and Pound in poetry, and Joyce and Proust in the novel, have sponsored programs of one sort or another whose aim has been to encourage a rejection of the legacy of Romanticism, with its inspirationist aesthetic, its cult of sincerity, its artlessness, and its confusions of art and religion. But, steady as this quarrel with the Romantic movement has been in our time, it is a family quarrel, and the fact remains that the great tradition of twentieth-century literature is, fundamentally, a product of the Romantic dispensation. As Robert Langbaum has recently observed,

> Whatever the difference between the literary movements of the nineteenth and twentieth centuries, they are connected . . . by their response to the same wilderness. That wilderness is the legacy of the Enlightenment, of the scientific and critical effort of the Enlightenment which, in its desire to separate fact from the values of a crumbling tradition, separated fact from all values–bequeathing a world in which fact is measurable quantity while value is man-made and illusory. Such a world offers no objective verification for just the perceptions by which men live, perceptions of beauty, goodness and spirit. It was as literature began in the latter eighteenth century to realize the dangerous implications of the scientific world-view that romanticism was born. It was born anew in at least three generations thereafter as men of genius arrived intellectually at the dead-end of the eighteenth century and then, often through a total crisis of personality, broke intellectually into the nineteenth. As literature's reaction to the eighteenth century's scientific world-view, romanticism connects the literary movement of the nineteenth and twentieth centuries.[18]

This recognition of the havoc wrought by Enlightenment iconoclasm did not lead the great English Romantics to an exacerbation of spirit so extreme as that which is often noticeable in their French and German

17. Hopper, *op. cit.*, p. 155.

18. Robert Langbaum, *The Poetry of Experience* (New York: Random House, 1957), p. 11-12.

contemporaries. We can, however, detect the signs of this unrest in Coleridge and in Wordsworth, and in Keats and Shelley. They all make us feel that for them the traditional archetypes and systems of faith had ceased to be effective any longer and that, as a result, in their dealings with the world, they were thrown back upon their own private resources. They had all felt what Keats called in *Lamia* "the touch of cold philosophy," and, as a consequence, they knew themselves to be deprived of that mythical machinery for the ordering of experience which writers in earlier periods of the tradition had been blessed in having; they knew themselves to be fated by the logic of their culture to bear, alone and unassisted, what Wordsworth called "the weight of all this unintelligible world." Thus, in works like "Tintern Abbey," the "Ode on Intimations of Immortality," "The Rime of the Ancient Mariner," "Adonais," the "Ode to the West Wind," and the "Ode to a Nightingale," these men attempted what Coleridge believed to be the poet's task, "of spreading the tone, the *atmosphere*, and with it the depth and height of the ideal world around forms, incidents, and situations, of which, for the common view, custom had bedimmed all the lustre, had dried up the sparkle and the dew drops."[19]

When we turn, however, to Continental Romanticism, particularly in France, and here not to such relatively early figures as Rousseau and Chateaubriand and Lamartine but to such later writers as Baudelaire and Rimbaud and Lautréamont—when we turn to this French Romantic tradition, we leave the elegiac temper of the English school and come to a new kind of intensity and a new kind of violence that point directly toward the *Angst*-ridden literature of the twentieth century. It was with this tradition in mind that the distinguished French critic Jacques Rivière remarked in his eaasy on "La Crise du concept de littérature" that "with Romanticism . . . the literary act began to be conceived as a kind of assault on the absolute, and its result as a revelation," the writer becoming a kind of "priest." Indeed, said Rivière, this whole literature is "a vast incantation toward the miracle."[20]

But not only does the artist working under the dispensation of Baudelaire and Lautréamont become a priest; he also becomes a kind of scientist, for wanting to rescue himself from the metaphysical void of his culture, he is so much in the grip of a passion for knowledge that the poetic process itself becomes not primarily a process of the artist's *making*, but rather a process of the artist's *discovering* the ultimate

19. S. T. Coleridge, *Biographia Literaria*, ed. J. Shawcross (London: Oxford University Press, 1907).

20. Jacques Rivière, "La crise du concept de littérature," *Nouvelle Revue Française*, 1 February, 1924.

frontiers of human existence and of there staking out his claim to dominion. Rimbaud, for example, in writing to his friend Paul Demeny, says:

> The first study for a man who wants to be a poet is the knowledge of himself, entire. He looks for his soul, inspects it, learns it. As soon as he knows it, he cultivates it: it seems simple. . . . But the soul has to be made monstrous, that's the point. . . .
>
> One must, I say, be a *seer*, make oneself a *seer*.
>
> The poet makes himself a seer through a long, a prodigious and rational disordering of *all* the senses. Every form of love, of suffering, of madness; he searches himself, he consumes all the poisons in him, keeping only their quintessences. Ineffable torture in which he will need all his faith and superhuman strength, the great criminal, the great sickman, the utterly damned, and the supreme Savant! For he arrives at the unknown! Since he has cultivated his soul—richer to begin with than any other! He arrives at the unknown: and even if, half crazed, in the end, he loses the understanding of his visions, he has seen them! Let him croak in his leap into those unutterable and innumerable things: there will come other horrible workers: they will begin at the horizons where he has succumbed.[21]

Now here we have an inner dislocation which this particular poet called a sacred disorder, but what is really signified is his having yielded to "an invasion of vertigo"[22] and lost his footing. So it is not surprising that he abandoned poetry in 1873 at the age of nineteen to spend the rest of his brief life in exotic adventure and in angry defiance of bourgeois Philistinism. Yet, despite Rimbaud's abdication from literature, his prophecy was borne out, and other laborers did come after him, "who began at the horizons where he had collapsed."[23] The particular horizon where he collapsed was the point at which his own desperate need, as an artist and as a man, for metaphysical and religious order collided with the spiritual void of the nineteenth century. And this is the precise horizon on which we may locate that great modern procession that includes, in addition to Baudelaire and Rimbaud and Lautréamont, such earlier writers as Hölderlin, Leopardi, and Vigny, and such later writers as Mallarmé, Valéry, Joyce, and Hart Crane, André Gide, André Malraux, St. John Perse, and many others. For all these, in the sense that I am claiming for the term, are Romantics: they are writers bent upon *improvising* perspectives and principles in terms of which a shape and a signifi-

21. Arthur Rimbaud, "Letters to Paul Demeny: 1871," *Prose Poems from the Illuminations*, trans. by Louise Varese (New York: New Directions, 1946), pp. xxvi-xxvii. Copyright 1946 by New Directions. Reprinted by permission of New Directions, Publishers.

22. Jacques Maritain, *Creative Inituition in Art and Poetry* (New York: Pantheon Books, 1953), p. 186, 189.

23. *Ibid.*

cance may be given to "the immense panorama" of modern experience, thus making it accessible to art. This is their passion and their chosen task, and it is their dedication to this that makes them candidates for the special kind of sainthood that the *avant-garde* has tended to produce in the modern period. In a way, they have been martyrized by the dislocations of the time, and, when we think of artists like Kafka and Hart Crane and Dylan Thomas and Malcolm Lowry, it does seem, indeed, that they have borne upon their own souls the stigmata of the bent and broken world to which they were committed by modern history.

This, therefore, is the first major observation to be made about the great classic tradition of contemporary letters: we must say that, in its tone and style and outlook, it is an incorrigibly Romantic tradition. We see this even in apparently so un-Romantic a figure as T. S. Eliot, who, to be sure, has made his way back to a classical tradition of religious faith and has found in Christian history the deepest inspiration for his work of the past twenty-five years. Yet the particular tradition of Christian faith in which Eliot has chosen to live—the tradition, say, of Origen and Dame Julian of Norwich and Jacob Boehme and St. John of the Cross—hardly strikes us as belonging to the great central tradition of Christian culture: it is very special and irregular, and its very reclamation by a contemporary Christian poet suggests that even his orthodoxy will, in its attainment, represent something of the same kind of improvisation that has tended generally to characterize the philosophic and religious stratagems of the modern artist.

But, now, a second major observation must be made of the modern tradition in literature, for we shall not fully comprehend it until we recognize it as a tradition which represents that particular late development of the Romantic movement which is an outgrowth of what Erich Kahler calls "the existentialist experience."[24] Not only, in other words, must we say that this is a Romantic literature; we must also say that it is an Existentialist literature as well. But when I denominate the central tradition in our literature as Existentialist, I do not intend to refer merely to certain recent writers, particularly in France, who have found a theoretical sanction for their vision in the doctrines of Existentialist philosophy. I use the term, rather, in a very much broader sense and intend it to define the literature of the last hundred years in which we find reflected an experience of existence as fundamentally and, perhaps even, essentially problematic.

This is an experience which it will doubtless be our first impulse to regard as having been occasioned by those ultimate exigencies in the history of the modern spirit to which Nietzsche called our attention in

24. Erich Kahler, *The Tower and the Abyss* (New York: George Braziller, Inc., 1957), pp. 168-175.

his announcement of "the death of God." But "the death of God," as a cultural fact of the modern age, is itself something whose fundamental cause, I believe, is to be sought in the "death of man" in our time, for this is the really primary fact in modern experience. What we confront, throughout the whole polity of modern society, is a tragic devitalization of the very concept of the person. The kind of life *en masse*, for example, that has been so distinctive of our period has been made possible by a system whose inner logic has necessitated a high degree of specialization in all fields of man's labor. And this, in turn, by a dreadful kind of inexorability, has accomplished what might even be said to be a mutation in human nature itself, in so far as the habit of requiring a man to justify himself by his ability to perform a special task has weakened in us the capacity to make the crucial distinction between the function and the human being who performs it. But not only has the distinction become a difficult one to make; the human act by which a man transcends his various social and economic functions has also, under the pressures of a commercialized culture, become an act that it is increasingly more difficult to perform. Many of the most thoughtful observers of modern life have noticed how the logic of a technocratic culture tends to reduce the concrete particularity of the unique human individual to a purely abstract and functional identity; and they have also noticed the gray anonymity of life that this reduction accomplishes. What every reporter on the present human condition has, indeed, to take into account is the sense men have today of being thrust into the nudity of their own isolated individual existence. Though "huddled together" in the great metropolises of the contemporary world "like dust in a heap," that which figures most prominently in their awareness is a sense of the world's vacancy, and the loss of which they are most acutely conscious is the loss of the real proximity of friends and neighbors. Life seems, as Karl Jaspers says, to have grown "indefinitely vast": it no longer has that "interlinkage" which holds it together, "so that it is not frittered away" and disintegrated into "the brief perspective of the [immediate] present."[25] A man has the function he performs for eight hours a day, and he has his bit of breathing-space somewhere in the urban or the suburban wilderness. But, as we are told in Mr. Eliot's "Choruses from 'The Rock' ":

> The desert is squeezed in the tube-train next to you,
> The desert is in the heart of your brother.[26]

---

25. Karl Jaspers, *Man in the Modern Age,* trans. by Eden and Cedar Paul (New York: Doubleday Anchor Books, 1957), p. 202.

26. T. S. Eliot, "Choruses from 'The Rock,' " *Collected Poems: 1909-1935* (New York: Harcourt, Brace, and World, 1936), p. 182.

So, though all the time we live closer and closer together in our great urban compounds, we find it more and more difficult to recognize one another or even to retain a sense of our own identities. And amidst this gray, dreary anonymity we know that we live in a world from which all the gracious marks of "presence" have been banished.

"Just as primitive man believed himself to stand face to face with demons and believed that could he but know their names he would become their master, so," says Karl Jaspers, "contemporary man [is] faced by . . . [something that is] incomprehensible, which disorders his calculations. . . . The nameless powers of Nothingness," he says, "are, in our world whence the gods have been driven forth, the analogy of the demons that confronted primitive man."[27] And this, I believe, is why men in the modern period have believed God to be silent and absent and even dead. This has been their conclusion because they have not lived out their days in real nearness to one another, and, not having known the gracious reality of "presence" in their relations with their neighbors, their imaginations have been unable to grasp the possibility of the world itself being grounded in a transcendent "Presence."

In such a world, where the human communion has been destroyed and man's condemnation is to an empty and unfertile solitude, what Gabriel Marcel calls *Presence*[28] appears to be an obsolescent relic of the past; not only does it appear that God is dead, but so too does it appear that an obituary notice is to be written memorializing the disappearance of man as well. In this "place of disaffection," as Mr. Eliot calls it, the only available dispensation seems to be that of loneliness and exile, and it is the sober acceptance of this icy alienation as the inescapable ground of human existence that constitutes that special modern sensibility which I am calling (after Erich Kahler) "the existentialist experience."

This is not an experience that is the sole property of those contemporary theorists of it whose program goes under the name of Existentialism. Their nineteenth-century predecessors were, to be sure, among the first to give it emphatic definition, and it first became a public fact in the Berlin lectures of Schelling (*Die Philosophie der Mythologie und der Offenbarung*) during the winter of 1841-1842 and in the later writings of men like Kierkegaard and Marx and Feuerbach and Nietzsche and Max Weber. But this is also an experience whose beginning is to be dated from the morning Baudelaire looked out upon the billboards of Paris—"that vast cemetery that is called a great city"—and felt an immense disgust. And not only do we find it in writers like Baudelaire

27. Karl Jaspers, *op. cit.*, p. 191.

28. Gabriel Marcel, *The Mystery of Being* (Chicago: Henry Regnery Co., 1951), vol. I, chapters IX and X; vol. II, chapter I.

and Rimbaud and Dostoievski and Strindberg, but we also find it in artists like Cézanne and Van Gogh, and the American Albert Pinkham Ryder. These were all men who belonged to that nineteenth-century vanguard of revolutionaries distinguished for the clarity and courage with which they acknowledged the bitter facts of alienation and estrangement as the central facts of modern existence. And when, as Paul Tillich says, "the nineteenth century came to an end" on 31 July 1914,[29] the existentialist experience ceased to be the experience of a sensitive minority and became the dominant experience of the age. In this century it has furnished the perspectives of the philosophic tradition established by such thinkers as Berdyaev and Shestov and Heidegger and Jaspers and Sartre and Marcel; it is the experience one feels in Stravinsky's *Pétrouchka*, in Schoenberg's *Pierrot Lunaire*, in Alban Berg's *Wozzeck*, in Bartok's *Second Quartet*, and in much of the great music of our time; and it is also the experience that has been painted into many of the canvases of such classic moderns as Picasso and Rouault and the early de Chirico, or of such recent artists as Willem de Kooning and Jackson Pollock and Hans Hofmann.

Now it is this strain of sensibility that is central in much of twentieth-century literature: it is what we recognize in such poets of verse as Rainer Maria Rilke and Hart Crane and Robert Penn Warren and Gottfried Benn and in such poets of the novel as Conrad and Kafka and Faulkner and Malraux. Indeed, as Lionel Trilling has remarked, "There is scarcely a great writer of our own day who has not addressed himself to the ontological crisis, who has not conceived of life as a struggle to be—not to live, but to be."[30] And what one feels to be formative in much of the representative literature of our period is a deep need for a deep restoration of confidence in the stoutness and reliability and essential healthiness of the things of earth. The trauma that has been suffered is the trauma that is inflicted upon the imagination when it appears that both God and man are dead.

So the narrative that is at the center of our literature is a narrative of estrangement and alienation: the story that is told is a story of our abandonment "in some blind lobby . . . or corridor of Time. . . . And in the dark," says Penn Warren, "no thread."[31] No thread. And we are given some measure of how emphatic is the insistence upon our lostness by the apocalypticism and the hyperaesthesia of the literary imagination

29. Paul Tillich, *The Courage to Be* (New Haven: Yale University Press, 1952), p. 137, 172.

30. Lionel Trilling, *The Opposing Self* (New York: Viking Press, 1955), p. 140, 88.

31. Robert Penn Warren, *Brother to Dragons* (London: Eyre and Spottiswoode, 1953), p. 7.

in our day, "its feeling," as Richard Chase says, "that no thought is permissible except an extreme thought: that every idea must be directly emblematic of concentration camps, alienation, madness, hell . . .; that every word must bristle and explode with the magic potency of our plight."[32]

In our own American tradition, the figure of William Dean Howells as a novelist has fallen into what is well-nigh a complete eclipse, and we may partly understand the reason for this by remembering the observation of Howells that was made many years ago by Henry James, when he said: "He is animated by a love of the common, the immediate, the familiar, and the vulgar elements of life, and holds that in proportion as we move into the rare and strange we become vague and arbitrary. . . ."[33] When we re-read today books like *The Rise and Fall of Silas Lapham*, or *A Hazard of New Fortunes*, or *A Modern Instance*, we realize that, with his customary acuteness, James put his finger exactly on what is one of Howells's primary qualities. So it is no wonder that the contemporary reader finds it so difficult to enter into a happy and reciprocal relation with his work, for, as Professor Trilling has reminded us, "we consent to the commonplace [only] as it verges upon and becomes the rare and the strange": we "want something that has affinity with the common, the immediate, the familiar . . . [but] we like them represented in their extremity to serve as a sort of outer limit of the possibility of our daily lives, as a kind of mundane hell."[34]

All the great charismatic seers of modern literature from Baudelaire to Kafka and from Pirandello to Faulkner have, in one way or another, wanted us to understand that we are lost in a dark wood and that, in this maze, what is least trustworthy is the common, the immediate, the familiar. Thus the motion the modern artist has often performed before the revolving universe has been a motion of recoil. Sometimes, like Rimbaud, he has fallen in love with what Jacques Maritain calls "the blind glitter of nothingness"[35] and made of his art a kind of incantatory magic. Or, like the author of *Finnegans Wake*, sometimes he has decided himself to be God and to create *ex nihilo* a universe of his own. On occasion, his retreat, like Mallarmé's, has been into *la poésie pure*, or, like the early Hemingway or the Dos Passos of the *U.S.A.* trilogy, it has been into the neutral factuality of naturalistic documentation. The recoil may have been into the subjectivistic perspectives of a Proust or a Virginia

32. Richard Chase, "Christian Ideologue" (a review of Basil Willey's *Nineteenth Century Studies)*, *The Nation* (8 April 1950), p. 330.

33. Henry James, "William Dean Howells," *The American Essays* (New York: Vintage Books, 1956), p. 152.

34. Trilling, *op. cit.*

35. Maritain, *op. cit.*

Woolf, or into that distress which provokes the belch of disgust expressed, say, in Jean-Paul Sartre's *La Nausé*. But, various as the configurations are, it can, nevertheless, be said that many of the major literary artists of our time, whether they knew it or not, have had as their patron saint not St. Athanasius, but Dionysius the Areopagite, for, in their dealings with the body of this world, their Way has been not the Way of Affirmation but the Way of Rejection. They have not known, in other words, the kind of confidence in the world and in temporal reality that was managed in happier moments in the literary tradition.

Those Roman Catholic apologists who explain this attrition in terms of the anti-sacramentalism of a Protestant ethos are doubtless right in part—but they are right only in part, for the authentic sacramentalism of the Christian faith has also been obscured by what has often been the theological and cultural obscurantism of post-Tridentine Romanism. Nor can we also forget the role played in this development by the deep fears generated by the continual expansion of the universe mapped out by modern science and modern cosmology. Back in the seventeenth century, Pascal was already conscious of the anxiety caused by contemplating "the infinite immensity of spaces" revealed by the new science, and, in what is one of the great expressions of the modern consciousness, he said: "The eternal silence of these infinite spaces frightens me." And, of course, far more frightening than the universes of modern physics have been the perils of historical existence itself, which has tended increasingly in the modern period to involve a kind of global insecurity hitherto unexperienced. But by far the deepest cause of the despondency and sense of alienation in modern literature is to be found in the collapse of any real certainty that what is Radically and Ultimately Significant is not absolutely secluded from that which is only provisionally significant in nature and in history. To the men of our age God seems, as Heidegger says, to be "withholding" Himself: He seems to be absent and perhaps even dead. And, as a consequence, our journey through the world does itself seem to be a terribly uncertain and perilous journey: as Stanley Hopper puts it, "the familiar trails to reality are swallowed up in thickets of confusion: the spoors are thickly overlaid.[36] And the artist's motion of recoil before this dark and threatening wood is but type and example of the deep mistrust with which modern man faces the indigence and privation of the world of finite, historical existence.

W. H. Auden tells us that Kafka bears to our own age the kind of

36. Stanley R. Hopper, "On the Naming of the Gods in Hölderlin and Rilke," in *Christianity and the Existentialists*, ed. Carl Michalson (New York: Charles Scribner's Sons, 1956), p. 156.

relation Dante bore to his, and a part of his meaning is, I am certain, that, whereas the hero of Dante's poem is a pilgrim and the movement of the poems "from low to high . . . [or] from dark to light,"[37] the hero of the Kafkan fable is a man who, at the end of his journeying, is no nearer the Castle than he was at the beginning and who remains forever quavering in the dungeon of his dereliction. In the one case, we have the Christian drama of rebirth and redemption, and, in the other, we have a story of the soul's exclusion from the Courts of the Most High and of the despair by which it is overtaken in its abandonment and isolation—the story, in other words, that forms the characteristic judgment of the human condition rendered by the existentialist imagination in modern literature.

Ours is, then, an "extreme" literature which plunges us into "extreme" situations. Conrad's Decoud, Kafka's K., Gide's Lafcadio, Malraux's Kyo, Faulkner's Joe Christmas, and Penn Warren's Jeremiah Beaumont are all men who have been "thrown into a world without [their] willing it and with no place prepared for [them]."[38] Their life has to be lived at a great distance from whatever are the sources of ultimate meaning, and, as a consequence, the salient stigmata of the modern hero are to be seen in his scepticism and in his despondency and alienation. But the miracle that occurs in the existentialist universe of a Conrad or a Kafka or a Malraux or a Faulkner is that, through the grace of some power that is unnamed and perhaps unknown, this scepticism and this despondency are prevented from so completely encircling the hero as to undo his humanity. Which is to say that the modern hero, in his great moments, has had what Paul Tillich calls "the courage of despair"—the courage, that is, despite everything that is problematic and uncertain in his world, to affirm his humanity. And since, despite all the nihilism that is in modern literature, this is a courage which is an expression of a kind of faith—faith itself, as Tillich says, being simply "the state of being grasped by the power of being-itself"[39]—it is not surprising, therefore, that the redefinition in our time of classical traditions of faith has often been deeply informed by this whole body of testimony. The Orthodox thinker Nicolas Berdyaev, the Roman Catholics Romano Guardini and Jacques Maritain, and the Protestant theologian Paul Tillich are representative of many other leading strategists of contemporary religious thought who have been alert to the fact that, if the high forms of faith are once again to be made to appear at least *possible* for us, their interpre-

---

37. Mark Van Doren, "The Divine Comedy," *The Noble Voice* (New York: Holt, Rinehart, Winston, 1946), p. 213.

38. Albert Votaw, "The Literature of Extreme Situations," *Horizon*, Vol. XX, no. 117 (September, 1949), p. 155.

39. Tillich, *op. cit.*

tation must itself be informed by the kind of awareness that comes from facing the distresses of life without any of the supports and consolations of religious faith. And so, in the attentiveness with which the religious community today is often listening to our poets and novelists and dramatists, we may discern some earnest of the reconstructive role that may yet be played by modern negation and denial.

SELECTED READINGS

Analysis of social movements may be found in Seymour M. Lipset, *Agrarian Socialism* (Berkeley, Calif.: University of California Press, 1950); Daniel Bell (ed.), *The New American Right* (New York: Criterion Books, 1955); James H. Tafts, "Liberal Movements in the United States–Their Methods and Aims," *International Journal of Ethics*, 1936. The following are general texts: Ralph H. Turner and Lewis M. Killian, *Collective Behavior* (Englewood Cliffs, N.J.: Prentice-Hall, Inc., 1957); Rudolf Heberle, *Social Movements: An Introduction to Political Sociology* (New York: Appleton-Century-Crofts, Inc., 1951). Sociological analysis can be profitably applied to the historical perspective. For this purpose the following chapters are recommended from Daniel Aaron (ed.), *American in Crisis* (New York: Alfred A. Knopf, 1952): Chapter II, Richard B. Morris, "Insurrection in Massachusetts"; Chapter VI, C. Vann Woodward, "John Brown's Private War"; Chapter VIII, Richard Hofstadter, "Manifest Destiny and the Philippines."

An interesting study of change in social structure is indicated in Eugen Pusić, "The Family in the Process of Social Change in Yugoslavia," *Sociological Review* (University College of North Staffordshire, England), New Series 5, 1957.

For analysis of the society-self relation in art see Alan Lomax, "Musical Style and Social Context," *American Anthropologist*, 1959; J. L. Fischer, "Art Styles and Cultural Cognitive Maps," *American Anthropologist*, February, 1961; Rudolf Arnheim, "Perceptual Abstracts and Art," *Psychological Review*, 1947, and, by the same author, "A Review of Proportion," *The Journal of Aesthetics and Art Criticism*, 1955. Works of interest by art historians are Arnold Hauser, *The Philosophy of Art History* (New York: Alfred A. Knopf, 1959), and, by the same author, *Social History of Art* (New York: Alfred A. Knopf, 1951); Walter Abell, *The Collective Dream in Art* (Cambridge: Harvard University Press, 1957). Abell's book is highly provocative for the social scientist. It seeks to apply the Freudian terminology to collective tensions in the histories of societies and to trace these collective tensions to forms and sequences in art styles.

8 *Postulates and Models*

THE READINGS in this book have indicated the complex relations between the individual and his society. They are a sample of a growing literature, but our knowledge of these complex relations is far from complete. And it is likely that, as Helen Merrell Lynd implies, the social scientist has tended to foreshorten his view in the interest of scientific order and a sense of progress. Our mid-century posture as social scientists must include a willingness to improve our postulates and to recognize the provisional nature of our operational theory.

The readings in this section concentrate on postulates about man's "domain of demands" and the adequacy of the theoretical models applied to his behavior.

Helen Merrell Lynd, "Thinking from Parts to Wholes," raises for evaluation the method of seeking truth through the division of the object of study. "The necessity to specify shades into a theory of atomism," she states, "if it includes the implicit assumption that the smaller and more isolable the units into which phenomena can be broken down the clearer and more precise specifications can be, and the closer we can come to reality. It is this implicit assumption that has characterized much of the development of Western science and that is currently open to question."

William L. Kolb, "Freedom and Theoretical Models in Social Science," assumes that "A social scientist is free to employ any model of man he chooses, so long as it is capable of ordering empirical data. . . ." He feels that an analysis of human values requires a postulate of the "conditioned freedom" of man and he examines the significance of such a postulate for sociological theory.

A. H. Maslow, "Cognition of Being in the Peak Experiences," calls attention to a type of cognition for which his knowledge of psychology had not prepared him. He calls this, "Cognition of Being," or "B-Cognition." He finds that in B-Cognition ". . . the experience of the object tends to be seen as a whole, as a complete unit, detached from relations, from possible usefulness, from expediency, and from purpose." He states that ". . . Western psychology . . . assumes that human needs, fears, and interests must always be determinants of perception." Maslow says that he considers this view ethnocentric in part ". . . because it arises so clearly as an unconscious expression of the Western world outlook. . . ."

His findings indicate that the ". . . normal perceptions of self-actualizing people . . . *can be relatively ego-transcending, self-forgetful, egoless.*" (Italics in original.)

Rudolf Arnheim, in his delightful article "The Robin and the Saint," reminds us of another dimension of man. He feels that ". . . intuitive knowledge of the nature and function of images . . ." is "a universal possession of the human mind," although it can be weakened by "unfavorable cultural conditions."

Georg Simmel, in "The Adventure," defines a type of experience which has "a self-sufficient form as though defined and, held together by an inner core." He compares the work of art and the adventure and concludes that in both of them ". . . the whole of life is somehow comprehended and consummated." Simmel's analysis thus supports the studies by Arnheim and Maslow and suggests that the creative faculty is a normal part of self process. This kind of evidence gives point to the suggestions on method made by Lynd and Kolb.

a) OPERATIONAL MODELS

HELEN MERRELL LYND

Thinking from Parts to Wholes

IN OUR STUDY of personality and society we characteristically work from parts to wholes, attempting to discover discrete items of behavior, then adding them together and trying to find relations among them. It is taken for granted that the units accessible to understanding

Reprinted from Helen Merrell Lynd, On Shame and the Search for Identity, *by permission of the author and the publisher, Harcourt, Brace and World, Inc., 1958, pp.*

are series of elements, items, or particulars that can be classified into groups. Part and whole are, of course, both relative concepts; everything is a part relative to something more comprehensive and a whole relative to something less so. But until recently a strong tendency in Western thought has been to assume that truth is to be found by breaking down observed phenomena into smaller and smaller parts and measuring these parts more and more accurately. This has been truer of psychology than of sociology and perhaps anthropology, since psychology sought more rigorously to model itself on the methods of the natural science of the nineteenth century, while such sociologists as Herbert Spencer and Auguste Comte were more influenced by what they thought were the sweeping conclusions of the natural sciences.

Some psychologists believe that the sequence of thinking from supposedly discrete entities to larger wholes is no longer dominant, that the differences between atomistic and holistic psychology have been largely reconciled or resolved in favor of holistic or *Gestalt* concepts.[1] In the writings of many contemporary sociologists there is an effort to distinguish and combine concepts of different degrees of inclusiveness such as the individual, his immediate social group, and the wider society. And certainly the vocabulary of psychology has in the last fifteen or twenty years included more terms referring to larger units of study.[2] But the writings of both academic and psychoanalytic psychologists suggests that the actual shift in ways of thinking may not have been as great as the new terms would seem to indicate. We may talk of holism, of field theory, of the necessity of seeing details in a *Gestalt* and still continue to think in atomistic ways.

The emphasis on discrete entities as either the given or as that which it is most important to discover has a long history in Western thought. If an observation of Aristotle's did not fit into a named class of phe-

---

74-83. [Reprinted as On Shame and the Search for Human Identity, *New York: Science Editions (John Wiley and Basic Books), 1962.] This book describes experiences of shame as peculiarly revealing of the self and points out that they have been too narrowly related to guilt or neglected altogether in research. The reasons for this neglect it finds in theories of psychological and moral scarcity that underlie dominant contemporary methods of personality study and that need to be supplemented by wider and more flexible ways of viewing personality if we are to gain understanding of pervasive experiences such as shame. The passage quoted outlines one characteristic of contemporary study of personality.*

1. See, for example, A. H. Maslow, *Motivation and Personality*, Harper, 1954, p. xi and Chap. XI.

2. See discussion of the different uses of molar and molecular and of holistic concepts, pp. 126-32. [Helen M. Lynd, *On Shame and the Search for Identity*, New York: Harcourt, Brace, and World, 1958].

nomena, he created a new classification. Aristotelian logic is embedded in our concepts and in our language.

European languages in general begin with a subject-noun whose action is expressed in an active verb. Some apparently permanent element is separated from the general process, treated as an entity, and endowed with active responsibility for a given occurrence. This procedure is so paradoxical that only long acquaintance with it conceals its absurdity.[3]

Hume revived an earlier tradition besides providing a prototype for contemporary positivism in his insistence that we can know only the separate elements of experience. On this ground he based his denial of the existence of a self.

There are some philosophers who imagine we are every moment intimately conscious of what we call our *self*. . . .

For my part, when I enter most intimately into what I call *myself*, I always stumble on some particular perception or other, of heat or cold, light or shade, love or hatred, pain or pleasure. I never can catch *myself* at any time without a perception, and never can observe anything but the perception. When my perceptions are removed for any time, as by sound sleep, so long am I insensible of *myself*. . . . They [mankind] are nothing but a bundle or collection of different perceptions.[4]

Hume could not discover the self because he was looking for another element or separate perception like heat or cold; his method of observation and analysis precluded the possibility of reaching a more comprehensive concept.[5] Thus to Hume the concepts of shame and the sense of identity as pervasive experiences would have been without basis in reality and without valid meaning.

The logic of John Stuart Mill, in the wake of Hume, tended to treat all psychological problems as soluble by an atomistic, associationist psychology. F. H. Bradley revolted against this form of atomism, the analysis of a judgment into detachable terms that are prior to propositions. He maintained that a thought is a functional unity, possessing distinguishable features but not composed of detachable pieces, and that a proposition cannot be said to be true or false because of self-consistency, but must have objective reference.[6]

---

3. Lancelot L. Whyte, *The Next Development in Man,* Holt, Rinehart, Winston, 1948, p. 67.

4. David Hume, *Treatise on Human Nature,* Everyman ed., Vol. I, pp. 238-40.

5. Cf. Solomon E. Asch, *Social Psychology,* Prentice-Hall, 1952, p. 280.

6. See Gilbert Ryle, Introduction, in A. J. Ayer and others, *The Revolution in Philosophy*, Macmillan, 1956, pp. 6, 7. Gottlob Frege and F. H. Bradley distinguished psychology sharply from logic and philosophy.

A distinction must be made here between atomism and specification. Atomism refers to the assumption that the universe is composed of simple, indivisible, and minute units externally related to each other. Specification refers to the necessity of saying as clearly as we can what it is that we are investigating. The necessity to specify shades into a theory of atomism if it includes the implicit assumption that the smaller and more isolable the units into which phenomena can be broken down the clearer and more precise specifications can be, and the closer we can come to reality. It is this implicit assumption that has characterized much of the development of Western science and that is currently open to question.

The terms determinate and indeterminate variables have come to be used in psychological and social-scientific writing to signify those units that are regarded for purposes of a particular study as fixed and under control and those that are regarded as not under control and therefore subject to testing and experiment. Whatever terms we use we must make clear what we are starting with, what we are trying to find out, what we regard as under control, and what is not under control but "free" to respond for purposes of a particular study. The necessity of such distinctions is not in question. What is in question is what kinds of phenomena may be habitually excluded from study by those items that are customarily singled out for control and for study; what is excluded by starting, to the extent that we usually do, with the small and discrete and supposedly fixed items, and demanding clarity and precision in such items. Much depends upon what questions we ask, what we consider as givens in an inquiry, and what is to be discovered. We cannot know whether a proposition is true or false without knowing, not only its relation to the external world, but what question it is trying to answer.

The assumption that understanding proceeds by means of first seeking the discrete, supposedly unchanging elements into which a phenomenon under study can be analyzed and only later turning attention to the changes going on in the elements and to the relations among them is still very much with us. Sumner's statement that "from the first acts by which men try to satisfy needs each act stands by itself and looks no further than the immediate satisfaction"[7] is out of date, if at all, in its manner of expression rather than in its underlying thought.

The methods of John Whiting are a particularly marked, but not an uncharacteristic, example of the use of this assumption. A scientific hypothesis is to him a tentative statement of the relation between two separate units or events; in validating a hypothesis it is necessary to iso-

7. William Graham Sumner, *Folkways,* Ginn and Company, 1906, p. 3.

late antecedent and consequent, and in the study of personality and culture understanding is reached by correlation of such isolates. Units of individual behavior are sought; and having started out with such separate units as given he reaches, by a chain of circular reasoning, the conclusion that "the practices of a society for one system of behavior are almost entirely independent of its practices with respect to other systems of behavior"; "aspects of child training practices . . . grow . . . out of antecedents specific to each system of behavior."[8] Integration of personality and culture in theory takes place after an initial assumption of separation.

For Parsons and Shils in their study that looks toward a general theory of human behavior[9] the place to start is with the isolation of certain specified units of behavior, regarded as if they were completely independent of each other and unchanging.[10] This assumption of separation and changelessness is necessary in order to meet their requirements of a good theory. Only after the study of the state of a system at a given moment has been completed should the study of the network of relations and of change in time be undertaken. The units of study are unaltered when viewed as isolated and unchanging and when viewed as related and in process of change. "There is . . . no difference between the variables involved in description of the state of a system and analysis of its processes. The difference lies in how the same variables are used."[11]

It is recognized that this separation and disregarding of change is an abstraction from the actual behavior of actual human beings, but it is looked upon as an abstraction necessary for scientific study. It is an inconvenience for science that the way human beings do behave interferes with this treatment of units of behavior as separate and static. In outlining ways to study the effect of maternal punishment on the aggression of the child and the effect of aggression on the punishment, Robert R. Sears says:

> Logically, and practically, a good theory requires that antecedents and consequents be entirely independent of one another. It would be most satisfactory if the child did not influence the mother's behavior, and if we could then say something about the effect of punishment on later behavior.[12]

The fact that the behavior of mother and child cannot empirically be

8. John W. M. Whiting and Irwin L. Child, *Child Training and Personality: A Cross-Cultural Study*, Yale University Press, 1953, pp. 8, 9, 10, 16, 117, 35; also pp. 50-4.

9. Talcott Parsons and Edward A. Shils, *Toward a General Theory of Action*, Harvard University Press, 1951, pp. 6, 476, 481-3.

10. Robert R. Sears, "Social Behavior and Personality Development," in *ibid.*, p. 476.

11. Parsons and Shils, *op. cit.*, p. 6.

12. Sears, *op cit.*, p. 476.

so isolated from each other creates, as Sears is careful to state, a difficult research problem.

Parsons in his *Social System* and Parsons and Shils in their later study discuss the concepts of equilibrium, of process, and of dynamics—all of which present difficulties to any investigator. Parsons' definition of equilibrium as a "boundary-maintaining" system[13] seems to me useful in emphasizing the necessity of at least a minimum of adaptation, self-preservation, and continuity if a phenomenon is to remain recognizably itself. Process seems to be used in the more usual sense of any changes occurring in a phenomenon or in related phenomena over a period of time, and in a somewhat more specialized sense as "any way or mode in which a given state of a system or of a part of a system changes into another state."[14] There is recognition that the word dynamic sometimes carries unstated assumptions, that dynamic refers particularly to motives or to development or sometimes to unconscious processes.[15] But Parsons refers to most social systems as "dynamically changing,"[16] without making entirely clear what his use of dynamic adds to the concept of process or change.

It is easier to observe many objects or events as if they were unchanging than to observe the processes in which they are always involved. But it does not follow from this relative ease of observation that equilibrium is a more normal or basic or important aspect of a phenomenon or system of phenomena than is change.[17] Parsons and Shils recognize that all individual and group behavior is constantly changing and that the dynamics (the energy or causal factors) of change is sooner or later necessary for any study of behavior; and Parsons is at pains to defend his structural-functional theory of society from charges of being static.[18] But it is not without significance that factors making for maintaining equilibrium come first in this analysis and factors making for change second and that there is assumed to be "no difference between the variables involved in description of the state of a system and analysis of its processes."[19]

One question raised by this way of thinking is whether logical com-

13. Talcott Parsons, *The Social System*, The Free Press of Glencoe, Inc., 1951, p. 481.

14. *Ibid.*, p. 201.

15. Sears, *op. cit.*, p. 472.

16. Parsons, *op. cit.*, p. 133.

17. See Kurt Goldstein on this point and further discussion of process, pp. 133-40 [Helen M. Lynd, *op. cit.*].

18. *Ibid.*, p. 535. Cf. Parsons and Shils' statement that equilibrium can be moving, not static, *op. cit.*, p. 107).

19. Parsons and Shils, *op. cit.*, p. 6.

pleteness is a desirable aim at this stage of our empirical knowledge. Study of change may interfere with logical completeness. Process is less readily observed in some phenomena, objects, or events than in others. But change in time can never be ignored or forgotten or added on as a relatively extraneous factor; it is always present. What are called structures in biology, for example, may be regarded as slow processes of long duration, what are called functions as more rapid processes of short duration.[20]

If the separate atoms or items linked together furnish manifestly inadequate explanations of human behavior, the tendency is not to re-examine the method but to create new links in the chain. Thus to independent variables and dependent variables are added hypothetical intervening variables; ". . . the need system is to be thought of as a set of interconnecting compartments, each compartment corresponding to a differentiated need."[21] It is possible as an outcome of the present habits of thought to speak of the need of a "*rapprochement*" between the "*field* of personality, *on the one hand,*" and the "*field* of perception, *on the other.*"[22] (Italics mine.)

All this suggests that our training inclines us to comprehend a totality of relations or a continuing process of change only after it has first been broken up into items or smaller categories. We give names to forms, structures, and functions rather than to more diffused, changing experiences.

Dorothy Lee calls this preoccupation with proceeding from parts to wholes, from separate items to integration, from isolated events to cause-and-effect sequences and changes, a lineal codification of reality that differs from the nonlineal codifications of reality employed by certain other cultures.[23] She describes our way of constantly acting in terms of

20. See Ludwig von Bertalanffy, *Problems of Life: An Evaluation of Modern Biological Thought*, Watts and Co., 2d ed., 1952.

21. Edward C. Tolman, "A Psychological Model," in Parsons and Shils, *op. cit.*, p. 319. "Intervening variables" are said by the persons who use this term to be directly derived from the empirical data and to be required by the data as principles of explanation, whereas "hypothetical constructs" are more independent productions not so directly derived from the data. There may be something to be said for the view that one man's intervening variable is another man's hypothetical construct. It all depends upon what, in view of one's training and postulates, one believes can be directly derived from empirical data as a necessary principle of explanation.

22. Else Frenkel-Brunswick, "Personality Theory and Perception," in Robert R. Blake and Glenn V. Ramsey, eds., *Perception: An Approach to Personality*, Ronald Press, 1951, p. 356.

23. Cf. discussion of Sapir's, Whorf's, and Hoijer's theories of the way the various patterns of language lead to the stressing of certain aspects of reality and ignoring of others differently in different societies, pp. 171-81 [Helen M. Lynd, *op. cit.*].

an implied line (in *drawing* a conclusion, *tracing* a relationship, *leading to* conclusions or a goal, taking *a course* of action, following the direction of an argument).[24] She contrasts this parts-to-whole, lineal characteristic of our thinking with the thought patterns of other peoples who select different aspects of reality for emphasis: the Ontang Javanese have words for emotional experiences but not for observed forms or functions; the Trobriands emphasize a patterned whole, not causal relationships or steps toward a climax;[25] the Wintu regard the given as an unpartitioned mass rather than as a series of particulars, and the individual as a differentiated part of society rather than society as a plurality of individuals.[26] A lineal codification of reality with stress on discrete items undoubtedly has been a major factor in the development of Western science. But it may be that making other kinds of experience accessible to understanding, and further development of science itself, requires an expansion of this way of thought.

Post-quantum developments in physics and recent work in biology suggest the inadequacy of the simpler lineal cause-and-effect concepts of the nineteenth century. Much psychological—perhaps less sociological—thought, however, still follows the concepts of an earlier physics and biology. We tend to take for granted separate events and objects and then attempt to trace connections and relations among them.

This parts-to-whole, lineal approach applied to the study of personality means that parts of the personality are regarded as separate units and then, the separation having been initially assumed, the problems of relation and integration are posed. The earlier segmenting of the personality into sensation, perception, and will, or listed traits and instincts has been replaced in Freudian and neo-Freudian thinking by segmenting into id, ego, and superego; unconscious, preconscious, and conscious. But the newer divisions, also, are often used as if they were discrete and isolable.

Anna Freud and other contemporary Freudians have come to take for granted the existence of id, ego, and superego as separate entities, and then go through elaborate explanations as to how these separate existences are related to each other. So distinct are they that Anna Freud

24. Dorothy Lee, "Lineal and Nonlineal Codifications of Reality," *Psychosomatic Medicine,* Vol. 12, No. 2, May 1950, pp. 91-2.

25. *Ibid.*, pp. 90, 91, 92, 97.

26. Dorothy Lee, "Linguistic Reflection of Wintu Thought," *International Journal of American Linguistics,* Vol. X, No. 4, Oct. 1944, pp. 181 and 185, and "Notes on the Conception of Self among the Wintu Indians," *Journal of Abnormal and Social Psychology,* Vol. 45, No. 3, July 1950. Gordon Allport, Henry A. Murray, Kurt Lewin, Kurt Goldstein, and others raise similar questions about this kind of cause and effect, this part-to-whole sequence which will be discussed later.

can say, "the analyst . . . when he sets about the work of enlightenment . . . takes his stand at a point equidistant from the id, the ego, and the super-ego."[27] The "ego" ceases to be a metaphor or a part of a hypothesis and becomes an entity "independent of the emotions," a distinct and separate part of the personality.[28]

Ways of studying personality with less emphasis on the autonomy of separate parts, more on the functioning whole, will be discussed in the next chapter [of *Shame and the Search for Identity*[29]]. It must be borne in mind, however, that the study of the whole does not make the study of subsystems unnecessary. Finer specification continues to be important. The point is that relations should be as much taken for granted and regarded as basic in the personality as separate items.

A similar assumed apartness and then laborious putting together occurs in our way of studying the individual *and* society. Here we are still influenced by post-Renaissance thinking, which takes as given separate individual human atoms and then poses as a problem how they can be related in society; by the Hobbesian view, which sees society as an aggregate of self-contained individuals, assimilated through some external instrument such as the common law. The separateness is assumed; the relationship is to be constructed. We discuss the necessity of combining individual behavior and social behavior into a single theoretical system[30] and the effect of culture on personality.[31] This separation is not accepted

27. Anna Freud, *The Ego and the Mechanisms of Defence*, International Universities Press, 1946, p. 30.

28. Anna Freud says: "All through childhood a maturation process is at work which . . . aims at perfecting [ego] functions, at rendering them more and more objective and *independent of the emotions* until they can become as accurate and reliable as a mechanical apparatus." ("Indication for Child Analysis," *Psychoanalytic Study of the Child*, Vol. I, 1945, p. 144. Italics mine.) Adelaide McF. Johnson comments on Anna Freud's view of the ego as a separate entity: "Is . . . not [Anna Freud's phrase 'the human ego by its very nature'] the logical error of petitio principii . . . in which a definition which has not been proved is smuggled into the sequence of an argument? 'By its very nature . . .' is an arbitrary postulation of what remains to be proved. Apparently Anna Freud assumed that the something within the ego itself, independent of outside influences and parental attitudes (and presumably, independent of heredity), is operating." ("Some Etiological Aspects of Repression, Guilt, and Hostility," *Psychoanalytic Quarterly*, Vol. XX, No. 4, Oct. 1951, p. 513.)

Erikson points out that the view that the ego can become independent of the emotions and like a mechanical apparatus reflects the mechanistic concepts of cause and effect of an earlier science. (Erikson, "Ego Development and Historical Change," p. 390.)

29. Helen M. Lynd, *op. cit.*

30. Sears, *op. cit.*, p. 468.

31. Whiting and Child, *op. cit.*, p. 1.

without question. The phrasing "personality *in* culture" is beginning to replace "personality *and* culture."[32] But, for people trained as many of us are, it is still difficult to think in terms other than those of separate individual atoms linked together in society.

A special instance of atomistic, lineal thinking is the stress on polarities, opposite ends of a scale, mutually exclusive opposites in Plato's sense, forms of thought used almost axiomatically in much psychological writing. Ernest Jones notes Freud's constant proclivity toward dualistic ideas; any kind of pluralism was alien to him. Throughout his professional life, Freud tended to think in terms of polarities: subject-object, the polarity of reality; pleasure-unpleasure, an economic polarity; active-passive, a biological polarity.[33]

Literary and artistic pursuits, says Melvin H. Marx, are at the "opposite end of the scale" from scientific method.[34] Books on personality abound in parallel columns of supposedly antithetical descriptive terms, and the word versus is frequently used to separate paired terms that are regarded as opposed rather than complementary to each other. We find such supposed antitheses in the use of active vs. passive, gratifying vs. noxious, need-gratifying vs. need-blocked, subject vs. object, pleasure vs. pain, dominance vs. submission, love vs. hate, friend vs. enemy, masculine vs. feminine.[35]

32. "Culture and personality," say Kluckhohn and Murray, "is as lopsided as biology and personality." (Clyde Kluckhohn and Henry A. Murray, *Personality in Nature, Society, and Culture,* Alfred A. Knopf, 1948, pp. 62-3.)

33. Ernest Jones, *Sigmund Freud,* Hogarth Press, Vol. II, 1955, pp. 356-8.

34. Melvin H. Marx, ed., *Psychological Theory: Contemporary Readings,* Macmillan, 1951, p. 13.

35. See, for example, Freud, "The Predisposition to Obsessional Neurosis" (1913), *Collected Papers,* Vol. II, (London: The Hogarth Press and The Institute of Psycho-Analysis, 1948) p. 128; Parsons and Shils, *op. cit.,* pp. 5, 9; Frenkel-Brunswick, *op. cit.,* p. 359; John Dollard and Neal E. Miller, *Personality and Psychotherapy: An Analysis in Terms of Learning, Thinking, and Culture,* McGraw-Hill, 1950, p. 103.

WILLIAM L. KOLB

Images of Man and the Sociology of Religion

EMPIRICAL KNOWLEDGE of man requires more than empirical method for its pursuit. It requires the presupposition that the world is real, important, and knowable. It further requires some image of man and his status in the world, so that criteria of significance for the selection and ordering of data can be developed. Such images are in part empirical but they are also in part composed of nonempirical presuppositions and assumptions about the nature of man. Within the autonomous activity of pure empirical science, the images of man and the presuppositions they embody occupy the status of heuristic devices to be accepted solely in terms of their success in ordering the data of human experience within the framework of public and repeatable investigation. A social scientist is free to employ any model of man he chooses, so long as it is capable of ordering empirical data and so long as he is willing to relinquish it when it can be shown that some other image orders the data in a superior fashion. At the same time, because the scientist is a man with commitments of his own that involve some image of man and because society is made possible because of shared commitments that involve some image of man, there is inevitably a deep psychological connection between the images of man in the social sciences, the images of man held by social scientists as committed participants in the affairs of their society, and the image of man at the root of a society's fundamental value orientations. Perhaps there would be no logical necessity for this if social scientists never acted in other roles and if the social sciences were never used in society, but the social scientist does tend to act toward other people on the basis of his scientific conception of them. The social sciences are used, and to use them is to act on the basis of their presuppositions about man. As an individual responsible to his own conscience and to the conscience of society, the social scientist cannot lightly ignore these connections.

I

The image of man dominant in current sociology and social psychology is that of the person determined, within the limits set by a permissive biological inheritance, by society and culture. Complete determinism is presupposed in this image, and a psychological determinism that would view the personality as a dynamic system in its own right is subordinated to societal and cultural determinism. Even where there is a claim that the personality is treated as an autonomous system, what is given to psychological determinism is taken way by diminishing the specificity of biological needs, by minimizing psychological needs other than those which are the result of internalizing culture, and by stressing consistency both as a functional requirement of motivating conformity to culturally defined means of pursuing culturally defined ends and as a postulated focus for the striving of the dynamic self.[1]

One of the consequences of the use of this image of man is the fact that the term *freedom* does not often appear in sociological literature as applying either to the human will or to the existence of a range of institutionalized significant choices. Now the structural phenomena that have in the past been designated by the term are not necessarily neglected in sociology, but neither are they treated from the point of view of significant choice. There is little doubt that, in the minds of the actors who make up our society, the values of equality and liberty and the institutions that implement these values are related to certain presuppositions with respect to man and the freedom of his will. According to Niebuhr:

> The social and political freedoms which modern democratic communities accord the person express the belated convictions of modern communities, gained after desperate struggles, that the community must give the person a social freedom which corresponds to the essential freedom of his nature.[2]

The mind of the sociologist is not too different from that of his lay brother; the reason he does not treat seriously the structures of freedom as structures of freedom is that he approaches his discipline with the presupposition that man does not have freedom of the will.

Additional evidence of this presupposition is to be found in the fact that when sociologists do struggle to define freedom within the frame-

1. See, for example, Kingsley Davis, *Human Society*, New York: The Macmillan Company, pp. 195-254, especially pp. 238-241.

2. Reinhold Niebuhr, "Freedom," *A Handbook of Christian Theology*, New York: Living Age Books, 1958, p. 141.

work of the discipline, its meaning is changed. There is a direct logical connection between the image of man in orthodox sociological theory and the conception of freedom embodied in the following statement from a review by Arthur K. Davis of Robert A. Nisbet's *Quest for Community:*

> A sociological definition of freedom . . . would run more like this: freedom is a subjective feeling of personal well being which results from the objective fact of living in an effectively functioning society. A society functions effectively to the degree that its social structure is integrated, that it successfully meets its problems of internal and external change, that it socializes new members, satisfies or reconciles their needs and expectations, etc. The point is that a number of concrete patterns of societal organization can meet this abstract definition of freedom. It is entirely possible that among them is Nisbet's bogey, the totalitarian community—once the latter has been stabilized or routinized.[3]

If sociologists and others were to accept this definition of freedom, its consequences when employed by them as actors rather than as observers would seem clear. Yet its connection with a totally deterministic image of man is apparent, and I see no way in which such an image can be restricted to social science in its pure form, once it is completely established there.[4] In this type of model it appears that culture and society have endured forever and that it is the eternal fate of the person to be contained within the process of socialization and the structure of statuses and roles. So long as his minimal biological needs and internalized cultural needs are met adequately by the appropriate institutionalized processes and provided he has been successfully socialized, he will conform. Universal qualities and needs of man which might lead to deviation even in a perfectly consistent sociocultural structure are for the most part ignored. Some attention is paid to the fact that the desire for

3. Arthur K. Davis, "Review of Robert A. Nisbet, *Quest for Community*," *American Sociological Review*, 18 (August, 1953), pp. 443-44.

4. There are several replies made to the argument advanced above, some of which may be logically valid, but none of which seem to me to be psychologically and socially valid: (a) models are not necessary at all, for all we do is establish empirical correlations among observable phenomena; (b) models are necessary in science, but one need not use the same model in science that one uses in everyday life; (c) all that is real is the observable, so that models are nothing more than constructs useful in ordering the data, and even within the same science one can use different models for ordering different ranges of data. I have yet to see a single case in the social sciences where one of these arguments has been adhered to when social science is being applied or when a model is being seriously challenged in scientific controversy. This may mean simply that human beings cannot live up to the rigorous demands of science, or it may mean that scientists as human beings of necessity believe that their constructs refer to something real.

power, prestige, and wealth is a disruptive force and calls for control by institutions and consensus; but control of this force is considered theoretically as a secondary function of these elements in the maintenance of the society. The fact that in almost all empirical cases such force has had a large part to do with the shaping of values and institutions is passed over.[5] Just as serious is the failure within this frame of reference to provide a genuine place for the creative deviant who transcends the causal matrix, either by criticism even within a consistent sociocultural situation that meets both his internalized cultural needs and his biological needs or, having been pushed to creativity by cultural contradiction, by creation that is to some degree discontinuous with the conditions of its emergence. In the general statement that constitutes the opening chapter of *Toward a General Theory of Action* and is signed by Talcott Parsons, Edward A. Shils, Gordon W. Allport, Clyde Kluckhohn, Henry A. Murray, Robert R. Sears, Richard C. Sheldon, Samuel A. Stouffer, and Edward C. Tolman is found this affirmation:

> Some actors possess, to a high degree, the potentialities of elaborating their own goals and standards, accepting the content of institutional role-expectations but simultaneously modifying and adding something new to them. These are the creative personalities whose conformity or alienation is not mainly motivated by a need-disposition to accept or reject the given institutional role-expectations, but rather by the need to discover, elaborate, and conform with their own ego-ideal.[6]

This is an admirable statement and gives notice of due attention to be paid to man the creator, although apparently the ability to transcend the clutch of culture is restricted to a few. What needs to be emphasized, however, is that this individual is nowhere to be found in the elaboration of this theoretical position, which has had so much impact on American sociology. Rather the stress is purely on the need-disposi-

5. See the controversy between C. Wright Mills and Talcott Parsons in the former's *Sociological Imagination,* New York: Oxford University Press, pp. 25-49, and the latter's "The Distribution of Power in American Society," in his *Structure and Process in Modern Societies,* New York: The Free Press, 1960, pp. 199-225. In this controversy Parsons treats power as a facility of an already established society integrated by an already existing value system and set of institutions, thus ignoring the role of power in the establishment of value systems and institutions as well as playing down its ability to "pervert" such values and institutions after they are established. Mills, equally a determinist, makes values and normative patterns simply legitimations of a system of power. See also William L. Kolb, "Values, Politics, and Sociology," *American Sociological Review,* 25 (December, 1960), pp. 966-969.

6. "Some Fundamental Categories of the Theory of Action: A General Statement," in Talcott Parsons and Edward A. Shils, eds., *Toward a General Theory of Action,* Cambridge, Mass.: Harvard University Press, 1951, p. 20.

tions to conform or to deviate and upon the constradictions in institutional structure that have influence on such need-dispositions.[7]

II

If we can seriously entertain the hypotheses that the free institutions of modern society are intimately linked with the presupposition of man's essential freedom and that the images of man prevalent in social science inevitably have an impact on the presuppositions contained in the consensus underlying such institutions, then it would appear incumbent upon us to inquire whether the deterministic presuppositions of sociological orthodoxy are indeed necessary for sociology and whether they are indeed the best presuppositions and image for the ordering of sociological data. In making such an inquiry, I should like also to examine what might be involved in using an image of man drawn from the Judaic-Christian strand of the Jewish-Greek-Christian tradition.[8] The present section will be used to set forth briefly the central aspects of this latter image.

The first, and most central element, in the Judaic-Christian image of man is the concept of human freedom, or perhaps better, the concept of the conditioned—but not determined—will, which may be used to point to both human freedom and the limits within which it exists. Freedom, in this image, is an ineradicable primitive experience of the self by the self that one does within and sometimes beyond limits choose without determination, without chance, and with responsibility. It does not consist only of the absence of external constraint as some soft determinists have argued; rather, it implies the rejection of any determinism that places the human self *totally* within a web of invariant relations, whether those relations exist among external elements of the environment or among the internal elements of personality. Nor does freedom consist in uniqueness, transcendence, or unpredictability as others have argued, for it can be observed by the self, conceived by the observer, generalized about, incorporated into the scientific analysis of limits and conditions, and to some degree predicted, either by relating it conceptually to conditioning elements or through sympathetic insight. It can be translated into sociology or any other social science as a concept that the observer

7. Parsons and Shils, "Values, Motives, and Systems of Action," *ibid.*, pp. 47-275; Talcott Parsons, *The Social System*, New York: The Free Press, 1951.

8. Although the image of man to be set forth below is drawn largely from the writings of theologians in the Jewish and Christian traditions, it is also to be found in part in the writings of such atheistic writers as Albert Camus.

uses to help in the ordering of his data; as such a concept, freedom consists of the presupposition that no act is ever totally determined and that every act insofar as it is not limited and conditioned consists of responsible choice.

The second major dimension of the Judaic-Christian image of man concerns certain universal conditions of man's situation and the needs that are generated thereby. It is implied in this conception of man that all men live their lives under the threat of meaninglessness and that they relate to one another either in a relationship of love and responsibility or in one of manipulation and control. Because of the threat of meaninglessness, man is forced to relate himself to some entity which in its absoluteness is capable of overcoming meaninglessness. From the point of view of the scientific observer, this entity must be considered nonempirical because no object insofar as it is capable of being described in the public language of science possesses this absoluteness. Moreover, meaninglessness can be fully overcome only if the actor orients himself as a free agent in love directed toward an experienced nonempirical free agent that creates, sustains, and loves him. Only if meaninglessness is fully overcome, can the actor relate himself to other men in a relationship of responsible love.

The third major dimension of the Judaic-Christian image of man is that while such a double orientation to a nonempirical free agent and other men is an actual possibility, it has such slight probability that it has been called the impossible possibility. The result of this failure is the inevitable occurrence in all societies of lovelessness among men and the presence in all religions, ultimate value systems, and social institutions of elements of self-centeredness, manipulation, and perversion of genuine commitment. No act, no value, no commitment, no institution is without the element of self-concern or self-enlargement; yet no act, no value, no commitment, no institution is without its element of genuineness.

The fourth and final major dimension of this image of man is constituted by its orientation to the reason and finiteness of man. It refuses to make man so finite that he is totally absorbed in the network of cause and effect, but it recognizes the limits on his freedom placed by nature, by culture, and by his own emotional processes. It recognizes ignorance, error, and irrationality, but it refuses to conceive of free commitment to the nonempirical as irrationality, because it goes beyond reason and beyond the empirical. Further, it seeks the thread of self-centeredness throughout the cumulative effects of culture and of irrationality.

This then is the image of man I would compare with that of sociological orthodoxy. The use of this image in sociological analysis and research is not a substitute for the investigation of empirical data, but like all other models is a heuristic starting point for such an investigation. Like all other models it must be tested against its ability to order the data gathered in such investigations and to cover wider ranges of data than those covered by other models.

III

Although the Judaic-Christian image of man may be used as a model in any area of social investigation requiring the concept of selfhood, it is perhaps particularly relevant in the study of the sociology of religion and, within that discipline, in the investigation of the nature and function of religion and ultimate value systems in the securing of societal integration and cohesion. I shall argue in the following that functional theorists have been forced by what they have taken to be the crucial empirical evidence to develop a theory of religion and ultimate values that is not compatible with the orthodox, deterministic image of man currently employed in systematic sociology and that this theory is compatible with the Judaic-Christian image of man set forth above.

Insofar as any human society is integrated through other than coercive means, it tends to be characterized by a system of shared ultimate moral values. In the last twenty-five years of American sociology an older theory of the significance of such shared values has been replaced by a newer theory. The older tradition held that population size, density, and growth, the development of technology, and the subsocial process of competition sufficed to create a human "community" constituted by a functionally integrated division of labor and a set of habits capable of sustaining this integrated system. Shared moral values have a role to play as an additional source of stabilization and integration after the division of labor has come into being.[9]

Such a conception of the nature and role of ultimate values sees the source of values in the habits created by the competitively developed division of labor, in that when something happens to upset the equilibrium established by these habits, the members of the community are forced to become conscious of the habits and to translate them through

9. "In human societies a division of labor based upon a diversity of occupations and enforced by economic competition performs the function, which in the plant community or other biotic associations is performed by symbiosis. There is, however, or there presently emerges in both animal and human societies, the necessity for a more stable form of association than that which either biotic or economic competition and cooperation is sufficient to produce." Robert E. Park, "Symbiosis and Socialization," in *Human Communities*, New York: The Free Press, 1952, p. 258.

the process of symbolic interaction into moral norms. These norms then come to be strengthened and rationalized by systems of religious belief, attitude, and ritual.[10]

The fundamental question here is whether competition among human beings is essentially analogous to competition among other forms of animal life and hence susceptible to being conceived as a subsocial process existing in the absence of normative control. The functional theorist believes that the nature of the human self as it emerges into self-awareness and the awareness of others precludes this possibility. Because of the existence of cognitive culture, men's desires increase in scope and intensity, so that unless they are normatively controlled, the natural state of man is that of social conflict—not subsocial competition.[11]

In fairness to the older tradition, it should be pointed out that it recognized that as man's behavior reaches the social level of symbolic interaction, competition tends to become conflict. It continued to stress the idea, however, that the biotic or the analogous-homologous economic struggle for existence continues as a subsocial process of competition creating and sustaining a division of labor. In contrast the functional theorist holds that when men interact at the level of the significant symbol, the biotic struggle for existence simply becomes one dimension of the social struggle for culturally defined objects. If competition exists, it exists as a social process created by one mode of the normative control of conflict. Thus any division of labor or any human society and its functional integration presupposes a set of moral values. The problem of the moral integration of the ends and means of social action and interaction is present from the beginning of social life. A functionally integrated society, whether cooperative or competitive, requires the presence of moral consensus for its creation and maintenance.

Now the theory of values held by the older tradition and opposed by the functionalists is only one of several theories that insist that the

10. This theory has been most explicitly formulated by E. B. Reuter and C. W. Hart in their *Introduction to Sociology*, New York: McGraw-Hill Book Company, 1933, pp. 144-157.

11. Talcott Parsons first pointed this out in his discussion of Durkheim in *The Structure of Social Action*, New York: McGraw-Hill Book Company, 1937, pp. 313-314. This aspect of the functional theorist's image of man seems closer to the Judaic-Christian image than to the image of modern orthodoxy; and as a matter of fact Parsons's image of man in *The Structure of Social Action* is in many respects closer to the Judaic-Christian image than the one he has employed in his later writings. Functionalists, however, have continued to use this particular aspect as indicating the *need* for controlling shared values, but then overestimate the independent and controlling power of such values by underestimating the power of self-interest to pervert value systems after they exist and even during the process of their coming into existence.

content of ultimate value systems and indeed their very existence are in some way derivable from the needs, interests, and motives of men as they relate to the objects and sources of satisfaction available in the empirical world. It has been a common trait of these theories to recognize that in the eyes of the actors holding a particular system of values, the system is always anchored in some nonempirical object capable of inspiring attitudes of awe, reverence, and respect.[12] But it is an equally common trait of these theories that each finds some way of denying the significance of the anchorage of ultimate values in religious commitment. In opposition to all these theories, the functional theory of ultimate values takes the religious dimension of religio-moral integration seriously and denies that ultimate moral values can be derived from the empirically oriented interests of men.

Although this argument against the other theories of ultimate values has never become fully explicit, the reasons for the functionalist rejection of the idea that ultimate values can be derived from men's empirically oriented interests can be inferred from fragmentary statements in their writings. Thus, for example, in the writings of Kingsley Davis there is a clearly implied denial that the central normative elements are merely rationalizations of an order established through power or the pursuit of economic interest, for they are pictured as being capable of subordinating "Other ends, and above all those that relate to the individual's own satisfactions taken distributively. . . ."[13] It is equally clear from his writing that ultimate ends and values are not the products of rational thought or simple projections of psychological preferences. If one takes seriously their integrative and direction-setting functions, it is apparent that they represent a selection from the paths left open by the structure of a natural situation and are not syntheses rationally derivable from a set of directly adaptive technical norms. There is no intrinsic psychological hierarchy of desires that will as a

12. Some of the functional theorists themselves have recently confused this point by suggesting that ultimate moral commitments are not always associated with a nonempirical object. This error seems to be due to identifying the nonempirical with the supernatural or to confusing the fact that not all nonempirical objects are associated with moral commitments. The confusion is compounded when remnants of religion, like those of Judaism and Christianity in the United States, are made the focus of the sociology of religion and the actual nonrational, nonempirical faith of a society is not treated as a faith. Under those circumstances it certainly appears that moral values are unconnected with religion. We must become reaware of the fact that the nonempirical is not necessarily a "god" in the popular sense of that term. It may be a master race, a process of history, progress, any object natural or supernatural to which is attributed qualities that transcend observation by the scientific method.

13. Kingsley Davis, *op. cit.*, p. 143.

matter of emotional preference give such common ends the power to control the pursuit of wealth, prestige, and power; there is no rational method by which the actor can be convinced that he should subordinate his powerfully motivated individual desires to such limited common ends over a long period of time. Finally, the ultimacy of such values—the fact that there are no ends and values above them and that they are able to inspire the attitudes of awe, reverence, and respect necessary for subordinating other ends—is based on the actor's orientation to and interests in a nonempirical object capable of invoking such attitudes and investing the values with the same capability.[14]

Unfortunately the functionalist critique of other theories of ultimate values does not resolve the issue. It is not enough to say that values cannot originate in the way these schools of thought have claimed and that they must appear to the actor to be anchored in the realm of the nonempirical. The functionalist must himself say how he thinks ultimate values originate.

Actually functionalists have shown a peculiar reluctance to deal with the origin of ultimate values. Parsons in *The Structure of Social Action* has recognized that the analytical priority of such values over society in that the very coming into being of a society is dependent upon a system of shared values means that it is more proper to speak of society as being a moral phenomenon than it is to speak of morality being a societal phenomenon.[15] Yet in Parsons' later writings this problem is dropped, and the focus of the theory is placed on already existing societies with already existing shared value systems, the process of socialization, and the processes of social control. The only reference I can find to the origin of values is the following:

> Moral standards are not logical deductions from systems of belief or manifestations of systems of expressive symbols nor do they derive from cognitive or appreciative standards. They depend in part on such systems, but they draw on all the elements of cognitive, cathectic, and evaluative selection from the alternatives of action. The important alternatives (which define the problems of action) emerge for the actor when he, armed with his cognitive and cathectic symbols and standards, directly confronts the relevant situation with all its functional exigencies. As he develops general methods for making choices among these alternatives, he thereby gains a new set of superordinate standards. These are moral value standards.[16]

This paragraph, however, is never developed as a theory of the origin of values, but rather the stress in the whole section on personality is

14. *Ibid.*, pp. 141-145, 509-545.

15. Parsons, *The Structure of Social Action*, *op. cit.*, pp. 390-391.

16. Parsons and Shils, *op. cit.*, pp. 171-172.

on the provision of such moral standards to the person by the culture and the society. So also in *The Social System* Parsons stresses the integrative function of ultimate values and takes the position that religious beliefs give cognitive significance to these values, but he evades the problem of origins by stating that this relationship between religion and values holds ". . . not in the sense that either the sentiments or the cognitive beliefs have causal priority but that they tend to be integrated with one another and that this integration is apparently related to the stabilization of the system."[17] I suggest that the reason for the avoidance of the problem of value origins is that it simply cannot be handled through the use of the orthodox image of man. This is best illustrated by the difficulties experienced by Kingsley Davis, the one functionalist, to seriously grapple with the issue. Davis attempts to account for the origin of ultimate values on the basis of their functional necessity, such necessity being viewed within the context of the evolutionary struggle for existence: "in the struggle for existence against nature and in the struggle between one human society and another, only those groups survived and perpetuated their culture which developed and held in common among their members a set of ultimate ends."[18] He adds that "They must, therefore, arise as a cultural emergent. They must spring from the dynamics of communicative interaction in a group that maintains itself by cultural adaptation."[19] This explanation is vulnerable on two counts. In the first place, the theories that the functionalists oppose do not deny that values emerge within a social and cultural matrix; the problem is how they emerge if they cannot be rationally derived from empirical interests and if they do not constitute rationalizations of such interests. In the second place, the fact that they are functionally necessary for survival does not explain their origin, but is only an explanation of why existing societies are all characterized by such values. In the biological theory of evolution, natural selection does not account for the origin of adaptive traits but only for the elimination of the organisms not possessing the traits. The function that an item performs is no explanation of its origin or its persistence, unless the psychological mechanisms involved can be demonstrated or at least hypothesized. While societal needs make the cultural emergence of ultimate value systems necessary and human communication makes them possible, the psychological analogue of biological mutation implied in Davis' natural selection analogy is missing. I am convinced that it cannot be supplied without the

17. Parsons, *The Social System, op. cit.*, p. 369.

18. Kingsley Davis, *op. cit.*, p. 144.

19. *Ibid.*, p. 526.

recognition of the autonomy of the religious realm and without the presupposition of the "conditioned will" within that realm. With such recognition and presupposition supplied by the Judaic-Christian image of man, there is a possible answer—indeed, an answer given by Max Weber and accepted by Parsons in his earlier writing on Weber but not compatible with the image of man in present-day system theory.

Although Parsons has not in his recent writing stressed this contribution of Max Weber, he called attention to it in the *Structure of Social Action.*[20] The logical starting point of Weber's analysis of religion is the fact that the universal conditions of man's existence create within him a need for "meaning." Man as a self-conscious creature is aware of the finiteness and contingency of his own existence. Confronted with the facts of death and suffering and the uncertainty of human affairs, he is forced to inquire into the meaning of the world, not as a casual spectator but as a passionate seeker. Whatever meaning can be found cannot be discovered by the methods of empirical knowledge.

The answer to the question of meaning is elaborated in different ways by different men, but two universal generalizations can be made about the answer. The first of these, accepted by most functional theorists of religion, is that there are certain universal foci around which the answer centers: the nature of the universe; the nature of man; the nature of man's relation to man; the nature of time, history, and the empirical world; the nature of the nonempirical world, and the nature of man's orientation toward both the empirical and nonempirical worlds. Within the system of concepts and attitudes organized around these foci are the answers to the problems of finiteness, suffering, and evil. The second generalization, the crucial one for our purposes, is that while the universal conditions and the historical conditions of man's existence pose the problem of meaning, determine that all men shall make religious responses, and *condition* the content of those responses, *they do not determine* the content that constitutes the answer to the problem. Parsons has the following to say about Weber's massive comparative studies of the religions and social structures of modern society, China, India, and ancient Judaism:

As a generalized result of these studies, he found that it was not possible to reduce the striking variations of pattern on the level of religious ideas in these cases to any features of an independently existent social structure or economic situation, though he continually insisted on the very great importance of situational factors in a number of different connections. These factors, however, served only to pose the problems with which great movements of religious thought have been concerned. But the distinctive cognitive patterns were only

20. *Op. cit.*, pp. 500-694.

understandable as a result of a cumulative tradition of intellectual effort in grappling with the problems thus presented and formulated.[21]

The core of any set of religious ideas and attitudes created by man in his state of conditioned freedom concerns the realm of the nonempirical because the problem of meaning cannot be answered through rational thought or with reference only to the empirical world. The realities of the empirical world, the needs of men and of societies, the nature of the empirical environment, however, all receive definitions in the complex of religious beliefs and attitudes, so that they derive their meanings from these definitions. Further these ideas define ends that refer to both the empirical and the nonempirical worlds and the means that may be employed. Thus, Parsons, in contrast to the statement of his cited earlier, points out that for Weber the religious ideas with which he is concerned are the source of ultimate values:

> They are rather rationalized interpretations of the meaning of the world including a complete metaphysical system. Out of these fundamental metaphysical postulates, then, is to be derived what meaning the world *can* have for man, and from this, in turn, what his ultimate values can "meaningfully" be.[22]

Here then is the more specific answer we have been seeking to the question of the source of ultimate values. Religion, defined broadly as man's reverent and respectful orientation to the nonempirical, no matter how that nonempirical is defined by the actor, is not only the anchorage and justification for the ultimate moral values of a social group, it is the source of such values. Out of man's responses to the nonempirical world, that he has had to conceive, but the content of which he has conceived in conditioned freedom, come the ultimate goals which he pursues. This is the body of theory with which the functional theorist of values may face the challenge not only of the traditional sociologists, but also of the instrumentalists, the Machiavellians, the Marxists, and others. But it is a body of theory that is possible only if one employs an image of man that presupposes conditioned human freedom, rather than determinism, and a recognition of the limits of human rationality and empiricism without reducing responses that transcend those limits to the finiteness of irrationality determined by affective impulses—in other words, what I have called the Judaic-Christian image of man.[23]

21. Talcott Parsons, "The Theoretical Development of the Sociology of Religion," in *Essays in Sociological Theory*, New York: The Free Press, 1949, p. 62.

22. Talcott Parsons, *The Structure of Social Action*, *op. cit.*, p. 668.

23. The treatment of religion within this framework may free us from several unnecessary limitations on the definition of religion within the functional approach:

IV

There remains to be discussed briefly a few of the longer range implications of the use of the Judaic-Christian image of man in the sociology of religion and values and in sociological theory and research generally.

First, I suggest that a sociology of religion and values using the Judaic-Christian image of man raises the question of the ambiguities and stresses in varying modes of social integration based on different religions and value systems. This problem must be approached in light of the double presupposition that (1) the nature of man is such that only by relating himself to a loving, creating, and sustaining nonempirical object and to other men in responsible affection can his need for meaning be met and (2) he always fails to establish such relations. Now such a statement as this does not imply that orientation to other nonempirical objects and the resultant systems of ultimate values do not produce social integration or even that they cannot generate a certain amount of affectional solidarity. Moreover, given these presuppositions, even men who orient themselves to such a nonempirical object will do so incompletely, even to the extent that the religious belief and attitude system through which they orient will contain elements of self-centeredness and self-serving error. Nevertheless, the idea of a society integrated by agape and oriented toward such a nonempirical entity in full faithfulness can be used as an objectively possible but empirically improbable model of social integration from which empirically probable constructed types of integrated and disintegrated societies can be described and accounted for in terms of mode, manner, and degree of deviation and resultant consequences.

The modes and manner of falling away from such a model are innumerable, as are the historical forms of the human situation that constitute the occasion for deviation, but it is possible to indicate only one

---

We can now recognize (1) that while all ultimate *moral* value systems have their roots in some religion, not all religions give rise to value systems that include morality—the world may simply be rejected; (2) religion may be a social phenomenon in the same sense that an individual is social but it is not a societal phenomenon and need not be a group phenomenon; (3) a religion may fail to integrate a society not only because it opposes an older system of moral values, but because it does not give rise to any system of moral values, because it is not shared, or because the content of the moral values created are not such as to prevent conflict; (4) all religion is not an attempt to resolve the problem of social disruption, although social disruption may be one of the forms that creates the problem of meaning, the answer to which need not be something which will create social order.

of the most common. Like the Marxist, the sociologist using the Judaic-Christian image of man is not surprised when a set of religious beliefs is subtly transformed into a rationalization of the economic interests of a social class or even when it contains elements of such rationalization in its very process of formation. Unlike the orthodox functionalist he is unlikely to treat power only or primarily in its instrumental relation to a set of values shared by the members of a society. Yet he will not easily order the data through the presupposition that all religion is nothing but a rationalization of class interest or that power is only an instrument of class domination. The sociologist using the Judaic-Christian image of man will, like Richard Niebuhr, write the *Kingdom of God in America* as well as *The Social Sources of Denominationalism.*

Second, the use of the Judaic-Christian image of man will call into question the whole use of the social system frame of reference, at least as the sole frame of reference for sociology. Society will be seen primarily as a value-realizing system rather than simply a boundary-maintaining system in which values are viewed from the point of view of their contribution to boundary maintenance. Moreover, society will be treated not as the central system of reference, but as an instrumentality through which men attempt to achieve their values. Such an approach will treat social system maintenance as one problem among others and will relate the processes of social control and socialization to the total individual in a very different way, thus opening the way to viewing innovation, conflict, and change within a very different perspective.

Third, the use of the Judaic-Christian image of man in sociology raises once again the theological and religious question of whether experiences of and beliefs about the nonempirical are at least partially valid and whether some are more valid than others. This is not a scientific question, but it presses on the scientist as well as others.

Finally, the use of the Judaic-Christian image of man in sociology will once again permit the discipline to see man, conditioned heavily though he may be, accepting in partial freedom the risks, liabilities, and responsibilities of his life. It should make more difficult the use of sociological knowledge primarily for purposes of manipulation. The functional theory of religion has been used to justify religion on the grounds of its social usefulness as a tool used by the self or by others to tie the person into society or to balance his personality. The grounding of the functional theory of religion in the Judaic-Christian image of man should cast doubt not on whether religion should be used in such a manner but on whether it can be so used. It is my belief that the extension of the use of the Judaic-Christian image of man into all areas of sociological theory will show that the empirical data of human life can be ordered in such a way as to be more effectively grasped. At the same time this extension will offer one way in which the postulate of fact that lies behind the value of institutional freedom in Western society may be supported. If we believe that men are free by nature, we can support an institutional structure of freedom, and a sociology that recognizes human freedom can itself serve its original purposes of enlightenment and emancipation.

b) ASSUMPTIONS ABOUT THE NATURE OF MAN

A. H. MASLOW

Cognition of Being in the Peak Experiences

A. Introduction

SELF-ACTUALIZING PEOPLE, those who have come to a high level of maturation, health, and self-fulfillment, have so much to teach us that sometimes they seem almost like a different breed of human beings. But, because it is so new, the study of the exploration of the highest reaches of human nature and of its ultimate possibilities and aspirations is a difficult and tortuous task. It has involved for me the continuous destruction of cherished axioms, the perpetual coping with seeming paradoxes, contradictions, and vaguenesses and the occasional collapse around my ears

Reprinted from The Journal of Genetic Psychology, *1959, pp. 43-66, by permission of the author and the journal.*

Presidential Address, Division 8, A.P.A., Chicago, Sept. 1, 1956.

I wish to thank James Klee, Frances Wilson Schwartz, and Harry Rand for helping me with this paper.—THE AUTHOR

of long established, firmly believed in, and seemingly unassailable laws of psychology. Often these have turned out to be no laws at all but only rules for living in a state of mild and chronic psychopathology, and fearfulness, of stunting and crippling, and immaturity which we don't notice because most others have this same disease that we have.

Most frequently, as is typical in the history of scientific theorizing, this probing into the unknown first takes the form of a felt dissatisfaction, an uneasiness with what is missing long before any scientific solution becomes available. For instance, one of the first problems presented to me in my studies of self-actualizing people was the vague perception that their motivational life was in some important way different from all that I had learned. I first described it as being expressive rather than coping, but this wasn't *quite* right as a total statement. Then I pointed out that it was unmotivated rather than motivated, but this statement rests so heavily on which theory of motivation you accept, that it made as much trouble as help. In a more recent paper, I have contrasted growth-motivation with deficiency-need motivations which helps, I think, but isn't definitive enough yet, because it doesn't differentiate Becoming from Being. In this address, I shall propose a new tack (into a psychology of Being) which should include and generalize the three attempts already made to put into words somehow, the observed differences between the motivational and cognitive life of fully developed people and of most others.

This analysis of states of Being (temporary, non-striving, purposeless, self-validating, end-experiences and states) emerged first from a study of the love-relations and sexual experiences of self-actualizing people, and then of other people as well, and finally from dipping into the theological and philosophical literatures. It became necessary to differentiate two types of love. The one is love that comes from ordinary love-need, what Fenichel calls love as the need for narcissistic supplies, for gratification of a deficiency of love. It can therefore be conveniently called deficiency-love (D-love). It is typically and normally found in children and adolescents (of whatever age) in our culture.

But this creates a paradox. Self-actualizing people, by definition gratified in their basic needs, including the love need, should cease loving and wanting love, if the only determinant of love were the basic love-need. But the finding is that they are *more* loving people than the average, rather than *less* loving, especially from the point of view of being able to give love as well as to receive it. The attempt to understand this led to the formulation of another form or type of love, closely akin to what the theologians have called Agapean love, or Godly love, and which the psychoanalysts have named object-love and never described further. It is a love for the essence of or the Being of the other person, in the style that Scheler has described, quite apart from what he can give the lover, a love for the person in himself rather than for what we can get from him, detached, altruistic, admiring, unneeded, unselfish. It is love for another person because he is what he is, rather than because he is a need-gratifier.

In this state of love for the Being of the other person or object, I found a particular kind of cognition for which my knowledge of psychology had not prepared me but which I have since seen well described by certain writers on esthetics, religion, and philosophy. This I shall call Cognition of Being, or for short, B-Cognition. This is in contrast to cognition organized by the deficiency needs of the individual, which I shall call D-Cognition. The B-lover is able to perceive realities in the beloved to which others are blind, i.e., he is more acutely and penetratingly perceptive.

This paper is an attempt to generalize in a single description some of these basic cognitive happenings in the B-love experience, the parental experience, the mystic or oceanic, or nature experience, the aesthetic perception, the creative moment, the therapeutic or intellectual insight, the orgasmic experience, certain forms of athletic fulfillment. These and other moments of highest happiness and fulfillment I shall call the peak-experiences.

This is then a chapter in the Positive or Ortho-Psychology of the future in that it deals with fully functioning and healthy human beings, and not alone with normally sick ones. It is therefore not in contradiction to Psychology as a Psychopathology of the Average; it transcends it and can in theory incorporate all its findings in a more inclusive and comprehensive structure which includes both the sick and the healthy, both deficiency, Becoming and Being.

B. B-Cognition in Peak Experiences

I shall present one by one now in a condensed summary, each of the characteristics of the cognition found in the generalized peak-experience, using the term cognition in an extremely broad sense.

1. *In B-Cognition the experience or the object tends to be seen as a whole, as a complete unit, detached from relations, from possible usefulness, from expediency, and from purpose.* It is seen as if it were all there was in the universe, as if it were all of Being, synonymous with the universe.

This contrasts with D-Cognition, which includes most human cognitive experiences. These experiences are partial and incomplete in ways that will be described below.

We are reminded here of the absolute idealism of the 19th century, in which all of the universe was conceived to be a unit. Since this unity could never be encompassed or perceived or cognized in any other fashion by a limited human being, all actual human cognitions were perceived as necessarily part of Being, and never conceivably the whole of it.

2. *When there is a B-Cognition, the percept is exclusively and fully attended to.* This may be called "total attention," or as Schachtel has called it, "focal attention." What I am trying to describe here is very akin to fascination or complete absorption. In such attention the figure becomes *all* figure and the ground, in effect, disappears, or at least is not importantly perceived. It is as if the figure were isolated for the time being from all else, as if the world were forgotten, as if the percept had become for the moment the whole of Being.

Since the whole of Being is being perceived, then all those laws obtain which would obtain if the whole of the cosmos could be encompassed at once. I shall discuss this further below.

This kind of perception is in sharp contrast to normal perception. Here the object is attended to simultaneously with attention to all else that is relevant. It is seen imbedded in its relationships with everything else in the world, and as *part* of the world. Normal figure ground relationships hold, i.e., both the ground and the figure are attended to, although in different ways. Furthermore in ordinary cognition, the object is seen not so much *per se* but as a member of a class, as an instance in a larger category. This kind of perception I have described as "rubricizing," and again would point out that this is not so much a full perception of all aspects of the objects or person being perceived, as it is a kind of taxonomy, a classifying, a ticketing off into one file cabinet or another.

To a far greater degree than we ordinarily realize, cognition involves also placing on a continuum. It involves a kind of automatic comparing or judging or evaluating. It implies higher than, less than, better than, taller than, etc.

B-Cognition is quite different. It may be called non-comparing cognition or non-evaluating or judging cognition. I mean this in the sense in which Dorothy Lee has described the way in which certain primitive peoples differ from us in their perceptions.

A person can be seen per se, in himself and by himself. He can be seen uniquely and idiosyncratically, as if he were the sole member of his class. This is what we mean by perception of the unique individual, and this is, of course, what all clinicians try to achieve. But it is a very difficult task, far more difficult than we are ordinarily willing to admit. However, it can happen, if only transiently, and it does happen characteristically in the peak experience. The healthy mother, perceiving her infant in love, approaches to this kind of perception of the uniqueness of the person. Her baby is not quite like anybody else in the world. It is marvelous, perfect, and fascinating (at least to the extent that she is able to detach herself from Gesell's norms and comparisons with neighbors' children).

Concrete perceiving of the whole of the object implies, also, that it is seen with "care." Contrariwise, "caring" for the object will produce the sustained attention, the repeated examination that is so necessary for perception of all aspects of the object. The caring minuteness with which a mother will gaze upon her infant again and again, or the lover at his beloved, or the connoisseur at his painting will surely produce a more complete perception than the usual casual rubricizing which passes illegitimately for perception. We may expect richness of detail and a many sided awareness of the object from this kind of absorbed, fascinated, fully attending cognition. This contrasts with the product of casual observation which gives only the bare bones of the experience, an object which is seen in only some of its aspects in a selective way and from a point of view.

3. While it is true that all human perception is a product of the human being and is his creation to an extent, still we can make some differentiation between the perception of *external objects as relevant to human concerns and as irrelevant to human concerns.* Self-actualizing people are more able to perceive the world as if it were independent not only of them but also of human beings in general. This also tends to be true of the average human being in his highest moments, i.e., in his peak experiences. He can then more readily look upon nature as if it were there in itself and for itself, and not simply as if it were a human playground put there for human purposes. He can more easily refrain from projecting human purposes upon it. In a word, he can see it in its own Being rather than as something to be used, or something to be afraid of, or to be reacted to in some other human way.

As one example, let us take the microscope which can reveal to us as we look at histological slides either a world of per se beauty or else a world of threat, danger, and pathology. A section of cancer seen through a microscope, if only we can forget that it is a cancer, can be seen as a beautiful and intricate and awe-inspiring organization. A mosquito is a wondrous object. Viruses under the electron microscope are fascinating objects (or, at least, they *can* be if we can only forget their human relevance).

B-Cognition, because it makes human-irrelevance more possible, enables us thereby to see more truly the nature of the object in itself.

4. One difference between B-Cognition and average cognition which

is now emerging in my studies, but of which I am as yet uncertain, is that repeated *B-cognizing seems to make the perception richer.* The repeated experiencing of a face that we love or a painting that we admire makes us like it more, and permits us to see more and more of it in various senses. This we may call intra-object richness.

But this so far contrasts rather sharply with the more usual effects of repeated experiencing, i.e., boredom, familiarization effects, loss of attention and the like. I have found to my own satisfaction—although I cannot prove it to anyone else—that repeated exposures to what I consider a good painting will make the painting look more beautiful to people preselected as perceptive and sensitive, while repeated exposures to what I consider a bad painting will make it look less beautiful.

In this more usual kind of perception, where so frequently the initial perception is simply a classification into useful or not useful, dangerous or not dangerous, repeated looking makes it become more and more empty. The task of normal perception which is so frequently anxiety-based or motivation-determined, is fulfilled in the first viewing and thereafter the object or person, now that it has been catalogued, is simply no longer perceived. Poverty shows up in repeated experiencing; so, also, does richness. Furthermore not only does poverty of the percept show up in repeated looking, but also the poverty of the beholder.

I am becoming more convinced that one of the main mechanisms by which love produces a profounder perception of the intrinsic qualities of the love object than does non-love, is that love involves fascination with the love-object, and therefore repeated and intent and searching looking, seeing with "care." Lovers can see potentialities in each other that other people are blind to. Customarily we snicker and say "Love is blind," but we must now make room for the possibility that love may be under certain circumstances more perceptive than non-love. Of course this implies that it is possible in some sense to perceive potentialities which are not yet actual. I do not think that this is as difficult a research problem as it sounds. The Rorschach test in the hands of an expert is also a perception of potentialities which are not yet actualized. I think this is a testable hypothesis in principle.

5. American psychology, or more broadly, Western psychology, in what I consider to be an ethnocentric way, assumes that human needs, fears, and interests must always be determinants of perception. The "New Look" in perception is based upon the assumption that cognition must always be motivated. The further assumption is implied that cognition is a coping, instrumental mechanism, and that it must to some extent be egocentric. It assumes that the world can be seen *only* from the vantage point of the interests of the perceiver and that the experience

must be organized around the ego as a centering and determining point.

I consider this point of view ethnocentric not only because it arises so clearly as an unconscious expression of the Western world outlook, but also because it involves a persistent and assiduous neglect of the writings of philosophers, theologians, and psychologists of the Eastern world, particularly of the Chinese, Japanese, and Hindus, not to mention Western writers like Goldstein and Angyal.

My findings indicate that in the normal perceptions of self-actualizing people and in the more occasional peak experiences of average people, *perception can be relatively ego-transcending, self-forgetful, egoless.* It can be unmotivated, impersonal, desireless, unselfish, not needed, detached. It can be object-centered rather than ego-centered. That is to say, that the perceptual experience can be organized around the object as a centering point rather than being based upon the ego. It is as if they were perceiving something that had independent reality of its own, and was not dependent upon the beholder. It is possible in the aesthetic experience or the love experience to become so absorbed and "poured into" the object that the self, in a very real sense, disappears. Some writers on aesthetics, on mysticism, on motherhood, and on love have gone so far as to say that in the peak experience we may even speak of identification of the perceiver and the perceived, a fusion of what was two into a new and larger whole, a super-ordinate unit. This could remind us of some of the definitions of empathy and of identification, and, of course, at once opens up the possibilities of research in this direction.

6. *The peak experience is felt as a self-validating, self-justifying moment which carries its own intrinsic value with it.* That is to say it is an end in itself, what we may call an end-experience rather than a means-experience. It is felt to be so valuable an experience, so great a revelation, that even to attempt to justify it takes away from its dignity and worth. This is universally attested to by my subjects as they report their love experiences, their mystic experiences, their aesthetic experiences, their creative experiences, and their bursts of insight. Particularly with the moment of insight in the therapeutic situation does this become obvious. By virtue of the very fact that the person defends himself against the insight, it is therefore by definition painful to accept. Its breaking through into consciousness is customarily crushing to the person. And yet, in spite of this fact, it is universally reported to be worth while, desirable, and wanted. Seeing is better than being blind, even when seeing hurts. It is a case in which the intrinsic self-justifying, self-validating worth of the experience makes the pain worth while. Not only do my subjects attest to this finding but so, also, do the numerous writers on

aesthetics, religion, creativeness, and love. Uniformly they describe these experiences not only as valuable intrinsically, but as *so* valuable that they make life worth while by their occasional occurrence. The mystics have always affirmed this great value of the great mystic experience which may come only two or three times in a lifetime.

The contrast is very sharp with the ordinary experiences of life, especially in the West, and, most especially, for American psychologists. Behavior is so identified with means to ends that by many writers the words "behavior" and "instrumental behavior" are taken as synonymous. Everything is done for the sake of some further goal, *in order to* achieve something else. The apotheosis of this attitude is reached by John Dewey in his theory of value, in which he finds no ends at all but only means to ends. Even this statement is not quite accurate because it implies the existence of ends. Rather to be quite accurate he implies that means are means to other means, which in turn are means, and so on ad infinitum.

The peak experiences are for my subjects ultimate goals of living and the ultimate validations and justifications for it. That the psychologist should by-pass them or even be officially unaware of their existence, or what is even worse, in the objectivistic psychologies, deny a priori the possibility of their existence as objects for scientific study, is incomprehensible.

7. In *all the common peak experiences, or at least in those which I have studied, there is a very characteristic disorientation in time and space.* This goes so far that it would be more accurate to say that in these moments the person is outside of time and space subjectively. For instance, in the creative furor, the poet or artist becomes oblivious of his surroundings, and of the passage of time. It is impossible for him when he wakes up to judge how much time has passed. Frequently he has to shake his head as if emerging from a daze to rediscover where he is.

But more than this is the frequent report especially by lovers of the complete loss of extension in time. Not only does time pass in their ecstasies with a frightening rapidity so that a day may pass as if it were a minute but also a minute so intensely lived may feel like a day or a year. It is as if they had, in a way, some place in another world in which time simultaneously stood still and moved with great rapidity. For our ordinary categories, this is of course a paradox and a contradiction. And yet this is what is reported and it is therefore a fact that we must take account of. I see no reason why this kind of experiencing of time should not be amenable to experimental research. The judgment of the passing of time in peak-experience must be very inaccurate. So, also, for consciousness of surroundings. This, too, must be much less accurate than in normal living and, therefore, can be researched with.

8. I have been much impressed with the implications of my findings for a psychology of values. I find them very puzzling and yet so uniform that it is necessary not only to report them but also to try somehow to understand them. To start at the end first, *the peak experience is only good and desirable, and is never evil or painful or undesirable.* The experience is intrinsically valid and the experience is perfect, complete, and needs nothing else. It is sufficient to itself. It is felt as being intrinsically necessary and inevitable. It is just as good as it *should* be. It is reacted to with awe, wonder, amazement, humility, and even reverence, exaltation, and piety. The word sacred is occasionally used to describe the person's reaction to it.

The philosophical implications here are tremendous. If, for the sake of argument, we accept the thesis that in the peak experience the nature of reality *may* be seen more clearly and its essence penetrated more profoundly, then this is almost the same as saying what so many philosophers and theologians have affirmed, that the whole of Being is only neutral or good, and that evil or pain or threat is only a partial phenomenon, a product of not seeing the world whole and unified.

Another way of saying this is to compare it with one aspect of the concept of God which is very widespread in many religions. Those Gods who can contemplate and encompass the whole of Being and who therefore understand it, must see it as good, just, inevitable, and must see "evil" as a product of limited vision and understanding. If we could be God-like in this sense then we, too, out of universal understanding would never blame or condemn or be disappointed or shocked. Our only possible emotions would be pity, charity, kindliness, and perhaps sadness for the shortcomings of the other. But this is precisely the way in which self-actualizing people react to the world, and in which *all* of us react in our peak moments. I remind you that this is precisely the way in which all psychotherapists *try* to react to their patients. We must grant, of course, that this god-like, universally tolerant, and accepting attitude is extremely difficult to attain, probably even impossible in a pure form, and yet we know that this is a relative matter. We can approximate it more closely or less closely and it would be foolish to deny the phenomenon simply because it comes rarely and impurely. Though we can never be gods in this sense, we can be more godlike or less godlike.

In any case the contrast with our ordinary cognitions and reactions is very sharp. Ordinarily we proceed under the aegis of means-values, i.e., of usefulness, desirability, badness or goodness, of suitability for a purpose. We evaluate, judge, condemn, or approve. We react to the experience in personal terms and perceive the world in reference to ourselves and our ends, thereby making the world no more than means to our ends. This is the opposite of being detached from the world, which means in turn that we are not really perceiving *it*, but perceiving ourselves in it. We perceive then in a deficiency-motivated way and can therefore perceive only D-values. This is different from perceiving the whole world, or that portion of it which in the peak experience we take as surrogate for the world. Then and only then can we perceive *its* values rather than our own. These I call the values of Being, or for short, the B-values. These are the same as Robert Hartman's "intrinsic values."

These B-values are so far as I can make out at this point, (*a*) wholeness, integration, unity, and interconnectedness; (*b*) necessity, perfection, completeness, and inevitability; (*c*) aliveness, good functioning, spontaneity, and process; (*d*) richness, intricacy, and complexity; (*e*) beauty, awe-fulness; (*f*) goodness, rightness, desirability; (*g*) uniqueness, idiosyncrasy, and expressiveness; (*h*) effortlessness, ease of achievement, lack of strain or striving; and finally (*i*) occasionally, but not always, an element of humor or playfulness.

Not only is this, then, a demonstration of fusion and unity of the old trinity of the true, the good, and the beautiful, but it is more than that. I have elsewhere reported my finding that truth, goodness, and beauty are in the normal person only fairly well correlated with each other, and in the neurotic even less so. It is only in the healthy and mature human being, in the self-actualizing, fully functioning person that they are so highly correlated that for all practical purposes they may be said to fuse into a unity. I would now add that this is also true for other people in their highest moments, i.e., in their peak experiences of love, of sex, of creativity, of aesthetic perception, of religious or mystic experience, and of insight and understanding.

This finding, if it turns out to be correct, is in direct and flat contradiction to one of the basic axioms that guides all scientific thought, namely, that the more objective and impersonal perception becomes, the more detached it becomes from value. Fact and value have almost always (by intellectuals) been considered to be antonyms and mutually exclusive. But perhaps the opposite is true, for when we examine the most ego-detached, objective, motivationless, passive cognition, we find that it claims to perceive values directly, that values cannot be shorn away from reality and that the most profound perceptions of "facts" are tinged with wonder, admiration, awe and approval, i.e., with value.

9. Normal experience is imbedded in history and in culture as well as in the shifting and relative needs of man. It is organized in time and in space. That is to say it is part of larger wholes and therefore is relative to these larger wholes and frames of reference. Since it is felt to depend upon man for whatever reality it has, then if man were to disap-

pear, *it,* also, would disappear. Its organizing frames of reference shift from the interests of the person to the demands of the situation, from the immediate in time to the past and the future and from the here to the there. In these senses experience and behavior are relative.

Peak experiences are from this point of view more absolute and less relative. Not only are they timeless and spaceless in the senses which I have indicated above, not only are they detached from the ground and perceived more in themselves, not only are they relatively unmotivated and detached from the interests of man, but they are also perceived and reacted to as if they were in themselves, "out there," as if they were perceptions of a reality independent of man and persisting beyond his life. It is certainly very difficult and also very dangerous scientifically to speak of relative and absolute and I am quite aware that I am walking into a semantic swamp. And yet I am compelled by the many introspective reports of my subjects to report this differentiation as a finding with which we psychologists will ultimately have to make our peace. These are the words that the subjects themselves use in trying to describe experiences which are essentially ineffable. *They* speak of "absolute," *they* speak of "relative," and it is my duty to report it.

Again and again we ourselves are tempted to this kind of vocabulary, for instance, in the realm of art. A Chinese vase may be perfect in itself, may be simultaneously 2000 years old and yet fresh in this moment, universal rather than Chinese. In these senses at least it is absolute, even though also simultaneously relative to time, to the culture of its origin, and to the aesthetic standards of the beholder. Is it not meaningful also that the mystic experience has been described in almost identical words by people in every religion, every era, and in every culture. No wonder Aldous Huxley has called it "The Perennial Philosophy." The great creators, let us say as anthologized by Brewster Ghiselin, have described their creative moments in almost identical terms, even though they were variously poets, chemists, sculptors, philosophers, and mathematicians.

The concept of absolute has made difficulty partly because it has almost always been permeated with a static taint. It is now clear from the experience of my subjects that this is not necessary or inevitable. Perception of an aesthetic object or a beloved face or a beautiful theory is a fluctuating, shifting process but this fluctuation of attention is strictly *within* the perception. Its richness can be infinite and the continued gaze can go from one aspect of the perfection to another, now concentrating on one side of it, now on another. A fine painting has many organizations, not just one, so that the aesthetic experience can be a continuous though fluctuating delight as it is seen, in itself, now in one way, now in another. Also it can be seen relatively in one moment, absolutely in the next. We needn't struggle over whether it is *either* relative *or* absolute. It can be both.

10. Ordinary cognition is a very active process. It is characteristically a kind of shaping and selection by the beholder. *He* chooses what to perceive and what not to perceive, he relates it to his needs and fears and interests, he gives it organization, arranging and re-arranging it. In a word, he works at it. Cognition is an energy consuming process. It involves alertness, vigilance, and tension and is, therefore, fatiguing.

B-Cognition is much more passive and receptive than active although, of course, it never can be completely so. The best descriptions that I have found of this "passive" kind of cognizing comes from Eastern philosophers especially from Lao-Tse and the Taoistic philosophers. Krishnamurti has an excellent phrase to describe my data. He calls it "choiceless awareness." We could also name it "desireless awareness." The Taoistic conception of "let be" also says what I am trying to say, namely, that perception may be undemanding rather than demanding, contemplative, rather than forceful. It can be humble before the experience, non-interfering, receiving rather than taking, it can let the percept be itself. I am reminded here, also, of Freud's description of "free floating attention." This, too, is passive rather than active, selfless rather than egocentric, dreamy rather than vigilant, patient rather than impatient. It is gazing rather than looking, surrendering and submitting to the experience.

I have also found useful a recent memorandum by John Shlien on the difference between passive listening and active, forceful listening. The good therapist must be able to listen in the receiving rather than the taking sense in order to be able to hear what is actually said rather than what he expects to hear or demands to hear. He must not impose himself but rather let the words flow in upon him. Only so can their own shape and pattern be assimilated. Otherwise one hears only one's own theories and expectations.

As a matter of fact we may say that it is this criterion, of being able to be receiving and passive, that marks off the good therapist from the poor one of whatever school. The good therapist is able to perceive each person in his own right, freshly and without the urge to taxonomize, to rubricize, to classify and pigeon hole. The poor therapist through a hundred years of clinical experience may find only repeated corroborations of the theories which he learned at the beginning of his career. It is in this sense that it has been pointed out that a therapist can repeat the same mistakes for 40 years and then call it "rich clinical experience."

An entirely different, though equally unfashionable, way of communicating the feeling of this characteristic of B-cognition, is to call it, with D. H. Lawrence and other Romantics, non-voluntary rather than volitional. Ordinary cognition is highly volitional and therefore demanding, prearranged, and preconceived. In the cognition of the peak-experience, the will does not interfere. It is held in abeyance. It receives and doesn't demand. We cannot command the peak-experience. It happens *to* us.

11. *The emotional reaction in the peak experience has a special flavor of wonder, of awe, of humility before the experience.* This sometimes has a touch of fear (although pleasant fear) of being overwhelmed. My subjects report this in such phrases as "This is too much for me." "It is more than I can bear." "It is too wonderful." The experience may have a certain poignancy and piercing quality which may bring either tears or laughter and which may be paradoxically akin to pain, although this is a desirable pain which is often described as "sweet." This may go so far as to involve thoughts of death in a peculiar way. Not only my subjects but many writers on the various peak experiences have made the parallel with the experience of dying, that is an eager dying. A typical phrase might be: "This is too wonderful. I don't know how I can bear it. I could die now and it would be all right." Perhaps this is in part a hanging on to the experience and a reluctance to go down from this peak into the valley of ordinary existence. Perhaps it is in part, also, an aspect of the profound sense of humility, smallness, unworthiness before the enormity of the experience.

12. Another paradox with which we must deal, difficult though it is, is found in the conflicting reports of perception of the world. *In some reports, particularly of the mystic experience or the religious experience or philosophical experience, the whole of the world is seen as a unity, as a single rich entity. In other of the peak experiences, most particularly the love experience and the aesthetic experience, one small part of the world is perceived as if it were for the moment all of the world.* In both cases the perception is of unity. Probably the fact that the B-cognition of a painting or a person or a theory retains all the attributes of the whole of Being, i.e., the B-values, derives from this fact of perceiving it as if it were all that existed at the moment.

13. In another paper I have tried to demonstrate the substantial difference between the cognition that abstracts and categorizes (rubricizing) and the fresh cognition of the concrete, the raw, and the particular. This is the sense in which I shall use the terms abstract and concrete. They are not very different from Goldstein's terms. There I pointed out also that most of our cognitions (attendings, perceivings, rememberings, thinkings, and learnings) were abstract rather than concrete. That is, we mostly categorize, schematize, classify, and abstract in our cognitive life.

We do not so much cognize the nature of the world as it actually is, as we cognize the organization of our own inner world outlook. Most of experience is filtered through our system of categories and rubrics, as Schachtel has also pointed out in his classical paper, "On Childhood Amnesia and the Problem of Memory." I was led to this differentiation by my studies of self-actualizing people, *finding in them simultaneously the ability to abstract without giving up concreteness and the ability to be concrete without giving up abstractness.* This adds a little to Goldstein's description because I found not only a reduction to the concrete but also what we might call a reduction to the abstract, i.e., a loss of ability to cognize the concrete. Since then I have found this same exceptional ability to perceive the concrete in good artists as well, even though not self-actualizing. More recently I find this same ability in ordinary people in their peak moments. They are then more able to grasp the percept in its own concrete idiosyncratic nature.

Since this kind of idiographic perceiving has customarily been described as the core of aesthetic perceiving, as for instance by Northrop, they have almost been made synonymous. For most philosophers and artists, to perceive a person concretely, in his intrinsic uniqueness is to perceive him aesthetically. I prefer the broader usage and think that I have already demonstrated that this kind of perception of the unique nature of the object is characteristic of *all* peak experiences, not only the aesthetic one.

I find it useful to understand the concrete perceiving which takes place in B-Cognition as a perception of all aspects and attributes of the object simultaneously or in quick succession. Abstracting is in essence a selection out of certain aspects only of the object, those which are of use to us, those which threaten us, those with which we are familiar, or those which fit our language categories. Both Whitehead and Bergson have made this sufficiently clear, as have many other philosophers since. Vivanti has phrased it well when he pointed out that abstractions to the extent that they are useful, are also false. In a word, to perceive an object abstractly means *not* to perceive some aspects of it. It clearly implies selection of some attributes, rejection of other attributes, creation or distortion of still others. We make of it what we wish. We create it. We manufacture it. Furthermore, extremely important is the strong tendency in abstracting to relate the aspects of the object to our linguistic system. This makes special troubles because language is a secondary rather than a primary process in the Freudian sense, because it deals with external reality rather than psychic reality, with the conscious rather than the unconscious. It is true that this lack can be corrected to some extent by poetic language but in the last analysis much of experience is ineffable and can be put into no language at all.

Let us take for example the perception of a painting or of a person. In order to perceive them fully we must fight our tendency to classify, to compare, to evaluate, to need, to use. The moment that we say this man is, e.g., a foreigner, in that moment we have classified him, performed an abstracting act and, to some extent, cut ourselves off from the possibility of seeing him as a unique and whole human being, different from any other one in the whole world. In the moment that we approach the painting on the wall to read the name of the artist, we have cut ourselves off from the possibility of seeing it with complete freshness in its own uniqueness. To a certain extent then what we call *knowing*, i.e., the placing of an experience in a system of concepts or words or relations, cuts off the possibility of full cognizing. Herbert Read has pointed out that the child has the "innocent eye," the ability to see something as if he were seeing it for the first time (frequently he *is* seeing it for the first time). He can then stare at it in wonder, examining all aspects of it, taking in all its attributes, since for the child in this situation, no attribute of a strange object is any more important than any other attribute. He does not organize it; he simply stares at it. In the similar situation for the adult, to the extent that we can prevent ourselves from only abstracting, naming, placing, comparing, relating, to that extent will we be able to see more and more aspects of the many sidedness of the person or of the painting. Particularly I must underline the ability to perceive the ineffable, that which cannot be put into words. Trying to force it into words changes it, and makes it something other than it is, something else *like* it, something similar, and yet something different that *it* itself.

It is this ability to perceive the whole and to rise above parts which characterizes cognition in the various peak experiences. Since only thus can one know a person in the fullest sense of the words, it is not surprising that self-actualizing people are so much more astute in their perception of people, in their penetration to the core or essence of another person. This is also why I feel convinced that the ideal therapist, who presumably should be able as a professional necessity, to understand another person in his uniqueness and in his wholeness, without presupposition, ought to be at least a fairly healthy human being. I maintain this even though willing to grant unexplained individual differences in this kind of perceptiveness, and that also therapeutic experience can itself be a kind of training in the cognition of the Being of another human being. This also explains why I feel that a training in aesthetic perceiving and creating could be a very desirable aspect of clinical training.

14. *At the higher levels of human maturation, many dichotomies, polarities, and conflicts are fused and resolved.* Self-actualizing people are simultaneously selfish and unselfish, Dionysian and Apollonian, individual

and social, rational and irrational, fused with others and detached from others, and so on. What I had thought to be straight line continua, whose extremes were polar to each other and as far apart as possible, turned out to be rather like circles or spirals, in which the polar extremes came together into a fused unity. So also do I find this as a strong tendency in the full cognition of the object. The more we understand the whole of Being, the more we can tolerate the simultaneous existence and perception of inconsistencies, of oppositions, and of flat contradictions. These seem to be products of partial cognition, and made away with cognition of the whole. The neurotic person, seen from a godlike vantage point, can then be seen as a wonderful, intricate even beautiful unity of process. What we normally see as conflict and contradiction and dissociation can then be perceived as inevitable, necessary, even fated. That is to say if he can be fully understood, then everything falls into its necessary place and he can be aesthetically perceived and appreciated. All his conflicts and splits turn out to have a kind of sense or wisdom. Even the concepts of sickness and of health may fuse and blur when we see the symptom as a pressure toward health, or see the neurosis as the healthiest possible solution at the moment to the problems of the individual.

15. *The person at the peak is godlike not only in senses that I have touched upon already but in certain other ways as well, particularly in the complete and loving and uncondemning acceptance of the world and of the person,* however bad he may look at more normal moments. The theologians have long struggled with the terrible task of reconciling sin and evil and pain in the world with the concept of an all-powerful, all-loving, all-knowing God. A subsidiary difficulty has been presented by the task of reconciling the necessity of rewards and punishments for good and evil with this concept of all-loving, all-forgiving God. He must somehow both punish and not punish, both forgive and condemn.

I think we can learn something about the resolution of this dilemma from the study of self-actualizing people and from the comparison of the two broadly different types of perception discussed so far, i.e., B-perception and D-perception. B-perception is a momentary thing ordinarily. It is a peak, a high spot, an occasional achievement. It looks as if all human beings perceive most of the time in a deficiency way. That is, they compare, they judge, they approve, they relate, they use. This means that it is possible for us to perceive another human being alternately in two different ways, sometimes in his Being, as if he were the whole of the universe for the time being. Much more often, however, we perceive him as a part of the universe and related to the rest of it in many complex ways. When we B-perceive him, *then* we can be all-loving, all-forgiving, all-accepting, all-admiring, all-understanding. But these are precisely the attributes assigned to most conceptions of God. In such moments we can then be godlike in these attributes. For instance, in the therapeutic situation we can relate ourselves in this loving, understanding, accepting, forgiving way to all sorts of people whom we normally fear and condemn and even hate—murderers, pederasts, rapists, exploiters, cowards.

It is extremely interesting to me that all people behave at times as if they wanted to be B-cognized. They resent being classified, categorized, rubricized. Ticketing off a person as a waiter or a policeman or a dame instead of as an individual often offends. We all want to be recognized and accepted for what we are in our fullness, richness, and complexity. If such an acceptor cannot be found among human beings, then the very strong tendency appears to project and create a godlike figure.

Another kind of answer to the "problem of evil" is suggested by the way in which our subjects "accept reality" as being-in-itself, in its own right. It is neither *for* man nor is it *against* him. It just is impersonally what it is. An earthquake which kills poses a problem of reconciliation only for the man who needs a personal God who is simultaneously all-loving and omnipotent and who created the world. For the man who can perceive and accept it impersonally and uncreated it presents no ethical or axiological problem, since it wasn't done "on purpose," to annoy him. He shrugs his shoulders and if evil is defined anthropocentrically, he simply accepts evil as he does the seasons and the storms. Of course it is much harder to achieve this attitude with human actions which are hurtful to him, but it is occasionally possible, and the more matured the man is, the more possible it is.

16. *Perception in the peak moment tends very strongly to be idiographic.* The percept, whether a person or the world or a tree or work of art, tends to be seen as a unique instance, and as the only member of its class. This is in contrast to our normal nomothetic way of handling the world which rests essentially on generalization and on an Aristotelian division of the world into classes of various sorts, of which the object is an example. The whole concept of classification rests upon general classes. If there were no classes the concepts of resemblance, of equality, of similarity and of difference would become totally useless. One cannot compare two objects which have nothing in common. Furthermore for two objects to have something in common means necessarily abstraction, e.g., such qualities as redness, roundness, heaviness, etc. But if we perceive a person without abstracting, if we insist upon perceiving all his attributes simultaneously and as necessary to each other, then we no longer can classify. Every whole person from this point of view or every

painting or every bird or flower becomes the sole member of a class and must therefore be perceived idiographically.

17. *One aspect of the peak-experience is a complete, though momentary, loss of fear, anxiety, inhibition, defense, and control, a giving up of renunciation, delay, and restraint.* The fear of disintegration and dissolution, the fear of being overwhelmed by the "instincts," the fear of death and of insanity, the fear of giving in to unbridled pleasure and emotion, all tend to disappear or go into abeyance for the time being.

It may be thought of as pure gratification, pure expression, pure elation. But since it is "in the world," it represents a kind of fusion of the Freudian "pleasure principle" and "reality principle." It is therefore still another instance of the resolution of normally dichotomous concepts at higher levels of psychological functioning.

We may therefore expect to find a certain "permeability" in people who have such experiences commonly, a closeness and openness to the unconscious, and a relative lack of fear of it.

C. Other Changes in the Person

In addition to all these changes in the cognition of the world (including attitudes toward it), all sorts of other changes occur in the person in the peak experience and afterward.

For one thing, not only the world but also he himself becomes more a unity, more integrated, and self-consistent. This is another way of saying that he becomes more completely himself, idiosyncratic, unique. And since he is so, he can be more easily expressive and spontaneous without effort. All his powers then come together in their most efficient integration and coordination, organized and coordinated much more perfectly than usual. Everything then can be done with unusual ease and lack of effort. Inhibition, doubt, control, self-criticism, diminish toward a zero point and he becomes the spontaneous, coordinated, efficient organism, functioning like an animal without conflict or split, without hesitation or doubt, in a great flow of power that is so peculiarly effortless, that it may become like play, masterful, virtuoso-like. In such a moment, his powers are at their height and he may be startled (afterwards) by his unsuspected skill, confidence, creativeness, perceptiveness, and virtuosity of performance. It is all so easy that it can be enjoyed and laughed with. Things can be dared that would be impossible at other times.

To put it simply, he becomes more whole and unified, more unique and idiosyncratic, more alive and spontaneous, more perfectly expressive and uninhibited, more effortless and powerful, more daring and courageous (leaving fears and doubts behind), more ego-transcending and self-forgetful.

But these are almost the same as the list of B-values already described above. Which is to say that as the essential Being of the world is felt by the perceiver to be cognized, so also does he concurrently come closer to his own Being, or to being himself, or to self-actualization, or to perfection in his own kind, etc. As the experience becomes more unified, so does he also become more unified, as it becomes richer, so does he, as it becomes more itself, so does he as well, and so on. He and the world become more like each other as they both move toward perfection. Perhaps this is what is meant by the well-known fusion of lovers, the becoming one with the world in the mystic experience, the feeling of absorbed fusion and unity with the work of art in the aesthetic experience, the feeling so often reported by our great creators that their words take hold of them and practically write themselves as if they were being dictated, the great philosophical insights in which one becomes *part* of the unity one experiences and merged into it. This is what Angyal is talking about in part, when he speaks of the trend to homonomy. Also relevant here is my conclusion that just those qualities which describe a good painting (Wilson's criteria) also describe the good human being, i.e., the B-values of wholeness, uniqueness, aliveness, richness, etc.

May I now attempt briefly to put all of this in another frame of reference which is more familiar to you, the psychoanalytic. Secondary processes deal with the real world outside the unconscious. Logic, science, common sense, good adjustment, enculturation, responsibility, planning, rationalism are all secondary process techniques. The primary processes were first discovered in neurotics and psychotics and then in children, and only recently in healthy people. The rules by which the unconscious works can be seen most clearly in dreams. Wishes and fears are the primary movers, the Freudian mechanisms, the primary techniques. The well adjusted, responsible, common sense man who gets along well in the real world must usually do this in part by turning his back on his unconscious and denying and repressing it.

For me, this realization came most keenly when I had to face the fact about 15 years ago that my self-actualizing subjects, picked because they were very mature, were at the same time, also childish. I called it "healthy childishness," a "second naïveté." It has since been recognized by Kris and the ego-psychologists as "regression in the service of the ego," not only found in healthy people, but finally conceded to be a *sine qua non* of psychological health. Balint has recognized love to be a regression (i.e., the person who can't regress can't love). And, finally, the analysts agree that inspiration and great (primary) creativeness comes partly out of the unconscious, i.e., is a healthy regression, a temporary turning away from the real world.

Now what I have been describing here may be seen as a fusion of ego, id, super-ego, and ego-ideal, of conscious and unconscious, of primary and secondary processes, a synthesizing of pleasure principle with reality principle, a regression without fear in the service of the greatest maturity, a true integration of the person at *all* levels.

D. Redefinition of Self-Actualization

In other words, any person in any of the peak experiences, takes on temporarily many of the characteristics which I found in self-actualizing individuals. That is, for the time they become self-actualizers. We may think of it as a passing characterological change if we wish, and not just as an emotional-cognitive-expressive state. Not only are these his happiest and most thrilling moments, but they are also moments of greatest maturity, individuation, fulfillment—in a word his healthiest moments.

This makes it possible for us to redefine self-actualization in such a way as to purge it of all its static and typological shortcomings, and to make it less a kind of all-or-none pantheon into which some rare people enter at the age of 60. We may define it as an episode, or a spurt in which the powers of the organism come together in a particularly efficient and intensely enjoyable way, and in which he is more integrated and less split, more open for experience, more idiosyncratic, more perfectly expressive or spontaneous, or fully functioning, more creative, more humorous, more ego-transcending, more independent of his lower needs, etc. He becomes in these episodes more truly himself, more perfectly actualizing his potentialities, closer to the core of his Being.

Such states or episodes can, in theory, come at any time in life to any person. What seems to distinguish those individuals I have called self-actualizing people, is that in them these episodes seem to come far more frequently, and intensely and perfectly than in average people. This makes self-actualization a matter of degree and of frequency rather than an all-or-none affair, and thereby makes it more amenable to available research procedures. We need no longer be limited to searching for those rare subjects who may be said to be fulfilling themselves most of the time. In theory at least we may also search *any* life history for episodes of self-actualization, especially those of artists, intellectuals and other especially creative people, of profoundly religious people, and of people experiencing great insights in psychotherapy, or in other important growth experiences.

E. The Question of External Validity

So far I have described a subjective experience in a phenomenological fashion. Its relationship to the external world is another matter altogether. Just because the perceiver *believes* that he perceives more truly and more wholly, is no proof that he actually does so. The criteria for judging the validity of this belief ordinarily lie in the objects or persons perceived or in the products created. They are therefore, in principle, simple problems for correlational research.

But in what sense can art be said to be knowledge? The aesthetic perception certainly has its intrinsic self-validation. It is felt as a valuable and wonderful experience. But so also are some illusions and hallucinations. And furthermore you may be aroused to an aesthetic experience by a painting which leaves me untouched. If we are to go at all beyond the private, the problem of external criteria of validity remains, just as it does with all other perceptions.

The same can be said for loving perception, for the mystic experience, for the creative moment, and for the flash of insight.

The lover perceives in the beloved what no one else can, and again, there is no question about the intrinsic value of his inner experience and of the many good consequences for him, for his beloved, and for the world. If we take as an example, the mother loving her baby, the case is even more obvious. Not only does love perceive potentialities but it also actualizes them. The absence of love certainly stifles potentialities and even kills them. Personal growth demands courage, self confidence, even daring, and non-love from the parent or the mate produces the opposite, self doubt, anxiety, feelings of worthlessness and expectations of ridicule, all inhibitors of growth and of self-actualization.

All personological and psychotherapeutic experience is testimonial to this fact that love actualizes and non-love stultifies, whether deserved or not.

The complex and circular question then arises here "To what extent is this phenomenon a self-fulfilling prophecy" as Merton has called it. A husband's conviction that his wife is beautiful, or a wife's firm belief that her husband is courageous, to some extent *creates* the beauty or the courage. This is not so much a perception of something that already exists as a bringing into existence by belief. Shall we perhaps consider this an example of perception of a potentiality, since *every* person has the possibility of being beautiful and courageous? If so, then this is different from perceiving the real possibility that someone may become a great violinist, which is *not* a universal possibility.

And yet, even beyond all this complexity, the lurking doubts remain to those who hope ultimately to drag all these problems into the domain of public science. Frequently enough, love for another brings illusions, the perceptions of qualities and potentialities that don't exist, that are not therefore truly perceived but created in the mind of the beholder and which then rest on a system of needs, repressions, denials, projections, and rationalizations. If love can be more perceptive than non-love, it can also be blinder. And the research problem remains to nag us, when is which? How can we select out those instances in which perception of the real world is more acute? I have already reported my observations at the personological level, that one answer to this question lies in the variable of the psychological health of the perceiver, in or out of the love relationship. The greater the health, the more acute and penetrating the perception of the world, all other things being equal. Since this conclusion was the product of uncontrolled observation, it must be presented only as a hypothesis awaiting controlled research.

In general, similar problems confront us in aesthetic and intellectual bursts of creativeness, and also in the insight experiences. In both instances, the external validation of the experience is not perfectly correlated with phenomenological self-validation. It is possible for the great insight to be mistaken, the great love to disappear. The poem that creates itself in a peak experience may have to be thrown away later as unsatisfactory. Creation of a product that will stand up feels subjectively the same as the creation of a product that folds up later under cold, objective critical scrutiny. The habitually creative person knows this well, expecting half of his great moments of insight not to work out. All peak experiences feel like Being-experience but not all are truly so. And yet, we dare not neglect the clear hints that, sometimes at least, greater perspicuity and greater efficiency of cognition can be found in healthier people and in healthier moments, i.e., some peak-experiences *are* B-experiences. I once suggested the principle that if self-actualizing people can and do perceive reality more efficiently, fully and with less motivational contamination than we others do, then we may possibly use them as biological assays. Through *their* greater sensitivity and perception, we may get a better report of what reality is like, than through our own eyes, just as canaries can be used to detect gas in mines before less sensitive creatures can.

As a second string to this same bow, we may use ourselves in our most perceptive moments, in our peak-experiences, when, for the moment, *we* are self-actualizing, to give us a report of the nature of reality that is truer than we can ordinarily manage.

F. The After-Effects of Peak Experiences

Completely separable from the question of the external validity of cognition in the various peak experiences, is that of the after-effects upon the person of these experiences which in still another sense, may be said to validate the experience. I have no controlled research data to present to you. I have only the unanimous agreement of my subjects that there *were* such effects, my own conviction that there were, and the complete agreement of all the writers on creativeness, love, insight, mystic experience, and aesthetic experience. On these grounds I feel justified in making at least the following affirmations or propositions, all of which are testable.

1. Peak experiences have some therapeutic effects, in the strict sense of removing symptoms. I have at least two reports—one from a psychologist, one from an anthropologist—of mystic or oceanic experiences so profound as to remove neurotic symptoms forever after. Such conversion experiences are of course plentifully recorded in human history but so far as I know have never received the attention of psychologists or psychiatrists.

2. They change the person's view of himself in a healthy direction.

3. They change his view of other people and his relations to them in many ways.

4. They change more or less permanently his view of the world, or of aspects or parts of it.

5. They release him for greater creativity, spontaneity, expressiveness, idiosyncrasy.

6. He remembers the experience as a very important and desirable happening and seeks to repeat it.

7. The person is more apt to feel that life in general is worth while, even if it is usually drab, pedestrian, painful, or ungratifying, since beauty and goodness and excitement and honesty and truth and meaningfulness have been demonstrated to him to exist.

Many other effects could be reported that are ad hoc and idiosyncratic, depending on the particular person, and his particular problems which he considers to be solved or seen in a new light as the result of his experience.

I think that these after effects can *all* be generalized and a feeling for them communicated if the peak experience could be likened to a visit to a personally defined Heaven from which the person then returns to earth. Desirable after-effects of such an experience, some universal and some individual, are then seen to be practically inevitable.

And may I also emphasize, that such after-effects of aesthetic experience, creative experience, love experience, mystic experience, insight exexperience, and other peak experiences are taken for granted and commonly expected by artists and art educators, by creative teachers, by religious and philosophical theorists, by loving husbands, mothers, and therapists. As a matter of fact, they are a commonplace to all but psychologists.

References

Allport, G. *Becoming.* New Haven: Yale Univ. Press, 1955.

Balint, M. *Primary Love and Psychoanalytic Technique.* New York: Liveright, 1953.

Bucke, R. *Cosmic Consciousness.* New York: Dutton, 1923.

Bühler, C. "Maturation and Motivation." *Dialectica,* 1951, 5, 312-361.

Dewey, J. "Theory of Valuation." *Int. Encycl. Unified Science.* Chicago: Univ. Chicago Press, 1939.

Ghiselin, B. (*Ed.*). *The Creative Process.* Berkeley: Univ. California Press, 1952.

Goldstein, K. *The Organism.* New York: American Book, 1939.

Hartman, R. (Forthcoming book.)

Huxley, A. *The Perennial Philosophy.* New York: Harper, 1944.

———. *Heaven and Hell.* New York: Harper, 1955.

Klee, J. "The Absolute and the Relative." (Unpublished.)

Kris, E. *Psychoanalytic Explorations in Art.* New York: International Univ. Press, 1952.

Lee, D. *In* C. Moustakas (*Ed.*). *The Self.* New York: Harper, 1956.

Maslow, A. H. *Motivation and Personality.* New York: Harper, 1954.

———. "Deficiency Motivation and Growth Motivation." *In* R. M. Jones (*Ed.*). *Nebraska Symposium on Motivation 1955.* Lincoln, Nebraska: Univ. Nebraska Press, 1955.

Northrop, F. *The Meeting of East and West.* New York: Macmillan, 1946.

Perls, F., Hefferline, R., & Goodman, P. *Gestalt Therapy.* New York: Julian Press, 1951.

Rogers, C. *In* C. Moustakas (*Ed.*). *The Self.* New York: Harper, 1956.

Schachtel, E. "On Memory and Childhood Amnesia." *Psychiatry,* 1947, 10, 1-26.

Scheler, M. *The Nature of Sympathy.* London: Routledge & Kegan Paul, 1954.

Schwartz, F. (Forthcoming book.)

Shlien, J. (Unpublished memoranda.)

Sorokin, P. *The Ways and Power of Love.* Boston: Beacon Press, 1954.

Tillich, P. *The Courage to Be.* New Haven: Yale Univ. Press, 1952.

Vivanti, L. *A Philosophy of Potentiality.* London: Routledge & Kegan Paul, 1955.

Werner, H. *Comparative Psychology of Mental Development.* New York: Harper, 1940.

RUDOLF ARNHEIM

The Robin and the Saint: On the Twofold Nature of the Artistic Image

IN THE GARDEN of my mother's neighbor there is a birdfeeding station. The open box containing the seeds is protected by a wooden gable roof. Directly under the roof there stands on a console a small white figure of St. Francis, who thus presides over the feeding operations; and on the rim of the box there is attached a life-sized and realistically colored wooden robin, poised to dip into the feed. The feeding station is not a work of art, but it can serve to illustrate some aspects of the question: What is the place of art in the world of things?

A setting of flower beds harmonizes with the modest carpenter work of the neighbor but shows it up as a stranger also. The flowers, too, are in the backyard by the will of the man, but they are not his work. They are nature, partially surrendered. They dwell here by their own consent, and while the rectangular beds and the studied arrangements of colors indicate an autocratic order, there is an equally deliberate margin of freedom, a mitigation of the regularity, which alone enables the flowers to do their service. By the partial disorder that the flowers are permitted to create they reveal themselves as being truly grown, and it is this property of growth that makes them precious to man beyond anything of their kind he can fashion with his own hands.

Man cherishes the perfection of symmetry, pure curve, and clean color because it enables him to identify, relate, and understand what he sees. He himself can produce objects with such properties quite easily, but, although useful, they are only a mirror of his own mind and therefore do not offer the comfort of the flowers. The flowers testify to the eyes that order, indispensable for survival, is a principle of growth itself and that man, in needing and creating order, does not simply impose an

---

Reprinted from The Journal of Aesthetics and Art Criticism *(September, 1959), pp. 68-79, by permission of the author and the journal.*

This essay was read as the presidential address for the Division on Aesthetics at the sixty-sixth annual convention of the American Psychological Association in Washington, D.C., on September 1, 1958.

alien demand upon reluctant wilderness. Rather does he reveal his own kinship with nature by insisting upon an inherent property of nature.

Flowers, then, in order to serve as intermediaries between man and nature, must not only display perfection of form but also supply that admixture of irregularity through which growth is made visible. Irregularity, of course, is but a superficial symptom of growth. More essential for grown things is that their appearance is caused by the forces organizing the object internally. The symmetry of the flower is the outer expression of symmetrically distributed internal forces. The shapes of nature are not form applied to substance; we remember here Martin Heidegger's observation that the distinction of substance and form is derived from artifacts and does not hold for nature.[1]

The generating power of the internal forces, however, cannot be read off directly from the surface. A grown flower is hardly distinguishable from a well made glass flower. What *can* be seen is an indirect effect of such origin. Molded by a team of internal forces, the object of nature is under the influence of other equally local teams of forces, which may constitute neighboring objects. Thus the internally generated shape of a plant shows the interference of other plants, the wind, or the dominant position of the sun; and even within one plant the perfection of any leaf is hindered by the expansion of its neighbors. Such approximation and distraction of shape distinguish things of nature from successful manufacture since the craftsman is in complete and exclusive control of the objects he makes. In the artifact, irregularity—that is, modification of the intended shape—appears as a flaw, caused by the technical imperfection of tool or mind. Irregularity may also be understood as a virtue of the artifact when it recalls the diversity of antagonistic forces within the craftsman, who thereby creates in the manner of nature. Nature offers relief from the one-sidedness of man's own perfection. The flower, in particular, displays graciously the ideals of order and harmony animated by "life," that is, by the pushes and pulls of irregular interaction.

In the garden there is also a small bridge, which lets the neighbor walk across the creek. Being made of redwood, it accords with the surrounding plants by its material. But the rectangular shape of the boards is not grown by the wood; it is imposed by the will of man—form imposed upon substance. All straight edges are completely straight, and the slight curve of the handrails is completely symmetrical. All relations of angle and size conform to one totally realized design. No interference by forces of the environment is discernible.

Although the bridge appears to be untouched by its surroundings, it is not only the very product of forces outside of itself, but is visibly dedi-

1. Martin Heidegger, *Holzwege* (Frankfurt am Main, 1950), pp. 16-18.

cated to the service of such outer forces. The meaning of its existence derives entirely from man. We may say that the bridge displays itself to the eye as a track and a facility. It is a preserved track of man's crossing the creek—not a passive imprint, however, but a planned facility. Its visible shape incorporates man's presence in the past and in the future: it recounts his crossing in the past and foretells his return. The bridge is a tool of man, and therefore its shape can be understood only by whoever knows about man. In fact, even the very percept of the bridge, in order to be complete and correct, must include the presence of the absent bridge-crosser. Otherwise it is an enigmatic ornament.

The flower also is a tool, but a tool of the plant itself. It is perceived properly only if it is seen as a dispenser and receptor of pollen. Otherwise it, too, is an enigmatic ornament, which is precisely what man prefers to see in it. Without blushing he looks at the shamelessly exposed and immodestly colored sexual organ of the plant, and he goes so far in his misinterpretation as to enjoy in the sight of the flower the purity of purposelessness. As a thing of nature, the flower is innocent of man. At best, it tolerates his company. The bridge, being a tool, makes man visible even though he be away. The sight of the bridge is an invitation; that of the flower is more nearly an exclusion.[2]

Now for the birdfeeding station. Built of rectangular redwood boards like the bridge, it presents itself as an artifact. One hesitates, however, to call it a tool since its percept does not include actions of man to be performed by means of it. One part of it, the feed box, can be seen as a tool if man is thought of as feeding the birds; but even the box is more properly an opportunity donated by man for the birds to feed themselves—not a tool of the birds either, since they did not make the box as the plant made its flowers, but certainly a party to a transaction with the birds from which man has withdrawn. Whereas the bridge, by being so close to man, is relatively remote from nature, the feeding station joins with nature in its independence of man. Even so, it does not entirely ignore its maker: it "faces" man by its frontality.

The "inviting" gesture of this frontality will concern us later. For the moment, we notice in its symmetry the almost harsh intransigence of the man-made, self-contained artifact. More in particular, the triangular gable serves as a protective frame for the small figure of the saint, which, less geometrical and closer to nature, would otherwise be in danger of being taken as a part of nature. Although the little man resembles the

2. Bridge and flower may or may not have "valence." Valence means attractiveness. An object may be attractive because or even though it invites us, and it may be unattractive under the same conditions. It also may be attractive or unattractive because or even though it excludes us.

shapes of natural things, he clearly takes sides with his encasement. Placed precisely upon the central axis of the feeding station, the figure defines itself as an integral part of the wooden pattern; that is, it declares itself an artifact.[3] In addition, its fully front-face attitude repeats the frontality of the encasement and shuns any interaction with the environment, except for the curious gesture of "exposure," already noticed in the design of the feeding station as a whole.

The wooden robin, perched on the rim of the feed box, resembles the shapes of nature even more strongly than the figure of the saint. Yet, no attempt is made to protect it from such association. It is not framed by the gable nor does it conform to the symmetry of the construction. The bird is placed off center, which characterizes its present relationship to the feeding station as accidental and transitory.[4] And instead of facing the beholder frontally, it sits on the box obliquely, ready to take a peck at the feed.

The robin relates to the station as a visiting customer, an emissary of nature. At the very least, it is an intermediary between the solemnly symmetrical artifact and the creatures that come and go and grow about it—not unlike the painted figures of those occasional bystanders in the group compositions of Renaissance or Baroque art who point out the central scene to the public. Whereas, however, the figure of the pointing guide is located on the stage within the picture frame, being itself a part of the presentation it presents, the robin does not share the dwelling place of the saint. The bird is an outsider.

The fundamental difference between the robin and the saint is clearly expressed in their relation to size. We call the robin neither large nor small but "just right" since we judge it by the norm of the live species. The figure of the saint also is neither large nor small. However, if we call it "just right" we do so not by applying a yardstick for saints. Rather do we approve of its size as appropriate to the individual character and function of the figure itself and as accorded with the sizes of the other things around it. Curiously enough, this evaluation of size refers only to the figure as a visual object and to its function. We can say that, given

3. Edward Bullough notes that "unification of presentment," by which he means the compositional qualities of symmetry, opposition, proportion, balance, etc., increase "aesthetic distance" by distinguishing the object from the "confused, disjointed and scattered forms of actual experience" (*British Journal of Psychology*, 5 [1912], 87-118). It appears that such distance is not specific to aesthetic or, in fact, man-made objects, but separates typically "natural" things from shapes of high rationality, often associated with artifacts but also found in the "unnatural" orderliness of crystals or radiolaria.

4. Rudolf Arnheim, "Accident and the Necessity of Art," *Journal of Aesthetics and Art Criticism* (Sept. 1957), 18-31.

the size of the garden and the various plants in it, the "little" figure occupies just as much space as is its due. But as a portrait of a human being it is neither smaller than the trees nor larger than the flowers, nor indeed is it larger or smaller than the norm of the live species man. The figure can be compared with the objects of physical space only as what it is, not as what it represents, because as a representation it does not dwell in physical space.

The curious isolation of the figure is demonstrated when we ask: Is the saint larger or smaller than the robin? Obviously, it is neither. St. Francis in the mural of the Upper Church of Assisi is clearly and significantly taller than his "sisters, the little birds" (*sorores meae aviculae*), to whom he addresses his famous sermon. If we force the neighbor's St. Francis and robin into such a unitary scene we discover—almost with surprise—that the robin is large enough to serve the saint as a giant eagle or that the saint is a dwarf. Or we see the bird as too large or the man as too small. But these percepts are so disturbingly wrong that it is hard to produce them at all.

Notice that this perceptual incapacity of ours comes from cultural training. A child or savage would spontaneously see what we can barely force ourselves to see: "The bird looks at the little man!" For us, the two figures are unrelatable. If we look at the sight as a scene of nature, the saint becomes a white puppet. If we look at the saint as a representation, the robin becomes a nonexistent impurity—something like a fly crawling over a painting. The two views exclude each other. We cannot hold them simultaneously.

The isolation of the image of the saint from physical space corresponds to its isolation from time. The robin, as a robin, exists in time like the garden. It just arrived at the feeding box and will be elsewhere soon. The flowers are a state of transition from the bud to the scattered petals withering on the ground. In the creek flows the Heraclitic water; and even the bridge was made and is perishable. The saint also has such a past and present—but only as its wooden self. As an image *of* the saint it is outside of time. If the figure is seen as something of a kind with the robin it looks rigidly arrested, deprived of life. Seen as something of a kind with the saint, the robin drops out of time and becomes a figure, alien to life.

For too long, however, have we treated the wooden robin as though it were a real bird. That indeed it is when it deceives us: "Look, there is a robin feeding at the box!" But although its size, shape, color, and position are such as to make it resemble a real bird as much as possible, it would miss its purpose if it deceived longer than for a while. Only when the deception is uncovered does it show up as a patent triumph of human virtuosity. The deceptive bird proves the human artisan to be a match for nature or the divine creator. At the same time it reveals the inferiority of man by the let-down of the discovery that the bird is wooden after all. In short, the robin is "cute"—a useful word of the American vernacular, which means "being amusingly clever beyond one's own standards."

The wooden robin can be said to be an epitome of the work of art as it has been popularly understood since the Renaissance. The work of art is misinterpreted as a sleight of hand by which man cleverly duplicates nature for the purpose of entertainment. The skill is admirable but not quite serious, since its product is dispensable. In this conception, a piece of sculpture or painting replaces the material presence of a natural object by either being like it or existing instead of it. It is not really an image of another object, but a duplicate of it—a rival object. It is an image but it makes only its own properties visible. Therefore I shall call it a *self-image*.[5] The wooden bird does not say: Such is a robin! It *is* a robin, although a somewhat incomplete one. It adds a robin to the inventory of nature, just as in Madame Tussaud's Exhibition the uniformed guards, made of wax, are not intended to interpret the nature of their fellow guards but to increase weirdly the staff of the institution.[6]

Being an addition to nature, the self-image is most at home at the places where its prototypes belong. The wooden robin sits on the feed box, the waxed guard lounges in a corner of the Exhibition, the still life of fruit and fowl hangs in the dining room. Beautiful women in marble or oil populate the palaces and mansions. They supplement the wealth of their owners by offering the promise and partial fulfillment of actual consumption.

Around the year 1570, Paolo Veronese paints on the walls of the Villa Barbaro life-sized children and pages peeping through half-open doors. It is a virtuoso's feat, "cute," done with a smile and presumably as an ironical comment on the eagerness of the period to vie with nature and

5. The term should not be misunderstood to mean an image in which the maker or beholder represents or recognizes his own self.

6. The same example is used by E. H. Gombrich, who in his "Meditations on a Hobby Horse or the Roots of Artistic Form," in *Aspects of Form*, ed. L. L. Whyte (London, 1951), points out that "originally" images serve as substitutes. Speaking of portraits he mentions the "unwarranted assumption: that every image of this kind necessarily refers to something outside itself—be it individual or class. But no such reference need be implied if we point to an image and say 'this is a man.' Strictly speaking that statement may be interpreted to mean that the image itself is a member of the class 'man'" (p. 211). Thus he clearly holds the view I am here adopting. He seems to believe, however, that the "substitute"—which is what I call the self-image—is limited to an early conception, later replaced with the image as a representation of "something outside itself." This "change of function," it seems to me, does not and should not eliminate the earlier conception of the self-image, which continues to operate side by side with what later I call a "likeness."

supplement it. Toward the end of the eighteenth century, Goethe, in his essay *Der Sammler und die Seinigen*, tells of a man who engages several painters to make him meticulously exact copies of birds, flowers, butterflies, and shells. In an upstairs room behind a door, there is a life-sized portrait of the gentleman himself and his wife as they seem to enter the room—frighteningly real, as Goethe puts it, "partly by the circumstances and partly by the art" of the painter. Shortly before his death, the old friend of the arts has a plaster cast made of his face and hands. With the help of a wig and a damask housecoat a replica is produced, which, mounted on a chair, is kept behind a curtain. The ironical smile is in this story also, but only in the words of Goethe: it is ominously absent from the mind of the uncanny gentleman whom he is describing.

Less than a hundred years later, Auguste Rodin conceives the idea—fortunately blocked by the good sense of the burghers of Calais—of having his bronze figures of Eustache de St. Pierre and the six other citizens placed in single file directly on the pavement of the square in front of the Town Hall as though they were actually on their way to meet the English conqueror. "By almost elbowing them," says Rodin, "the people of Calais of today would have felt more deeply the tradition of solidarity which unites them to these heroes."[7]

This intermingling of art and the traffic of daily life is an aberration which proves that the intuitive knowledge of the nature and function of images—a universal possession of the human mind—can be fatally weakened by unfavorable cultural conditions. In the works of Rodin as well as those of other artists of the same historical period this deficiency manifests itself also in the absence of truly interpretive shape. As art degenerates into the material duplication of individual objects, the artifact threatens to invade nature and thereby causes the nightmares of what might be called the Pygmalion complex, traceable in the literature of the period (Wilde's *Portrait of Dorian Gray*, Meyrink's *Golem*, Zola's *L'Oeuvre*, d'Annunzio's *La Gioconda*, Pirandello's *Come Tu Mi Vuoi* and *Sei Persone in Cerca di un Autore*). In these novels and plays, the creations of painting, sculpture, and fiction acquire the physical reality of psychotic hallucinations while at the same time human beings vainly try to attain the perfection and immortality of images.

In a materialistic culture, whose natural sciences are concerned with the exact physical qualities of things and capable of reproducing them faithfully, self-images tend to be accurate and complete. They serve the purposes of material consumption and interaction. A recent newspaper advertisement offered a hot-water bottle in the shape of a well known movie actress dressed in two bits of bathing suit. Made of pink plastic and presenting the lady in a pose of chaste surrender, the image adds the

7. Auguste Rodin, *On Art and Artists* (New York, 1957), p. 103.

touch and temperature qualities of the human flesh to visual resemblance and thereby carries duplication to a new height. Nevertheless the figure is only twenty-two inches in length—partly, we suppose, for practical reasons but also because the reduced size conceals somewhat the otherwise unveiled obscenity of the bedtime gift, which, in the words of the advertisement, is "guaranteed to bring a smile and warmth to Father, Fiancé, Friend or Foe." We notice that deviations from the accuracy of duplication do not necessarily interfere with the functions of the self-image and, in fact, may enhance its suitability.

This observation holds for most images. Only under particular cultural conditions must they be deceptive replicas. *We call an object a self-image when we find that it visibly expresses its own properties. Its functions derive from the properties it reveals.* That it can do so without being a strict duplicate is demonstrated by the capacity of children to treat a stick as a horse and a stuffed bag as a baby. These toys have been a puzzle to theorists, who have asserted that the child is capable of creating within himself the "illusion" of dealing with a real horse or baby—an obvious absurdity since such delusions would make it necessary for us to diagnose the child as insane. The theory, a sibling of the naturalistic schools of art, presupposes that identification requires mechanically complete replication.[8] But no conception of identity could mislead the psychologist more than the assumption that two things are either totally identical or not identical at all. The existential uniqueness of the individual object is negligible compared with the fact that all things are experienced as being identical to some extent with all others. Identity, in other words, is a matter of degree.[9] The stick is a horse because—for the purposes of the play situation—it has enough of the horse's properties. The statements "the stick is a horse" and "the stick is not a horse" do not contradict each other.

The North American Indians who told the explorer Catlin that his portrait sketches of their chiefs were "a little alive"[10] asserted correctly that images not only represent, but *are* what they represent. All images tend to be treated as self-images, and as such they share some of the powers of their prototypes. A photograph of my father *is*, in a diminished way, my father. To tear it up would be a diminished form of murder. The wooden robin is a gift of real birdiness to the feeding station, and

8. Here again compare the enlightening remarks of Gombrich, *op. cit.*

9. An object or creature, far from being only an exclusive *id-entity*, is experienced and treated by us as a syndrome of general properties and categories, partial images of other things or beings, etc. In the extreme case, a person's identity may consist for us in nothing but one general property, e.g., in his being a waiter or an intruder.

10. Lucien Lévy-Bruhl, *How Natives Think* (London, 1926), p. 46.

the figure of St. Francis actually spreads peace, sympathy, and the solidarity of the creatures through the garden. A framed caricature of Daumier's on the wall subtly poisons the room by the presence of an ingeniously potent distortion. When these effects are no longer felt, that is, when the image ceases to be perceived as a self-image, art is no longer whole.

The self-image is treated as identical with its prototype when it possesses attributes of the prototype pertinent to the given situation. Its other, deviating attributes may enhance its suitability and power. The golden calf is a calf in spite of being golden, and the shiny rare metal adds powerful splendor to the fetish. The neighbor's St. Francis is painted all over with white lacquer, which decreases its resemblance to a live Franciscan monk but enhances the purity and unworldliness of the figure; and its smallness is in keeping with the delicacy of its saintliness and the limited function allotted to it in the garden, which is not a place of worship. We note here that the expressive qualities of perceptual appearance—shape, size, color, etc.—serve the self-image to create, define, and enhance the powers it exerts.

Back in the neighbor's garden, we examine the figure of the saint more closely. Earlier we described the difference between the flowers as things of nature and the bridge as a man-made tool. The flowers were said to be experienced as being grown, existing by themselves and for their own purpose. The bridge had the appearance of an artifact and of a track and facility of man. How about the figure of the saint? First of all, is it perceived as being grown like a flower? It does not deceive us, as the robin might, but on the other hand it does not appear shaped for and by the use of man. Even its frontality, by which it displays itself to the eyes of the beholder, can be perceived as its own initiative, rather than an arrangement made by man for his convenience. The little figure has the independence of a flower: its properties exist to the end of its own being. We are using here an observation of Heidegger's, who remarks that the work of art in its self-sufficient appearance is like the "self-grown and unentreated" things of nature.[11] In fact, even more independent than the flowers, the figure does not tolerate any modifications of its form through neighboring powers. Such interferences introduce the environment into the percept of the flower, which thereby becomes a part of the continuity of nature. The figure, on the other hand, is completely itself and therefore alone.

11. Heidegger, *op. cit.*, p. 18: "Trotzdem gleicht das Kunstwerk in seinem selbstgenügsamen Anwesen eher wieder dem eigenwüchsigen und zu nichts gedrängten blossen Ding."

However, a thing of nature or an artifact acquires a new dependence upon man when it is treated as an image of a higher order, namely as what I will call a *likeness.* It becomes a statement about objects and properties beyond itself. As a self-image, too, the object is a statement, but a statement it makes about its own powers. We say, it expresses itself. When treated as a likeness, the object is made (or found to be) an image of things transcending itself. Its being an image becomes a means to an end, and only man can make it become that. A self-image possesses the properties of other things as parts of its own identity. The golden calf is a calf. It does not point to other calves. Only man can make it do that by treating it as a likeness.

Even as a likeness, however, the object is not necessarily a tool although it is used as one, because an object is classified as a tool only when its usability is viewed as the cause of its being what it is. A likeness, therefore, is a tool only to the extent to which it appears as having been made for the purpose of being used as a likeness. Granted that the frontality of the saint, which appeared as an accommodating gesture of the figure's own initiative in the self-image, is perceived as a facility provided by man for his convenience when the figure functions as a likeness. But on the whole, even as a likeness it tends to preserve a large measure of that self-sufficiency which distinguishes a flower from a hammer.

A likeness, then, is an object treated as a statement about other objects, kinds of object, or general properties, which are recognized in the object. The figure of the saint, in addition to being its own moderately powerful self, is also a portrait of the son of the merchant Bernardone, who lived in Assisi in the thirteenth century. Looking more closely, we notice that no attempt has been made to render the individual features of the historical Francisco, but that he, in turn, has been used to portray the saintliness of saints. In the last analysis, the figure represents those disembodied qualities of peace, harmony, and love, which we found emanate from it as a self-image.

Now, when the figure is viewed as a likeness and the flowers around it are not, the distinction must be expressed by such means as the symmetrical wooden frame, and the saint appears as a stranger, unrelatable in space and time. As far as he is a self-image, no such estrangement exists. The wooden St. Francis, diminished perhaps, but fully present as a feeble power, diffuses bliss as the flowers spread their scent and resides as the highspot of the Creation among and above his minor brothers and sisters. But removed from them by the wooden frame, he tends to change curiously into a mere transition to something beyond himself.

As the transformation occurs, the perceptual properties of the object change function. In the mere self-image they serve, we said, to create, define, and enhance the powers exerted by the object. They are, as it were, consumed by the task of creating the nature of the object. The darkness of the thundercloud disappears in supplying the cloud with the adjective "threatening." The whiteness of the saint is an aspect of his visible saintliness and a source of his beneficial power. Heidegger says about tools: "The stone is used and consumed in the making of the tool, e.g., of the axe. It disappears in the serviceability."[12] This relationship changes to its opposite when the object is treated as a likeness. Employed to illustrate universal qualities, the object now appears as the vehicle of its properties. The thundercloud presents darkness; the saint becomes the carrier of whiteness.

This prominence of the expressive qualities must not be confused with the separation of percepts from their meaning, often mistakenly described as the aesthetic attitude. The dark mass in the sky can cease to be a thundercloud and become an interestingly shaped patch of blue color harmoniously related to the orange streaks painted around it by the sun. The saint can become a small column of whiteness, a stimulating contrast to the meandering greens around it. This disengagement of vision from its biological duty as a discoverer of meaning—far from being aesthetic—is a serious disease, which can ruin the efficiency and self-respect of whole generations of artists. The view is spread by innocent art educators and has all but succeeded recently in perverting the nature of what is known as abstract art.[13]

It cannot be denied, however, that even by treating objects as pure likenesses we are courting the danger of alienation. Whereas the stoniness of the axe disappears by making the stone axe sharp and hard, stoniness assumes prominence in a statue of Henry Moore when the sculptured block is viewed as a likeness of sharpness and hardness; and since the stone is in addition a likeness of a human being the qualities portrayed through its being human combine with those of its stoniness in an intriguing counterpoint of forces. As the observer focuses upon this rather abstract contrapuntal pattern, with his eyes adapted, as it were, to infinity, the tangible stone figure all but dissolves.

Undoubtedly, the capacity to see objects as likenesses is a sublimation

12. Heidegger, *op. cit.*, p. 34.

13. Genuine abstract art is not a game of shapes and colors. It makes statements just as any other art. It does not represent objects of nature but carries expressive properties, which, in the self-image, endow the abstract piece of sculpture or painting with the powers of harmony, aggressiveness, frivolity, solemnity, or whatever their nature may be. Treated as a likeness, abstract art makes statements about these same qualities as universal forces.

of vision, a privileged accomplishment of the human species. It enables us to roam beyond the particulars toward the mothers of all existence. At the same time the image becomes ever emptier as we proceed from the individual to the universal. Being a complex, particular creature himself, man recognizes himself only in what is complex and particular so that in his pursuit of the universal he risks losing either it or himself. Also since he can only contemplate the universal but not act upon it, he tends to lapse into inactivity, which in turn will distort his contemplation. In the extreme case, a person will perceive all things only as what they stand for, not as what they are, which will transform the world of beings into one of apparitions and destroy his own foothold within the world.

We are driven to the conclusion that full vision requires us to treat the object as a self-image and a likeness at the same time. To deal with the object as nothing but an image of its own self is an elementary form of vision, accessible even to animals. It belongs to the early state of mind in which experiences can be understood only as related to the present and its extensions into the past and future. At that stage, the expressive perceptual qualities of the object appear as its own powers, and it is to them that we respond when we interact with the object. Art serves here to render the perceptual properties of the object pure, clear, and intense. It makes the object visibly itself.

To deal with the object as nothing but a likeness is a later development. It occurs when the human mind withdraws from interaction with the here and now and reserves itself for the contemplation of the universals. At that stage, art plays down the material existence of the object and treats it as a mere statement about fundamentals. The expressive qualities are given dominance over the object carrying them.

When in full sight, the object is completely and personally present in the world of the eye-witness. It possesses the powers of its appearance, which are not only visible but affect the witness and must be reacted to by him.[14] At the same time, the powers of the object appear as manifestations of universal forces so that by dealing with the object the witness deals with existence in general. The savage who treats the object only as itself is as remote from full vision as the critic who only judges it.

What has been said here applies to objects of nature as well as to artifacts. What, then, is art? Art is what makes the expressive properties

14. Even though the self-image dwells as an object among objects inside the world of action, all sensible civilizations provide for the distinction between things of nature and effigies, that is, between what is alive physically and what is alive only perceptually. Humans do not intermingle with the images they make but set them off by special appearance, location, or ceremony.

of the object perceivable. Nature applies art, and so does man, who is one of nature's products. Originally nature does not aim at visibility. It achieves it as a by-product through the external manifestation of the generating forces within the object. But visibility provokes the creation of eyes, and with the existence of eyes nature begins to take account of its visibility. The history of evolution tells us that the flowering plants or angiosperms, inventors of advertising color, develop in correspondence with the kingdom of insects. Color, shape, and behavior of animals are influenced by the visual information they supply or conceal. The same is true for almost anything man does or makes. A recent illustration is the use of color in factories for the purpose of distinguishing objects from the background, classifying machine parts according to their functions, warning of dangerous contact, and also making the workroom a clean-looking and cheerful place.

For most things, to take their visibility into account is a part of their coping with life in the physical world. Man seems to be the only creature to have invented objects that operate exclusively through being looked at. Many of these objects indicate their function by their "frontality"—sculpture often has a principal view and paintings display their content within the frontal plan. The self-image, by its visual properties, transmits its powers, which play their part in man's practical life. Note here that even works of art have not commonly been among the objects made exclusively for the purpose of being seen. The images of gods and rulers were placed in temples, tombs, palaces in order to exert certain powers, quite regardless of whether they were seen or not; in fact, they were often kept invisible. This is a fundamental difference between much art of the past and our modern paintings and sculpture, which are meant to act only through being seen.

As a pure likeness, the image fulfils its purpose by referring to matters outside of the present situation. For this reason, the purpose of the pure likeness is a puzzle to the innocent. Albert Michotte, asserting that we learn what things are by what they do, reports that one of his children at the age of three or four asked what the paintings on the walls of the living rooms were for, and after receiving an explanation exclaimed: "Mais alors, les tableaux, ce n'est rien!"[15] No such comment is likely to have been elicited by the statue of Pallas Athene in a Greek

15. Albert Michotte, *La perception de la causalité* (Louvain, 1946), p. 3. The purpose of the pure likeness seems to remain a puzzle also to some aestheticians even to our day. "There is nothing that one can do *with* a painting," explains Etienne Gilson in his recent book *Painting and Reality* (New York, 1957), p. 118, "except look at it. What distinguishes tools and instruments from a work of art is . . . that their final cause lies outside themselves. Not one of them is made for its own sake." The work of art allegedly *is* made for its own sake. *Alors, ce n'est rien!*

temple since it was very much of a self-image and as such performed action and was reacted to. The pure likeness, unrelated in space and time to its environment, requires a beholder who is able to cut his own ties in space and time. To the object that is not in full sight corresponds an observer incapable of full vision. Such alienation is quite different from the attitude of a man who, moved by the course of his life into the presence of an object whose powers answer his demands or destroy his hopes, pauses to contemplate life itself in the image of its pregnant manifestation.

The true work of art, then, is more than a statement floating adrift. It occupies, in the world of action, a place suitable to the exercise of its powers. It cannot be alone. Primitively it performs only as a thing among other things. At its most human, it rules as an embodied statement over a world in which every tool, every flower, and every rock also speaks as itself and through itself. We find it perhaps in the tea room, in the Japanese garden. The backyard of my mother's neighbor, I am afraid, lies somewhat behind.

GEORG SIMMEL

The Adventure

Each segment of our conduct and experience bears a twofold meaning: it revolves about its own center, contains as much breadth and depth, joy and suffering, as the immediate experiencing gives it, and at the same time is a segment of a course of life—not only a circumscribed entity, but also a component of an organism. Both aspects, in various configurations, characterize everything that occurs in a life. Events which may be widely divergent in their bearing on life as a whole may nonetheless be quite similar to one another; or they may be incommensurate

"*Das Abenteuer*," Philosophische Kultur. Gesammelte Essays *([1911] 2nd ed.; Leipzig: Alfred Kröner, 1919), pp. 7-24. Used by permission of Else Simmel, M.D.*

Translated by David Kettler, in Kurt H. Wolff (ed.), Georg Simmel, 1858-1918: A Collection of Essays, with Translations and a Bibliography *(Columbus, Ohio: Ohio State University Press, 1959). Reprinted by permission of the published.*

in their intrinsic meanings but so similar in respect to the roles they play in our total existence as to be interchangeable.

One of two experiences which are not particularly different in substance, as far as we can indicate it, may nevertheless be perceived as an "adventure" and the other not. The one receives the designation denied the other because of this difference in the relation to the whole of our life. More precisely, the most general form of adventure is its dropping out of the continuity of life. "Wholeness of life," after all, refers to the fact that a consistent process runs through the individual components of life, however crassly and irreconcilably distinct they may be. What we call an adventure stands in contrast to that interlocking of life-links, to that feeling that those countercurrents, turnings, and knots still, after all, spin forth a continuous thread. An adventure is certainly a part of our existence, directly contiguous with other parts which precede and follow it; at the same time, however, in its deeper meaning, it occurs outside the usual continuity of this life. Nevertheless, it is distinct from all that is accidental and alien, merely touching life's outer shell. While it falls outside the context of life, it falls, with this same movement, as it were, back into that context again, as will become clear later; it is a foreign body in our existence which is not somehow connected with the center; the outside, if only by a long and familiar detour, is formally an aspect of the inside.

Because of its place in our psychic life, a remembered adventure tends to take on the quality of a dream. Everyone knows how quickly we forget dreams because they, too, are placed outside the meaningful context of life-as-a-whole. What we designate as "dreamlike" is nothing but a memory which is bound to the unified, consistent life-process by fewer threads than are ordinary experiences. We might say that we localize our inability to assimilate to this process something experienced by imagining a dream in which it took place. The more "adventurous" an adventure, that is, the more fully it realizes its idea, the more "dreamlike" it becomes in our memory. It often moves so far away from the center of the ego and the course of life which the ego guides and organizes that we may think of it as something experienced by another person. How far outside that course it lies, how alien it has become to that course, is expressed precisely by the fact that we might well feel that we could appropriately assign to the adventure a subject other than the ego.

We ascribe to an adventure a beginning and an end much sharper than those to be discovered in the other forms of our experiences. The adventure is freed of the entanglements and concatenations which are characteristic of those forms and is given a meaning in and of itself.

Of our ordinary experiences, we declare that one of them is over when, or because, another starts; they reciprocally determine each other's limits, and so become a means whereby the contextual unity of life is structured or expressed. The adventure, however, according to its intrinsic meaning, is independent of the "before" and "after"; its boundaries are defined regardless of them. We speak of adventure precisely when continuity with life is thus disregarded on principle—or rather when there is not even any need to disregard it, because we know from the beginning that we have to do with something alien, untouchable, out of the ordinary. The adventure lacks that reciprocal interpenetration with adjacent parts of life which constitutes life-as-a-whole. It is like an island in life which determines its beginning and end according to its own formative powers and not—like the part of a continent—also according to those of adjacent territories. This factor of decisive boundedness, which lifts an adventure out of the regular course of a human destiny, is not mechanical but organic: just as the organism determines its spatial shape not simply by adjusting to obstacles confining it from right and left but by the propelling force of a life forming from inside out, so does an adventure not end because something else begins; instead, its temporal form, its radical being-ended, is the precise expression of its inner sense.

Here, above all, is the basis of the profound affinity between the adventurer and the artist, and also, perhaps, of the artist's attraction by adventure. For the essence of a work of art is, after all, that it cuts out a piece of the endlessly continuous sequences of perceived experience, detaching it from all connections with one side or the other, giving it a self-sufficient form as though defined and held together by an inner core. A part of existence, interwoven with the uninterruptedness of that existence, yet nevertheless felt as a whole, as an integrated unit—this is the form common to both the work of art and the adventure. Indeed, it is an attribute of this form to make us feel that in both the work of art and the adventure the whole of life is somehow comprehended and consummated—and this irrespective of the particular theme either of them may have. Moreover, we feel this, not although, but because, the work of art exists entirely beyond life as a reality; the adventure, entirely beyond life as an uninterrupted course which intelligibly connects every element with its neighbors. It is because the work of art and the adventure stand over against life (even though in very different senses of the phrase) that both are analogous to the totality of life itself, even as this totality presents itself in the brief summary and crowdedness of a dream experience.

For this reason, the adventurer is also the extreme example of the ahistorical individual, of the man who lives in the present. On the one hand, he is not determined by any past (and this marks the contrast between him and the aged, of which more later); nor, on the other hand, does the future exist for him. An extraordinarily characteristic proof of this is that Casanova (as may be seen from his memoirs), in the course of his erotic-adventurous life, every so often seriously intended to marry a woman with whom he was in love at the time. In the light of his temperament and conduct of life, we can imagine nothing more obviously impossible, internally and externally. Casanova not only had excellent knowledge of men but also rare knowledge of himself. Although he must have said to himself that he could not stand marriage even two weeks and that the most miserable consequences of such a step would be quite unavoidable, his perspective on the future was wholly obliterated in the rapture of the moment. (Saying this, I mean to put the emphasis on the moment rather than on the rapture.) Because he was entirely dominated by the feeling of the present, he wanted to enter into a future relationship which was impossible precisely because his temperament was oriented to the present.

In contrast to those aspects of life which are related only peripherally —by mere fate—the adventure is defined by its capacity, in spite of its being isolated and accidental, to have necessity and meaning. Something becomes an adventure only by virtue of two conditions: that it itself is a specific organization of some significant meaning with a beginning and an end; and that, despite its accidental nature, its extraterritoriality with respect to the continuity of life, it nevertheless connects with the character and identity of the bearer of that life—that it does so in the widest sense, transcending, by a mysterious necessity, life's more narrowly rational aspects.

At this point there emerges the relation between the adventurer and the gambler. The gambler, clearly, has abandoned himself to the meaninglessness of chance. In so far, however, as he counts on its favor and believes possible and realizes a life dependent on it, chance for him has become part of a context of meaning. The typical superstition of the gambler is nothing other than the tangible and isolated, and thus, of course, childish, form of this profound and all-encompassing scheme of his life, according to which chance makes sense and contains some necessary meaning (even though not by the criterion of rational logic). In his superstition, he wants to draw chance into his teleological system by omens and magical aids, thus removing it from its inaccessible isolation and searching in it for a lawful order, no matter how fantastic the laws of such an order may be.

The adventurer similarly lets the accident somehow be encompassed by the meaning which controls the consistent continuity of life, even though the accident lies outside that continuity. He achieves a central feeling of life which runs through the eccentricity of the adventure and produces a new, significant necessity of his life in the very width of the distance between its accidental, externally given content and the unifying core of existence from which meaning flows. There is in us an eternal process playing back and forth between chance and necessity, between the fragmentary materials given us from the outside and the consistent meaning of the life developed from within.

The great forms in which we shape the substance of life are the syntheses, antagonisms, or compromises between chance and necessity. Adventure is such a form. When the professional adventurer makes a system of life out of his life's lack of system, when out of his inner necessity he seeks the naked, external accidents and builds them into that necessity, he only, so to speak, makes macroscopically visible that which is the essential form of every "adventure," even that of the non-adventurous person. For by adventure we always mean a third something, neither the sheer, abrupt event whose meaning—a mere given—simply remains outside us nor the consistent sequence of life in which every element supplements every other toward an inclusively integrated meaning. The adventure is no mere hodgepodge of these two, but rather that incomparable experience which can be interpreted only as a particular encompassing of the accidentally external by the internally necessary.

Occasionally, however, this whole relationship is comprehended in a still more profound inner configuration. No matter how much the adventure seems to rest on a differentiation within life, life as a whole may be perceived as an adventure. For this, one need neither be an adventurer nor undergo many adventures. To have such a remarkable attitude toward life, one must sense above its totality a higher unity, a super-life, as it were, whose relation to life parallels the relation of the immediate life totality itself to those particular experiences which we call adventures.

Perhaps we belong to a metaphysical order, perhaps our soul lives a transcendent existence, such that our earthly, conscious life is only an isolated fragment as compared to the unnamable context of an existence running its course in it. The myth of the transmigration of souls may be a halting attempt to express such a segmental character of every individual life. Whoever senses through all actual life a secret, timeless existence of the soul, which is connected with the realities of life only as from a distance, will perceive life in its given and limited wholeness as an adventure when compared to that transcendent and self-consistent fate. Certain religious moods seem to bring about such a perception.

When our earthly career strikes us as a mere preliminary phase in the fulfillment of eternal destinies, when we have no home but merely a temporary asylum on earth, this obviously is only a particular variant of the general feeling that life as a whole is an adventure. It merely expresses the running together, in life, of the symptoms of adventure. It stands outside that proper meaning and steady course of existence to which it is yet tied by a fate and a secret symbolism. A fragmentary incident, it is yet, like a work of art, enclosed by a beginning and an end. Like a dream, it gathers all passions into itself and yet, like a dream, is destined to be forgotten; like gaming, it contrasts with seriousness, yet, like the *va banque* of the gambler, it involves the alternative between the highest gain and destruction.

Thus the adventure is a particular form in which fundamental categories of life are synthesized. Another such synthesis it achieves is that between the categories of activity and passivity, between what we conquer and what is given to us. To be sure, their synthesis in the form of adventure makes their contrast perceptible to an extreme degree. In the adventure, on the one hand, we forcibly pull the world into ourselves. This becomes clear when we compare the adventure with the manner in which we wrest the gifts of the world through work. Work, so to speak, has an organic relation to the world. In a conscious fashion, it develops the world's forces and materials toward their culmination in the human purpose, whereas in adventure we have a nonorganic relation to the world. Adventure has the gesture of the conqueror, the quick seizure of opportunity, regardless of whether the portion we carve out is harmonious or disharmonious with us, with the world, or with the relation between us and the world. On the other hand, however, in the adventure we abandon ourselves to the world with fewer defenses and reserves than in any other relation, for other relations are connected with the general run of our worldly life by more bridges, and thus defend us better against shocks and dangers through previously prepared avoidances and adjustments. In the adventure, the interweaving of activity and passivity which characterizes our life tightens these elements into a coexistence of conquest, which owes everything only to its own strength and presence of mind, and complete self-abandonment to the powers and accidents of the world, which can delight us, but in the same breath can also destroy us. Surely, it is among adventure's most wonderful and enticing charms that the unity toward which at every moment, by the very process of living, we bring together our activity and our passivity —the unity which even in a certain sense *is* life itself—accentuates its disparate elements most sharply, and precisely in *this* way makes itself the more deeply felt, as if they were only the two aspects of one and the same, mysteriously seamless life.

If the adventure, furthermore, strikes us as combining the elements of certainty and uncertainty in life, this is more than the view of the same fundamental relationship from a different angle. The certainty with which—justifiably or in error—we know the outcome, gives our activity one of its distinct qualities. If, on the contrary, we are uncertain whether we shall arrive at the point for which we have set out, if we know our ignorance of the outcome, then this means not only a quantitatively reduced certainty but an inwardly and outwardly unique practical conduct. The adventurer, in a word, treats the incalculable element in life in the way we ordinarily treat only what we think is by definition calculable. (For this reason, the philosopher is the adventurer of the spirit. He makes the hopeless, but not therefore meaningless, attempt to form into conceptual knowledge an attitude of the soul, its mood toward itself, the world, God. He treats this insoluble problem as if it were soluble.) When the outcome of our activity is made doubtful by the intermingling of unrecognizable elements of fate, we usually limit our commitment of force, hold open lines of retreat, and take each step only as if testing the ground.

In the adventure, we proceed in the directly opposite fashion: it is just on the hovering chance, on fate, on the more-or-less that we risk all, burn our bridges, and step into the mist, as if the road will lead us on, no matter what. This is the typical fatalism of the adventurer. The obscurities of fate are certainly no more transparent to him than to others; but he proceeds as if they were. The characteristic daring with which he continually leaves the solidities of life underpins itself, as it were, for its own justification with a feeling of security and "it-must-succeed," which normally only belongs to the transparency of calculable events. This is only a subjective aspect of the fatalist conviction that we certainly cannot escape a fate which we do not know: the adventurer nevertheless believes that, as far as he himself is concerned, he is certain of this unknown and unknowable element in his life. For this reason, to the sober person adventurous conduct often seems insanity; for, in order to make sense, it appears to presuppose that the unknowable is known. The prince of Ligne said of Casanova, "He believes in nothing except in what is least believable." Evidently, such belief is based on that perverse or at least "adventurous" relation between the certain and the uncertain, whose correlate, obviously, is the skepticism of the adventurer—that he "believes in nothing": for him to whom the unlikely is likely, the likely easily becomes unlikely. The adventurer relies to some extent on his own strength, but above all on his own luck; more properly, on a peculiarly undifferentiated unity of the two. Strength, of which he is certain, and luck, of which he is uncertain, subjectively combine into a sense of certainty.

If it is the nature of genius to possess an immediate relation to these secret unities which in experience and rational analysis fall apart into completely separate phenomena, the adventurer of genius lives, as if by mystic instinct, at the point where the course of the world and the individual fate have, so to speak, not yet been differentiated from one another. For this reason, he is said to have a "touch of genius." The "sleepwalking certainty" with which the adventurer leads his life becomes comprehensible in terms of that peculiar constellation whereby he considers that which is uncertain and incalculable to be the premises of his conduct, while others consider only the calculable. Unshakable even when it is shown to be denied by the facts of the case, this certainty proves how deeply that constellation is rooted in the life conditions of adventurous natures.

The adventure is a form of life which can be taken on by an undetermined number of experiences. Nevertheless, our definitions make it understandable that one of them, more than all others, tends to appear in this form: the erotic—so that our linguistic custom hardly lets us understand by "adventure" anything but an erotic one. The love affair, even if short-lived, is by no means always an adventure. The peculiar psychic qualities at whose meeting point the adventure is found must be added to this quantitative matter. The tendency of these qualities to enter such a conjuncture will become apparent step by step.

A love affair contains in clear association the two elements which the form of the adventure characteristically conjoins: conquering force and unextortable concession, winning by one's own abilities and dependence on the luck which something incalculable outside ourselves bestows on us. A degree of balance between these forces, gained by virtue of his sense of their sharp differentiation, can, perhaps, be found only in the man. Perhaps for this reason, it is of compelling signficance that, as a rule, a love affair is an "adventure" only for men; for women it usually falls into other categories. In novels of love, the activity of woman is typically permeated by the passivity which either nature or history has imparted to her character; on the other hand, her acceptance of happiness is at the same time a concession and a gift.

The two poles of conquest and grace (which manifest themselves in many variations) stand closer together in woman than in man. In man, they are, as a matter of fact, much more decisively separated. For this reason, in man their coincidence in the erotic experience stamps this experience quite ambiguously as an adventure. Man plays the courting, attacking, often violently grasping role: this fact makes one easily overlook the element of fate, the dependence on something which cannot be predetermined or compelled, that is contained in every erotic experience. This refers not only to dependence on the concession on the part of the other, but to something deeper. To be sure, every "love returned," too, is a gift which cannot be "earned," not even by any measure of love—because to love, demand and compensation are irrelevant; it belongs, in principle, in a category altogether different from a squaring of accounts—a point which suggests one of its analogies to the more profound religious relation. But over and above that which we receive from another as a free gift, there still lies in every happiness of love—like a profound, impersonal bearer of those personal elements—a favor of fate. We receive happiness not only from the other: the fact that we do receive it from him is a blessing of destiny, which is incalculable. In the proudest, most self-assured event in this sphere lies something which we must accept with humility. When the force which owes its success to itself and gives all conquest of love some note of victory and triumph is then combined with the other note of favor by fate, the constellation of the adventure is, as it were, preformed.

The relation which connects the erotic content with the more general form of life as adventure is rooted in deeper ground. The adventure is the exclave of life, the "torn-off" whose beginning and end have no connection with the somehow unified stream of existence. And yet, as if hurdling this stream, it connects with the most recondite instincts and some ultimate intention of life as a whole—and this distinguishes it from the merely accidental episode, from that which only externally "happens" to us. Now, when a love affair is of short duration, it lives in precisely such a mixture of a merely tangential and yet central character. It may give our life only a momentary splendor, like the ray shed in an inside room by a light flitting by outside. Still, it satisfies a need, or is, in fact, only possible by virtue of a need which—whether it be considered as physical, psychic, or metaphysical—exists, as it were, timelessly in the foundation or center of our being. This need is related to the fleeting experience as our general longing for light is to that accidental and immediately disappearing brightness.

The fact that love harbors the possibility of this double relation is reflected by the twofold temporal aspect of the erotic. It displays two standards of time: the momentarily climatic, abruptly subsiding passion; and the idea of something which cannot pass, an idea in which the mystical destination of two souls for one another and for a higher unity finds a temporal expression. This duality might be compared with the double existence of intellectual contents: while they emerge only in the fleetingness of the psychic process, in the forever moving focus of consciousness, their logical meaning possesses timeless validity, an ideal significance which is completely independent of the instant of consciousness in which it becomes real for us. The phenomenon of adventure is such that its abrupt climax places its end into the perspective of its beginning. However, its connection with the center of life is such that it is to be distinguished from all merely accidental happenings. Thus "mortal danger," so to speak, lies in its very style. This phenomenon, therefore, is a form which by its time symbolism seems to be predetermined to receive the erotic content.

These analogies between love and adventure alone suggest that the adventure does not belong to the life-tyle of old age. The decisive point about this fact is that the adventure, in its specific nature and charm, is a *form of experiencing*. The *content* of the experience does not make the adventure. That one has faced mortal danger or conquered a woman for a short span of happiness; that unknown factors with which one has waged a gamble have brought surprising gain or loss; that physically or psychologically disguised, one has ventured into spheres of life from which one returns home as if from a strange world—none of these are necessarily adventure. They become adventure only by virtue of a certain experiential tension whereby their substance is realized. Only when a stream flowing between the minutest externalities of life and the central source of strength drags them into itself; when the peculiar color, ardor, and rhythm of the life-process become decisive and, as it were, transform its substance—only then does an event change from mere experience to adventure. Such a principle of accentuation, however, is alien to old age. In general, only youth knows this predominance of the process of life over its substance; whereas in old age, when the process begins to slow up and coagulate, substance becomes crucial; it then proceeds or perseveres in a certain timeless manner, indifferent to the tempo and passion of its being experienced. The old person usually lives either in a wholly *centralized* fashion, peripheral interests having fallen off and being unconnected with his essential life and its inner necessity; or his center atrophies, and existence runs its course only in isolated petty details, accenting mere externals and accidentals. Neither case makes possible the relation between the outer fate and the inner springs of life in which the adventure consists; clearly, neither permits the perception of contrast characteristic of adventure, viz., that an action is completely torn out of the inclusive context of life and that simultaneously the whole strength and intensity of life stream into it.

In youth, the accent falls on the process of life, on its rhythm and its antinomies; in old age, it falls on life's substance, compared to which experience more and more appears relatively incidental. This contrast between youth and age, which makes adventure the prerogative of youth, may be expressed as the contrast between the romantic and the historical spirit of life. Life in its immediacy—hence also in the individuality of its form at any one moment, here and now—counts for the romanitc attitude. Life in its immediacy feels the full strength of the current of life most of all in the pointedness of an experience that is torn out of the normal run of things but which is yet connected with the heart of life. All such life which thrusts itself out of life, such breadth of contrast among elements which are penetrated by life, can feed only on that overflow and exuberance of life which exists in adventure, in romanticism, and in youth. Age, on the other hand—if, as such, it has a characteristic, valuable, and coherent attitude—carries with it a historical mood. This mood may be broadened into a world view or limited to the immediately personal past; at any rate, in its objectivity and retrospective reflectiveness, it is devoted to contemplating a substance of life out of which immediacy has disappeared. All history as depiction in the narrower, scientific sense originates in such a survival of substance beyond the inexpressible process of its presence that can only be experienced. The connection this process has established among them is gone, and must now, in retrospect, and with a view to constructing an ideal image, be re-established by completely different ties.

With this shift of accent, all the dynamic premise of the adventure disappears. Its atmosphere, as suggested before, is absolute presentness—the sudden rearing of the life-process to a point where both past and future are irrelevant; it therefore gathers life within itself with an intensity compared with which the factuality of the event often becomes of relatively indifferent import. Just as the game itself—not the winning of money—is the decisive motive for the true gambler; just as for him, what is important is the violence of feeling as it alternates between joy and despair, the almost touchable nearness of the daemonic powers which decide between both—so the fascination of the adventure is again and again not the substance which it offers us and which, if it were offered in another form, perhaps would receive little heed, but rather the adventurous form of experiencing it, the intensity and excitement with which it lets us feel life in just this instance. This is what connects youth and adventure. What is called the subjectivity of youth is just this: The material of life in its substantive significance is not as important to youth as is the process which carries it, life itself. Old age is "objective"; it shapes a new structure out of the substance left behind in a peculiar sort of timelessness by the life which has slipped by. The new structure is that of contemplativeness, impartial judgment, freedom from that unrest which marks life as being present. It is all this that makes adventure alien to old age and an old adventurer an obnoxious or tasteless phenomenon. It would not be difficult to develop the whole essence of adventure from the fact that it is the form of life which in principle is inappropriate to old age.

Notwithstanding the fact that so much of life is hostile to adventure, from the most general point of view adventure appears admixed with all practical human existence. It seems to be an ubiquitous element, but it frequently occurs in the finest distribution, invisible to the naked eye, as it were, and concealed by other elements. This is true quite aside from that notion which, reaching down into the metaphysics of life, considers our existence on earth as a whole, unified adventure. Viewed purely from a concrete and psychological standpoint, every single experience contains a modicum of the characteristics which, if they grow beyond a certain point, bring it to the "threshold" of adventure. Here the most essential and profound of these characteristics is the singling out of the experience from the total context of life. In point of fact, the meaning of no single part of life is exhausted by its belonging in that context. On the contrary, even when a part is most closely interwoven with the whole, when it really appears to be completely absorbed by onflowing life, like an unaccented word in the course of a sentence—even then, when we listen more closely, we can recognize the intrinsic value of that segment of existence. With a significance which is centered in itself, it sets itself *over against* that total development to which, nevertheless, if looked at from another angle, it inextricably belongs.

Both the wealth and the perplexity of life flow countless times from this value-dichotomy of its contents. Seen from the center of the personality, every single experience is at once something necessary which comes from the unity of the history of the ego, and something accidental, foreign to that unity, insurmountably walled off, and colored by a very deep-lying incomprehensibility, as if it stood somewhere in the void and gravitated toward nothing. Thus a shadow of what in its intensification and distinctness constitutes the adventure really hovers over every experience. Every experience, even as it is incorporated into the chain of life, is accompanied by a certain feeling of being enclosed between a beginning and an end—by a feeling of an almost unbearable pointedness of the single experience as such. This feeling may sink to imperceptibility, but it lies latent in every experience and rises from it—often to our own astonishment. It is impossible to identify any minimal distance from the continuity of life short of which the feeling of adventurousness could not emerge—as impossible, to be sure, as to identify the maximal distance where it must emerge for everyone. But everything could not become an adventure if the elements of adventure did not in some measure reside in everything, if they did not belong among the vital factors by virtue of which a happening is designated a human experience.

Similar observations apply to the relation between the accidental and the meaningful. In our every encounter there is so much of the merely given, external, and occasional that we can, so to speak, decide only on a quantitative basis whether the whole may be considered as something rational and in some sense understandable, or whether its insolubility as regards its reference to the past, or its incalculability as regards its reference to the future, is to stamp its whole complexion. From the most secure civic undertaking to the most irrational adventure there runs a continuous line of vital phenomena in which the comprehensible and the incomprehensible, that which can be coerced and that which is given by grace, the calculable and the accidental, mix in infinitely varied degrees. Since the adventure marks one extreme of this continuum, the other extreme must also partake of its character. The sliding of our existence over a scale on which every point is simultaneously determined by the effect of our strength and our abandonment to impenetrable things and powers—this problematic nature of our position in the world, which in its religious version results in the insoluble question of human freedom and divine predetermination, lets all of us become adventurers. Within the dimensions into which our station in life with its tasks, our aims, and our means place us, none of us could live one day if we did not treat that which is really incalculable as if it were calculable, if we did not entrust our own strength with what it still cannot achieve by itself but only by its enigmatic cooperation with the powers of fate.

The substance of our life is constantly seized by interweaving forms which thus bring about its unified whole. Everywhere there is artistic forming, religious comprehending, the shade of moral valuing, the interplay of subject and object. There is, perhaps, no point in this whole stream where every one of these and of many other modes of organization does not contribute at least a drop to its waves. But they become the pure structures which language names only when they rise out of that fragmentary and confused condition where the average life lets them emerge and submerge and so attain mastery over life's substance. Once the religious mood has created its structure, the god, wholly out of itself, it is "religion"; once the aesthetic form has made its content something secondary, by which it lives a life of its own that listens only to itself, it becomes "art"; once moral duty is fulfilled simply because it is duty, no matter how changing the contents by means of which it is fulfilled and which previously in turn determined the will, it becomes "morality."

It is no different with adventure. We are the adventurers of the earth; our life is crossed everywhere by the tensions which mark adventure. But only when these tensions have become so violent that they gain mastery over the material through which they realize themselves—only then does the "adventure" arise. For the adventure does not consist in a substance which is won or lost, enjoyed or endured: to all this we have access in other forms of life as well. Rather, it is the radicalness through which it becomes perceptible as a life tension, as the rubato of the life process, independent of its materials and their differences—the quantity of these tensions becoming great enough to tear life, beyond those materials, completely out of itself: this is what transforms mere experience into adventure. Certainly, it is only one segment of existence among others, but it belongs to those forms which, beyond the mere share they have in life and beyond all the accidental nature of their individual contents, have the mysterious power to make us feel for a moment the whole sum of life as their fulfillment and their vehicle, existing only for their realization.

SELECTED READINGS

The selection from Lynd appears in *On Shame and the Search for Identity*, (New York: Harcourt, Brace, and World, 1958.) See also A. H. Maslow, *Motivation and Personality* (New York: Harper and Brothers, 1954), and Clemens E. Benda, *The Image of Love* (New York: Free Press, 1961). Bruno Bettelheim, *The Informed Heart: Autonomy in a Mass Age* (New York: The Free Press, 1960), examines the relations of society and self in the concrete setting of a prison camp. A book of ever-increasing relevance to the issues considered in this section is Paul Schilder, *Goals and Desires of Man* (New York: Columbia University Press, 1942). For an able attack on the Freudian view of man and a resolute defense of human autonomy, see Otto Rank, *Beyond Psychology* (New York: Dover Publications, Inc., 1941), especially Chapter I.

Existential psychiatry has a strong interest in the definition of Being. Rollo May has been an articulate spokesman for this approach. See Rollo May (ed.), *Existence: A New Dimension in Psychiatry and Psychology*.

Other relevant books of readings are Harold H. Anderson (ed.), *Creativity and Its Cultivation* (New York: Harper and Brothers, 1959), and Morris I. Stein and Shirley J. Heinze (eds.), *Creativity and the Individual* (New York: The Free Press, 1960), which consists of summaries of selected literature in psychology and psychiatry.

List of Contributors

Abel, Theodore F. Sociologist. Professor and Chairman of the Department of Sociology and Anthropology at Hunter College.

Arnheim, Rudolph. Professor of Psychology at Sarah Lawrence College.

Back, Kurt W. Associate Professor in the Department of Sociology and Associate Professor of Medical Sociology in the Department of Psychiatry at Duke University.

Becker, Howard S. Sociologist. Research Associate with Community Studies, Inc., in Kansas City, Missouri.

Ben-David, Joseph. Professor, Department of Sociology, The Hebrew University, Jerusalem.

Biblarz, Arturo. Teaching Assistant in the Department of Anthropology and Sociology at the University of California, Los Angeles.

Brim, Orville G., Jr. Sociologist and Assistant Secretary with the Russell Sage Foundation.

Burchinal, Lee G. Sociologist. Associate Professor in the Department of Economics and Sociology at Iowa State University.

Campbell, Ernest Q. Sociologist. Associate Professor in the Department of Sociology and Anthropology and Research Associate in the Institute for Research in Social Science at the University of North Carolina.

Christensen, Harold T. Professor and Chairman of the Department of Sociology at Purdue University.

Clark, Burton R. Associate Research Sociologist at the Center for the Study of Higher Education at the University of California, Berkeley.

Clarke, Alfred C. Sociologist. Associate Professor in the Department of Sociology and Anthropology at Ohio State University, Columbus.

Cloward, Richard A. Sociologist. Associate Professor of Social Work at the New York School of Social Work at Columbia University.

Coates, Charles H. Assistant Professor in the Department of Sociology at the University of Maryland and Co-Director of the Russell Sage Foundation Project in Military Sociology.

Coker, Robert E., Jr. Professor in the Department of Public Health Administration of the School of Public Health at the University of North Carolina and Director, Study of Choice of Specialties in Medicine, University of North Carolina.

Davis, Fred. Sociologist. Project Director, Studies of Career Development in Nursing, School of Nursing, Medical Center, University of California, San Francisco, and Chairman, Bay Area Forum for Social Science Studies in the Health Fields.

Dinitz, Simon. Associate Professor in the Department of Sociology at Ohio State University and Research Associate, Department of Psychiatry, at the Columbus Psychiatric Institute and Hospital.

Donnelly, Thomas G. Research Associate at the Urban Studies Center, University of North Carolina.

Donohue, George A. Associate Professor in the Department of Sociology and Extension Sociologist and Director of Extension Research, University of Minnesota.

Dynes, Russell R. Sociologist. Associate Professor in the Department of Sociology and Anthropology at Ohio State University.

Empey, LaMar T. Associate Professor in the Department of Sociology at Brigham Young University and Director of the Provo Experiment in Delinquency Rehabilitation.

Gardner, Bruce. Professor in the Department of Child Development and in the Department of Psychology at Iowa State University and Research Editor for the *Journal of Nursery Education.*

Geer, Blanche. Sociologist. Research Associate with Community Studies, Inc., in Kansas City, Missouri.

Gold, Martin. Assistant Professor in the Department of Psychology at the University of Michigan and Study Director, Research Center for Group Dynamics at the Institute for Social Research.

Goldsen, Rose, K. Sociologist. Associate Professor in the Department of Sociology and Anthropology at Cornell University.

Goode, William J. Professor in the Department of Sociology at Columbia University and on the Board of Governors of the Bureau of Applied Social Research.

Hawkes, Glenn R. Professor of Psychology and Chairman of the Department of Child Development at Iowa State University.

Inkeles, Alex. Professor of Sociology in the Department of Social Relations and Director of Studies in Social Relations at the Russian Research Center at Harvard University.

Kanin, Eugene. Instructor in the Department of Sociology at Purdue University.

Kirkpatrick, Clifford. Professor in the Department of Sociology at Indiana University.

Klineberg, Otto. Professor in the Department of Psychology at Columbia University.

Kolb, William L. Sociologist. Fred B. Hill Professor of Sociology and Anthropology and Chairman of the Department at Carleton College.

Larsen, Otto N. Associate Professor in the Department of Sociology at the University of Washington and Director of the Institute for Sociological Research at the University of Washington.

Lee, Dorothy. Anthropologist. Lecturer on Social Relations at Harvard University.

Levine, Gene Norman. Sociologist. Research Associate at the Bureau of Applied Social Research at Columbia University and Lecturer at the School of General Studies, Columbia University. Lecturer at the School of Social Work at Adelphi College.

Lipset, Seymour Martin. Professor of Sociology at the University of California, Berkeley.

Litwak, Eugene. Sociologist. Associate Professor at the School of Social Work of the University of Michigan.

Lynd, Helen Merrell. Professor of Social Philosophy at Sarah Lawrence College.

McEwen, William J. Assistant Professor in the Department of Environmental Medicine and Community Health at the State University of New York College of Medicine.

Mack, Raymond W. Associate Professor and Chairman in the Department of Sociology at Northwestern University.

Mahony, Frank J. Anthropologist with the United States Trust Territory of the Pacific Islands. Community Analyst, USOM to Somalia, Somalia Republic.

Martin, James G. Associate Professor of Sociology at Northern Illinois University.

Maslow, Abraham H. Professor of Psychology at Brandeis University.

Medalia, Nahum Z. Sociologist in the Division of Air Pollution for the Public Health Service in Washington, D.C.

Messinger, Sheldon L. Associate Research Sociologist at the Center for the Study of Law and Society at the University of California, Berkeley.

Middleton, Russell. Associate Professor in the Department of Sociology at Florida State University.

Mills, Theodore M. Associate Professor in the Department of Sociology and Director of the Interaction Laboratory at Yale University.

Murphy, Raymond J. Assistant Professor of Sociology in the Department of Anthropology and Sociology and Assistant Research Sociologist in the Institute of Industrial Relations at the University of California, Los Angeles.

Murray, Ellen. Juvenile Probation Officer.

O'Dea, Thomas F. Sociologist. Associate Professor in the Department of Political Philosophy and Social Science at Fordham University.

Paul, Benjamin. Director of the Social Science Program in the Department of Public Health Practice in the School of Public Health at Harvard University.

Pellegrin, Ronald. Professor of Sociology and Director of the Institute for Community Studies at the University of Oregon.

Pettigrew, Thomas F. Assistant Professor of Social Psychology in the Department of Social Relations at Harvard University.

Phillips, Bernard S. Assistant Professor in the Department of Sociology and Anthropology at Boston University.

Putney, Snell. Assistant Professor in the Department of Sociology at Florida State University.

Reckless, Walter C. Professor of Sociology and Director, Research Project on Delinquency at Ohio State University.

Reeder, Leo G. Associate Professor in the Department of Preventive Medicine and Public Health, School of Medicine, at the University of California Medical Center in Los Angeles and Lecturer in the Department of Anthropology and Sociology.

Reina, Ruben E. Assistant Professor of Anthropology and Assistant Curator, American Section, of the University Museum at the University of Pennsylvania.

Rosenberg, Morris. Sociologist. Social Science Analyst in the Laboratory of Socio-Environmental Studies at the National Institute of Mental Health and Professorial Lecturer at American University.

San Juan, Ophelia. Member of Filipino research team working with editor, 1954-1955.

Scott, Nathan A., Jr. Associate Professor of Theology and Literature in the Divinity School of the University of Chicago. Literary Editor of *The Christian Scholar* and member of the Editorial Board of *The Journal of Religion.*

Seeman, Melvin. Professor of Sociology in the Department of Anthropology and Sociology at the University of California, Los Angeles.

Simmel, Georg (1858-1918). German philosopher, sociologist. Held professorships at the University of Berlin and University of Strasbourg. Published works on philosophy, philosophy of history, sociology. A major influence on American sociology.

Stoodley, Bartlett H. Professor of Sociology in the Department of Sociology and Anthropology at Wellesley College.

Suchman, Edward A. Adjunct Professor of Medical Sociology at Columbia University and Director of Social Science Activities for the Department of Health in New York City.

Sussmann, Leila A. Assistant Professor in the Department of Sociology and Anthropology, Wellesley College and Project Director for the Social Science Research Center at the University of Puerto Rico.

Thompson, James D. Professor and Chairman of the Department of Sociology and Director of the Administrative Science Center at the University of Pittsburgh.

Vogt, Evan Z. Professor in the Department of Anthropology at Harvard University and Curator of Middle American Ethnology in the Peabody Museum.

Warriner, Charles K. Associate Professor of Sociology in the Department of Sociology and Anthropology at the University of Kansas.

Westie, Frank R. Associate Professor in the Department of Sociology at Indiana University.

White, Martha Sturm. Education and Career Guidance Associate at the Institute for Independent Study at Radcliffe College and Lecturer in the Department of Psychology at Boston University.

Williams, Robin M., Jr. Professor of Sociology in the Department of Sociology and Anthropology at Cornell University.

Yellin, Seymour. Assistant Professor of Sociology in the Department of Sociology and Anthropology at Washington Square College, New York University.

Index

n beside page number indicates the reference is in a footnote
r beside page number indicates the reference is in recommended readings